N. J. Enfield and Bernard Comrie (Eds.)
Languages of Mainland Southeast Asia

Pacific Linguistics

Managing editor
Bethwyn Evans

Editorial board members
Wayan Arka
Mark Donohue
Nicholas Evans
Gwendolyn Hyslop
David Nash
Bill Palmer
Jane Simpson
Andrew Pawley
Malcolm Ross

Volume 649

Languages of Mainland Southeast Asia

—

The State of the Art

Edited by
N. J. Enfield and Bernard Comrie

DE GRUYTER
MOUTON

ISBN 978-1-5015-1589-7
e-ISBN (PDF) 978-1-5015-0168-5
e-ISBN (EPUB) 978-1-5015-0170-8
ISSN 1448-8310

Library of Congress Cataloging-in-Publication Data
A CIP catalog record for this book has been applied for at the Library of Congress.

Bibliographic information published by the Deutsche Nationalbibliothek
The Deutsche Nationalbibliothek lists this publication in the Deutsche Nationalbibliografie;
detailed bibliographic data are available on the Internet at http://dnb.dnb.de.

© 2017 Walter de Gruyter Inc., Berlin/Boston
This volume is text- and page-identical with the hardback published in 2015.
Cover image: Sơn La Province, Vietnam (photo by N. J. Enfield)
Printing and binding: CPI books GmbH, Leck
♾ Printed on acid-free paper
Printed in Germany

www.degruyter.com

Contents

N. J. Enfield and Bernard Comrie
Mainland Southeast Asian languages: State of the art and new directions —— 1

Part 1: Language relatedness in MSEA

Martha Ratliff
Word-initial prenasalization in Southeast Asia: A historical perspective —— 31

Paul Sidwell
Local drift and areal convergence in the restructuring of Mainland Southeast Asian languages —— 51

Marc Brunelle and James Kirby
Re-assessing tonal diversity and geographical convergence in Mainland Southeast Asia —— 82

James A. Matisoff
Re-examining the genetic position of Jingpho: Putting flesh on the bones of the Jingpho/Luish relationship —— 111

Part 2: Boundaries of the MSEA area

Mathias Jenny
The far West of Southeast Asia: 'Give' and 'get' in the languages of Myanmar —— 155

Mark W. Post
Morphosyntactic reconstruction in an areal-historical context: A pre-historical relationship between North East India and Mainland Southeast Asia? —— 209

David Gil
The Mekong-Mamberamo linguistic area —— 266

Hilário de Sousa
The Far Southern Sinitic languages as part of Mainland Southeast Asia —— 356

Part 3: Defining the sesquisyllable

Becky Butler
Approaching a phonological understanding of the sesquisyllable with phonetic evidence from Khmer and Bunong —— 443

Pittayawat Pittayaporn
Typologizing sesquisyllabicity: The role of structural analysis in the study of linguistic diversity in Mainland Southeast Asia —— 500

Part 4: Explorations in MSEA morphosyntax

Mark J. Alves
Morphological functions among Mon-Khmer languages: Beyond the basics —— 531

Roger Blench
The origins of nominal classification markers in MSEA languages: Convergence, contact and some African parallels —— 558

Alice Vittrant
Expressing motion: The contribution of Southeast Asian languages with reference to East Asian languages —— 586

Indexes

Subject index —— 633
Author index —— 641
Place index —— 643
Language index —— 646

N. J. Enfield and Bernard Comrie
Mainland Southeast Asian languages
State of the art and new directions

1 Mainland Southeast Asia and its people

Mainland Southeast Asia (hereafter: MSEA) can be broadly defined as the area occupied by present day Cambodia, Laos, Peninsular Malaysia, Thailand, Myanmar, and Vietnam, along with areas of China south of the Yangtze River. Also sometimes included are the seven states of Northeast India, and—although here the term 'mainland' no longer applies—the islands from Indonesia and Malaysia running southeast to Australia and West Papua (see Map 1).

There are no exact borders around the MSEA area. Different scholars draw lines in different places. But there is nevertheless a core (Comrie 2007: 45). MSEA is always taken to include Indochina—Vietnam, Laos, and Cambodia—together with Thailand, and, usually, Peninsular Malaysia and part or all of Myanmar (see Map 2).

This book covers the broader scope of Greater MSEA, with several chapters moving beyond the core area of Indochina and Thailand, in all directions; see chapters in this book by Vittrant and by Jenny on Myanmar (cf. Bradley 1995; Watkins 2005), by Post on Northeast India (cf. Morey and Post 2008, 2010; Hyslop, Morey, and Post 2011, 2012, 2013), by Gil on Insular Southeast Asia (cf. Adelaar and Himmelmann 2005; Blust 2013a, b), and by de Sousa on Southern China (cf. Bauer 1996; Ansaldo and Matthews 2001; Chappell 2001).

MSEA is a tropical and sub-tropical area with rugged and well-forested hills and river systems running from higher altitudes in the northwest to the plains and deltas of the south. Among the biggest rivers are the Mekong, the Brahmaputra, the Red River in North Vietnam, the Salween and Irrawaddy rivers in Myanmar, the Pearl and Yangtze rivers in China, and the Chaophraya in central Thailand. The lower reaches of these river systems are well-fertilized plains, which have attracted people partly because of the mobility the environment affords, but also because of the suitability for paddy rice farming. Paddy farming, in which rice plants are kept continually flooded as they grow, requires management of water via systems of dikes and channels (Hartmann 1998). This method is significantly more productive than upland dry-field methods, and can support larger populations (Bellwood 1992: 90). It also reduces biodiversity.

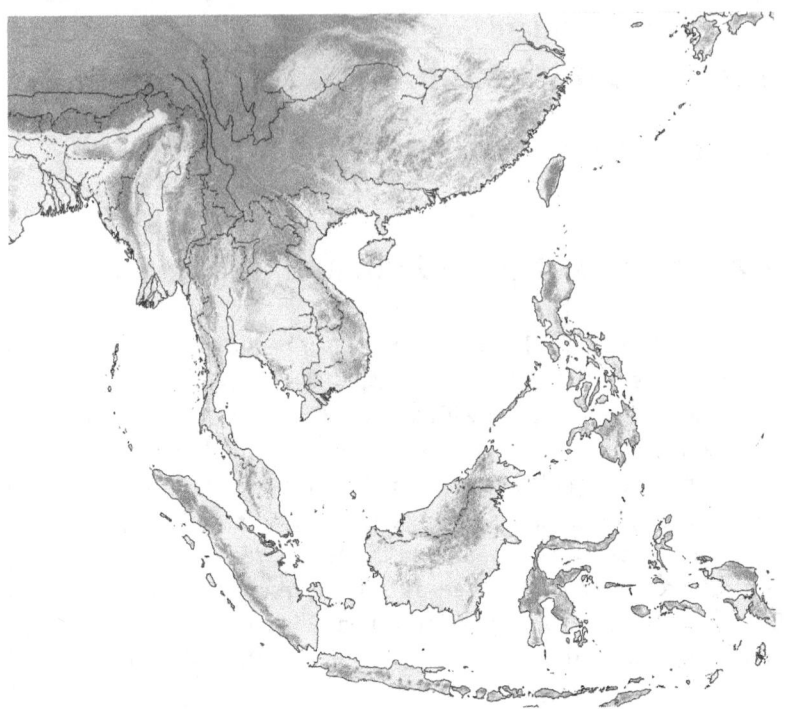

Map 1: Greater mainland Southeast Asia: present day Cambodia, Laos, Peninsular Malaysia, Thailand, Myanmar, and Vietnam, along with China south of the Yangtze River, Northeast India, and Insular Southeast Asia.

MSEA has seen a long and complex history of human movement, contact, and diversification. Evidence from genetics and archaeology suggests that there has been human activity in the area since some 40,000 years ago, when conditions were very different from today. At around 20,000 years ago, global sea levels were 120m lower than now (Chappell and Shackleton 1986; Tooley and Shennan 1987), implying different possibilities for human movement and livelihoods. Then, one could walk on dry land in a straight line from the site of present-day Ho Chi Minh City to Kuala Lumpur, and then in another straight line to Bali and again up to Brunei (Voris 2000; Oppenheimer 2011; White 2011). While a fair amount is known from bioarchaeological evidence about more recent human activity in the pre-agricultural period (Oxenham and Tayles 2006), the time horizon of comparative linguistics is limited to the last few thousand years (for recent reviews, see Enfield 2011a). Just behind that horizon are the beginnings of agriculture in MSEA some 4000 or so years ago.

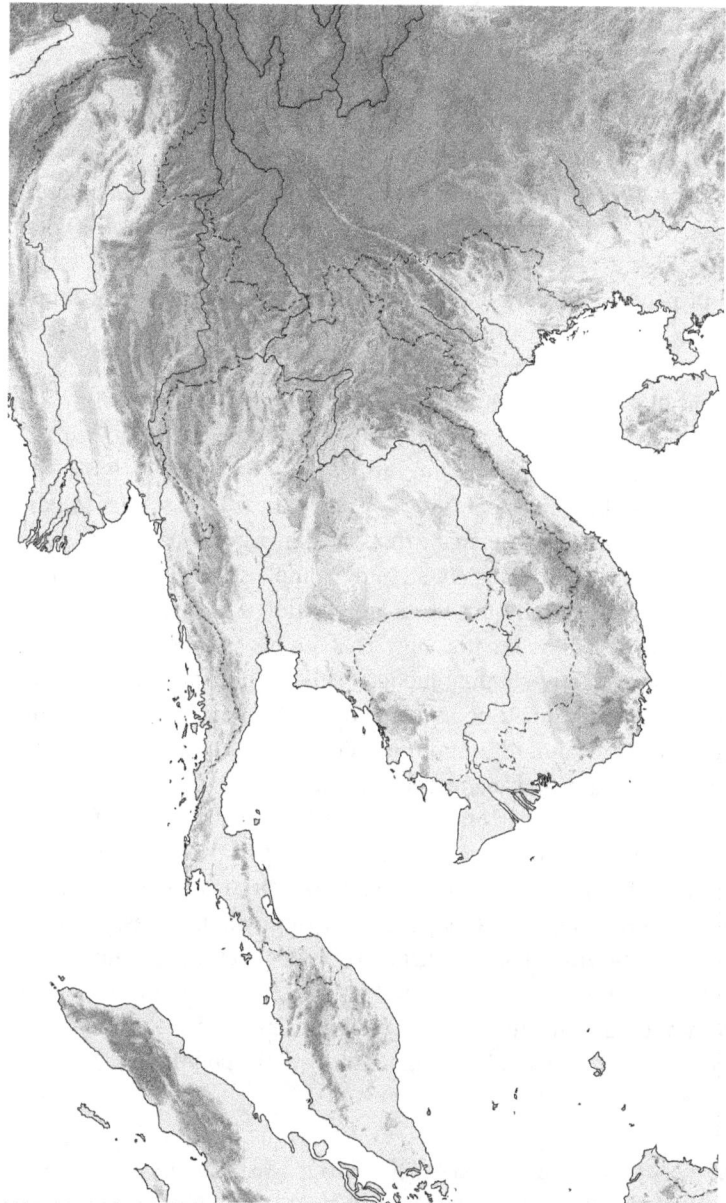

Map 2: Core mainland Southeast Asia: present day Cambodia, Laos, Vietnam, Thailand, and neighbouring parts of China, Malaysia, and Myanmar.

A widely accepted view is that the people of MSEA once spoke Austroasiatic languages in a 'continuous distribution', and that this distribution was 'broken up by the historical expansions of the Chinese, Tai, Vietnamese, Burman and Austronesian (Malay and Cham) peoples' (Bellwood 1992: 109; cf. Sidwell and Blench 2011: 338 and passim; Post 2011). By what mechanism did this take place? Some have argued that modern ethnolinguistic diversification in MSEA was associated with demic diffusion (Bellwood 1992; Blust 1994; Higham 2002; Edmondson and Gregerson 2007). This implies the incoming migration of groups of people who rely on agriculture, and who can thereby support large populations. The incomers replace less populous and less powerful existing forager populations (Ammerman and Cavalli-Sforza 1971; Cavalli-Sforza, Menozzi, and Piazza 1993; Nichols 1992).[1] An alternative to demic diffusion is cultural diffusion, whereby resident populations remain in place, but adopt new practices and ways of speaking. According to O'Connor (1995: 987), 'there is no direct evidence that an actual influx of immigrants ever displaced earlier peoples' in MSEA. He argues instead that an 'agricultural paradigm' is what diffused, bringing with it a 'society-shaping complex' (see Jonsson 2011, 2014 for discussion). For other critiques of the application of a demic diffusion model in MSEA see White (2011) on the view that hunter-gatherer communities have played a central role in shaping modern MSEA ethnographic diversity, and Fix (2011) on the genetics of ethnolinguistic diversification, in which he presents an alternative to the standard account of demic diffusion in the Malay Peninsula, with a model he calls *trickle-effect colonization*.

Regardless of whether one thinks the historical process of peopling and ethnolinguistic diversification in MSEA was driven primarily by the spread of people or by the spread of ideas—here, more work is needed—the modern distribution of ethnolinguistic groups is clear. In lowland areas, populations are denser, more culturally and linguistically homogeneous, and more closely affiliated with state political power. In upland areas, populations are sparser, more culturally and linguistically diverse, and have limited if any access to infrastructure, education, or power. The dominant lowland populations are clearly dis-

---

[1] Demic diffusion is the spread of genes. It is usually associated with the outcomes of migration. In world history, this has often involved the movement of groups who have adopted agriculture, and who are therefore more populous and viable than those (e.g., hunter-gatherers) who are resident in the area being entered. Demic diffusion may be associated with population displacement or replacement, but this need not necessarily be the case. There may be genetic admixture between an incoming population and a resident population, such that some fraction of the genes of the resident population survives. We are grateful to Mark Stoneking and Dan Dediu for clarification of these points.

tinct from each other in terms of political identity ('the Thai' vs. 'the Lao' vs. 'the Khmer', etc.), but the upland minority populations that straddle these nations have something in common: they are politically and geographically marginalized.

The upland areas in which many MSEA minorities live are conjoined in a single, elongated area, crossing political borders and encompassing 'virtually all the lands at altitudes above roughly three hundred meters all the way from the Central Highlands of Vietnam to northeastern India' (Scott 2009: ix). This area has been referred to as *Zomia*, a term coined by Van Schendel (2002) in making the point that arbitrary research areas can be constructed and reified by 'academic politics', as he puts it (cf. Michaud 2010). Van Schendel's proposal of a Zomia area is a conceptual exercise, useful because it counteracts the politically sanctioned alternatives. The term has gained some recognition (though ironically not without danger of creating the reification it was warning against; Jonsson 2011, 2014), particularly due to Scott (2009). According to Scott, it is not that the inhabitants of Zomia simply share the fate of having been marginalized by states. Instead, he argues, they share a cultural distaste for being governed: they have chosen to remain isolated from central government control.

We do not have space in this introduction for more on the detailed history of human activity—peopling and migration, social contact and cultural shift, state formation and avoidance, war and peace—in MSEA. For further information, see Tarling (1993), Scott (2009), and Enfield (2011a).

2 Mainland Southeast Asian languages

The degree of linguistic diversity in MSEA (i.e., the number of languages per square km) is high (Enfield 2011b), and it is highest in upland areas. Lower language density in lowland areas is likely related in part to geographical factors and their implications for the nature of social networks (see Nettle 1999). In historical demographic processes of the kinds noted above, formerly diverse lowland communities in MSEA have become homogenized by a combination of two processes. One process was ethnolinguistic shift. Some groups stayed where they were but stopped passing on their languages and identities to their children, instead adopting the languages and identities of new dominant groups. This process can be observed all over MSEA today. Another process was out-migration, typically to more isolated hill areas (Scott 2009). Geographical isolation is a force that still promotes language diversity in the region, where former diversity of lowland areas is on its last legs. Many of the lowland languages are heavily endangered or extinct (Enfield 2006, Bradley 2007, Suwilai 2007). This is quickened by effects of the concentration of political power of modern nation states in the lowlands. In recent decades, processes of language standardization in MSEA nations (Simpson 2007) have helped to heavily reduce language diversity.

The languages of MSEA are from five major language families: Sino-Tibetan, Tai-Kadai, Hmong-Mien, Austroasiatic, and Austronesian.[2] There are nearly 600 distinct languages spoken in greater MSEA.[3] If we exclude the China and India data, thus representing the core MSEA area, the number of languages is about half this amount; see Table 1.

Table 1: A breakdown of numbers of languages in MSEA, separated into language families.

	Core MSEA	Greater MSEA
Austroasiatic	122 (44%)	138 (24%)
Sino-Tibetan	74 (26%)	288 (49%)
Tai-Kadai	51 (18%)	93 (16%)
Austronesian	25 (9%)	26 (4%)
Hmong-Mien	8 (3%)	38 (7%)
Total	280	583

The very high linguistic diversity (i.e., the number of languages) in northeast India and southern/southwestern China adds dramatically to the number of languages included in the area. It also reverses the relative proportion of Sino-Tibetan and Austroasiatic languages.

The MSEA area is unusual in global terms in that there is good agreement among scholars as to the basic language family affiliation of known languages. There are unresolved issues about lower level subgroupings and there are unre-

---

[2] The Andamanese languages are located just outside MSEA as defined here; though we note with interest new work on these lesser-known languages: see Abbi's recent reference grammar (2012) and dictionary (2013) of Great Andamanese.
[3] Data are from glottolog.org, accessed in May 2014. Many thanks to Harald Hammarström for his input and assistance. Core MSEA was defined for this count as Cambodia, Laos, Myanmar, Thailand, and Vietnam; Greater MSEA included this, along with Peninsular Malaysia, areas of India east of 90 degrees (i.e., the states of Arunachal Pradesh, Nagaland, Manipur, Mizoram, Assam, Meghalaya, and Tripura) and China south of the Yangtze river (specifically, the provinces of Zhejiang, Jiangxi, Hunan, Guizhou, Yunnan, Guangxi, Guangdong, Fujian, and Hainan).

solved hypotheses about possible macro-groupings. But for every known language, scholars agree as to which of the five main language families it fits into. This is unusual firstly because it means that each language's basic affiliation is apparently uncontroversial, and secondly because it suggests that there are no language isolates (Blench 2011: 125-126).[4] For a survey of the historical linguistic background, see Sidwell (2013).

Following is a list of some of the typological features that characterize MSEA languages (drawing mostly from Enfield 2005: 186-190, 2011b: 69-70; see further references there):

Sound system features

- Large vowel systems (it is sometimes difficult to determine how many vowels a system has; there are alternative analyses of features such as diphthongs and phonation splits).
- Common underlying structure of vowel phoneme system (often 9-place, symmetrical; hi-mid-low by front-central-back).
- Long versus short vowel distinctions.
- Many more consonants are possible in initial position than in final position; syllables have an initial-and-rhyme structure.
- Preference for one (major) syllable per word, with many languages featuring minor syllables or pre-syllables in an iambic pattern (see chapters of this volume by Pittayaporn, Butler, Post, and Brunelle and Kirby).
- Lexical contrast is marked by laryngeal features including pitch and phonation type, often in combination; tone systems are complex (number of tones ranges from 4 to 15 in number, with counts for a language differing depending on the analysis chosen); phonation type systems usually distinguish two registers, e.g., 'clear' versus 'breathy'; lexically contrastive pitch and phonation type are strongly correlated in functional and historical terms.
- Gap in voiced stop series at velar place of articulation (no voiced 'g').

---

4 Not considered in this chapter are sign languages. The sign language used in Ban Khor, Thailand (Nonaka 2004) appears to be an isolate, and there are surely more of its kind. Among spoken languages in MSEA there is Kenaboi, now extinct, and known only from two early 20th century word lists. Hajek (1998) refers to Kenaboi as 'unclassified' but does not call it an isolate. Benjamin (2006) summarizes and analyses the available data as far as is possible. His view is that Kenaboi is 'a specially-invented form of speech', a 'taboo-jargon' associated with forest collecting trade. Kenaboi had large proportions of both Austroasiatic and Austronesian vocabulary, along with some unexplained forms. The data are too tenuous to establish whether it was an isolate or not.

Morphosyntax-semantics system features

- No inflectional morphology (no case, gender, number, or definiteness marked on noun phrases, no agreement or tense-marking on verbs); note that *derivational* morphology is widespread and sometimes highly productive in Austroasiatic languages of MSEA (see Alves this volume).
- Open class items—mostly nouns and verbs—serve functions that are expressed by dedicated functional morphemes (including bound morphology) in other languages, e.g., nominals as prepositions, verbs as aspect markers, comparative markers, adversative passive markers, and valence-changing devices (Clark and Prasithrathsint 1985; Kölver 1991; Ansaldo 1999).
- Widespread use of verb serialisation (meaning a range of different kinds of predicative structures that use combinations of verbs), with a rich array of types and functions in each language (Bisang 1991).
- Order of major constituents of the clause tends to be relatively flexible within languages, sensitive to pragmatic factors (though verb-object constituent order is dominant); noun phrases tend to be left-headed, and may have discontinuous constituents, especially when classifiers are involved.
- Zero anaphora: noun phrases may be ellipsed when their referents are contextually retrievable (this combined with flexibility in constituent order results in quite variable surface options; for a case study see Enfield 2007: 271-284).
- Extensive use of topic-comment structure in clauses.
- Large set of labile or ambitransitive verbs, especially of the causative/inchoative or unaccusative type (e.g., Lao *hak2* can mean transitive 'snap' or intransitive 'is/has been snapped').
- Rich inventories of sentence-final particles that make subtle distinctions in sentence type, stance, evidentiality, and combinations thereof.
- Rich inventories of ideophones (or 'expressives') and other expressive forms, including rhyming four-syllable expressions, and productive elaborative rhyming devices.
- Numeral classifiers and related systems of nominal classification (see Blench this volume).
- Complex pronominal systems, with multi-level social-deictic meanings.

Some of the most noteworthy commonalities among MSEA languages concern their *lack* of marking of certain semantico-grammatical categories. Most notably, as remarked upon in the list above, the languages almost entirely lack inflectional morphology in the usual sense of that term (i.e., including agreement, case, gender/number/definiteness on noun phrases, tense-marking on verbs). For an overview of selected national languages, see Comrie (1990), while Goddard (2005) presents a more topic-oriented approach; see also Vittrant and Watkins (forthcoming).

3 Linguistics of MSEA: New developments

This book presents new developments in linguistics of the MSEA area, but it is not our intention to offer a general or comprehensive review of all current work. In this section, we briefly discuss a few ways in which MSEA linguistics has progressed in recent years.

3.1 Conferences and publications

The community of scholars working on MSEA linguistics is steadily growing. The South East Asia Linguistic Society (SEALS)—founded by Martha Ratliff and Eric Schiller at Wayne State University, Detroit, in 1990—will hold its 25th annual meeting in 2015. Prior to 2009, proceedings of SEALS meetings were published in edited volumes. Since then they have appeared in the open-access *Journal of the Southeast Asian Linguistics Society* (for which, see http://www.jseals.org/). The SEAlang Projects website (http://www.sealang.net) is an invaluable resource that makes accessible a range of primary and secondary sources on MSEA languages. Other regular publishing venues for research on MSEA languages include the journals *Mon-Khmer Studies* (an open-access journal, see http://www.mksjournal.org/) and *Linguistics of the Tibeto-Burman Area* (see http://sealang.net/sala/ltba/htm/index.htm). Some recent interdisciplinary explorations of ethnolinguistic diversification have focused on languages of MSEA and neighbouring places (e.g., Sagart, Blench, and Sanchez-Maras 2005; Enfield 2011a). The last 10 years have seen the publication of multiple landmark overviews of MSEA language families, including Tai-Kadai (Diller, Edmondson, and Luo 2008), Sino-Tibetan (Thurgood and LaPolla 2003; cf. Matisoff 2003a), Austroasiatic (Jenny and Sidwell in press; cf. Shorto 2006), and the Austronesian languages of MSEA (Thurgood 1999; Grant and Sidwell 2005; Larish 2005; Blust 2013b: 70-75).

3.2 New descriptive work

A key measure of progress in an area is the production of reference materials based on new empirical research.[5] Full-sized descriptions of MSEA languages published since the turn of the century include grammars of Semelai (Kruspe 2004), Jahai (Burenhult 2005), Garo (Burling 2004), Deuri (Jacquesson 2004), Mongsen Ao (Coupe 2007), Lao (Enfield 2007), Anong (Sun and Liu 2009), Hainan Cham (Thurgood, Thurgood, and Li 2014), Turung (Morey 2010), the Tai languages of Assam (Morey 2005), Lisu (Yu 2007), Thai (Higbie and Thinsan 2003; Iwasaki and Ingkaphirom Horie 2005) and Cambodian (Haiman 2011). Numerous grammars have been completed as PhD dissertations; just in the area of northeast India, for example, see grammars of Galo (Post 2007), Atong (van Breugel 2014), and Karbi (Konnerth 2014). Sketches or partial descriptions have appeared on languages including Pacoh (Alves 2006), Kri (Enfield and Diffloth 2009), and Arem (Ferlus 2014), and detailed descriptions have appeared of specific domains of grammar such as phonetics/phonology; see for example Watkins (2002) on Wa and Coupe (2003) on Ao. Major dictionaries of minority languages are less abundant; two notable examples are Watkins (2013) on Wa and Svantesson et al. (2013) on Kammu Yùan. An important preoccupation of descriptive linguistics globally is the documentation of endangered languages; for excellent examples of new empirical work with this orientation in the MSEA context, see Morey (2005, 2010; see also Suwilai 1998, 2008).

A significant amount of new data and analysis from MSEA languages has become available on most if not all domains of interest to linguists, and on most if not all language families and sub-areas of MSEA. As just one example, here we mention the Aslian languages of Peninsular Malaysia. In the last decade or so, we have seen the publication of typological overviews of the Aslian languages as a group (Matisoff 2003b), new reference grammars (Kruspe 2004; Burenhult 2005), other descriptive materials (Burenhult and Wegener 2009; Wnuk forthcoming), new interdisciplinary research on the history and diversification of ethnolinguistic subgroups (Burenhult, Kruspe, and Dunn 2011; Dunn et al. 2011; Bulbeck 2011; Fix 2011; Oppenheimer 2011; Dunn, Kruspe, and Bu-

---

[5] We mention here only a selection of those recent materials that are published in English, though we note that a substantial descriptive literature on MSEA languages is being published in other languages, including Chinese, French, Indonesian, Thai, and Vietnamese (for some examples, see: Bo 2002; Bon 2014; Buakaw 2012; Chen 2005; Gai 2002; Giaphong 2004; Kosaka 2000; D. Li 2003, 2004; Y. Li 2003; Lidz 2010; Mao, Zongwu, and Yunbing Li 2002, 2007; Mayuree 2006; Ploykaew 2001; Samarina 2011; Seng Mai 2012; Shee 2008; Shintani 2008; Srisakorn 2008; Wayesha 2010).

renhult 2013), and field research on the psychological implications of semantic systems that are indigenous to Aslian languages and world views (Burenhult and Majid 2011; Majid and Burenhult 2014; Wnuk and Majid 2014). Not only is this breadth and depth of new work improving our basic understanding of MSEA languages and their socio-historical contexts, it is also helping to balance our perspective on the MSEA area, with effects on our image of what a Southeast Asian language is typically like (see below). The availability of new descriptive materials means that we can progress in the field by testing existing proposals and by continuously expanding the scope of our work (see Pittayaporn 2009 for a good illustration of this point).

3.3 New methods

As new methods in linguistic research are being developed and applied in linguistics globally, so they are being developed and applied in mainland Southeast Asia. In phonetics and phonology, for example, new instrumental and computational technologies are rapidly transforming the realms of possibility in data collection and analysis, both by making new kinds of measurement possible, and by making the equipment smaller and more portable for fieldwork; see Edmondson and Esling (2006: 172-175) for the use of laryngoscopy to study the phonetics of breathy vocal register in Jianchuan Bai (spoken in Yunnan), and Brunelle (2009) for the use of electroglottography to study register in Cham dialects in Vietnam (see also Brunelle, Nguyễn, and Nguyễn 2010 on Northern Vietnamese). Newly-developed statistical techniques are being applied with interesting results: in historical linguistics, probability-based bioinformatic techniques are being used for exploring cladistic representations of language relatedness (see for example Burenhult, Kruspe, and Dunn 2011); and in areal typology, statistical modelling is being used to test dependencies among phonological features, language history, and language contact (Brunelle and Kirby this volume). In lexical and grammatical work, new field methods are being applied in the exploration of semantic fields, in a range of functional and conceptual domains (see, for example Burenhult 2006; Wnuk and Majid 2014; Enfield 2015). There is an increasing interest in combining methods in order to further our knowledge of the area's languages, for example in the interdisciplinary collaborations of historical work (Sagart et al. 2005; van Driem 2007; Enfield 2011a). And computational power is being exploited in building larger and better databases of, or including, MSEA languages (Dryer and Haspelmath 2013; Donohue et al. 2013).

3.4 Historical-comparative linguistics

Research in historical-comparative linguistics continues apace in MSEA. At the level of sub-grouping, advances are being made in all the major language families. Old hypotheses are being tested with new data and techniques, and new hypotheses are being put forward. The appearance of new data, in particular, has made an important difference, enabling, for example, Pittayaporn (2009) to propose a new reconstruction of Proto-Southwestern-Tai phonology, Sidwell (2009) to offer an improved account of vowels in Proto-Mon-Khmer, and Matisoff (this volume; cf. Matisoff 2003a) to re-examine the place of the Jingpho language within Tibeto-Burman. In research on historical Hmong-Mien, Ratliff (2010) has recently provided an assessment of previous work and offers substantial new reconstructions, with consideration of their implications. Historical Austroasiatic has seen substantial developments, including a suspension of the assumption of a highest-level split between Munda and Mon-Khmer. It is no longer widely assumed that 'Mon-Khmer languages' represent descendants of a single ancestor language below Proto-Austroasiatic (although the term is still useful with the meaning 'non-Munda Austroasiatic languages'; for a range of perspectives on this, see discussion in Sidwell and Blench 2011; Diffloth 2011; Sagart 2011; and Van Driem 2011). Similarly, in Sino-Tibetan linguistics, assumptions are being questioned. For example, recent reconsiderations of the position of Chinese in the family have assigned it to a lower-level subgroup rather than the standard placement as a high major branch; more subgroups of Sino-Tibetan are identified, and the time-depth of reconstructed proto-Sinitic is pushed back to well before Old Chinese (Blench and Post 2013; Van Driem 2013).

3.5 Language in social life

Numerous lines of work in linguistics deal with the role of language in social life. An important theme in recent work in MSEA is the sociolinguistics of language endangerment, and associated issues including language protection and revitalization; for an example, see Phattharathanit (2012) on identity maintenance in Lanna (cf. Bradley 2007, Suwilai 2007). Research on linguistic politeness continues, mostly in relation to national languages, and with reference to the languages' elaborated systems of social deixis, for example in their systems of personal pronouns, and the pragmatic alternatives that effectively create open class systems for person reference (Cooke 1968; Haas 1969; Luong 1990; Enfield 2015: Ch. 5). The more complex documented systems of person reference are those belonging to the major literate languages of the area, including Thai, Cambodian, Vietnamese, and Burmese (Cooke 1968). There has been recent work in this domain on languages including Lao (Enfield 2007: Ch. 5, 2015: Ch. 5). On Vietnamese, see Sophana (2008) on politeness strategies, and Sidnell and Shohet (2013) on avoidance strategies (see also Luong 1988). Linking social life to central concerns of historical linguistics and typology, there has been recent work on sociolinguistic conditions for borrowing (Alves 2009); for similar work see Thurgood (2010) comparing two varieties of Cham with the Tibeto-Burman language Anong. A new line of work in MSEA is conversation analysis; Enfield (2013) presents several case studies of Lao language in conversation; Hạ (2010, 2013) presents studies of Vietnamese conversation with a focus on the role of prosody, for example in repair and backchannelling (see also Umaporn 2007 on backchannelling in Mon).

3.6 Changing perceptions

Like in any area, linguistics in MSEA is subject to preconceptions. As soon as an idea becomes something of an orthodoxy it is right to revisit and question it. We are pleased that several chapters in this book raise and sometimes challenge certain assumptions about the linguistics of this area.

3.6.1 The idea of a typical MSEA language

Comrie (2007: 45) finds that, on measures taken using data from the *World Atlas of Language Structures* (Haspelmath et al. 2005), 'Thai turns out to be the most typical of the three major national languages of Mainland Southeast Asia considered here.'[6] This conclusion is shared by Dahl (2008). This of course does not mean that Thai is the most typical of all MSEA languages, although this is often assumed to be the case. The national languages of the area are the better-described and better-known languages, and they happen to share many typological features that characterize Thai, such as a tendency for monosyllabicity, a lack of productive affixation, and an elaborate numeral classifier system. But there are many MSEA languages whose properties differ from these and many other properties found in Thai and other national languages like Vietnamese. In

---

[6] The idea that a language may be 'typical' of an area seems to be an intuitive one, but the relevant sense in which a language can be said to be typical is seldom defined.

fact, many languages of the area lack these features. Within MSEA linguistics one's view of what is typical may depend on one's academic background, and, especially, on which language one worked on first, or has worked on most, in one's research career. If, for example, one's earliest and most in-depth work on MSEA languages was on Lao (as is the case with the first author here), then languages like Lao and Thai would seem typical. They are typologically very similar to other major languages like Vietnamese. Another researcher's background would suggest otherwise. The viewpoint professed by our colleague Gérard Diffloth is that a typical MSEA language lacks lexical tone, has complex phonotactics including syllable-initial consonant clusters, and has productive derivational morphology, quite a contrast from the oft-cited set of features of MSEA languages (see Henderson 1965; Capell 1979; Suwilai 1987; Kruspe 2004; cf. Alves 2001, this volume). The problem with treating the area's major national languages as reference points is not only that they are a tiny sample but that they are known to be not like the rest, due to factors including (1) they are spoken by very large, often urbanized populations, (2) they are spoken as second languages by large sections of the population, (3) they are official languages, used in major education systems, media and broadcasting, and legal documents.

3.6.2 Nominal classification

MSEA is often cited in typologies of nominal classification as an area that has numeral classifiers (cf. Grinevald 2000; Aikhenvald 2000). Recent research shows that systems of nominal classification in MSEA can be more complex than this. They not only contain the classic numeral classifier type, consisting of a large set of classificatory nominals that are used whenever something is being numerated, but also systems that resemble the *noun class* systems found widely in Africa and the Amazon, and ancillary systems that resemble numeral classifiers but which are involved in the use of more simple modifiers such as demonstratives and specifiers. Enfield (2007: 119-156) shows that in Lao there are in fact four distinct grammatical systems of nominal classification, of which numeral classifiers are one (see Blench this volume).

3.6.3 Sesquisyllables

Researchers of the sound structure of words in MSEA languages often refer to the idea of 'sesquisyllables' and even the property of 'sesquisyllabicity'. This term was introduced by Matisoff (1973) to refer to the 'one-and-a-half syllable' form of words found in many MSEA languages (see Henderson 1952; Shorto 1960, and the chapters by Butler and by Pittayaporn in this volume). The term has not always been applied in an exact or consistent way. In a narrow sense, it can refer specifically to a syllable with schwa epenthesis between elements of an initial consonant cluster; that is, a syllable whose onset is phonologically /CC/ but phonetically [CᵊC]. In a broad sense, it can refer to any word that has an iambic structure, with the main stressed syllable coming at the end. Consider the following three words in Kri (Enfield and Diffloth 2009): /cakaaŋ/ [caka:ŋ] 'to measure something by handspans', /ckaaŋ/ [cᵊka:ŋ] 'a hand span', and /caaŋ/ [ca:ŋ] 'buttress of a tree' (or /kaaŋʔ/ [ka:ŋʔ] 'chin/jaw'). In the broad sense, both /cakaaŋ/ [caka:ŋ] and /ckaaŋ/ [cᵊka:ŋ] are sesquisyllabic, while in the narrow sense, only /ckaaŋ/ [cᵊka:ŋ] is. In this book we include two chapters—those by Butler and by Pittayaporn—that make a significant advance here not only by insisting that we be consistent and precise in the use of such terms, but by turning to empirical and theoretical accounts in order to offer motivated solutions, making the intuitive idea of sesquisyllabicity accountable to current theory and data in theoretical phonology and articulatory phonetics. Butler calls for more thoughtful consideration of the terms, and seeks to make progress by holding certain phonological ideas of syllable structure accountable to phonetic behaviour that can be experimentally tested. Pittayaporn takes a broader comparative approach to the problem, offering a typology of sesquisyllabic languages, defining the distinct meanings that this term can have.

3.6.4 Tone phonetics and phonology

An oft-cited feature of MSEA languages is that many of them are tone languages. When asked what this means, most linguists would agree with Yip (2002:1): 'A language is a "tone language" if the pitch of the word can change the meaning of the word.' But as linguists of MSEA languages since Henderson (1952, 1965, 1967) have insisted, it is wrong to think that *pitch* is the sole or defining feature of a tone system in MSEA (see the chapters by Brunelle and Kirby and by Sidwell in this volume; see also Abramson and L-Thongkum 2009): 'It is important to recognize that pitch is frequently only one of the phonetic components of "tone" as a phonological category. ... A phonological tone is in our area very frequently a complex of other features besides pitch—such as intensity, duration, voice quality, final glottal constriction and so on.' (Henderson 1967: 171). From this perspective, while tone and phonation type are sometimes considered to be distinct phonological organizations, they should instead be treated as instances of a single sound system property insofar as they each involve the use of laryngeal features for lexical contrast. Pitch contours, distinctions in phonation, and other glottalic effects are all produced in the larynx, by the vocal folds, and are all articulatorily independent of segmental speech sounds produced with the lips, teeth, and tongue (i.e., consonants). Tone and phonation are intimately bound, and not essentially distinct. For this reason we recognize that the sound system of an MSEA 'tone' language such as Vietnamese is not of a different species from that of a classical MSEA 'register' or 'phonation type' language such as Kri (Enfield and Diffloth 2009). Most systems that are identified as one or the other (in phonological terms) actually display properties of both (in phonetic terms).

3.6.5 MSEA as a linguistic area

In research on areal linguistics, a great deal of new empirical and conceptual work from around the world has improved our understanding of historical processes of ethnolinguistic diversification, contact, and convergence, while at the same time some of the basic tenets of areal linguistics have come under question (Stolz 2002; Muysken 2008). MSEA has been widely regarded as a classic linguistic area with close parallelism in structure between neighbouring languages that have no demonstrable common ancestor (see Henderson 1965; Capell 1979; Clark 1989; Matisoff 1991; Bisang 1991; Enfield 2005; Comrie 2007; Dahl 2008; Vittrant and Watkins forthcoming). The cause of this parallelism is widely assumed to be language contact. While several chapters in this volume examine typological parallels across language families and interpret these as evidence of effects from language contact, the chapters by Sidwell, Ratliff, and Brunelle and Kirby call for caution in jumping to that conclusion. If neighbouring but unrelated languages share typological features this can also be a result of parallel language-internal development (cf. Thurgood 1998; Enfield 2005). That possibility is equally deserving of consideration, and so the idea that convergence is due to contact should not be assumed without question.

4 Summary preview of this book

We have organized the 13 chapters of this book into four parts, as follows.

Part 1: Language relatedness in MSEA. The four chapters of Part 1 address the issue of language relatedness, which can be either a result of contact, or of shared inheritance of features from a common ancestor. Three of the chapters address a central problem for areal linguistics discussed in the last section, namely the overly seductive nature of language contact as an explanation for parallel structure observed in languages which are not genealogically related. Careful case studies are presented, each in a domain of phonology. Ratliff shows that word initial prenasalization can emerge independently in unrelated languages from common causes in syllable-level processes ('front-end collapse', related to sesquisyllabicity, treated in Part 3). Sidwell makes the point with regard to cases of tonogenesis/registrogenesis and their systemic relation to syllable structure. Brunelle and Kirby explore the example of tone typology and the parallel occurrence of tonogenesis in the languages of the area, making the case that language-internal processes are at work. In the last chapter of Part 1 on language relatedness, Matisoff addresses the issue of determining internal relations between subgroups of a language family, with a fine-grained case study of the relationship between Jingpho and the Luish group of languages.[7]

Part 2: Boundaries of the MSEA area. Part 2 explores ways in which the borders of an MSEA linguistic area may be rightly thought to extend beyond the core MSEA area shown in Map 1, above; it brings four chapters together that look at extensions in four directions: Jenny to the west in Myanmar, Post to the north west in India, Gil to the south east in Insular Southeast Asia and West Papua, and de Sousa to the north and north east in China.

Part 3: Defining the sesquisyllable. In Part 3, two chapters concentrate on the category of 'sesquisyllabicity', a widely-used term, but one that is often vague or ambiguous in meaning. Both Butler and Pittayaporn raise the bar considerably, insisting that the term be used in a way that is grounded in theory, experimentation, and clear definitions, rather than meaning something roughly like 'has iambic syllables'. Pittayaporn proposes a typology of sesquisyllabic languages.

Part 4: Explorations in MSEA morphosyntax. Part 4 offers explorations in the morphosyntax of MSEA languages: Alves surveys the rich morphological marking found in Mon-Khmer languages of core MSEA (i.e., non-Munda languages of the Austroasiatic family); Blench examines the origins of nominal classification, responding to a new understanding of this domain as being richer than merely numeral classifiers, and looking at underlying processes by

---

[7] Note that there is an online-only appendix to Matisoff's chapter, available at the book's webpage: http://www.degruyter.com/view/product/449361

means of a comparison with some African languages; and Vittrant looks into the semantico-grammatical typology of motion event expression, assessing the contribution of MSEA languages to the global typology of motion events.

These studies are of course just a thin slice of the rich, diverse, and substantial work that is currently being produced in MSEA linguistics. But we think that the chapters of this book convey a sense of the state of the art in this field, of where MSEA linguistics is at, and where it is heading. And while much progress has been made, there is of course much to be done. There are hundreds of languages in the area, and thousands of research questions that need answering. We have much to look forward to in the coming years of research on the languages of mainland Southeast Asia.

Acknowledgements

We gratefully acknowledge financial support from the Max Planck Institute for Evolutionary Anthropology (Department of Linguistics), the Max Planck Institute for Psycholinguistics (Language and Cognition Department), and the European Research Council (through grant 240853 'Human Sociality and Systems of Language Use'). The editors co-convened a conference on the book's theme, held at MPI EvA in Leipzig, 29 November to 1 December, 2012. We are grateful to Julia Cissewski and Claudia Bavero for their organizational assistance in Leipzig, and to Julija Baranova for her help in Nijmegen. We thank Maarten van den Heuvel for his tireless and brilliant formatting and technical assistance in preparing the manuscript for publication, and Angela Terrill at Punctilious Editing (http://www.punctilious.net/) for first-class copy-editing and indexing. For comments and suggestions on a draft of this introduction, we thank Roger Blench, Jeremy Collins, Mark Donohue, David Gil, Pittayawat Pittayaporn, Mark Post, Martha Ratliff, and Paul Sidwell. Finally, we thank all the contributing authors for their patience and input, as well as all those who attended and contributed to the workshop, especially Christian Bauer, Walter Bisang, and Niclas Burenhult.

References

Abbi, Anvita. 2012. *Dictionary of the Great Andamanese language: English - Great Andamanese - Hindi*. Delhi: Ratna Sagar.
Abbi, Anvita. 2013. *A grammar of the Great Andamanese language: An ethnolinguistic study*. Leiden: Brill Academic.

Abramson, Arthur S. & Theraphan L-Thongkum. 2009. A fuzzy boundary between tone languages and voice-register languages. In G. Fant, H. Fujisaki & J. Shen (eds.), *Frontiers in phonetics and speech science*, 149-155. Bejing: The Commercial Press.

Adelaar, Alexander & Nikolaus P. Himmelmann. 2005. *The Austronesian languages of Asia and Madagascar*. London: RoutledgeCurzon.

Aikhenvald, Alexandra Y. 2000. *Classifiers: a typology of noun categorization devices*. Oxford: Oxford University Press.

Alves, Mark J. 2001. What's so Chinese about Vietnamese? In Graham W. Thurgood (ed.), *Papers from the Ninth Annual Meeting of the Southeast Asian Linguistics Society*. 221–242. Phoenix: Arizona State University.

Alves, Mark J. 2006. *A grammar of Pacoh: A Mon-Khmer language of the central highlands of Vietnam* (Shorter Grammars). Canberra: Pacific Linguistics.

Alves, Mark. J. 2009. Sino-Vietnamese grammatical vocabulary and sociolinguistic conditions for borrowing. *Journal of the Southeast Asian Linguistics Society* 1. 1–9.

Ammerman, A. J. & L. L. Cavalli-Sforza. 1971. Measuring the rate of spread of early farming in Europe. *Man* 6(4). 674–688.

Ansaldo, Umberto. 1999. *Comparative constructions in Sinitic: areal typology and patterns of grammaticalisation*. Stockholm: Stockholm University dissertation

Ansaldo, Umberto & Stephen J. Matthews. 2001. Typical Creoles and simple languages: The case of Sinitic. *Linguistic Typology* 5(2/3). 311–24.

Bauer, Robert S. 1996. Identifying the Tai substratum in Cantonese. In *Pan-Asiatic linguistics: Proceedings of the Fourth International Symposium on Languages and Linguistics* V, 1806-1844. Bangkok: Mahidol University.

Bellwood, P. 1992. Southeast Asia before prehistory. In N. Tarling (ed.), *The Cambridge history of Southeast Asia: from early times to c. 1800* (Vol.1). New York: Cambridge University Press.

Benjamin, Geoffrey. 2006. Hervey's "Kenaboi": lost Malayan language or forest-collecting taboo jargon? Manuscript.

Bisang, Walter. 1991. Verb serialization, grammaticalization and attractor positions in Chinese, Hmong, Vietnamese, Thai and Khmer. In Hansjakob Seiler & Waldfried Premper (eds.), *Partizipation: Das sprachliche Erfassen von Sachverhalten*, 509–62. Tübingen: Gunter Narr Verlag.

Blench, Roger. 2011. The role of agriculture in the evolution of Mainland Southeast Asian language phyla. In N.J. Enfield (ed.), Dynamics of human diversity: The case of mainland Southeast Asia, 125–152. Canberra: Pacific Linguistics.

Blench, R. & M. W. Post. 2013. Re-thinking Sino-Tibetan phylogeny from the perspective of North East Indian languages. In N. Hill & T. Owen-Smith (eds.), *Trans-Himalayan linguistics*, 71–104. Berlin: Mouton de Gruyter.

Blust, Robert. 1994. The Austronesian settlement of Mainland Southeast Asia. In Karen L. Adams & Thomas John Hudak (eds.), *Papers from the Second Annual Meeting of the Southeast Asian Linguistics Society*, 25–83. Tempe, AZ: Arizona State University.

Blust, Robert. 2013a. Southeast Asian islands and Oceania: Austronesian linguistic history. In Peter Bellwood (ed.), *The encyclopedia of global human migration. Volume 1: Prehistory*. Oxford: Wiley-Blackwell.

Blust, Robert. 2013b. *The Austronesian languages (revised edition)*. Canberra: Asia-Pacific Linguistics.

Bo, Wenze. 2002. *A study of Mulao*. Beijing: The Nationalities Press.

Bon, Noëllie. 2014. *Une grammaire de la langue stieng, langue en danger du Cambodge et du Vietnam*. Lyon: Université Lumière Lyon 2 dissertation.
Bradley, David. 1995. *Studies in Burmese languages* (Papers in Southeast Asian Linguistics 13). Canberra: Pacific Linguistics.
Bradley, David. 2007. Language endangerment in China and Mainland Southeast Asia. In Matthias Brenzinger (ed.), *Language diversity endangered* (Trends in Linguistics: Studies and Monographs), 278–302. Berlin: Mouton de Gruyter.
Breugel, Seino van. 2014. *A grammar of Atong*. Leiden: Brill.
Brunelle, Marc. 2009. Contact-induced change? Register in three Cham dialects. *Journal of the Southeast Asian Linguistics Society* 2. 1–22.
Brunelle Marc, Nguyễn Duy Dương & Nguyễn Khắc Hùng. 2010. A laryngographic and laryngoscopic study of Northern Vietnamese tones. *Phonetica* 67. 147-169.
Buakaw, Supakit. 2012. *A phonological study of Palaung dialects spoken in Thailand and Myanmar, with focuses on vowels and final nasals*. Bangkok: Mahidol University doctoral dissertation.
Bulbeck, David. 2011. Biological and cultural evolution in the population and culture history of Homo sapiens in Malaya. In N.J. Enfield (ed.), *Dynamics of human diversity: The case of mainland Southeast Asia*, 207–255. Canberra: Pacific Linguistics.
Burenhult, Niclas. 2005 *A grammar of Jahai*. Canberra: Pacific Linguistics.
Burenhult, Niclas. 2006. Body part terms in Jahai. *Language Sciences* 28. 162–180.
Burenhult, Niclas, N. Kruspe & M. Dunn. 2011. Language history and culture groups among Austroasiatic-speaking foragers of the Malay Peninsula. In N.J. Enfield (ed.), *Dynamics of human diversity: the case of Mainland Southeast Asia*, 257–275. Canberra: Pacific Linguistics.
Burenhult, Niclas & Asifa Majid. 2011. Olfaction in Aslian ideology and language. *The Senses and Society* 6(1). 19–29.
Burenhult, Niclas & Claudia Wegener. 2009. Preliminary notes on the phonology, orthography and vocabulary of Semnam (Austroasiatic, Malay Peninsula). *Journal of the Southeast Asian Linguistics Society* 1. 283–312.
Burling, Robbins. 2004. *The language of the Modhipur Mandi (Garo). Volume I: Grammar*. New Delhi: Bibliophile South Asia.
Capell, Arthur. 1979. Further typological studies in Southeast Asian languages. In Nguyen Dang Liem (ed.), *South-East Asian linguistic studies* (Vol. 3), 1–42. Canberra: Pacific Linguistics.
Cavalli-Sforza, L., P. Menozzi & A. Piazza. 1993. Demic expansions and human evolution. *Science* 259(5095). 639–646.
Chappell, Hilary. 2001. Language contact and areal diffusion in Sinitic languages. In Alexandra Y. Aikhenvald & R. M. W. Dixon (eds.), *Areal diffusion and genetic inheritance: Problems in comparative linguistics*, 328–57. Oxford: Oxford University Press.
Chappell, J. & N. J. Shackleton. 1986. Oxygen isotopes and sea level. *Nature* 324(6093). 137–140.
Chen, Guoqing. 2005. *Kemieyu yanjiu* [A study of Kemie]. Beijing: Minzu chubanshe.
Clark, Marybeth & Amara Prasithrathsint. 1985. Synchronic lexical derivation in Southeast Asian languages. In Suriya Ratanakul & Suwilai Premsrirat (eds.), *Southeast Asian linguistic studies presented to André-G. Haudricourt*, 34–81. Bangkok: Mahidol University.
Clark, Marybeth. 1989. Hmong and areal South-East Asia. In David Bradley (ed.), *Papers in Southeast Asian Linguistics No.11, Southeast Asian Syntax*, 175–230. Canberra: Pacific Linguistics.

Comrie, Bernard (ed.). 1990. *The major languages of East and South-East Asia*. London: Routledge.
Comrie, Bernard. 2007. Areal typology of mainland Southeast Asia: what we learn from the WALS maps. In Pranee Kullavanijaya (ed.), *Trends in Thai linguistics* [Manusya Special Issue 13], 18–47. Bangkok: Chulalongkorn University.
Cooke, Joseph R. 1968. *Pronominal reference in Thai, Burmese and Vietnamese*. Berkeley: University of California Press.
Coupe, A.R. 2003. *A phonetic and phonological description of Ao: a Tibeto-Burman language of Nagaland, north-east India*. Canberra: Pacific Linguistics.
Coupe, A. R. 2007. *A grammar of Mongsen Ao*. (Mouton Grammar Library 39). Berlin: Mouton de Gruyter.
Dahl, Östen. 2008. An exercise in 'a posteriori' language sampling. *Sprachtypologie Und Universalienforschung* 61(3). 208–20.
Diffloth, Gérard. 2011. Austroasiatic word histories: boat, husked rice and taro. In N.J. Enfield (ed.), *Dynamics of human diversity: The case of mainland Southeast Asia*, 295–313. Canberra: Pacific Linguistics.
Diller, Anthony V. N., Jerold A. Edmondson & Yongxian Luo. 2008. *The Tai-Kadai languages*. London: RoutledgeCurzon.
Donohue, Mark, Rebecca Hetherington, James McElvenny & Virginia Dawson. 2013. *World phonotactics database*. Canberra: Australian National University. http://phonotactics.anu.edu.au. (accessed July 2014).
Driem, George van. 2007. Austroasiatic phylogeny and the Austroasiatic homeland in light of recent population genetic studies. *Mon-Khmer Studies* 37. 1–14.
Driem, George van. 2011. Rice and the Austroasiatic and Hmong-Mien homelands. In N.J. Enfield (ed.), *Dynamics of human diversity: The case of mainland Southeast Asia*, 361–390. Canberra: Pacific Linguistics.
Driem, George van. 2013. Trans-Himalayan. In Nathan Hill & Tom Owen-Smith (eds.), *Trans-Himalayan linguistics*. Berlin: Mouton De Gruyter.
Dryer, Matthew S. & Martin Haspelmath (eds.). 2013. *The World Atlas of Language Structures Online*. Leipzig: Max Planck Institute for Evolutionary Anthropology. http://wals.info. (accessed July 2014).
Dunn, Michael, Niclas Burenhult, Nicole Kruspe, Sylvia Tufvesson & Neele Becker. 2011. Aslian linguistic prehistory: A case study in computational phylogenetics. *Diachronica* 28(3). 291–323.
Dunn, Michael, Nicole Kruspe & Niclas Burenhult. 2013. Time and place in the prehistory of the Aslian languages. *Human Biology* 85. 383–399.
Edmondson, Jerold A. & John H. Esling. 2006. The valves of the throat and their functioning in tone, vocal register and stress: laryngoscopic case studies. *Phonology* 23(2). 157-191.
Edmondson, Jerold A. & Kenneth J. Gregerson. 2007. The languages of Vietnam: Mosaics and expansions. *Language and Linguistics Compass* 1(6). 727–749.
Enfield, N. J. 2005. Areal linguistics and mainland Southeast Asia. *Annual Review of Anthropology* 34. 181–206.
Enfield, N. J. 2006. Languages as historical documents: The endangered archive in Laos. *South East Asia Research*, 14(3), 471-488.
Enfield, N. J. 2007. *A grammar of Lao*. (Mouton Grammar Library 38). Berlin: Mouton de Gruyter.

Enfield, N. J. (ed.). 2011a. *Dynamics of human diversity: the case of mainland Southeast Asia*. Canberra: Pacific Linguistics.

Enfield, N. J. 2011b. Linguistic diversity in mainland Southeast Asia. In N. J. Enfield (ed.), *Dynamics of human diversity: The case of mainland Southeast Asia*, 63–80. Canberra: Pacific Linguistics.

Enfield, N. J. & Gérard Diffloth. 2009. Phonology and sketch grammar of Kri, a Vietic language of Laos. *Cahiers de Linguistique - Asie Orientale* 38(1). 3–69.

Enfield, N. J. 2013. *Relationship thinking: Agency, enchrony, and human sociality*. New York: Oxford University Press.

Enfield, N. J. 2015. *The utility of meaning: What words mean and why*. Oxford: Oxford University Press.

Ferlus, Michel. 2014. Arem, a Vietic language. *Mon-Khmer Studies* 43(1). 1–15.

Fix, Alan. 2011. Origin of genetic diversity among Malaysian Orang Asli: An alternative to the demic diffusion model. In N.J. Enfield (ed.), *Dynamics of human diversity: The case of mainland Southeast Asia*, 277–291. Canberra: Pacific Linguistics.

Gai, Xingzhi. 2002. *A study of Tanglang*. Beijing: The Nationalities Press.

Giaphong, Suchada. 2004. *Plang grammar as spoken in Huay Namkhun village, Chiang Rai province*. Bangkok: Mahidol University MA thesis.

Goddard, Cliff. 2005. *The languages of east and southeast Asia*. Oxford: Oxford University Press.

Grant, Anthony & Paul Sidwell. 2005. *Chamic and beyond: studies in mainland Austronesian languages*. Canberra: Pacific Linguistics.

Grinevald, Colette. 2000. A morphosyntactic typology of classifiers. In Gunter Senft (ed.), *Systems of nominal Classification*, 50–92.

Hạ, Kiều Phương. 2013. Prosodic means in repair initiation as an activity in Northern Vietnamese conversation. In D. Hole & E. Löbel (eds.), *Linguistics of Vietnamese - an international survey*, 35–54. Berlin & New York: De Gruyter Mouton.

Hạ, Kiều Phương. 2010. Prosody of Vietnamese from an interactional perspective: ờ, ừ and vâng in backchannels and requests for information. *Journal of the Southeast Asian Linguistics Society* 3(1). 56–76.

Haas, Mary Rosamond. 1969. Sibling terms as used by marriage partners. *Southwestern Journal of Anthropology* 25(3). 228–235.

Haiman, John. 2011. *Cambodian: Khmer*. (London Oriental and African Language Library 16). Amsterdam: John Benjamins.

Hajek, John. 1998. Kenaboi: an extinct unclassified language of the Malay Peninsula. *Mon-Khmer Studies* 28. 137–149.

Hartmann, John. 1998. A linguistic geography and history of Tai Meuang-Fai (Ditch-Dike) techno-culture. *Language and Linguistics* 16(2). 67–101.

Haspelmath, Martin, Matthew S. Dryer, David Gil & Bernard Comrie (eds.). 2005. *The World Atlas of Language Structures*. Oxford: Oxford University Press.

Henderson, Eugénie. J.A. 1952. The main features of Cambodian pronunciation. *Bulletin of the School of Oriental and African Studies* 14. 149–174.

Henderson, Eugénie. J.A. 1965. The topography of certain phonetic and morphological characteristics of South East Asian languages. *Lingua* 15. 400–434.

Henderson, Eugénie J.A. 1967. Grammar and tone in South East Asian languages. *Wissenschaftliche Zeitschrift der Karl-Marx-Universität Leipzig* 16(1/2). 171–178.

Higbie, James & Snea Thinsan. 2003. *Thai reference grammar: The structure of spoken Thai.* Bangkok: Orchid Press.
Higham, C. 2002. *Early cultures of mainland Southeast Asia.* Bangkok: River Books.
Hyslop, G., S. Morey & M. W. Post (eds.). 2011. *North East Indian linguistics Vol. 3.* New Delhi: Cambridge University Press India.
Hyslop, G., S. Morey & M. W. Post (eds.). 2012. *North East Indian linguistics Vol. 4.* New Delhi: Cambridge University Press India.
Hyslop, G., S. Morey & M. W. Post (eds.). 2013. *North East Indian linguistics Vol. 5.* New Delhi: Cambridge University Press India.
Iwasaki, Shoichi & Preeya Ingkaphirom Horie. 2005. *A reference grammar of Thai.* Cambridge: Cambridge University Press.
Jacquesson, François. 2004. *Le deuri: Langue tibéto-birmane d'Assam.* Leuven & Paris & Dudley, MA: Peeters.
Jenny, M. & P. Sidwell (eds.). forthcoming 2015. *Handbook of the Austroasiatic languages.* Leiden: Brill.
Jonsson, Hjorleifur. 2011. Ethnology and the issue of human diversity in Mainland Southeast Asia. In N.J. Enfield (ed.), *Dynamics of human diversity: The case of mainland Southeast Asia*, 109–122. Canberra: Pacific Linguistics.
Jonsson, Hjorleifur. 2014. *Slow anthropology: Negotiating difference with the Iu Mien.* Ithaca, NY: Cornell Southeast Asia Program Publications.
Konnerth, Linda. 2014. *A grammar of Karbi.* Eugene, OR: University of Oregon dissertation.
Kosaka, Ryuichi. 2000. *A descriptive study of the Lachi Language: Syntactic description, historical reconstruction and genetic relation.* Tokyo: Tokyo University of Foreign Studies doctoral dissertation.
Kölver, Ulrike. 1991. Local prepositions and serial verb constructions in Thai. In Hansjakob Seiler & Waldfried Premper (eds.), *Partizipation: das sprachliche Erfassen von Sachverhalten*, 485–508. Tübingen: Narr.
Kruspe, Nicole. 2004. *A grammar of Semelai.* Cambridge: Cambridge University Press.
Larish, Michael D. 2005. Moken and Moklen. In Nikolaus P. Himmelmann & Alexander Adelaar (eds.), *The Austronesian languages of Asia and Madagascar*, 513–533. London: RoutledgeCurzon.
Lebar, F., G. Hickey & J. Musgrave. 1964. *Ethnic groups of Mainland Southeast Asia.* New Haven: HRAF Press.
Li, Daqin. 2003. *A study of Geman.* Beijing: The Nationalities Press.
Li, Daqin. 2004. *Sulong Yu yanjiu* [A study of Sulong]. Beijing: Minzu Chubanshe.
Li, Yongsui. 2003. *A study of Sangkong.* Beijing: The Nationalities Press.
Lidz, Liberty A. 2010. A descriptive grammar of Yongning Na (Mosuo). University of Texas at Austin doctoral dissertation.
Luong, H. V. 1988. Discursive practices and power structure: Person-referring forms and sociopolitical struggles in colonial Vietnam. *American Ethnologist* 15(2). 239–253.
Luong, H. V. 1990. *Discursive practices and linguistic meanings: The Vietnamese system of person reference.* Amsterdam: John Benjamins.
Majid, Asifa & Niclas Burenhult. 2014. Odors are expressible in language, as long as you speak the right language. *Cognition* 130(2). 266–270.
Mao, Zongwu & Yunbing Li. 2002. *A study of Jiongnai.* Beijing: Central Nationalities University Press.

Mao, Zongwu & Yunbing Li. 2007. *Younuoyu Yanjiu* [A study of Younuo]. Beijing: Minzu University of China Publishing House.

Matisoff, James A. 1973. Tonogenesis in Southeast Asia. In Larry M. Hyman (ed.), *Southern California occasional papers in Linguistics, No. 1*, 72–95. Los Angeles: University of Southern California.

Matisoff, James A. 1991. Areal and universal dimensions of grammatization in Lahu. In Elizabeth Closs Traugott & Bernd Heine (eds.), *Approaches to grammaticalization*, 383–453. Amsterdam: John Benjamins.

Matisoff, James A. 2003a. *Handbook of Proto-Tibeto-Burman*. Berkeley: University of California Press.

Matisoff, James A. 2003b. Aslian: Mon-Khmer of the Malay Peninsula. *Mon-Khmer Studies* 33. 1-58.

Mayuree, Thawornpat. 2006. *Gong: An endangered language of Thailand*. Bangkok: Mahidol University doctoral dissertation.

Michaud, Jean (ed.). 2010. Editorial – Zomia and beyond. [Special Issue]. *Journal of Global History* 5(2). 187–214.

Morey, Stephen. 2005. *The Tai languages of Assam - a grammar and texts*. Canberra: Pacific Linguistics.

Morey, Stephen. 2010. *Turung - a variety of Singpho language spoken in Assam*. Canberra: Pacific Linguistics.

Morey, Stephen & M. W. Post (eds.). 2008. *North East Indian linguistics* (Vol. 1). New Delhi: Cambridge University Press India.

Morey, Stephen & M. W. Post (eds.). 2010. *North East Indian linguistics* (Vol. 2). New Delhi: Cambridge University Press India.

Muysken, Pieter. 2008. *From linguistic areas to areal linguistics*. Amsterdam: John Benjamins.

Nettle, Daniel. 1999. *Linguistic diversity*. Oxford: Oxford University Press.

Nichols, Johanna. 1992. *Linguistic diversity in space and time*. Chicago: Chicago University Press.

Nonaka, Angela M. 2004. The forgotten endangered languages: Lessons on the importance of remembering from Thailand's Ban Khor Sign Language. *Language in Society* 33(5). 737–767.

O'Connor, Richard A. 1995. Agricultural change and ethnic succession in Southeast Asian states: A case for regional anthropology. *The Journal of Asian Studies* 54(4). 968–996.

Oppenheimer, Stephen. 2011. MtDNA variation and southward Holocene human dispersals within Mainland Southeast Asia. In N.J. Enfield (ed.), *Dynamics of human diversity: The case of mainland Southeast Asia*, 81–108. Canberra: Pacific Linguistics.

Oxenham, Marc & Nancy Tayles. 2006. *Bioarchaeology of Southeast Asia*. New York: Cambridge University Press.

Phattharathanit Srichomthong. 2012. Identity maintenance in Lanna (Northern Thai). *Journal of the Southeast Asian Linguistics Society* 5. 67-84.

Pittayaporn, Pittayawat. 2009. Proto-Southwestern-Thai: A new reconstruction. *Journal of the Southeast Asian Linguistics* Society 2. 119–143.

Ploykaew, Pornsawan. 2001. *Samre grammar*. Bangkok: Mahidol University doctoral dissertation.

Post, Mark W. 2007. *A grammar of Galo*. Melbourne: La Trobe University dissertation.

Post, Mark W. 2011. Prosody and typological drift in Austroasiatic and Tibeto-Burman: Against "Indosphere" and "Sinosphere". In S. Srichampa, P. Sidwell & K. J. Gregerson (eds.), *Aus-*

troasiatic studies: Papers from International Conference on Austroasiatic Linguistics (ICAAL4) [Mon-Khmer Studies Special Issue 3], 198–211. Canberra: Pacific Linguistics.

Ratliff, Martha. 2010. *Hmong-Mien language history*. (Studies in Language Change 8). Canberra: Pacific Linguistics.

Sagart, Laurent, Roger Blench & A. Sanchez-Mazas (eds.). 2005. *The peopling of East Asia: putting together archaeology, linguistics and genetics*. New York: RoutledgeCurzon.

Sagart, Laurent. 2011. The Austroasiatics: east to west or west to east? In N.J. Enfield (ed.), *Dynamics of human diversity: The case of mainland Southeast Asia*, 345–359. Canberra: Pacific Linguistics.

Samarina, Irina. 2011. *Jazyki gelao: Materialy k sopostavitel'nomu slovarju kadajskich jazykov* [Gelao languages: materials for a comparative dictionary of Kadai languages]. Moskva: Academia.

Scott, James C. 2009. *The art of not being governed: An anarchist history of upland Southeast Asia*. New Haven, CT: Yale University Press.

Schendel, Willem van. 2002. Geographies of knowing, geographies of ignorance: jumping scale in Southeast Asia. *Environment and Planning D: Society and Space* 20(6). 647–668.

Seng Mai, Ma. 2012. *A descriptive grammar of Wa*. Chiang Mai: Payap University MA thesis.

Shee, Naw Hsar. 2008. *A descriptive grammar of Geba Karen*. Chiang Mai: Payap University MA thesis.

Shintani, Tadahiko. 2008. *The Palaung language: the comparative lexicon of its southern dialects*. Tokyo: Research Institute for Languages and Cultures of Asia and Africa (ILCCA).

Shorto, H. L. 1960. Word and syllable pattern in Palaung. *Bulletin of the School of Oriental and African Studies* 23(3), 544-557.

Shorto, H. L. 2006. *A Mon-Khmer comparative dictionary*. (Edited by Paul Sidwell). Canberra: Pacific Linguistics.

Sidnell, Jack & Merav Shohet. 2013. The problem of peers in Vietnamese interaction. *Journal of the Royal Anthropological Institute* 19(3). 618–638.

Sidwell, Paul. 2009. Proto-Mon-Khmer vocalism: Moving on from Shorto's "Alternances." *Journal of the Southeast Asian Linguistics Society* 1. 205–214.

Sidwell, Paul. 2013. Southeast Asian Mainland: linguistic history. In Peter Bellwood (ed.), *The encyclopedia of global human migration Volume 1: Prehistory*, 259–268. Oxford: Wiley-Blackwell.

Sidwell, Paul & Roger Blench. 2011. The Austroasiatic Urheimat: the southeastern riverine hypothesis. In N.J. Enfield (ed.), *Dynamics of human diversity: The case of mainland Southeast Asia*, 315–343. Canberra: Pacific Linguistics.

Simpson, Andrew (ed.). 2007. *Language and national identity in Asia*. Oxford: Oxford University Press.

Sophana Srichampa. 2008. Patterns of polite expressions in Vietnamese. *The Mon-Khmer Studies Journal* 38. 117–147.

Srisakorn, Preedaporn. 2008. *So (Thavung) grammar*. Bangkok: Mahidol University dissertation.

Stolz, Thomas. 2002. No Sprachbund beyond this line! On the age-old discussion of how to define a linguistic area. In Paolo Ramat & Thomas Stolz (eds.), *Mediterranean languages: Paper from the MEDTYP Workshop, Tirrenia, June 2000*, 259–281. Bochum: Universtätsverlag Dr. N. Brockmeyer.

Sun, Hongkai, & Guangkun Liu. 2009. *A grammar of Anong: Language death under intense contact.* [edited translation and annotation, with the translation, editing, annotation and expansion by Graham Thurgood, Fengxiang Li, and Ela Thurgood]. (Languages of the Greater Himalayan Region). Leiden: Brill.

Suwilai Premsrirat. 1987. *Khmu, a minority language of Thailand*. Canberra: Pacific Linguistics.

Suwilai Premsrirat. 1998. Language maintenance and language shift in minority languages of Thailand. In Kazuto Matsumura (ed.), *Studies in endangered languages: Papers from the International Symposium on Endangered Languages, Tokyo, November 18-20 1995*, 191–211. Tokyo: Hituzi Syobo.

Suwilai Premsrirat. 2007. Endangered languages of Thailand. *International Journal of the Sociology of Language* 186. 75-93.

Suwilai Premsrirat. 2008. Orthography development: A tool for revitalizing and maintaining ethnic minority languages. *Journal of Language and Culture* 26. 18–34.

Svantesson, Jan-Olof, Raw Kam, Kristina Lindell & Håkan Lundstrom. 2013. *Dictionary of Kammu Yuan language and culture*. Honolulu: University of Hawai'i Press.

Tarling, N. 1993. *The Cambridge history of Southeast Asia: from early times to c. 1800* (Vol. 1). Cambridge University Press.

Thurgood, Graham. 1998. The development of the Chamic vowel system: the interaction of inheritance and borrowing. In David Thomas (ed.), *Papers in Southeast Asian Linguistics No. 15: Further Chamic Studies*, 61–90. Canberra: Pacific Linguistics.

Thurgood, Graham. 1999. *From ancient Cham to modern dialects: two thousand years of language contact and change*. Honolulu: University of Hawai'i Press.

Thurgood, Graham. 2010. Hainan Cham, Anong, and Eastern Cham: Three languages, three social contexts, three patterns of change. *Journal of Language Contact - VARIA* 3. 39–61.

Thurgood, Graham & Randy J. La Polla. 2003. *The Sino-Tibetan languages*. London: Routledge.

Thurgood, Graham, Ela Thurgood & Fengxiang Li. 2014. *A grammatical sketch of Hainan Cham: History, contact, and phonology*. Berlin: Mouton de Gruyter.

Tooley, M. J. & Ian Shennan (eds.). 1987. *Sea level changes*. Oxford: Blackwell.

Umaporn, Sungkaman. 2007. Backchannel response in Mon conversation. *Mon-Khmer Studies* 37. 67–85.

Vittrant, Alice & Justin Watkins (eds.). forthcoming. *Mainland South East Asia linguistic area: The languages*. Boston & Berlin: De Gruyter.

Voris, Harold K. 2000. Maps of Pleistocene sea levels in Southeast Asia: Shorelines, river systems and time durations. *Journal of Biogeography* 27(5). 1153–1167.

Watkins, Justin. 2002. *The phonetics of Wa. Experimental phonetics, phonology, orthography and sociolinguistics*. Canberra: Pacific Linguistics.

Watkins, Justin (ed.). 2005. *Studies in Burmese linguistics*. Canberra: Pacific Linguistics.

Watkins, Justin. 2013. *Dictionary of Wa* (2 vols). Leiden: Brill.

Wayesha, Ahsi James. 2010. *A phonological description of Leinong Naga*. Chiang Mai: Payap University MA thesis.

White, Joyce C. 2011. Cultural diversity in Mainland Southeast Asia: a view from prehistory. In N.J. Enfield (ed.), *Dynamics of human diversity: The case of mainland Southeast Asia*, 9–46. Canberra: Pacific Linguistics.

Wnuk, Ewelina. forthcoming. Semantic specificity in verbs of perception in the context of ethnobiology in Maniq. Nijmegen: Radboud University.

Wnuk, Ewelina & Asifa Majid. 2014. Revisiting the limits of language: The odor lexicon of Maniq. *Cognition* 131(1). 125–138.

Yip, Moira. 2002. *Tone*. (Cambridge Textbooks in Linguistics). Cambridge: Cambridge University Press.

Yu, Defen. 2007. *Aspects of Lisu phonology and grammar, a language of Southeast Asia*. Canberra: Pacific Linguistics.

Part 1: **Language relatedness in MSEA**

Martha Ratliff
Word-initial prenasalization in Southeast Asia

A historical perspective

1 Introduction

In Eugénie Henderson's seminal (1965) article on the Southeast Asian linguistic area based on 59 languages, word-initial prenasalization (#NC) is included as a relatively weak areal feature. This chapter examines the distribution and sources of prenasalization in Southeast Asia and revisits the question of whether or not word-initial prenasalization is a diagnostic feature of the mainland Southeast Asian linguistic area. My study shows that although word-initial prenasalization is not represented in the national languages Vietnamese, Thai, Lao, or Burmese—and is only represented by /mC-/ initials in Khmer[1]—it is well-represented in other languages of the Austroasiatic, Hmong-Mien, Tibeto-Burman, and Sinitic families, and is attested, although less well-represented, in Tai-Kadai. It is also represented in Austronesian and Papuan languages to the east. It thus appears to be a much better areal feature than Henderson's early study suggests.

The object of the present study is not limited to word-initial prenasalized stops as unitary phonemes, and so my conclusion about prenasalization as an areal feature differs from that of a recent study of phonemic prenasalization in Southeast Asia by Donohue and Whiting (2011), who found prenasalized phonemes much more robustly attested in New Guinea than in mainland Southeast Asia.[2] As a historical linguist, I expect the phonological status of this particular feature to change, either through natural processes of fusion and simplification,

---

[1] Phnom Penh Khmer does not have a full series of initial prenasalized stops with nasals at every place of articulation. Surin Khmer (Northern Khmer) spoken in Thailand, however, has a wider range of word-initial prenasalized stops (Chantrupanth 1978).

[2] This study also differs from Maddieson (1984), an analysis of phoneme inventories, in which phonemic prenasalization is reported for only 19 of the 317 languages in the UPSID database. Eight of the 19 are languages of Southeast Asia, including New Guinea (only two, Sedang and Hakka, are spoken in mainland Southeast Asia); 6 are African, 3 South American, 1 Australian, and 1 Mesoamerican.

or through extension by transfer in language contact situations. Accordingly, I follow Henderson in considering initial prenasalization whatever its status: morphological, phonemic, or phonetic. The nasal element in the present study may thus be (1) a syllabic nasal preceding a stop-initial root, (2) the first element of a cluster, (3) part of a complex unitary stop phoneme that contrasts with other types of stop, (4) the product of the hyper-voicing of a voiced stop, or (5) a nasal phoneme followed by a brief oral stop closure.[3] It also appears that the primary historical source of word-initial prenasalization in Southeast Asia is the process whereby an initial light syllable is reduced, giving rise to consonant clusters. This process is reflected in the presence of both a prenasalized voiced and a prenasalized voiceless stop series in some Southeast Asian languages. The occurrence of word-initial prenasalization is therefore inextricably linked to studies of iambic (light-heavy) word prosody and prefixation as areal characteristics of Southeast Asia. Finally, word-initial prenasalization, while rare cross-linguistically, extends beyond mainland Southeast Asia to the west, north, and east, and thus is useful in re-thinking the geographical extent of the Southeast Asia linguistic area, a question addressed by other contributors to this volume as well.

Although word-initial prenasalized stops are familiar to linguists studying languages of Southeast Asia, New Guinea, Africa, and some parts of Central and South America, more significant for typological and areal studies is the fact that word-initial prenasalized stops seem to be absent from other areas: Europe, the Middle East, Northern Asia, as well as most of North America. As others have pointed out (e.g., Thomason 2000; Comrie 2007), it is difficult to use unmarked features—the existence of a /t/ phoneme, for example—to delineate a linguistic area since they can be expected either to occur, or arise naturally, in any part of the world. The study of a marked feature with limited distribution is thus valuable for our common project of bringing the picture of the mainland Southeast Asia linguistic area up to date.

Of the 59 languages in Henderson's study, only 12 are characterized by prenasalized initials, and some of these she reports as having only restricted pre-

---

[3] I do not include consideration of word-medial or word-final prenasalization, however. The nasal portion of a word-medial NC can be interpreted either as the coda of the preceding syllable or as ambisyllabic, and a word-final NC forms a natural sequence from the more sonorant nasal to less sonorant oral stop consonant at the end of the syllable. Initial prenasalization, however, violates the Sonority Sequencing Principle that favours a gradation of increasing sonority from the left edge to the nucleus of a syllable, and decreasing sonority from the nucleus to the right edge of a syllable (Selkirk 1984). It is thus much rarer than either word-medial or word-final prenasalization.

nasalization, e.g., limited to a single prefix (Kachin), or to a reading style (Tibetan). The best-represented groups in her study are Austroasiatic, Austronesian, and Papuan. She observes, "A striking feature of this preliminary investigation has been the seeming concentration of putative areal characteristics in the New Guinea group of languages and in the tribal languages of South Vietnam. In the present state of our studies it would be premature to speak either of 'confluence' or of 'dissemination' in this connection but it may be helpful to think in terms of 'concentration areas'" (1965: 432). The mainland Southeast Asia/New Guinea connection has been insightfully explored with respect to prenasalization and areality by Donohue and Whiting (2011), and is addressed in terms of other shared features in the work of David Gil on the "Mekong-Mamberamo" linguistic area (this volume).

Thanks largely to three valuable sources—Chan (1987) for Sinitic, Namkung (1996) for Tibeto-Burman, and the Sidwell and Cooper SEAlang Mon-Khmer Dictionary (Sidwell and Cooper n.d.)—as well as my own knowledge of Hmong-Mien languages, the map that results from the present study adds substantially to Henderson's more limited set and shows the importance of southern China as the central locus for the feature on the mainland (see de Sousa, this volume, on southern China as part of Southeast Asia).

In the sections to follow, I will first give a brief overview of the distribution of word-initial prenasalized stops by family in Southeast Asia. I will then discuss both the synchronic status of these onsets and their historical sources, and will consider the importance of this information to the establishment of initial prenasalized stops as a linguistic feature of Southeast Asia. Finally, I will discuss the relationship between prenasalized stops and some other well-known features of Southeast Asian languages.

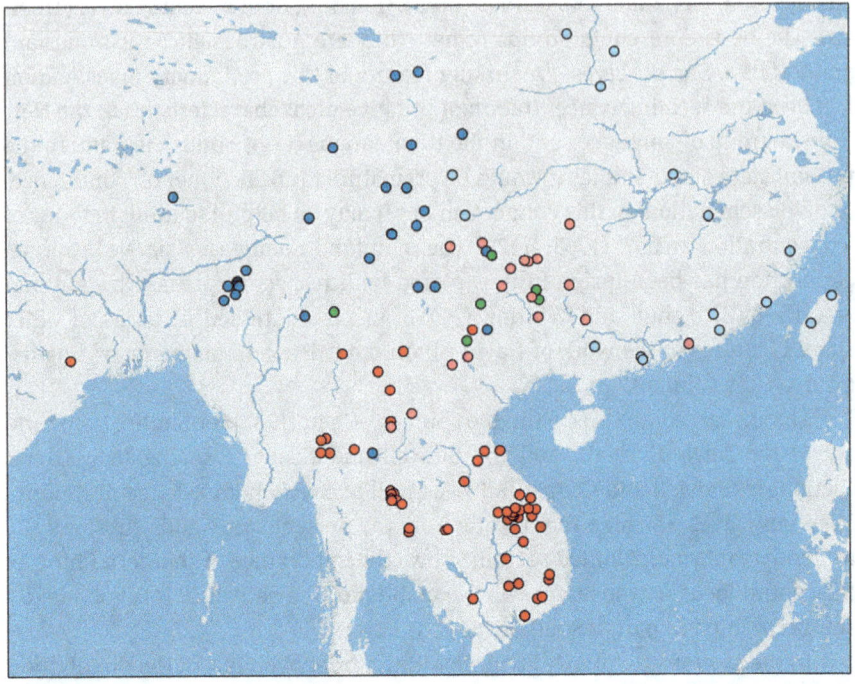

Fig. 1: Map of locations of languages with word-initial prenasalized stops by language family.[4] Legend: Pink: Hmong-Mien, Red: Austroasiatic, Light blue: Sinitic, Dark blue: Tibeto-Burman, Green: Tai-Kadai

---

4 Dots represent separate sources rather than separate languages. Latitude and longitude coordinates for Austroasiatic and Hmong-Mien languages were provided by the Center for Research in Computational Linguistics, Bangkok; latitude and longitude coordinates for the other languages were determined by the author. The map was created using the Linguist List LL-MAP Program and the following sources: Bertrais 1979; Blust 2009; Chan 1987; Edmondson and Yang 1988; Edmondson and Solnit 1997; Heimbach 1979; Henderson 1965; Hsiu 2014; Lyman 1974; Maddieson 1984; Namkung 1996; Niederer 1997; Ostapirat 2000; Pan 2004; Pucilowski 2011; Sidwell and Cooper (see http://sealang.net/monkhmer/dictionary for information about original sources); Wang 1988; Wang and Mao 1995; Zhou and Burusphat 1996.

2 Geographical distribution by family

Initial prenasalized stops are found widely in modern-day Austroasiatic languages, the family whose speakers have occupied mainland Southeast Asian for the longest time. They are best attested in languages of the central groups Bahnaric, Katuic, Khmuic, and Monic, as well as in languages of the Palaungic group to the north. They occur, but less richly, in the more peripheral groups as well: Vietic to the east (Vietnamese lacks this feature), Pearic and Khmeric to the south and Aslian further south in the Malay peninsula. They commonly occur in all places of articulation: to take examples from three different subfamilies, Rölöm Mnong (Bahnaric) has *mb-, nd-, ɲɟ-, ŋg-* (Blood 2005), Kui (Katuic) has *mp-, nt-, ɲc-, ŋk-* (Prasert 1978), and Central Nyah Kur (Monic) has *mp-, mb-, nt-, nd-, ɲc-, ŋk-* (L-Thongkum 1984). Initial NCs are just one type of onset cluster among many in a family famous for its "sesquisyllabic" word structure of a initial light syllable followed by a heavier final syllable (Matisoff 1973: 86).[5]

Only a few Tai-Kadai languages spoken in southern China have initial prenasalized stops. Maonan in the Kam-Tai subfamily (Edmondson and Yang 1988: 147) has initial prenasalized stops at four places of articulation, and most varieties of Southwestern Gelao in the Kra subfamily have developed prenasalized stops (Ostapirat 2000: 26-33). Two other languages show just a trace of prenasalization. Mangshi (Dehong Dai) is a variety of Shan (Kam-Tai) with post-stopped /m/ [m^b] (and /l/, [l^d]), similar to some southern Sinitic languages (Edmondson and Solnit 1997b: 350). Wang (1988: 130) reports that Sui (Kam-Tai) has sub-phonemic prenasalization: in reference to /b/ and /d/, he writes "It is a special feature of their articulation to carry a slight, simultaneous prenasal sound." The largest and best-known languages in this family—Thai, Lao, and Zhuang—do not have initial prenasalized stops, however, which may give the impression that Tai-Kadai languages do not have this feature so well-attested in other families of Southeast Asia. It may be of significance that both Thurgood (1988) and Matisoff (1988) have reconstructed prenasalized stops for Tai-Kadai subgroups (Proto-Kam-Sui and Proto-Hlai, respectively).

Hmong-Mien languages have had prenasalized initial stops for a long time, although in some branches of the family they have now simplified to either simple oral stops or simple nasals. Correspondences involving these complex initials make clear that Proto-Hmong-Mien had a three-way contrast of *mp-, *mph-, *mb- (taking the labial place of articulation as representative) at six

---

[5] See the chapters by Butler and by Pittayaporn in this volume, where the concept of the sesquisyllable is re-examined and contested in various ways.

places of articulation,[6] as well as prenasalized stops in clusters with medial liquids: *mbr- *mbl- (Ratliff 2010). Prenasalization is best preserved in the Jiongnai language and in West Hmongic languages such as Hmong/Mong, A-Hmao, and A-Hmø spoken in northern Southeast Asia and in southern China (Yunnan, western Guizhou, southeastern Sichuan, and the Guangxi-Zhuang Autonomous Region). White Hmong of Laos and Thailand, for example, has the following prenasalized stop onsets: mp-, mpʰ-, mpl-, mplʰ-, nt-, ntʰ-, nts-, ntsʰ-, nt̪-, nt̪ʰ-, ɲc-, ɲcʰ-, ntʃ-, ntʃʰ-, ŋk-, ŋkʰ-, ɴq-, ɴqʰ-. In these languages the voiceless, voiceless aspirated, and voiced series are still distinct, despite the fact that *p- and *b- (and *mp- and *mb-) have merged: the merger triggered a tone split into an "upper" and a "lower" tone register, which makes the voicing of the original stop clear. In North Hmongic languages (varieties of Xiong or Xong), prenasalization is retained only before ancient voiceless stops; ancient prenasalized voiced stops are now simple nasals. In East Hmongic, the prenasalized voiceless stops have lost the nasal and are now simple voiceless stops, and the prenasalized voiced stops have lost the oral stop and are now simple nasals. In modern-day Mienic languages, all ancient prenasalized stops are now simple voiced stops.

In addition to initial prenasalization as a retention of a distinctive stop series in the protolanguage, there is another recent source for initial prenasalized stops in at least one Hmongic language. Ho Ne [hɔ nte], also called She, spoken in Guangdong Province to the north of Hong Kong, has post-stopped nasals much like those reported for neighbouring Sinitic languages (see below). The autonym for these people frequently appears in the literature as "Ho Nte", which raises the predictable oral stop portion of the nasal to phonemic status. We know that this is a recent development in Ho Ne because the name means "mountain people", [nte] deriving from Proto-Hmongic *næn^A 'person/people'. None of the cognates of this word across the family contains an oral stop (Mao and Meng 1986; Ratliff 1998).

Sinitic languages do not immediately come to mind as a group characterized by word-initial prenasalized stops. But according to Chan (1987: 73), the "post-stopping of nasals is ... fairly widespread among the modern Chinese dialects". Most #NCs in this group are post-stopped nasals (#N^C) rather than prenasalized stops, and thus do not contrast with simple nasals. In Southern Min languages, however, word-initial prenasalized voiced stops (#^{N}C), usually

---

[6] One is a manner distinction that behaves like a place distinction in terms of cross-cutting contrasts. The six series are labial, dental/alveolar, dental/alveolar affricate, palatal, velar, and uvular.

represented phonologically as voiced stops, are found; they contrast phonetically and sometimes phonemically (as in Chaozhou) with simple nasals (Chan 1987: 88-91). The fact that most Sinitic #NCs are post-stopped nasals rather than prenasalized stops is immaterial to the analysis of initial prenasalization as an areal feature: if this is a feature that spread from speakers of prenasalizing languages to Chinese through language shift, the character of the feature in L1 could well have been different than it was in L2. A nasal-stop sequence would have been reproduced out of the materials at hand.

Most important for the analysis of initial prenasalized stops as an areal feature is the geographical distribution of post-stopped nasals within China. Post-stopped nasals are not an exclusively southern feature of Chinese, but rather a western and southern feature of Chinese. And the presence of post-stopped nasals in Northwestern Mandarin varieties spoken in Shanxi and Shaanxi provinces extends the geographical reach of this feature to the north far from our area of interest, mainland Southeast Asia. Moving counter-clockwise, post-stopped nasals have been reported for Sinitic varieties from Northwest Mandarin, down through varieties of Southwest Mandarin in Sichuan, to the southern groups Kejia, Yue (spoken in Guangdong Province where the post-stopped nasals of the Hmongic language Ho Ne are also attested, see above), and Min. They have not been reported, or have been reported only sporadically, for the more easterly and northeasterly contiguous groups Xiang, Gan, Wu, Southeast Mandarin, and Northern Mandarin (Chan 1987: 81-92). Chan reports that there is evidence for post-stopped nasals going back to the 8th century, e.g., during the Tang dynasty, loanwords to Japanese with post-stopped nasals were borrowed as words with voiced stops (Chan 1987: 101-104). True prenasalized stops (^{N}C rather than N^C) have been reconstructed for the Proto-Min subgroup of Sinitic by Norman (1986),[7] and Baxter and Sagart have reconstructed nasal pre-initials (among other pre-initials) for Old Chinese, some of which have survived as such in loanwords to Hmong-Mien languages (Baxter and Sagart 2014: 115).

About a quarter of the Tibeto-Burman languages in Namkung (1996), a collection of phonological inventories drawn from 170 Tibeto-Burman language descriptions, have initial prenasalized stops, either as part of a stop series, as initial clusters, or as the sequence of an initial syllabic nasal and a stop-initial syllable. These languages are distributed widely across branches of the family

---

[7] However, Baxter and Sagart (2014: 112) believe that the Northern Min "softened" stops that Norman explains as the trace of earlier prenasalization are due rather to the existence of an earlier presyllable (not necessarily one with a nasal onset), and that the intervocalic context accounts for the character of these stops.

and across Asia—from India to Tibet to China, and into northern Southeast Asia. Prenasalized stops are best represented in languages of the Kamarupan, Himalayish, Qiangic, and Loloish groups (Matisoff 2003: 121-126). Of special interest is the way prenasalized stop series, in the languages that have them, pattern in contrast to other stop series. Some languages have more than one series of prenasalized stops: for example, the Qiangic languages Ersu, Lüsu, Muya, and Namuyi, all spoken in Sichuan Province China, have both a prenasalized voiceless aspirated series and a prenasalized voiced series (in some languages these are analysed as phonemes and in others as clusters). Of the greater number that have a single prenasalized series, there are two general patterns: (1) the prenasalized series contrasts with three others—plain voiceless, voiceless aspirated, and voiced, e.g., Rengma (Eastern Naga, Kamarupan), Zhaba (Qiangic), Yi (Northern Loloish), or (2) the prenasalized series contrasts with only a plain voiceless series and a voiceless aspirated series, e.g., Amdo Tibetan (Himalayish), Xixia (Qiangic), and Sangkong (Southern Loloish). In the latter type, the prenasalized stops appear to fill the role of a voiced series, although they need not have been derived from voiced stops. In the case of Geman (Kamarupan), however, the voiced stops and affricates are described as phonetically voiced prenasalized stops (Sun et al. 1980, 1991).

In the large Austronesian (AN) family, "[m]ost AN languages outside Taiwan allow phonetic sequences of nasal + homorganic obstruent either within a morpheme or across a morpheme boundary" (Blust 2009: 214). Several of these allow word-initial prenasalized stops as well, including Kambera, Muna, Rotinese, Fijian, Javanese, and Malagasy. The Austronesian Chamic languages spoken in Cambodia, Vietnam and China (Hainan Island) are the only Austronesian languages of mainland Southeast Asia (linguistically, Hainan Island shows closer ties to the mainland than to insular Southeast Asia). Since Chamic languages have been restructured under the influence of mainland Southeast Asian languages, they might be expected to have developed prenasalized initials if this is indeed a contact feature for the Southeast Asian mainland linguistic area.[8] This is apparently not the case. The original disyllabic words of Chamic languages have shortened to monosyllabic words yielding initial stop-liquid

---

[8] "In the last 2000 years, the Chamic languages of Vietnam have undergone radical restructuring in the canonical shape of their words, major changes in their consonantal and vocalic phonological inventories, and, in some cases, even in the basic structure of their phonological systems" (Thurgood 1999: 5).

clusters, but these reductions have not yet led to the formation of nasal-stop clusters (Thurgood 1999: 93-99).[9]

Perhaps most important for our purposes is the answer to the following question: Do prenasalized initials show up in families that straddle the line that defines mainland Southeast Asia only on the mainland Southeast Asian side of that line? If initial prenasalization were indeed a mainland Southeast Asian convergence feature, this would be our expectation. The evidence on this question is mixed. We can observe that the post-stopped nasals of Sinitic languages appear most reliably in the south; no post-stopped nasals are reported for Wu, Xiang, or the Southeast Mandarin groups of Sinitic to the north of the post-stopping Southwest Mandarin, Kejia, and Yue groups. However, they do occur in some Northwest Mandarin dialects as far north as Shanxi and Shaanxi provinces (Chan 1987: 81-92).[10] To the west, the Austroasiatic and Tai-Kadai languages of India do not have prenasalized initials,[11] but several Tibeto-Burman languages of Nagaland and Manipur in India do. Then there is the robust extension of the prenasalization area to insular Southeast Asia and New Guinea to the east. The geographic extent of the prenasalization area is thus considerably larger than mainland Southeast Asia. Nonetheless, mainland Southeast Asia forms the centre of the prenasalization area (see map, Figure 1).

3 Phonological status and historical sources

3.1 Phonological status

Initial prenasalized stops are presented in grammars and language sketches variously as combinations of a syllabic nasal and a consonant (N.C), as consonant clusters (NC), as complex unitary stop phonemes (^{N}C), or as post-stopped nasals (N^C). These descriptions vary with respect to transcription convention,

---

9 Orthographies for the Chamic language Rade make it appear that the language has prenasalized stops, but this is because the intervening schwa is not represented (Thurgood 1999: 270-271).
10 However, Chan quotes Scott (1973: 290) as saying that the Southwest dialect of Mandarin spoken in Yibin, Sichuan Province might "be classified as plosives with nasalization." She notes that no description of a similarly strong stop element in an N^C- onset has been made of any northern dialect (Chan 1987: 84). The signal of this feature is therefore strongest in the south.
11 According to the SEAlang Mon-Khmer Dictionary, #*mC*- appears in only two words in the Austroasiatic language Khasi spoken in the Meghalaya state in India.

phonological analysis, and even the extent to which phonetic detail or a phonological analysis is provided at all, so it is difficult to compare these objects in detail across languages. With only a few exceptions (Chen 1987, Sarvestani 2012), acoustic analyses of initial prenasalized stops are not presented. One must assume that phonological patterning, the expectations of linguists (as influenced by their training), and the intuitions of speakers primarily determine the way in which word-initial nasal-consonant sequences are represented in grammars, language sketches, and orthographies.[12]

Although the phonetics and phonology of prenasalized initials are important to the description of individual languages, a comparison of the phonological status of prenasalized initials from language to language is not relevant to their status as an areal feature of mainland Southeast Asia. This is because the relationship between a nasal and a following stop can change over time, and a synchronic description of a language will represent only one stage in the evolution of this relationship. These changes may take place rapidly, or a language may settle into one stage that persists over centuries. For example, a language that derives prenasalized initials from an initial light syllable with a nasal onset (either part of the root or a prefix) by a process of "front-end collapse" may go through the following stages: upon the loss of the reduced initial syllable vowel, the nasal may first stabilize as a syllabic nasal before it later adjoins to the following syllable in a cluster NV.C- > N.C- > NC-. This cluster may then be reanalysed as a complex unitary stop NC- > ^{N}C- before finally simplifying to either a C- or an N-. It is logical to think that any given language in the area that develops prenasalized initials in this particular way may represent one stage of the process (N.C, NC, or ^{N}C) at the same time as its neighbour represents either an earlier or later stage (or may have derived its prenasalized initials in a completely different way, see Section 3.2 below).

For example, as mentioned above, West and North Hmongic languages are characterized by word-initial prenasalized stops. Furthermore, all reconstructions of Proto-Hmong-Mien include three full series of initial prenasalized stops:

---

[12] The success of writing systems can provide indirect information about the status of prenasalized initials. Older, fluent White Hmong speakers, for example, report that they do not perceive their prenasalized initials as clusters, and find mastery of the romanized orthography which represents them as clusters difficult in this respect. Many prefer the native orthography "Pahawh Hmong", which symbolizes onsets and rimes rather than phonemes, and has different unrelated symbols for /p/, /pʰ/, /mp/, /mpʰ/, /mpl/, /mpʰl/, etc. (Smalley et al. 1990). In contrast, young heritage speakers whose first language is English have trouble perceiving and producing the initial nasal, which gives them a different problem with the romanized writing system.

voiceless, voiceless aspirated, and voiced (Purnell 1970; Wang and Mao 1995; Ratliff 2010). In some cases, the nasal element reflects an old presyllable (*mnɔk 'bird', *nmɛj 'to have') and in others the nasal element suggests the presence of an old prefix of inalienable possession (*mbræu 'ear', *mbruiH 'nose', *ɲʲuj 'mouth'), but in most cases no evidence remains of the source of these complex initials at a period that antedates the c. 2500-year-old protolanguage. We know, however, that initial prenasalized stops have developed in the following ways in Hmong-Mien:

*NC > NC   West Hmongic languages
*NC$_{[-voice]}$ > NC   North Hmongic languages
*NC$_{[-voice]}$ > C$_{[-voice]}$ East Hmongic languages
*NC$_{[+voice]}$ > N   North and East Hmongic languages
*NC > C$_{[+voice]}$ All Mienic languages

Subgroupings have been based in part on ancient prenasalized stop developments, most notably the major division between Hmongic and Mienic. This does seem to be a reliable diagnostic for this first-order split, since all Mienic languages, without exception, realize ancient prenasalized stops as voiced stops. However, given the inherently unstable nature of initial prenasalized stops, they have been susceptible to simplification on the Hmongic side as well, in the various ways noted above. I have observed that some Hmong-American college students (for whom English is dominant) do not consistently produce the nasal portion of a prenasalized stop, so find it difficult to write these words in the Romanized Popular Alphabet in which prenasalization is represented. Similarly, Chan reports the "optionality" of post-stopping in various Yue dialects spoken in the Guangxi–Zhuang Autonomous Region (Chan 1987: 86). In the Lolo-Burmese-Naxi subfamily of Tibeto-Burman, the western dialect of Naxi has prenasalized stops but the eastern dialect does not (Namkung 1996: 278-283), and the northern and eastern dialects of Yi have prenasalized stops but the southern, southeastern, western, and central dialects do not (Namkung 1996: 434-443).

3.2 Historical sources

Although it would be difficult to map initial nasal-consonant sequences according to their synchronic phonological status for the reasons given above, it may be that the historical sources of prenasalization can be mapped in a way that reveals something about language contact and change. This goal is now within reach due to the appearance in recent years of new work on the history of Asian and Southeast Asian languages and the changes that have taken place between reconstructed protolanguages and their descendants.

Word-initial nasal-consonant sequences arise in at least five ways, the first three of which I would categorize as "major" because they have the potential to give rise to a series of #NCs across all places of articulation. The other two I would categorize as "minor", since they occur sporadically, and do not give rise to regular patterns. The three major sources are (1) front-end collapse, described in Section 3.1 above, in which the residue of an old initial syllable or prefix attaches to the initial consonant of the following syllable; (2) post-stopping of nasals; and (3) voicing enhancement of voiced consonants, in which a lowered velum allows voicing to be maintained during the articulatory closure of a voiced stop. The minor sources are (4) stop excrescence between a nasal and a continuant, and (5) juncture reanalysis.[13] It should be possible to link each major type of development to patterns in the phonemic inventory, unless time and subsequent developments have obscured these patterns.

In languages that developed initial prenasalized stops by front-end collapse, we might expect to find a phonemic contrast between two series of prenasalized stops: a voiceless series and voiced series. Such a contrast could not develop from either post-stopping of nasals or voicing enhancement of voiced stops, since in neither case would there be a source for the contrast. A pair of contrastive prenasalized stop series could only come from sequences in which the stop portion of the primary (heavy) syllable had originally shown a voicing contrast: *N.C$_{[-voice]}$ and *N.C$_{[+voice]}$. Matisoff (2003:121ff) reports that a number of Tibeto-Burman languages, especially those in the Kamarupan and Qiangic groups, contrast prenasalized voiceless and prenasalized voiced stops, citing Rengma (Eastern Naga) as a prime example with /mp-/, /mph-/, and /mb-/, etc. (Matisoff 2003:16). This contrast is not uncommon in Austroasiatic languages: Bru, Katu, and Ngeq (Katuic) show the contrast, as do Alak, Sapuan, and Stieng (Bahnaric), and Nyah Kur (Monic) (Sidwell and Cooper n.d.). In addition, reconstructions of not only Austroasiatic and Tibeto-Burman, but also the monosyllabic languages of the Sinosphere (Tai-Kadai and Hmong-Mien, as well as Chinese itself) have been reconstructed with sesquisyllables rather than monosyllables. This helps give context for the reconstruction of a voicing contrast in initial prenasalized stops across the area: (1) Proto-Tibeto-Burman

---

13 Paul Sidwell (p.c.) suggested that another minor source of word-initial prenasalization in Austroasiatic languages could be the loss of an initial consonant in a #C<N>C- onset, where the nasal is an infix.

(Matisoff 2003) and Old Chinese (Baxter and Sagart 2014) have been reconstructed with nasal prefixes before both kinds of stops; (2) I have reconstructed both prenasalized voiceless and prenasalized voiced stops for Proto-Hmong-Mien (Ratliff 2010); (3) both series have been reconstructed for Proto-Austroasiatic by Shorto (2006), and for lower-level Austroasiatic subgroups Proto-Wa and Proto-Wa-Lawa by Diffloth (1980), and (4) an *mpr- vs. *mbr- contrast has been reconstructed for Proto-Kam-Sui by Thurgood (1988). The contrast between prenasalized voiceless and prenasalized voiced onsets across the area gives testimony to the fact that front-end collapse was the primary source of word-initial prenasalized stops in Southeast Asia.

In languages that developed initial prenasalized stops by post-stopping nasals, we should expect to find no contrast between simple nasals and post-stopped nasals. This is in fact the situation that Chan reports for those Sinitic languages that have word-initial post-stopped nasals: "Similar to most languages in the world, Chinese lacks a series of prenasalized stops contrasting with a series of plain stops on the one hand, and a series of plain nasals on the other in its phonological system." (Chan 1987: 73).

In languages that developed initial prenasalized stops the third way, by enhancing the voicing of voiced stops, we might expect to find three stop series—voiceless, voiceless aspirated, and prenasalized—but no simple voiced series. This is in fact a pattern encountered fairly widely (as in the Tibeto-Burman languages Amdo Tibetan, Xixia, and Sangkong mentioned above), but it cannot be attributed to the enhancement of voiced stops unless there is evidence that the prenasalized series developed recently: most languages of Southeast Asia that exhibit this pattern have merged original *p- and *b- in favour of /p-/, so that *b- could not have been the source of *mb- . Nonetheless, synchronic descriptions of some Southeast Asian languages that have voiced stops also report low-level prenasalization, such as the Austroasiatic language Jruq (Jacq 2002), the Tai-Kadai language Sui (Wang 1988: 130) and the Tibeto-Burman language Geman (Namkung 1996: 112), so we do not need to rely on a study of phoneme inventories alone to show that this kind of development has taken place.

Since stop excrescence and juncture reanalysis are dependent on highly specific phonological contexts (and since even in these contexts they only apply optionally), they should not give rise to a full series of prenasalized stops. Ostapirat (2011) has given an account of stop excrescence in Hmong-Mien that depends both on evidence for direction of borrowing and on the reconstruction of Old Chinese. He claims that certain words with *ml- in Old Chinese were borrowed by Proto-Hmong-Mien speakers as *mbl- : e.g. Old Chinese 稻 *m.lˤuʔ

'rice plant' > Proto Hmong-Mien *mbləu.[14] That juncture reanalysis has given rise to initial prenasalized stops in Hmong can be more securely exemplified. In the series of numerals for 20 through 29, the word for 'ten' in collocations meaning '20' (two-ten), '21' (two-ten-one), '22' (two-ten-two), etc. is prenasalized, /ŋkau⁸/, although elsewhere it appears as /kau⁸/. This is because the word for 'two' that precedes the numerals 20 through 29, /nɛŋ⁷/, ends in a /ŋ/ that has been reanalysed as part of the onset of the word for 'ten'. Another example of juncture reanalysis in Hmong involving a Chinese borrowing is /sɛŋ¹ ntsɯ³/ 'grandchild' from Chinese 孫子 sūn zi 'grandson'. Presumably these individual reanalyses were facilitated by the presence of full sets of prenasalized stops in the language.

It may be that all languages in those parts of the world where initial prenasalized stops are attested develop them primarily through reduction of root-initial material, i.e. front-end collapse. However, the fact that initial prenasalized stops may arise in other ways leaves this an open question.

4 Prenasalization and other Southeast Asian features

Word-initial prenasalization is a feature with obvious links to other mainland Southeast Asian structural features, which are in turn linked to each other. There could be no process of front-end collapse which led to monosyllabization and the formation of prenasalized stops and other complex onsets if words did not originally have an iambic prosodic structure, that is, if they were not typically composed of a light syllable followed by a heavy syllable. It is also well-known that when affixes occur in Southeast Asian languages they tend to be prefixes, although the preference for prefixes runs counter to a world-wide preference for suffixes (Bybee et al. 1990). The prefix-root word structure is clearly harmonic with the light-heavy makeup of Southeast Asian words. Finally, although the source of the nasal element in initial prenasalized stops is usually unrecoverable, we can tell in some cases that the nasal element was probably a prefix. For example, prenasalization occurs on the stative member of a few stative/transitive pairs of Chinese loanwords in Mien (Downer 1973) and a significant number of Hmong-Mien body part terms ('ear', 'nose', 'mouth', 'finger/toe', 'arm'). The same contrasts are clearer in Tibeto-Burman, for which a sta-

---

14 Old Chinese from Baxter and Sagart (2014), Proto-Hmong-Mien from Ratliff (2010).

tive/intransitive prefix on verbs and an "inalienably possessive" prefix on some body parts and kin terms must be reconstructed (Matisoff 2003: 117-121; Hartmann 2001). There is no need to discuss these related features of language structure here, as they are addressed in other chapters of this volume (see Pittayaporn this volume and Butler this volume) as well as in numerous other works on Southeast Asian language prosody (e.g., Matisoff 1989; Donegan and Stampe 2002; Brunelle and Pittayaporn 2012) and history (e.g., Edmondson and Solnit 1988, 1997a; Matisoff 2003; Sagart 1999).

The question arises of whether prefixation, sesquisyllabicity, and initial prenasalized stops should count as separate features in discussing the Southeast Asian linguistic area. They are certainly not independent in the same way that the features of the Balkan linguistic area—a high or mid central vowel, loss of the infinitive, postposed articles, a future with 'want', etc.—are independent. One could say that word structure (or prosodic structure) is the key areal feature, and a number of other features, including complex syllable onsets, derive from it. According to Thomason (2000: 316) there are four requirements for establishing a contact-induced linguistic area:

(1) Establish that there was contact intimate enough to permit contact-induced structural change.
(2) Find several *independent* [emphasis added] shared features in X and Y—ideally, features in different grammatical subsystems.
(3) Prove that the shared features were not present in pre-X.
(4) Prove that the shared features were present in pre-Y.

There are problems with both (2) and (3) above in this case. Contra (2), the Southeast Asian features of prefixation, sesquisyllabicity, and complex initial clusters are not independent (although they do involve different grammatical subsystems), and less directly, contra (3), most linguists agree that the language families of the area had prefixation in their protolanguages, one of the features in this related network of features, and more than one of the protolanguages had prenasalization as well. But initial prenasalization may still have been spread by contact in those cases where an internal front-end collapse explanation is not available. For example, was contact responsible for the realization of initial nasals as N^C- when these nasals were simple nasal consonants in the protolanguage? Micro-level studies of language contact situations between languages with and without initial prenasalization are needed to provide the answer.

5 Conclusion

The way in which word-initial prenasalization patterns in the languages of Southeast Asia reflects its most common source—front-end collapse. There is evidence that this kind of development from disyllables through sesquisyllables to monosyllables was replicated independently in all of the families of the area—a series of developments that itself is best explained as the result of contact and multilingualism. Therefore the distribution of word-initial prenasalization cannot be viewed separately from the distribution of word structure, iambic prosody, and the preference for prefixation over suffixation.

Speakers who inherited words with initial prenasalized stops, hearing prenasalized stops in the languages around them, would have had a supportive context for maintaining them, despite the sonority imbalance. Language contact may account for the spread of this feature in two ways: the development of post-stopped nasals from nasals in southern varieties of Chinese and the development of hyper-voiced (pre-nasalized) stops from voiced stops in languages such as Jruq (Austroasiatic), Sui (Tai-Kadai) and Geman (Tibeto-Burman) mentioned in Section 3.2 above.

This one feature extends west to northeast India, north into China, and east to the Pacific—especially across a band from the Sulawesi-Lesser Sunda region through New Guinea to Near Oceania (Donohue and Whiting 2011:111). Although southern China is arguably part of the mainland Southeast Asian linguistic area, post-stopped nasals in the Northwest varieties of Mandarin spoken in Shanxi and Shaanxi provinces are found well to the north of this part of China. The ancestral languages of all the families of mainland Southeast Asia, including Austronesian, occupied what is now southern China approximately seven to eight thousand years ago (Bellwood 2005; Sagart 2005), and their similarities in some respects may be explained by this fact. The geographical extension of this feature to New Guinea, where it is widely attested, may reflect migrations or trade routes that are even more ancient.

This leads to my final point: word-initial prenasalized stops appear to be a relatively old convergence zone feature of Southeast Asia. Prenasalized stops have been reconstructed for the ancestors of languages that no longer have them (Edmondson and Solnit 1988, 1997a; Matisoff 2003; Ratliff 2010; Baxter and Sagart 2014).[15] They survive in the smaller Southeast Asian languages, not in the national languages, with the exception of Standard Khmer, as mentioned

---

[15] Contra Donohue and Whiting (2011:107), who report that "...[Prenasalization] has not been conclusively reconstructed for any of the major language families attested in this region."

above, which has a limited number of them. Chan also observes that post-stopped nasals are not present in the most influential and widely-spoken dialects of Chinese—Standard Mandarin (Putonghua), Shanghainese and Standard Cantonese—and are thus an obscure and often neglected feature of Chinese (Chan 1987: 73). On the other hand, many familiar features of the mainland Southeast Asia linguistic area are found in the national languages, e.g., tones, monosyllabic words, numeral classifiers, SVO word order, serial verbs, and sentence-final discourse particles. Since national languages reach across wide areas through education, commerce, and government—and since for minority language speakers, fluency in a national language is highly advantageous if not necessary in the modern-day "linguistic ecology" of the area (Smalley 1994)—language contact now privileges features that characterize these languages. The area defined by the initial prenasalized stop seems to represent an earlier period when all language contact and feature-sharing occurred across small communities.

Acknowledgements

I would like to thank Bernard Comrie and Nick Enfield for their very helpful comments on an earlier version of this chapter. I have also benefited from discussions with John Haiman, Paul Heggarty, Larry Hyman, Weera Ostapirat, Pittayawat Pittayaporn, Paul Sidwell, and Graham Thurgood.

References

Baxter, William H. & Laurent Sagart. 2014. *Old Chinese: A new reconstruction*. Oxford: Oxford University Press.
Bellwood, Peter. 2005. Examining the farming/language dispersal hypothesis in the East Asian context. In Laurent Sagart, Roger Blench & Alicia Sanchez-Mazas (eds.), *The peopling of East Asia: Putting together archaeology, linguistics and genetics*, 17–30. London & New York: RoutledgeCurzon.
Bertrais, Yves. 1979 [1964]. *Dictionnaire hmong-français*. Bangkok: Sangwan Surasarang.
Blood, Evangeline. 2005. *Mnong-Vietnamese-English dictionary*. Manuscript.
Blust, Robert. 2009. *The Austronesian languages*. Canberra: Pacific Linguistics.
Brunelle, Marc & Pittayawat Pittayaporn. 2012. Phonologically-constrained change: The role of the foot in monosyllabization and rhythmic shifts in Mainland Southeast Asia. *Diachronica* 29(4). 411–433.

Bybee, Joan L., William Pagliuca & Revere D. Perkins. 1990. Asymmetries in affixation. In William Croft, Keith Denning & Suzanne Kemmer (eds.), *Studies in typology and diachrony for Joseph H. Greenberg*, 1–42. Amsterdam & Philadelphia: John Benjamins.

Chan, Marjorie. 1987. Post-stopped nasals in Chinese: An areal study. *UCLA Working Papers in Phonetics* 68. 73–119.

Chantrupanth, Dhanan. 1978. *Khmer (Surin) – Thai – English dictionary*. Bangkok: Chulalongkorn University.

Comrie, Bernard. 2007. Areal typology of Mainland Southeast Asia: What we learn from the WALS maps. *Manusya* 13. 18–47.

Diffloth, Gérard. 1980. The Wa languages. *Linguistics of the Tibeto-Burman Area* 5(2). 1–182.

Donegan, Patricia & David Stampe. 2002. South-East Asian features in the Munda languages: Evidence for the analytic-to-synthetic drift of Munda. In Patrick Chew (ed.), *Proceedings of the Twenty-Eighth Annual Meeting of the Berkeley Linguistic Society*, 111–120. Berkeley: Berkeley Linguistics Society.

Donohue, Mark & Bronwen Whiting. 2011. Quantifying areality: A study of prenasalization in Southeast Asia and New Guinea. *Linguistic Typology* 15. 101–121.

Downer, Gordon B. 1973. Strata of Chinese loanwords in the Mien dialect of Yao. *Asia Major* 18(1). 1–33.

Edmondson, Jerold A. & Quan Yang. 1988. Word-initial preconsonants and the history of Kam-Sui resonant initials and tones. In Jerold A. Edmondson & David B. Solnit (eds.), *Comparative Kadai: Linguistic studies beyond Tai*, 143–166. Dallas: Summer Institute of Linguistics & Arlington, TX: University of Texas.

Edmondson, Jerold A. & David B. Solnit (eds.). 1988. *Comparative Kadai: Linguistic studies beyond Tai*. Dallas: Summer Institute of Linguistics & Arlington, TX: University of Texas.

Edmondson, Jerold A. & David B. Solnit (eds.). 1997a. *Comparative Kadai: The Tai branch*. Dallas: Summer Institute of Linguistics & Arlington, TX: University of Texas.

Edmondson, Jerold A. & David B. Solnit. 1997b. Comparative Shan. In Jerold A. Edmondson & David B. Solnit (eds.), *Comparative Kadai: The Tai branch*, 337–359. Dallas: Summer Institute of Linguistics & Arlington, TX: University of Texas.

Hartmann, Helga. 2001. Prenasalization and preglottalization in Daai Chin, with parallel examples from Mro and Mara. *Linguistics of the Tibeto-Burman Area* 24(2). 123–142.

Heimbach, Ernest E. 1979. *White Hmong–English dictionary* (revised edition) (Linguistics Series 4, Data Paper 75). Ithaca: Cornell University

Henderson, Eugénie J. A. 1965. The topography of certain phonetic and morphological characteristics of South East Asian languages. *Lingua* 15. 400–432.

Hsiu, Andrew. 2014. Recordings of Mo Piu made in February, 2014.

Jacq, Pascale. 2002. Phonetic realisations of /ʔC/ and /hC/ word-initial sequences in Jruq (Loven). *Mon-Khmer Studies* 32. 25–53.

L-Thongkum, Theraphan. 1984. *Nyah Kur (Chao bon)-Thai-English dictionary* (Monic Language Studies, Vol. 2). Bangkok: Chulalongkorn University Printing House.

Lyman, Thomas Amis. 1974. *Dictionary of Mong Njua*. The Hague: Mouton.

Maddieson, Ian. 1984. *Patterns of sounds*. Cambridge: Cambridge University Press.

Mao Zongwu & Meng Chaoji. 1986. *Sheyu jianzhi* [A sketch of the She language]. Beijing: Nationalities Press.

Matisoff, James A. 1973. Tonogenesis in Southeast Asia. Consonant Types and Tone. In Larry M. Hyman (ed.), *Southern California Occasional Papers in Linguistics No. 1*, 71–95. Los Angeles: University of Southern California.

Matisoff, James A. 1988. Proto-Hlai initials and tones: A first approximation. In Jerold A. Edmondson & David B. Solnit (eds.), *Comparative Kadai: Linguistic studies beyond Tai*, 289–321. Dallas: Summer Institute of Linguistics & Arlington, TX: University of Texas.

Matisoff, James A. 1989. The bulging monosyllable, or the mora the merrier: echo-vowel adverbialization in Lahu. In J. Davidson (ed.), *South-East Asian linguistics: Essays in honour of Eugénie J.A. Henderson*, 163–197. London: School of Oriental and African Studies.

Matisoff, James A. 2003. *Handbook of Proto-Tibeto-Burman*. Berkeley: University of California Press.

Namkung, Ju (ed.). 1996. *Phonological inventories of Tibeto-Burman languages*. Berkeley, CA: University of California.

Niederer, Barbara. 1997. Notes comparatives sur le Pa-hng. *Cahiers de Linguistique Asie Orientale* 26(1). 71–130.

Norman, Jerry. 1986. The origin of the Proto-Min softened stops. In John McCoy & Timothy Light (eds.), *Contributions to Sino-Tibetan Studies*, 375–384. Leiden: E. J. Brill.

Ostapirat, Weera. 2000. Proto-Kra. *Linguistics of the Tibeto-Burman Area* 23(1). 1–251.

Ostapirat, Weera. 2011. Linguistic interaction in South China: The case of Chinese, Tai and Miao-Yao. Paper presented at an International Symposium, Historical Linguistics in the Asia-Pacific Region and the Position of Japanese. National Museum of Ethnology, Osaka, Japan, 30 July.

Pan, Ho-hsien. 2004. Nasality in Taiwanese. *Language and Speech* 47(3). 267–296.

Prasert, Sriwises. 1978. *Kui (Suai)-Thai-English dictionary*. Bangkok: Chulalongkorn University.

Pucilowski, Anna. 2011. Aspects of the phonetics and phonology of Ho. [Special Issue]. *Mon-Khmer Studies* 2. 154–174.

Purnell, Herbert C. Jr. 1970. *Toward a reconstruction of Proto-Miao-Yao*. Ithaca, NY: Cornell University dissertation.

Ratliff, Martha. 1998. Ho Ne (She) is Hmongic: One final argument. *Linguistics of the Tibeto-Burman Area* 21(2). 97–109.

Ratliff, Martha. 2010. *Hmong-Mien language history*. Canberra: Pacific Linguistics.

Sagart, Laurent. 1999. *The roots of Old Chinese*. Amsterdam & Philadelphia: John Benjamins.

Sagart, Laurent. 2005. Sino-Tibetan-Austronesian: An updated and improved argument. In Laurent Sagart, Roger Blench & Alicia Sanchez-Mazas (eds.), *The Peopling of East Asia: Putting together archaeology, linguistics and genetics*, 161–176. London & New York: Routledge Curzon.

Sarvestani, Karl Reza. 2012. Speech error evidence for homorganic nasal-oral initial clusters in Xong. Paper presented at the Miao-Yao Workshop, 45th International Conference on Sino-Tibetan Languages and Linguistics, Nanyang Technological University, Singapore, October 25.

Scott, N. C. 1973. The monosyllable in Szechuanese. In W. E. Jones & J. Laver (eds.), *Phonetics in linguistics*, 278–298. London: Longman.

Selkirk, E. 1984. On the major class features and syllable theory. In Mark Aronoff & Richard T. Oehrle (eds.), *Language sound structure: Studies in phonology*, 107–136. Cambridge: MIT Press.

Shorto, H. L. 2006. *A Mon-Khmer comparative dictionary* (Edited by Paul Sidwell). Canberra: Pacific Linguistics.

Sidwell, Paul & Doug Cooper. n.d.. SEAlang Mon-Khmer languages project dictionary. http://sealang.net/monkhmer/dictionary/ (Accessed 2013).

Smalley, William A. 1994. *Linguistic diversity and national unity: Language ecology in Thailand*. Chicago: University of Chicago Press.

Smalley, William A., Chia Koua Vang & Gnia Yee Yang. 1990. *Mother of writing: The origin and development of a Hmong Messianic script*. Chicago: The University of Chicago Press.

Sun, Hongkai, Lu Shaozun, Zhang Jichuan & Ouyang Jueya (eds.). 1980. *Menba, Luoba, Dengren de yuyan* [The languages of the Menba, Luoba, and Deng peoples]. Beijing: Social Sciences Press.

Sun, Hongkai, et al. 1991. *Zangmianyu yuyin he cihui* [Tibeto-Burman phonology and lexicon]. Beijing: Social Sciences Press.

Thomason, Sarah Grey. 2000. Linguistic areas and language history. In Dicky Gilbers, John Nerbonne & Jos Schaeken (eds.), *Language in Contact*, 311–327. Amsterdam: Rodopi.

Thurgood, Graham. 1988. Notes on the reconstruction of Proto-Kam-Sui. In Jerold A. Edmondson & David B. Solnit (eds.), *Comparative Kadai: Linguistic studies beyond Tai*, 179–218. Dallas: Summer Institute of Linguistics & Arlington, TX: University of Texas.

Thurgood, Graham. 1999. *From Ancient Cham to modern dialects: Two thousand years of language contact and change* (Oceanic Linguistics Special Publication No. 28). Honolulu: University of Hawai'i Press.

Wang, Dewen. 1988. A comparative study of Kam and Sui initial consonants. In Jerold A. Edmondson & David B. Solnit (eds.), *Comparative Kadai: Linguistic studies beyond Tai*, 129–141. Dallas: Summer Institute of Linguistics & Arlington, TX: University of Texas.

Wang, Fushi & Zongwu Mao. 1995. *Miaoyaoyu guyin gouni* [Reconstruction of the sound system of proto-Miao-Yao]. Beijing: Zhongguo shehui kexue chubanshe [China social sciences press].

Zhou, Guoyan & Somsonge Burusphat. 1996. *Language and cultures of the Kam-Tai (Zhuang-Dong) group: A word list*. Bangkok: Mahidol University.

Paul Sidwell
Local drift and areal convergence in the restructuring of Mainland Southeast Asian languages

1 Introduction

This paper takes as its point of departure the challenge mounted by Post (2011) to the broad characterization of MSEA languages as falling into "Indospheric" and "Sinospheric" convergence areas, advocated by the likes of Matisoff (1991), Bradley et al. (2003) and others. Post argues that while the Indosphere/Sinosphere model suggests that Indic and Sinitic linguistic contacts largely explain the typological divide observed in Mainland Southeast Asia, on the ground there are languages which are typologically more or less Indospheric or Sinospheric; these languages demonstrably lack a history of either the direct linguistic contacts or dominance/subordination relationships implied by the model. Building on the insights of Donegan and Stampe (1983, 2004, etc.), Post proposes a mechanism of prosodic convergence that does not require extensive bilingualism or other intensive linguistic interaction, but one that minimally relies upon speakers imitating without understanding the linguistic performance of others. Such a mechanism may account for diffusion of prosodic features, which can ultimately drive much more extensive restructuring, yet still falls within the scope of a contact driven explanatory model. One might characterize it as a linguistic "butterfly effect" whereby subtle changes may trigger cascades that ultimately manifest significant structural outcomes.

It strikes this writer that, while Post's hypothesis may well characterize some real linguistic history, in principle it may be difficult to test or to apply in a predictive manner. It is arguable that independent linguistic restructuring – Sapir's *Drift* (1921: 147-170) – is such a creature of general linguistic tendencies that parallel examples will occur with or without geographical or temporal proximity. Consequently, one would predict that suspiciously areal patterns of linguistic features will arise randomly, raising the general problem of how to test the role of contact (if any) to account for such patterns. All things being equal, contact is only one hypothesis among multiple possible causal factors.

In this modest contribution I add more grist to the mill by drawing attention to some examples of phonological restructuring among one notionally Indospheric plus several notionally Sinospheric languages that might otherwise be eminent candidates for explanation along the lines suggested by Post, except that the details in each case are strongly inconsistent with their areal contexts. This is interesting because it challenges us to consider how we can know what role — if any — contact has played. This is not to challenge the very notion of areality, but it does question the reasonableness of inferring historical linguistic contact as an explanation for linguistic outcomes that may appear to lack other strong motivation.

The general view is well captured by Enfield:

> MSEA is a site of long-term contact between languages of several major language families. This contact has resulted in extensive parallels in linguistic structure, making MSEA an illustrative case study for areal linguistics. (Enfield 2005: 198)

I do not take issue with this perspective, but I do caution against a simplistic approach to areal-typological analysis that lumps languages into groups according to proximity and identity of structural features without consideration of historical or other independent data that can confirm or otherwise lend support to a contact based explanation. In this context I draw special attention to the paper by Brunelle and Kirby in this volume that tests for statistical significance the geographical distributions of tonal languages in south east Asia, finding that in some cases apparently obvious correlations actually fail to pass conventional objective measures of significance, and leaving genealogy as the most important predictor of typology.

Close examination of various Austroasiatic (AA) data challenges a simple narrative of contact driven convergence; within various individual AA branches, even among close neighbours, one finds gross discrepancies in phonological restructuring, or neighbours which are restructuring in broadly parallel ways (e.g. Laven and Nyaheun towards monosyllables, Angkuic languages becoming tonal), and yet at a micro level are doing so by different paths. While the latter may arguably be characterized as structural convergence, the very real differences in how they play out are not readily explainable as contact driven. It can be more parsimonious to explain these phenomena as being examples of drift conditioned by commonly inherited features (the specific case of Laven and Nyaheun being rooted in historically iambic sesquisyllable structure). A clearer case of independent drift is found within Munda, where despite otherwise overwhelming areal pressure for stable multisyllabic words with simple (C)V(C) syllables, we find the counter example of Gta' with SEAsian type sesquisyllabic structure. Rather strikingly, the examples discussed in this paper involve small languages that are in clearly subordinate social positions to their larger neighbours, yet those dominant neighbours cannot be held to model the changes at stake. Instead of making these small languages more susceptible generally to areal pressures, it may be that their size is somehow connected to the apparent independence of their histories.

2 Two stories of atypical tonogenesis/registrogenesis

2.1 Angkuic

The Angkuic languages represent a Palaungic subgrouping within AA, spoken by small communities in Southern Yunnan and border areas (lumped with the Bulang nationality in Chinese scholarship). The group is named after the language identified as Āng-kú by Scott (1900).[1] Although Angkuic became known to scholars in the late 1800s, those early records are fairly brief and linguistically naive, and thus are not particularly useful. However, several Angkuic languages have been expertly documented and analysed in more recent times, and that work reveals a fascinating story of syllabic, segmental and tonal restructuring that runs counter to the immediate areal trends. Three languages are relevant here: U and Hu, discussed by Svantesson (1988, 1989, 1991), and Muak Sa'aak, more recently described in an MA thesis by Hall (2010). Both Svantesson and Hall analyse historical phonology and tonogenesis in the respective languages of their studies, while in this paper I integrate the analyses to offer a broad account of the development of Angkuic with special reference to tonogenesis.

A key insight relates to understanding the role of vowel length in the historical phonology; while the length contrast has been lost from two of the three languages – arguably under direct areal pressure – the feature is robustly if indirectly reflected in the tonal systems of all three, and contact can only be invoked as a marginal feature in tonogenetic history. This author has prepared a reconstruction of protoPalaungic phonology and lexicon, a working version of

---

[1] The name Āng-kú has not been subsequently reported, although Hall (2010) compares it to the contemporary Kon Keu (ISO KKN). Etymologically Āng-kú is likely to have meant something like 'the people'.

which can be accessed online at sealang.net/monkhmer.[2] The discussion that follows in respect of Angkuic draws directly upon that working reconstruction and the works of Svantesson and Hall mentioned above.

The Angkuic languages are readily recognized as a sub-group by reason of their sharing a so-called Germanic sound shift identified by Haudricourt (1965); historical voiceless stops became aspirated, while pPalaungic plain and implosive voiced stops merged to a single series of voiceless stops (see Table 1). Not only is this shift important for identifying the Angkuic group, it also removed the voicing (phonation) contrast normally associated with high/low tonogenetic series in AA languages (see Huffman 1985 for a general theory of tonogenetic development in AA languages conditioned by voiced initials). Assuming then that Angkuic tones arose in the absence of a voicing contrast, we might also invoke contact with tone languages — especially Shan, Tai Lue or Southwestern Mandarin — but this also problematic, as we see below.

Table 1: Angkuic 'Germanic' shift examples

pPalaungic	gloss	Muak Sa-aak	Hu	U	Lamet	Palaung
*pəɲ	'to shoot'	pʰɤɲ³	pʰɨɲ	pʰèt	pɨɲ	piɲ
*-taʔ	'tail'	k.tʰaː²	θatʰáʔ	satʰà	ntaʔ	səta
*kɔːn	'child'	kʰuan³	kʰɔ̀n	-	kɔn	kuən
*ɓiːl	'forget'	pil³	-	pìn	-	bir
*pldaːk	'palm (hand)'	pɯc² taːk¹	pʰltàk	ʔată̆ʔ	pltàːk	-
*gaːŋ	'house'	kaːŋ³	Kàŋ	káā	-	gaŋ
*gak	'to bite'	kak²	Kák	kàk	kàk	-

2.1.1 Hu: high/low tones

The simplest tone system among the Angkuic languages is that of Hu. Its origin is explained neatly:

> From a general phonological point of view, the most interesting phenomenon is the development of a two-tone system where the tones are not the reflexes of voiced/voiceless proto-initials, as is most often the case in Mon-Khmer two-tone (or two-register) languages. Instead, the tones are the reflexes of the long/short vowel opposition which existed in Proto-Palaungic (inherited from Proto-Mon-Khmer). As far as I know, no language with this kind of tonogenesis has been described before. (Svantesson 1991: 67)

---

[2] This is a work in progress, so consequently the online version may at any time lag behind the current state of the analysis, and this should be taken into account when accessing the site.

What Svantesson (1991: 75) shows is that the two phonological tones - high and low – show a strong relation to vowel length. This can be seen in the measurements of mean durations in Table 2:

Table 2: Hu tone/length correlations from Svantesson (1991: 75)

		Mean durations by rime
High tone	jám	126 ms
	páp	102 ms
	kák	117 ms
Low tone	jàm	200 ms
	kàp	120 ms
	ʔàk	188 ms

Svantesson's measurements show that vowel length distinctions have not completely levelled in Hu, and in many environments it is evident that etymological quantity contrasts are recoverable. The merger is most evident in the near minimal pair *páp, kàp*, which are separated by less than 20ms, while syllables with final nasals differ by 74ms, with low tone syllables consistently longer than their high tone counterparts. In terms of how length contrasts are realized in phonologically conservative AA languages, we lack the broad statistically robust datasets needed to make strong generalizations, but experience suggests that the long/short contrast is typically realized as something approximating a single versus double length quantity, which is frequently captured in transcription by scholars with a doubling of vowel glyphs. The Hu quantity differences are certainly somewhat narrowed, but we still see the low tone vowels are overall 68% longer than the high tone vowels.

That a high/low tone contrast should emerge from length differences has been remarked upon as being very unusual; Svantesson was not aware of any exact parallel, and more recently Kingston (2011) in a survey of tonogenesis could only nominate Western Lugbara (Nilo-Saharan) as another example. Svantesson (1991: 76) ponders the question, drawing attention to the apparently inherent intrinsic relation between shorter duration and higher pitch, suggesting that an earlier non-distinctive pitch difference could have acquired a functional load. It may also be significant that in respect of Köho/Sre (Manley, 1972) and Nyaheun (Davis, 1968), scholars have reported non-phonemic falling tones on long vowels.

In unrestructured AA languages (in the paradigm of Huffman 1985) the long vowels are less marked phonologically than the short, and neutralization of quantity is generally realized as lengthening; for a well understood example see the history of Sedang as analysed by Smith (1979) and elsewhere in this paper. One could speculate that if a falling tone was associated with long syllables, it is reasonable to suggest that the non-falling, that is a higher or even rising pitch contour over the historically short syllables may have been accentuated and phonologized as a marked tone. Consequently, it is tempting to propose reconstructing a proto-Angkuic stage with an emerging binary tone system. However, we need to consider other Angkuic data before moving forward with this idea.

2.1.2 U: high/low/falling/rising tones

The U language - closely related to Hu - was described and analysed in detail by Svantesson (1988). U has undergone even more extensive restructuring, with much more reduction of disyllables into monosyllables and associated segmental mergers than has Hu. Additionally, and more importantly here, U shows a four way high/low/rising/falling tonal system that does not map symmetrically onto the binary Hu system. In fact, according to Svantesson's analysis there are actually nine distinct tonal outcomes according to different rimes, which then sort out into an overall four-way tone system.

Putting aside two marginal cases, the broad picture of tonal development in U, with conditioning environments specified, is laid forth in Table 3:

Table 3: U tonal developments

		Examples: pPalaungic → U
pAngkuic short vowels: *V̆	→ V̀ /_C[son.]	*jam → jàm 'to die'
	→ V́ elsewhere	*gak → káʕ 'bite'
pAngkuic long vowels: *V:	→ V̂ /C[+son.] _	*ʔma:r → mâ 'field'
	→ V̆ /C[any] _C[-son.]	*hla:t → lăt 'to fear'
	→ V́ /C[-son.] _C[+son]	*kta:m → tʰám 'crab'
	→ V́ /C[-son.] V[+high] ∅	*ciʔ → ncʰí 'louse'
	→ V̀ /C[-son.] V[-high] ∅	*kaʔ → kʰà 'fish'

Dividing tonal outcomes in U according to the historical vowel length allows us to sort out otherwise overlapping/merging developments. For example, we see that historically short syllables have both high and low tone outcomes, depending on whether they have stopped or continuant codas. Additionally, historically long syllables have at least five distinct tonal outcomes, including high and low, superficially suggesting no connection with Hu tonogenesis. However, further analysis suggests that interactions between length, sonority of onsets, vowel height, and quality of codas readily account for the complex outcomes in U, with length playing a primary role.

However, with only Hu and U data, we are still left in an ambiguous position. There are no reasons beyond considerations of economy to suppose that the U system is more indicative of proto-Angkuic, and to suppose that Hu tones resulted from widespread mergers conditioned by the persistence of phonetic vowel length. Fortunately since recently we have been in a better position to address this with the availability of data on a third Angkuic language. An MA thesis on Muak Sa'aak (henceforth simply Muak) by Hall (2010) provides enough evidence to permit a broadly confident reconstruction of tonogenesis in Angkuic.

2.1.3 Muak Sa'aak: three tones plus length contrast

At the time Svantesson was writing in the 1980s/early 1990s, it seemed that only one Palaungic language had retained the historical AA vowel quantity distinction in all or most environments, namely Lamet (as described variously by Lindell et al. [1978] and Narumol Charoenma [1982]). Spoken in a pocket of Northern Laos surrounded by Khmu' and Tai speakers, Lamet never lost vowel length. Svantesson relied heavily on Lamet comparisons for his historical analyses of Hu and U. However, thanks to Hall's description, it is clear that Muak also more or less faithfully preserves the AA vowel quantity contrast, while also undergoing both the Angkuic Germanic sound shift and developing a tonal system also related to vowel quantity. Our Figure 1. shows the Muak vowel inventory, indicating contrastive length for all but two monophthongs: additionally there are three tones:

Close	i i:	ɯ ɯ:	u u:
Close-mid	e e:	ɤ ɤ:	o o:
Open	ɛ	a a:	ɔ
Diphthongs	ia		ua

Fig. 1: Muak Sa'aak vowel phonemes according to Hall (2010)

The three Muak tones are described by Hall as follows:

– Tone 1: low tone with tense phonation, not consistently creaky;

– Tone 2: so called "checked tone", high pitch on short open syllables and with stop codas, and falling pitch on long open syllables and with nasal codas;
– Tone 3: high falling tone occurring only with sonorant codas and open syllables ("live" syllables).

Other than the restriction against stop codas with Tone 3, all three tones occur across a broad range of environments that are difficult to characterize if one tries to account for the full synchronic distribution without considering etymology. There are also independent secondary changes that in some codas created new long syllables, such as by the loss of finals *-ʔ, *-h, and *-s. Additionally there is a huge cohort of Tai (apparently mostly Shan) loans that fills what would otherwise be many systematic gaps in the distribution of rimes. It is also quite striking to note that the strong influence of Shan and Tai Lue on Muak – repeatedly noted and illustrated by Hall – is not associated with the loss of vowel quantity in Muak, given that in Shan and Tai Lue length is only contrastive on /a/. Evidently multilingualism in and massive borrowing from languages that do not contrast vowel length may not be enough to condition a general shift in that direction (although admittedly the periods of time involved in these cases are not known).

If one removes from consideration the hundreds of Tai loanwords from Hall's Muak lexicon, important asymmetries emerge, a point commendably recognized by Hall but not followed through in the thesis. The list edited in this way allows us to more effectively isolate the tonogenetic conditions, and establish that there is a clear connection between etymological vowel length and tone in Muak, although it is not the only factor. The basic relations revealed by the analysis are presented in Table 4:

Table 4: Muak Sa'aak tonal developments

		pPalaungic	Hu	Muak Sa'aak
Tone 1: low	V̇ː / _ C[-voice]	*leːk	lèk	leːk¹ 'pig'
		*hɲaːp	-	ɲaːp¹ 'difficult'
		*lih	líh	liː¹ 'to exit'
		*-taːk	ntʰàk	tʰaːk¹ 'tongue'
		*kaːp	kʰàp	kʰaːp¹ 'chin'
		*ʔaːk	ʔàk	ʔaːk¹ 'hunting bow'
Tone 2: high allotone	V̇ / _ C[-voice]	*kuʔ	-	kʰu² 'body'
		*tiʔ	tʰíʔ	tʰi² 'hand, arm'
		*suk	θúk	suk² 'hair'
		*jɛt	-	jɛt² 'to extinguish'
		*gak	kák	kak² 'to bite'
Tone 2: falling allotone				Loanwords only
Tone 3: falling	V̂ / _ C[+voice]	*jam	jám	jam³ 'to die'
		*rim	ʁím	rim³ 'village'
		*ɓiːl	(pìn U)	pil³ 'forget'
		*jaːm	jàm	jaːm³ 'to weep'
		*ɗiəm	tèn	tian³ 'low'
		*gaːŋ	kàŋ	kaːŋ³ 'house'
		*ʔmaːr	mà	maːl³ 'field'
		*kɔːn	kʰɔ̀n	kʰuan³ 'child'

Commentary on tones:

Within Tone 1 historically long vowels are generally indicated; note that in case such as *lih* 'to exit' with final glottal fricative, the vowel was unmarked for length and was probably phonetically long.

Tone 2 is divided into two allotones by Hall, but the falling allotone is restricted to loanword vocabulary, so we can treat it as secondary. Lexicon in the high allotone of Tone 2 shows both long and short vowels, but is consistently marked by stopped finals, including the glottal stop which clearly persisted into pAngkuic (as shown by Hu comparisons) but was later lost in Muak.

Tone 3 shows both long and short vowels, but is marked by having historically voiced codas consistently.

The above data suggest a Hu-like long/short > high/low tonogenesis, plus a third category in which all voiced continuant finals conditioned a falling tone. The question is then whether the third category is a direct development or conceals a more complex past.

2.1.4 Proto-Angkuic tonogenesis reconstructed

In order to reconcile the various data reviewed here with a single account of Angkuic tonogenesis, I propose reconstructing four distinct phonetic tonal contours for pAngkuic which subsequently phonologized differently in pre-Hu-U and pre-Muak. The hypothesis is that while quantity conditioned whether the contours were generally high or low, coda voicing conditioned falling contours. This is laid out in Table 5.

Table 5: Proto-Angkuic phonetic tones

	Vowel short	Vowel long
- voiced coda	high	non-high
+ voiced coda	high falling	non-high falling

The hypothesis suggests that all tones in rimes with voiced codas become phonologized as a single falling tone in preMuak, while in pre-Hu the phonetic tonal contours did not phonologize, yielding a simple high/low system. Within U more complex developments occurred, and these can be accounted for broadly as voiceless initials conditioning higher tonal outcomes in long syllables with high vowels or sonorant finals, and voiceless finals conditioning rising tones in long syllables with sonorant initials. Given that voiceless segments generally correlate with tenser phonation/higher pitch these outcomes essentially reflect inherent linguistic tendencies, and do not require any unusual appeals to account for their motivation.

Table 6: Angkuic tonal evolution schematized

	pAnguic phonetic tones	Hu	U	Muak
Short vowel	CV́T	CV́T/N	CV́T	CV́T
	CV̌N		CV̌N	CV̌N
Long vowel	CV́:T	CV̀:T/N	NV̌Ø	CV̀:T
	CV̀:N		NV̌T	CV̀:N
			TV̌N	
			TV́[+high] Ø	
			TV̀[-high] Ø	

Ideally one would attempt to test this reconstruction by examining pitch traces of all three languages for signs of the supposed pAngkuic allotones. In any case, Svantesson's initial insight, that vowel length plays a special and unusual role in Angkuic tonogenesis, seems to be valid. We are presently compelled to reconstruct a general relationship between pitch and quantity in pAngkuic that was phonologized in ways that do not fit the 'typical' tonogenetic pathways associated with SEAsian languages. Neither do they fit more specifically with the restructuring paradigm of Huffman (1985) or the "Laryngeally based account" of Thurgood (2007) that broadly underpin our understanding of tonogenesis and orient our approach to the reconstruction of AA vocalism. Instead, Angkuic tonogenesis appears to reflect rather mundane phonetic tendencies, not immediately related to the structural properties of neighbouring languages. It may be sufficient to explain what has happened as internal change — grounded in articulatory and acoustic phonetics — without recourse to contact. On the other hand, the apparent rarity of tonal distinctions developing primarily from quantity differences suggests that there is more at stake than a straightforward case of independent drift. Muak speakers are using other tone languages, and borrowing heavily from them, and this may have played a role in the restructuring of Muak, although it is not clear exactly what this role may have been, beyond providing the source of the Tone 2 falling allotone.

2.2 North Bahnaric

The Bahnaric languages are spoken mainly in the central highlands of Vietnam and constitute perhaps the most internally diverse branch of AA. The languages are spread over three countries, where they are separated not only by topography but also by the (sometimes overlapping) areal influences of Vietnamese, Khmer, Thai/Lao, Chamic and the Katuic branch of AA. Despite the diverse influences from variously restructured and/or tonal languages, most Bahnaric tongues are relatively conservative, preserving the historical AA voice distinction in stops, and vowel systems that strikingly resemble, for example, that of Old Khmer before it was restructured (see Ferlus [1992] on the historical phonology of Khmer).

In this context, it is interesting that the North Bahnaric (NB) languages, a sub-group of around ten closely related speech varieties spoken in the vicinity of Kontum, evince an unusual[3] phonation (or "register") contrast that appears to correlate directly with historical vowel height distinctions, rather than con-

---

3 Arguably the closest parallel is in Pacoh, a Katuic language spoken roughly a hundred kilometres north of the NB area. Synchronic and diachronic aspects of Pacoh registers are discussed in, e.g. Diffloth (1982), Alves (2006), and Sidwell (2005). The parallel with NB registrogenesis is only partial, but shares important features especially in terms of the correlation between vowel aperture and phonation.

sonant phonation types, in contradiction to conventional models of registrogenesis.

The historical phonology of NB registers is discussed by Smith (1967, 1972, 1979) and further analysed by this writer (Sidwell, 1998). These studies allow us to sketch out what happened in terms of segmental changes, although the understanding of the articulatory, acoustic and perceptual mechanisms underlying the restructuring remains incomplete. Below I briefly outline our understanding of the historical vocalism, with reference to three key NB languages, contrasting this with what we know about the most important historical contact languages.

2.2.1 Rengao

According to Gregerson (1976), Rengao has a highly symmetrical inventory of 10 long and 10 short vowels, each divided into five lax and five tense, as shown in Figure 2:

long lax			long tense			short lax			short tense		
iː		uː				i		u			
			e_i		$^o u$				ɪ		ʊ
eː	əː	oː				e	ə	o			
			ɛː	aː	ɔː				ɛ	a	ɔ

Fig. 2: Rengao vowels (Gregerson 1976)

It is evident that the registers correlate directly with vowel height, such that tense vowels are lower, or have lower onsets compared to their apparent lax counterparts. From a purely phonological viewpoint one could treat either register or timbre as primary, and disregard the other. However, it is clear that these two features are closely linked, and it would be wrong to disregard the relationship. In an important paper arising from the 1973 ICAAL conference, Gregerson (1976) characterizes the articulatory correlates of the registers as shown in Figure 3:

	First Register (tense)	Second Register (lax)
resonance	sharply defined oral (clear)	deep pharyngeal
pharyngeal cavity	constricted	expanded
larynx	normal to high	lowered
tongue root	retracted	advanced
tongue blade	lowered	raised

Fig. 3: Articulatory correlates of Rengao registers

Of the above, the height of the tongue blade is clearly important, since it correlates directly with F1, which is the most important contributor to apparent vowel height. Significantly, Gregerson's model connects tongue blade height with the action of the tongue root and other gestures associated with manipulating pharyngeal cavity volume, and we will revisit this after discussing two other NB languages and the implications of the phonological correspondences between them.

2.2.2 Halang

Halang phonology as discussed by Cooper and Cooper (1966) has a breathy register which is only contrastive among the long vowels; the breathy short vowels are only slightly breathy such that timbre is clearly more salient. Also, their phonetic description of the allophones indicates some minor asymmetries in the phonetics of the mid and open vowels, but these are trivial. More significant is the aperture difference between the tense and lax diphthongs (Figure 4):

long lax		long tense		short lax		short tense	
iː	uː	iː	uː	ɪ	u		
eː		eː			ə		o
aː	ɔː	aː	ɔː			ɛ	a
iə	uə	ea	oa				

Fig. 4: Halang vowels (Cooper and Cooper 1966)

Although it appears that the register contrast is robust among the long monophthongs, it is also evident that among the diphthongs and short vowels there is a direct correlation between aperture and phonation that broadly parallels the situation in Rengao.

2.2.3 Sedang

Sedang has a strikingly different vocalism compared to other NB languages, although thanks to the comparative work of Smith (1967, 1972, 1979) we have a good understanding of how to relate Sedang phonology to the rest of NB. The vowel inventory is shown in Figure 5:

Monophthongs			Diphthongs				
i		u	iə	uə	io	uo	iɪ
e		o	eə	oə	eo		oɛ
ɛ	a	ɔ					
Vowels occur in two registers: tense/creaky & lax/modal							

Fig. 5: Sedang vowels (Smith 1979)

Broadly speaking, Sedang dramatically restructured its phonology, with outcomes that include:

– the loss of a quantity distinction in vowels, thanks to a general diphthongization of long vowels and lengthening of etymological short vowels;
– the general devoicing of voiced stops, and acquisition of new voiced stops by borrowing and cluster assimilation;
– the loss of final stops in tense syllables leading to frequent homophony;
– a general tensing of phonation such that modal (tense) syllables became creaky and breathy (lax) syllables became modal.

An effect of the above changes was that Sedang came to look very different from the rest of the group, but the changes are so regular that Sedang still provides a reliable witness for reconstructing historical vowel length, quality and register values. Of particular importance is the fact that, although the Sedang vowels occur generally across the registers, significant asymmetries emerge when historical mergers and loans are taken into account, and these confirm the correlations evident in the Rengao and Halang data.

2.2.4 Proto-North Bahnaric vowel-register correlation

Fortunately we are not solely reliant on NB data in order to investigate the history of registrogenesis within the subgroup. Sidwell (1998) offered a preliminary pBahnaric reconstruction: this was modified by Sidwell (2002) and further extended and refined by Sidwell (2011), and this foundation provides both a framework for analysis of the correspondences and a resource for etymological comparisons, and underlies the following discussion.

To begin with, the fact that Rengao and Halang effectively lack a register contrast among their short vowels immediately suggests that they have more or less simply failed to undergo registrogenesis or other significant restructuring, while something inherent to the long vowels was a significant factor in their later developments. Analysis indicates that the etymological high vowels (and more often than not mid vowels) are consistently reflected with lax phonation in NB daughter languages (breathy in Rengao and Halang, modal in Sedang). Conversely, reflexes of historically low vowels and diphthongs show tense register (modal in Rengao and Halang, creaky in Sedang where codas have not been dropped). To see this pattern clearly it is necessary to sort out the secondary restructuring of diphthongs among the languages. In Halang, *iə,*uə lowered to /ea, oa/, while *iː, *uː diphthongized to /iə, uə/, and short vowels in various environments lengthened, filling the space vacated by the newly diphthongized vowels. In Rengao *iə,*uə are reflected as tense monophthongs, in some environments becoming short. These patterns are exemplified in Table 7.

Table 7: Proto North Bahnaric high vowels and diphthongs

	North Bahnaric				CentralB	WestB	
gloss	Rengao	Halang	Sedang	pNB	Bahnar	Laven	pBahnaric
'mushroom'	bə̰tsi̤t	pəsi̤ːt	kəset	*psit	-	pseːt	*pseːt
'sky'	pli̤ŋ	pli̤ːŋ	plɛn	*pliŋ	plɛɲ	-	*pleːŋ
'banana'	pre̤ːt	pri̤ət	priət	*priːt	priːt	priət	*priːt
'to dig'	-	ci̤ər	ciəl	*ciːr	siːr	-	*ciːr
'tongue'	rəpɛt	rəpeat	rəpe	*lpiət	rəpjɛt	hpiat	*lpiət
'chicken'	ʔi̤ːr	ʔe̤ar	ʔi̤	*ʔiər	ʔjɛr	ʔiar	*ʔiər
'to push'	drṳt	drṳt	trɔt	*drut	drut	-	*drut
'fire'	ʔṳŋ	ʔṳŋ	ʔɔn	*ʔuŋ	ʔuɲ	ʔuŋ	*ʔuŋ
'axe'	co̤ːŋ	cṳəŋ	cuoŋ	*cuːŋ	suːŋ	cuːŋ	*cuːŋ
'smoke'	ɲo̤ːj	ʔɲṳəj	ŋoj	*ʔnuːj	ʔɲuːj	ʔɲuːj	*ʔɲuːj
'four'	puːn	poan	pṳn	*puən	pwan	puan	*puən
'to cut'	-	poat	poe	*puət	pwat	puat	*puət

Table 8 demonstrates the relationship between low vowels and tense register, although one should note that finding suitable examples of *ɛː is difficult, so I restrict the treatment to reflexes of *aː and *ɔː here.

Table 8: Proto North Bahnaric low vowels

gloss	North Bahnaric				CentralB	WestB	
	Rengao	Halang	Sedang	pNB	Bahnar	Laven	pBahnaric
'squirrel'	prɔːk	proak	proa	*prɔːk	prɔːk	prɔːk	*prɔːk
'tree'	lɔːŋ	ʔloaŋ	lo̰əŋ	*ʔlɔːŋ	ʔlɔːŋ	ʔlɔːŋ	*ʔlɔːŋ
'child'	kɔːn	koan	ku̯ən	*kɔːn	kɔːn	kuan	*kɔːn
'hungry'	məŋɔːt	məʔŋoat	məŋuə	*pŋɔːt	pəŋɔːt	pŋuat	*pŋɔːt
'navel'	klɔk	klɔk	klɔ	*klɔk	klɔk	klɔk	*klɔk
'back'	rɔŋ	rɔŋ	ro̰ŋ	*rɔŋ	hərɔŋ	-	*(k)rɔŋ
'water'	daːk	daːk	tea	*daːk	ɗaːk	daːk	*ɗaːk
'eagle'	klaːŋ	klaːŋ	kəklḛəŋ	*klaːŋ	klaːŋ	klaːŋ	*klaːŋ
'blood'	məhaːm	məhaːm	məhḛəm	*phaːm	phaːm	phaːm	*bhaːm
'to slap'	taːp	taːp	tea	*taːp	taːp	-	*taːp
'to hunt'	daŋ	daŋ	ta̰ŋ	*daŋ	-	daŋ	*daŋ
'trap'	dak	dak	Ta	*dak	ɗak	dak	*ɗak
'woodpecker'	təlɛh	təlɛh	təlḛjt	*təlɛh	təlɛh	-	*təlɛh
'to think'	kəcɛŋ	kəcɛŋ	təcḛŋ	*təcɛŋ	təcɛŋ	-	-

(† 'hook used to pick fruit from tops of trees')

More problematic are the correspondences reflecting historical mid vowels. In this regard it is especially important to consider the fate of the pB mid central vowels *əː and *ə; these are frequent in pB, and typically reflected as mid central vowels in Bahnaric languages, but typically there is no /əː/ vowel in NB languages, and usually short /ə/ is either absent or is functionally the lax equivalent of tense /a/ (effectively a tense/lax [ɐ] pair). Bahnaric *əː is reflected as a front vowel - mostly [eː ~ ɛː] - where it has variously merged with etymological *eː or been involved in a chain shift in which it displaced etymological *eː (merging to /i/ as in examples 'mushroom' and 'sky' above); in any case the reflexes are consistently lax, while the reflexes of *oː and *o are tense. Examples are given in Table 9.

Table 9: Proto North Bahnaric mid vowels

	North Bahnaric			pNB	CentralB	WestB	
gloss	Rengao	Halang	Sedang		Bahnar	Laven	pBahnaric
'leech'	plẹːm	plɛːm	pliəm	*plẹːm	pləːm	plʌːm	*pləːm
'beginning, stump'	tsẹːm	sɛːm	pəsiəm	*tsẹːm	təːm	tʌːm	*təːm
'answer'	tẹːl	tɛːl	tiəl	*tẹːl	təːl	tʌːl	*təːl
'crowded'	-	gədrạm	kram	*krạm	kədrəm	-	*krəm
'thick'	həbạl	həbạl	həbɔ	*həbạl	həbəl	kbəl	*-ɓəl
'to blow'	hluːm	hluːm	hlum̥	*hloːm	hloːm	kloːm	*k(h)loːm
'hot'	tuʔ	tuʔ	to	*toʔ	tɔʔ	ʔtoʔ	*toʔ
'to spit'	cuh	kəcuh	kəcow	*kcoh	kəsɔh	kcoh	*kcoh

While the examples given above illustrate only part of a larger more complicated history, they are strongly indicative of the historical processes that governed the evolution of NB vowel phonology. Broadly we see that, regardless of both vowel length, and the phonation of onset or coda consonants, vowels with historical quality /i, u, e, ə/ developed breathy phonation while historical /o, ɔ, ɛ, a, iə, uə/ became tense (with just a few exceptions involving /o/). This forces us to consider whether features related to vowel height can be related to phonation.

2.2.5 Proto-North Bahnaric registrogenesis in context

Much of our present understanding of tonogenesis and registrogenesis is well summed up in the recent works by Thurgood (2002, 2007) and Brunelle (2005) etc. Thurgood tabulates the phonetic correlates of register as follows:

Table 10: "The three most common register complexes" Thurgood (2007: 274)

	Tense Register	Unmarked	Breathy Register
original initials:	proto-voiceless		proto-voiced
voice quality:	tense (creaky)	modal (clear)	breathy
vowel quality:	lower (open);		higher (closed);
	more fronted vowels;		more backed vowels;
	tendency to diphthongization;		tendency to centralization;
	often shorter		often longer
pitch distinctions:	higher pitch		lower pitch
state of larynx:	larynx tense and/or raised		larynx lax and/or lowered
	(reduced supraglottal cavity)		(increased supraglottal cavity)

And recently Mortensen explains:

> It is well known that there is an association between phonation type and vowel quality. Specifically, breathy phonation requires a lowering of the larynx, which has the effect of lowering formants, especially F1 (Fagan 1988; Ladefoged and Maddieson 1996; Gordon and Ladefoged 2001; Brunelle 2005). This effect may give rise to either low-level allophonic splits or to more phonologically significant developments. (Mortensen 2006: 13)

Mortensen is correct that formant lowering associated with breathy phonation can give rise to significant developments, a point anticipated by Huffman (1985). But more important in this discussion is that apparently there was no trigger of the conventionally understood type (e.g. voicing of onsets with subsequent devoicing) which would have given rise to breathy phonation on vowels. The distribution of registers in NB is quite blind to onset voicing, or any other consonantal features, with the exception of the well understood much later secondary developments within Sedang. What seems to have occurred is that phonation differences inherently associated with vowel height differences became phonologized. This is unusual, as Kingston (2011: 2319) remarks (including register within a broad understanding of tone), "Tone splits from vowel height or ATR contrasts are decidedly rare."

Brunelle, discussing the correlations between register and vowel height remarks:

> A study of vowel quality in another Mon-Khmer language, Wa, shows no clear difference between registers (Watkins, 2002). This is not surprising, as vowel quality is the most variable correlate of register, varying from systems where there are no differences between the two registers to systems where vowel quality becomes the only register cue. For example, register has lost its phonemic status in Standard Khmer (Huffman 1978), after conditioning a two-way split of the vowel system, leaving the vowel space unusually over-

crowded. However, when register does condition vowel quality differences, the high register always has lower vowels than the low register. (Brunelle 2005: 165-6)

Elsewhere in his thesis Brunelle discusses the correlations between vowel timbre and register in Cham, and a significant relation between F1 and phonation:

Overall, the first formant of the high register (h) has higher frequency, which means that high register vowels tend to be more open. This is expected because the lengthening of the vocal tract due to the lowering of the larynx during the production of the low register results in lower formant frequencies, especially for F1. (Brunelle 2005: 187)

However, the general theory of registrogenesis, with which Brunelle is in concord, assumes that laryngeal lowering is connected with voicing, whereas in NB, words with voiceless onsets were just as likely to become breathy as those with voiced onsets. In order to reconcile these facts with our general theory of registrogenesis, we are forced to hypothesize that pre- or proto-NB speakers were articulating their high and mid-high vowels with a lowered larynx, conditioning breathy phonation, which then became analysed as a salient component of the bundle of features treated as +high.

The closest we have got so far to an explanation — one that has not been generally well received (e.g. see Brunelle 2005 for a critique) — is that of Gregerson (1976). In Gregerson's scheme, registers are modelled as primarily a function of tongue root advancement/retraction such that lax = [+ATR], tense = [-ATR], and the movement of the tongue root is assumed to have a direct association with the position of the tongue blade. For example, it is supposed that advancing the tongue root to enlarge the pharyngeal cavity in association with production of breathy voice inherently acts to raise the tongue blade and thus lower F1. Gregerson's theory gives primacy to the role of pharyngeal resonance in registers, and this runs directly counter to the primacy the standard model gives to the state of the larynx, but it does not discount an important role for ±ATR at the margins.

I speculate that speakers connected subtle acoustic correlates of an enlarged pharyngeal cavity with the lowered F1 characteristic of high vowels. Speakers augmented these features by further enlarging the cavity with lowering of the larynx, yielding a more breathy phonation. In due course the phonation quality feature came to dominate the perceptual character of high and mid-high vowels, and the register contrast was phonologized, facilitating subsequent and diverse vowel restructuring within the group.

Given the evident rarity of these NB developments (regardless of the correctness of the proposed reconstruction), one may speculate about the possible role of language contact. For example, we may wonder if NB speakers were in contact with register languages, and somehow mis-analysed what they were hearing and trying to pronounce, and carried over those new habits into their everyday speech. However, there is a serious difficulty with this idea, since we know that the development of registers in important neighbouring languages, principally Chamic and Khmer, occurred historically rather late, probably well after the bulk of their known lexical influence on NB occurred. The great areal de-voicing swept into Indo-China rather late, from the 1700s (e.g. Ferlus 2011) whereas Khmer and Chamic power was dramatically declining in the immediate region from the 1300s through 1500s, robbing us of a potentially convenient if expedient contact driven hypothesis.

3 Two stories of atypical syllable restructuring

3.1 Laven and Nyaheun: restructuring toward monosyllables

Laven and Nyaheun are two closely related West-Bahnaric languages spoken on the Boloven Plateau in southern Laos; the 1995 census counted around 40,000 Laven and 4,000 Nyaheun. Laven is described in some detail in Jacq's (2001) MA thesis, and the historical phonology of Laven and Nyaheun is analysed by Ferlus (1974) and Sidwell and Jacq (2003). A Nyaheun lexicon is published (Ferlus 1998) and the grammar is briefly discussed by Davis (1973). Further, I have personally collected field data on both languages. Although Laven and Nyaheun are closely related, they do not subgroup together, and phonological and syntactic differences are so extensive that there are strong barriers to mutual intelligibility. My own field observation is that mutual comprehension between the speakers is a function of multilingualism more than of linguistic similarity. Additionally, my understanding is that there was a previous tendency for Nyaheun speakers to use Laven as in inter-language, while more recently I observe Lao now dominantly employed in that purpose.

Both Laven and Nyaheun have restructured sesquisyllabic words into monosyllables, completely in the case of Nyaheun, and in a subset of sesquisyllabic lexicon in Laven. This is quite unlike anything that has occurred in Lao or any other known contact language of the immediate area. In fact, Lao and Khmer robustly maintain sesquisyllabic words, as do the Katuic languages of southern Laos which are the main other contact languages. Of course, Vietnamese and some Chamic languages have restructured sesquisyllables into monosyllables (see, for example Thurgood 1999, Brunelle 2005) but neither of these was geographically or temporally aligned to exert influence on the languages of the Boloven. What happened on the plateau in this respect was apparently quite local and specific.

Broadly, Nyaheun speakers restructured the entire lexicon into monosyllables, predominantly by two processes:

– Assimilation, changing clusters into geminates, and
– Lenition of prevocalic segments creating onsets with rising or plateaued sonority.

Laven, on the other hand, underwent a partial restructuring:

– Lenition of rhotic and sibilant clusters into simple or complex segments which begin with devoiced transitions (CC, CrC > hC~C̦),
– Loss of prenasalization yielding preglottalized onsets,
– Reduction in the prominence of minor syllable vowels.

The examples in Table 11 highlight the creation of geminated onsets in Nyaheun, which includes both oral stops and nasals. For Laven we see reduction where initials in clusters are historically glottal, palatal or stop+rhotic clusters. To illustrate the historical processes, comparisons are also offered for Brao (another West Bahnaric language), Proto-West Bahnaric (Sidwell and Jacq 2003), Khmer and Stieng (South Bahnaric):

Table 11: Laven-Nyaheun comparisons (1)

gloss	Laven	Nyaheun	Brao	pWBahnaric	other
'right (side)'	hmaː	mːaː	cəmaː	*cmaː	
'finger'	hpuac	pːuac	tərpuac	*trpuac	
'buttock'	hboːk	pːoːk	tərpɑk	*trboːk	Khmer trɑpouk
'bean'	htaːk	tːaːk	hntaːk	*hntaːk	Khmer sɑndaek
'turtle'	ʔtʌːk	tːeːk	ʔntəːk	*ʔntəːk	Khmer ʔɑndaək
'hoof'	kʲɟoːp	cːɔːp	-	*kɟ(ɔ/o)ːp	Stieng kənɟɔːp
'a small bean'	kɲɛː	ɲːɛː	-	*kɲɛː	

The Laven initial sequences written with initial /h/ represent preaspirated oral stops and partly devoiced nasals. The nasals are normal length but voicing commences about half way through the duration (these are described by Jacq 2001: 62-65). The Nyaheun geminates are quite long, with the stops around 200+ ms, and the nasals typically more than 300ms, actually a little more than twice as long as the equivalent unmarked segments.

Table 12: Laven-Nyaheun comparisons (2)

gloss	Laven	Nyaheun	Brao	pWBahnaric	other
'mortar'	tᵊpal	dwaw	təwa:w	*tʔpal	Khmer t ɓal
'crab'	kᵊta:m	gra:m	kəda:m	*kʔta:m	Khmer kɗa:m
'ghost'	kᵊsɔk	gjɔk	kəjak	*kʔsɔk	
'to wash'	hta:	hra:	səda:	*sʔta:	
'day'	tᵊŋaj	nɨe, ŋe:	təŋaj	*tŋaj	Khmer tŋaj
'year'	kᵊmɔ:	ŋwɔ:, m:ɔ:	kəmɑ:	*kmɔ:	Katu kamɑ:
'house'	n̥ə:m	n̥ra:m	hna:m	*sna:m	SurinKhmer sna:m

Table 12 shows Nyaheun words in which lenition of prevocalic segments creates sequences with rising sonority, although in some cases there are also doublets with geminated onsets. Where the historical initial was *s, the outcome in Laven is a partly devoiced onset. Where the initial is a stop there is not a great change, but it is noticeable that the epenthetic vowel which is normally a feature of these clusters is much less prominent than in other West Bahnaric languages, such as Brao. Also note that in several examples below, clusters are reconstructed with medial glottal stops; this was tentatively offered by Sidwell and Jacq (2003) to explain differential outcomes of structurally similar clusters in Laven and Nyaheun. These reconstructions deserve reassessment: perhaps they reflect a stratum of loans from Old/Middle Khmer, since it underwent a change in which prevocalic voiceless stops became implosives, which may or may not have been voiced (Ferlus 1992 dates the shift to implosion to the 13th~14th C).

It is apparent that Nyaheun continues to an extreme a tendency that is partly manifest in Brao, another West Bahnaric language. In Brao there is a limited lenition in which clusters of stop+stop and stop+fricative see the second element become a voiced approximant. Yet in Nyaheun all initial clusters that were not already of the type stop+approximant were restructured either to that pattern or into geminates.

How to characterize the phonological processes? In respect of Nyaheun we recognize that there has been a phonotactic simplification, such that only three types of onsets became permissible in the language: 1) single consonantal segments, 2) long level sonority (geminate), and 3) rising sonority voiced onsets (voiced stop/nasal+approximant). Where a voicing change has occurred, it has involved an increase in voicing. In contrast, Laven has increased the overall complexity of possible onsets. While retaining a large proportion of otherwise typically Mon-Khmer clustered onsets, it also restructured a marked subset of clusters into preaspirates and partly devoiced nasals. The effect of the restructuring was to depress sonority at the left edge of onsets, thus creating a rising sonority over the onset. This can be characterized as a fortition in restructured onsets.

In a broad sense we might say that both Laven and Nyaheun have been restructuring characteristically complex AA initials into more compact rising sonority onsets, consistent with broad SEAsian trends. Change was most dramatic in Nyaheun, to an extent that is directly comparable to, for example, Vietnamese, which is known to have radically reduced all clustered and sesquisyllabic onsets (e.g. Gage 1985, Ferlus 1992). Consistent with our established narrative of contact driven change, it is widely recognized that Vietnamese restructured in circumstances of prolonged intimate contact with (especially southern) Chinese (see Alves 2001 for a survey).

But no such history of prolonged contact conditioning phonological change can be invoked for either Nyaheun or Laven: both closely related and in intimate contact with each other for hundreds of years, they manifest very different phonological histories. There is nothing in the phonologies of Lao, Khmer, or other known contact languages that models the changes we have discussed above. Additionally we do know that especially Laven has been under very strong Lao influence for several hundred years.

3.1.1 Wider areal/historical context

There are good linguistic indications that the Boloven Plateau was closely integrated into the Angkorian Empire, but had little or no interaction with Champa (see Sidwell and Jacq 2003). Consequently, with the collapse of Angkorian power in the 1300s, the locals enjoyed considerable autonomy until the Laotians and Siamese began settling in and exerting control over the area in the 1700s. But in 1870 Harmand, the first European to visit the Boloven Plateau, was able to report that the Laven women were so culturally Laoisized that they dressed as Laos, wore their hair as Laos, and even used lipstick purchased in the markets of Pakse with money made from their plantations (Harmand 2002). Harmand also described meeting Nyaheun on the Plateau, and the sketchy details are consistent with the two groups living in close contact much as they do now.

It is apparent that language contact between Lao and Laven has been so extensive that we may almost characterize Laven as a relexified form of Lao; for example, a comparison of Lao clause structure as described by Enfield (2007: 171) and Laven as described by Jacq (2001) shows almost complete congruity. In fact, the minor discrepancies between the two descriptions vanish under close examination:

- the Laven future marker corresponds to the Lao irrealis marker,
- the positions immediately following Subject/Agent in Laven can be filled by particles and/or adverbials equivalent to Lao,
- although the Lao Achievement morpheme (*dajø*) slot has no equivalent in Jacq's Laven, I have heard Laven speakers use the equivalent (*bic* 'obtain/achieve') in the same way,
- many Laven functors and adverbs are borrowed from Lao or Isaan Thai, and greetings/leave takings are calqued (some of these are discussed by Jacq (2001)).[4]

However, Nyaheun presents a different situation, especially being much more flexible in word order. Compare Table 13:

Table 13: Variation in Nyaheun word order (recorded by Sidwell) compared to Lao and Laven

Obligatory Lao and Laven word order:						
S/A	Neg.	Asp.		Mod.	V(O)	
Available Nyaheun word orders:						
S/A	Neg.	Asp.		Mod.	V(O)	
	Neg.	Asp.	S/A	Mod.	V(O)	
		Asp.	S/A	Mod.	V(O)	Neg.
S/A		Asp.		Mod.	$V_{intrans}$	
		Asp.		Mod.	$V_{intrans}$	S

In my Nyaheun text collection I find many examples of Nyaheun clauses with distinctive word order, such as intransitive subjects after verbs, subject immediately before the modal and main verb so that negation and the aspectual marker precede the subject. Even the negator can be relegated to the end of the clause without it becoming a question marker as in Lao. So far as I can tell, this variability in Nyaheun word order does not impact on information structure, rather it facilitates considerable stylistic manipulation. For example, speakers value a 2-4 beat, especially with rhyming/alliterating pairs, often realized with reduplications, deletions and reordering elements within the generous constraints indicated above. This kind of flexibility is apparently not available in Laven, which is syntactically remodelled after Lao, an example of metatypy in the sense of Ross (2006).

---

[4] It can be somewhat confronting to first encounter Nyaheun greetings which translate literally as "You are not sick?" or "Aren't you dead yet?" (Davis 1973), while the Laven /hbai rip/ "good health" transparently calques the Lao /saba:j3 di:3/.

In other important ways both Laven and Nyaheun are untouched by Lao; there is no apparent accommodation to a Lao style tonal system, and the robustly complex vocalism and range of consonant articulations remain essentially intact without being collapsed to the simpler phonotactics of Lao. Apparently, Laven and Nyaheun have mixed for a considerable time, and both have been exposed to Lao, with Laven significantly affected, and in these conditions speakers have effected very different phonological and syntactic restructuring.

3.2 Gta' (Munda) creating initial clusters/sesquisyllables

Anderson (2008) presents a sketch grammar of Gta', a small Munda language of southern Orissa, India, with less than 4,500 speakers. Several varieties are spoken, including a Hill Gta' and a Plains Gta'. The language and people are also called Didayi or Didei. According to Anderson the classification is open to question, although it is generally regarded as belonging to the South Munda subfamily. A Didayi dictionary by Chatterji et al. is available electronically from the Stampe digital Munda archive.[5] Forms labelled Gta' in the discussion that follows are extracted from Anderson (2008) while Didayi forms are from Chatterji et al.

As Anderson reports, Gta' is phonotactically somewhat Mon-Khmer looking:

> Gta' is an unusual language from the perspective of syllable structure or phonotactics. It has an enormous number of 'clusters' found in word-initial position but a restricted number of consonants found in coda position. A small number of words with syllabic nasals and prenasalized stops may also be found.
> [.....]
> This feature of Gta' appears to be very similar to syllable structure constraints found in other AA languages that are distant relations of Gta'. However, rather than representing a retention of an archaic phonotactic feature directly inherited from Proto-Austroasiatic lost in all other Munda languages, this feature of Gta' is more likely to be a pseudo-archaism,[6] [....].
> Although, so-called sesquisyllabic words are found frequently in Mon-Khmer languages, their presence in Gta' arose through, among other processes, the loss of unstressed vowels in word-initial syllables. The specific form of the vowel found in such languages as Gutob or Remo is not predictable based on the Gta' form, but the reverse is largely true. (Anderson 2008: 684-5)

---

5 http://www.ling.hawaii.edu/austroasiatic/AA/Munda/Dictionaries/Gta_Chatterji
6 The term pseudo-archaism is being used here to mean a form or structure that superficially appears to reflect an older stage of the language but is in fact the outcome of changes that output forms which coincidentally appear archaic.

To illustrate something of these phonotactics before going further I present in Table 14 some lexical examples, with other South Munda comparisons and pMK (effectively pAA) reconstructions by Shorto (2006):

Table 14: Gta' monosyllables

Shorto (2006) PMK	Munda glosses	Gta'	Didayi	Remo	Gutob
*ɓa:r (#1562)	'two'	mbar	mbar	bar	ba:r-ɟu:
bri:ʔ (#181)	'uncultivated land'	Bri	-	biri	bjroŋ
*cɔʔ (#41)	'dog'	gsuʔ	gusu	guso:	gusoʔ
*ci(ə)m (#1324)**	'chicken'	gsæŋ	gesaiŋ	gi-siŋ	gi-siŋ
*cʔa:ŋ (#488)	'bone'	ncia	ncja	saŋ	sisaŋ
*ɗa:k (#274)	'water'	nɖiaʔ	ɖia	ɖag	da
*ɗak (#330)	'trap'	dnoʔ	-	ɖonok	-
*ɟla(i)ŋ (#740)	'long/tall'	clæʔ	-	sileŋ	sileɟ
*ɟmu:l (#1777)***	'seed'	cmu	-	sumu	-
*ɟru:ʔ (#172)	'deep'	Cri	ciri	siri	gaɽia
*ɟu(ə)ŋ (#5381)	'foot'	Nco	co	suŋ	susuŋ
*kaʔ (#16)	'fish'	haʔɽo	-	aʔ	aʔɖoŋ
*klaʔ (#197)	'tiger'	Ŋku	-	kisa:	gikkil
*ks(i)ʔ (#246)	'rope'	ghæʔ	-	gieʔ/gije	geʔ
*mat (#1045)	'eye'	mmwaʔ	moa	m'o:	mo:
*muh (#2045)	'nose'	mmu	mu	se:-mi	mi
*ris (#1927)	'root'	nɖræʔ	nɖrɛ	regi	-
*rk(aw)ʔ (#1820)	'uncooked rice'	rkoʔ	-	rŋku	rukuʔ
*ru(ə)j (#1534)	'fly'	n(d)rwe	conɖroe	-	uroj
*sɲiʔ (#37)****	'village'	Hni	hini	suŋ	-
*ti:ʔ (#66)	'hand'	nti, tti	ti	ti	titi
*tɲi:ʔ (#31)	'sun'	Sni	sini	siɲi	siŋgi ~ sĩĩ

* 'forest', ** 'bird'; *** 'to dibble'; **** 'house' (indicating PMK glosses that vary from the Munda values)

Anderson is confident that the phonological forms found in Gta' are secondary; note the quote above. There are also additional factors to consider:

- historically AA lexical items have clustered onsets in Gta', even when proto-forms did not, with gemination and prenasalization being common augments;
- the vowel system is very simple, including the lack of a length contrast in monophthongs.

The simple vocalism of Gta' continues an especially Munda characteristic, in particular the lack of length or diphthong contrasts that are otherwise fairly common elsewhere in AA and are readily reconstructed to deeper historical levels (e.g. Shorto 2006). The simplification of vocalism is connected with a general restructuring towards a CVC syllable canon in Munda, as explained by Donegan and Stampe (1983 and passim.). This restructuring also involved an extension of word structure as Munda became increasingly suffixing and thus ceased to show the consistent word final stress characteristic of conservative AA languages (although it is important to note that Munda languages still predominantly put stress on the second syllable of disyllabic words, with exceptions relating to Munda languages with quantity sensitive systems such as Mundari [Anderson, personal communication 6/10/2012]).

A general outcome of these tendencies within Munda was a prosodic shift that changed sesquisyllables and many monosyllables into disyllables, examples of which we see in the Didayi, Remo and Gutob columns in Table 14. This disyllabic stage must be reconstructed for pMunda, and consequently it is apparent that Gta' has restructured words of both CV´CV(C) and CV(C) types into CCV(C), in what seems to be a very local innovation.

Can the remodelling of Gta' be motivated by language contact? Anderson remarks that there is evidence of Remo influence, and borrowings from Dravidian, Desiya (the local Indic language) are also noted. None of these influences can be credited with providing a model for the changes in Gta', and we are left wondering how and why — in the face of evidently overwhelming areal pressure — Gta' restructuring took place. As is evident, it was not just a matter of losing unstressed vowels, but there was also a comprehensive addition of augments that created a general pattern of initial clusters/geminates that are not supported etymologically. Tentatively one could apply the theory of Donegan and Stampe in reverse (so to speak) and suggest that a restoration of consistent word final stress by loss of suffixing would favour a return to iambic sesquisyllabic structure by internal tendency: this alone would be a sufficient explanation.

4 Concluding remarks

Returning to the opening theme of considering Post's (2011) model of prosodic convergence that does not require extensive bilingualism or other intensive linguistic interaction, it seems to this writer that Post is seeking to somehow keep language contact as a causal factor in language change, even in cases where we see little evidence of it. In the case of structural convergence it may seem intuitively obvious that contact is an important factor, especially when geographical proximity is apparent, or at least historically plausible, but objectively it is merely one hypothesis among all the possible explanations that may be available. Languages undergo restructuring apparently spontaneously, in directions consistent with or somehow related to their existing typologies, and they may or may not be in proximity to, or in some relation with, other languages with parallel structures. Causal factors may be quite subtle, and difficult to definitively identify. Areal linguistics must be approached with considerable caution and an understanding that its results need to be based on reasonable models of linguistic interactions. It is timely to consider Enfield's observation that:

> Areal linguistics invites us to revise our understanding of the ontology of languages and their historical evolution, showing that the only units one needs to posit as playing a causal role are individual speakers and individual linguistic items. These unit types are mobile or detachable with respect to the populations they inhabit, arguing against essentialism in both linguistic and sociocultural systems. (Enfield 2005: 198)

Enfield's point draws attention to the fact that there are no inherent boundaries between languages, such that structures and habits may readily propagate among speakers in contexts of greater or lesser linguistic diversity, yet we still must recognize that speakers do make choices — consciously and unconsciously — that privilege speech forms with which they identify. While we must eschew essentialism, social groups defining themselves by their specific language use is normal, and we should not be surprised to observe changes emerging within a language (whether imported in some manner or generated internally) diffusing and evolving within the confines of that community.

In this paper I have discussed several examples of phonological restructuring in languages from across the breadth of the AA phylum. Each can be categorized within broad tendencies such as monosyllabism or tonogenesis that are considered typical of the SEAsian linguistic area. Diverse processes are yielding outcomes that are in some sense convergent, yet the role of contact – if any – is not clear. This challenges us to consider what areality is, and how useful is the idea, if we are to define it in terms of languages of a geographical region sharing common features without reference to how they came to share those features. The proximity of communities due to chance, combined with tendencies relating to common ancestry, may be expected to throw up apparent linguistic areas that have little to do with contact driven change.

Acknowledgements

This is a somewhat revised draft of paper read at the "Mainland Southeast Asian Languages: The State of the Art in 2012" meeting at the MPI for Evolutionary Anthropology, Leipzig, 29/11-1/12/2012. Many thanks are due to the organizers for running this important meeting, and for financially supporting various presenters, including the present writer, to attend. Also particular thanks are due to Nick Enfield and Bernard Comrie for their constructive remarks on drafts of this paper.

References

Alves, M. J. 2001. What's so Chinese about Vietnamese? *In:* Thurgood, G. W. (ed.), *Papers from the Ninth Annual Meeting of the Southeast Asian Linguistics Society*. Tempe: Arizona State University, Program for Southeast Asian Studies.
Alves, Mark. 2006. *A grammar of Pacoh: a Mon-Khmer language of the central highlands of Vietnam*. Canberra: Pacific Linguistics.
Anderson, G. D. S. (ed.). 2008. *The Munda languages*. London: Routledge.
Bradley, D., R. J. Lapolla, B. Michailovsky & G. Thurgood (eds.). 2003. *Language variation: papers on variation and change in the Sinosphere and in the Indosphere in honour of James A. Matisoff*. Canberra: Pacific Linguistics.
Brunelle, M. 2005. *Register in Eastern Cham: phonological, phonetic and sociolinguistic factors*. Ithaca: Cornell University dissertation.
Cooper, James & Nancy Cooper. 1966. Halang phonemes. *Mon-Khmer Studies* 4. 87–98.
Charoenma, Narumol. 1982. The phonologies of a Lampang Lamet and Wiang Papao Lua. *Mon-Khmer Studies* 11. 35–45.
Davis, J. J. 1968. Nyaheun phonemes. Bangkok: David Thomas Library.
Davis, J. J. 1973. Notes on Nyaheun grammar. *Mon-Khmer Studies* 4. 69–75.
Diffloth, Gérard. 1982. Registres, dévoisement, timbres vocaliques: leur histoire en Katouique. *Mon-Khmer Studies* 11. 47–82.
Donegan, Patricia & David Stampe. 1983. Rhythm and holistic organization of language structure. In J. Richardson, M. Marks & A. Chukerman (eds.), *Papers from the Parasession on the Interplay of Phonology, Morphology and Syntax*, 337–353. Chicago: Chicago Linguistic Society.
Donegan, Patricia & David Stampe. 2004. Rhythm and the synthetic drift of Munda. In Rajendra Singh (ed.), *The Yearbook of South Asian Languages and Linguistics*, 3–36. Berlin & New York: De Gruyter.
Enfield, N. J. 2005. Areal linguistics and Mainland Southeast Asia. *Annual Review of Anthropology* 34. 181–206.
Enfield, N. J. 2007. *A Grammar of Lao*. Berlin: Mouton de Gruyter.
Fagan, Joel L. 1988. Javanese intervocalic stop phonemes. *Studies in Austronesian Linguistics* 76. 173–202.

Ferlus, M. 1974. Délimitation des groupes linguistiques austroasiatiques dans le centre indochinois. *Asie du Sud-Est et Monde Insulindien* 5. 15–23.
Ferlus, M. 1992. Essai de phonétique historique du khmer. *Mon-Khmer Studies* 21. 57–89.
Ferlus, M. 1998. *Nhaheun-French-English lexicon*. München: Lincom Europa.
Ferlus, M. 2011. Toward Proto-Pearic: Problems and historical implications. In: Sophana Srichampa, Paul Sidwell, Kenneth Gregerson (eds.), *Austroasiatic Studies: papers from ICAAL4. Mon-Khmer Studies Journal Special Issue No. 3, part 1*. Dallas, Salaya & Canberra: SIL International, Mahidol University & Pacific Linguistics.
Gage, W. W. 1985. Vietnamese in Mon-Khmer perspective. In: Suriya Ratanakul, David. D. Thomas & Suwilay Premsrirat (eds.), *Southeast Asian Linguistic Studies Presented to André-G. Haudricourt*. Bangkok: Institute of Language and Culture for Rural Development, Mahidol University.
Gordon, M. & P. Ladefoged. 2001. Phonation types: a cross-linguistic overview. *Journal of Phonetics* 29. 383–406.
Gregerson, K. J. 1976. Tongue-Root and register in Mon-Khmer. In: Philip N. Jenner, Lawrence C. Thompson, Stanley Starosta (eds.), *Austroasiatic Studies*. Honolulu: University of Hawai'i Press.
Hall, E. 2010. *A phonology of Muak Sa-aak*. Chiang Mai: Payap University MA thesis.
Harmand, F. J. 2002. *Laos and the hill tribes of Indochina: Journeys to the Boloven Plateau*. Bangkok: White Lotus.
Haudricourt, A.-G. 1965. Mutation consonantique en Mon-Khmer. *Bulletin de la Société Linguistique de Paris* 60. 160–172.
Huffman, F. E. 1978. Synchronic evidence for the history of Khmer vowels. Paper presented at 2nd International Conference on Austroasiatic, Mysore (India) December 18–21, 1978.
Huffman, F. E. 1985. Vowel permutations in Austroasiatic languages. *Linguistics of the Sino-Tibetan Area: The State of the Art*. Canberra: Pacific Linguistics.
Jacq, P. 2001. *A description of Jruq (Loven): a Mon-Khmer language of the Lao PDR*. Canberra: Australian National University MA thesis.
Kingston, J. 2011. Tonogenesis. In: Marc van Oostendorp, Colin J. Ewen, Elizabeth Hume, Keren Rice (eds.), *Blackwell Companion to Phonology*. Hoboken: Wiley-Blackwell.
Ladefoged, P. & I. Maddieson. 1996. *The sounds of the world's languages*. Oxford: Basil Blackwell.
Lindell, K., J.-O. Svantesson and D. Tayanin. 1978. Two dialects of the Romeet (Lamet) language. *Cahiers de Linguistique, Asie Oriental* 4: 5–22.
Manley, T. M. 1972. *Outline of Sre structure*. Honolulu: University of Hawaii Press.
Matisoff, J. 1991. Sino-Tibetan linguistics: Present state and future prospects. *Annual Review of Anthropology* 20: 469–504.
Mortensen, D. 2006. Tonally conditioned vowel raising in Shuijingping Hmong. Handout from the LSA 80th Annual Meeting, Albuquerque, New Mexico. 6 January 2006.
Post, M. W. 2011. Prosody and typological drift in Austroasiatic and Tibeto-Burman: Against "Sinosphere" and "Indosphere". In: Sophana Srichampa, Paul Sidwell, Kenneth Gregerson (eds.), *Austroasiatic Studies: papers from ICAAL4. Mon-Khmer Studies Journal Special Issue No. 3*. Dallas, Salaya & Canberra: SIL International, Mahidol University & Pacific Linguistics.
Ross, M. D. 2006. Metatypy. In: Brown, K. (ed.), *Encyclopedia of language and linguistics* (2nd ed.). Oxford: Elsevier.

Sapir, E. 1921. *Language: An introduction to the study of speech,* New York: Harcourt, Brace and company.
Scott, J. G., J. P. Hardiman. 1900. *Gazetteer of Upper Burma and the Shan states 1.1,* Rangoon: Superintendent, Government Printing.
Shorto, H. L. 2006. *A Mon-Khmer comparative dictionary.* Canberra: Pacific Linguistics.
Sidwell, P. 1998. *A reconstruction of Proto-Bahnaric.* Melbourne: University of Melbourne dissertation.
Sidwell, Paul. 2002. *Proto North Bahnaric.* (Draft monograph circulated for comment but not published)
Sidwell, Paul. 2005. *The Katuic languages: classification, reconstruction and comparative lexicon.* Munich: Lincom Europa.
Sidwell, Paul. 2011. *Proto Bahnaric.* http://sealang.net/monkhmer/database/.
Sidwell, Paul & Pascale Jacq. 2003. *A handbook of comparative Bahnaric: Volume 1, West Bahnaric.* Canberra: Pacific Linguistics.
Smith, K. D. 1967. A phonological reconstruction of Proto Central North Bahnaric. *University of North Dakota SIL 1967 Workpapers.*
Smith, K. D. 1972. *A phonological reconstruction of Proto-North-Bahnaric.* Santa Ana, CA: Summer Institute of Linguistics.
Smith, K., D. 1979. *Sedang grammar.* Canberra: Pacific Linguistics.
Svantesson, Jan-Olof. 1988. U. *Linguistics of the Tibeto-Burman Area* 11. 64–133.
Svantesson, Jan-Olof. 1989. Tonogenic mechanisms in Northern Mon-Khmer. *Phonetics* 46. 60–79.
Svantesson, Jan-Olof. 1991. Hu - a language with unorthodox tonogenesis. In J.H.C.S. Davidson (ed.), *Austroasiatic languages, Essays in honour of H. L. Shorto*, 67–80. London: School of Oriental and African Studies, University of London.
Thurgood, G. 1999. *From Ancient Cham to modern dialects: two thousand years of language contact and change* (Oceanic Linguistics special Publications No. 28). Honolulu: University of Hawai'i Press.
Thurgood, G. 2002. Vietnamese and tonogensis. *Diachronica* 19: 333–363.
Thurgood, G. 2007. Tonogenesis revisited: revising the model and the analysis. In: Jimmy G. Harris, Somsonge Burusphat, James E. Harris (eds.), *Studies in Tai and Southeast Asian Linguistics.* Bangkok: Ek Phim Thai Co.
Watkins, J. 2002. *The phonetics of Wa: experimental phonetics, phonology, orthography and sociolinguistics.* Canberra: Pacific Linguistics.

Marc Brunelle and James Kirby
Re-assessing tonal diversity and geographical convergence in Mainland Southeast Asia

1 Introduction: Tone typology and contact-induced tonogenesis

Mainland Southeast Asia (MSEA) is often described as the quintessential *Sprachbund*, or language area, in which languages belonging to different language families converge as a result of contact (Alieva 1984; Enfield 2005). While we hold this to be true in a general sense, we suspect that there is little to be gained in arguing about what defines a language area or in determining the exact boundary of this language area (e.g., should it just include the mainland or insular Southeast Asia as well?). What seems much more interesting to us is to gain a better understanding of how convergence happens for specific features, especially phonological and phonetic ones. In this paper, we look in detail at a specific phonological feature, tone, and at two of its phonetic correlates, pitch and voice quality. Based on a database of 197 languages and dialects (Section 2), we assess the extent of tonal diversity in MSEA languages (Section 3) and construct a statistical model of the degree to which tonal inventories can be predicted on the basis of geographic proximity, genealogical relatedness and population size (Section 4).

Although it is generally agreed that MSEA languages are highly tonal, this characterization is often based on large national languages. Furthermore, there is often little attention paid to the types of phonetic properties that characterize tonal inventories. To our knowledge, the only systematic attempt to establish a topography of tone in Southeast Asia is Henderson (1965), who looked, among other features, at lexically contrastive pitch, phonation type, and combinations thereof. In this study, Henderson showed convincingly that tone is more prevalent on the mainland than in the archipelago and that phonation type plays a crucial role in MSEA lexical contrasts. However, because of the state of the field in 1965, Henderson's observations were only based on 31 MSEA languages, and she had limited access to phonetic data.

One motivation for the current study is to reassess Henderson's results based on an expanded sample of languages. Just like her, we have decided to focus on two phonetic properties of lexical tone: pitch, the usual suspect, and phonation type, which we will call voice quality. Other properties, such as rhyme duration, intensity and vowel quality, should ultimately be considered as well, but had to be left out as most existing phonetic/phonological studies of MSEA languages do not describe their tonal systems to this level of phonetic detail.

The second issue we address in this paper is the role of contact in tonogenesis. To our knowledge, the first piece of scholarly work that explicitly and comprehensively tackles the issue is Matisoff (1973). On the one hand, Matisoff recognizes that some languages are tone-prone, i.e. have structural characteristics that favour tonal development, like the loss of laryngeal contrasts (well established since Haudricourt 1954) or a trend towards monosyllabization. However, he also considers contact an important driving force. More specifically, Matisoff sees Chinese influence as a crucial factor in the development of tones in Tai-Kadai, Miao-Yao and Vietnamese:

> It seems likely that the development of true tones in Vietnamese was precipitated not only by influence from Chinese, but also from Siamese as well. This indicates that Tai (and Miao-Yao) acquired their tone systems from Chinese before Vietnamese did... (Matisoff 1973: 88).

This scenario is not without problems, however. How does a language "acquire" tone from a neighbour, even under intense contact? Pulleyblank (1986), who generally agrees with Matisoff, states the problem in the following way:

> How such a trend [i.e. tonogenesis] can spread across linguistic boundaries is an intriguing puzzle, on which I shall not venture to make any guesses (Pulleyblank 1986: 78).

To our knowledge, the only attempt to tackle this issue in more detail is Ratliff (2002), who proposes that Proto-Hmong-Mien must have borrowed Chinese loanwords at a time when neither language was tonal, and that they must have undergone tonogenesis in parallel. However, Ratliff generally accepts the view that contact played a role in the development of tonality in the Sinosphere.

More recently, there has been a proliferation of case studies suggesting that languages belonging to originally atonal families have developed or are developing tones under the influence of Tai-Kadai and Vietnamese. The following quote, chosen for its careful wording, illustrates the type of process that might be at play:

> Experimental findings and impressionistic observations imply that both languages, Suai and Pattani Malay, are pursuing different paths leading to phonological shifts from clear and breathy voice registers for the former, and the latter, from word-initial distinctive con-

sonant length, to a kind of prosodic salience. This could be a matter of a replacement by phonemic stress or accent, yet, given the close contact with Thai, a tone language, and the widespread bilingualism of the speakers of the two minority languages, we may have here a way station on the road to tonogenesis. (Abramson 2004)

The large-scale scenario that emerges from these accounts is that tone would have first developed in Chinese two thousand years ago. Tone-prone languages spoken in the southern Sinosphere, like the ancestors of Tai-Kadai, Miao-Yao and Vietnamese, would then have acquired tone under Chinese influence; contact with their modern daughters, such as Thai, Lao and Vietnamese, would similarly explain tonogenesis in smaller languages. This scenario suggests that tone convergence due to language contact is a force that has been affecting the shape of tone systems for centuries.

The role of this constant force in the distribution of tone languages in modern-day MSEA will be tested in Section 4.

2 The database

In order to support a quantitative analysis of tonal convergence, we constructed a database of 197 MSEA languages. Languages were included in the database if reliable descriptions were available, if they were spoken in one of the eight MSEA countries (Vietnam, Laos, Cambodia, Thailand, Burma, Malaysia and Singapore) and if they belonged to one of the five MSEA language families (Austroasiatic, Austronesian, Sino-Tibetan, Tai-Kadai and Hmong-Mien). For languages spoken in several countries, one variety per country was included in the database, as long as data was available about its tone system (for example, Mon is counted twice, as a language of Burma and as a language of Thailand). If a language has several varieties with different tone systems in the same country, all varieties for which data was available were included (for example, northern and southern Vietnamese are counted as two distinct varieties, along with other regional dialects, as they have different tone systems). Linguistic and geographical data were extracted from available descriptions. Population figures were based on national census figures, on *Ethnologue* or, when available, on information contained in linguistic descriptions. More details and proper acknowledgements are given in the database (available upon request).

For each variety included in the database, the following information was included:

Geographical, demographic and genealogical factors

- Language family: 87 Austroasiatic varieties (all Mon-Khmer), 19 Austronesian varieties, 40 Sino-Tibetan varieties, 43 Tai-Kadai varieties and 8 Hmong-Mien varieties. We have not subdivided languages into smaller groupings because of disagreement about subgroupings in some families and because our language sample is too small to create statistically meaningful subgroups.

- Population of the described variety, in number of speakers.

- The specific location, in longitude and latitude, of the variety described in the scholarly materials used in building the database. Whenever descriptions of varieties spoken at different locations were available, we chose to report the largest community.

- Total population of all the varieties of the same language, in number of speakers.

Phonological variables

- Number of contrastive tones: the number of lexically contrastive categories distinguished by differences in pitch and/or voice quality on the syllable bearing the largest number of such contrasts. As an illustration, Northern Vietnamese, which has six contrastive tones in open syllables and two contrastive tones on checked syllables, can be analysed as having six or eight tones. Here, we assume that the two checked tones can be analysed as allotones of two of the open tones and settle for a six tone analysis.

- Number of pitch units: the number of different pitch curves used to distinguish the contrastive tones described above, even if they are redundant with voice quality (as few descriptions provide this type of information or state explicitly which cue is primary).

- Number of voice qualities: the number of different voice qualities used to distinguish the contrastive tones described above, even if they are redundant with pitch (once again, few descriptions provide this type of information or state explicitly which cue is primary).

– Word type: The maximal "non-marginal" phonological stem after excluding Western, Pali and Sanskrit loanwords. There are three possible categories: monosyllabic, sesquisyllabic and polysyllabic.

To avoid confusion, we use the term *tone* only when referring to lexically contrastive units, whereas pitch units and voice quality are often redundant and thus cannot be characterized as contrastive or not. For instance, Mon-Khmer register languages typically have a contrast between a modal/high-pitched and a breathy/low-pitched register. In most cases, we do not know what is the primary contrastive cue and what is the redundant one, notwithstanding the fact that these two cues may not be fully distinct perceptually (Brunelle 2012). A register language of that type would thus be analysed as having two contrastive tones, two pitch units and two voice qualities.

The most difficult type of classification decision we had to make occurred when a tone system combined both contrastive pitch curves and voice quality units. We illustrate this with Northern Vietnamese, the language for which alternative classifications would yield the most important discrepancy. The Northern Vietnamese tone system has six tones in open syllables. These six tones consist of six distinct pitch curves and at least three surface voice qualities (or even more if we adopt a fine-grained typology like Nguyễn and Edmondson 1997). However, perceptual investigation reveals that not all of these properties are contrastive and that listeners seem to rely on a matrix of three relevant pitch shapes and two relevant voice qualities to distinguish the six tones (Brunelle 2009b). Depending on how we count, we could therefore have five (3+2) or six tones (3×2) in Northern Vietnamese, but more importantly, we could reduce its number of pitch and voice quality units to three and two, respectively, rather than the surface six pitch contours and three voice qualities that are commonly reported in the literature. We settled on the latter option for two reasons. First, the primary materials we relied on rarely provide the level of instrumental and experimental description that would be needed to do a strictly contrastive classification. Second, most of the languages that have two possible classifications happen to be Vietic and Northern Mon-Khmer (along with a handful of Tibeto-Burman languages). Thus, the more superficial type of classification increases the tonality of many Austroasiatic languages in contact with tonal languages of other families and maximizes the probability that our models will detect a geographical convergence effect (which, as we will see in Section 4, we still failed to uncover.)

Classification decisions aside, some factual errors and misinterpretations of previous work are bound to have crept in. Moreover, it is possible that some of the descriptions we relied on are erroneous or tacitly avoid discussing some aspects of tone systems. Voice quality, for instance, seems to have been generally ignored in descriptions of Tai-Kadai languages until very recently. We welcome help from language specialists interested in revising parts of our database.

3 The typology of tone in Mainland Southeast Asia

A first look at the database, as summarized in Figure 1, reveals that contrastive tone is found in the majority of MSEA languages, but that close to 20% of the languages of the area are atonal. Another 20% have an equal number of tones and voice qualities, and could therefore be treated as *register* languages (i.e. languages in which pitch and voice quality are redundant). Therefore, depending on how we categorize languages, up to 40% of the languages of the area do not have contrastive pitch. Another interesting observation is that among languages that have contrastive tone, 66% also employ more than one type of voice quality, a proportion that reaches 54% even if we exclude register languages. Note, however, that in most of these languages, only two voice qualities, modal voicing and glottalization/creakiness (or more rarely, breathiness), accompany the pitch-based contrast. Overall, the more pitch units a language employs, the more likely they are to be accompanied by differences in voice quality. One last observation is the relative rarity of languages with three tones, which merely reflects the history of the five language families spoken in the area: while Tai-Kadai and Hmong-Mien underwent a three-way tone split followed by a further two-way split, most of the Austronesian and Austroasiatic languages that have tonal contrasts only underwent a two-way split (Sino-Tibetan is more diverse and less reliably reconstructed). Based on the apparent cut-off at three tones, we could say that a little less than half of our sample is composed of languages that are atonal or weakly tonal, while a comparable number of languages have complex tone systems (4 tones or more).

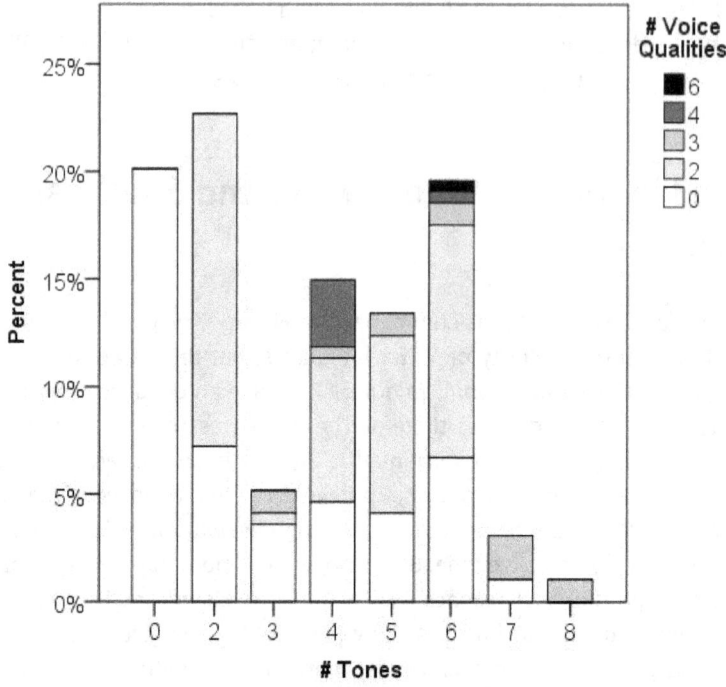

Fig. 1: Co-occurrence of tone and voice quality in Mainland Southeast Asian languages

We will now look at the geographical distribution of tone, pitch and voice quality, but before doing so, a look at the geographical distribution of language families is necessary. We see in Figure 2 that only Austroasiatic and Tai-Kadai are fairly well (though far from perfectly) distributed throughout the area. Sino-Tibetan is mostly found in the northwest, Austronesian in the south, and Hmong-Mien is concentrated in the north-central zone.

The geographical distribution of contrastive tone in MSEA is given in Figure 3. Atonal languages are more common in the south (the Malay Peninsula and southern Vietnam), while languages with large numbers of contrastive tones tend to be found in the north. There are notable exceptions, however, like highly tonal southern Thai dialects and a few atonal Mon-Khmer languages in northern MSEA. Overall, a comparison of Figures 2 and 3 reveals that there is a strong correlation between geography and language family: most atonal languages are Austroasiatic and Austronesian, two families that are mostly spoken in the south of the area of interest. We come back to this issue at the end of this section.

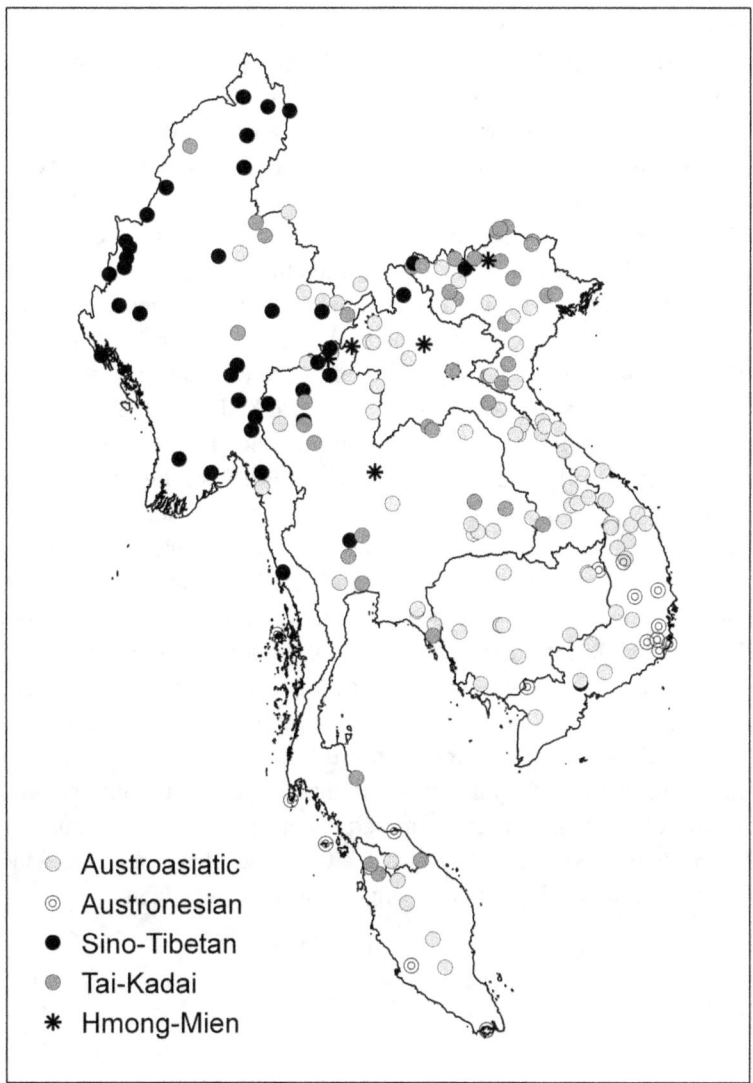

Fig. 2: Geographical distribution of language families in Mainland Southeast Asia

Figure 4 gives the geographical distribution of languages by number of pitch units. There is little difference between this map and the preceding, which simply confirms that contrastive lexical tones normally have a pitch component.

Figure 5 finally shows the distribution of voice qualities. Languages that lack linguistically relevant voice quality are once again concentrated in southern Vietnam and the Malay Peninsula. Languages with two voice qualities are found throughout MSEA. Larger numbers of voice quality types (3-4) seem more common in the north-east, with a maximum of 6 in Kri (Enfield and Diffloth 2009). Interestingly, there does not seem to be an obvious correlation between the prevalence of voice quality and language family, something we will test in more detail in Section 4.

Since geographical distribution and language family are not independent (language families are not equally distributed in MSEA), we need to look at the types of tone systems attested in the different families. Figure 6 groups tone systems into four types and gives their relative proportion in each family. We can first see that atonal languages are exclusively found in Austroasiatic and Austronesian languages. All Hmong-Mien, Tai-Kadai and Sino-Tibetan languages found in MSEA exhibit some form of tone. These results might seem trivial, but they clearly illustrate some regularities: first, the proportion of Austroasiatic languages that have developed tones is not negligible: even if we exclude register systems, which are most certainly a development internal to Mon-Khmer, 36% of Austroasiatic languages are now tonal. Second, languages that belong to families with atonal ancestors (Austroasiatic and Austronesian) can become tonal, but languages with tonal ancestors do not lose their tones altogether. Note, however, that this directional bias is not a universal in the strong sense: register, is occasionally "restructured" into complex vowel systems in Austroasiatic and Austronesian (Huffman 1976; Lee 1977), and although we do not have cases of complete neutralization of pitch contrasts in MSEA, reductions of pitch inventories through mergers are common: for instance, Southern Vietnamese dialects have merged the tones *hỏi* and *ngã* and most Tai languages have merged some of the original six tone categories.

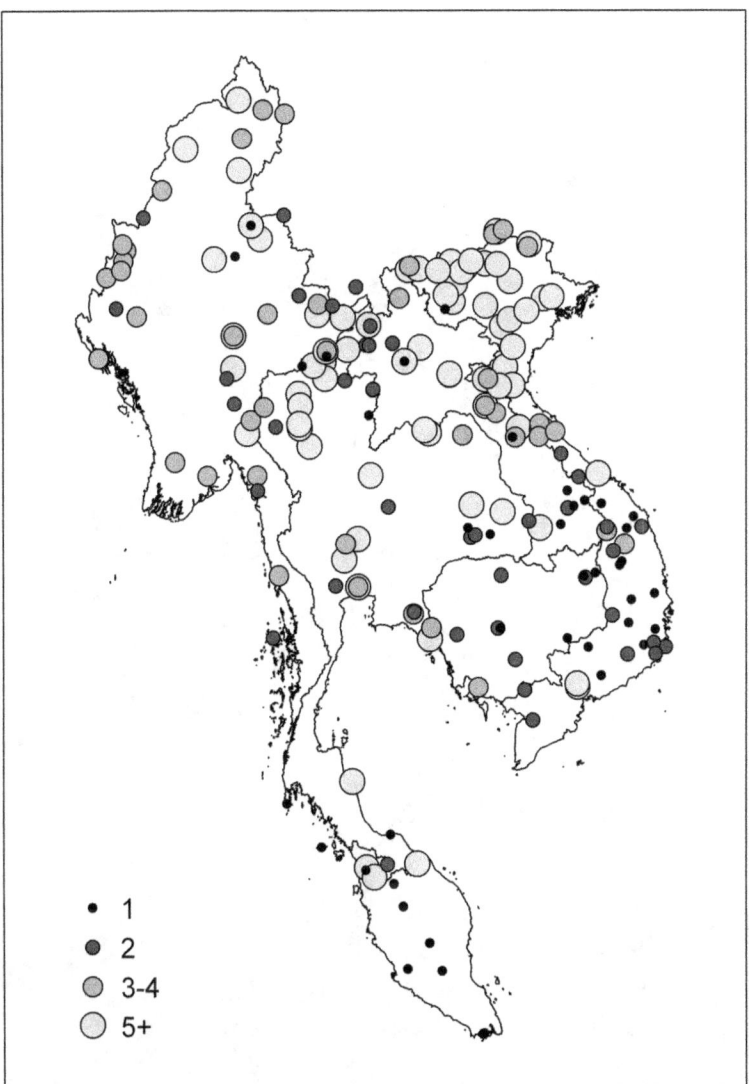

Fig. 3: Number of tones per language

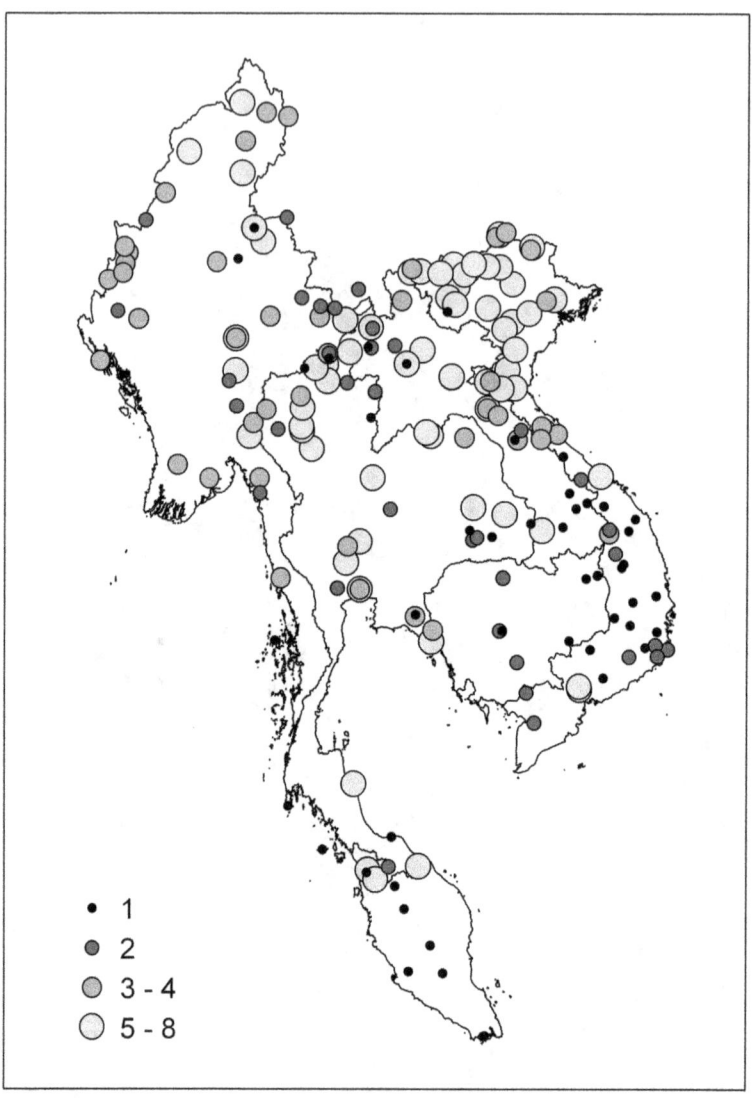

Fig. 4: Number of different pitch units per language

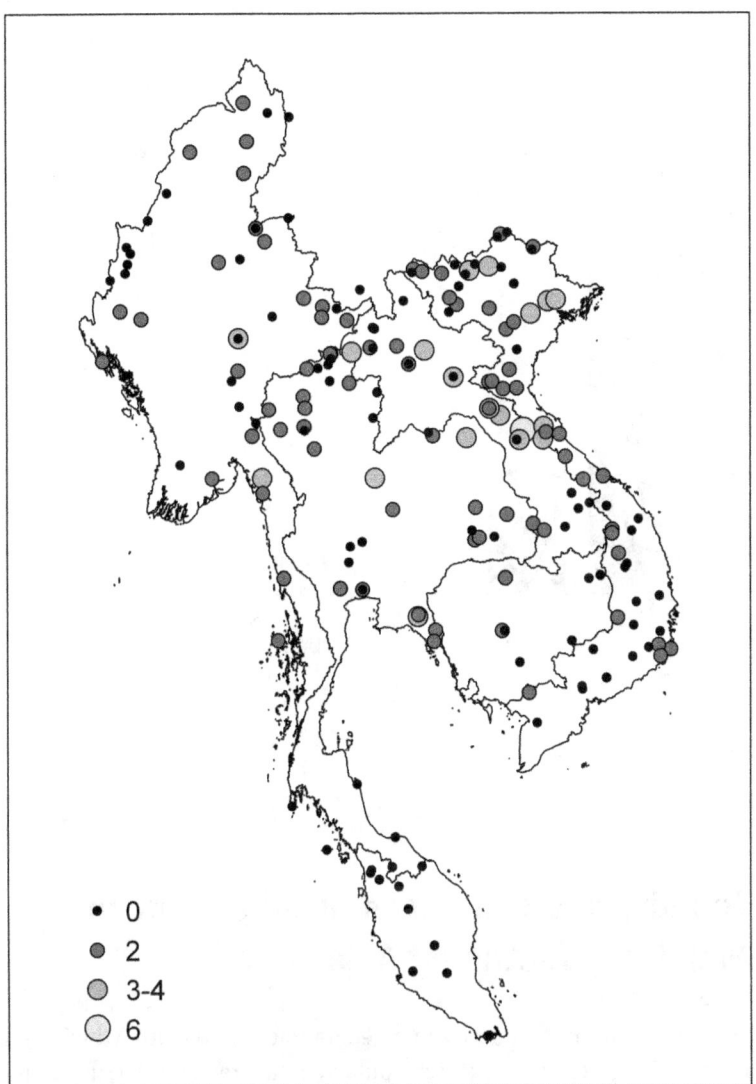

Fig. 5: Number of voice qualities per language

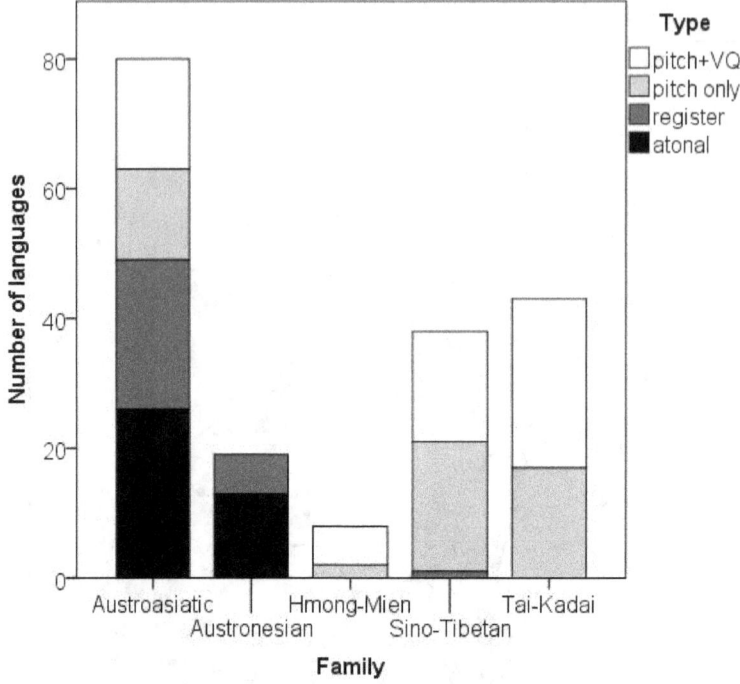

Fig. 6: Tonality type, per family

4 Tonality and contact-induced change in Mainland Southeast Asia

In this section, we try to determine if geographical proximity, which we use as an admittedly imperfect proxy for contact, is a predictor for the number of tones, pitch units and voice qualities found in a language. We are expecting that if contact plays a role in tonal convergence, *all other things being equal*, then neighbouring languages should be more similar than distant languages. We are working on two assumptions:

1. The influence of the mass media and of the institutions promoting national languages (schools, military service, etc.) is recent enough that they are probably relatively ineffective in isolated communities.

2. Population movements have been limited enough in most of the area in the recent past (since the Tai southward migrations) that conclusions based on the current geographical location of modern language communities can be projected a few centuries into the past. We know that this assumption is inaccurate in the case of Hmong-Mien languages and of some refugee communities in Northern Thailand, but statistical tests reveal that this does not affect our results significantly.

There are also limitations to the models we are using, which are either due to the unavailability of data or to practical implementation issues:

1. Our measurement of geographic distance is based on specific geographic coordinates (points) rather than areas speaking the given variety (polygons). However, the geographic smooths we are using (see Section 4.1) are sensitive to the types of topographical features that slow down or speed up communication (e.g. mountain ranges, rivers, etc.).

2. Some variables, like population size, would be better factored in as relative variables defined for each pair of languages. Due to the relative sparseness of the dataset, this is not feasible using our current approach.

4.1 Modelling the effects of geography with Generalized Additive Models

How can we model differences in tonal inventories as a function of distance? Perhaps the simplest idea would be to include latitude and longitude as predictors in a linear model, but this approach places severe and wholly inappropriate restrictions on the kinds of geographic effects that can be modelled. In particular, such an approach provides no way to capture potentially local areas of tonal convergence, nor can it take into account the potentially disruptive influence of topography. If we are to take seriously the hypothesis of areal effects on tonal inventories, a more sophisticated technique will be necessary.

Here we follow recent work in statistical dialectometry (Wieling et al. 2011; Wieling 2012) in making use of the generalized additive model (GAM) framework

(Hastie and Tibshirani 1990; Wood 2006). A GAM is a type of statistical model very much like classical multiple linear regression, but with the ability to capture non-linearities in the way that a predictor variable influences the response variable. The use of simple linear regression with latitude and longitude as predictors would only allow us to capture hypothetical linear effects—for instance, that the degree of influence one language exerts upon another is related to the Euclidean distance between those languages, as measured by the shortest path between them on a map. While this may be true in some cases, one can easily imagine scenarios where it is inappropriate: two languages may be spoken in villages that are only a few miles apart as the crow flies, but separated by an impassable mountain range or valley. Similarly, the effects of Euclidean distance between two languages could be mitigated if they both lie along a major trade route (e.g. a river). Using GAMs, we can construct a model that is sensitive to this type of topographic variation.[1]

As a first pass, we built a GAM to predict the number of tones based on the (potentially non-linear interaction of) latitude and longitude. The plot in Figure 7, created using the R package mgcv (Wood, 2006), shows the results. Lighter greys represent areas where the model predicts languages to have fewer tones, while darker areas represent regions of greater tonality.

Figure 7 captures the same information as Figure 3: it indicates that, broadly speaking, the area of greatest tonality is northern Vietnam, while in the southern regions (southern Vietnam and Malay Peninsula) there are fewer tones. Importantly, there do not appear to be any dark regions surrounded by lighter ones, or vice versa, suggesting that languages in close geographic proximity tend to have similar numbers of tones (although they may still differ in other aspects of their tonal inventory). Although this might suggest a potentially strong effect of contact on tonal inventories, the following sections will demonstrate that there does not appear to be a geographical influence on the distribution of tone that is independent of language family.

---

[1] While it is possible to include non-linear (parabolic or otherwise polynomial) predictors in a standard multiple regression, their shapes need to be specified in advance. The GAM framework provides a principled means of determining the shapes of these components automatically; see Wood (2006) for details.

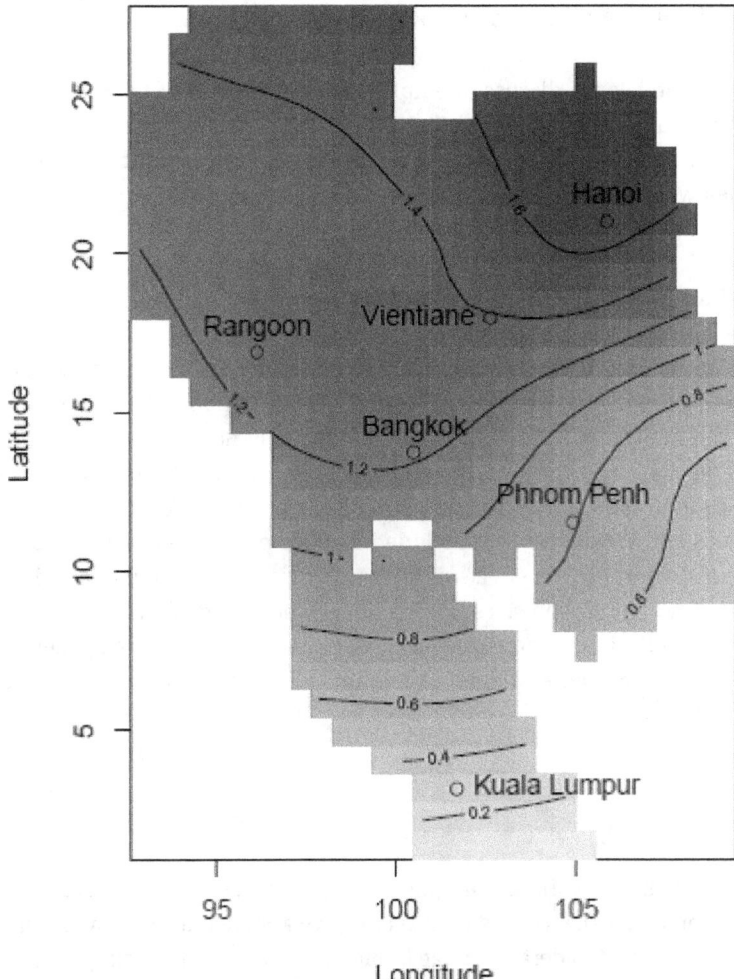

Fig. 7: Contour plot of geographic effects on number of tones. Lighter greys indicate areas of fewer tones, darker greys areas with more tones. Black lines show isoglosses; the numbers indicate the logarithm of the predicted number of tones for the bounded area.

4.2 Modelling the size of the tonal inventory

The first set of models we discuss attempt to predict the size of tonal inventories. Due to partially missing information on several languages, only 175 of the languages in the database were used as data points in the statistical analyses described below.[2]

4.2.1 Model predictors

In addition to the non-linear 'smooth' term representing geographic proximity (henceforth GEOGRAPHY), we considered a subset of the variables from the database described in Section 2. These included language FAMILY, the local population size (POPLOCAL) and the total population size (POPTOTAL) along with the language's canonical WORDTYPE (mono-, sesqui-, or polysyllabic). Of these predictors, FAMILY and WORDTYPE were included as fixed-effect predictors; we also considered models where the effects of geography were potentially affected by the local and total population sizes (for instance, where a small language community has little effect on a large one, even if the two languages are spoken in the same location, or where a large population affects a small one despite a large distance).

4.2.2 Results

Because our dependent variable (number of tones) takes on successive non-negative integer values (i.e. counts from 0 to 8), we assumed it to follow a Poisson distribution.[3] We considered a range of models, starting with a simple model containing just a single predictor (FAMILY or WORDTYPE), then adding predictors and checking if their inclusion resulted in a justified increase in model complexity.

Table 1 lists the coefficients and associated statistics of our final model, which has an adjusted R^2 of 0.678. This model contains two predictors, FAMILY

---

[2] It would have been possible to include up to 186 languages for some of the models (like those that do not factor in population), but since this has little effect on the overall results, we have favoured a uniform approach that allows easy statistical comparison of the models.

[3] In particular, we employed generalized additive Poisson regression models using a logarithmic link function, with smoothing parameters estimated using the method of restricted maximum likelihood (REML).

and WORDTYPE; the base levels are Austroasiatic for FAMILY and monosyllabic for WORDTYPE. As we used a logistic link function, the estimates are logarithms, but it is simple to transform them into integer estimates. For example, the predicted number of tones for a polysyllabic Sino-Tibetan language is exp(1.3408) + exp(0.4818) − exp(0.4446) = 3.88, while for a monosyllabic Austronesian language the estimate is exp(1.3408) − exp(0.6091) = 1.98.

Table 1: Significant parametric coefficients and associated statistics for the final model, predicting number of tones from FAMILY (base level: Austroasiatic) and WORDTYPE (base level: monosyllabic). Estimates give the logarithm of adjustment to the intercept predicting the number of tones, with positive estimates indicating increases relative to the intercept and negative estimates indicating decreases (see text).

	Estimate	Std. error	z-value	p-value
(Intercept)	1.3408	0.1315	10.193	<0.0001
Family=Austronesian	-0.6091	0.2173	-2.803	<0.01
Family=Hmong-Mien	0.6052	0.1875	3.227	<0.01
Family=Sino-Tibetan	0.4818	0.1410	3.418	<0.001
Family=Tai-Kadai	0.3891	0.1481	2.628	<0.01
Wordtype=sesquisyllabic	-0.5554	0.1414	-3.928	<0.0001
Wordtype=polysyllabic	-0.4446	0.1608	-2.764	<0.01

Despite the fact that word shapes are not evenly distributed across the five language families under consideration (see Table 2), models containing a predictor for WORDTYPE always resulted in a significant reduction in deviance. This model is consistent with the descriptive generalizations to be gleaned from our database and from previous scholarship: the number of tones tends to be inversely correlated with complexity of canonical word shape (i.e., monosyllabic languages tend to have more tones than sesquisyllabic or polysyllabic languages). As such, Hmong-Mien and Tai-Kadai languages tend to have large tonal inventories, and Austroasiatic and Austronesian languages tend to have small tone inventories (typically register systems) or to be non-tonal.

Table 2: Distribution of word type by family.

	Wordtype		
Family	Monosyllabic	Sesquisyllabic	Polysyllabic
Austroasiatic	10	62	4
Austronesian	1	10	9
Hmong-Mien	8	0	0
Sino-Tibetan	5	7	24
Tai-Kadai	34	1	0

That our best-fitting model is reasonably reflective of empirical realities allows us to have some measure of confidence in its predictions, as well as its status vis-à-vis alternative models. In particular, in none of the alternative models we considered did GEOGRAPHY emerge as a significant predictor; while a model containing GEOGRAPHY, FAMILY and WORDTYPE is not significantly worse than a model without the GEOGRAPHY smooth term (adjusted $R^2=0.675$), the smooth term itself did not reach significance (see Table 3). We also considered a model in which the effect of geographic proximity was modulated by population size (POPLOCAL or POPTOTAL), in order to capture a potential asymmetry in degree of influence (whereby a language with a large population could exert a greater influence on a nearby language with a small population); neither model was superior to one containing a non-linear geographic predictor only.

However, as was seen in Figure 2, language families in our database are not evenly distributed throughout mainland Southeast Asia. As this is unlikely to be an artefact of our sample, we considered the possibility that GEOGRAPHY could function as an equally good predictor as FAMILY (i.e., that both variables encode similar information about tonal distributions). Indeed, in a model including just WORDTYPE and the smooth term for GEOGRAPHY, the latter emerges as a significant predictor ($\chi2 = 24.88$, $p<0.001$), but a likelihood-ratio test determines that this model is inferior to the model containing FAMILY and WORDTYPE, explaining less overall variance ($R^2=0.603$ vs 0.678).

Table 3: Coefficient estimates and associated statistics for a model containing the predictors GEOGRAPHY, FAMILY (base level: Austroasiatic) and WORDTYPE (base level: monosyllabic). Estimates give the logarithm of adjustment to the intercept predicting the number of tones, with positive estimates indicating increases relative to the intercept and negative estimates indicating decreases.

Parametric coefficients:

	Estimate	Std. error	z-value	p-value
(Intercept)	1.3132	0.1413	9.296	<0.0001
Family=Austronesian	-0.5136	0.2274	-2.258	<0.05
Family=Hmong-Mien	0.5798	0.1978	2.931	<0.01
Family=Sino-Tibetan	0.4471	0.1661	2.691	<0.01
Family=Tai-Kadai	0.3676	0.1554	2.365	<0.05
Wordtype=sesquisyllabic	-0.5282	0.1455	-3.631	<0.001
Wordtype=polysyllabic	-0.3770	0.1754	-2.150	<0.05

Approximate significance of smooth terms:

	edf	Ref. df	χ^2	p-value
Geography	2.004	2.088	2.903	0.247

Based on these results, we infer that any influence of geographic proximity on the number of tonal contrasts in a MSEA language, independent of genealogical affiliation, is likely to be fairly small.

4.3 Pitch and voice quality inventories

We also explored a number of similar models to see how well the number of pitch categories or voice qualities in a language could be predicted on the basis of the variables in our database. The same factors were tested as for the number of tones, except that the number of voice quality units (NBVQ) was also tested as a predictor for the number of pitch categories, and the number of pitch categories (NBPITCH) was tested as a predictor for the number of voice qualities.

The best model for predicting pitch units includes FAMILY, WORDTYPE and NBVQ as significant predictors (R^2= 0.722). As we can see in Table 4, it is overall very similar to the model for tonal contrasts (Table 1), but the significant NBVQ term also shows that there is a slight positive correlation between voice quality and pitch. This reflects the common finding that voice quality tends to be accompanied by redundant pitch variations, especially in register systems. Once again, GEOGRAPHY was not a significant predictor in any of the nested models we compared.

Table 4: Significant parametric coefficients and associated statistics for the best-fit model predicting number of pitch units from FAMILY (base level: Austroasiatic), WORDTYPE (base level: monosyllabic) and NBVQ. Estimates give the logarithm of adjustment to the intercept predicting the number of pitch units, with positive estimates indicating increases relative to the intercept and negative estimates indicating decreases.

Parametric coefficients:

	Estimate	Std. error	z-value	p-value
(Intercept)	1.13291	0.15913	7.119	<0.0001
Family=Austronesian	-0.51268	0.22420	-2.287	<0.05
Family=Hmong-Mien	0.42815	0.19674	2.144	<0.05
Family=Sino-Tibetan	0.45891	0.14815	3.098	<0.01
Family=Tai-Kadai	0.32919	0.14967	2.199	<0.05
Wordtype=sesqui	-0.72077	0.14509	-4.968	<0.0001
Wordtype=poly	-0.50725	0.16640	-3.048	<0.01
NbVQ	0.13194	0.05289	2.495	<0.05

All the models we built for predicting the number of voice qualities had a low explanatory power (R^2 of at most 0.23). The only interesting observation here is that in all these models, NBPITCH is the only significant factor. A look at coefficients reveals that an increase of one pitch unit results in a similar increase in number of voice qualities, which reflects the fact that languages with large numbers of pitch units are more likely to make use of voice quality in their tone systems than languages with smaller pitch inventories, all other things being equal. On the other hand, the factors that do well in predicting the number of tones or the number of pitch units (FAMILY and WORDTYPE) fail to predict the number of voice qualities found in a language.

4.4 The 'idea' of tone

One could also imagine that contact spreads the 'idea' of tone, rather than influencing the number of tonal categories directly (an idea proposed by Benedict 1996 in a paper whose conclusions are otherwise not supported by our results). This would be the case if the chance of a language phonologizing previously predictable pitch variation was higher if its speakers were bilingual in a language that already made use of contrastive pitch (the same scenario may hold for voice quality). For instance, Eastern Cham, which is in contact with tonal Vietnamese, seems to have a register system that is more pitch-based (though not exclusively) than Western Cham, a language of Cambodia that is not in contact with languages making use of contrastive pitch (Brunelle 2009a). Perhaps this is due to familiarity with contrastive pitch, and it is plausible that given enough time and a little chance, Eastern Cham could develop a two-way contrast based exclusively on pitch.

We explored this possibility by recoding all languages in our database as tonal or atonal. Here, we depart from the definition of tone used in the rest of the paper in that a language was designated as tonal if it employs at least two different pitch units that are not redundant with voice quality, a criterion meant to exclude from consideration canonical register systems. Table 5 shows that by this definition, the only family that exhibits any meaningful variation is Austroasiatic. Hmong-Mien is entirely tonal, Austronesian is entirely atonal, Tai-Kadai is tonal, except for Cao Lan, which is treated as an atonal register language, and the only atonal Sino-Tibetan language is Chin Daai.

Table 5: Number of atonal and tonal languages per family (186 languages for which we have Word type data)

Family	Number of atonal languages	Number of tonal languages
Austroasiatic	54	24
Austronesian	20	0
Hmong-Mien	0	8
Sino-Tibetan	1	36
Tai-Kadai	1	42

Since Austroasiatic is the only language that exhibits variation, a statistical model would have to factor in interactions, something for which we do not have enough observations. However, a further look at tonal Austroasiatic languages reveals that this group contains both languages which could have borrowed the idea of tone from neighbouring languages, and languages that do not seem to have immediate tonal neighbours:

Languages with tonal neighbours

- 10 Vietic languages, 8 of which are varieties of Viet-Muong which probably have the same tonal ancestor and have not developed tones independently
- 4 Khmuic languages, including two closely-related Khmu dialects.
- 3 closely related Palaungic languages which probably have not developed tones independently
- Mang

Languages without tonal neighbours

- 2 varieties of Khmer that have developed marginal tone through the loss of medial /r/ (possibly a single tonogenetic event)
- 2 Bahnaric languages (Southern Jeh and Koho—the tonal status of the latter is uncertain)
- 1 Aslian language (Kensiu)
- 1 Pearic language, that could probably be described as a complex register language (Samre)

Although our available data does not contain enough observations to support a robust statistical model, the hypothesis that contact spreads the idea of tone in a way independent of genealogical relationship is not clearly supported by our sample.

5 Discussion

On the basis of the typological survey and statistical analyses outlined above, four main findings are worth highlighting:

1. *MSEA is tonally diverse, and dichotomous tonal classifications give an erroneous impression of homogeneity.* As shown in Section 3, 20% of the languages of the area are atonal and 20% have register systems. The 60% of tonal languages are not homogeneous but exhibit a wide range of diversity, from simple two-tone systems based exclusively on pitch to complex tone systems combining a large number of contrastive pitch units and voice qualities.

2. *The phylogenetic signal for tone is extremely strong.* In all models we considered except those accounting for the number of voice qualities, FAMILY emerged as a significant predictor of the number of categories under investigation (number of tonal categories, number of pitch units, presence/absence of tone).

3. *Although FAMILY and WORDTYPE are closely related, the best models always included both factors*, indicating that both explain at least partially independent portions of the observed variance. This seem to confirm Matisoff's (1973) view that there is a causal relation between monosyllabization and tonality. However, this causal relationship is still ill-understood. It could stem from two sources: either the loss of presyllables is accompanied by the transfer of some of their contrastive properties onto the main syllable (like the spirantization and voicing of medial obstruents in Việt-Mường described in Ferlus 1982), or monosyllables are for some reason intrinsically more likely to neutralize laryngeal contrasts in onsets and codas. Unfortunately, the former is rarely attested or reconstructed and no solid phonetic scenario seems to support the latter.

4. *When FAMILY is included in the model there is no independent effect of GEOGRAPHY*. While this could change in a model with more sophisticated geographic terms (e.g. elevation, travel distance, etc.), we suspect, based on the current results, that any influence of geographic proximity on the size of the tone inventory is likely to be extremely small.

These findings suggest to us that there is no wide scale force that directly pushes languages to become tonally similar to their neighbours. By and large, neighbouring languages tend to have similar tone systems because they are related, not because they are in contact. Of course, this does not mean that there are never cases of contact-induced tonogenesis. Indeed there are cases where contact is the obvious explanation for tonality, but they are not cases of convergence proper. For example, in Mal, Tai loanwords bear a special tone that distinguishes them from native vocabulary (Chommanad 2010). Furthermore, as we are using synchronic tonal inventories as a proxy for the effects of contact, we might be overlooking past cases of tonal convergence. However, on the basis of the current survey, we submit that there is no evidence for broad, areal convergence of tonality, independent of genealogical affiliation.

Based on this result, what should we do with celebrated cases of contact-induced tonogenesis, like Vietnamese (Haudricourt 1954) or Tsat (Maddieson and Pang 1993; Thurgood 1993)? A first explanation is that these languages may have undergone an exceptionally intensive and long-lasting contact that goes beyond the diffuse and large-scale geographical effect measured here. We know that these conditions were probably met in the case of Vietnamese (Taylor, 1983), although we have little reliable information about Tsat history (Brunelle accepted). A second possibility is that some of these languages underwent tonogenesis independently of contact. This certainly happened to Chinese, allegedly the first East Asian language to have undergone tonogenesis, and to a number of languages spoken in atonal environments, like two independent subgroups of languages of New Caledonia (Rivierre 1993), the ancestor of Athapaskan languages (Kingston 2004), Seoul Korean (Silva 2006; Kirby 2010) and Balsas Nahuatl (Guion et al. 2010). Therefore, contact-independent tonogenesis should occasionally happen in Mainland Southeast Asia as well.

A question that immediately comes to mind, and that was frequently asked by audiences when presenting preliminary versions of this work is "if the role of contact is so limited why are so many MSEA languages tonal?". While this is not a trivial question, we believe it can only be answered after considering a few issues:

a) First of all, as shown in Section 3, MSEA tone systems are not homogeneous. The wide tonal diversity found in MSEA languages suggests that even if there was convergence, it would probably operate at a subtler level than a mere tonal/atonal dichotomy. Furthermore, while MSEA seems more tonal than average, there seem to be other language areas with comparable degrees of tonality. While, there is to our knowledge no other systematic survey of tone in a specific language area, a look at WALS (Maddieson 2011) and at the World Phonotactic Database (Donohue et al. 2013) suggests that West Africa, Papua and perhaps Mesoamerica, are also highly tonal, both in the sense that tone languages are thick on the ground and that the tone systems themselves are highly complex. That MSEA is tonally exceptional in any meaningful way still remains to be demonstrated.

b) Second, an underlying assumption behind this question is that even if there is no obvious convergence effect in modern languages, there must have been some convergence between the tone systems of the ancestors of Chinese, Hmong-Mien and Tai-Kadai (see Section 1 for explicit claims). While reconstructions of Proto-Tai and Proto-Hmong-Mien tone systems (Pittayaporn 2009; Ratliff 2010) suggest strong similarities with Chinese, with three tones in open syllables, it is important to insist that we know very little about the sources of these three tones and that current reconstructions do not allow us to date or locate their development. Therefore, while tone convergence in the Sinosphere cannot be excluded, it is at the moment a speculative scenario, and, in any case, its underpinnings are mostly unknown. Moreover, while the five modern MSEA language families are uncontroversially recognized, it is possible that they are distantly related (see articles in Enfield 2011 for an overview of recent competing scenarios), and that tone, or tone-proneness, is partly traceable to common ancestors.

c) Thirdly, it is important to recognize that tone languages are not present to an especially great degree in the two MSEA families that do not have tonal ancestors. MSEA Austronesian languages are either atonal or registral, and MSEA Austroasiatic languages exhibit the full range of tonal behaviour (atonal, registral, pitch+voice quality, pitch only). Crucially, since Austroasiatic can probably be reconstructed with an onset voicing contrast on the verge of being phonologized into register, its descendants are expected to have evolved in various directions independently of contact, because a register contrast can easily be lost, preserved or reinterpreted as a primarily pitch contrast.

We should finally consider the possibility that contact has no direct effect on tone, but that word shape is affected by contact and in turn affects tonality (in fact, the link between word type and tonality is supported by our results). Such scenarios would seem in line with some of the ideas raised in Matisoff (1973). Unfortunately, since the only language families that exhibit significant variation in word shape are Sino-Tibetan and Austroasiatic, a well-adapted model would require the inclusion of interactions, something for which we lack sufficient observations to test at present. More generally, while it is possible to imagine scenarios in which speakers of an atonal language become familiar with tone in their second language and then phonologize pre-existing pitch variations in their native language, it is not obvious why fluency in a monosyllabic L2 would prompt speakers to drop syllables in their native language. Complex scenarios involving simultaneous monosyllabization in two languages are possible (with the possible involvement of stress-shifts: Donegan and Stampe 2004; Brunelle and Pittayaporn 2012), but they do not explain why a polysyllabic/sesquisyllabic language would become monosyllabic after coming in contact with an already monosyllabic language. There are obviously interesting questions and possible answers here, but they are beyond the scope of this paper.

6 Conclusion

The database presented in this study allows us to obtain a finer-grained typology than that presented in Henderson (1965). Pitch and voice quality are both important tonal cues in MSEA languages, but the tone systems that result from the combination of these cues are very diverse, ranging from register systems (simple or complex) to tone systems based on either only pitch or a combination of pitch and voice quality. Moreover, contrary to stereotypical views, a significant proportion of MSEA languages are atonal: 20% of the languages in our database are atonal, and depending on how we treat voice register languages, this figure could go up to 40%. The geographical distribution of tonality is also clearly skewed. Languages tend to have the most tones (and pitch units) in northern MSEA (especially Northern Vietnam) and least in southern Vietnam and Peninsular Malaysia, with a smooth gradient in between. Interestingly, this geographical effect is not statistically significant and seems to be an artefact of linguistic affiliation and word shape.

Voice quality on the other hand, seems largely random. Language family and word shape do not account for it, nor does geography. The only factor that explains the presence of voice quality distinctions, even if weakly, is the number of pitch units: languages that have many pitch categories tend to accompany them with voice quality distinctions, probably for reasons of contrast maximization.

The second type of conclusion reached in this paper is essentially a series of negative results. While these may appear unexciting, they are nonetheless important as they challenge current views of contact and change. First of all, it seems that population size does not have a clear effect on the tendency that a language has to look like its neighbours. Thus it cannot be said that small languages are more prone to become tonally similar to their neighbours. Second, the absence of geographical effect suggests that there is no systematic large-scale effect of contact on tone inventories: all else being equal, unrelated neighbouring languages do not tend to have tonal inventories of similar size. Similarly, languages do not seem to borrow the idea of tone from their neighbours: that is, the likelihood of a language phonologizing pitch variations into tones does not seem to depend on the tonality of neighbouring languages. Our results suggest a single clear trend in terms of tone change: in MSEA, atonal languages can become tonal, but tonal languages rarely become atonal (and the few attested cases belong to the subset of register languages). In the end, only two factors predict the degree of tonality of MSEA languages: the language family to which the language belongs, which suggests that tonality is largely inherited, and word shape (independently of family). While this finding suggests to us a potentially more complicated scenario in which geographic proximity exerts an indirect influence on tonality, the mechanism(s) driving word shape convergence would need to be spelled out in more detail before assessing such a proposal.

We would like to conclude by insisting that our models should not be interpreted as evidence that there has never been any form of contact-induced (or contact-favoured) tonogenesis in MSEA. It is possible that such effects occur at a very local level (although an inspection of residuals from our statistical models did not reveal any such effect), or that only the inclusion of sociolinguistic factors like intensity or duration of contact would allow them to emerge. We believe that the burden of proof falls on the proponents of such effects (we are planning to test such models ourselves), and we think that it is worth insisting that since tonogenesis does occur in languages that are not in contact with tonal languages, it would be expected to occasionally occur in languages that have tonal neighbours even if contact were to play no role at all.

Acknowledgements

We would like to thank Martijn Wieling and Dan Dediu for their thoughtful comments on our implementation of the statistical models, audiences at the MPI workshop and at BLS 39 for their feedback (special thanks to James Matisoff, whose ideas we seem to keep returning to), Pittayawat Pittayaporn for his help with the coding of the Tai-Kadai languages in the database, and Phạm Thị

Thanh Hiền for her help with cartographical software and geographic projections.

References

Abramson, A. 2004. Towards prosodic contrast: Suai and Pattani Malay. In B. Bel & I. Marlien (eds.), *Proceedings of the International Symposium on tonal aspects of languages: Emphasis on tone. Social Sciences*, 1335. Beijing: Chinese Academy of Social Sciences, Institute of Linguistics.

Alieva, N. F. 1984. A language-union in Indo-China. *Asian and African Studies* XX. 11–22.

Benedict, P. K. 1996. Interphyla flow in Southeast Asia. *The Fourth International Symposium on Language and Linguistics*, 1579–1590. Bangkok: Mahidol University.

Brunelle, M. 2009a. Contact-induced change? Register in three Cham dialects. *Journal of Southeast Asian Linguistics* 2. 1–22.

Brunelle, M. 2009b. Tone perception in Northern and Southern Vietnamese. *Journal of Phonetics* 37. 79–96.

Brunelle, M. 2012. Dialect experience and perceptual integrality in phonological registers: Fundamental frequency, voice quality and the first formant in Cham. *Journal of the Acoustical Society of America* 131(4). 3088–3102.

Brunelle, M. accepted. Revisiting the expansion of the Chamic language family: Acehnese and Tsat. In A. Griffiths, A. Hardy & G. Wade (eds.), *New research in Cham studies: an international conference*. Singapore: Institute of Southeast Asian Studies.

Brunelle, M. & P. Pittayaporn. 2012. Phonologically-constrained change: The role of the foot in monosyllabization and rhythmic shifts in Mainland Southeast Asia. *Diachronica* 29(4). 411–433.

Chommanad, I. 2010. Tai loanwords in Mal: A minority language of Thailand. *Mon-Khmer Studies* 39. 123–136.

Donegan, P. & D. Stampe. 2004. Rhythm and the synthetic drift of Munda. In R. Singh (ed.), *The Yearbook of South Asian Languages and Linguistics*, 3–36. New Delhi: Thousand Oaks.

Donohue, M., R. Hetherington, J. McElvenny & V. Dawson. 2013. World phonotactics database. Canberra: Department of Linguistics, The Australian National University. http://phonotactics.anu.edu.au. (last accessed 09-04-2014).

Enfield, N. J. 2005. Areal linguistics and Mainland Southeast Asia. *Annual Review of Anthropology* 34. 181–206.

Enfield, N. J. 2011. *Dynamics of human diversity*. Canberra: Pacific Linguistics.

Enfield, N. J. & G. Diffloth. 2009. Phonology and sketch grammar of Kri, a Vietic language of Laos. *Cahiers de linguistique - Asie orientale* 38(1). 3–69.

Ferlus, M. 1982. Spirantisation des obstruantes médiales et formation du système consonantique du vietnamien. *Cahiers de linguistique - Asie orientale* 11. 83–106.

Guion, S. G., J. D. Amith, C. S. Doty & I. A. Shport. 2010. Word-level prosody in Balsas Nahuatl: The origin, development, and acoustic correlates of tone in a stress accent language. *Journal of Phonetics* 38(2). 137–166.

Hastie, T. & R. Tibshirani. 1990. *Generalized additive models*. London: Chapman & Hall.

Haudricourt, A. 1954. De l'origine des tons en viêtnamien. *Journal Asiatique* 242. 69–82.

Henderson, E. 1965. The topography of certain phonetic and morphological features of Southeast Asian languages. *Lingua* 15. 400–434.
Huffman, F. 1976. The register problem in fifteen Mon-Khmer languages. *Austroasiatic Studies Part 1* (Oceanic Linguistics special publications 13). 575–589.
Kingston, J. 2004. The phonetics of Athabascan tonogenesis. In K. Rice & S. Hargus (eds.), *Athabascan prosody*, 137–184. Amsterdam: John Benjamins.
Kirby, J. 2010. *Cue selection and category restructuring in sound change*. Chicago: University of Chicago dissertation.
Lee, E. W. 1977. Devoicing, aspiration, and vowel split in Haroi: Evidence for register (contrastive tongue-root position). In D. D. Thomas, E. W. Lee & N. Đ. Liêm (eds.), *Papers in Southeast Asian Linguistics Volume 4, Chamic Studies*, 87–104. Canberra: Pacific Linguistics.
Maddieson, I. 2011. Tone. In M. S. Dryer & M. Haspelmath (eds.), *The World Atlas of Language Structures Online*. Munich: Max Planck Digital Library. http://wals.info/feature/13 (last accessed 09-04-2014).
Maddieson, I. & K.-F. Pang 1993. Tone in Utsat. In J. Edmondson & K. Gregerson (eds.), *Tonality in Austronesian languages*, 75–89. Honolulu: University of Hawai'i Press.
Matisoff, J. 1973. Tonogenesis in Southeast Asia. In L. Hyman (ed.), *Consonant types and tone* (Southern California Occasional Papers in Linguistics No. 1), 71–96. Los Angeles: University of Southern Colombia.
Nguyễn, V. L. & J. Edmondson. 1997. Tones and voice quality in modern northern Vietnamese: Instrumental case studies. *Mon-Khmer Studies* 28. 1–18.
Pittayaporn, P. 2009. *Phonology of Proto-Tai*. Ithaca, NY: Cornell University dissertation.
Pulleyblank, E. G. 1986. Tonogenesis as an index of areal relationships in East Asia. *Linguistics of the Tibeto-Burman Area* 19(1). 65–82.
Ratliff, M. 2002. Timing tonogenesis: Evidence from borrowing. *Proceedings of the Twenty-Eight Annual Meeting of the Berkeley Linguistics Society: Special Session on Tibeto-Burman and Southeast Asian Linguistics*, 29–41.
Ratliff, M. 2010. *Hmong-Mien language history*. Canberra: Pacific Linguistics.
Rivierre, J.-C. 1993. Tonogenesis in New Caledonia. In J. A. Edmondson & K. Gregerson (eds.), *Tonality in Austronesian languages*, 155–173. Honolulu: University of Hawai'i Press.
Silva, D. J. 2006. Acoustic evidence for the emergence of tonal contrast in contemporary Korean. *Phonology* 23(2). 287–308.
Taylor, K. 1983. *The Birth of Vietnam*. Berkeley: University of California Press.
Thurgood, G. 1993. Phan Rang Cham and Utsat: Tonogenetic themes and variants. In J. Edmondson & K. Gregerson (eds.), *Tonality in Austronesian languages*, 91–106. Honolulu: University of Hawai'i Press.
Wieling, M., J. Nerbonne and R. H. Baayen. 2011. Quantitative social dialectology: Explaining linguistic variation geographically and socially. *PLOS ONE* 6(9). e23613.
Wieling, M. 2012. *A quantitative approach to social and geographical dialect variation* (Groningen Dissertations in Linguistics 103). Groningen: University of Groningen dissertation.
Wood, S. 2006. *Generalized additive models: An introduction with R*. Boca Raton: Chapman & Hall.

James A. Matisoff
Re-examining the genetic position of Jingpho*

Putting flesh on the bones of the Jingpho/Luish relationship

1 Introduction

As one of the best studied minority Tibeto-Burman (TB) languages, with approximately three quarters of a million speakers in northernmost Burma and adjacent regions of China and India, Jingpho[1] has long been recognized as being of key importance for understanding the internal relationships of the TB family. Several reasonable hypotheses have been proposed about Jingpho's closest relatives, and the time now seems ripe to evaluate them. This paper will briefly discuss five other subgroups of TB in connection with this problem: Bodo-Garo (= Shafer's "Barish"), Northern (or Northeastern) Naga (often referred to as "Konyak"), Nungish, Lolo-Burmese, and Luish. Thanks to copious new data on two Luish languages, it will now be possible to focus on that hitherto obscure branch of the family with much greater precision than before.

Any subgrouping enterprise in such a teeming linguistic area as E/SE Asia runs up against the eternal problem of distinguishing between similarities due to genetic relationship from those due to contact. All of our TB subgroups have been subject to pressure, ranging from slight to overwhelming, from coterritorial languages. We may recognize contact situations of two types:

(a) Extra-TB → TB, i.e. the influence of a non-TB language on a TB group. This is often relatively easy to detect, e.g. the influence of Tai on Jingpho, Nungish, and Luish.[2]

---

* The full version of this chapter appeared in Linguistics of the Tibeto-Burman Area, Vol. 36.2 (2013), pp. 15-95. It includes three Appendices, one evaluating Burling's SAL grouping, one giving a sketch of Jingpho phonology, and, most importantly, 45 pages of Jingpho/Luish cognates, some 75 of which are indicative of a special Jingpho/Luish relationship. These appendices are available at the book's webpage: http://www.degruyter.com/view/product/449361
1 Formerly known as "Kachin". The autonym Jingpho is also spelled "Jinghpaw" or "Jingphaw." In India, a dialect of this language is known as "Singpho".
2 See below Sections 2.2, 3.1, and 4.2.1.

(b) Intra-TB (TB ¹ → TB ²), i.e. the influence of one TB group on another. In the present context we will have to deal with two major donor languages: Burmese (especially the dialect of Arakan State, known as Marma), and Jingpho itself. Burmese has had some influence on Nungish and Jingpho, but a particularly strong influence on Luish (both Kadu and Sak). Jingpho in turn has exerted powerful pressure on Nungish (e.g. Rawang) and on Burmish (Atsi, Maru, Lashi, Achang, Bola).[3]

1.1 Benedict's unorthodox anti-Stammbaum

Recognizing the geographic centrality of Jingpho in the TB area, as well as the fact that it seems to have special areas of similarity with several other subgroups of TB, Benedict (1972: 6) offered an unorthodox type of family tree, where all branches of the family (except Karenic) are seen to radiate out from Jingpho at the centre. See Figure. 1.

1.2 The Sal hypothesis: Jingpho, Bodo-Garo, Northern Naga

Some sort of special relationship among Jingpho, Northern Naga, and Bodo-Garo has been posited ever since the *Linguistic Survey of India* (1903–28) lumped them together as "Bodo-Naga-Kachin". This closeness, whether due to genetic or contact factors, was noted in Benedict (1972).[4] Benedict goes on to give the two most "striking" lexical examples of this special relationship: distinctive roots for SUN and FIRE (Table 1):[5]

---

[3] These Burmish groups are still considered by Chinese linguists to belong to the Jingpho (or "Kachin") nationality.
[4] "The 'Naked Naga' (Konyak) languages of the northern Assam-Burma frontier region...are most profitably compared with Bodo-Garo, though some of the easternmost members of the group...show points of contact with Kachin. Chairel, an extinct speech of Manipur...is best grouped with Bodo-Garo and Konyak" (1972: 607). As we shall see, it now seems clear that Chairel belonged to the Luish group.
[5] These forms actually represent general TB roots, although their "semantic centre of gravity" is elsewhere (see *tsyar and *b-war, below Appendix III Section 4). The most widespread TB etyma for these concepts are *nəy and *may, respectively.

Table 1: 'Sun' and 'fire' in Jingpho, Northern Naga, and Bodo-Garo

	PTB	Kachin (Jingpho)	Namsang (N.Naga)	Moshang (N.Naga)	Garo (Barish)	Chairel (Luish)
'sun'	*tsyar	dźān	san	śar	sal	sal
'fire'	*b-war	ʔwàn	van	var	waʔl	phal

In 1983, R. Burling, a distinguished specialist in the Bodo-Garo group, developed this idea in detail, generalizing Benedict's example of the distinctive etymon for SUN by dubbing Bodo-Garo, Northeastern Naga, and Jingpho collectively "the Sal languages". Later, on the basis of classic data on Sak (Bernot 1967) and Kadu (Brown 1920), he suggested that Luish belongs in the "Sal group" as well, and observed that Sak's "special similarities to Jingphaw are obvious" (Burling 2003: 178). For an elaboration of this hypothesis, see Figure 6, below.

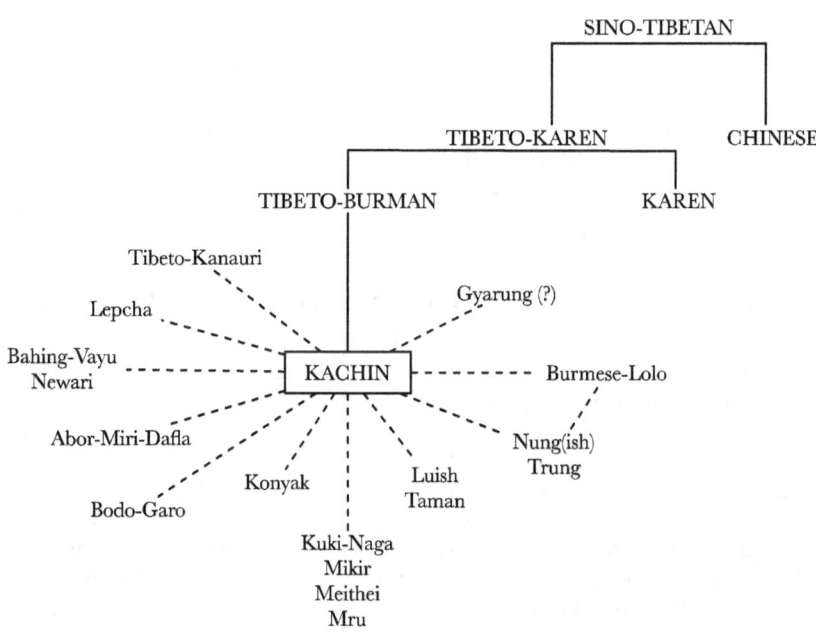

Fig. 1: Benedict's "Schematic chart of ST groups" (Benedict 1972: 6)

However, a close re-examination of Burling's evidence[6] seems to show that while the Bodo-Garo/Northern Naga relationship seems quite solid,[7] the connection of either of them to Jingpho is much more tenuous and distant. A large proportion of the putative *Sal*-specific etyma are actually general TB roots, with cognates in other branches of the family. Burling himself was aware that this would someday be demonstrated: "I have no doubt that a fair number of the cognate sets that I offer, even those that now seem most solid, will finally turn out to have cognates outside the *Sal* group, but the collective weight of the examples I have collected seems to me to demand an explanation" (1983: 15).

As for the "obvious" similarities between Jingpho and Luish, we shall try to make them more precise, thanks to copious modern data on the two principal surviving Luish languages, Sak (Huziwara 2008) and Kadu (Sangdong 2012).

2 The position of Nungish

In Vol. VII of *Sino-Tibetan Linguistics*,[8] Benedict quotes the opinion of the Editor of the *Linguistic Survey of India* on the genetic position of Nungish (Grierson 1928, Vol. I, Part 2, p.24): "Grierson (p. 24) refers to Nungish as a language transitional between Kachin and Lolo, and this view in general has been confirmed." In Benedict (1972: 5) the fifth among Benedict's "seven primary divisions or nuclei of Tibeto-Burman" is listed as #5 "Burmese-Lolo (perhaps also Nung)".[9]

However, Nungish has usually been linked more closely to Jingpho than to Lolo-Burmese. The Rawang, who live in the far north of Kachin State, are considered to be "Kachin" by the Burmese government. In Matisoff (2003: 5) I posited a "Jingpho-Nungish-Luish" group as one of the primary branches of TB,

---

6 See Appendix I.
7 A particularly good reason for positing a special connection between Bodo-Garo and Northern Naga is their characteristic pair of etyma for HAND and FOOT, which differ only in that HAND ends in a velar while FOOT is an open syllable. (Scattered languages elsewhere, e.g. in Tani, have this too.) See Burling (1983: 10) and Section 6, below.
8 Shafer and Benedict (1937-41: vi-vii).
9 In a more modern formulation, Benedict would probably have distinguished between the relatively conservative "Burmish" branch of Lolo-Burmese and the phonologically much more eroded "Loloish" (= Yi) branch. Nungish resembles Burmish much more than it does Loloish. The loose ethnonym "Kachin" has been applied to Burmish groups like the Atsi (=Zaiwa), Maru (=Langsu), and Lashi (=Leqi) by both the Chinese and Burmese governments. For more discussion of the relationship between Nungish and LB, see Section 2.3, below.

without any explicit justification.¹⁰ Fortunately I have been set straight on this matter by Randy LaPolla, the leading Western authority on Rawang: "My view has been that Rawang is not really close to Jinghpaw, there are just a lot of loanwords and calque structures because all Rawang people are considered Kachins and almost all speak Jinghpaw. Jingphaw seems to me a lot closer to Luish."¹¹

LaPolla (p.c., *ibid.*) emphasizes the internal diversity of Nungish, a relatively small group numerically, but boasting "70 or more language varieties in at least six major clusters." The profusion of overlapping Nungish language names testifies to this complexity. According to LaPolla, there is no clear difference among Nung, Dulong/Trung, Rawang, and Anong, since these names are rather indiscriminately applied to what is really just "a crisscrossing dialect chain". No doubt it is because of this unruly diversity that no one has yet ventured to reconstruct Proto-Nungish, or to create a conventional Stammbaum to diagram its internal relationships.

At any rate one thing is clear: Nungish definitely doesn't belong in the "Sal" group; its word for SUN is *nam* (LaPolla 1987, #53).

The Nungish languages are rather conservative phonologically, preserving such features as final liquids (e.g. Rw. *war⁵³* 'fire/burn', *mul³³* 'body hair') and voiceless sonorants, usually from previous combinations of the *s- prefix and the root-initial (e.g. Anong *hwar* 'fire/burn', *n̥o³¹iuŋ⁵⁵* 'remain/stay', *m̥i⁵⁵ŋu³¹* 'begin', *n̥u⁵⁵ŋu³¹* 'weave', *ŋɛ³¹ŋu³¹* 'scales'). It is worth noting that neither of these features is preserved in Jingpho, where final *liquids have become -*n*, and where voiceless sonorants are absent, undoubtedly partially because the *s- prefix has been protected by schwa, so that it is realized as a minor syllable, *šə- ~ dźə-*.

2.1 Variational patterns in Nungish

(a) Between medial -i- and -u-

Nungish seems to be a stronghold of this type of variation, which is pervasive through much of TB,¹² e.g.:

---

10 I am grateful to Carol Genetti for pointing this out to me (p.c. Feb. 2012), since her observation was the motivation for writing the present paper!
11 E-mail p.c., Aug. 16, 2012. For more on the Jingpho/Nungish relationship, see below Section 2.4.
12 See Matisoff (2003: 493–505). This variation is also highly typical of Bodo-Garo.

'name' Rawang bɯŋ³¹ / Anong biŋ
'sleep' Trung yɯp⁵⁵ / Anong yɨp
'warm' Dulong lɯm⁵³ / Nung (Rawang) lim
'year' Anong ɳɯŋ³¹ / Dulong niŋ⁵⁵

(b) Between homorganic final stops and nasals

'black' Dulong naʔ⁵⁵ / Anong ɳi³³xa⁵⁵naŋ⁵⁵
'braid' Dulong blat⁵⁵ / Anong ban⁵⁵sɛ³¹
'branch' Dulonghe aŋ³¹kɔʔ⁵⁵ / Rawang dəgaŋ³¹
'bury' Dulong lɯp⁵⁵ / Anong lɨm⁵⁵
'carve' Dulong gap⁵⁵ / Nung ʔgam⁵⁵
'cloud' Dulong ɹɯ³¹mɯt⁵⁵ / Anong io³¹mɯn⁵⁵
'teach' Dulong sɯ³¹lap⁵⁵ / Anong sɿ³¹lam⁵⁵
'thresh' Rawang am³³thap / Nung tham⁵⁵u³¹

(c) (Diachronic) change of initial nasal to a stop

'name' PTB *r-miŋ > PNungish *b(r)iŋ ⋊⋉ *b(r)uŋ
(e.g. Trung aŋ³¹bɹɯŋ⁵³, Dulong aŋ⁵⁵bɹiŋ⁵³)

A similar development has occurred in loans from Tai:

'insect/worm' Rw. bəlɯŋ³³ (cf. Si. məlɛɛŋ)

(d) (Synchronic and diachronic) variation in position of articulation of nasal initials

'corpse' PTB *s-maŋ > Nung maŋ³¹ / Rawang ənaŋ
'ear (of grain)' PTB *s-nam > Dulong aŋ⁵⁵nam⁵⁵ / Anong mɛn⁵⁵
'eye' PTB *s-mik > Dulong mjɛʔ⁵⁵ / Rawang nɛ³³, Anong ñi dzɯŋ⁵⁵
'mind/temper' PTB *m-yit > Anong mit ~ nit
'nail' PTB *m-tsin ⋊⋉ *m-tsyen > Rw. nyin (Jg. ləmyīn)

(e) (Diachronic) intrusive medials via metathesis

In at least two cases, LaPolla (1987) explains the development of a liquid glide in Dulong/Trung in terms of metathesis from the PTB *r- prefix:

'dream' PTB *r-maŋ > Dulong (Dulonghe) mlaaŋ⁵⁵, Dulong (Nujiang) mlaŋ⁵⁵ (#82)
'name' PTB *r-miŋ > Proto-Nungish *b(r)iŋ ⋊⋉ *b(r)uŋ (#179) [See (c) above]

2.2 Nungish and Tai

Judging from the 130 or so Nungish classifiers listed in such sources as LaPolla's *Rawang Glossary* (2003), Sun Hongkai et al. (1991), and Dai and Huang (1992), there seems to be a great profusion of classifiers in Rawang. This is a Tai-like characteristic, and very unlike Jingpho, where classifiers are rare.

Among the lexical items borrowed from Tai into Nungish, we may mention:

'fish'	Trung *ŋa⁵⁵plaʔ⁵⁵*
	/This is a TB/Tai hybrid (PTB **ŋya* 'fish' + Tai (cf. Si. *plaa*) 'fish'./
'fruit'	Rawang *nəm-si*
	/The 1ˢᵗ syllable is from Shan 'water' (cf. Si. *ná(a)m*); the immediate source of the Rawang form is Jg. *nàm-sì* (2ⁿᵈ syll. < PTB **sey* 'fruit'). The connection between FRUIT and WATER is also found in Chinese *shuǐguǒ* 水果 ./
'garden'	Rw. *son³³* (cf. Si. *sŭan*)
'insect/worm'	Rw. *bəluɯ³³* (cf. Si. *məlɛɛŋ*)
'wear on head/hat'	Dulong *mɔʔ⁵⁵* (cf. Si. *mùak*)

There is one case where an apparent Tai loan is actually a native lexical item:

'rain'	Trung *nǎm⁵³zaʔ⁵⁵*
	/Here the 1ˢᵗ syllable is not from Tai 'water', but is rather from the native Nungish root *nam* 'sun; meteorological phenomenon'. (LaPolla 1987:#53)/

2.3 Nungish and Lolo-Burmese

LaPolla is dubious about any close connection between Nungish and LB, given the phonological conservativeness of Rawang (and the lack of it in Lolo-Burmese),[13] and also because of the complex and apparently ancient morphological patterns in Rawang.[14]

---

[13] We should distinguish here between the Burmish and Loloish branches of LB, since Burmish is much more conservative phonologically.
[14] LaPolla has discussed these patterns in a long series of insightful articles, including LaPolla (2004), (2008a), (2008b), (2008c) and (2010).

Nevertheless there are many Nungish/LB cognates, which indicates to me that Nungish and Lolo-Burmese, while definitely belonging to different TB subgroups, are fairly close to each other in the context of the whole family.

Table 2 shows some of the more interesting Nungish/LB comparisons:

Table 2: Nungish/LB cognates

	Lolo-Burmese	**Nungish**
'bean'	*s-nuk^H	Trung $a^{31}n\mathfrak{d}\mathcal{P}^{55}$; Anong $a^{31}nu^{55}$
'black/deep'	*s-nak^H 'black' (Lh. nâʔ); *ʔnak̚ 'deep' (Lh. nâ)	Trung (Dulong) naʔ^{55} 'black', na^{43} 'deep'
'blind'	Lh. mêʔ-cú	Rw. nɛ^{33} dəzɯʔ
	/ Lh. mêʔ and Rw. nɛ^{33} mean 'eye'; Lh. cú 'tightly closed; puckered'. The Lahu high-rising tone implies a glottalized initial and a final stop) There is also an apparent cognate in Kadu: míkcē./	
'cat'	Lh. mɛ́-ni	Nung (Dai and Huang 1992) mɯ^{31}n̠i^{31}
'chaff'	*pway² (WB phwâi, Lh. phî)	Rw. am^{33}phal^{31}; Dulong waʔ^{55}pi^{53}
	/Rawang provides evidence for *-l in this root./	
'charcoal'	Lh. ší-g̈əʔ [cf. Jg. ǹ-ráʔ]	Dulong mɯ^{31}ɹap^{55}; Nung n̠i^{31}xi^{55}
	/Cf. PTB *g-rap 'fireplace', but that etymon became Lh. g̈ɔ̀ʔ 'hearth; household; fireplace rack'. The Lahu voiced velar fricative seems to favour the centralization and raising of -a- to -ə-, so these could well be internal Lahu allofams: g̈əʔ ⤨ g̈ɔ̀ʔ. The nasal prefix appears in its fullest form in Dulong mɯ^{31}-; it is reduced to a syllabic nasal in Jg. ǹ-, and is probably also represented by Nung n̠i^{31}. As in the Lahu compound mû-qhɔ̂ 'smoke', the morphemic source of this syllable is *maw 'sky; atmospheric phenomenon'. The 1st syllable of the Lahu form seems to be related to the 2nd syllable of the Nungish form (Lh. ší-g̈əʔ / Nung n̠i^{31}xi^{55}); since the Lahu and Nung tones are very similar, it is possible that this syllable has been borrowed by both languages from a common source./	
'foot'	*krəy¹ (WB khre; Lh. khɨ)	Trung xrai^{55}; Anong xɛ^{35}
'gall'	*ʔgrəy¹ (WB khre; Lh. kɨ)	Trung tɕi^{31}xɹi^{55}
'garden/ fence'	*kram¹ (WB khram; Lh. kho)	Nung (Dai and Huang 1992) dʑa^{31}ham^{35}

	Lolo-Burmese	**Nungish**
'morning/ tomorrow'	Lh. *šɔ́-pɔ́* 'tomorrow'	Dulong *sɯ³¹raaŋ⁵⁵*; Rw. *əʃaŋ⁵³* 'morning'

/We can here reconstruct a Loloish/Nungish binome, **syaŋ-braŋ*, where the 1ˢᵗ syllable < PTB **syaŋ* ¹⁵, and the 2ⁿᵈ syllable < PTB **b-raŋ* 'dawn; morning'. Benedict posits a prefixed form **s-raŋ* to account for Trung *sraŋ* (1972: 72, n. 224), but these data show that a full compound is involved, not merely a prefixed root./

'pair'	**dzum³* (Lh. *cɛ̀*)	Dulong *dzŭm⁵⁵*
'pillow'	**m-kum²* (Lh. *ú-gɛ̂*)	Anong *məkhim*; Dulong *mɯ³¹kum⁵⁵*

/The nasal prefix is preserved overtly in Nungish, and indirectly by the voiced Lahu initial./

'pine'	WB *thâŋ-rû* [Jg. *məràu*]	Anong *śəru*
'poor'	Lh. *hā*	Anong *di³¹ɕa³¹*; Rw. *dəʃa³¹*
'prefix'	**ʔaŋ¹-* ⋉ **ʔak-*	Dulong *aŋ⁵³* '3p. pronoun'

/The Nungish 3p. pronoun *aŋ* undoubtedly reflects the same etymon as the *aŋ-* prefix ubiquitous in Loloish (Lahu *ɔ̀-*, Bisu and Pyen *aŋ-*, Phunoi *ā-*), as well as in other languages like Mikir. In Dulong it also functions as a prefix: *aŋ³¹-mul* 'hair', *aŋ³¹-niŋ* 'year', *aŋ³¹-śi⁵⁵* 'fruit'. See Matisoff (2003:109, 522)./

'price'	**pəw²* (WB *ʔəphûi*, Lh. *ɔ̀-phû*)	Trung *aŋ³¹pɯ⁵³*; Anong *dəphü*
'raw'	**džim²* (Lh. *ɔ̀-cî*)	Anong *ɕa⁵⁵dzim⁵⁵*, *əzim*
'scales (weight)'	**kyi:n* (Lh. *chɨ̀*)	Dulong *ci⁵⁵*
'scatter (as seeds)'	PLB **swan²* ⋉ **swat*	PTB **sywar*
		Rawang *wɯn*

/WB *swan* ⋉ *swân*; Lahu *šē* 'scatter seed' < PLB **swan²* ⋉ *šêʔ* 'pour' < PLB **swat*. Since Rawang preserves both **-r* and **-l* in native words, *wɯn* may be a borrowing from PLB **swan*. Both Lahu and Chinese show final nasal ⋉ stop allofamy in this root (cf. Chinese 散 < OC **sân* [Karlgren 1957: 156a-b] ⋉ 撒 < OC **sât* [Karlgren [1923] 1974 #767]), as does Kadu (*sē* 'pour water, as from a kettle' ⋉ *sét* 'scatter seed'). See Matisoff (2003: 394–5)./

'sparrow/ bird'	**n-tsya¹* (WB *ca*, Lh. *jà* 'sparrow')	Anong/Nung *tɕha⁵⁵*, Rw. *sa* 'bird'

---

15 The Lahu high-rising tone suggests an intermediate stage **syaʔ-braŋ*; the sibilant initial and glottal final would then provide the proper environment for "glottal dissimilation"; see Matisoff 1970.

	Lolo-Burmese	Nungish
	/Cf. Spanish *pájaro* 'bird' vs. Fr. *passereau* 'sparrow'./	
'set(of sun)'	*$g(l)im$ ⚭ *$g(l)um$ (Lh. $qè$)	Trung $glɔm^{53}$; Nung $dʑim^{55}$
'stretch out'	*$tšan^3$ (WB *can'*, *chan'*; Lh. *che*)	Trung $t'san^{53}$, Dulong $tɕa:n^{55}$
'sweet'	*$kyəw^1$ (WB *khyui*; Lahu *chɔ*)	Anong $khɹn^{53}$; Trung $dʑɯ^{53}$
'tears'	*m-$brəy^1$ (Mpi m^4pi^6)	Trung $mɛ^{55}pi^{53}$; Nung (Dai and Huang 1992) $phɹn^{55}$
	/The LB prefix is undoubtedly a reduction of PLB *s-*myak* 'eye', which appears overtly in the 1ˢᵗ syllable of the Trung form./	
'testicles/ virility'	*$səw^2$ (WB *sûi*, Lh. *šɔ̄*)	Rw. $sɯ^{33}$ 'male genitals'
'tired/ thirsty'	PLB *ban^2 < PTB *bal 'tired'	Trung bal^{55}, Dulong $ba:n$ 'thirsty'
'turn over'	*m-*pup* (Lh. $phû?$)	Dulong $ɔʔ^{55}$
'vegetable'	*$ʔgyak$	Dulong $dzɯ^{31}gwaʔ^{55}$
'warm/glad'	*lum^1 (Lh. *lɛ̀* 'warm')	*lum^1 (Lh. *lɛ̀* 'warm')
	Lh. *ha-lɛ̀* 'happy'	Anong $a^{31}lim^{31}ʂi^{55}$, Trung $a^{31}lɯ̃p^{55}ɕɯ^{31}$, Trung Nujiang $ɹ^{31}lɯm^{53}$ 'glad'
	/Both Lahu and Nungish have undergone the same semantic development from WARM to HAPPY. The 1ˢᵗ syllable of Lahu *ha-lɛ̀* < PLB *s-la^3 'spirit, soul'. When the spirit is warm, one is happy./	

2.3.1 Burmese loans into Rawang

Quite distinct from the above examples are a number of relatively recent loanwords from Burmese into Rawang, e.g. (Table 3):

Table 3: Recent loans from Burmese into Rawang

	Written Burmese	Modern Burmese	Rawang
'butter'	*thâw-pat*	*thɔ̀bá?*	$thɔ^{33}bat$
'festival'	*pwây*	*pwê*	$bwɛ^{53} \sim bɔi^{31}$
'happy'	*pyau*	*ɔ*	$byo^{33}\,wɛ^{33}$
'peacock'	*ʔu-dâuŋ*	*ʔu-dāū*	$u^{31}dɔŋ^{33}$
'prison'	*thauŋ*	*thāu*	$thoŋ^{31}$
'slippers'	*bhi-nap ~ phi-nap*	*phəna?*	*phənat*

2.4 Nungish and Jingpho

As indicated above (Section 2), expert opinion seems now to be firmly of the view that the perceived closeness of Jingpho and Rawang is due to contact, rather than to any especially close genetic relationship.[16] Among the lexical items which Rawang has borrowed from Jingpho are words which Jingpho itself had borrowed, either from Burmese or from Shan (see, e.g. FRUIT, above Section 2.2).

Table 4 shows a few examples of Jingpho loans into Rawang:

Table 4: Jingpho loans into Rawang

	Jingpho	Rawang
'brick'	wùt	wut
	/The Jg. form is borrowed from Burmese: WB ʔut./	
'early morning/ tomorrow'	mənàp 'early morning'	nap ni^{33} 'tomorrow'
	/Other languages reflect *m-nak, e.g. WB mənak, Lh. tê nàʔ (Matisoff 2003: 326)./	
'flower'	nàm-pàn	nam^{31}ban^{33}
'God'	kərài-kəsàŋ	gərai^{31}-gəʃaŋ^{31}.
	/For the connection between the first element of the Jg. form and the copular morpheme *ray, see Matisoff (1985)./	
'net'	sùm-gòn	ʃam^{33}gon^{53}
'place'	šərà	ɕəra^{31}
'rabbit'	pràŋtái	braŋ^{31}dai^{33}
	/This is a widespread areal word, found also in Lolo-Burmese and Luish./	
'tobacco'	lùt; məlùt	məlɯt
	/Cf. also Dulong nɯt^{55}./	
'tomb'	lùp	Dulong tɯ^{31}lɯp^{55}
'vulture'	làŋ-dà	Dulong laŋ^{31}da^{31}
	/This is another areal word, of Mon-Khmer origin./	

---

16 Among the important structural differences between Jingpho and Nungish are the near absence of numeral classifiers in Jingpho vs. their profusion in Nungish (Section 2.2); and the great degree of sesquisyllabicity in Jingpho as opposed to its relative rarity in Nungish (Section 5.2.1).

In SILVER and HORSE, Rawang has borrowed the Jg. *gu'm-* prefix:

'silver'	gùm-phrò	gəm³¹soŋ³¹
'horse'	gùm-rà ~ gùm-ràŋ	gɯm³¹raŋ³¹

/Note that the Jingpho and Rawang tones are the same in these prefixes. The Jg. variant with final nasal is characteristic of the Hkauri dialect./

3 Other aspects of Jingpho's interrelationships

3.1 Jingpho and Tai (Shan)

There is a large Shan element in the Jingpho lexicon[17]. Most of these words were identified already in Hanson ([1906] 1954). Some of these Shan items were themselves from Burmese, and in turn some of these were originally from Indo-Aryan (Pali/Sanskrit), constituting borrowing chains across several language families, e.g.:

Pali	→	Burmese	→	Shan	→	Jingpho	→	Rawang.
IA		TB		Tai		TB		TB

Table 5 shows a few examples of Tai loanwords into Jingpho:

Table 5: Tai loanwords into Jingpho

	Tai	Jingpho
'bazaar'	Shan *gát*	*gát*
'difficult'	Si. *jâak*	*yàk* 'difficult'; *ʔəyàk* 'difficulty'
	/The borrowed status of this word is immediately apparent, since in native words *-k > Jg. -ʔ (e.g. PIG *pʷak > Jg. wàʔ; EYE *s-mik > Jg. myìʔ)./	
'high/deep'	Si. *sŭuŋ*; Shan *sʰuŋ*	*sùŋ*
'rice plant'	Si. *khâaw*	*khàw*
'rope'	Si. *chîak*; Shan *jìk*	*jìk*

---

17 For a sketch of Jingpho phonology, see Appendix II. For a recent illuminating study of Jingpho dialects, see Kurabe (2013). The classic Jingpho dictionary of Hanson ([1906] 1954) has now been superseded by Maran (ca. 1985), unfortunately still unpublished.

	Tai	Jingpho
'teak'	Si. *máj-sàk*	*mài-sàk*
'turtle'	Si. *tàw*	*tāw-kok*[55]
	/This Tai word has also been borrowed into Lahu: *tɔ́-qú*./	

3.2 Jingpho and Lolo-Burmese

Perhaps because Jingpho and Burmese were the first TB languages I ever studied, I have wondered for a long time whether there was any special relationship between them.[18] Comparison of the tone systems of Jingpho and LB (Matisoff 1974, 1991) was inconclusive (except for a certain weak correlation between Jingpho high tone /x́/ and PLB Tone *2). I am now persuaded that the LB/Jingpho relationship is no closer than that between any two major subgroups of Tibeto-Burman.

Yet there has been massive contact between Jingpho and the Burmish branch of Lolo-Burmese. Many Burmish languages are known both by Jingpho and Chinese names, e.g. Atsi, Maru, and Lashi are Jingpho language names corresponding to Chinese Zaiwa, Langsu, and Leqi, respectively. Chinese taxonomy considers these Burmish groups to be part of the Jingpho nationality.

Table 6 shows a few loanwords of Indic origin which came into Jingpho by way of Burmese:

Table 6: Indic loanwords in Jingpho

	Written Burmese	**Jingpho**	**Other**
'camphor'	*pərut*	*pəyúk*	
'life/age'	*ʔəsak*	*əsàk*	Kadu *asák* [DS]
'ocean'	*səmúddara*	*nammukdəra*	
	/The Jg. form is a Burmese/Tai hybrid, with the 1st syllable remodelled after Tai *nam* 'water'./		
'unhappiness/misery'	*dukkha*	*dùk-khàʔ*	

Modern Jingpho must now be borrowing from Burmese without restraint.

---

[18] I am even guilty of coining a term "Jiburish" to cover Ji(ngpho), Bur(mish) and (Lolo)ish collectively. For a previous study of the place of Jingpho in TB, see Burling (1971).

4 Luish: an obscure branch of TB coming into focus

The Linguistic Survey of India grouped Andro, Sengmai, Chairel, and Kadu/Ganan into the "Lūi Group" (Grierson 1904, Vol. III, Part 3, p.43); to these have been added Sak (= Cak = Chak = çak),[19] spoken both in northern Arakan (Rakhine Province, Burma) and in the Chittagong Hill Tracts of Bangladesh (formerly E. Pakistan). Lucien Bernot, who studied Sak in E. Pakistan in the 1960's, refers to these languages and ethnicities as "Loi",[20] while Shafer and Benedict have preferred "Luish" (see Benedict 1972: 6). However, it seems preferable to come up with a new name for this group, since *loi* is said to be the Meithei (Manipuri) word for 'slave; dependent'.[21] The Kadu (= Kantu), who are thought to have once been a dominant group in northern Burma,[22] are now concentrated in the Sagaing Division of Katha District, in the Chindwin Valley. Their autonym is also Sak or Asak. Since Sak and Kadu are the most important surviving members, there seems no reason not to rename this group as something like Asakian or Kantu-Sak.[23]

Although these languages have been the object of sporadic study since the mid-19th century,[24] it is only very recently that full length lexical, phonological, and grammatical treatments of the two major representatives of the group have become available. Two splendid doctoral dissertations, by Huziwara Keisuke (Kyoto University, 2008) on the Sak of Bangladesh, and by David Sangdong (La Trobe University, 2012) on Kadu, have now made it possible both to undertake systematic phonological comparisons within Luish, and to better evaluate its affiliations with other subgroups of Tibeto-Burman.

---

19 See also Grierson (1921). To add further to the nomenclatural proliferation, this group is also known by the Modern Burmese pronunciation of WB *sak*, namely [θɛʔ], transliterated either as *Thek* or (misleadingly) as *Thet*.
20 This name was first used in McCullough (1859), who wrote it "Loee".
21 The dominant Meithei group has swept away many smaller languages of Manipur, including Andro, Sengmai, and Chairel, which have all become extinct.
22 It may well be that pressure from Kadu caused the Taman language (see Brown 1911) of the upper Chindwin valley to become extinct. Luce surmises that the Asakian languages "once spread over the whole north of Burma, from Manipur perhaps to northern Yunnan" (1985: 36).
23 Löffler (1964) already referred to this group as "Sakisch".
24 See, e.g. McCulloch (1859); Houghton (1893); Bernot (1967); Löffler (1964); Luce (1985).

4.1 Luish phonologies

4.1.1 Kadu

The arrival of the Chins into the Chindwin Valley in the early second millennium A.D. challenged the dominant position of the Kadu in northern Burma; their decline was then definitively sealed by the Shan, who flooded Burma when Yunnan was seized by the Mongols in the 13th century. Naturally enough, the influence of Burmese and Shan on Kadu is very strong.[25]

Kadu syllable canon:

$$\text{T}$$
$$(C_i)(G) \ V \ (C_f)$$

Kadu tones: (Sangdong 2012: 81–89)

HIGH	55 ~ 44 ~ 45 ~ 44	v́	
MID	33 ~ 22	v̄	(This is lexically the most common tone.)
LOW	22 ~ 11	v̀	

Huziwara has recently shown that this three-way contrast also occurs in stopped syllables.
Minimal tonal triplets:

sín	'spicy'	sīn	'iron'	sìn [HK]	'heart' [DS], ʔəsʰèn
há	'red'	hā	'bitter'	hà	'five'
káp	'shoot'	kāp	'peel'	kàp	'prepare'

---

25 Sangdong (2012: 27–28) cites a wonderful judgment on this matter by Houghton 1893: "Who the Kadu were originally remains uncertain, but now they are little more than Burmese and Shan half-breeds with traces of Chin and possibly Kachin blood. If they ever had a distinct language it is now extinct or has been modified so much by all its neighbors as to be little better than a kind of Yiddish."

C_i:	p	t		k [26]		V:	i		u
	p^h	t^h		– [27]					
			tɕ				e		o
			tɕʰ						
		s [28]	ɕ		h		ɛ		ɔ [29]
		s^h							
	m	n	ɲ	ŋ				a	
	w	l	j					ai [30]	

| C_f: | -p | -t | -k | -ʔ | G: | -w- | -y- [31] |
| | -m | -n | -ŋ | | | | |

Fig. 2: Kadu Consonants and vowels [32]

4.1.1.1 Sesquisyllabicity [33]

Kadu is highly sesquisyllabic. As in Sak (below), the most common minor syllable is *a-*, followed in order of frequency by *ka-*, *ta-*, *sa-*, *pa*, *na-*, and *ma-*. Rare ones include *ha-*, *la-*, *wa-*, *ya-*, *za-*, and *ca-*. Kadu even has words with two minor syllables, e.g. *takalāt* 'root'. This is not uncommon in TB, e.g. Tangkhul *khəmələk* 'lick', WT *brgyad* 'eight', but we need a term for such a word – "doubly sesquisyllabic"?

---

26 /k/ and /ŋ/ do not occur before front vowels.
27 *Kh-* occurs mostly in loanwords from Burmese. Huziwara observes (p.c. 2012) that in some cases Kadu *kh-* is also found in loanwords from Shan (e.g. 'parrot' Kadu *makʰɛ́* < Shan *nok⁵khew¹*), and also as the result of sandhi (e.g. *-hán* 'again' becomes *-kʰán* after checked syllables.
28 In his practical orthography, Sangdong uses "z" for the phoneme /s/, and "s" for its aspirated homologue, /sʰ/, an unusual sound that also occurs in Mod Bs and Shan.
29 In Sangdong's practical orthography, the vowels /ɛ/ and /ɔ/ are written with the digraphs "eu" and "au", respectively, with the tonemark written over the "u". In the comparative portion of this paper (Appendix III) these digraphs have been replaced with the proper phonemic symbols, e.g. 'monkey' *kweú* /kwɛ́/; 'jump' *phaúk* /pʰɔ́k/.
30 Sangdong and Huziwara agree that *-ai* occurs before *-ʔ* and *-ŋ*, but Sangdong claims it also occurs in open syllables, which Huziwara denies.
31 The glides *-w-* and *-y-* occur mostly in loans from Burmese.
32 Adapted from Sangdong (2012: 47 ff, 95).
33 See Sangdong "Minor syllables" (2012: 98–104).

4.1.2 Sak/Cak/Chak

Huziwara calls his language "Chakku" (= Chak = Sak). Everyone agrees that this Luish language is quite distinct from that of another group in the Chittagong Hills Tracts called "Chakma", which is Indo-Aryan, a rather divergent form of Bengali, but written in a Burmese-type script.[34] Bernot surmises that the Cak (= Sak) had lived in Central Burma for at least eight centuries, and that they migrated from Arakan to the Chittagong area in relatively recent times. The dialects of the two regions are mutually intelligible, and intermarriage occurs between the groups. There are 2000–3000 Sak in Bangladesh, where Huziwara did his research. The Sak share the Chittagong Hills with ten other minority populations: besides the Indo-Aryan Chakma and Tangchangya, there are Central Chins (Mizo, Pangkhua, Bawm), Southern Chins (Khumi, Khyang), a Barish language (Tripura = Kokborok), Mru (close to the Chin group, but unclassified), and most importantly, Marma (= Arakanese). Huziwara is especially careful to identify the innumerable Marma words that have made their way into the Sak lexicon (2008: 857–917).

Huziwara recognizes two subdialects of Bangladeshi Sak: that of Baishari District (on which his work is based) and that of Naikyongchari District. There are only relatively slight differences between them, e.g. B. *ny-* / N. *y-* ('weaken' B. *ŋyó*, N. *yó*); B. *ky-* / N. *tɕ-* (e.g. 'sweet' B. *kyi*, N. *tɕi*).

Sak syllable canon :

$$\text{(Cə)(Ci) (G) V (Cf)}^{\text{T}}$$

Sak tones:
LOW   v   (longer, comparatively lower pitch)
HIGH   v́   (shorter, comparatively higher pitch)

G = glides (-*w*-, -*y*-, -*r*-); -*l*- only occurs in loanwords where Marma has *hl*-; -*w*- also occurs mostly in loanwords from Marma (2008: 68). Medial -*y*- occurs only after labials and velars (2008: 74). There is also a glide -*v*- which only occurs before /u/, and which is realized phonetically as a syllabic [ʏ].[35] There are also a few Marma loanwords with the double glide -*yw*-.

---

[34] See especially Löffler (1964).
[35] There is a somewhat analogous phenomenon in Lahu; see below Section 4.2.2.

C_f = final consonants (-ŋ, -ʔ). All scholars agree on these two. But Luce (1985) also recognized -k -t -n; Löffler (1964) also noted -k and -p; while Bernot (1967) recorded -h and -f. Evidently the final consonants other than -ŋ and -ʔ are hard to hear and/or on the way out. See Section 5.1.1 below.

C_i:	p	t		k	V:	i	ɨ		ɯ	u
	ph	th		kh						
	b	d		g		e		ə		o
		c								
		ch					a			
		j								
	ɓ	ɗ								
	s	ʃ								
	v				G:	-w-			-r-	-y-
	m	n		ŋ	C_f:	-ŋ			-ʔ	
	l	r								
	w	y								

Fig. 3: Sak consonants and vowels (Huziwara 2008: 19, 63, 77; see also Huziwara 2002)

4.1.2.1 Sesquisyllables

Huziwara (2010) has devoted a whole article to Sak prefixes. He recognizes 8 minor syllables. The most common of them appears to be *a-*, which shows dissimilatory tonal variation according to the tone of the major syllable: *a-* before HIGH tone (e.g. *atáʔ* 'branch') vs. *á-* before LOW tone (e.g. *átaʔ* 'leaf'). The other prefixal syllables, in rough order of frequency, are: *sə-* (which pre-verbally occasionally has causative meaning: e.g. *pyoʔ* 'disappear'/*səbyoʔ* 'lose'; *pru* 'appear'/*səbru* 'put something into view'); *pə-, mə-, hə-, kə-, rə-,* and *tə-*.

4.1.3 The fate of PTB *velars in Luish

(a) The regular development of PTB *k- is Luish h- (Table 7):

Table 7: PTB velars in Luish

	PTB	Jingpho	Kadu	Sak
'bile'	*m-kri-t	khrī		ʔáha
'bitter'	*b-ka	khá	hā	ha
'borrow'	*s-kəy		hē	hɯ
'branch'	*s-kaːk		hàk	ʔáhaʔ
'chin/jaw'	*m/s-ka	ǹ-khá	ahà	ʔəhəɓɯ́ʔ
'crow'	*ka	ù-khā	ūhá	ʔuhá
'door'	*m-ka	ñ-khā		ʔahá
'dove'	*m-krəw	khrū-dû	[khō] [36]	bəhrîʔ
'hole'	*g/kuŋ	ǹ-khūn		ʔahúŋ
'pillow'	*m-kum	bùŋ-khúm		ʔúʔ-huŋ
'smoke'	*kəw	khú ⊗ khùt	[khó] [37]	vaiŋ-hvu
'weep'	*krap	khràp	hāp	hraʔ

(b) In at least one root, dialects of Sak show k- ⊗ h- variation, indicating that the sound-change *k- > h- was still in progress (Table 8):

Table 8: k- ⊗ h- variation in Sak

	PTB	Jingpho	Sak
'head'	*m/s-gaw	khàʔ-khú	ʔahú [HK],
'upstream'			ăhwu² [Luce 1985, Bawtala dial.];
			uk'u [Luce 1985, Dodem dial.]

(c) In a few other roots with voiced or nasal initials, Luish retains original velars (Table 9):

---

[36] This form is also a loan from Burmese (Mod. Bs. *khou*).
[37] This Kadu form is a loan from Burmese (Mod. Bs. *ʔəkhôu*). Still another case is DANCE, where Kadu *káʔ* is evidently borrowed from Bs. *ka'* (< PLB *s-ka³*).

Table 9: Original velars retained in Luish

	PTB	Jingpho	Kadu	Sak
'earth'	*r-ga	gá	kā	kəjá?
'five'	*b/l-ŋa	məŋā	[hà < Shan]	ŋá-hvú
'hot'		kā	ká	ká 'hot', ʔaká 'roast'

(d) Morphophonemically there is also interplay in Kadu between velars and h-. In two-syllable sequences where S¹ ends in -t or -k and S² begins with h-, the h- is realized as aspirated [kʰ]: kát 'run' + háng 'again' > kátkháng; yōk 'eat' + háng > yōkkháng (Sangdong 2012: 59).

(e) In two cases Kadu t- is found to correspond to Sak k(y)- before -i (Table 10):

Table 10: Kadu t- corresponds with Sak k(y)- before -i

	PTB	Proto-Luish	Kadu	Sak
'penis'	*ti-k	*ti	tí	ʔakyí ~ atyí [38]
'sweet'	*twəy	*ti	tī	kyi

4.1.4 Kadu (and Ganan) infixation

There is an infix in Kadu, transcribed as -al- by Sangdong (2012: 158–60) and pronounced as -əl-, which is used (non-productively) especially for nominalizing verbs, e.g. mɛ́ 'good' ("meú") > məlɛ́ 'goodness' ("maleú"). As Sangdong observes, this infixational process is responsible for creating secondary minor syllables, as in the first vowel of "goodness".

Sometimes this infix can disguise a valid cognate, e.g. Kadu salaú 'oil' is from PTB *sa:w (Benedict 1972: #272), though this was not recognized by Benedict, probably because the form was lacking in his sources. (The closely related Ganan language, recorded recently by Huziwara, also has an infixed form here: sʰəlɔ́.)

---

[38] Luce (1985) records ătyí from the Bawtala dialect.

Other examples include:

'branch'	həlàk (n.); hàk is the Kadu classifier for branches, and is directly cognate with WB ʔəkhak.
'flesh/skin'	Huziwara (p.c. 2012) derives Kadu məla 'flesh' from ma, which in Ganan and Sak means 'classifier for animals', and is probably related to the Sak 3rd person pronoun ʔáma.
'hatch'	Sak has puʔ, while Kadu has a doublet pok 'hatch' ⋈ pəlok 'nest' (< PTB *puk; see Matisoff (2008: #16).
'leaf'	Sak has ʔátaʔ, while Kadu has an infixed form talāt (< tāt). Other languages have lateral initials and final -p (Jg. làp, PNN *lap [French 1983: 510]).
'meat'	Kadu has a doublet sān ⋈ salān, while Sak ʔásaiŋ reflects the simple root (< PLu *san < PTB *dzya-n [see Appendix III]). Here as well, Ganan has developed an infixed form (sʰəlan [HK, p.c. 2013]), leading to the possibility that this infix should be reconstructed for Proto-Luish.
'two'	kalìng (Huziwara reconstructs PLu *kìŋ).

There are no doubt quite a few more hidden examples of this infix, so that all Kadu forms with medial -al- should be looked at carefully, e.g. 'head/sky' Kadu halang (? < *haŋ).

However, in other cases a Kadu lateral looks like it is part of the root, not an infix:

'rain/cloud/sky'	Huziwara (2012: #202) reconstructs PLu *hráŋ on the basis of Kadu həláŋ, Sak hráŋ 'rain' and Andro/Sengmai harʌng 'sky'.[39]
'root'	Kadu has təklat, but Sak has ʔákraiʔ, justifying a PLu reconstruction *k-rat.

---

[39] However, Huziwara does consider the Kadu -əl- to be an infix here. He observes that PLu *r- drops without trace in Kadu and Ganan, and supposes that a lateral was infixed after the loss of *r-, with the initial h- treated as a prefix: *h-ráŋ > háŋ > həláŋ. In Andro, PLu *r is preserved if it is not a part of the root, but dropped otherwise (p.c., Huziwara).

4.2 Luish and linguistic groups other than Jingpho

4.2.1 Tai → Luish

I have identified a few Tai loans into Luish, but there are likely to be many more to find. All the Kadu numerals from 5–10 are from Shan, and have been so since the early 20th century (Brown 1920). For reference, Table 11 shows the numerals from 1–10 in several languages of interest. (The Sak numerals from 3–10 seem particularly close to those of Jingpho.)

Table 11: Numerals in several languages

	Jingpho	Kadu	Sak	Rawang	PNNaga
'one'	ləŋâi	tèn-à [DS] [40] tèn-na [HK]	hvú-wa [41]	thiʔ	tse / kla
'two'	ləkhôn	kalìng-tên	níŋ-hvú	əni⁵³	-ni
'three'	məsūm	sóm-tèn	súŋ-hvú	əʃum³¹	sum
'four'	məlī	pí-tèn	prî-hvú	əbi³¹	bə-ləy
'five'	məŋā	Tai	ŋá-hvú	phə ŋwa³¹	bə-ŋa
'six'	krúʔ	Tai	kruʔ-hvú	ətɕhuʔ/kruʔ	tə-ruk
'seven'	sənìt	Tai	səniŋ-hvú	ʃəɯt	n(y)it
'eight'	mətsát	Tai	ʔácaiʔ-hvú	əʃat	tə-gyat [42]
'nine'	krúʔ	Tai	təhvú-hvú	dəgɯ³¹	tə-gə:w
'ten'	šī	Tai	sî-hvú	thiʔ sɛ⁵³	ro:k / bo:n

A random Tai loanword into Luish:

'bedbug'   Kadu *hàt* < Shan *hat* (cf. Siamese *r̯yat*). This Tai word has also been borrowed into Lahu as *hâʔ* (Matisoff 1988: 1107). [43]

---

40 The second syllable is glossed as 'one' in Sangdong (2012: 237). Kadu must thus be added to the short list of languages that has this root for ONE (Aka/Hruso *a*; Qiang Taoping *a²¹*; Qiang Mawo *a*). See Matisoff (1995: 132 [Section 3.154]). Fu Jingqi (p.c. 2012) pointed out to me that this root is also attested in Baic: Jianchuan *a³¹*, Bijiang *a⁴²* (Xu and Zhao 1984: 173).
41 The Sak second syllable must also mean 'one'.
42 This is the reconstruction given in French (1983: 482), but this seems to be a "teleo-reconstruction" based on PTB *b-r-gyat. The actual Naga forms cited point rather to PNN *tsat or *tsyat.
43 Huziwara (p.c. 2013) notes that in his data the forms for 'bedbug' are *hap* in both Kadu and Ganan.

4.2.1.1 Ichthyonyms

Fish names in Kadu frequently have the prefixal morpheme *pa-*, e.g. *pacīsá* 'loach'; *pazīngzú* 'dwarf fish'; *pasàt* 'carp'; *patùn* 'eel' (Sangdong 2012: 100– 101). This is clearly a loan from Tai (cf. Si. *plaa* 'fish'), which regularly occurs as the first syllable in Tai names for fish.

4.2.2 Luish and Lolo-Burmese

These two branches of TB are not particularly closely related at all. There is, however, one phonological phenomenon which Sak shares with Lahu and other Loloish languages: affrication of consonants before /-u/. In Lahu this only happens with labial initials, but in Sak it occurs after other points of articulation as well:

'elephant'	ʔukvú	
'grind'	thvu	
'help'	kvú	
'insect'	ʔápvu	/cf. Lahu **pû**, phonetically [*pfû*]/
'porcupine'	pədvu	
'rat'	kəyvu	
'smoke'	vaiŋ hvu	
'snake'	kəhvú	
'steal'	kvu	

But there is an exception:

'dig'   thu

There are a number of Kadu doublets comprising both native Kadu and Burmese loans as shown in Table 12:

Table 12: Native Kadu and loans from Burmese

	Native	Loans from Burmese
'boat'	halí	lē
'moon/month'	satá	láq [DS], lá [HK]

Huziwara devotes 60 pages (2008: 857–917) to listing loanwords and cognates between Marma (Arakanese) and Sak. A tiny sample of these hundreds of items is listed in Table 13:

Table 13: Loanwords and cognates between Marma (Arakanese) and Sak

	Written Burmese	Marma	Sak
'advantage/profit'	ʔəmrat	ʔəmraiʔ	ʔáməraiʔ
'brain'	ʔû-hnok	ʔŭhnɔʔ	ʔúnóʔ
'carry on shoulder (w. pole)'	thâm	tháiŋ	tháiŋ
'fox'	— —	khéwa	ʃówa
'gold'	hrwei	ʃwe	ʃwe
'hoof'	khwa	khwa	khwa
'open'	phwaŋ'	phwǒŋ	phwáŋ
'hit'	tî	tí	tí
'ice'	re-khâi	rəkhé	rəkhé

A number of these words are ultimately of Indic origin (Table 14):

Table 14: Loans of Indic origin

	Pali/Skt	Written Burmese	Marma	Sak
'body'	khandhaa	khandha	khaiŋtha	kaiŋtha
'distress'	dukkha	dukkha'	douʔkhă	dúʔkhá
'heart/mind'	citta	cit	coiʔ	cíʔ
'sugar'	śarkarā-	sakra	θəgrá	səgrá

4.2.3 Luish and Nungish

Sangdong, who is a native speaker of Rawang, finds (2012: 39) that any connection between Nungish and Luish is "less promising" than the Jingpho/Luish relationship, and one can only agree with him!

However, here are a few examples of closely similar cognates between Luish and Nungish:

'lung'	Sak ʔasésuʔ	Rawang rəʃɯ^{53}
'sesame'	Kadu sanàn	Nung sənam
'smoke'	Sak vaiŋ-hvu	Trung mɯ^{31}ɯ^{55}, Anong mə ö, Rawang məyɯ^{53}

'squirrel'	Kadu *cīlāng*	Nung *dzɿ³¹thaŋ⁵⁵*
'thread'	Sak *rɿ*	Dulong *tsɯ³¹ri⁵⁵/³³*
'wither'	Sak *ŋyɯ*	Anong *ŋyö*

5 Jingpho and Luish

Positing a special relationship between Jingpho and Luish is not a new idea, as witness the fourth of the seven major groupings of TB languages listed in Benedict (1972: 5):

"Kachin; perhaps also Kadu-Andro-Sengmai (Luish) and Taman."

Burling (2003: 178) believes in it too: "Bernot's own data on Sak [1967] are the best that is available on any of these languages, and its special similarities to Jinghpaw are obvious." How much more "obvious" this becomes with all our new data!

5.1 Comparative phonological summary

An outline of Jingpho phonology appears below as Appendix II. Table 15 summarizes some of the salient phonological features of Kadu and Sak, and compares them to those of Jingpho. As implied by the chart, Kadu will prove to be better for reconstructing earlier finals, while Sak will be better for reconstructing initials:[44]

---

[44] This is rather analogous to the situation in Hmong-Mien, where Hmongic is better for reconstructing earlier initials, but Mienic is better for reconstructing finals, i.e. Sak : Hmongic :: Kadu : Mienic.

Table 15: Some phonological features of Kadu and Sak compared to Jingpho

	Kadu	**Sak**	**Jingpho**
C$_i$'s	only 2 series (plain, aspirated)	4 series (plain, aspirated, voiced, imploded)	4 series (plain, aspirated, voiced, glottalized)
C$_f$'s	-p -t -k -ʔ	-ʔ [45]	-p -t -ʔ (-k)
	-m -n -ŋ	-ŋ	-m -n -ŋ
Initial clusters	none	yes	yes
Rhotic initials	no	yes	yes
Numerals	< Tai above 4	TB preserved	TB preserved
Sesquisyllabic	yes	yes	yes

5.1.1 Variation in final stops

A word about final stops in Jingpho, Kadu, and Sak. In general, Jingpho is much more conservative than the Luish languages in its preservation of original final consonants.[46] Final stops seem no longer to have reliably distinct points of articulation in Luish,[47] to the point where Huziwara admits that he has often been obliged to browbeat his Kadu informants in order to get them to pronounce, e.g. -p rather than -t or -ʔ.[48] Where Sangdong records Kadu final -k, Huziwara has -ʔ. We may note the following types of discrepancies involving Jingpho and/or Luish final stops:

a) Jingpho open syllable / Luish -k

fly (n.) Jg. *matšî* 'small winged insects': Kadu *pazèk* [DS]; *pəsíʔ* [HK] : Sak *pacíʔ* / But in this case Jg. does have an allofam with the proper final: *tšíʔ-kròŋ* 'mosquito' / 'husk (of rice)' Jg. *námkhó*: PLuish **hók* > Kadu *yəháuʔ*, Sak *yaʔhóʔ*

---

45 The Dodem dialect of Sak recorded by Luce (1985) has -k as well.
46 An exception to this generalization is that PTB *-k has regularly become Jg. -ʔ. Modern Jingpho words with -k are loans from Shan or Burmese.
47 The same sort of evolution is characteristic of Modern Burmese, where all the final stops of Written Burmese have been reduced to -ʔ, while all the final nasals have lost their points of occlusion, leaving nasalized vowels.
48 See the discussion of BEDBUG (Section 4.2.1).

(b) Jingpho -ʔ / Sak -ŋ

'stingy/miserly'   Jg. mədžìʔ: Sak kəjíŋ

(c) Jingpho -p / Luish -p ~-t

'bear (n.)'   Jg. tsáp : Kadu kəsʰàp [HK], kasát [DS]
'bubble'   Jg. khùm-bòp : PLuish *Cót > Kadu sʰəpɔ́t, Sak ʔasəɓóʔ
'leaf'   Jg. làp : Kadu talāt [DS], təlap ~ tətap [HK], Sak ʔátaʔ

(d) Jingpho -t / Kadu -k

'deer (sambhur)'   Jg. khyì-tút : PLuish *kᴴ-juk > Sak kəjuʔ, Ganan kəsàuʔ
/Here it is Jingpho that has innovated. This etymon is reconstructed as PTB *d-yuk [Benedict 1972: #386] on the basis of forms like Mizo sa-zuk, Mikir thidźok./

(e) Jingpho -p / Kadu -k

'calf (of leg)'   Jg. bòp, ləbòp : PLuish *t-pók > Kadu təpáuʔ [HK], təpók [DS]

(f) Other -t / Luish -t ~ -k

'vagina'   PTB *b(y)at : PLuish *pak > Kadu paʔ; Sak ʔápaʔ [HK], ăpɛt [Luce 1985, Dodem dialect]

It should also be pointed out that a number of etyma show variation in final stops at the PTB level, e.g. 'suck/breast' PTB *dzyuk ⋈ *dzyut ⋈ *dzyup.

Kadu shows a similar uncertainty with respect to the position of articulation of final nasals, e.g. 'sesame' PTB *s-nam > Kadu sanàn [DS], but also recorded as sʰənàm [HK].

5.2 Morphological similarities and differences between Jingpho and Luish

5.2.1 Sesquisyllabicity

It seems to me that "degree of sesquisyllabicity" is an important criterion for comparison among subgroups. Both Jingpho and Luish are highly sesquisyllabic, while Nungish seems only slightly so.[49] Bodo-Garo and Northern Naga prefer compounding to prefixation; in Lolo-Burmese sesquisyllables do exist, but are extremely rare.

5.2.2 Morphological parallelism in the triple allofams for 'eat/food/rice'

Both Jingpho and Luish display a three-member word family built on the basic PTB root *dzya* 'eat', with the allofam in -*n* meaning 'meat/food', and the allofam in -*t* meaning 'cooked rice' (Table 16):[50]

Table 16: PTB word family **dzya* 'eat' in Jingpho and Luish

		Jingpho	Kadu	Sak	Other
'eat'	*dzya	šá		sa	WB câ
'meat/food'	*dzya-n	šàn	salān	ʔásaiŋ	WT zan 'food'
'rice (cooked)'	*dzya-t	šàt	sàt	kvúsaiʔ	Lp. zot 'graze'

However, partially similar allophony in this root is also found in Tangkhulic (*tsa* 'eat', *tsaat* 'cooked rice'). See also Proto-Tani *do* 'eat' (Sun 1993: 160), a root which appears in suffixed form in Kachai (Tangkhulic) *ʔa-dot* 'cooked rice' (Mortensen 2012).

---

[49] Although LaPolla does observe that "Dulong often preserves the proto-prefixes as separate syllables" (1987: 2). Examples include 'grandchild' PTB *b-ləy > Dulong phəli³³; 'pillow' *m-kum > Rawang əgɔ məkhim; 'chin/jaw' PTB *m-ka > Rw. məkha⁵³.
[50] See Matisoff (2003: 440).

5.2.3 Sibilant causative prefix

Jingpho has quite a productive causative prefix, *šə-* ⋊ *jə-* (the latter variant occurring before aspirates and sibilants), which descends from the well-known PTB **s-* prefix with the same function (see Matisoff 2003: 100–102). The same prefix occasionally shows up in Luish as well[51]:

'emerge'   Jg. *prū* 'emerge', *šəpróʔ* 'bring out, exhume'
            Sak *pru* 'emerge', *səbru* 'put out'

5.2.4 Verb pronominalization

So-called "verb pronominalization", a type of "head marking" where morphemes in the VP indicate the person and number of the subject and/or object of the sentence, is characteristic of several branches of TB, to the point where some scholars (e.g. DeLancey 2013) are sure this feature should be reconstructed for PTB.

Jingpho does have such agreement marking to signal the person and number of the subject, although it is nowhere nearly as complicated as, e.g., the systems of the Kiranti languages of Eastern Nepal, where pronominalization reaches its apogee. On the Luish side, there seems to be no evidence at all for verbal agreement. Huziwara (2008) has a section (2.15.1.1; p. 37) entitled "Personal suffixes marked in the verb-phrase",[52] which consists of exactly three words: *"Toku ni nasi."* ("Not especially; not particularly.") This is accompanied by a footnote which suggests a possible distant survival of some sort of agreement system, although Huziwara does not seem to really believe it.[53]

Given the lexical closeness I hope will have been demonstrated between Jingpho and Luish, it seems significant that the two groups should differ in this important respect. To me it indicates that verb pronominalization, like tonogen-

---

[51] Note the different rhyme in the Jingpho causative form.
[52] Dousi-ku ni hyouzi sareru ninshou setuzi.
[53] "However, certain particles which mark the directionality of the action, i.e. *-Xaiŋ* 'benefactive venitive', *-Xaŋ* and *-Xa* 'andative' might descend from the personal suffixes that are hypothesized for PTB, respectively from **-n* '2nd person', **-ŋ* '1st person', and **-a* '3rd person'." ("X" is a morphophonemic symbol which stands for various assimilatory variations in the shape of the particles: Huziwara [ibid.] 420–3, 424–6). However, HK has now abandoned this speculation (p.c. 2012).

esis, is a phenomenon which can easily arise independently in different branches of TB.

5.3 Obstruentization/dentalization of laterals: a key phonological isogloss

A particularly striking phonological development in a few TB languages involves the development of prefixed *lateral initials into secondary dental stops. Before having access to this new Luish data, I had discussed eleven TB etyma that illustrate this phenomenon (Matisoff 2010). When Luish is added to the mix, the parallels between Jingpho and Luish become obvious indeed! Of my 11 etyma, five show obstruentization in Jingpho and/or Luish, with three showing it in both groups, one in Jingpho but not in Luish, and one in Luish but not in Jingpho (Table 17).[54]

Table 17: Obstruentization in Jingpho and Luish

		Jingpho	Kadu	Sak	N.Naga	Other
'hand'	*g-lak	tá?, lətá?	tāk	təhú	Nocte dak	WT lag-pa

/In Jingpho, after *l > t, there was reprefixation by lə- (< *lak). Bernot (1967: 243) cites Sak (Pakistan) la? ñɯ 'index finger'. This looks like a survival of the general TB root, but HK points out that this is evidently a borrowing from Marma la?-hŋyú (cf. WB lak-hŋûi). The usual Luish word for 'arm/hand' is tahu, where the 1st syllable is very likely an unstressed allomorph of tak./

		Jingpho	Kadu	Sak	N.Naga	
'leaf'	*s-la(p)[55]	làp	talāt [DS] talap [HK]	?áta?	PNN *lap [French 1983: 510]	

/The Kadu form contains the -al- infix (above 4.12)./

---

54 Furthermore, three of the five also show obstruentization in Northern Naga. On the other hand, none of my eleven etyma show obstruentization in Bodo-Garo (except for Garo ste 'abdomen' < *s-lay ⋊ *s-ta:y 'navel'). In this respect Jingpho is closer to Northern Naga than it is to Bodo-Garo. Obstruentization of laterals is not characteristic of Nungish, any more than it is of Lolo-Burmese.

55 For the *s- prefix, cf. Magar hla, Dhimal hla-ba.

		Jingpho	Kadu	Sak	Other
'lick'	*s/m-lyak	tá?, mətá?	tāk	ʔáta?	WT ldag, Tangkhul mɔlek
		/Other languages (e.g. Akha myà?) show preemption by the nasal prefix./			
		Jingpho	Kadu	Sak	Other
'moon'	*s-la	šətā, tā	satá[DS] sʰətá [HK]	sədá	WT zla-ba; Meithei tha
		/Benedict's reconstruction *sgl- (1972: 42, n.137) is needlessly complicated. Interestingly, Meithei also has a stop here./			
'navel'	*s-lay dāi, šədāi		ʔásəlu		PNN *ta:y (French 1983: 525), Garo ste 'abdomen'

WEAVE is a somewhat analogous etymon, which shows interchange between r- in Nungish (e.g. Rawang ra?) and in Lolo-Burmese, e.g. WB rak, Lh. yà? < PLB *rak^L), but a dental stop in most other TB languages (e.g. WT ḥthag-pa). This has been explained variously by a proto-cluster (Matisoff 1972: #192, reconstructs PTB *d-rak), and ascribed by Benedict to an Austro-Tai prototype (1972: 19, n.69). Jingpho has a doublet dà? ⋊⋉ wà?, while Luish and Northern Naga have stops: Kadu tàk, Sak ta?, PNN *tak (French 1983: 578).

MORTAR is a rather similar case, this time illustrating the hardening of a fricative to a stop. While Nungish, as well as Mizo and Garo, have s-, and the PLB reconstruction is *ts- (> WB chum, Lh. chɛ), Jingpho and Luish have dental stops, as does most of Northern Naga, leading to a reconstruction something like *(t)sum > *tum:

Table 18: 'Mortar'

Rawang	Mizo	Garo	WB	Lahu	Jingpho	Kadu	Sak
dɔŋ³¹sɯm³³	sum	sam	chum	chɛ	thùm	thōn[DS], tʰom [HK]	thuŋ

Northern Naga also has dental stops (Yogli thim, Moshang thum, Nocte thʌm), except for Chang šʌm (French 1983: 523).

COCKROACH, reconstructed hesitantly by Huziwara as PLuish *s-Cíp (?) (2008: #296), with unspecified initial consonant, shows internal variation within in Luish between intervocalic -l- and -d-: Kadu sʰəlíp, but Sak sɨdî?.

As I observed at the end of "The dinguist's dilemma" (Matisoff 2010), the very sporadicity of l/d or l/t interaction is a consequence of its basis in articulatory fact. Sound changes which are based on universal articulatory tendencies may be activated at any time, so may paradoxically appear to be sporadic in their operation. But in this case the sporadicity may be somewhat localized within the TB family!

6 Conclusions

Working on this paper has brought home to me with particular clarity the crudeness of the traditional family-tree model of linguistic relationships,[56] especially in a complex contact area like Southeast Asia. Any valid language family will show overlapping points of similarity: phonological, lexical, and grammatical isoglosses. Subgrouping depends on how many of these isoglosses reinforce each other—how many strands of similarity combine to become a rope or a cable, as it were. No single criterion suffices. Along with purely lexical matches, we might use such features as obstruentization of laterals, verb pronominalization, triple allofams of the root for EAT (with -n and -t suffixes), the sibilant causative prefix, etc.

At the present state of our knowledge, all we can do is rely on our gut impressions as to degrees of interrelationship. Here are mine, for what they are worth:

(a) Bodo-Garo and Northeastern Naga do indeed share a special relationship, as witness the "curious series" of characteristic roots for HAND and FOOT, where the forms are virtually identical except for the presence of a final element in HAND (see Benedict 1972: 34, n. 108) (Table 19)
(b) In general, Jingpho seems closer to Luish than to any other TB subgroup.
(c) The connection between Jingpho and Northern Naga seems stronger than that between Jingpho and Bodo-Garo.
(d) Contrary to my previous view (Matisoff 2003: 5), I no longer consider Jingpho to be particularly close to Nungish, since the lexical similarities between them seem to be due to borrowing.
(e) Lolo-Burmese seems closer to Nungish than to Jingpho.

---

56 This of course was also the view of Benedict. See Figure 1, above.

Table 19: 'Arm/hand' and 'foot'

	'arm/hand'	'foot'
Bodo-Garo:		
Garo	dźak	dźa
Dimasa	yau	ya
Northern Naga:		
Tableng	yak	ya
Tamlu	lak	la
Banpara	tśak	tśia
Namsang	dak	da
Moshang	yok	ya
Luish:		
Chairel	lak	la
Tani:		
Miri	əlak	əle
Dafla	əla	al

At any rate, we Tibeto-Burmanists should not be discouraged by the fact that the higher-order subgrouping of our family is still problematic. After 200 years of intensive research, similar uncertainties still exist for Indo-Europeanists. While some IE subgroups are demonstrably each other's closest relatives (e.g. Baltic and Slavic), many conundrums remain: e.g. is Italic closer to Greek or to Celtic? This uncertainty was captured long ago by O. Schrader (1906–07), who used a diagrammatic representation rather like the logician's "Venn diagrams", which show by means of overlapping circles the extent of the areas of similarity among different entities. See Figure 4.

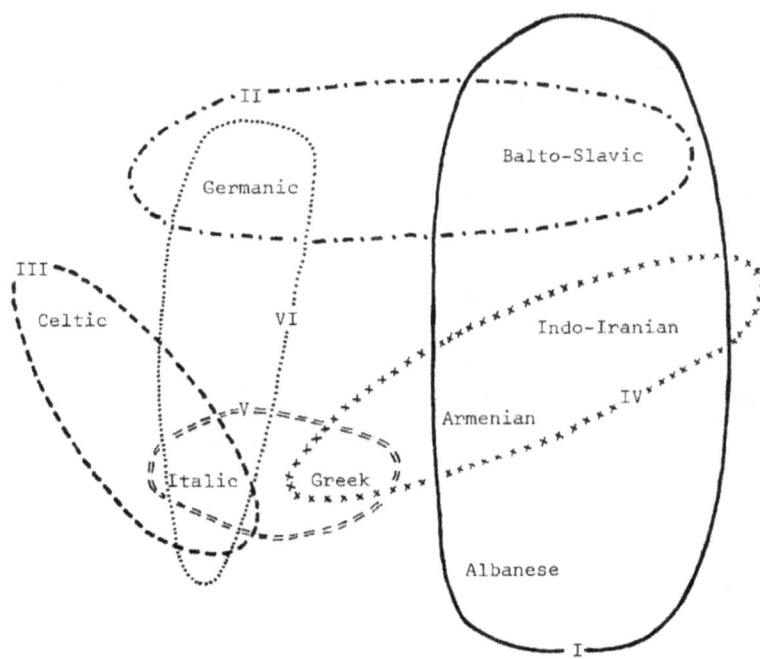

I. Sibilants for velars in certain forms.
II. Case-endings with [m] for [bh].
III. Passive-voice endings with [r].
IV. Prefix ['e-] in past tenses.
V. Feminine nouns with masculine suffixes.
VI. Perfect tense used as general past tense.

Fig. 4: Some Overlapping Features of Special Resemblance among the Indo-European Languages Conflicting with the Family-Tree Model (adapted from O. Schrader, in Bloomfield 1933, p. 316)

Despite the above caveats, it seems useful to adapt here the Asakian Stammbaum suggested by Huziwara (2012: Section 2.3). See Figure 5.

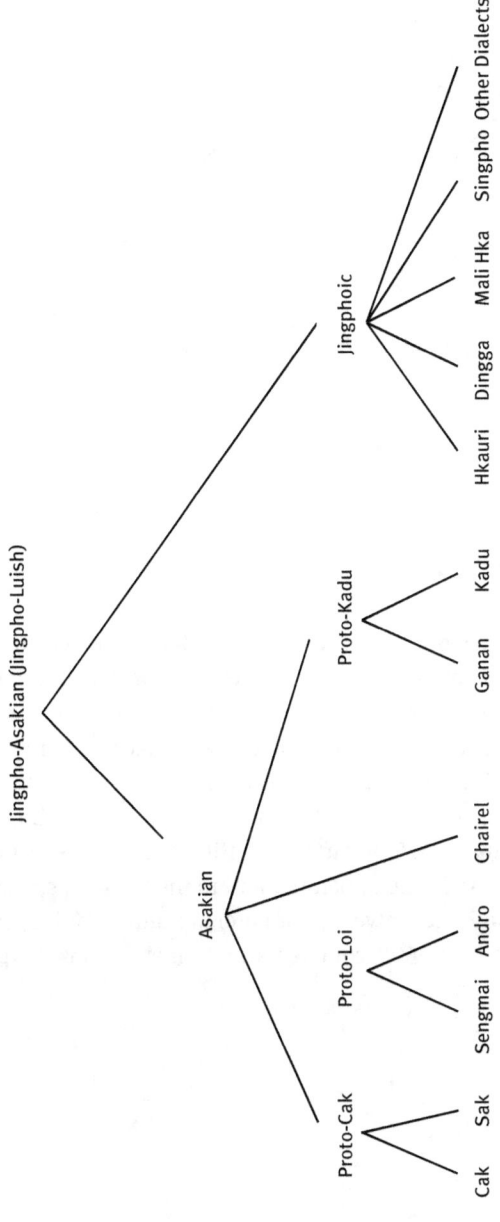

Fig. 5: Jingpho-Asakian Stammbaum

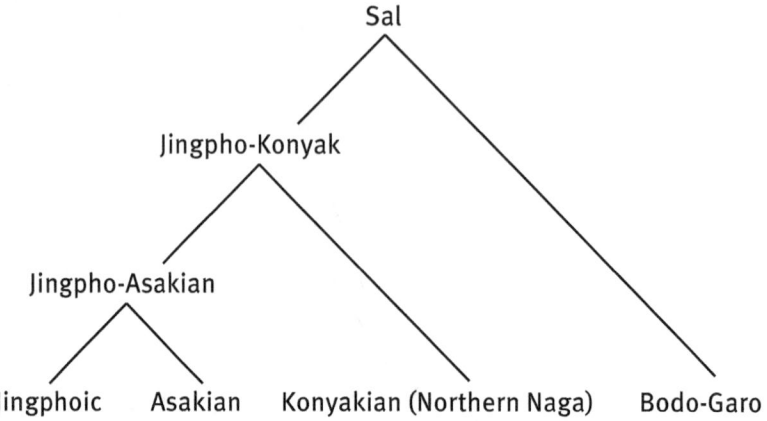

Fig. 6: Elaboration of the *Sal* Hypothesis

Acknowledgements

This material is based upon work supported by the National Science Foundation under Grant #1028192, and by the National Endowment for the Humanities under Grant #PW-50674-10. A previous version of this paper was first presented at the 45th International Conference on Sino-Tibetan Languages and Linguistics at Nanyang Technological University in Singapore (Oct. 2012), then at the Max Planck Institute in Leipzig (Nov. 2012). My thanks to Daniel Bruhn, John B. Lowe, and especially Chundra A. Cathcart for creating the spreadsheet displaying the etymologies included in the appendix, and to the Asakian specialist Dr. HUZIWARA Keisuke of the Kobe University of Foreign Studies for his extraordinary feedback, including some 500 comments and emendations on previous versions.

Abbreviations

A ⋈ B	A and B are allofams; A and B belong to the same word-family
A	Andro
B.	Baishari (subdialect of Bangladeshi Sak)
C_i	Initial consonant
C_f	Final consonant
Clf	Classifier
DS	David Sangdong
G	Ganan; glide
GEN	A general Tibeto-Burman root, appearing both in Jingpho and Luish
IA	Indo-Aryan
ICSTLL	International Conference on Sino-Tibetan Languages and Linguistics
HK	Huziwara Keisuke
JAM	James A. Matisoff
Jg.	Jingpho
LB	Lolo-Burmese (= Yi-Burmese = Burmese-Lolo)
Lh.	Lahu
Lp.	Lepcha
Mand.	Mandarin
Mod.Bs.	Modern Burmese
N	Noun or New
N.	Naikyongchari (subdialect of Bangladeshi Sak)
[N]	New etymology
OB	Old (=Inscriptional) Burmese
OC	Old Chinese
PCC	Proto-Central-Chin (Button 2011)
PCK	Proto-Central-Karen (Theraphan 2013)
PK	Proto-Karen (Jones 1961)
PKC	Proto-Kuki-Chin (VanBik 2009)
PLB	Proto-Lolo-Burmese
PLJ	Proto-Luish and Jingpho only
PLJ+	Proto-Luish and Jingpho special similarity, but also attested elsewhere
PLO	Proto-Luish only
PLTB	Proto-Luish and elsewhere in TB, but not in Jingpho
PLu	Proto-Luish (= Proto-Asakian)
PNN	Proto-Northern-Naga (French 1983)

PTani	Proto-Tani (J. Sun 1993)
PTB	Proto-Tibeto-Burman
PTk	Proto-Tangkhulic (Mortensen 2012)
Rw.	Rawang
Se	Sengmai
SEA	Southeast Asia
Si.	Siamese (= Standard Thai)
TB	Tibeto-Burman
V	vowel; verb
V_i	intransitive verb
V_t	transitive verb
WB	Written Burmese
WT	Written Tibetan

References

Benedict, Paul K. 1972. *Sino-Tibetan: a Conspectus*. Contributing Editor, James A. Matisoff. Cambridge: Cambridge University Press.

Bernot, Lucien. 1967. *Les Cak: contribution à l'étude ethnographique d'une population de langue loi*. Paris: Editions du Centre National de la Recherche Scientifique.

Bloomfield, Leonard. 1933. *Language*. New York: Holt, Rinehart and Winston.

Brown, R. Grant. 1911. The Tamans of the Upper Chindwin, Burma. *Journal of the Royal Anthropological Institute* 41. 305–317.

Brown, R. Grant. 1920. The Kadus of Burma. *Bulletin of the School of Oriental and African Studies* 1(3). 1–28.

Burling, Robbins. 1971. The historical place of Jinghpaw in Tibeto-Burman. *Occasional Papers of the Wolfenden Society on Tibeto-Burman Linguistics* (Vol. II), 1–54.

Burling, Robbins. 1983. The Sal languages. *Linguistics of the Tibeto-Burman Area* 7(2). 1–32.

Burling, Robbins. 2003. The Tibeto-Burman languages of Northeastern India. In Graham Thurgood and Randy LaPolla (eds.), *The Sino-Tibetan Languages*, 169–191. London & New York: Routledge.

Button, Christopher. 2011. *Proto Northern Chin*. (STEDT Monograph #10). Berkeley: University of California.

Coupe, Alexander R. 2012. Overcounting numeral systems and their relevance to subgrouping in the Tibeto-Burman languages of Nagaland. *Language and Linguistics* 13(1). 193–220.

Dai Qingxia, Xu Xijian, Shao Jiacheng, and Qiu Xiangkun. 1983. *Jinghpo Miwa Ga Ginsi Chyum* [Jǐng-Hàn Cídiǎn 景漢辭典] Jingpho-Chinese Dictionary. Kunming: Yunnan People's Publishing Co.

Dai Qingxia and Huang Bufan (eds.). 1992. *Zang-Mian yuzu yuyan cihui*. [A Tibeto-Burman Lexicon.] Beijing: Central Institute of Minorities.

DeLancey, Scott. 2013. Second person verb forms in Tibeto-Burman. Paper presented at the 46th International Conference on Sino-Tibetan Languages and Linguistics, Hanover, NH: Dartmouth College, August 10.
French, Walter T. 1983. *Northern Naga: a Tibeto-Burman Mesolanguage.* New York: City University of New York dissertation.
Grierson, Sir George A. 1921. Kadu and its relatives. *Bulletin of the School of Oriental Studies* 2. 39–42.
Grierson, Sir George A. and Sten Konow, eds. 1903–28. Linguistic Survey of India. 11 vols. Calcutta: Office of the Superintendent of Government Printing.
Hanson, Ola. 1954 [1906]. *A Dictionary of the Kachin Language.* Rangoon: Baptist Board of Publication.
Houghton, Bernhard. 1893. The Kudos of Katha and their vocabulary. *Indian Antiquary* 22. 129–136.
Huziwara, Keisuke. 2002. Chakku-go no onsei ni kansuru kousatu. [A phonetic analysis of Cak] *Kyoto University Linguistic Research* [Kyouto Daigaku Gengogaku Kenkyuu] 21:217–273.
Huziwara, Keisuke. 2008. *Chakku-go no kizyutu gengogakuteki kenkyuu* [A descriptive linguistic study of the Cak language]. Kyoto: Kyoto University dissertation.
Huziwara, Keisuke. 2010. Cak prefixes. In Dai Zhongming and James A. Matisoff (eds.), *Zang-Mian-yu yanjiu sishi nian* [Forty Years of Sino-Tibetan Studies], 130–145. Harbin: Heilongjiang University Press.
Huziwara, Keisuke. 2012. *Rui sogo no saikou ni mukete* [Toward a reconstruction of Proto-Luish]. Manuscript.
Jones, Robert B. 1961. *Karen Linguistic Studies*. Berkeley and Los Angeles: University of California Press.
Karlgren, Bernhard. 1974 [1923]. Analytic Dictionary of Chinese and Sino-Japanese. New York: Dover Publications.
Karlgren, Bernhard. 1957. Grammata Serica Recensa. *Bulletin of the Museum of Far Eastern Antiquities* (Stockholm) 29(1). 1–332.
Kurabe, Keita. 2013. A preliminary report on Dingga phonology: a new dialect of Jingpho. Paper presented at ICSTLL 46, Hanover, NH: Dartmouth College, August 10.
LaPolla, Randy J. 1987. Dulong and Proto-Tibeto-Burman. *Linguistics of the Tibeto-Burman Area* 10(1). 1–43.
LaPolla, Randy J. 2003. *Rawang Glossary*. Manuscript.
LaPolla, Randy J. 2004. Reflexive and middle marking in Dulong/Rawang. *Himalayan Linguistics 2* (on-line journal), December, 2004.
LaPolla, Randy J. 2008a. Nominalization in Rawang. *Linguistics of the Tibeto-Burman Area* 31(2). 45–66.
LaPolla, Randy J. 2008b. Relative Clause Structures in the Rawang Language. *Language and Linguistics* [special issue on relative clause structures edited by Henry Y. Chang] 9(4). 797–812.
LaPolla, Randy J. 2008c. 'Transitivity harmony' in the Rawang language of northern Myanmar. In L. de Beuzeville and P. Peters (eds.), *From the Southern Hemisphere: Parameters of Language Variation*. E-Proceedings of the 2008 Conference of the Australian Linguistics Society (University of Sydney, 2–4 July, 2008), 1–9.
LaPolla, Randy J. 2010. Hierarchical person marking in the Rawang language. In Dai Zhaoming (ed.), *Forty Years of Sino-Tibetan Language Studies: Proceedings of the 40th International*

Conference on Sino-Tibetan Languages and Linguistics (Dec. 2010), 107–113. Harbin: Heilongjiang University Press.

Löffler, Lorenz G. 1964. Chakma und Sak: ethnolinguistische Beiträge zur Geschichte eines Kulturvolkes. *Internationales Archiv für Ethnographie* 50(1). 72–115.

Luce, Gordon H. 1985. *Phases of Pre-Pagán Burma: Languages and History* (2 Volumes). Oxford & New York: Oxford University Press.

Maran, LaRaw. ca. 1985. *A Dictionary of Modern Spoken Jingpho*. Bloomington, Indiana. Manuscript.

Matisoff, James A. 1970. Glottal dissimilation and the Lahu high-rising tone: a tonogenetic case-study. *Journal of the American Oriental Society* 90(1). 13–44.

Matisoff, James A. 1972. *The Loloish Tonal Split Revisited*. Berkeley: Center for South and Southeast Asia Studies, University of California, Berkeley.

Matisoff, James A. 1974. The tones of Jinghpaw and Lolo-Burmese: common origin vs. independent development. *Acta Linguistica Hafniensia* 15(2). 153–212.

Matisoff, James A. 1978. *Variational Semantics in Tibeto-Burman*. Philadelphia: Institute for the Study of Human Issues.

Matisoff, James A. 1985. God and the Sino-Tibetan copula, with some good news concerning selected Tibeto-Burman rhymes. *Journal of Asian and African Studies* (Tokyo) 29. 1–81.

Matisoff, James A. 1988. *The Dictionary of Lahu*. Berkeley: University of California Press.

Matisoff, James A. 1991. Jiburish revisited: tonal split and heterogenesis in Burmo-Naxi-Lolo checked syllables. *Acta Orientalia* 52. 91–114.

Matisoff, James A. 1995. Sino-Tibetan numerals and the play of prefixes. *Osaka: National Museum of Ethnology Research Reports* 20(1). 105–252.

Matisoff, James A. 2000. An extrusional approach to *p-/w- variation in Tibeto-Burman. *Language and Linguistics* (Taipei) 1(2). 135–186.

Matisoff, James A. 2003. *Handbook of Proto-Tibeto-Burman: system and philosophy of Sino-Tibetan reconstruction*. Berkeley: University of California Press.

Matisoff, James A. 2008. *The Tibeto-Burman Reproductive System*. Berkeley: University of California Press.

Matisoff, James A. 2010. The dinguist's dilemma: regular and sporadic d/l interchange in Sino-Tibetan and elsewhere. In Tim Thornes, Erik Andvik, Gwendolyn Hyslop and Joana Jansen (eds.), *Functional-Historical Approaches to Explanation: a Festschrift for Scott DeLancey*, 83–104. Amsterdam: John Benjamins.

McCulloch, W. 1859. *Account of the Valley of Munnipore and of the hill tribes, with a comparative vocabulary of the Munnipore and other languages*. Calcutta: Bengal Printing Co.

Mortensen, David R. 2012. Database of Tangkhulic Languages. (unpublished). Accessed via STEDT database <http://stedt.berkeley.edu/search> on 2012-09-26.

Sangdong, David. 2012. *A Grammar of the Kadu (Asak) Language*. Bundoora: La Trobe University dissertation.

Schrader, Otto. 1906–07. Sprachvergleichung und Urgeschichte. 3rd edition, Jena. English translation of the 2nd edition, entitled Prehistoric Antiquities of the Aryan Peoples (London, 1890).

Shafer, Robert and Paul K. Benedict. 1937–41. *Sino-Tibetan Linguistics, Volumes 6–7: Digarish-Nungish*. (Unpublished typescript, 15 Volumes, bound as 14.). Berkeley: University of California.

Sun, Hongkai, et al., eds. 1991. *Zang-Mian-yu yuyin he cihui* [Tibeto-Burman Phonology and Lexicon]. Beijing: Chinese Social Sciences Press.

Sun, Jackson Tianshin. 1993. *A Historical-Comparative Study of the Tani (Mirish) Branch in Tibeto-Burman*. Berkeley: University of California dissertation.
Theraphan, Luangthongkum. 2013. *A View on Proto-Karen Phonology and Lexicon*. Manuscript. Bangkok: Chulalongkorn University.
VanBik, Kenneth. 2009. *Proto-Kuki-Chin: a reconstructed ancestor of the Kuki-Chin languages*. (STEDT Monograph #8). Berkeley: University of California.
Xu Lin and Zhao Yansun. 1984. *Bai-yu Jianzhi* [Outline Grammar of the Bai Language]. Beijing: People's Publishing Co.

Part 2: **Boundaries of the MSEA area**

Mathias Jenny
The far West of Southeast Asia

'Give' and 'get' in the languages of Myanmar

1 Introduction

Southeast Asia has been established as a linguistic area at least since Henderson (1965) and has received a fair amount of interest by linguists, as can be seen in the regular appearance of publications devoted to the field. Despite the fact that there are a number of specific areal studies in Southeast Asian languages, general typological overviews of the area are still rare. Specific studies on Southeast Asia include Henderson (1965) on phonology and morphology, Matisoff (2004) on semantics, Clark (1989) on syntax, and Bisang (1992) and Enfield (2003) on grammaticalization paths of verbs. Paper-length general overviews of linguistic features of the languages of Southeast Asia are Comrie (2007) and Enfield (2005). One common trait of almost all studies of Southeast Asian languages is that they do not include the languages of Myanmar (Henderson 1965 being a rare exception here). This exclusion of the western fringes of Southeast Asia may be attributed to a number of reasons. On the practical side, most of the languages of present-day Myanmar are not (yet) well described, and field research in the area has been difficult or impossible for over 40 years. Also, the material that is available, especially on the Tibeto-Burman languages (apart from Karenic varieties) suggests a rather different typological profile from the one found further to the east. The general verb-final clause structure of the Tibeto-Burman languages stands in contrast with the predominantly verb-medial structure of what can be called "core Mainland Southeast Asia", comprising languages belonging mainly to the Austroasiatic, Tai-Kadai, Hmong-Mien, and Austronesian families. The best known languages of Myanmar are thus superficially closer to the languages of South Asia, which led Masica (1976:183) to include Burmese as a (peripheral) member of the South Asian Sprachbund, stating that there is "a profound hiatus between India and Southeast Asia beyond Burma". In a recent study, Vittrant (2011) asks whether Burmese is linguistically part of (Mainland) Southeast Asia. Like Masica (1976), Vittrant (2011) looks only at Burmese, leaving aside the other languages spoken in present day Myanmar. Unlike Masica (1976), Vittrant (2011) concludes that Burmese shares enough features with Southeast Asian languages to be included in this linguistic area.

In the present study I look at two constructions widespread in Southeast Asian languages, in a number of languages of Myanmar, including Burmese varieties and minority languages belonging to three different families. The constructions under investigation are the grammatical functions of the verbs 'give' and 'get', the latter of which has been described and analysed in detail by Enfield (2003) in Southeast Asian languages. The main focus is on the (core Southeast Asian) preverbal functions of these two verbs, which are 'permissive/jussive causative' and what Enfield (2003) describes as 'result of prior event' respectively. In postverbal position, the functions are 'benefactive' and 'possibility/ability' respectively. As argued in Jenny (2009) for the case of 'get', I take the preverbal and postverbal functions as independent grammatical developments, rather than different stages of a single linear development, as proposed by Haiman (1999) for Khmer (see also Enfield's [2001] critique of Haiman). The grammatical use of 'give' and 'get', though a solid feature of Mainland Southeast Asian languages, is not restricted to this area (see Heine and Kuteva 2002 for a broader cross-linguistic overview of the grammatical uses of the lexemes discussed here). Parallel constructions are found in many languages of Myanmar and all the way through Northeast India up to Nepal. In accordance with the different syntactic structures of the languages west of Mainland Southeast Asia, the respective constructions may appear in forms seemingly radically different from what has been described for Southeast Asian languages. However, the underlying semantics exhibit close parallels, certainly enough to identify and compare the expressions across the boundaries of syntactic differences. The fact that similar lexemes are used to express similar grammatical meanings over a vast area from Southeast Asia to South Asia may suggest either independent language internal developments along cognitively plausible lines, or some kind of language contact in the distant past, possibly a chain of contact scenarios. We are in no position at the present stage of knowledge to decide in favour of one explanation or the other, nor exclude the possibility of internal development reinforced by language contact.

The geographical areas which display grammatical uses of 'give' and 'get' are not completely coextensive, with 'get' apparently more widespread than permissive/jussive 'give'. Still the constructions and underlying conceptual semantics seem to be related, and they are transparent enough to be replicated in languages that lack one or both of them. We are, in the case of Southeast Asia in general, and Myanmar in particular, not dealing with a single uniform linguistic convergence area, but rather a series of small scale contact scenarios alongside larger scale areas of influence. It can be shown that regionally or nationally dominant languages, such as Burmese, Mon and Shan, exercised influence on subordinate vernaculars, while locally dominant languages may induce changes in otherwise superordinate languages, as can be seen in Mon influence on southern varieties of Burmese (see Næss and Jenny 2011).

In the following sections I will present data and analyses of 'give'-constructions (Section 2) and 'get'-constructions (Section 3), before summing up the findings and presenting a synthesis thereof in Section 4.

2 Grammatical functions of 'give'[1]

2.1 Short note on 'benefactive' and 'causative' constructions

Benefactive constructions are constructions that use some grammatical means, morphological or syntactic, to introduce an additional participant who prototypically benefits in some way from the state of affairs described by the predicate. Different languages employ different coding strategies in benefactive expressions, most commonly case marking on the beneficiary, adpositions, secondary (or serial) verbs, or applicativizing verbal derivation (Zúñiga and Kittilä 2010). In most Southeast Asian languages, postverbal 'give' is used to introduce a beneficiary to a state of affairs, either in core serialization as in Thai and Khmer (Bisang 1992:366-367, 424-425), or root (or nuclear) serialization as in Mon (Jenny 2005: 213-214). Benefactives can have different concrete readings, not all of which are necessarily present in all benefactives. Kittilä (2010) distinguishes plain beneficiary, deputative beneficiary and recipient beneficiary as basic types, following Van Valin and LaPolla (1997), while Jenny (2010) describes a further distinction between direct, indirect, and additional benefactive in Thai: the distinction is neutralized if no overt beneficiary is present and postverbal 'give' expresses that the activity is carried out for the benefit of someone else.

Caused events are encoded in various ways in languages around the world. Different types of causatives can be found also within individual languages, often with semantic differences. Causative constructions can be lexical, with special verbs expressing caused events; morphological, usually with an affix on the verb; periphrastic, that is involving a causative auxiliary; or biclausal, in-

---

[1] I use the glosses 'give' and 'get' as cover terms for the respective verbs with basic semantics denoting a transfer of control over an object in the languages of the area under discussion. It is evident that this label does not imply that the semantics of these lexemes are identical either to the English verb nor to each other in all respects and extensions, including syntactic and collocational possibilities.

volving two clauses, one of which expresses the causation, the other the caused event. In terms of semantics, the causation can be direct or indirect, and the causee can retain or lose control over the caused event. There is some correlation between the different factors, though not an absolute one (see Dixon and Aikhenvald 2000: 74-78). Syntactically, causative expressions are transitive or ditransitive. The causer is assigned the A role, and the causee receives different syntactic roles in different languages. Most commonly it is demoted to direct object (P) and receives formal object marking (Comrie 1989: 165-184). For recent comprehensive accounts of the typology of causative constructions, see Song (1996) and Dixon and Aikhenvald (2000).

A number of languages in the area under discussion make use of morphological causatives. These languages belong mainly to the Tibeto-Burman, Austronesian and Austroasiatic families, with Indo-Aryan languages in the far west of the area. In many cases these morphological causatives have lost their productivity and survive only as fossilized lexemes. Periphrastic causatives tend to replace the older morphological ones, often with initially less grammaticalized meanings. The types of causatives found in Southeast Asia and adjacent areas include all types found cross-linguistically, though not all languages make use of all types. The strongly isolating languages like Thai and Vietnamese exhibit, besides lexical causatives, only periphrastic and biclausal causatives, while other Austroasiatic and Tibeto-Burman languages have lexical, morphological, as well as periphrastic causatives. The latter are often morphologized, with the auxiliaries becoming verbal affixes.

2.2 Grammatical uses of 'give' cross-linguistically

A ditransitive verb with a basic meaning corresponding roughly to 'give' is found in most, if not all languages (see Newman 1996 for a detailed discussion, on which this paragraph is based). In some languages this is the sole ditransitive verb. In more formal terms, the typical meaning of this lexeme can be expressed as "a giver A transfers control over an object (T) to a recipient (G)". Prototypically the transfer is done with the hands of the giver, and it often involves a transfer of possession. The giver wilfully instigates the transfer, by which the thing leaves his sphere of control and enters the recipient's sphere of control. The effect is also prototypically benefactive to the recipient. It goes without saying that any aspect of the semantics of the verb 'give' can be different in a given language, or that different verbs can be used to express similar states of affairs. In German, for example, the verb *geben* 'give' is used to express the act of passing control over an object to a recipient, without entailing transfer of possession. The transfer of possession of an object, without monetary exchange, is expressed by the unrelated verb *schenken* 'give as a present'. While the former is neutral as to the benefactive factor, the latter is commonly used only with objects that are seen as desirable to (or desired by) the recipient. The giver as wilful instigator of the transfer is foregrounded and coded as A, as is the transfer of control expressed by the verb. Either the object given/theme (T) or the recipient (G) can be marked as P, based on language specific syntactic rules.

The semantics taken as basic here are given in a schematic representation in (1). These can be taken as starting point for the grammatical functions of the verb involved in different languages in Southeast Asia and adjacent regions,.

(1) A passes control over T to G.

Given this semantic structure, it is a short step to metaphorically extend the use of the verb 'give' in the sense that T is not necessarily a concrete object, but rather a state of affairs. If a giver passes the control over a state of affairs to a recipient, this leads to an interpretation as enablement or permission, or as obligation. The responsibility of the state of affairs (SoA=T) is transferred from A to G, with the concrete interpretation varying in individual languages. The extended function can be represented as in (2).

(2) A passes control over SoA to G.

The verb 'give' is thus a semantically transparent source of permissive and jussive expressions, with the source of permission or obligation foregrounded and syntactically coded as A. If this use is further grammaticalized, 'give' can end up as general marker of (usually indirect) causation (see Schulze 2011 for a cross-linguistic sample of 'give' constructions). If the grammatical extension goes even further, it can lead to 'give' as a marker of change of subject and/or purpose, as can be seen for example in Lao (Enfield 2007: 423-425) and Mon (Jenny 2005: 127-128, 207-213).

Another source of the indirect causative function of 'give' is found in many languages around the world, including modern German, namely 'A gives G (a T) to V'. We can call this a contextual extension of the situation, where control over T is passed to G so G can do something with T. In this case, the original semantics of 'give' are still present, as in example (3a), less so in example (3b), where a logical theme can be imagined nonetheless, in this case most likely 'reason' or similar. That the causative function of 'give' is not fully grammaticalized in German can be seen from the fact that it is restricted to a smallish number of verbs, as the ungrammatical example (3c) shows.

(3) German

a. Ich   gab   ihr   ein   Buch   zu   lesen.
   1SG.NOM   give.PST.1SG   3SG.F.DAT   one.N   book   to   read.INF
   'I gave her a book to read.'

b. Das   gibt   mir   zu   denken.
   that.N give.PRS.3SG   1SG.DAT   to   think.INF
   'That makes me think.'

c. *Sie   gab   ihm   zu   gehen.
   3SG.F.NOM give.PST.3SG   3SG.M.DAT   to   go.INF
   intended: 'She made him go.'

Similar constructions to example (3) are found in Jinghpaw (Myitkyina), described in Section 2.5.2, where causative 'give' occurs only with a concrete object handed to the recipient (or causee). For a recent study of 'give' + infinitive constructions expressing causative situations in Russian, Polish, and Czech see von Waldenfels (2012).

2.3 General Southeast Asian patterns

2.3.1 Full verb 'give'

The ditransitive full verb 'give' appears in different constructions in the languages of Southeast Asia. In Thai and Khmer, the normal word order is Agent-Verb-Theme-Recipient (AVTG) with simple themes and AVGT with complex themes.[2] Quantifier expressions belonging to the theme regularly follow the recipient, irrespective of whether the theme is an overt NP or not. The two possibilities are shown in examples (4) and (5).

---

2 By simple themes is meant themes that consist of a one-word expression, or a non-modified noun, while complex themes consist of complex NPs including modifiers or multi-word expressions in general.

(4)　Thai
　　kháw **hây** (ŋɤn)　phŏm maː　sɔ̌ːŋ rɔ́ːy　bàːt.
　　3　give money 1M　come two hundred baht
　　'He gave me two hundred baht.'³

(5)　Thai
　　XX **hây** khun mâːk kwàː　khwaːm-sùk.
　　XX give 2　much more.than NML-happy
　　'XX gives you more than happiness.'
　　(from an advertisement signboard)

In other languages, such as Mon, the theme regularly follows the recipient, as seen in (6).

(6)　Mon
　　dɛh **kɒ** ʔuə lòc mùə.
　　3　give 1SG text one
　　'He gave me a book.'

2.3.2 Postverbal 'give' - benefactive and general applicative

Postverbal 'give' is found in most if not all languages of Southeast Asia, denoting an activity that is carried out for the benefit of another person, more rarely an animal. The verbal predicate may be transitive, as in (7) and (8), or intransitive, as in (9). In the former case, a literal reading with 'give' is possible, depending on the context and the semantics of the verb and the object/theme. This reading is not available with the transitive predicate in (8) and the intransitive predicate in (9).

(7)　Thai
　　nák.riən ʔaw　năŋ.sɯ̌ː maː　**hây** khruː.
　　student take book　come give teacher
　　'The student brought a book for the teacher.'

---

3 For the use of the directional *maː* 'come' as spatial-temporal V2 see Jenny (2001: 132f).

(8) Burmese

hlá.tan	sho	té	kaun θei?	tɕhi?	tɛ	sho
PN	say	NFUT.DEP	body very	love	NFUT	say

ta	ko	lɛ̀	θí	**pê**	pa	ʔòun.
NFUT.NML	OBJ	ADD	know	give	POL	still

'Please (do me the favour and) know also that the one called Hla Tan loves (you) very much.'

(FL.MinLouq; corpus of spoken Burmese)

(9) Thai

hàːk	cam.pen	khâː	cà?	taːy	**hây**	ʔeŋ	dây.
if	necessary	1FAM	IRR	die	give	2FAM	get

'If (it is) necessary, I can/am ready to die for you.'

(Jenny 2010: 385)

Formally, the secondary verb 'give' may be adjacent to the main verbal predicate (nuclear serialization), as in (10), or it may be separated from it by an intervening object/theme (core serialization), as in (11).

(10) Mon

dɛh	**ràn**	**nèŋ**	kʋ	ʔuə	lòc	mùə.
3	buy	CAUS.come	give	1SG	text	one

'He bought me a book.'

(11) Khmer

ʔoːpùk	**tɛ̀ɲ**	siəv.phr̆u	**ʔaoy**	khɲom.
father	buy	book	give	1

'Father bought me a book.'

(Bisang 1992: 424)

The interpretation can be plain benefactive or deputative benefactive, depending on the context, as seen in (12a) and (12b).

(12) Thai
    a. thâː   khun   wâːŋ   phǒm   càʔ   sɔ̌ːn   phaːsǎː
       if   2   free   1M   IRR   teach   language
       thay   **hây**   khun.
       Thai   give   2
       'If you have time, I will teach you Thai.'

    b. thâː   khun   mây   wâːŋ   phǒm   càʔ   sɔ̌ːn
       if   2   NEG   free   1M   IRR   teach
       phaːsǎː   thay   **hây**   khun.
       language   Thai   give   2
       'If you don't have time, I can teach Thai for you.'
       (Jenny 2010: 384)

2.3.3 Interverbal 'give' - purposive and adverbial; 'dummy causative'

If 'give' occurs in the construction V1 GIVE V2,[4] the normal interpretation is that 'activity 1 is carried out in order to bring about the state of affairs 2', that is, 'give' receives an adverbial or purposive reading. This is seen in examples (13) and (14), respectively.

(13) Vietnamese
    bây.giờ   tôy   phải   về   nhà   **cho**   nhanh.
    now   1SG   must   return house give   quick
    'Now I have to go home quickly.'
    (Bisang 1992: 322)

(14) Thai
    thaːn   **hây**   ʔìm   náʔ   khráp.
    eat   give   full   EMPH POL
    'Eat your fill, sir.'

---

4 V2 can be any predicative element and is not restricted to verbal expressions.

If the main verb is a desiderative or prohibitive expression, the function of the interverbal 'give' is what Enfield (2009: 811) calls 'dummy causative', indicating a change of subject from the first to the second predicate. This construction is seen in (15) and (16).

(15) Mon
ʔəmè hùʔ mòc **kɒ** kon wɔ̀ɲ məŋèh kwan.
mother NEG DES give child play outside village
'The mother doesn't want her child to play outside the village.'

(16) Thai
yà: **hây** mǎ: khâw bâ:n.
PROH give dog enter house
'Don't let the dog into the house.'

There is no difference between dummy causative and desiderative/prohibitive causative in many languages. Sentence (15) can alternatively be translated as 'the mother doesn't want to let her child play outside the village'. As both desiderative and prohibitive markers are verbal (in some Southeast Asian languages only diachronically), the dummy causative function may in fact be a secondary development from desiderative and prohibitive causative expressions. The interverbal use of 'give' is less widespread than both the postverbal and preverbal varieties, though obviously very common in the languages of the core area.

2.3.4 Preverbal 'give'

Preverbal (or more accurately preclausal) 'give' is widespread in Southeast Asia to encode permissive and in some languages also jussive causative expressions. This can be seen as an extension of the basic semantics: 'transfer of control over object to recipient' to 'transfer of control over state of affairs/event to causee', as outlined above in (1) and (2). The linguistic data suggest that this was indeed the path of extension, rather than from purposive to causative, as suggested by Song (1996: 86f). The pattern A GIVE CAUSEE V, with both transitive and intransitive V, is found in all regions of Southeast Asia and South China. Examples (17) and (18) illustrate the permissive causatives in Maonan, a Kam-Sui (Tai-Kadai) language in southern China. In Maonan the recipient (G) usually precedes the theme (T), though the word order VTG is also possible (Lu 2008: 242). The caused event thus takes the normal position of the theme.

(17) Maonan
man2 **ʔnaːk7** ɦe2 paːi1 jaːn1 man2.
3SG give 1SG go house 3SG
'He let me go to his house.'
(Lu 2008: 254)

(18) Maonan
lja3 kam3 **ʔnaːk7** man2 na4 khaːu3.
wife not give 3SG consume wine
'His wife does not let him drink wine.'
(Lu 2008: 254)

Parallel constructions are found abundantly in languages belonging to all families spoken in (core) Southeast Asia, including Hmong and Cham, as seen in examples (19) and (20). In Hmong, either of two verbs can be used, namely *pub* 'give as a present' or *muab* 'give, hand over', apparently with no semantic difference.

(19) Hmong
Nws txiv tsis **pub/muab** nws mus
3 male not give 3 go
'Her father won't let her go.'
(Clark 1989: 203)

(20) Phan Rang Cham
min əmɛɛʔ MəKaam oh **pràỳ** naaw.
but mother PN NEG give go
'But Kam's mother would not let her go.'
(Thurgood 2005: 508; glosses adapted)

The pattern found in many languages of Southeast Asia may suggest a connection between the different positions of 'give' with respect to the main lexical verb. Looking at Thai expressions like the ones given in (21a-c), it is easy to derive one from the other, taking the benefactive as point of departure, as it is the most widespread construction involving 'give' in Southeast Asian languages.

(21) Thai

    a. *mê: sɯ́: khənŏm **hây** lû:k.*
       mother buy sweets give offspring
       'The mother bought sweets for her child.'

    b. *mê: sɯ́: khənŏm **hây** lû:k kin.*
       mother buy sweets give offspring eat
       'The mother bought sweets for her child to eat.' ('so that the child may eat')

    c. *mê: **hây** lû:k kin (khənŏm).*
       mother give offspring eat sweets
       'The mother lets the child eat sweets.'

Though the superficial similarity of the constructions and the conceptual plausibility of a grammaticalization path from benefactive to purposive to causative are obvious, there are good reasons not to see them as different stages of a single development. First, the similarity is not absolute. In the construction in (21a), the beneficiary can be optionally marked by the dative preposition *kàp* or *kɛ̂:*, which is not possible in (21b) and (21c). In (21b) and (21c), the verb *hây* 'give' can be negated, which is not possible in (21a). The P argument of a transitive main verb, as in (21a), obligatorily functions as P argument of both the main verb and 'give'. In (21b), there is no restriction on the reference of the P of the first and second main verbs, while the P argument (if any) of the first verb is coreferential with the T argument of 'give'. In (21c), 'give' may take an argument different from the argument of the verb in the caused event, in which case 'give' receives its literal reading, as in 'the mother gave her child money to buy food'. Apart from these syntactic differences, the presence of a number of languages that have only the patterns in (21a) and (21c), but not the 'intermediary' stage in (21b) further proves the independence of the three constructions. At least in one language, namely Shan, the form of the benefactive (*pěn*) is different from the purposive and causative *(hɯɯ).*

2.4 Patterns in Myanmar

2.4.1 Burmese

Standard Burmese uses *pè* 'give' as full verb and as benefactive secondary verb. The basic ditransitive pattern of the lexical verb is AGTV, with the recipient (G) obligatorily case marked by postpositional *ko*. While standard Burmese does not have preverbal causative 'give', this function is found frequently in colloquial style in southern and central Myanmar. In Upper Myanmar (Mandalay and Sagaing region), this usage is not completely unknown, but considered southern (or 'Mon') style and nonstandard (cf. Okano 2005; Næss and Jenny 2011). Here postverbal *khàin* 'order' is regularly used for both permissive and jussive causative expressions, while in central and southern colloquial Burmese a distinction is made between jussive postverbal *khàin* 'order' and permissive preverbal *pè* 'give'. Compare the examples given in (22) to (24) from standard and colloquial Burmese.

(22) Burmese (standard)
ʔəme θà ko zè θwà **khàin** tɛ.
mother son OBJ market go order NFUT
'The mother allows/tells her son to go to the market.'

(23) Burmese (colloquial)
ʔəme θà ko zè θwà **khàin** tɛ.
mother son OBJ market go order NFUT
'The mother tells her son to go to the market.'

(24) Burmese (colloquial)
ʔəme θà ko zè **pè** θwà tɛ.
mother son OBJ market give go NFUT
'The mother allows her son to go to the market.'

The structure of the expression in (24) is atypical for Burmese, suggesting a structure AGVT, with the caused event as theme of the verb 'give'. This suggests a foreign, presumably Mon, origin of this construction as an instance of pattern replication without adapting the syntax of the source to the target language. The contact scenario is outlined in Section 2.5 below. Synchronically, the construction *pè*+V in colloquial Burmese can be analysed as a causative verb, but the negator *mə-* can occur either before the main verb or, less commonly, before the causative *pè* 'give', which is evidence against a one-word analysis.

While Burmese uses the indigenous construction with postverbal causative in control expressions with different subjects and in prohibitive constructions, the construction with preverbal 'give' is possible in both cases, giving a desiderative or prohibitive causative reading. This difference, which is not possible in core Southeast Asian languages, including Mon (the putative source of the Burmese construction) is illustrated in examples (25) and (26), both of which merge in Mon in the sentence in (27).

(25) Burmese (standard/colloquial)
 tɕənɔ θú   ko   mə-θwà **se**   tɕhin phù.
 1M   3.DEP OBJ   NEG-go CAUS DES   NEG
 'I don't want him to go.'

(26) Burmese (colloquial)
 tɕənɔ θú   ko   **pè**   mə-θwà tɕhin phù.
 1M   3.DEP OBJ   give NEG-go DES   NEG
 'I don't want to let him go.'

(27) Mon
 ʔuə hùʔ mòc **kɒ**   dɛh ʔa.
 1SG NEG DES give 3   go
 'I don't want him to go.' or 'I don't want to let him go.'

Burmese (including colloquial Burmese) does not use 'give' to introduce purposive adverbial expressions or a change of subject in control constructions, as is found in the languages of core Southeast Asia, a fact that further underpins the view that the construction is a (recent?) result of language contact and not grammaticalized to the extent that it is in Thai, Khmer, and Vietnamese, for example. This further shows that the development of the causative function is independent of the purposive function, as argued above.

2.4.2 Karen

Karen is a group of Tibeto-Burman languages that at some point of their development changed the basic word order from verb final to verb medial, presumably under influence from neighbouring languages. In Kayah Li the lexical verb *dá* 'give' (Solnit 1997: 314) is used as preverbal causative marker (Solnit 1997: 65). Unlike in the standard Southeast Asian pattern, Karen uses 'give' to causativize the verb directly, rather than the clause, resulting in the pattern A give-V CAUSEE. The causee appears as object of the causative verb complex, rather than the subject of the caused event. The Kayah Li construction is thus similar to the construction found in colloquial Burmese described above. Examples illustrating the ditransitive and causative constructions in Kayah Li are given in (28) and (29).

(28) Kayah Li
ʔa lɛ **dá** lū ʔíkwa tə=phre tə=phō rʌ.
3 descend give 3OBV stick one=CL.HUM one=CL.BLOOM PTCL
'He came down and gave each a stick.'
(Solnit 1997: 314)

(29) Kayah Li
vē **dá** cwá ne to.
1SG give go 2SG NEG
'I won't let you go.'
(Solnit 1997: 65)

In Sgaw (Moulmein), 'give' as lexical verb is expressed by *yéʔ*, while the causative expressions are formed by preverbal *dɯʔ*, probably cognate with Kayah Li *dá*. Relevant examples are given in (30) and (31).

(30) Sgaw
tɯnéʔ təʔ=blɔ́ sɔpa báʔ **yéʔ** ñáʔlíʔ=phó
then one=time king hit give Nyali=little
lɔ́ ʔəʔ=phómúʔθəʔdá lɔ.
to 3SG=youngest.daughter CFP
'Then one time the king had to give Nyali his youngest daughter.'
(adapted from Jones 1961: 212)

(31) Sgaw

tə?.bá? **dɯ?** lɛ di? (?ɔ) tə?=ye.
NEG CAUS go yet (3S) NEG=good
'Don't let him go yet.'
(adapted from Jones 1961: 53)

The Kayah Li verb 'give' and Sgaw causative *dɯ?* probably go back to a Proto-Tibeto-Burman root **ter/*s-ter* 'give, CAUSATIVE' (Matisoff 2003: 399, 615), which appears in Lai Chin in expressions like *tlaak-**tèr*** 'cause to fall', *kaŋ?-**tèr*** 'cause to burn', *ril?-**tèr*** 'cause to roll' (see also Peterson 2003: 418), and in Tibetan as ***stér**-ba* 'to give, bestow, grant, concede, allow, let, permit' (Jäschke 1977 [1881]: 222). The development in Karen can be summarized as in (32).

(32) PTB **ter* 'give, permit' → Kayah Li *dʌ́* 'give, let > CAUS', Karen *dɯ?* 'let, CAUS'.[5]

This suggests that the connection between 'give' and causation is old in the Tibeto-Burman family, though it has been lost (and later reintroduced) in Burmese and a number of other languages, including some Jinghpaw varieties, as seen below in Section 2.5.

2.4.3 Shan

In Shan, the inherited verb meaning 'give' is *hɐɯ* (cognate with Thai *hây*), which is used in the standard language (literary Shan) only as preverbal (or preclausal) permissive/jussive causative. It has been replaced as a full verb as well as in postverbal (benefactive) function by *pěn* 'give', earlier 'share'. The pattern with the lexical verb *pěn* 'give' is AVGT. The different patterns found in Shan are given in examples (33) to (35).

---

[5] The original word for 'give', *dɯ?*, in Karen is replaced by a new word, *yé?*, similar to the situation in Shan, where *hɐɯ* CAUS < 'give' is replaced by *pěn* 'give' < 'share', see Section 2.4.3

(33) Shan (Hsihsaing)
   kĕu **pĕn** mén sà.ʔók.
   1SG give 3SG book
   'I gave him a book.'

(34) Shan (Hsenwi chronicle)
   sĕŋ pɤn thăm **hɐɯ** wa cɐu.phâ cɐu.náŋ
   if 3PL ask CAUS say lord lady
   khĕu hɔ̆ŋ kwà ʔàn kɔ̆n hɔ̆.
   PL call go count rafter palace
   'If someone should ask, let them tell him that the lord and the lady called them to count the rafters in the palace.'

(35) Shan (Shan conversation guide for Thai)
   yɔ́m **pĕn** ʔít nuɯŋ cɔ̀ŋ lɐi nɛ̀.
   decrease give little.bit one Q get Q
   'Can you reduce (the price) for (me) a little bit.'

In some varieties of Shan, *pĕn* has replaced *hɐɯ* also in preverbal causative function. This is shown in example (36) from Anisakhan village, near Pyin U Lwin. The same extension of *pĕn* 'give' to causative function is also found in the area south of Taunggyi (data from Hsihsaing).

(36) Shan (Anisahkan)
   kĕu ʔèm **pĕn** mén nɐŋ.
   1SG NEG give 3SG sit
   'I don't let him sit.'

Interverbal 'give' occurs in Shan in the form *hɐɯ*, also in varieties that have replaced this verb by *pĕn* in other contexts. Its use seems to be restricted to (purposive) causation and dummy causatives and it is not found in more general adverbial expressions. Relevant examples are given in (37) and (38), the former of which would use *hây* 'give' in Thai to introduce the adverbial expression (see (14) above).

(37) Shan (Hsihsaing)
kǐn ʔɯ̀m-ʔɯ̀m ná.
eat full-RED EMPH
'Eat your fill.'

(38) Shan (Hsihsaing)
ʔèm khɯɯ **hɯɯ** mén hét kăn kăŋ khún.
NEG want CAUS 3 do work middle night
'I don't want him to work during the night.'

2.4.4 Mon

Mon behaves very much like the languages of core Southeast Asia with respect to the use of 'give' in all three positions. The verb *kɒ* 'give' is used as a full lexical verb, and as a postverbal benefactive marker, as well as in preverbal position. In interverbal position its use is, at least in Mon varieties spoken in Myanmar, restricted to the 'dummy causative' function. It does not introduce purposive adverbial expressions.

Already Old Mon inscriptions of the 11th century show the permissive causative use of <kil> 'give', as illustrated in (39).

(39) Old Mon
tirta toʔ tluṅ sak ḍeḥ **kil** lop sṅi.
heretic PL come NEG 3 give enter house
'The heretics come (but) they don't let them enter the house.'
(Kubyaukgyi)

In modern Mon, the structure remains unchanged, as seen in (40).

(40) Modern Mon
dɛh **kɒ** (poy) dac mɔ̀ŋ ha.
3 give 1PL ride stay Q
'Would they let (us) ride?'
(WW2nc_mn)

In Old Mon, the form <or> 'cause, command' is used both for jussive and permissive causatives, while <kil> 'give' seems to be restricted to permissive contexts. Example (41) is the last sentence of the Myazedi inscription, showing the permissive use of <or>. The parallel text in Burmese in (42) has postverbal <ciy>, corresponding to modern Burmese *se* 'command > CAUS'. Interestingly, the Pyu version of the same sentence, given in (43), seems to use postverbal <pả:> 'give' to express the permissive causative notion, though the Pyu language is still not very well understood and the exact structure of the sentence is unclear.

(41) Old Mon
 yaṅ ñirñāc kyek trey mettey
 FR.NP NML.see holy.object holy PN
 laḥ **or** ḍeh go?.
 PROH cause 3 get
 'Don't let him get the sight of the holy Buddha Metteya.'
 (Myazedi inscription)

(42) Old Burmese
 arimittiyā purhā skhaṅ a phū ra **ciy.**
 PN buddha lord NEG behold get cause
 'Let him not be able to behold the Lord Buddha Ariya Metteya.'
 (Myazedi inscription)

(43) Pyu
 medeyạ dạ.ḅa: dị chí: tí tmū
 PN excellent(?) sight(?) get LOC presence
 ma **pả:** che cho:.
 NEG give PRS OPT(?)
 'May he never be permitted to approach the presence of the lord Buddha Ariya Metteya.'
 (Myazedi inscription; Taw Sein Ko and Duroiselle 1919: 63; Shafer 1943: 337)

In modern Mon jussive causatives can alternatively be expressed by preverbal *ciəʔka* 'use, order', and occurrences of permissive use of preverbal *kɒ* 'give' may be more frequent. But *kɒ* 'give' is also used in jussive contexts, as the following example (44) shows, where the first instance is permissive, the second one rather jussive. In example (45), the context only permits a jussive reading. Modern Mon thus has a marked form for jussive causative expressions, *ciaʔka* 'use, order', and a general form covering both permissive and jussive causatives, *kʊ* 'give', while the reverse situation held in Old Mon, with a dedicated permissive causative <kil> 'give' and a general form <ʔor> 'cause, command'.

(44) Modern Mon

*dɛh   hùʔ   **kʊ**   dun   ciaʔ   pɤŋ   dɔə   hənoɲ   pùh,   dɛh*
3   NEG   give   cook   eat   cooked.rice   LOC   shade   NEG   3
*hùʔ   kəmʋə   lɔ́   pùh,   dɛh   **kʊ**   dun   ciaʔ*
NEG   cover.with.roof deposit   NEG   3   give   cook   eat
pɤŋ   dɔə   prɔ̀ə.
cooked.rice   LOC   rain

'They (the Japanese) wouldn't let us cook under the trees, they didn't make a roof, they had us cook our rice in the rain.'
(WW2nc_mn)

(45) Modern Mon

*əmè   dɛh   **kʊ**   mɔ̀ŋ   phɛ̀ə   mɔ̀ŋ   kɤ̀ʔ   ʔəyɤ̀k   həcam   hnam.*
mother   3   give   stay   school   Mon   get   age   eight   years
*ʔəmè   dɛh   **kʊ**   mɔ̀ŋ   toə,   ʔəmè   dɛh   hʊm,   ʔuə   hʊm,   ʔuə   kəliəŋ*
mother   3   give   stay   finish   mother 3   speak   1SG   speak   1SG   return
mɔ̀ŋ   phɛ̀ə   həmɛ̀ə   plɔn   noŋ.   dɛh   hʊm,   hùʔ   kɤ̀ʔ   raʔ.
stay   school   Burmese again   ASRT   3   speak   NEG   get   FOC

'My mother had me go to the Mon school when I was eight years old. She had me stay there and my mother said, I said I'm going back to the Burmese school. She said no, you can't.'
(KM_SR)

The ditransitive structure in Mon is AVGT, the causative structure is 'A give CAUSEE V'. The causee thus takes the place of the G argument, and the caused event appears as theme. The resulting construction is biclausal in Mon. The causee remains subject (S or A) of the caused event, as shown by the choice of non-causative directionals. Directionals associated with causative predicates regularly take the causative form if the patient is the argument that is moved by the event described by the main predicate, as seen in (46). This is not the case in periphrastic causative expressions, as seen in (47).

(46) Modern Mon
 ʔəmè **kəwac** **phyao** **na** kon.ŋàc.
 mother CAUS.walk CAUS.return CAUS.go child
 'The mother made the child walk back (home).'

(47) Modern Mon
 ʔəmè **kʋ** kon.ŋàc kwac **cao** **ʔa.**
 mother give child walk return go.
 'The mother let the child walk back (home).'

For a more detailed account of 'give' in Mon, including its development, see Jenny (2005: 207-215).

2.4.5 Palaung

Palaung, an Austroasiatic language (or rather a group of languages) spoken in northern Myanmar as well as across the border in Thailand and China, has *dɛːh* 'give' as a full verb as well as preverbal causative marker. The ditransitive pattern is AVGT; the causative marker occurs in preclausal position, between the causer and the causee, with the caused event following the causee, like the theme follows the recipient. The function as purposive and dummy causative marker is not found in the data available to the author and awaits clarification as more data and grammatical descriptions of Palaung are being produced. The following examples (48) and (49) illustrate the ditransitive and causative constructions, with (50) an intermediary example, *dɛːh* 'give' having both causative and its literal meaning.

(48) Palaung
 dɛːh ɔː raleːh lă uː kuː.
 give 1SG husband good one CL
 'Give me a good husband.'
 (Milne 1921: 170)

(49) Palaung

*maː ʌːn raːt deː **dɛːh** ʌːn dɯːɛ lăchɔ̆p shɛːŋ.*
mother 3SG steal self give 3SG bring ring gem
'Her mother secretly let her bring rings and gems.'
(Milne 1921:174)

(50) Palaung

*khuːn phiː leːh **dɛːh** ʌːn hɔːm pleː briː ʃiːn.*
master ghost descend give 3SG eat fruit forest ripe.
'The great spirit came down and gave her ripe jungle fruit to eat.'
(Milne 1921: 146)

Judging from the available data, the Palaung structures correspond closely to the structures found in Mon, both in form and function. There is a marked and probably relevant difference from the syntax of the corresponding constructions in Austroasiatic languages further east, such as Khmer and Vietnamese. Palaung is also strikingly similar to Shan, which in turn differs in syntax from the closely related Thai in the core area of Southeast Asia. That Shan is an important dominant contact language of Palaung is also evidenced by the large number of Shan words in the Palaung lexicon.

2.5 Contact scenarios

Core Southeast Asia is not only a large convergence area or Sprachbund, but it also consists of a number of small scale contact scenarios. The same is obviously true for Myanmar, which, in spite of being a political entity with more or less strong centralized control by the ethnically dominant Burmese in the peripheral areas, is home to a large number of local languages. Some of these languages function as lingua francas in their immediate context, leading to influence on the subordinate local languages. In the following, two of these contact scenarios are outlined. While one can often argue that language change is the result of language internal development rather than contact, in the two scenarios described in Sections 2.5.1 and 2.5.2, language contact is likely to have led to the constructions found in Burmese and Mon, as will be detailed below.

2.5.1 Mon and Burmese

Whereas Mon was used as literary (and possibly official) language in the Burmese kingdom of Bagan during the 11th century, it ceased to be a politically and culturally dominant language in Myanmar at least since the 16th century, when the last Mon kingdom fell to the expanding Burmese empire. Ever since the 14th century Middle Mon period, Mon was exposed to increasing Burmese influence, which led to a partial restructuring of the language (see Jenny 2011, forthc.). Although Mon is a subordinate language on the national level, it is the language of prestige at least in some social groups on the local level in some areas. In these areas, large numbers of original L2 speakers of Burmese influenced the structure of Burmese (see Næss and Jenny 2011). One possible feature of Mon in Burmese, that spread beyond the immediate area of Mon influence, is the use of causative preverbal 'give' in colloquial Burmese. The following points suggest that the Burmese construction is indeed a pattern replication of a Mon model, though not as recent an innovation as suggested by Okano (2005).

i. The construction does not conform to general Burmese syntax.
ii. It is less widespread, both functionally and geographically, than in other languages of the area.
iii. The construction is fully transparent in Mon and in Burmese, facilitating the replication even across typological boundaries.
iv. The construction is prominent in Mon (and other languages of Southeast Asia).
v. The construction fills a conceptual gap in standard Burmese (permissive causative) which is presumably more acutely felt by bilingual speakers in their L2.

Mon is (or was until recently) the language of the majority in Mon State and adjacent areas in southern Myanmar. Although most Mon are fluent bilingual speakers of Mon and Burmese, their Burmese variety shows Mon influence to varying degrees in phonology and syntax, and to a lesser extent in vocabulary. Bilingual speakers tend to make use of the whole repertoires of their linguistic possibilities in what Matras (2009: 240-243) calls 'creative pivot matching'. A speaker chooses the most efficient (or temporarily most activated) construction to achieve his communicative goal and fills it with the vocabulary appropriate in the present speech context. In the course of this process, a mismatch between construction and lexicon may occur, that is, the speaker chooses the construction of one language and fills it with vocabulary of the other. The expected result of a Mon-Burmese pivot match for a permissive causative expression is exactly what we find in colloquial Burmese preverbal 'give'.

The possibilities of Burmese *pè* 'give' are more restricted than the constructions available in Mon. Burmese allows, besides the use as full lexical verb, only postverbal benefactive and preverbal permissive (very rarely jussive) causative *pè* 'give.' There is no dummy causative or purposive use of 'give' in Burmese. This can be seen as evidence of incomplete contact-induced grammaticalization, as postulated by Heine and Kuteva (2005: 117-122). According to this theory, an element in the replica or target language undergoes grammaticalization along the same path as the corresponding element in the source language, but does not achieve the same degree of grammaticalization. Assuming a hypothetical grammaticalization path from causative to dummy causative to purposive, we can assume that Burmese stopped after the first stage of grammaticalization.

Another, more likely explanation of the different extent of grammatical uses of 'give' in Mon as source language and Burmese as target language, lies in the above mentioned gap in the Burmese system felt by speakers of Mon with Burmese as L2. Formal Burmese has a semantically neutral periphrastic causative form with postverbal *se*. The original semantics of *se* are probably 'order, command', but this meaning is not available to present day speakers. The use of *se* in colloquial Burmese is restricted to desiderative and prohibitive contexts, the functions covered by dummy causatives in Mon. Purposive adverbial expressions in colloquial Burmese are formed either by deverbal derivation of the secondary (subordinate) predicate, or by the postverbal purposive marker *ʔaun* 'so that'. Jussive causatives are formed in the colloquial language with *khàin* 'order, command' as postverbal secondary verb, the jussive semantics of which are transparent in the modern language. In spite of this semantic transparency, *khàin* 'order > CAUSATIVE' is used in Upper Myanmar as general causative marker, including permissive. In contact with Mon, where a distinction can be made between permissive 'give' and jussive 'order', the underspecificity of Burmese is felt as a conceptual gap, which is filled via replication of the Mon pattern. As the gap concerns only the permissive function of 'give', not the other functions it has in Mon, this was the only function to be replicated in Burmese. Additionally, the jussive semantics of Burmese *khàin* 'order, command' are closer to Mon *ciəʔka* 'use, order', with which it is usually associated, than to the general causative marker *kɒ* 'give'. As *ciəʔka* 'use, order' is restricted to jussive causative contexts in Mon, so is *khàin* 'order, command' in contact varieties of Burmese. In other words, the unmarked form of Burmese, *khàin*, was identified with the (semantically similar) marked form in Mon, *ciəʔka*, and was replaced by a calque of the unmarked form of Mon, preverbal 'give'.

One interesting outcome of the replication of the preverbal causative 'give' construction in Burmese is the emerging distinction between change of subject in control and prohibitive expressions and desiderative and prohibitive permissive causative, which is not possible in Mon and other languages of core Southeast Asia. This leads to a conceptual gap in the system of Mon in contact with Burmese, Burmese having the means to make a difference not available in Mon, as seen in examples (51) and (52), both of which are rendered identically in Mon, as seen in (53).

(51) Burmese (colloquial)
tɕənɔ θú   ko   θwà khàin tɛ.
1M   3.DEP OBJ go   order NFUT
'I tell him to go.'

(52) Burmese (colloquial)
tɕənɔ θú   ko   pè   θwà tɛ.
1M   3.DEP OBJ give go   NFUT
'I allow him to go.'

(53) Mon
ʔuə kɒ   dɛh   ʔa.
1SG give 3   go
'I let him go.' = 'I allow him to go.', 'I tell him to go.'

Why this gap is not regularly filled by some sort of replication of Burmese patterns in Mon remains to be explained. Possibly it is gaps in the L2 of bilingual speakers that tend to be felt as deficient rather than gaps in their L1, a hypothesis that needs to be confirmed by more data from this and other contact situations.

2.5.2 Shan and Jinghpaw

Another contact scenario is found in northern Myanmar, where Shan serves as lingua franca (besides Burmese) in a vast area not only within the boundaries of the Shan State. Further north, in Kachin State, Jinghpaw varieties are the most widespread languages. Jinghpaw as spoken in the area of Myitkyina makes very restricted use of causative preverbal 'give', mostly in expressions that involve a physical handing over of some object to a recipient to do something with it. In Turung, a Jinghpaw variety spoken in Assam, only postverbal 'give' occurs as purposive and benefactive marker (see Morey 2010: 408-409). There are no occurrences of preverbal causative 'give'. Also in Jinghpaw spoken in China, the grammatical uses of 'give' seem to be restricted to postverbal benefactive and, as extension thereof, malefactive (see Peng and Chappell 2011). The ditransitive and extended ditransitive-causative patterns in Myitkyina Jinghpaw are given in (54), and (55) and (56) respectively.

(54) Jinghpaw (Myitkyina)[6]
 ndai laika-buk ɕi phe ʤɔʔ ya re.
 this book-paper 3SG OBJ give give SP
 'Give him this book.'

(55) Jinghpaw (Myitkyina)
 ndai laika-buk ɕi phe ʤɔʔ thi na i.
 this book-paper 3SG OBJ give read FUT Q
 'Will you let him read this book?'

(56) Jinghpaw (Myitkyina)
 ɕi n-ʤɔʔ ɕa.
 3SG NEG-give eat
 'He doesn't let (me) eat it.'

If no actual act of giving is involved, the use of ʤɔʔ 'give' is excluded and the regular causative marker must be used. This also holds for dummy causative expressions, as seen in examples (57) and (58).

---

[6] The Jinghpaw data was collected in 2012 with native speakers in two locations. The phonology of these two varieties still needs to be worked out, and the transcription used here is preliminary, with no indication of tones.

(57) Jinghpaw (Myitkyina)
 ɕi phe sa ɕəkhun na i.
 3SG OBJ go CAUS FUT Q
 'Will you let him go?'

(58) Jinghpaw (Myitkyina)
 ɕi phe n-kam sa **khun** na ai.
 3SG OBJ NEG-want go CAUS FUT SP
 'I don't want him to go.'

Another Jinghpaw variety, spoken in the area of Muhse on the Myanmar-China border, shows a different picture. Muhse is a commercial hub in the area, with a very mixed and multilingual population. Besides Burmese and Chinese, Shan has an important, though not official, status in the area. In the variety of Jinghpaw spoken here, preverbal ʥɔʔ 'give' can be used in all contexts as preverbal causative, including dummy causative constructions. The structure of the construction is identical to the one found in Myitkyina Jinghpaw, but its function is extended to new contexts. The examples (59) to (63) illustrate the Muhse Jinghpaw variety with the same sentences as given above (54) - (58) for Myitkyina Jinghpaw. Apart from the extended use of preverbal 'give', Muhse Jinghpaw also shows a reordering in the demonstrative-noun complex, with the demonstrative following the noun, as in Shan, but unlike Myitkyina Jinghpaw (and unlike Chinese, the other major contact language in the area).

(59) Jinghpaw (Muhse)
 laika ndei ɕi phe **ʥɔʔ** ʔo.
 book this 3SG OBJ give IMP
 'Give him this book.'

(60) Jinghpaw (Muhse)
 laika ndei ɕi phe **ʥɔʔ** thi na kun.
 book this 3SG OBJ give read FUT Q
 'Will you let him read this book?'

(61) Jinghpaw (Muhse)
ɕi n-dʑɔʔ ɕa ai.
3SG NEG-give eat SP
'He doesn't let me eat it.'

(62) Jinghpaw (Muhse)
ɕi phe dʑɔʔ sa na kun.
3SG OBJ give go FUT Q
'Will you let him go?'

(63) Jinghpaw (Muhse)
ɕi phe n-kam dʑɔʔ sa ai.
3SG OBJ NEG-want give go SP
'I don't want him to go.'

Jinghpaw has a productive causative construction marked by postverbal (shə)khun, which in Muhse Jinghpaw seems to have been replaced by preverbal dʑɔʔ 'give'. As there is no conceptual gap in the Jinghpaw system that was filled by replication of a Shan pattern, other explanations have to be sought in this contact situation than the ones given above in the case of Mon and Burmese contact. More data on the languages spoken in the Muhse area and on the social factors involved are needed, but the contact between Shan and Jinghpaw obviously is very intense, leading to a more thorough mixture of the systems, as is also shown by the reordering of demonstrative and nouns.

2.6 Beyond Myanmar

Causative 'give' is also found in languages further to the west, such as Mongsen Ao (Tibeto-Burman, Northeast India) and Kham (Tibeto-Burman, Nepal). The respective structures involve a nominalized main verb, which functions as object of a finite form of 'give'. Relevant examples are given in (64) to (66).

(64) Mongsen Ao
nì   nə   kə-ni   wa-ì-pà?   **khi?-ù?**.
1SG AGT   1SG.POSS-wife   go-IRR-NML   give.PST-DEC
'I let my wife go.' [she wanted to go]
(Coupe 2007: 196)

(65) Mongsen Ao
nì   nə   niŋ   tʃàɹ li   á-hŋá?   phà?-ì-pa?   **khi?-ù?**.
1SG AGT 2PL.POSS son DAT   NRL-fish   catch-IRR-nml   give.PST-DEC
'I let your son catch fish.' or 'I gave fish to your son to catch.'
(Coupe 2007: 197)

(66) Kham
je-lai   wazə geda: lã:-wo   ŋa-**ya**-ci-zya.
you.PL-OBJ   only grain take-NML   1SG-give-2PL-CONT
'I am permitting only you (pl) to take grain.'
(Watters 2002: 333)

Similar constructions with postverbal 'give', though with no morphology to indicate a distinction of the syntactic status of the main verb and the causative marker, are found in Lahu, but only with intransitive bases, as seen in example (67).

(67) Lahu (Matisoff 1973: 247)
   nà pî 'hurt s.o.'
   ši pî 'kill'
   pə̀ pî 'bring to an end'

Transitive verbs combined with postverbal *pî* 'give' regularly get a benefactive reading, as in other languages of the area. The interpretation of postverbal *pî* 'give' in Lahu thus depends on the transitivity of the main predicate. This serves to avoid ambiguity where no morphology is available to keep postverbal causatives and benefactives apart. Compare the benefactive expression in Kham in (68), which also involves postverbal 'give' (in a reduced form and glossed as BEN by Watters), but with different morphology from the causative construction.

(68) Kham

    no-e   *ŋa-lai*   *o-bənduk* *sətaĩ-d-y-ã:-ke-o.*
    he-ERG me-OBJ 3SG-gun show-NF-BEN-1SG-PFV-3SH
    'He showed me his gun.' (lit. 'showing gave')
    (Watters 2002: 249)

A number of Tibeto-Burman languages of Northeast India and presumably Northwest Myanmar exhibit a causative prefix which appears to be related to the verb 'give'. These cases still need an explanation, as there are no obvious neighbouring languages with preverbal causative 'give', that can be seen as a source of contact influence. I list two of these cases here to complete the picture without attempting to give an analysis, awaiting further data on the languages in the Myanmar-Northeast India area.

Angami Naga (Giridhar 1980: 66-67, Matisoff 2003: 132)

Examples of verbs with causative prefix *pê-* are given in (69).

(69) *krâ* → *pêkrâ* 'cause to cry'
    vó → *pêvó* 'cause to go'
    šī → *pêšī* 'cause to know, inform'

In addition, some kinds of adverbs are also formed with prefix *pê-* (presumably from *piê* 'give'), as in (70) (Giridhar 1980: 83).

(70) *vī* → *pêvī* 'well'
    soù → *pêsoù* 'deeply'
    khrō → *pêkhrō* 'be down' → 'down'

In some cases the forms receive a redundant *biê-*, presumably 'give', as seen in (71).

(71) *tsə̄* 'be small' → *pêtsə̄* = *biêpêtsə̄* 'cause to be small'

The full verb 'give' is illustrated in examples (72) and (73).

(72) â puō rākā kriê può kêtsē **pié** â tsɔ̀.
 1SG father rupee hundred one send give 1SG give (?)
 'My father sent me hundred rupees.'
 (Giridhar 1980: 46) piêtsɔ̀ 'give'

(73) nō rākā può **pié** â tsâ rô.
 2SG rupee one give 1SG give (?) COND
 'If you give me one rupee...'
 (Giridhar 1980: 77)

Mikir (Grüssner 1978)

Grüssner lists the following morphemes related to the causative formations in Mikir.

(74) /pī-/   'give' (p. 205)
 /pa᷄-/ - /pe᷄-/ 'causative' (pp. 93-94)

He illustrates the causative and double causative forms as in (75), but there are no examples of these forms in actual use, so that nothing can be said about the syntactic structure of the causative (or ditransitive) constructions in this language.

(75) mē 'good' → pe-mē 'make better, improve'
 thì 'die' → pe-thì 'kill' → pa-pe-thì 'let kill'
 ti 'egg' → pa-ti 'lay eggs' → pa-pa-ti 'let lay eggs'

3 Grammatical functions of 'get'

3.1 Short note on get → modal

The same state of affairs that is expressed by 'give' can be expressed, with reversed perspective, by a transitive verb with the basic meaning 'get' (Enfield 2003 prefers the gloss 'acquire' as basic meaning). In this case, it is the recipient which is foregrounded and coded as A, while the giver or source remains unspecified (and usually unexpressed). The schematic representation of the semantics of 'get' is given in (76).

(76) A receives control over O (from source S).

One widespread grammaticalized function of the verb 'get' in Southeast Asian languages is something along the lines 'X performs/can perform an activity V because of some earlier state of affairs' (Enfield 2003: 290-319). This earlier state of affairs that leads to or enables the occurrence of the situation described by the main verb of the clause is backgrounded, but understood to be present and relevant. The schematic representation of the extended use is given in (77).

(77) A receives control over SoA.

If A gains control or responsibility over a state of affairs, he is either allowed or obliged to perform the activity. In this case, unlike in constructions with 'get' in its literal meaning, the source cannot be overtly expressed in the clause. In a number of languages of Southeast Asia, there is a difference between preverbal and postverbal 'get' (Enfield 2003). Modals that originate in a lexical verb meaning 'get, acquire' are also found in northern Europe (e.g. English *get to V* and *have got to* V, and Swedish *få* 'get, may, must'). It is not clear how close the correspondence between the 'get' constructions in northern Europe and Southeast Asia is. Van der Auwera et al. (2009) propose the term "acquisitive modality" for the various grammaticalized functions of 'get', a label that is based on the lexical origin rather than the actual function of the modal. In the present context, it is especially the preverbal form (in core Southeast Asian languages) that is relevant, as it corresponds to the preverbal causative function of 'give' in a number of features. Postverbal 'get' is better analysed as a grammaticalized serial verb or resultative verb compound, extended from expressions like 'take and get' or 'look for and get' (cf. Jenny 2005: 215-228; 2009) and not connected to the preverbal use of 'get' (but see Haiman 1999 for a different view). The parallelism between 'give' and 'get' constructions, though not perfect, shows striking similarities in the languages of the greater Southeast Asian area. The spread zones of the two constructions are to a large extent coextensive and the two constructions can be seen as related phenomena or parallel grammaticalizations. Apparently 'get' constructions are more widespread to the West of Southeast Asia, including standard Burmese and older stages of the language.

3.2 General Southeast Asian patterns

The general pattern of Southeast Asian constructions involving grammatical uses of pre- and postverbal 'get' has been comprehensively described by Enfield (2003). Two main construction types are found in the verb medial languages of Southeast Asia, namely A GET V (P) and A V GET, the latter in some languages with a difference according to the position of the P argument, A GET P V and A GET V P. The postverbal constructions usually express a general possibility or absence of any obstacles for A to carry out V, or more generally, the possibility for V to come about. Preverbal 'get', on the other hand, is more difficult to describe semantically. Probably all functions can be reduced to (or derived from) the basic notion given by Enfield (2003: 290-319) as 'result of prior event', that is, a state of affairs comes about because of a prior state of affairs. This can be seen as a description of a caused event or state of affairs, with the causing event backgrounded. In this sense, the constructions with preverbal 'get' are connected with constructions with preverbal causative 'give'. As in the case of 'give', many languages also have interverbal 'get' expressing adverbial notions. The different patterns with 'get' are described and illustrated in the following subsections.

3.3 Postverbal 'get' - from resultative verb compound to general possibility

In many Southeast Asian languages, activity verbs do not necessarily include the outcome of the activity, but denote the wilful act by the A argument. The result of the activity can optionally be expressed by a resultative verb. Similarly, the addition of a negated resultative verb indicates that the activity was not carried out with success. This kind of construction, which is known as 'resultative verb compound' (RVC), is a common feature also of Chinese (see Li and Thompson 1981: 54-70). In example (78) from Thai, only the addition of the resultative verb *cɤ:* 'find, meet' indicates that the activity of looking for the object was successful. Similarly, *kin* 'consume' in (79a) does not necessarily entail the actual consumption of the bread, but rather the act of trying to achieve the goal of eating something. The result can easily be cancelled by addition of a negated resultative verb, as in (79b).

(78) Thai

    *phûən hǎː   nǎŋ.sɯ̌ː   **cɤː** léːw.*
    friend seek book   find NSIT
    'The friend has (looked for and) found the book.'

(79) Thai

    a. *phǒm kin   khənǒm.paŋ.*
       1M   consume bread
       'I'm eating bread.'

    b. *phǒm kin   khənǒm.paŋ **mây loŋ**.*
       1M   consume bread   NEG go.down
       'I cannot eat bread.' ('trying to eat bread, it doesn't go down (my throat).')

One resultative verb compound pattern, namely V + 'get', has been generalized and its use extended to contexts where no actual obtainment of an object is involved. This has led to postverbal 'get' being used as general indicator of successful completion of an activity and general marker of possibility to carry out an activity. Postverbal 'get' is in most Southeast Asian languages a free form which can occur on its own and may be separated from the main lexical verb by other elements, such as objects and the negation particle.

3.4 Interverbal 'get' - adverbial

Between two predicative elements, the second of which can be either a verb or an adverbial expression, 'get' frequently conveys the meaning that the activity denoted by the first verb is carried out with the result or to the extent described by the second predicating element. This function has been described by Enfield as "descriptive complementation" (2003: 250-289). Relevant examples are given in (80) to (82).

(80) Thai

    *khǎw yùː kruŋthêːp **dây** sǎːm piː léːw.*
    3HUM stay PN   get three year NSIT
    'He has been in Bangkok for three years.'

(81) Thai
*fəràŋ   khon níː   phûːt thay **dây** diː.*
foreigner CL   PROX   speak Thai get good
'This foreigner can speak Thai well.'

(82) Thai
*mêː   diː.cay thîː   lûːk   sɔ̀ːp   **dây** thîː-nùŋ.*
mother happy SUB offspring take.exam get ORD-one
'The mother is happy that her child got the best grade in the exam.'

3.5 Preverbal patterns

Preverbal 'get' is described differently in the languages of Southeast Asia, including indigenous textbooks and grammars. One common notion that is associated with it is past tense. This definition of preverbal 'get' is used for example in traditional Thai grammars, though its actual use does not entail the notion of past tense. The position taken here is the one postulated by Enfield (2003: 290-319), according to which preverbal 'get' (or 'acquire' in Enfield's analysis) denotes an event that comes about because of an earlier event or 'event as result of a prior event'. This implies that preverbal 'get' denotes an event which is caused, whether directly or indirectly. Different concrete interpretations are found in different languages, some of which can lead to past tense implicature. If an event is enabled or facilitated by a prior event, it is most likely placed in the past and it most likely came about. In some languages, including Thai, negated preverbal 'get' is used to mark wide scope negation, often associated with negated past. Relevant examples are given in (83) to (85).

(83) Kmhmu Cwang
*gaang ô' yat   pè'   ôm, ô' **bwan**   klyoong ôm hwa.*
house 1 be.at next.to river 1 RSLT.PRR.EVNT swim river often
'My house is close to the river, (so) I get to go swimming often.'
(Enfield 2003: 298; RSLT.PRR.EVNT = 'get')

(84) Hmong
   kuv **tau**   mus Mis.Kuj.
   1   RSLT.PRR.EVNT go America
   'I went to America.' or 'I got to go to America.'
   (Enfield 2003: 299)

(85) Thai
   phŏm **yaŋ mây dây** kin khâ:w.
   1M   yet NEG get eat rice
   'I haven't eaten yet.'

In the last example, the collocation of negated preverbal 'get' with *yaŋ* 'yet' regularly gets the interpretation of negated past/perfect tense. This pattern is widespread in Southeast Asian languages, as is the use of negated preverbal 'get' to express wide-scope or contrastive negation, as in (86).

(86) Thai
   mây dây pay thîəw,   pay tham ŋa:n.
   NEG get go go.for.fun go do work
   'I'm not going there for fun, I'm going to work.' (tense neutral)

Preverbal 'get' is a bound form which cannot occur on its own in a one word utterance, though it may be separated from the main lexical verb by the verbal negator, depending on the scope of the negation. In many cases preverbal 'get' shows phonological reduction, which is realized variously in different languages as reduced vowel length, loss of tone or register, and/or neutralization of the vowel. This phonological reduction is not attested in postverbal uses of the same lexeme, a fact that reflects the general phrase-final stress pattern of Mainland Southeast Asian languages. The fact that preverbal 'get', unlike postverbal 'get', cannot occur as the sole predicate of an utterance and does not have all properties of a complement-taking verb (Enfield 2003: 154-156), suggests that it has progressed far on the grammaticalization path.

3.6 Patterns in Myanmar

3.6.1 Burmese

In Burmese, only postverbal *yá* 'get' occurs, but it appears in two different syntactic constructions and covers (at least) three different functions (see Jenny 2009). The first of the two structures is with *yá* 'get' as free morpheme in a subordinate construction, the two clauses linked by the general subordinator *ló* 'that, because' in colloquial Burmese, and by the sequential marker *ywé* 'and then, therefore' in formal Burmese. This construction has the general possibility reading, as in (87) and (88).

(87) Burmese
θu di sa.ʔouʔ yu ló **yá** tɛ.
3 this book take SUB get NFUT
'He can take this book.' (lit. 'taking this book, he gets it.')

(88) Burmese
tɕanɔ θwà ló **yá** là.
1M go SUB get Q
'May I go?'

In these examples, the form *yá* 'get' is a free morpheme in the sense that it is separated from the main lexical verb by the subordinator *ló* and, if present, the preverbal negator *mə-*, and that it can appear on its own, as in a short answer to (88), given in (89).

(89) Burmese
yá tɛ.
get NFUT
'Yes.' (lit. 'can, may')

The negated form of this construction is V *ló* NEG *yá*, 'cannot V', may not V', as in (90).

(90) Burmese
θu di né θwà ló mə-**yá** phù.
3 this day go SUB NEG-get NEG
'He cannot go today.'

In some varieties of colloquial Burmese the subordinator *ló* may be dropped. The negated form is in these varieties V NEG *yá*.

In the second construction, 'get' appears in the immediate postverbal position. In this case *yá* 'get' is a bound morpheme, that is, it cannot be separated from the main verb by the negator or any other element, and it cannot occur on its own in a short answer. The reading of this construction is normally as obligative 'must, have to', especially when connected with the future marker *mɛ*. Examples are given in (91) and (92).

(91) Burmese
mənɛʔ.phyan tɕənɔ yangoun θwà **yá** mɛ.
tomorrow 1M PN go get FUT
'I'll have to go to Yangon tomorrow.'

(92) Burmese
θu di sa.ʔouʔ phaʔ **yá** mə=là?
3 this book read get FUT=Q?
'Does he have to read this book?' (colloquial also 'can he read this book?')

The shortest possible answer to (92) is given in (93), with both the main verb and the postverbal 'get'.

(93) Burmese
phaʔ **yá** mɛ.
read get FUT
'Yes.' (lit. 'has to read')

The negation of the bound form NEG-V *yá* can have either a possibility or an obligation reading, depending on the context. A third reading, corresponding closely to the core Southeast Asian negated preverbal 'get', is favoured in the construction NEG-V *yá θè* 'not V yet', which implies a past tense reading and does not necessarily involve possibility or obligation. Example (94) just states that the event of eating has not yet come about, independent of the reasons, though possibility or obligation are possible readings. In example (95) with the subordinate construction, only the possibility reading is available.

(94) Burmese
    tɕənɔ thəmìn   mə-sà   **yá** θè phù.
    1M   cooked.rice NEG-eat get yet NEG
    'I haven't eaten yet.'

(95) Burmese
    tɕənɔ thəmìn   sà ló mə-**yá** θè phù.
    1M   cooked.rice eat SUB NEG-get yet NEG
    'I cannot eat yet.'

The different construction types and different readings of postverbal 'get' in Burmese suggest different origins, corresponding to the preverbal and postverbal constructions in the verb-medial core Southeast Asian languages. The Burmese subordinate construction corresponds to the postverbal 'get', and the Burmese bound morpheme 'get' is close in function and form to preverbal 'get' in the other languages, which is also bound in the sense that it cannot occur on its own.[7] The obligative meaning in Burmese is semantically compatible with the core Southeast Asian reading as 'event caused by prior event'.

3.6.2 Karen

Kayah Li has the full verb *nì* 'get, come to have' as in (96), which is used also as a postverbal resultative compound in nuclear serialization as in (97), and as a marker of general possibility (98). The adverbial function (descriptive complementation) is illustrated in (99).

---

[7] I take the term 'preverbal get' to include the functions of Burmese bound *yá*.

(96) Kayah Li
ʔa **nì** kā́ ʔamē tə-phre rʌ.
3   get COM wife one-CL PTCL
'He got a wife.'
(Solnit 1997: 132)

(97) Kayah Li
ʔa déhā́ **nì** kā́ lū ʔikē du ɔ.
3   ask get COM 3.OBV blanket big TAG
'He got (by asking) a big blanket from them, huh?'
(Solnit 1997: 132)

(98) Kayah Li
ʔíbe **nì** vā.
speak get sure
'Sure you can say (it).'
(Solnit 1997: 133)

(99) Kayah Li
ʔa ʔírɛ **nì** sō nā́
3   work get three day
'He worked (as much as) three days.'
(Solnit 1997: 133)

Similar patterns are found in Bwe (Henderson 1997 vol. 2: 258-260): $nĭ^ʔ$ 'get, obtain', V $nĭ^ʔ$ 'succeed in doing, manage to do, happen to do'. The situation in other Karen varieties, especially Sgaw and Pwo spoken further away from core Southeast Asia in the Irrawaddy Delta of Myanmar, needs further investigation.

3.6.3 Shan

In Shan, postverbal *lɐi* 'get' denotes a general possibility, as illustrated in examples (100) to (102). The preverbal negator *ʔèm* 'not' occurs before the main verb or before the postverbal modal, with no obvious difference in meaning. The special negator *pèi* 'not yet' is regularly placed before the main verb.

(100) Shan (Anisahkan)
   nəŋ kém.nĕi ʔèm **lɐi**.
   sit   here   NEG get
   '(You) may not sit here.'

(101) Shan
   ʔèm yɔ̀m   **lɐi** yêu   kha.
   NEG reduce get   finish POL
   'I cannot reduce (the price) anymore.'
   (Shan conversation guide for Thai)

(102) Shan (Anisahkan)
   pèi   tɕĭn **lɐi**.
   not.yet eat   get
   '(We) cannot eat yet.'

Preverbal *lɐi* 'get' is used to express either obligation, usually in combination with the future marker *tĕ*, as in (103) and (104), or more generally an event as a result of a prior event, as in (105). This example is taken from a popular song about the approaching New Year's day, when the people return to their village, one of the rare occasions allowing them to meet their friends and secret lovers.

(103) Shan (Anisahkan)
   tĕ   **lɐi** kwà.
   FUT get   go
   '(I will) have to go.'

(104) Shan
   tĕ   **lɐi** khì   ká   lĕŋ kwà ʔɔ.
   FUT get   ride car red go   SP
   '(You) have to take the red bus.'
   (Shan conversation guide for Thai)

(105) Shan
  tĕ **lɐi** hĕn khúan yêu.
  FUT get see return finish
  'I will soon see you again.'
  (from a popular song)

With the negator *pèi* 'not yet', it denotes negated past/perfect tense, as in (106).

(106) Shan (Anisahkan)
  pèi **lɐi** tɕĭn.
  not.yet get eat
  '(I) haven't eaten yet.'

The adverbial function of *lɐi* 'get' as descriptive complementation in Shan is illustrated in (107) and (108).

(107) Shan (Hsihsaing)
  mɛ́n yù wéŋ **lɐi** sɔ̆ŋ pĭ yêu.
  3 stay town get two year finish
  'He has been living in town for two years already.'

(108) Shan (Hsihsaing)
  mɛ́n phyè lik **lɐi** ti-nuɯŋ.
  3 answer text get ORD-one
  'He got the best grade in the exam.'

3.6.4 Mon

In Mon, *kɤ̀ʔ* 'get' is used as full lexical verb, as in (109).

(109) Mon
  dɛh **kɤ̀ʔ** nèŋ sənat pɔn həkʊʔ.
  3 get CAUS.come gun four CL
  'They got four guns.' (WW2nc_mn)

Postverbal functions are firstly, a resultative verb compound (RVC) indicating the successful completion of an act, and secondly, a general possibility to carry out an act. The former can be seen as the origin of the latter, which is probably a reanalysis and generalization of the former function. Syntactically there is a difference between the two functions, as the RVC *kɤʔ* 'get' occurs between the main verb and the object, as in (110), while the modal follows the verb and object, as in (111). In (110), the original meaning 'get' is still present, which is not the case in (111).

(110) Mon

 cəpan rɔ̀p ***kɤʔ*** lɔ̂ [ʔənkəlòc] hə-ʔʊt.
 Japanese catch get deposit English ADV-all
 'The Japanese caught them (the British) all.'
 (WW2nc_mn)

(111) Mon

 ŋuə nɔʔ ʔa phɛ̀ə hùʔ ***kɤʔ***.
 day PROX go school NEG get
 'I cannot go to school today.'

Preverbal *kɤʔ* 'get' fits Enfield's (2003) definition of 'event as result of prior event', as seen in (112). The first event, the listeners being quiet, enables the second, the speaker telling a story, which in turn leads to the third event, the listeners listening or being able to listen. In (113), the causing event or situation is only given as the year 1303 (1941/42).

(112) Mon

 mɔ̀ŋ hɛt-hɛt nah, ***kɤʔ*** lèə kʊ pom, ***kɤʔ*** kəlɛŋ.
 stay quiet-RED EMPH get tell give story get listen
 'Be quiet now, I'll tell you a story (so you can listen).'
 (frog_mon01)

(113) Mon

 pʊəʔ-klɔm-pʊəʔ ***kɤʔ*** cʊp pəŋaʔ kɔʔ.dot nɔʔ.
 three-hundred-three get arrive PN PN PROX
 'In 1303 they arrived in Panga and Kawdot.' (WW2nc_mn)

Negated preverbal *kɤʔ* 'get', especially together with postverbal *nɛm* 'yet', regularly gets negated past/perfect reading, as in (114).

(114) Mon
   *pʊəʔ-klɔm-pʊəʔ   dɛh **hùʔ kɤ̀ʔ** cao   **nɛm** pùh ɓʊt   dɛh*
   three-hundred-three 3   NEG get return yet NEG about 3
   kyaʔ raʔ.
   lose FOC
   'In 1303 they hadn't returned yet, but they had all but lost (the war).'
   (WW2nc_mn)

The adverbial function is illustrated in (115), where *kɤ̀ʔ* 'get' introduces the amount of the result reached in the activity described by the main predicate.

(115) Mon
   *kao.mɔ̀n   mɔ̀ŋ phɛ̀ə   **kɤ̀ʔ** mùʔ.ciʔ   tan.*
   PN   stay school get how.many grade
   'Up to what grade did you go to school?'
   (KM_SR)

Unlike in Shan, preverbal 'get' in Mon is never used to express an obligation. For a more detailed account of the development and uses of Mon *kɤ̀ʔ* 'get', see Jenny (2005: 215-228).

3.6.5 Palaung

The full verb use of *bɤːn* 'get' is illustrated in (116), where the contextually appropriate translation is 'win'.

(116) Palaung
   *ʌːn   **bɤːn** dɔːɛt thiː geː.*
   3SG   get   all   bean 3PL
   'He won all their beans.'
   (Milne 1921: 168)

There are apparently no postverbal occurrences of *bɤːn* 'get' in Palaung. In preverbal position it expresses possibility and obligation, depending on the context. Relevant examples from Milne's grammar are given in (117) to (120). In (119), there is no obvious possibility/ability or obligation in the context. The event can here be seen as a result of some prior event, such as arrangements made by the elders, as found in the other languages of Southeast Asia.

(117) Palaung
ɔː **bɤːn** ɔː lɔh.
1SG get 1SG go
'I must go.'
(Milne 1921: 76)

(118) Palaung
ʌːn **bɤːn** deː iːt.
3SG get self sleep
'He could sleep.'
(Milne 1921: 76)

(119) Palaung
ʌːn ka **bɤːn** deː gwaːi jɔːm ɛː, ʌːn mɤːh biː mɤːŋ-koːn.
3SG NEG get self live follow 1PL 3SG be person land-human
'It cannot stay along with us, it is a human being of the world of men.'
(Milne 1921: 156)

(120) Palaung
ʌːn **bɤːn** diː lɛː.
3SG get FUT marry
'He will marry her.'
(Milne 1921: 172)

Palaung preverbal *bɤːn* 'get' covers all the functions of Burmese postverbal *yá* 'get', and Shan pre- and postverbal *lɐi* 'get'. This may be a case of convergence in the semantics, but not in the syntax of the respective constructions. Especially striking is the obligative function of Palaung and Shan preverbal, and Burmese postverbal 'get', a use hardly found in the languages further east (cf. Enfield 2003: 142, 147-148). Mon, which otherwise shows a large degree of convergence with Burmese, does not have the obligative use of preverbal 'get'.

3.6.6 Other languages of Myanmar

In Jinghpaw "the potential mood is expressed by the verb *lu*, to possess (implying ability to perform)" (Hertz 1902: 17). The more common translation of *lu* is 'get, come to have', which is used in the glosses here. The examples given by Hertz show *lu* 'get' as marker of possibility and obligation, as in (121) to (123).

(121) Jinghpaw
 *ngai kǎlaw **lu** ai.*
 1SG do get PRS
 'I can do.'
 (adapted from Hertz 1902: 17)

(122) Jinghpaw
 *ngai kǎlaw **lu** na.*
 1SG do get FUT
 'I shall be able to do.'
 (adapted from Hertz 1902: 17)

(123) Jinghpaw
 *nang dai ni rong de sa **lu** na.*
 2SG this day court LOC go get FUT
 'You must go to the court today.'
 (adapted from Hertz 1902: 17)

A similar situation is found in Turung, a close relative of Jinghpaw spoken in Assam (Morey 2010). Here postverbal *lu* 'get' is "aspectual, conveying whether the action of that verb is achieved or not" (Morey 2010: 403). The verb 'get' can also "have the sense of ability, possibility" (Morey 2010: 404), in which case it can take the preverbal negator *n-*, as in (124).

(124) Turung

    *mreyng sang n-**lu**.*

    village enter NEG-get

    'I could not enter the village (because I did not find time).'

    (Morey 2010: 404)

3.7 Beyond Myanmar

Modal functions of 'get' are also found in languages further apart, such as Kham in Nepal. The meaning here, as seen in examples (125) and (126), is given as 'be permitted', which makes clear the functional connection with permissive 'give'. According to the morphological structure of Kham, the main predicate, that is the predicate describing the event that is permitted, occurs in the nominalized form and thus appears as the object of *dəi-* 'get'.

(125) Kham

    *ŋa: ba-o   ŋa:-**dəi**-ke.*

    I   go-NML   1S-get-PFV

    'I am/was allowed to go.'

    (Watters 2002: 334)

(126) Kham

    *ao-lai   lã:-wo   ma-**dəi**-si-i.*

    this-OBJ   take-NML   NEG-get-DETRANS-IMPFV

    'It's not permitted to take this.'

    (Watters 2002: 334)

The Kham example suggests that the modal function of 'get' is indeed related to the permissive causative function of 'give', and that these constructions are far more widespread, areally and perhaps within the Tibeto-Burman family, than core Southeast Asia. More data is needed from languages in South Asia and other areas to complete the picture.

4 Conclusions

4.1 Summary of findings

We have seen in the preceding sections that constructions involving the verbs 'give' as causative and 'get' as 'event result of prior event' are widespread not only in core Southeast Asia, but further to the west in Myanmar and beyond. The areas where the two constructions are used are partly, but not exactly coextensive, with 'get' constructions more common in the languages of Myanmar than 'give' causatives. At least in two documented cases, colloquial (southern) Burmese and Muhse Jinghpaw, the 'give' causative has apparently been introduced by contact with neighbouring languages where the construction is firmly established, as the construction does not conform to the general typological (word order) profile of the receiving languages. In most languages of the area both constructions are semantically and syntactically transparent, facilitating the transfer to other languages in contact situations. Of special interest in this overview are the constructions corresponding to preverbal 'give' and 'get' in the verb-medial languages of Southeast Asia. In most of the verb-final Tibeto-Burman languages of Myanmar 'give' and 'get' appear only in postverbal position, partly merging the functionally distinct pre- and postverbal 'give' and 'get' in the verb-medial languages. Similar constructions are also found in the languages further south, on the Malay peninsula (e.g. Aslian, colloquial Malay) and north of core Southeast Asia (e.g. Chinese), further showing that the phenomena discussed here are more widespread than core Southeast Asia. The semantic and syntactic transparency of the constructions certainly is a facilitating factor in their spread.

4.2 Connection between transfer/obtainment of (control over) object with grammatical functions

The conceptual extension of 'transfer of control over object to recipient' to 'transfer of control over situation' is a small step. This extension explains the permissive/jussive uses of 'give', which in some cases have been further expanded to general causative function. Similarly, the verb 'get' describes the obtainment of an object or the control/responsibility over an object. In a conceptual extension paralleling the one seen in 'give', 'get' comes to describe the obtainment of the control or responsibility over a situation. The actual interpretation varies among the languages, ranging from 'have the opportunity to V' to 'have to V', among others. All functions found in the languages under investigation can be taken as going back to an underlying 'event as result of prior event' (Enfield 2003: 290ff), with various language-specific extensions or semantic concretizations.

4.3 Connection between 'give' and 'get' constructions

This basic meaning as 'event result of prior event' of grammatical 'get' suggests a firm connection with the causative uses of 'give'. Semantically, 'give' and 'get' can be used to describe the same situation with a change in perspective. If A gives B a book, B gets a book. Similarly, if A lets B eat, B gets to eat (cf. Jenny 2005: 223). 'Get' describes a caused event with the causing event and the causer backgrounded, while 'give' describes the caused event with the cause or causing event, including the causer, foregrounded. This parallelism is found in many languages in Southeast Asia and beyond, as in Kham (see Sections 2.6 and 3.7 above). The parallelism is evident also syntactically, in some languages more than in others, though there are also differences.[8] The syntactic and semantic transparency of the constructions involved may lead to a felt paradigmatic gap in the languages that have only one (or none) of the two constructions in contact situations with languages which have both constructions, as in the case of Mon and Burmese. This paradigmatic gap, together with the felt conceptual gap (e.g. the lack of permissive as distinct from jussive causative), may eventually lead to the adaptation of the missing construction in the target language.

4.4 Micro areas and areal convergence

While Southeast Asia has been established as a linguistic convergence area, many features spread beyond the geographic boundaries of the region. The languages of Myanmar have not received the attention they deserve in most studies on Southeast Asia, and the area between the Salween and Chindwin valleys in fact can be seen as a transitional zone between Southeast and South Asia. Nevertheless, many languages of Myanmar show strong connections with

---

8 While preverbal 'get' cannot stand alone, preverbal 'give' can in many, but not all, languages of Southeast Asia, be used as a one-word utterance. 'Give' can thus be taken to be less grammaticalized.

what I call core Southeast Asia. Not much is known about how the Southeast Asian convergence area came about, or how what today is Myanmar fits in the picture, but a number of documented small scale contact scenarios, such as Shan and Jinghpaw in Muhse, suggest that the spread of features went through a chain of contact situations, at least as one possibility. The case of the replication of preverbal 'give' in colloquial Burmese, which spread from southern Myanmar up to many areas also in Upper Myanmar and found its way into the written language at least in the modern colloquial style, shows that it is not always the politically or economically dominant language that is the source of contact induced change. Low-prestige Mon is the most likely source of the Burmese construction, with L2 speakers of Burmese innovating and initiating the propagation, which was then taken over by L1 speakers of Burmese.

While the languages of core Mainland Southeast Asia show hardly any variation in the patterns of grammatical functions of 'give' and 'get', the situation further west is less uniform. This variety of constructions allows the investigation of ongoing contact scenarios and spread of the constructions to new areas. From this observation, insight can be gained that also helps to explain the development of the situation in core Mainland Southeast Asia, which presents itself as a rather opaque block in this respect. The present study is a first step towards disentangling the complex linguistic situation in the Southeast Asian convergence area, including small-scale local convergence regions. More data from more languages in the Myanmar area are needed, and will certainly become available in the near future, as a result of the ongoing political changes in Myanmar.

Abbreviations

A	Agent-like argument in transitive clause	NF	Non-future
ADD	Additive	NFUT	Non-future
ADV	Adverbial	NML	Nominal(izer)
AGT	Agentive	NOM	Nominative
ASRT	Assertive	NSIT	New situation
BEN	Benefactive	OBJ	Object
CAUS	Causative	OBV	Obviative
CFP	Clause final particle	OPT	Optative
CL	Classifier	ORD	Ordinal number

COM	Comitative	P		Patient-like argument in transitive clause
COND	Conditional	PFV		Perfective
CONT	Continuous	PL		Plural
DAT	Dative	PN		Proper name
DEC	Declarative	POL		Politeness marker
DEP	Dependent	POSS		Possessive
DES	Desiderative	PROH		Prohibitive
DETRANS	Detransitivizer	PROX		Proximative demonstrative
EMPH	Emphatic	PRS		Present
ERG	Ergative	PST		Past
F	feminine	PTCL		Particle
FAM	Familiar	PTB		Proto-Tibeto-Burman
		Q		Question particle
FOC	Focus	RED		Reduplication
FR.NP	Fronted noun phrase	RSLT.PRR.EVNT		Result of prior event
FUT	Future	S		Sole argument in intransitive clause
G	Recipient/goal-like argument in ditransitive clause	SG		Singular
HUM	Human	SOA		State of Affairs
IMPFV	Imperfective	SP		Sentence particle
INF	Infinitive	SUB		Subordinator
IRR	Irrealis	T		Theme/less patient-like argument in ditransitive clause
LOC	Locative	TAG		Tag question
M	Male	V		Verb
N	Neuter	3SH		Third person singular human
NEG	Negation			
NRL	Non-relational prefix			

References

Adelaar, Alexander & Niklaus P. Himmelmann (eds.). 2005. *The Austronesian languages of Asia and Madagascar.* London & New York: Routledge.
Auwera, Johan van der, Petar Kehayov & Alice Vittrant. 2009. Acquisitive modals. In Lotte Hogeweg, Helen de Hoop & Andrej Malchukov (eds.), *Cross-linguistic semantics of tense, aspect, and modality*, 271–302. Amsterdam & Philadelphia: John Benjamins.
Bisang, Walter. 1992. *Das verb im Chinesischen, Hmong, Vietnamesischen, Thai und Khmer.* Tübingen: Gunter Narr.
Comrie, Bernard. 1989. *Language universals and linguistic typology* (2nd edition). Oxford: Blackwell.
Dixon, R. M. W. & Alexandra Y. Aikhenvald. 2000. Introduction. In R. M. W. Dixon & Alexandra Y. Aikhenvald (eds.), *Changing valency. Case studies in transitivity*, 1–29. Cambridge: Cambridge University Press.
Clark, Marybeth. 1989. Hmong and areal South-East Asia. In David Bradley (ed.), *South-East Asian syntax*, 175–230. Canberra: Pacific Linguistics.
Comrie, Bernard. 2007. Areal typology of Mainland Southeast Asia: what we learn from the WALS maps. *Manusya Special Issue* 13. 18–47.
Coupe, A. R. 2007. *A grammar of Mongsen Ao.* Berlin & New York: Mouton de Gruyter.
Enfield, N. J. 2001. Remarks on John Haiman, 1999. Auxiliation in Khmer: the case of Baan. *Studies in Language* 23(1). 149–172.
Enfield, N. J. 2003. *Linguistic epidemiology. Semantics and grammar of language contact in Mainland Southeast Asia.* London & New York: RoutledgeCurzon.
Enfield, N. J. 2005. Areal linguistics and Mainland Southeast Asia. *The Annual Review of Anthropology* 34. 181–206.
Enfield, N. J. 2007. *Grammar of Lao.* Berlin & New York: Mouton de Gruyter.
Enfield, N. J. 2009. 'Case relations' in Lao, a radically isolating language. In Andrej Malchukov & Andrew Spencer (eds.), *The Oxford handbook of case*, 808–819. Oxford: Oxford University Press.
Giridhar, P. P. 1980. *Angami grammar.* Mysore: Central Institute of Indian Languages.
Grüssner, K. H. 1978. *Arleng Alam, die Sprache der Mikir: Grammatik und Texte.* Wiesbaden: Steiner.
Haiman, John. 1999. Auxiliation in Khmer - the case of Baan. *Studies in Language* 23(1). 149–72.
Heine, Bernd & Tania Kuteva. 2002. *World lexicon of grammaticalization.* Cambridge: Cambridge University Press.
Heine, Bernd & Tania Kuteva. 2005. *Language contact and grammatical change.* Cambridge: Cambridge University Press.
Henderson, Eugénie J. A. 1965. The topography of certain phonetic and morphological characteristics of South East Asian languages. *Lingua* 15. 400–34.
Henderson, Eugénie, J. A. 1997. *Bwe Karen dictionary. With texts and English-Karen word list* (Two vols. edited by Anna J. Allott). London: SOAS.
Hertz, H. F. 1902. *A practical handbook of the Kachin or Chingpaw language.* Rangoon: Government Printing.
Jäschke, H. A. 1977 [1881]. *A Tibetan-English dictionary.* London & Henley: Routledge & Kegan Paul.

Jenny, Mathias. 2001. The aspect system of Thai. In Karen H. Ebert & Fernando Zúñiga (eds.), *Aktionsart and aspectotemporality in non-European languages*, 97–140. Zurich: ASAS.
Jenny, Mathias. 2005. *The verb system of Mon*. Zurich: ASAS.
Jenny, Mathias. 2009. Modality in Burmese: 'may' or 'must' - grammatical uses of yá 'get'. In *Journal of the Southeast Asian Linguistics Society* 1. 111–126.
Jenny, Mathias. 2010. Benefactive strategies in Thai. In Zúñiga & Kittila (eds.), *Benefactives and malefactives. Typological perspectives and case studies*, 377–92. Amsterdam & Philadelphia: John Benjamins.
Jenny, Mathias. 2011. Burmese syntax in Mon - external influence and internal development. In Sophana Srichampa, Paul Sidwell & Kenneth Gregerson (eds.), Austroasiatic Studies: papers from ICAAL4 [Special issue]. *Mon-Khmer Studies* 3. 48–64.
Jenny, Mathias. forthcoming. The Mon language: recipient and donor between Burmese and Thai. To be published in *Journal of Language and Culture*, Mahidol University: Thailand.
Jones, Robert B., Jr. 1961. *Karen linguistic studies*. Berkeley & Los Angeles: University of California Press.
Kittilä, Seppo. 2010. Beneficiary coding in Finnish. In Zúñiga & Kittila (eds.), *Benefactives and malefactives. Typological perspectives and case studies*, 245–70. Amsterdam & Philadelphia: John Benjamins.
Li, Charles N. & Sandra A. Thompson. 1981. *Mandarin Chinese. A functional reference grammar*. Berkeley: University of California Press.
Lu, Tian Qiao. 2008. *A grammar of Maonan*. Boca Raton: Universal Publishers.
Masica, Colin P. 1976. *Defining a linguistic area*. Chicago: University of Chicago Press.
Matisoff, James A. 1973. *The grammar of Lahu*. Berkeley: University of California Press.
Matisoff, James A. 2003. *Handbook of Proto-Tibeto-Burman*. Berkeley: University of California Press.
Matisoff, James A. 2004. Areal semantics - is there such a thing? In A. Saxena (ed.), *Himalayan languages*, 347–393. Berlin & New York: Mouton de Gruyter.
Matras, Yaron. 2009. *Language contact*. Cambridge: Cambridge University Press.
Milne, Mary L. H. 1921. *An elementary Palaung grammar*. Oxford: Clarendon Press.
Morey, Stephen. 2010. *Turung*. Canberra: Pacific Linguistics.
Næss, Åshild & Mathias Jenny. 2011. Who changes language? Bilingualism and structural change in Burma and the Reef Islands. *Journal of Language Contact* 4. 217–49.
Newman, John. 1996. *Give. A cognitive linguistic study*. Berlin & New York: Mouton de Gruyter.
Okano, K. 2005. The verb 'give' as causativiser in colloquial Burmese. In J. Watkins (ed.), *Studies in Burmese linguistics*, 97–104. Canberra: Pacific Linguistics.
Peng, Guozhen & Hilary Chappell. 2011. Ya[33] 'give' as a valency increaser in Jinghpo nuclear serialization. *Studies in Language* 35(1). 128–167.
Peterson, David. 2003. Hakha Lai. In Thurgood, Graham & Randy J. LaPolla (eds.), *The Sino-Tibetan languages*, 409–426. London & New York: Routledge.
Schulze, Wolfgang. 2011. *On instances of causative/passive homonymy*. Manuscript, downloaded from http://www.lrz.de/~wschulze/causpass.pdf (accessed 19 April 2012).
Shafer, R. 1943. Further analysis of the Pyu inscriptions. *Harvard Journal of Asiatic Studies* 7(4), 313–366.
Solnit, David. 1997. *Eastern Kayah Li. Grammar, texts, glossary*. Honolulu: University of Hawai'i Press.
Song, Jae Jung. 1996. *Causatives and causation. A universal-typological perspective*. London & New York: Longman.

Taw Sein Ko & Charles Duroiselle. 1919. *Epigraphia Birmanica* (Vol. 1,1). Rangoon: Government Printing.

Thurgood, Graham. 2005. Phan Rang Cham. In Alexander K. Adelaar & Nikolaus Himmelmann (eds.), *The Austronesian languages of Asia and* Madagascar, 489–512. London: Routledge.

Van Valin, Robert jr. & Randy LaPolla. 1997. *Syntax. Structure, meaning and function*. Cambridge: Cambridge University Press.

Vittrant, Alice. 2011. Aire linguistique Asie du Sud-Est continentale: le birman en fait-il partie? *Moussons* 16(1). 7–38.

von Waldenfels, Ruprecht. 2012. *The grammaticalization of give + infinitive. A comparative study of Russian, Polish, and Czech*. Berlin & New York: Mouton de Gruyter.

Watkins, Justin (ed.). 2005 *Studies in Burmese linguistics*. Canberra: Pacific Linguistics.

Watters, David E. 2002. *A grammar of Kham*. Cambridge: Cambridge University Press.

Zúñiga, Fernando & Seppo Kittilä. 2010. Introduction. In Fernando Zúñiga & Seppo Kittilä (eds.), *Benefactives and malefactives. Typological perspectives and case studies*, 1–28. Amsterdam & Philadelphia: John Benjamins.

Mark W. Post
Morphosyntactic reconstruction in an areal-historical context

A pre-historical relationship between North East India and Mainland Southeast Asia?

1 Introduction

North East India is an ethnolinguistic crossroads located at the intersection of South, East, and Southeast Asia (Figure 1). Geographically, culturally and linguistically, it is an exceptionally diverse region, in which the soaring glaciered peaks of the Eastern Himalaya contrast with the vast Brahmaputra river floodplain, and in which animist hunter-forager groups can be found in close proximity with Tibetan monasteries and modern South Asian urban economies. An untold number of villages of widely-varying socio-cultural makeup and productive strategies is found in between. Linguistic diversity in North East India is similarly high, with languages of the Tibeto-Burman, Indo-European, Austroasiatic and Tai-Kadai families represented, possibly in addition to a number of language isolates. Typologically, North East Indian languages exhibit features common to both the South Asian and Mainland Southeast Asian linguistic areas, albeit in different ways and to different degrees, depending on the particular language.

With its geographical location in North East India as a background, this chapter focuses on the morphosyntactic evolution of the Tani languages, a subgroup of Tibeto-Burman languages primarily spoken in the central part of the Eastern Himalayan region. The primary goal of the chapter will be to compare some aspects of the modern-day grammars of Tani languages with their reconstructed ancestor Proto-Tani, in the context of the present-day morphological typologies of both South Asian and Mainland Southeast Asian languages. Its primary argument will be that, while present-day Tani languages exhibit typological features that suggest closer alignment with a greater South Asian linguistic area (henceforth SA), Proto-Tani was typologically closer to the languages of modern-day Mainland Southeast Asia (henceforth MSEA). Assuming, then, that a typological shift from basic MSEA-alignment to basic SA-alignment might indeed have occurred in the history of Tani languages, we will then ask what implications this might have for the reconstruction of regional pre-history.

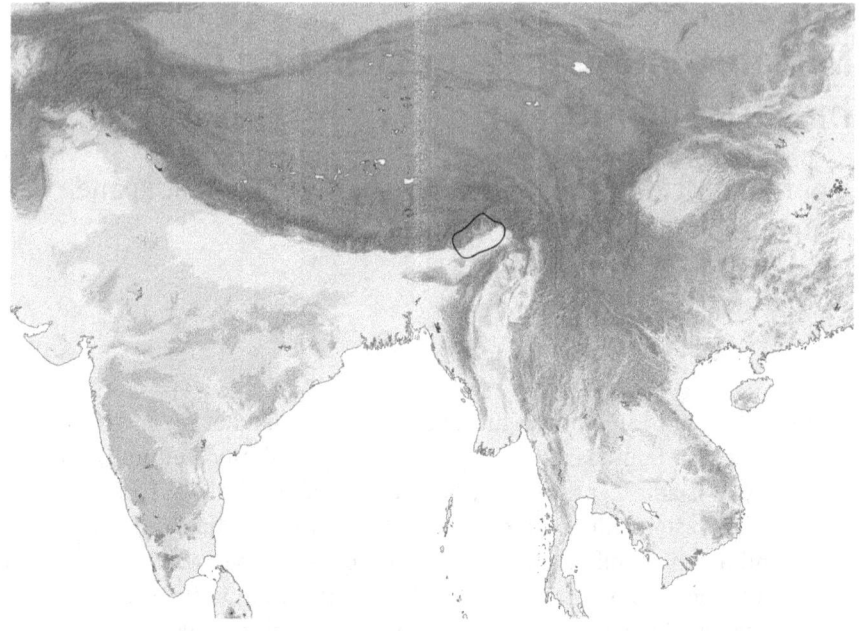

Fig. 1: Location of the Tani languages in the context of South and Southeast Asia

Four non-exclusive possibilities will be considered:

(1) there might have been a contact corridor linking the Eastern Himalaya with MSEA, which fostered typological convergence in earlier times, and which has since been disrupted.
(2) ancestors of the speakers of modern-day Tani languages might have migrated to their present location from somewhere in MSEA, bringing MSEA language typology with them.
(3) the Tani languages might be genealogically aligned with one or more Tibeto-Burman languages of MSEA, with the reconstructed MSEA-like typology of Proto-Tani thus assigned to an earlier common ancestor.

(4) the typology exhibited by Proto-Tani, and (by implication) by MSEA languages more generally, is in essence a creoloid typology[1], which might have developed independently in the two regions in question; under this view, no special contact or genealogical relationships need be assumed.

The present chapter will not take a strong position in favour of any of the four possibilities outlined above. However, it will suggest that available data seem to support hypothesis (4) relatively well.

2 Areal-typological preliminaries

2.1 South Asia and Mainland Southeast Asia as "linguistic areas"

South Asia and Mainland Southeast Asia have long been identified as "linguistic areas", understood loosely as "geographical area[s] in which, due to borrowing and language contact, languages of a region come to share certain structural features" (Campbell 2001 [1998]: 299-300).[2] South Asia is one of the earliest-recognized linguistic areas (Emeneau 1956; Masica 1976), and Mainland Southeast Asia is one of the most strikingly consistent (Enfield 2001; Matisoff 2001; Enfield 2005; Comrie 2007). The South Asian linguistic area roughly comprises the whole of the Subcontinent, including the vast majority of present-day India

---

[1] Here and throughout this chapter, the term "creoloid" is used in the sense of a language which has undergone simplification due to extensive and imperfect adult learning (McWhorter 2007); more extensive discussion will be found in Section 5.4.
[2] The term "linguistic area" is controversial. Several definitions have been advanced (e.g. Sherzer 1976: 760), while at least two authors have argued against criterial definitions of linguistic areas, and in favour of studying the specific processes which may give rise to *perceptions* of linguistic areas in various contexts, but which are ultimately diverse in kind (Campbell 2006; Stolz 2006). Here, no attempt will be made to defend a particular definition of the term "linguistic area", nor will we defend references to the SA and MSEA regions as "linguistic areas" in relation to any particular definition thereof. Instead, the term is used in a heuristic sense, simply to indicate that there are at least some linguistic features which are endemic to each of the geographical areas mentioned herein, which span genealogical linguistic boundaries, and which correlate with the occurrence of population contacts. The assumption made here, which, again, no attempt is made to defend, is that cross-family feature-sharing is likely to have resulted at least in part from population-level diffusion of innovations as a result of language contact in the areas discussed (Enfield 2003).

and Bangladesh, and extending into Pakistan and the Himalayan region. The Mainland Southeast Asian linguistic area comprises nearly all of present-day Thailand, Cambodia, Laos and Vietnam, and extending well into southern China and eastern Burma [Ref maps of SA and MSEA, ideally general to the volume]. Within both South and Mainland Southeast Asia, we find convergence among languages from distinct families; in South Asia, we find convergence among languages from the Indo-Aryan, Dravidian, Austroasiatic and Tibeto-Burman families, while within Mainland Southeast Asia convergence spans the Tai-Kadai, Austroasiatic, Hmong-Mien, Austronesian and, again, Tibeto-Burman families.

Typologically, South Asian languages tend to exhibit the following set of features: morphological agglutination with many fusional features, a polysyllabic phonological word, trochaic (strong-weak) metre, an absence of lexical tone, verb-final clause constituent order, a robust "finiteness asymmetry" in the sense of Bisang (1995), including participial and clause-chain constructions, as well as auxiliary verbs, and morphological inflections for agreement, gender, number, case, and tense-aspect-modality. A simple example from Hindi which illustrates most of these features is given in (1).

(1) Hindi
vivek-ne   kitaab paṛh-nii   chaah-ii.
Vivek-ERG   book.F read-INF.F   want-PFV.F.SG
'Vivek wanted to read the book.'
(Bhatt 2005: 760; transcription regularized by this author)

By contrast, Mainland Southeast Asian languages tend to exhibit the following set of features: a morphologically isolating/analytical profile, with short, mainly monosyllabic and sesquisyllabic basic word structures, iambic (weak-strong) metre, lexical tone systems with anywhere from two to six or more categorical contrasts, more frequent verb-medial clause constituent order, lack of a robust finiteness asymmetry – instead emphasizing structures which are formally unmarked for finiteness or subordination, such as verb serialization – and lack of morphological inflections for agreement, gender, number, case and TAM. A simple example from Lao illustrating most of these features is given in (2).

(2) Lao
jaak⁵   qòòk⁵   paj   som²   suan³.
want   exit   go/ABL appreciate garden
'(She) wanted to go out and appreciate the garden.'
(adapted from Enfield 2007: 428; numerals are tone category markers)

2.2 Typological differences within language families. Or, straddling the SA and MSEA linguistic areas

As noted above, some language families are represented in both the South Asian and Mainland Southeast Asian regions. For example, most Austroasiatic languages fall both geographically and typologically within Mainland Southeast Asia, whereas the Munda branch is geographically and typologically aligned with South Asia (Donegan and Stampe 2004).[3] However, no regional family is as famously divided as is Tibeto-Burman. Within Tibeto-Burman, several subgroups, such as West Himalayish and Newaric, can be typologically aligned to the Indo-Aryan languages to which they are areally proximate, while more easterly Tibeto-Burman languages such as Lahu, Karen and Jingpho are in many ways closer to the Mainland Southeast Asian norm. This broad division among Tibeto-Burman languages was noticed long ago by Matisoff (1990, inter alia), who coined the terms "Indosphere" and "Sinosphere" to refer to the South Asian and Mainland Southeast Asian convergence zones respectively. Later popularized by a number of other authors (Bradley, LaPolla et al. 2003; Enfield 2005), Matisoff's Indosphere and Sinosphere labels explicitly attribute the differing typological characteristics of many Tibeto-Burman languages and subgroups to language contact; specifically, influence from Indo-Aryan and Sinitic languages, respectively. An example from Newar, an Indospheric language spoken in central Nepal, is contrasted with an example from Lahu, a Sinospheric language spoken in northern Thailand and southwest China in (3)–(4). Note that in Newar, the number of morphemes per word is higher than in Lahu, and similar to the Hindi example (1). Similarly, Newar exhibits fusional inflectional characteristics, a finiteness asymmetry, and polysyllabic words, lacking tone. On the other hand Lahu, like Lao, shows several lexical tones, has monosyllabic words with few or no inflections, lacks a finiteness asymmetry, and modifies

---

[3] Khasian languages are slightly more difficult to place in relation to South and Mainland Southeast Asia, about which more below.

temporal-aspectual structure via functional variants of lexical words and particles (again compare (2) above).

(3) Dolokha Newar
janta   pokhara   ū-i   manpar-ai   jur-a.
1.SG.DAT   Pokhara   go-INF   like-BV   happen-3.SG.PST
'I want to go to Pokhara.'
(adapted from Genetti 2007: 421)

(4) Lahu
qay   gâ   jɔ   ve   yò.
go   want   ever   NZR/COP   DECL
'I have wanted to go.'
(adapted from Matisoff 1973a: 333)

2.3 North East India as an ethnolinguistic crossroads

North East India (henceforth NEI) presents an interesting challenge to the division of the Asian continent into distinct linguistic (or cultural) areas. Lying directly at the intersection of South Asia, Mainland Southeast Asia, and East Asia (specifically, Southwest China), NEI displays geographical, linguistic, and cultural affinities with all of these regions. NEI as a region is best defined by the diversity that results from this dynamic mixture and broad range of affinities. At the same time, however, it is clear that significant levels of language contact, and a certain amount of areal convergence, are found here as well, even to the extent that NEI itself has occasionally been described as a "linguistic area" (Moral 1997). A full description of the geography, culture and languages of NEI lies outside the scope of this chapter (some description can be found in Burling (1965; 2003) and in Post (2011c)); however, some background will be useful to help contextualize the Tani languages in relation to NEI, as well as to SA and MSEA, in terms of their ethnolinguistic context and language typology.

North East India is generally viewed as comprising the six Indian hill states of Arunachal Pradesh, Nagaland, Manipur, Mizoram, Tripura and Meghalaya (and sometimes also Sikkim), as well as the plains of Assam. At various historical times, Assam has been dominated by Shan Tai speakers (Gohain 1999), the Tibeto-Burman Bodo-Garo speakers (DeLancey 2013) and the Eastern Indo-Aryan speakers of the present day; speakers of many other languages, primarily from Tibeto-Burman groups (Karbi, Mising, Singpho, etc.), can be found in various areas within the broad Assam plains. Other than Meghalaya, whose eastern half is dominated by Austroasiatic speakers of the Khasian group, the hill states are traditionally dominated by a huge variety of hill tribes.⁴ In western Meghalaya, we find Bodo-Garo languages such as Garo and A'tong, in Tripura Kok-Borok (increasingly supplanted by the Eastern Indo-Aryan language Bengali), in Mizoram we find Kuki-Chin languages such as Mizo, in Manipur we find Meithei spoken amidst a huge variety of distinct Kuki-Chin languages and dialects thereof, and in Nagaland we find the highly diverse "Naga" languages, whose precise subgrouping and position in Tibeto-Burman remains to be fully worked-out (Coupe 2011).

The remaining state of Arunachal Pradesh is by far the most diverse and least well-studied of any North East Indian region, and indeed of any part of the continent of Asia [Ref Map of Arunachal Pradesh]. Constituting a sort of miscellaneous remainder, after the rest of North East India had been partitioned into states, Arunachal Pradesh was first dubbed the "North East Frontier Agency" (NEFA) after Indian independence in 1947, and administered externally from Shillong (Elwin 2005 [1957]). A highly mountainous region, Arunachal Pradesh hosts East Bodish groups in the west (culturally and linguistically aligned with Bhutan and southeastern Tibet), and Tangsa, Singpho, Nocte, Wancho and Khamti Tai groups in the east (culturally and linguistically aligned with Tibeto-Burman and Tai groups of northern Burma). In between we find a highly diverse group of hill tribes, whose Tibeto-Burman affiliation has long been assumed (e.g. Shafer 1955). In most cases, however, this assumed genealogical alignment remains to be systematically substantiated (Blench and Post 2012). Caution dictates that we must therefore keep open the possibility that some of these languages could be non-Tibeto-Burman, whether language isolates, or perhaps representing a heretofore unrecognized language phylum or phyla (Post and

---

4 The term "tribe" and especially "hill tribe" is considered problematic in some literatures and in some parts of the world, and the traditional "hills/plains" division has been questioned in the context of Mainland Southeast Asia (Walker 2006). Certainly, terms such as these are generalizations, in which exceptions can be found. However, as generalizations, they provide an insightful broad stroke characterization of correlations among geographical concentration, material culture, social organization and ethnolinguistic identity in the North East Indian region, and identical or similar terms are accordingly used self-referentially and with pride by most North East Indian tribal people themselves (apparently without awareness that such terms might be considered derogatory in other parts of the world); indeed, several North East Indian autonyms mean something like "hill people" (e.g. *Adi* < PT *ʔa-di* 'PFX-mountain', *Idu ~ Madə* < PSiang **ma-dɛ* 'person-mountain', *Nyishi* < PT **mi-ɕiŋ* 'person-streamhead/origin'). In many North East Indian hill tribal cultural areas, the more mountainous one's region is, the more prestigious is one's group. Therefore this characteristically North East Indian usage of the term "hill tribe" is the usage followed in this chapter.

Blench 2011). These languages include (moving from west to east) the Mey (Sherdukpen) cluster, including Sartang, Chug and Lish, the Aka and Miji groups, including Bangru, the possibly related Bugun and Puroik (Sulung), the Siangic group of Koro and Milang, the possibly related Digarish languages Idu and Digaru, and finally Miju, which may be affiliated with TB groups of northern Burma; none of these languages are well described, and most are to some extent endangered. In the central region, we find the Tani languages, about which more in the next section.

Typologically, it is impossible to characterize the North East Indian region as a whole. The Austroasiatic Khasian languages exhibit SVO clause constituent order, with an iambic prosody and proclitics betraying their Mon-Khmer genealogical affiliation (Nagaraja 1993). Similarly, the relatively recently-arrived North East Indian Tai languages are exactly that; few or no signs of departure from the Southern Tai norms mark any putative convergence to the South Asian linguistic area.[5] Certain innovations in the Eastern Indo-Aryan language Assamese suggest influence from local non-Indo-Aryan substrates; for example, Assamese lacks the characteristically Indic dental/retroflex contrast, merging both to an alveolar, and Assamese has gained a comparatively small but nonetheless functional classifier system (Chowdhary 2012) and a reduced and serial-verb-like conjunctive participial system (Post 2005a); in principle, all of these traits might be explainable in terms of influence from neighbouring Bodo-Garo languages (Kiryu 2009).

Nonetheless, in terms of morphological typology, the majority of Tibeto-Burman languages spoken in North East India, including almost all of the languages spoken in Arunachal Pradesh state (excluding the far-eastern Tai and Singpho languages, for example), have been described as "Indospheric" (Matisoff 1991b: 485), a characterization with which Post (2011c) has basically agreed. In general, trochaic rhythm and suffixation dominate among Tibeto-Burman languages of NEI. Words tend to be polysyllabic and morphologically complex, and tone systems are either simple or not found. Constituent order is overwhelmingly predicate-final, and a finiteness asymmetry predominates. These features are more clearly-represented in the northern parts of North East India than they are along some parts of the Burma border (for example, Mizo); but as rough generalizations, they tend to hold.

---

5 *Contra* Kanittanan (1986), who had selectively presented evidence of a putative SVO > SOV shift in Khamti Tai; see Morey (2006). Note however that Morey (2013) presents evidence of convergence in argument-marking patterns among both North East Indian Tai languages and certain Tibeto-Burman languages, to which they are areally proximate.

2.4 The Tani languages: Genealogical and geographical context

In the remainder of this chapter, we will focus most closely on the Tani languages, a fairly compact and homogeneous subgroup of Tibeto-Burman languages spoken in North East India, specifically in the central part of Arunachal Pradesh state and in northern Assam (Sun 2003; Post 2012).[6] We first present a brief background description.

While its status as a Tibeto-Burman subgroup was convincingly established by Sun (1993), the position of the Tani languages within Tibeto-Burman remains uncertain; no other language or subgroup has yet been demonstrated to be directly-relatable at a post-Proto-Tibeto-Burman level.[7] However, the internal relations of Tani languages seem reasonably clear in their basic outlines (Figure 2). The primary distinction within Tani is between "Western Tani" languages clustering around the Subansiri River (WT) and "Eastern Tani" languages clustering around the Siang river (ET). These languages share both genealogically-inherited traits, as well as those acquired and diffused via extensive regional language contact. For this reason, some geographically central languages such as Galo, Bokar, Bori and Minyong tend to display traits from both Western and Eastern Tani branches (Post 2013c), even to the extent that the viability of a genealogically-based subgrouping of the Tani languages has been questioned (Post 2013a). The highly aberrant Milang language may not fall within Tani proper, as was suggested by Post and Modi (2011), but may instead have been strongly influenced by contact with Eastern Tani languages.

---

[6] A small number of Tani languages is also spoken across the modern-day border with Tibet; very little information about them is currently available.

[7] Sun (1993) suggests that the closest relatives of the Tani languages may be the "Digarish" languages Idu and Digaru. More recently, Modi (2013) has suggested that a hypothetical Tani-Digarish relationship might be better substantiated if Tani and Digarish are independently co-ordinated with Milang. However, since we continue to lack comprehensive and reliable descriptions of Digarish languages, such hypotheses remain speculative.

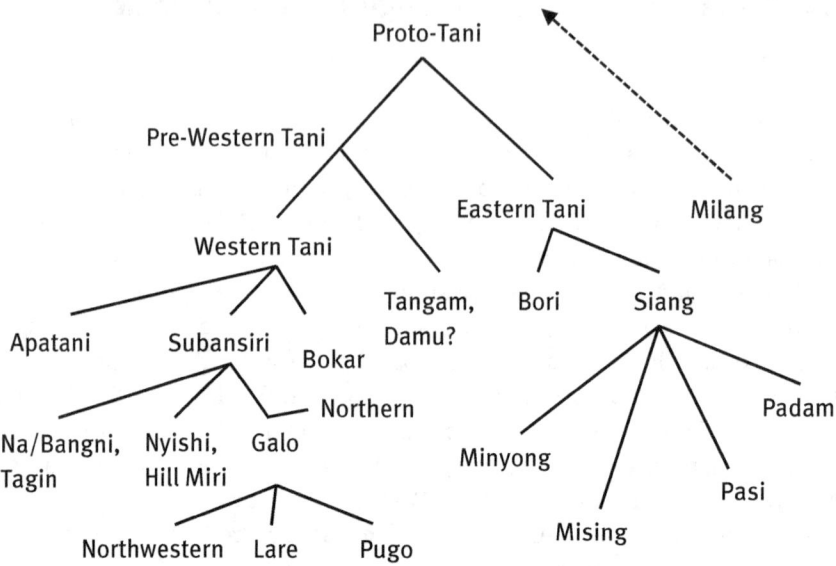

Fig. 2: Provisional Tani *Stammbaum*, based on Post (2013a)

Given their areas of geographical concentration (Figure 3), speakers of Tani languages have experienced high levels of contact with Indo-European languages in modern times, especially Assamese (in Assam and Assam-bordering regions), Hindi (in Arunachal Pradesh) and Indian English; bilingualism is high in most Tani-speaking areas, and lexical borrowing and constructional calquing in multiple domains are both very common. The northern border with Tibet is currently closed, making any large-scale present-day contact with Bodic and Sinitic languages impossible; however, more northerly Tani languages such as Tangam are in contact with Bodic languages spoken on the Indian side of the modern-day border with Tibet. These exhibit evidence of more extensive pre-modern contacts in the form of nativized loanwords (author's field notes).[8] Pre-modern contacts between Tani speakers and speakers of Bodic languages on a larger scale cannot be excluded; however, very little can be said on this topic at the present moment, at least, due to the inherent difficulty of distinguishing contact effects from common inheritance at deeper time-depths.

---

8 It seems certain that Tani languages spoken on the Tibetan side of the present-day international border are in contact with Sinitic and Bodic languages, however we continue to lack any reliable data of any scale concerning these languages and their speakers.

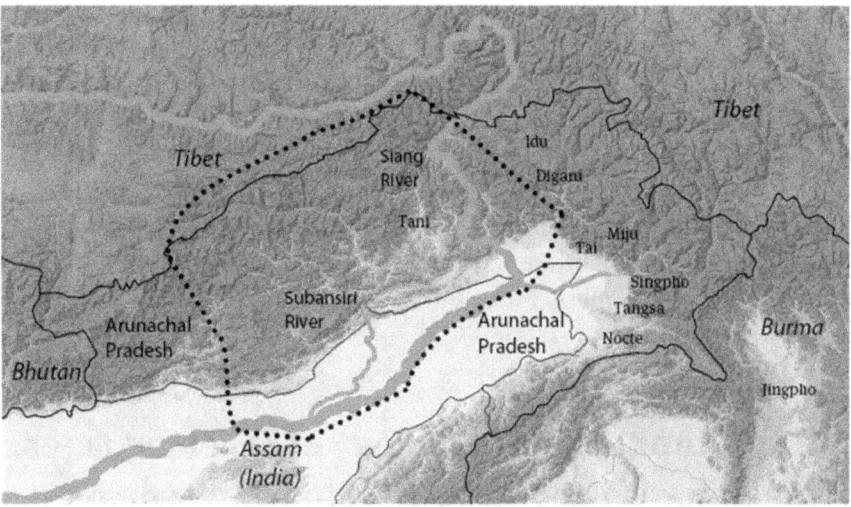

Fig. 3: Immediate geographical location of the Tani languages

It is difficult to assess the nature of pre-modern language contact between Tani languages and the many non-Tani languages spoken in the immediate region. On the eastern fringe of the Tani area we find speakers of Idu and Digaru, on the western fringe we find speakers of Sulung (Puroik), Miji (including Bangru), Aka and Koro, while to the south we find speakers of Bodo. All of these languages are presumed to be Tibeto-Burman by most scholars (e.g. Bradley 1997), however the precise nature of the relationships of these languages to more well-established Tibeto-Burman subgroups such as Bodic and Lolo-Burmese remains to be systematically demonstrated (Blench and Post 2012). Since modern times, Hindi has functioned as a lingua franca among most local populations, although its rise in the region is very recent – something on the order of 40-50 years (Modi 2005). Use of Assamese as a lingua franca is more common in the Assam plains and the plains-bordering areas of Arunachal Pradesh. There is clear evidence of intensive contact between Milang speakers and speakers of Tani languages proper (Post and Modi 2011), and we might imagine that more such local contact situations may have obtained in earlier times. However, again due to an ongoing lack of comprehensive and reliable descriptions for any non-Tani languages in the region, it remains impossible to distinguish contact effects from possible common genealogical inheritance.

Broadly speaking, the Tani languages can be said to constitute a small "spread zone" in the sense of Nichols (1992: 16-21): an area of low structural diversity, high mutual intelligibility and seemingly low time-depth, in which the speakers are socially dominant within their region.[9]

Culturally, speakers of Tani languages are aligned with the hill tribal populations of Mainland Southeast Asia (Burling 1965), with wood-and-bamboo raised house construction, a traditionally animist belief system, hillside swidden cultivation including grains and proto-grains such as Job's Tears (*Coix lacryma-jobi*) balanced with hunting, trapping and foraging, and limited animal domestication (pigs, dogs and chickens).

3 The morphological typology of Tani languages: Modern-day and reconstructed antecedents

3.1 Preliminaries

This section focuses on some typological characteristics of Tani languages, with a focus on morphology. Following a general overview, each subsection will discuss an area of the grammar (e.g. "relational marking"), and present data from the Western Tani branch – generally represented by the Lare dialect of Galo – and from the Eastern Tani branch – generally represented by Upper Minyong. Before proceeding, a few methodological points should be raised concerning the use of Galo and Minyong as representative languages, and about the nature of "Proto-Tani" as it is conceived of for the purpose of this chapter.

As discussed in Section 2.4, Sun (1993) proposed a bifurcation of the Tani languages into two primary branches – Western Tani and Eastern Tani (WT and ET). The primary evidence was a set of four phonological innovations, supplemented by twenty-five lexical isoglosses. Sun's reconstruction of Proto-Tani phonology was in turn conducted on the basis of five "key languages", three Western Tani and two Eastern Tani: Apatani, Bangni, Bokar (WT), and Padam and Mising (ET) (occasionally supplemented by information from other, more

---

[9] It is important to note here that due to restrictions on non-indigenous settlement within the Eastern Himalayan region, which were imposed by the British, and which to a large extent remain in place today, indigenous groups enjoy a degree of autonomy and social dominance relative to non-indigenous groups which is relatively rare in the Himalayan region (Elwin 2005 [1957]).

sparsely-documented languages). In principle, then, a grammatical reconstruction should proceed along similar lines, by identifying grammatically conservative "key" languages, and/or by co-ordinating reconstructions from both Tani branches.

Unfortunately, due to an ongoing lack of comprehensive and reliable descriptions of most Tani languages, such a thoroughgoing comparative reconstruction of Proto-Tani grammar is presently impossible. Nevertheless, the existing data are sufficient to enable us to identify most core aspects of Tani morphosyntax, at least, including data from languages of most major branches of the Tani group: these include Apatani, Galo (Northwestern, Lare and Pugo dialects), Tangam, Minyong, Milang, and to an extent Bangni and Tagin.[10] Furthermore, data found in other published sources, such as Tayeng (1990) and Tayu (2010), while they may at times be less comprehensive and/or uneven in quality, are at least sufficient to enable an indication that particular features are at least roughly comparable to or radically different from data over which we have better control. For example, the presence or absence of primary predicate aspect-markers in a given source is generally evident, even though the entire paradigm of aspect-markers, and their precise functional values, may not be clear.

In this chapter, we will be less concerned with the precise characterization of a punctual "proto-language" than we will be with the overall character of changes that have occurred between the ancestral stages of Tani languages and Tani languages of the present day. As such, we will not be conducting an exhaustive comparative reconstruction of Proto-Tani, and use of the Western and Eastern Tani languages Galo and Minyong is not framed as a claim that Galo or Minyong are grammatically conservative exemplars of their respective branches, nor that they are necessary or sufficient to the reconstruction of any particular aspect of Proto-Tani morphosyntax. Instead, they are provided as rough illustrations of the overall character of Tani morphosyntax, the history of which is perhaps as amenable to internal reconstruction as it is to comparative reconstruction.

Finally, it should be noted that no claim is made here regarding the precise time-depth of any reconstructed feature; this is particularly true of internally-reconstructed features, which potentially correspond to languages of any given antiquity. Again, since this chapter's target is the overall character of changes that have occurred over an unspecified period of pre-historical time, identifica-

---

10 Milang data is from Yankee Modi, Bangni data from Jackson Sun, and Tagin data is from Kepor Mara; all other data are from this author's field notes.

tion of a particular reconstructed feature with a particular proto-language is as unnecessary as it probably is impossible. That being the case, while the term "Proto-Tani" or "PT" will be used when referring to common-ancestral stages of the Tani languages, this should not necessarily be taken as limited to the immediate common ancestor of Tani languages; in principle, reconstructed features could date from a much earlier language or languages.

With these caveats in place, the following subsections next outline some of the common features of modern Tani languages, and their most likely prehistorical antecedents.

3.2 Background: Broad characteristics of the Tani languages

The Tani languages, as described by Sun (1993) and continued by Sun and Post (2014), have the following broad typological characteristics.

In terms of phonology, Tani languages tend to have six or (more often) seven vowels, and to have fairly small consonant inventories (Sun 1993: Section 2.2); WT languages tend to preserve PT onsets (and onset clusters) better than ET languages do, while ET languages tend to preserve PT syllable codas better. Phonological words in modern-day Tani languages are minimally monosyllabic, but tend strongly to be disyllabic (Post 2006). There is a pervasive weight asymmetry in Tani languages, with heavy syllables treated as more prominent than light syllables for stress and tone-assignment purposes (Post and Tage 2013); this weight asymmetry is straightforwardly reconstructible to PT (Sun 1993: Section 2.3). In general, rhythm in the subgroup is characterized by a trochaic (strong-weak) metre. Languages from both WT and ET groups exhibit lexical tone, and although many also do not, two factors suggest that tone is a conservative rather than an innovative feature of Tani languages: first, we find no correlation between segmental or syllabic features and lexically-assigned tone categories, which would argue against recent tonogenesis in Tani languages. Second, in the few Tani languages for which tone has been well-described (primarily, Apatani and Galo, though to an extent also Upper Minyong), lexical tone categories tend to align fairly well (though not perfectly) (Post 2005b). The actual number of lexically-assigned tone categories in Tani languages tends to be small – generally, two – and the functional load of lexical tones in Tani languages tends to be small (particularly in Eastern Tani languages). Finally, the interactions between tone and metrical features can be extensive, rendering prosodic description complex. In sum, while the available evidence suggests that two tone categories will eventually be reconstructible to

Proto-Tani, we are not yet at the stage where this can be convincingly accomplished.

Syntactically, Tani languages are prototypically verb-final, and exhibit a prototypical topic-comment information structure in the clause. Argument ellipsis is common, as is postpositional relational marking; core arguments are primarily disambiguated via accusative marking of definitely-referential grammatical objects; agentive marking has not been attested. As in many Tibeto-Burman subgroups, nominalization is pervasive, and forms relative clause and complement clause structures, in addition to other subordinate clause types (Post 2011b). A finiteness asymmetry is well-expressed via these and other non-final constructions, including adverbial subordination and clause chain constructions (Post 2009). A rich set of constituent-final particles code propositional-act functions such as evidentiality, stance and mood.

The primary focus of this chapter will be morphological typology. Morphologically, Tani languages tend to be strongly agglutinating-to-polysynthetic. They exhibit relatively few fusional characteristics. Lexical compounding is rich in several domains, with various types of N-V compounds also potentially interpretable as incorporation. Lexical derivations are rich, particularly in predicate-formation, and TAM inflections are also numerous. However, there is no morphological agreement, and no nominal inflections for case, number, gender, etc. The following sections will present and exemplify some of these features in more detail.

3.3 Categories

All modern Tani languages exhibit a distinct lexical category "noun"; nouns can stand underived as head of a noun phrase, while members of other lexical classes must be nominalized to do so (5)–(6). Similarly, verb roots can head a final predicate, whereas nouns cannot (7).

(5) Galo, WT   Minyong, ET
     ɲíi gó   ami ko
     [ɲiigo]$_{NP}$ [ami ko]$_{NP}$
     person IND   person IND
     'a person'   'a person'

(6) Galo, WT Minyong, ET
    dónam gó *donam ko*
    [dó-nam go]_{NP} [do-nam ko]_{NP}
    eat-NZR IND eat-NZR IND
    'some food' 'some food'

(7) Galo, WT Minyong, ET
    dotó (*ɲii to) *doto (*ami to)*
    dó-tó ɲii-to do-to ami-to
    eat-PFV person-PFV eat-PFV person-PFV
    'ate' (*'personed') 'ate' (*'personed')

Accordingly, there seems to be good evidence for reconstructing nouns and verbs to PT.

The status of adjectives is more complex. Generally speaking, adjectives are defined in modern Tani languages by their unique ability to occur as both copula complement and head of a predicate; this is not the case for either nouns or verbs (Post 2006) (8)-(9).

(8) (Galo, WT)
    adɨ́r ə́! *ŋó adɨ̀r dù.*
    ʔadɨr ə ŋó ʔadɨr-**dùu**
    tired COP 1.SG tired-IPFV
    'How tired (I am)!' 'I'm tired.'

(9) (Minyong, ET)
    apeŋ ə! *ŋo apee duŋ.*
    apeŋ ə ŋo apeŋ-**duŋ**
    tired COP 1.SG tired-IPFV
    'How tired (I am)!' 'I'm tired.'

A large number of modern Tani adjectives exhibit a reflex of PT prefix **ʔa-*, with most others being lexical compounds (Section 3.5). Most likely, this prefix was a nominalizer (Wolfenden 1929). If it was, then it looks as though modern-day Tani adjectives derive from nominalized verbs; the copula construction would have arisen first as a predicate nominal, with the predicate construction possibly becoming available later as a result of categorical reanalysis (Post 2006). This scenario would suggest that adjectives were aligned with verbs at the PT stage; many remnants of this earlier distribution can still be found. In (10), note that the cognate root from Galo ʔadɨ̀r 'tired' (9) also occurs as an intransitive verb (the adjectival meaning appears to be a metaphorical extension).

(10) Galo, WT
dɨ̀rdùu
dɨ̀r-dùu
break.long-IPFV
'It's broken.'

Similarly, there is mixed evidence for the occurrence of adverbs at the PT stage. Manner adverbs in modern Tani languages tend to be derived via a dative-cognate postposition from adjectives, forming an adverbial phrase; for example, Minyong *kampo pə* 'good-looking DAT/AVZR' 'nicely; beautifully'. Time adverbs are typically compounds of nominal roots together with another root of an unknown earlier categorical status; for example, in Tangam (Pre-WT) *kaʔɲi* 'last year', *ɲi-* reflects PT **ɲiŋ* 'year', while *kaʔ-* may reflect PT **kan>kon* 'other (one)'. Time and manner constructions accordingly offer little basis for reconstruction of a lexical adverb class to the PT stage. A small number of simplex forms with mostly emphatic meanings are found widely in Tani, and could support reconstruction of a small, possibly closed, and overall somewhat marginal adverb class to the PT stage; however, most are not cognate across WT and ET languages, suggesting later innovations. One of the few such terms which possibly can be reconstructed is **ruŋ* 'definitely'.

Classifiers seem to be a Tani innovation – they are not found in Milang, for example (Post and Modi 2011) – however, among nuclear Tani languages, classifiers are well-expressed, and can be straightforwardly reconstructed as simplex monosyllables to the PT stage. A few examples given by Sun (1993) are **tiŋ* 'CLF: GROUP (OF ANIMALS)', **soŋ* 'CLF: LONG, SLENDER', **buŋ* 'CLF: LONG, HOLLOW' and **tak* 'CLF: FRAGMENT OF SPHERE'; since most modern Tani languages exhibit dozens of mostly cognate classifiers, many more classifiers will eventually be reconstructed to the PT stage.

Ideophones are poorly-described in the Tani languages. However, they have been attested in Galo, Minyong, Pasi, as well as in small numbers in Tangam. Accordingly, there is likelihood that ideophones will be reconstructible to the PT stage. In all Tani languages for which ideophones have been attested, the construction is headed by a 'say' verb, usually in non-final form, with the lexical main verb following. Ideophones often have non-canonical segmental properties, and few if any seem cognate across Tani languages. Accordingly, it would seem that ideophones are likely to be able to be reconstructed as a category as well as a construction to the PT stage, but would be subject to innovation and replacement in the later languages.

(11) Galo, WT
 "cubúk!" əmlà oĺik kàa.
 cubúk ə́m-làaó-lĭk-káa
 sound.of.silent.entry.into.water say-NF fall.from.height-INSERT-PF
 'He sliced 'cubuk!' into the water.'

Constituent-final particles are a well-attested category in all known modern Tani languages, although again due to much cross-branch and cross-language variation, it is difficult to reconstruct more than a handful to the PT stage. Some of the best attested are *ju(kə) 'REP', *di 'WONDER', *pa/ə 'INFR' and *la 'CQ'; typically, these occur sentence-finally, but they may also follow noun phrases in a variety of constructions.

Finally, although again reconstruction is difficult in this case due to descriptive incompleteness, well-described Tani languages exhibit systems of typically semi-reduplicative elaborate expressions. For example, Galo mə́ə-kín mə́ə-mín 'think-muddled think-RDUP' 'confused' or móo-kòp móo-lòp 'cheek-dent cheek-RDUP' 'sunken-cheeked'. Productivity in the modern languages is limited, although distribution across word classes is wide; in the preceding examples from Galo, the initial formatives are a transitive verb root and a noun root respectively. Accordingly, while a description of their precise distribution awaits further comparative research, it is likely that elaborate expressions of some kind were found in Proto-Tani.

To summarize this section, the lexical categories of noun and verb are reconstructed to Proto-Tani; adjectives are seemingly aligned with verbs at the PT stage, and adverbs are apparently a marginal category at best. Classifiers are well-represented in PT, as are constituent-final particles. Ideophones and elaborate expressions are also reconstructible as categories, although their inventories may be largely secondary.

3.4 Nominal inflection: Case, person, number and gender

3.4.1 Person-indexing on the predicate ("agreement")

No grammaticalized person-indexing features ("agreement") have been attested in any modern Tani language; examples (12)–(13) show that Galo and Minyong verbs do not change form depending on the person of the subject or object.

Unlike in some Tibeto-Burman subgroups (e.g. Kiranti), no verb stem alternations are available to support reconstruction of agreement.

(12) Lare Galo, WT
ŋó ˀacín dorə́. nó ˀacín dó-rə́. bɨ̀ɨ nòm dəmrə́...
ŋó	ˀacín	dó-rə́.	nó	ˀacín	dó-rə́.	bɨ̀ɨ	nó-m̀
1.SG	cooked.rice	eat-IRR	2.SG	cooked.rice	eat-IRR	3.SG	2.SG-ACC

'I'll eat. You'll eat. S/he'll beat you...'

(13) Upper Minyong, ET
ŋo ˀama doye. no ˀama doye. bɨ nom dəmye...
ŋo	ˀama	do-ye.	no	ˀama	do-ye.	bɨ	no-m	dəm-ye...
1.SG	cooked.rice	eat-IRR	2.SG	cooked.rice	eat-IRR	3.SG	2.SG-ACC	beat-IRR

'I'll eat. You'll eat. S/he'll beat you...'

Many Tani languages (primarily in the WT branch) have so-called "conjunct/disjunct" or "egophoric" aspectual inflections, which is sometimes described as a type of "person-marking" system (Bickel 2000). Post (2011a; 2013b) has shown that egophoricity does not function as a grammaticalized person index in Tani languages, but instead as a semantic index of experiential knowledge. It is possible, and indeed likely, that some sort of egophoric marking will be reconstructible as a feature of PT inflections, or more likely, of their historical source forms (Section 3.6.2), but this would not seem to bear on the reconstruction of agreement per se. In sum, the PT predicate appears to have been free of grammaticalized person-indexing features.

3.4.2 Relational marking

Relational marking of non-pronominal noun phrases is primarily postpositional in all attested Tani languages; morphological inflection for nominal case is seemingly unattested. While relational postpositions typically phonologically depend on – and can phonologically merge with – a leftward noun phrase constituent, the nature of that constituent may vary according to the structure of a noun phrase. Thus, while the Galo Accusative postposition forms a phonological constituent with 'dog' and 'CLF-two' in (14) and (16) respectively, we can see that it remains a grammatical constituent of the noun phrase in both cases.

(14) Lare Galo, WT
ŋó ˀĩkìə̀m tutó.
ŋó   ˀikìi=ə̀m   tú-tó.
1.SG   dog=ACC   kick-PFV
'I kicked the dog.'

(15) Upper Minyong, ET
ŋo ˀəki əm tuto.
ŋo   ˀəki   əm   tu-to.
1.SG   dog   ACC   kick-PFV
          [N   POS]ₙₚ
'I kicked the dog.'

(16) Lare Galo, WT
ŋó ˀikìi dôrɲə̀m tutó.
ŋó   ˀikìi   dór-ɲì=ə̀m   tú-tó.
1.SG   dog   CLF:ANIMAL-two=ACC   kick-PFV
'I kicked the two dogs.'

(17) Upper Minyong, ET
ŋo ˀəkii dorɲi əm tuto.
ŋo   ˀəkii   dor-ɲi   əm   tu-to.
1.SG   dog   CLF:ANIMAL-two   ACC   kick-PFV
          [N   CLF-NUM   POS]ₙₚ
'I kicked the two dogs.'

No segmental alternations among nominal stems exist which would support reconstruction of a morphological case alternation to an earlier Tani language. Accordingly, morphological case on nouns is not a reconstructible feature of PT. The following set of relational postpositions appears to be reconstructible to PT (Table 1):

Table 1: PT relational markers

Form	Value
*lo	LOC
*pa ~ *pə	DAT
*ka ~ *kə	GEN
*m(i)	ACC ~ NAGT

Morphological case *is* frequently found on Tani pronouns. However, two factors suggest that Tani pronominal case is an innovation which is reconstructible to sequences of pronoun and/or noun and postposition. First of all, the forms of the pronominal case markers are in many cases identical to, or can easily shown to descend from, the postpositional relational markers given in Table 1. Second, intervening formatives in the complex (dual and plural) pronouns – as well, as, potentially, in the innovated third person pronoun – can be reconstructed to nominal roots and, ultimately, to lexical nouns (Table 2).

Table 2: Selected Galo and Minyong Accusative pronouns, with PT reconstructions

Form	Galo	Minyong	PT	Composition
1.SG.ACC	ŋó-m̀	ŋo-m(ə)	*ŋo mɨ	1 ACC
1.DL.ACC	ŋuɲì-m̀	ŋoɲi-m(ə)	*ŋo ɲi mɨ	1 two ACC
1.PL.ACC	ŋunù-m̀	ŋolu-m(ə)	*ŋo luŋ mɨ	1 group ACC
3.SG.ACC	mɨ̀-əm ~ bɨ̀-m̀	bɨ-m(ə)	*ba *hɨ mɨ	3 self ACC

If this account proves tenable, then morphological case is most likely not reconstructible to any subclass of Tani nouns, except perhaps as innovations in the pronoun set at a relatively shallow time-depth. At the earliest time-depth, all relational markers are postpositions.

3.4.3 Number and gender

In many (though not all) Indian descriptions of Tani languages, number and gender – as well as case – are treated as nominal inflectional categories, just as they typically are in Indo-Aryan languages (e.g. Prasad, Sastry et al. 1991: 50-53). In fact however, most forms which have been described either as "gender suffixes" or "plural markers" are not inflectional operators, but are instead themselves nominals, whether compounded roots or functional words. Table 3 shows that putative "gender suffixes" such as *nə-* and *bo-* are in fact nominal roots with the meanings 'mother; female' and 'father; male'; when prefixed, the resulting words have exactly these meanings, while when compounded to another root – in this example, the root *kii-* 'dog' – the resulting word indicates a female or male of the species.

Table 3: "Gendered" compound nouns in Galo and Minyong

	'mother; female'	'father; male'	'dog'	'bitch'	'male dog'
Galo	ʔanə̀	ʔabó	ʔikìi	kiinə̀	kiibò
Minyong	ʔanə	ʔabo[11]	ʔəki	kiinə	kiibo

Similarly, most Tani languages have forms which function to augment a referenced quantity, and which are sometimes described as "plural markers". In fact, they are themselves nouns, which can typically function both as referential modifiers and as noun phrase heads. Examples from Galo are given in (18)–(19).

(18) Galo, WT
 rɨbâa gaddə̀...
 rɨbàa **gadə̀**=ə
 CLAN **group**=TOP
 'The Ribas (particular group *or* in general)...'

(19) Galo, WT
 hɨ̂g gâdə hɨgɨ̂...
 hɨgɨ **gadə̀** hɨgɨ
 SPRX.IND **group** SPRX.IND
 'This group here...'

The lexemes actually employed in this category tend to vary widely in Tani languages[12], suggesting that most if not all represent secondary developments in this function. In sum, morphological number and gender are not reconstructible to PT; instead, lexical compounding and use of functional modifying nominals seem to be found throughout the family, and may be reconstructible as morphosyntactic features if not in all cases as a set of forms.

3.5 Basic word structures

This section discusses basic word-formation processes in the Tani languages. The processes found in the Tani languages are similar to those found in many

---

[11] In Minyong, this form refers to a male (father) animal only. Human fathers require the kin term *ʔabu*. Galo has a different alternation *ʔapó* 'male animal', *ʔabó* 'father (human or animal)'
[12] For example, for the post-nominal 'group' modifier, Minyong has *kɨdɨŋ*, Padam has *kɨdar*, and Tangam has *meru*, none of which seem cognate with Proto-Galo *gadɨ*.

other Tibeto-Burman languages, in their basic outlines at least.[13] In modern Tani languages, the minimal lexical word consists of a single simplex morpheme (e.g. Galo *ɲii* 'person' < PT **mi*); however, the vast majority of Tani lexemes are morphologically complex, whether in synchronic or diachronic senses. The most common basic structures of nouns and adjectives are [PFX-ROOT] and [ROOT-ROOT], as illustrated in Table 4.

Table 4: Some Tani N/ADJ word structures

Minyong	Galo	Proto-Tani	Gloss	Structure
ʔanə	ʔanə̀	*ʔa-nə	'mother; mature female'	PFX-ROOT
bottə	ʔattə̀	*ʔa-tə	'big'	PFX-ROOT
ʔəki	ʔikìi	*ʔa-k(w)i	'dog'	PFX-ROOT
tabɨ	tabə́	*ta-bɨ	'snake'	PFX-ROOT
hɨmyo	hoɲò	*ɕa-myo	'tiger'	PFX-ROOT
myotə	ɲotə̀	*myo-tə	'tiger (alt.)' < 'tiger-big'	ROOT-ROOT
myonə	ɲonə̀	*myo-nə	'tigress' < 'tiger-female'	ROOT-ROOT
kinə	kiinə̀	*k(w)ii-nə	'bitch' < 'dog-female'	ROOT-ROOT
bɨtə	bɨtə̀	*bɨ-tə	'king cobra' < 'snake-big'	ROOT-ROOT

Another important aspect of Tani noun and adjective formation is classification, which follows a 'GENERIC-SPECIFIC' (or 'TYPE-EXEMPLAR') template (Figure 4). The resulting classificatory "word families" can be large (Table 5):

---

[13] Much of what follows here was discussed in Post (2006), but is recapitulated here for completeness.

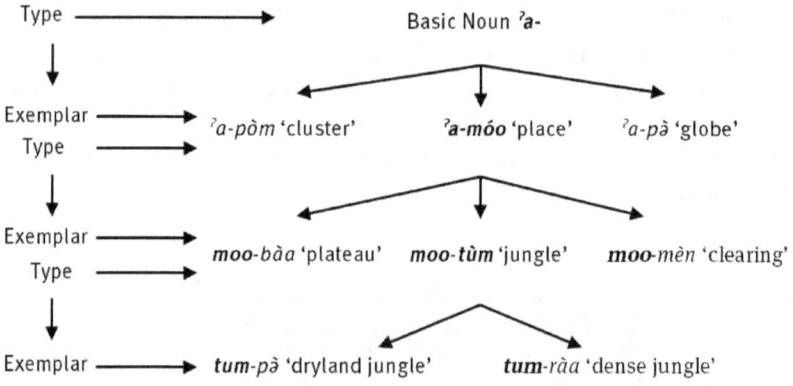

Fig. 4: Classificatory word formation in Galo (from Post (2012))

Table 5: Word family based on the initial class root *lɨ-* 'stone' (from Post (2006))

Term	Gloss
lɨ̀càk	'pebble'
lɨ̀mĩk	'gravel'
lɨ̀mìk	'algae'
lɨ̀tàk	'giant boulder'
lɨ̀kàa	'igneous rock'
lɨ̀pùu	'marble'
lɨ̀nà	'boulder'
lɨ̀pùm	'stone pile'
lɨ̀tòr	'hard stone'
lɨ̀jàa	'soft stone'
lɨ̀kàr	'turquoise'
lɨ̀cùm	'jade'
lɨ̀pà	'sharpening stone'
lɨ̀kà	'onyx'
lɨ̀cĩk	'cooking tripod'

In modern Tani languages, the constituents of a [PFX-ROOT] or [ROOT-ROOT] lexical compound tend to be morphologically bound, in the sense that they cannot be meaningfully pronounced independently of their morphological context.¹⁴ However, there are strong suggestions that these compositions were at one time productive, and that the constituent lexical roots would at one time have been potentially free lexical words. For one thing, we see from sets such as those in Figure 4 and Table 5 that the roots in question are semantically consistent, both in their specific denotations and in their common occurrence within a semantically unified set. For another, we can see from differential lexicalizations across Tani languages that there was at one time variability in how such compositions could be formed. For example, consider Apatani *lèndáa* 'road; path', Galo *bədàa* 'road; path' and Mising *lambə* 'road; path', which share the same three formatives arranged in different compositions.

An indication of how productive prefixation and compounding might have looked at an earlier stage in Tani languages comes from *classifier expressions*. Classifier expressions are grammatical word-level compositions found in most if not all Tani languages, in which a bound classifier root is compounded to one of the bound numeral roots 'one' through 'six' and 'ten' (sometimes also 'hundred'), in that order: [CLFR-NUMR] (20). In most languages (Tangam is an exception in this regard), numerals 'seven' through 'nine' cannot participate in this construction; instead, they must appear in the syntactic construction [CLF NUM] (21). It seems clear that the modern-day morphological composition in (20) derives from the same proto-syntax that is still represented in (21).

(20) Galo, WT
 ʔikìi dôrɲ gò
 ʔikìi dór-ɲì   go   (< *ʔa-k(w)i*dor *ɲi *ko)
 dog   CLF:ANIMAL-two IND PFX-dog CLF:ANIMAL two IND)
 N   CLFR-NUMR   ART
 'two dogs'

(21) Galo, WT
 ʔikìi ʔadór kân gò
 ʔikìi ʔadór   kanə̀ go
 dog   CLF:ANIMAL   seven IND
 N   CLF   NUM   ART
 'seven dogs'

---

14 Note that this is not a phonological restriction. Morphologically simplex and monosyllabic phonological words do occur in most if not all Tani languages (again cf. Galo *ɲíi* 'person' < PT *mi*); however, such words appear to be specially licensed for a simplex morphological structure in the Tani lexicon. Phonologically-identical roots which are not specially licensed to occur as lexical words cannot do so.

Similar phenomena occur at the right edge of an NP. Tani languages all display a hybrid (and cross-linguistically rare-seeming) word type with both referential and relational functions: a *demonstrative postposition*. These clearly derive from earlier sequences of demonstrative and postposition, i.e. from morphological fusions of earlier syntactic formations. In some Eastern Tani languages, we can easily tease them apart, such that they could in principle be viewed as phonologically fused (perhaps the postpositions are enclitic) but syntactically distinct (cf. Minyong in Table 6). In Western Tani languages, this is typically impossible due to a series of irregular phonological innovations. Overall, however, it is abundantly clear that proto-sequences of adjacent monosyllabic syntactic words have fused into disyllabic grammatical words.

(22)   Galo, WT
       ˀə́rᵊk tə̀ kekkáa, mootûm loî?
       ˀərə́k   **tə̀**   kéK-káa   mootùm   **lo** =(ə)î
       [pig   DST.UP]ₛ   [flee-PF]ₚᵣₑ_D   [jungle   LOC]ₒ_BL=TAG
       'That pig up there ran away, into the jungle, right?'

(23)   Galo, WT
       tôl hottə̂m cìn, ŋunù...kaapâa beetù.
       tolò   hotə̀=**ə̀m**   cìn   ŋunù   káa-pàa-bée=tú
       DST.UP.LOC   elephant=TOP.ACC   ADD   1.PL   look-ATTN-EPF=EMPH(<Asm)
       'We also saw the elephant up there.'

Table 6: Tani demonstrative postpositions and their internal composition (selection)

Minyong	Galo	Value	Form. 1	Value	Form. 2	Value
təlo	tolò	'DST.UP.LOC'	*tə	'DST.UP'	*lo	'LOC'
bəlo	bolò	'DST.DOWN.LOC'	*bə	'DST.DOWN'	*lo	'LOC'
ˀəlo	alò	'DST.SLEV.LOC'	*ˀa ~ *ˀə	'DST.SLEV'	*lo	'LOC'
holo	holò	'SPRX.LOC'	*ɕo	'SPRX.LOC'	*lo	'LOC'
haˀa	həmbə̀	'SPRX.SEMB'	*ɕa	'SPRX.SEMB'	*pa ~ *pə	'DAT'

Similar observations have already been made regarding pronouns. Comparing Table 2 with Table 7, we can see that the entire Tani pronoun set derives from the sequence [PRO QNOM POSP] (where "QNOM" is a quantifying nominal, generally 'two' to form the dual and 'group' to form the plural). A few vestiges of the proto-syntax in this case remain in some modern languages; in example (24) from Michi-Bamin Apatani, we see that the numeral root source of the pan-Tani pronominal dual ɲi 'two' is independently reflected in a nominal-coordinating marker 'both'.

Table 7: Proto-compositionality of Tani pronouns

		sg	dl	pl
1	Galo	ŋó	ŋuɲì	ŋunù
	Minyong	ŋo	ŋo-ɲi	ŋo-lu
	Proto-Tani	*ŋo	*ŋo ɲi	*ŋo luŋ
	Proto-gloss	'I'	'I two'	'I group'
2	Galo	nó	nuɲì	nunù
	Minyong	no	no-ɲi	no-lu
	Proto-Tani	*no	*no ɲi	*no luŋ
	Proto-gloss	'you'	'you two'	'you group'

(24) Michi-Bamin Apatani, WT
 tagêe là catûu ɲì ziró caanè.
 tàgée   là   càtúñ   **ɲi**   zírò   càa-nè.
 NAME   and   NAME   **both(<two)** PLACE   ascend-PFV(<NZR+ANTR)
 'Tage and Catu both went up to Ziro.'

In conclusion, while the majority of words in modern Tani languages are polysyllabic and morphologically complex, it appears that the majority derive from earlier syntactic compositions of simplex, monosyllabic lexical words.

3.6 Predicate structure

The modern-day Tani predicate can be expansive, with as many as seven or eight morphemes, in addition to a compounded or incorporated nominal,[15] constituent-final particles and, in some though not all languages, a final copula predicator somewhat like a Jingpho "sentence-final word" (Dai and Diehl 2003: 407).

---

15 Depending on how one chooses to analyse it. In a nutshell, these nominals are potentially distinct syntactic words, typically representing a grammatical object, which immediately precede a predicate with no referential or relational marking, and with generic rather than specific reference.

(25) Pagro Mising, ET
 kironbɨ oŋosogaptiladuŋai
 kiron=bɨ   oŋo=soo-gap-ti-la=duŋ-ai
 NAME=3.SG   fish=pull-STUCK-PERS-NF=COP.IPFV-ANTR
 'Kiron had been catching fish.'

Excluding peripheral elements, the basic structure of a Tani final predicate word typically divides neatly into three position classes: a bound root, one or two obligatory inflections, and from one to as many as three or four "optional" derivations Figure 5.

$$[[\text{ROOT} - (\text{PDER}_{1\text{-}4})]_{\text{STEM}} - \text{PINFL}_{1\text{-}2}]_{\text{WORD}}$$

Fig. 5: Structure of a Galo final predicate (somewhat simplified, PDER = predicate derivation, PINFL = predicate inflection)

3.6.1 Predicate derivations

Tani predicate derivations have been discussed fairly extensively by Post (2010); here we present only a brief summary overview.

Tani predicate derivations are:

a) morphologically bound
b) prosodically dependent
c) optional (non-inflectional)
d) predicate stem-expanding
e) semantically rich/complex
f) highly productive
g) often homophonous with lexical roots (usually but not always, verb roots)
h) often translated by independent lexemes in other languages

Example (26) illustrates the use of five Galo predicate derivations (in **bold**) in two predicates.

(26) Galo, WT
buɲɲə̀...kɨrkí ə̀m...ləkkôk paalà...
buɲì=ə   kɨrkíi=ə̀m   lə̀k-**kók-pàa**-là(a)
3.DL=TOP   window(<Asm)=ACC   slide-OPEN-ATTN-NF
kaabôk bîhⁱ tò.
káa-**bók-bì-hí**-tó
look-DOWN/SOUTH-DCOL-REFL-PFV
'They two **got** the window to slide **open** and looked **down as a pair**.'

Predicate derivations in all Tani languages for which any amount of data exists appear to form very large sets – at least three hundred for any given language – and appear to be fully productive, subject to semantic compatibility restrictions. Table 8 simply illustrates the productivity of predicate derivations in Galo; any of the verb roots on the left can combine freely with any of the predicate derivations on the right.

Table 8: Productivity of predicate derivations (Galo, WT) (from Post 2010)

Verb root	Predicate derivation
ʔín- 'go'	-mèn 'PLAYFULLY'
dám- 'beat'	-càa 'UPWARD/TO NORTH'
jùp- 'sleep'	-bə́ə 'CONTINUOUSLY'
hí- 'die'	-hí 'AUTONOMOUS/REFLEXIVE'

Functionally, predicate derivations tend to modify the predicate with Manner, Result, Directional Modality or Aspectual/Aktionsart-related information, to modify the valence of a predicate (increase, decrease or semantic role > syntactic argument reassignment), and/or to change the word class of a predicate (typically, nominalization or adjectivalization of a verb). Thus in (26), we find modification for Result and Aktionsart in the first predicate and for Direction and Valence change in the second (a fuller set of illustrative examples may be found in Post 2010).

In the majority of cases, the functional values of Tani predicate derivations can be straightforwardly mapped onto the serial verb constructions that are commonly (perhaps universally) found in languages of Mainland South East Asia. A cursory comparison of Galo predicate derivations with Thai post-head serial verbs is given in Table 9.

Table 9: Functional subclassification of Galo predicate derivations, compared with Thai serial verbs; note that the "functions" listed are not necessarily mutually-exclusive, for either language; for example, 'Direction' could in both languages be simultaneously understood as a type of 'Result'

Function	Galo	Thai	Gloss
Manner	ʔín-**mèn**	dəən **lên**	'stroll (walk as play)'
Result	dó-**nám**	kin (hâj) **mòt**	'eat all up'
Direction	gá-**càa**	piin **khɨ̂n**	'climb up'
Valence change	mèn-**zí**	bɔ̀ɔk **hâj**	'tell to/for someone'
Aspect/aktionsart	ʔín-**báə**	dəən **jùu**	'(be) walk(ing) continuously'
Modality	dó-**làa**	kin **dâj**	'can eat'

From the perspective of a synchronic description of modern-day Tani languages, it is important to reiterate that Tani predicate derivations are not identifiable as syntactic words. While it is generally possible to isolate and to ask (for example) a Thai speaker the "meaning" of "words" such as *lên*, *mòt* and *khɨ̂n* in Table 9, Galo speakers do not permit isolation and translation of formatives such as *mèn-*, *nám* and *càa-* in the same way. Nonetheless, if we continue to assume, as was suggested in Section 3.5, that modern-day bound roots in Tani languages should reconstruct at some stage to lexemes, then it seems entirely reasonable to suppose that the origin of Tani predicate structure is in verb serialization; the functional values and linear positions of most formatives appear to have been retained, despite the evident change in their morphological status.

3.6.2 Predicate inflections

All final Tani predicates obligatorily terminate with a predicate inflection: a negator -*ma(ŋ)*, a TAM marker, or both, in that order (27).

(27) Lare Galo
  ŋó ʔimmáa rə́!
  ŋó ʔín-**máa-rə́**
  1.SG go-NEG-IRR
    ROOT[-NEG-TAM]INFL
  'I'm not going to go!'

Most Tani languages have from around six to ten core inflections, depending on the language as well as on the analysis of certain formatives. Generally speaking, though, the core set of pan-Tani inflections includes a Negator -*ma(ŋ)*, an

Irrealis marker *-rje*, three Imperfectives and one or two Perfectives. All of these transparently reconstruct to verb roots which still occur in most of the modern languages. In most if not all cases, these are either existential verbs, or positional verbs which are used as locative existentials.[16] (Table 10).

Table 10: Tani predicate inflections and their lexical sources

Domain	Galo	Minyong	Proto-Tani	Value	Source
Negation	-máa	-maŋ	*maŋ	NEG	'lack; not have'
Imperfectives	-dùu	-duŋ	*duŋ	IPFV	'sit; be (at)'
	-dóo	-do	*do	STAT	'lie down; be (at)'
	-dàk	-dak	*dak	COS	'stand; be (at)'
Perfectives	-tó	-to	*to	PFV	'discard' (?)
	-káa	-kai	*ka	PF	'have/exist'
Irrealis	-rá	-je	*rje	IRR	'live/exist'

The grammaticalization pathway by which Tani existential verbs became predicate inflections seems clear. Depending on the language, many Tani existentials function as clause-final predicators, a type of copula function. This is true of languages from the WT branch such as Apatani (28), and of ET languages such as Mising (29). It is important to note in both of these examples that the existential verb is not itself marked by one of the predicate inflections listed in Table 10; this distinguishes existential predications from the prototypical Tani final predicates schematized in Figure 5 above.[17]

(28) Tajang Apatani, WT
ŋɨkɨ́ póosá dó.
ŋɨkɨ́   póosá   **dó**
1SG.GEN   money(<Asm)   **exist.inanimate**
'I have money.'

---

[16] The only exception might be the Perfective *to, whose etymology is uncertain. The only semantically plausible candidate etymology that has been adduced is *to 'discard', which is of course not a prototypical existential verb (although it does seem to be a plausible Perfective source more generally). This question awaits further study.

[17] The anterior inflection -*ai* appears to be a much older form whose grammaticalization in this position predates the existentials in Table 10
. Speculatively, however, it too may have an ultimate existential source, if it descends from the hypothesized Proto-Tibeto-Burman copula *way (Matisoff 1985). This too awaits further study.

(29) Pagro Mising, ET
kironbɨ oŋosogaptɨladuŋai
kiron=bɨ   oŋo=soo-gap-tɨ-la=**duŋ**-ai
NAME=3.SG   fish=pull-STUCK-PERS-NF=**COP.IPFV**-ANTR
'Kiron had been catching fish.'

The copula source of Tani predicate inflections becomes even clearer when we look at the position of Tani negation, which is suffixal. As it turns out, a seemingly cognate negator /*ma(-C) /is pre-head in the vast majority of Tibeto-Burman languages and subgroups, being either prefixal as in Kham (Watters 2002 : Section 5.5.1), or proclitic as in Burmese (Okell 1969: Section 2.16), or else a free auxiliary with rightward scope, as in Lahu (Matisoff 1973a: Section 4.411). In Tani languages, the negative suffix can terminate a final predicate at the right edge; or, if the predicate is further inflected, then negation appears between the stem and other inflections. Considering the negative suffix almost certainly derives from a pre-head operator, it seems clear that this modern-day morphological concatenation would reconstruct to a proto-syntax in which the negator had rightward scope over a final copula or auxiliary (30).[18]

(30) Lare Galo
ŋó ʔimmáa rə́!   (< *ŋo *ʔin *maŋ=*rje)
ŋó   ʔin-**máa-rə́**
1.SG   go-**NEG-IRR**
          ROOT[-NEG-TAM]INFL
'I'm not going to go!'

In sum, Tani predicate inflections could be reconstructed as a set of clause-final predicators (i.e. copulas), with the negator presumably occurring as a copula prefix or proclitic. The modern-day Root-Negation-Inflection morphology would have resulted from re-morphologization of the predicate syntax as a single grammatical word.

---

18 A handful of other Tibeto-Burman subgroups, primarily in the Northeast Indian region, also have a suffixal negator which, however, in most cases either is or has fused with a following existential verb. Tani is perhaps the only Tibeto-Burman subgroup with a direct suffixal reflex of pre-head *ma(-C). Further discussion and exemplification may be found in Post (2014).

3.7 Propensity predicates

The preceding sections Section 3.5–Section 3.6 demonstrated how the basic structures of nouns, adjectives and predicates can be analysed as morphologizations of an earlier syntactic construction. A number of predicate subtypes can be similarly analysed as deriving from syntactic constructions with particular sets of properties. Many of these are Tani-particular, and shed little light on the present discussion. However, it will be useful to consider at least one type of predicate, called "propensity predicates" here, in the context of a comparison with South and Mainland Southeast Asian languages.

In a nutshell, "propensity predicates" in Tani languages have the etymological[19] root structure [BODY PART-PROPENSITY TERM]. An illustrative set from Galo is first given in Table 11.

Table 11: Propensity predicates in Lare Galo, WT

Term	Gloss	Root 1	Root 2
dumcì	'aching, of head'	dúm- 'head'	cì- 'be in pain'
ɲɨgrâm	'lazy-eyed'	ɲɨ́k- 'eye'	râm- 'look askance'
iikúm	'numb-toothed'	íi- 'tooth'	kúm- 'drunk; senseless'
gomzùp	'closed-mouthed'	góm- 'mouth (NW); speech'	zùp- 'closed'
pumzàp	'flat-nosed'	púm- 'nose'	zàp- 'flat'
ləpèe	'cramped, of legs'	là- 'leg/foot'	pèe- 'tired; cramped'

Propensity predicates have the morphosyntactic status of a single grammatical word; lexically, they might be alternately analysable as adjectives or as stative verbs, but that point is not relevant to the present discussion. What is important is to note that a propensity predicate stands as the base of a morphological predicate word, inflected with a predicate inflection (Section 3.6.2) as in (31). The resulting intransitive predicate takes a single Experiencer argument which is unmarked for case, zero being the canonical marking of main clause subjects in Tani languages (31)–(33).

---

19 Use of "etymological" here is intended to suggest the fact that while the underlying compositions given here were once actively-formed and meaningful, in the modern languages they are no longer actively-formed. The constituent roots of a propensity predicate may be active constituents of other constructions in the language, or they may not be.

(31) Lare Galo, WT
ŋó dûmcì dùu.
ŋó   dumcì-dùu
[1SG]s [ache.head-IPFV]PRED
'I have a headache.'

(32) *ŋôk dûmcì dùu.
ŋó-kə̀   dumcì-dùu
1SG-GEN ache.head-IPFV

(33) *ŋôp dûmcì dùu.
ŋó-pə̀   dumcì-dùu
1SG-DAT ache.head-IPFV

Morphosyntactically, Tani propensity predicates seem clearly to derive from an earlier structure in which the body part root stood as a syntactically unmarked, predicate-adjacent noun; schematically, [N1 N2 PRED].

(34) reconstructed PT
*ŋo *dum *ki *duŋ.
1SG head ache exist
[N1 N2   [V   COP]PRED]
'I have a headache.'

If this reconstruction is correct, it looks very much like an *external possession* construction, of the type identified for Chinese by Chappell (1999). In a Chinese external possession construction, the possessor is expressed as "second subject" of an "unaccusative" verb whose "primary subject" is inalienably-possessed.

(35) Mandarin Chinese
wǒ   xīn   hán.
1SG   heart cold
POSR   POSD PRED
'I felt discouraged.' (example from Chappell (1999))

Such expressions are common throughout Mainland Southeast Asian languages, and have been identified as "Psycho-collocations" by Matisoff (1986) and "Proprioceptive-state expressions" by Iwasaki (2002), among others (Clark

1996; Enfield 2007: 94ff). The tendency of MSEA-type constructions to be of the form [N1 V N2] no doubt reflects the prototypical MSEA verb-medial syntax.[20] Whatever the syntactic order of N2 vis-à-vis the predicate, N1 is crucially unmarked throughout MSEA languages; this differs from the South Asian (or Indo-European) type, in which the experiencer in a compound body part-experience noun is typically either marked in the genitive or dative (36).

(36)   Hindi, IA
       mujhē   sira-darda hai.
       1.DAT   head-ache   COP
       'I have a headache.' (lit., 'To me is a headache.')

Interestingly, the PT construction [N1$_{Expr}$ N2$_{BodP}$ PRED$_{Stat}$] appears to have been reintroduced in at least some modern Tani languages (37), even making use of propensity predicates (38).

(37)   Lare Galo, WT
       ŋó ˀakíə gookàa.
       ŋó   ˀakíi=ə   gòo-káa.
       1SG   belly=TOP   swell-PF
       POSR   POSD   PRED
       'My belly swelled.'

(38)   Lare Galo, WT
       ŋó dumpóo dûmcì dùu.
       ŋó   dumpóo   dumcì-dùu.
       1SG   head   ache.head-IPFV
       POSR   POSD   PRED
       'I have a headache (in my head).'

To summarize, monosyllabic, analytical body part expressions of the form [N1$_{Expr}$ N2$_{BodP}$ PRED$_{Stat}$], in which N1 is an unmarked Experiencer, N2 is a body part noun and PRED is an intransitive state predicate, are reconstructed to Proto-Tani.

---

20 Close resemblance between Tani and Chinese syntax in this construction is most likely due to historical verb-final clause constituent ordering in Chinese, but since this point is regarded as controversial (Peyraube 1996), we can leave it aside in the present context.

3.8 Interim conclusion

Preceding sections have argued for a broad-stroke reconstruction of Proto-Tani along the following lines:

Phonologically, Proto-Tani would have had seven vowels (monophthongs), two tones, initial/rhyme phonotactics, and monosyllabic-to-sesquisyllabic phonological word structures. Morphologically, Proto-Tani was basically isolating/analytical, strongly prone to compounding, had few or no morphological derivations, and had no morphological case, no agreement, no number, no gender, with few if any morphological TAM inflections. Most reconstructed Proto-Tani constructions appear to have been syntactic compositions of simplex, monosyllabic words. Clause constituent order was verb-final, information structure was Topic-Comment, relational marking was postpositional, and alignment accusative. The Proto-Tani predicate would have made extensive use of verb serialization, together with a set of sentence-final copula predicators, with pre-posed negation. There would have been constituent-final particles, external possession of the verb-final type, and large sets of numeral classifiers.

We now return to the areal context of Tani languages, briefly canvassed in Section 2.

4 Areal comparisons: Mainland Southeast Asia and South Asia

As was briefly mentioned above, there is little agreement regarding the definition of linguistic areas in general. It then follows that there would also be lack of agreement concerning the nature of linguistic features that should be criterial to definition of a linguistic area. With regard to South Asia, the major effort to date has been Masica (1976). Masica focused primarily on relatively unique defining features, i.e. features (such as retroflex consonants) which to him defined the Subcontinent to the exclusion of neighbouring areas. For Mainland Southeast Asia, Enfield (2005) had a different focus, namely on features shared across genealogical groups which are found throughout the area, whether or not they appear to be exclusive to the area or also found among any neighbours.[21] Enfield's approach also differs from Comrie (2007), who shifts the focus from a

---

[21] For example, Sinitic languages (particularly in the Southeast) seem to share a large majority of Enfield's defining MSEA features.

possibly biased set of hand-picked features to a more general and area/family-neutral feature set. While the motivation for Comrie's emphasis on general feature-sets is clear and his critique of feature-picking well-taken, one might nonetheless object that the only truly non-biasing feature set is an exhaustive set, i.e. one which can be used to define and characterize any human language. Since such an exhaustive linguistic feature set is lacking, the present chapter we will continue Enfield's (2005) practice of defining a particular linguistic area in terms of features which subjectively appear to be characteristic of the area inasmuch as they are shared among genealogically distinct languages, without regard to factors such as area-exclusivity, proneness for diffusion, or area/family-independence.

We might therefore begin a comparative study by simply adopting Enfield's (2005: 186-190) set of characteristically MSEA linguistic features, with a few additions as cited.

Phonology

1. large (9) simple vowel systems (smaller in north)
2. diphthongs
3. initial/rhyme phonotactics (constraints on permissible final segments, fewer finals in north)
4. monosyllabic to sesquisyllabic (vowel neutralization in sesquisyllable)
5. tone ~ register (phonation type) gives lexical contrasts (more in north)
6. iambic stress (if any) (Donegan and Stampe 1983)

Morphology

7. isolating/analytical
    a. one morpheme per word
    b. few or no derivations
    c. phrase is relevant "unit of meaning" at clause level
8. no morphological case
9. no person-indexing ("agreement")
10. no grammaticalized tense-marking
11. no grammaticalized number
12. no grammaticalized gender
13. aspect given verbally
14. relator nouns (nouns with adposition-like functions)
15. lack of explicit nominalizing/subordinating morphology

Lexicon

16. elaboration (rhyming, alliteration...)
17. ideophones
18. "pronouns" with many register distinctions
19. prevalence of compounding
20. numeral classifier system
21. appositional noun phrase structure (most noun phrase operators come from lexical nouns)
22. adjectives like verbs (Comrie 2007: 41)

Syntax

23. variable word order
    a. topic-comment
    b. argument ellipsis
24. typically verb-medial
25. sentence-final particles
26. topic-comment body-part constructions (e.g. 'you heart cold' ~ 'you cold heart') (this chapter)
27. serial verb constructions (this chapter)

The scope of this paper will not permit a full accounting of these features with respect to the South Asian linguistic area, nor even for any given putatively representative South Asian language. However, on the basis of data and discussion in Masica (1976: 187-190), supplemented by data and discussion in Cardona and Jain (2003), we can at least draw up a simplified schematic for comparative purposes. This is presented in Table 12. Here, note that certain features are compressed or re-labelled for ease of presentation; for example, Enfield's features 7a-c above are compressed into a single "morphology" value, while features 23 and 24 "variable word order" and "typically verb-medial" are compressed into "order" with values "(variable) SOV" and "(variable) SVO".

Table 12: South Asian and Mainland Southeast Asian languages compared for features given by Enfield (2005)

Area	Feature	S. Asia	MSEA
Phonology	Vowels	7~11	9
	Diphthongs	few	many
	Phonotactics	balanced	onset-rhyme
	Syllabism	poly	mono
	Tone	no	yes
	Rhythm	trochaic	iambic
Morphology	Morphology	agglutinating	isolating
	Morph. case	yes	no
	Agreement	yes	no
	Number	yes	no
	Gender	yes	no
	TAM	yes	no
	Aspect verbal	no	yes
	Relator nouns	few	yes
	NZR/SUB	yes	no
Lexicon	Elaboration	no	yes
	Ideophones	no	yes
	Semantic PRO	no	yes
	Compounding	mixed	yes
	NUM CLF	no	yes
	Appositional NP	no	yes
	Adj like V	no	yes
Syntax	Order	V-final	most V-medial
	Topic-comment	no	yes
	SFP	no	yes
	External Poss.	no	yes
	SVC	no	yes

Table 12 suggests very few overlaps between South and Mainland Southeast Asian languages in relation to the given feature set; this is to be expected, of course, to the extent that this feature set was explicitly chosen for the purpose of identifying the MSEA linguistic area.

However, our interest here is in situating the early and modern Tani languages in relation to these two linguistic areas, in terms of the values given. Excluding a few possibly irrelevant parameters (e.g. size of vowel inventory), as well as some others for which Proto-Tani reconstruction is currently impossible (e.g. rhythmic profile), and re-ordering the feature set to show degrees of overlap rather than thematic areas, we are left with the following Table 13.

Table 13: Proto-Tani and modern Tani languages compared with South Asian and MSEA languages in terms of a subset of Enfield's (2005) defining MSEA feature values[22]

Feature	S. Asia	Modern Tani	Proto-Tani	MSEA
Order	(var.) SOV	var. SOV	SOV	most var. SVO
Diphthongs	few	no	no	yes
Semantic PRO	no	no	no	yes
NZR/SUB	yes	yes	yes?	no
Adj like V	no	no	yes	yes
SVC	no	no	yes	yes
Phonotactics	balanced	balanced	onset-rhyme	onset-rhyme
Syllabism	poly	poly	mono	mono
Morphology	agglutinating	agglutinating	isolating	isolating
TAM	yes	yes	no	no
Aspect verbal	no	no	yes	yes
Tone	no	mixed	yes	yes
Morph. case	yes	on PRO only	no	no
Topic-comment	no	mixed	yes	yes
Agreement	yes	no	no	no
Number	yes	no	no	no
Gender	yes	no	no	no
Elaboration	no	yes	yes	yes
Ideophones	no	yes	yes	yes
NUM CLF	no	yes	yes	yes
SFP	no	yes	yes	yes
External Poss.	no	yes	yes	yes
Appositional N	no	yes	yes	yes
Compounding	mixed	yes	yes	yes

The comparison in Table 13 suggests at least two things:

First, it suggests that Proto-Tani was typologically what we might call a "peripheral" Mainland Southeast Asian language. PT contrasts with the MSEA prototype in terms of most frequent clause constituent order, being SOV rather than the usual SVO – however this is generally true of MSEA Tibeto-Burman languages, such as most Lolo-Burmese languages and Jingpho; only Karenic is exceptional among MSEA Tibeto-Burman languages in exhibiting SVO order (Dryer 2008). PT also differs from MSEA languages in having fully grammaticalized pronouns, with no semantic basis or register distinctions, and in nearly, or possibly completely, lacking diphthongs. This is very much unlike MSEA Tibeto-

---

[22] Note that in the "Proto-Tani" column, "no" values should be interpreted as meaning "cannot be reconstructed" rather than "did not exist".

Burman languages such as Lahu (Matisoff 1973a). However, PT agrees with the MSEA prototype with respect to nearly every other feature.[23]

Second, Table 13 suggests that modern Tani languages are more similar to South Asian languages in a number of important respects. Unlike Proto-Tani, modern Tani adjectives are well-distinguished from verbs. In addition, modern Tani languages lack serial verb constructions, instead having a robustly-marked finiteness asymmetry. Onset-rhyme syllabicity has eroded, and phonological words are most often polysyllabic, with some languages having also lost tone. Morphological case distinctions have emerged on pronouns, and a grammaticalized subject pervades a number of constructions, despite the continuing relevance of Topic-comment information structure at the clause level. Perhaps most notably, however, the grammatical word has become strongly agglutinative, with earlier auxiliary verbal aspects and serial verb constructions developing into large sets of morphological derivations and morphological TAM inflections.

This is obviously a broad stroke characterization; many details are necessarily elided and any number of the statements made above might be individually challenged or qualified with respect to any given SA or MSEA language. Nonetheless, the overall character of a shift seems apparent: while Proto-Tani was more similar to MSEA languages, modern Tani languages have shifted closer to the SA norm – particularly with respect to their morphological typology.

Assuming, then, that such a shift might have taken place in the history of Tani languages, we next turn to ask what this might mean in terms of the reconstruction of regional pre-history.

5 What might it mean for regional pre-history?

In this section we consider four mutually non-exclusive scenarios which might explain the MSEA alignment of Proto-Tani and the subsequent shift to closer SA alignment of modern Tani languages. These are: (1) Proto-Tani might genealogically subgroup with one or more MSEA Tibeto-Burman languages (2) Tani speakers might have originated in the MSEA Tibeto-Burman region, and have migrated to their present area of concentration (3) there may have been an early contact corridor linking the Eastern Himalaya and MSEA region, which has

---

[23] The existence and morphological status of nominalizers/subordinators is uncertain at the PT stage; it is possible that they were independent syntactic particles, as in Lahu, but we must leave this aside for the present.

since been disrupted (4) PT and MSEA languages both exhibit a creoloid typology; they may appear typologically similar for this reason, rather than because of sharing any early genealogical or contact relationships.

5.1 Does Tani subgroup with MSEA TB languages?

There is little doubt that Tani genealogically aligns with Tibeto-Burman languages, hence little doubt that Tani ultimately shares a common ancestor with MSEA Tibeto-Burman languages such as Lahu, Lisu, Burmese, and Jingpho at some level. Typologically also, we find a large number of features shared between Proto-Tani and the TB languages of Northern Burma. In particular, we note the existence of serial verb constructions, cognate prefixal or proclitic negation, cognate grammaticalized pronouns, and, in Jingpho at least, the existence of sentence-final existential predicators which closely resemble the reconstructed Proto-Tani predicate syntax (though with the additional feature of agreement) (39)–(40).

(39) Lahu, Lolo-Burmese
    lâ   pɔ̂ʔ   chɛ̀ʔ   câ   pà   šē   ve   cê.
    tiger jump bite   eat finish ADVS NZR QUOT
    'The tiger jumped (out) and bit (into them) and ate (them) all up!'
    (Matisoff 1991a:411)

(40) Jingpho, Kachinic
    ŋai³³   lai³¹ka³³ thi   ŋa³¹   ŋ³¹ŋai³³
    1SG   book   read be.doing 1SG.SUB.DECL
    'I am reading.'
    (Dai and Diehl 2003: 408)

However, there are no clear indications that Tani languages are likely to subgroup with Lolo-Burmese and/or Kachinic at any post-Proto-Tibeto-Burman stage. Although it is true that no systematic studies of the possibility have been conducted, indications are that cognate percentages are very low; accordingly,

Tani languages are not aligned with Lolo-Burmese or Kachinic in any of the standard subgrouping schemes (Matisoff 1991b; Bradley 1997; van Driem 2013).[24]

To summarize, while the possibility of a post-PTB Tani-Lolo-Burmese-Kachinic relationship cannot be ruled out, current scholarship does not point to its likelihood.

5.2 Were there North-Westward migrations?

As was briefly mentioned in Section 5.1, we find a number of typological similarities between reconstructed Proto-Tani typology and the typology of Northern Burma-area TB languages such as (in particular) Jingpho. Although a close genealogical relationship between them was considered implausible, the possibility remains that typological similarities could have been the result of contact. Is it possible, then, that Proto-Tani speakers were found in or near to the Northern Burma cultural-linguistic area, and may have migrated North-Westward to their area of present concentration?

Material culture makes this seem plausible. Tani groups have a fairly uniform material culture which falls closely in line with the Mainland Southeast Asian hill tribal norm. Raised houses are traditionally constructed from wood and bamboo, with palm leaf, grass or plantain fibre roofing (Figure 6). Domestic animals include the pig, chicken, dog and mithun (*Bos frontalis*, a type of gaur); virtually all other animals are hunted for meat. Swidden cultivation of multiple grain and some legume crops is universally practiced, while terraced paddy cultivation has spread to the area only recently. Cultivation is balanced with extensive foraging of wild plants, concentrating on several varieties (such as taros) which are endemic to the MSEA region (Blench in press). Tani are traditionally animist, with virtually no evidence of pre-modern influence from larger organized religions.

Modern Tani cultures remain notoriously ill-equipped for cold-climate lifestyles. Despite the occurrence of snowfall in or near some Tani areas (such as the Tangam, Bokar and Na areas), Tani cultures traditionally lack almost any sort of footwear, prefer loincloths to leggings, have no tradition of exploiting furs, feathers or wools for clothing (instead typically burning the furs of hunted animals off in a fire), almost never insulate dwellings, and recount in oral histo-

---

[24] While very much a work-in-progress, the current "best guess" is that Tani languages may subgroup with the nearby Siangic and/or Digarish languages (Sun 1993; Modi 2013). However, the possibility of shared features due to language contact must also be considered here.

ries having obtained cold-weather items such as blankets and coats via trade with Tibetans in earlier times (nowadays, such items are generally obtained in Assam. Most often, these are Chinese goods imported circumlocuitously via Singapore and Kolkata rather than via the closed border with Tibet only about ten kilometres away (Figure 7).

Fig. 6: Raised wood, bamboo and plantain fibre houses in *Moobuk* (*Peki-Modi*) village, Milang tribe, Upper Siang District, Arunachal Pradesh, India

Fig. 7: Minyong man in traditional attire, Riga Village, Upper Siang District, Arunachal Pradesh, India

Clearly, then, Tani cultures align with hill-tribal groups of the Mainland Southeast Asian region rather than with highland Himalayan groups of the Tibetosphere such as the East Bodish or with Indospheric groups such as the Newar. However, this does not necessarily count as evidence of a Northwesterly Proto-Tani migration into the Eastern Himalaya. Burling (2007a) has criticized the tendency among some linguists to imagine that entire populations of language-speakers ever "migrate", en masse, from one geographical location to another, bringing their language with them and leaving no residue behind. Instead, what we more typically find is *language* spread, often accompanying "micro-migrations" of populations (Huber 2012), mergers with pre-existing populations, and shifts in ethnic profile and identity as a result (Burling 2012). Furthermore, we might note Blench and Post's (2013) claim that the especially high levels of linguistic diversity that are found in the Eastern Himalayan region suggest if anything that Tibeto-Burman peoples might have *originated* in the Eastern Himalayan region and diffused outward, rather than having migrated into it. In short, while it is not impossible that at least some Tani speakers may have migrated north-westward from the Northern Burma region, we would probably need at least some positive evidence from remnant populations or transitional languages before asserting that it was most likely this way rather than (for example) the other way around.

To summarize this section, cultural and linguistic typological evidence are both *compatible* with the hypothesis that Proto-Tani speakers might have originated in the Northern Burma region. However, neither seems to constitute positive evidence in favour of this hypothesis.

5.3 Was there a contact corridor?

Enfield (2005: 182) explicitly links areal feature-sharing in MSEA to "social contact among hundreds of speech communities speaking languages from at least five major language families. The result has been extensive diffusion of linguistic structure leading to massive structural convergence among the languages". If this is the case, then might the Eastern Himalaya have at one point been part of this area of diffusion?

If we simply look at a language map, a contact corridor seems plausible – why not? – the geographical distances appear small, and there is plenty of evidence of language contact on a small scale along the way (Figure 8).

But when we consider topography, it seems unlikely. East/west contact is very rare in this region. This is because topography declines rapidly from north to south (from average 6000m to average 300m above sea level over a distance of around 150km), with the result that rivers flow north to south through deep valleys. This means that the resulting north-south mountain spurs present obstacles which, while not insurmountable in principle, in practice typically reduce direct population contacts to a tiny trickle (Post 2013c). Thus, despite the fact that Idu speakers live only about two or three kilometres from Milang speakers as the crow flies, the mountain spur that separates them is so daunting and dangerous that earlier Idu-Milang contacts tended to be circumlocuitous. Both communities used the language of their common neighbour the Padam as a contact language, with the result that little if any mutual influence on one another's languages can be detected (Post and Modi 2011; Modi 2013). It is for these reasons that linguistic diversity in the Eastern Himalaya exists on a largely East-West rather than North-South basis.[25] The south-flowing river valleys mostly constitute convergence zones, while the resulting mountain spurs discourage east-west contacts and lead to population isolation and language divergence.

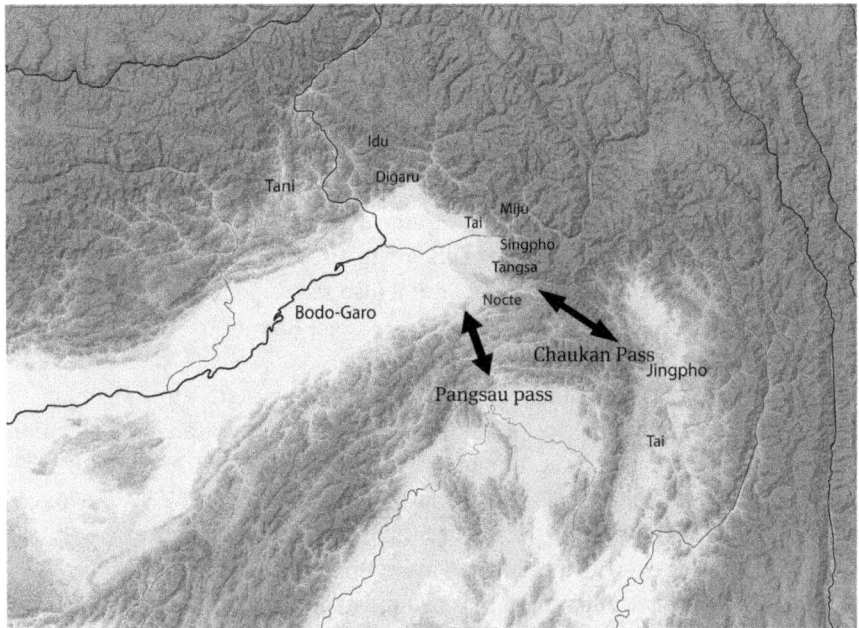

Fig. 8: A contact corridor between Northern Burma and the Eastern Himalaya?

---

25 These statements primarily apply to the Eastern Himalayan region as far as the Lohit River. It is true that the Lohit presents East/West contact opportunities with modern-day Northern Burma, and we do nowadays find related communities - such as the Tai Khamti - on both the Indian and on the Burmese sides of the Eastern Himalayan spurs. However, we should also note Shakespear's (1914) summary of late-19th century British exploration of the region, in which he notes that the primary avenue of population contacts, Chaukan Pass, was reported as dangerous at the best of times, and only passable at all from November to March - the rest of the year being blocked by landslides or snowfall. Given the relative remoteness of the modern-day Tani area from the Lohit Valley or Chaukan Pass, it would seem a stretch indeed to imagine any direct population contacts along this route.

Accordingly, any Tani participation in a greater MSEA contact area extending outward from the Northern Burma area would have to have been indirect, probably via plains-based populations who would either have been Bodo-Garo, Austroasiatic, or Indo-Aryan-speaking, depending on time-depth. If this is so, little would seem to be gained by comparing Proto-Tani, Jingpho, and Lolo-Burmese typologies directly.

To summarize, the likelihood of Proto-Tani having been part of an east-west contact corridor linking it directly to the MSEA area seems remote. If anything, links through contact would have to have been indirect, via a great number of intermediary languages of differing typological profiles.

5.4 Is this a creoloid typology?

The preceding sections have each considered possibilities that the MSEA-like typology of Proto-Tani might have been due to direct factors such as genealogical relationships or language contact. But it also seems possible that Proto-Tani might exhibit a MSEA-like typology for the indirect reason that both Proto-Tani and most languages of Mainland Southeast Asia are in essence *creoloids* – languages whose morphosyntactic structures have been significantly simplified due to extensive and imperfect adult language learning, typically in a situation of high language contact and language shift (McWhorter 2007; Trudgill 2009; Gil this volume). If this were true, it might imply that PT and MSEA languages shared similar formative circumstances; however, it would lead to few if any implications for the reconstruction of a broader regional prehistory.

This hypothesis would entail that two things are probably the case: (1) that MSEA-type typologies are indeed essentially creoloid typologies (2) that circumstances which normally foster the development of creoloid languages were indeed found in the histories of MSEA/Tani-speaking populations. A full substantiation of these points with respect to MSEA languages lies well beyond the scope of this chapter, and it is in any case not the goal of this chapter to argue for this or any other pre-historical scenario in particular.[26] Instead, we might simply review some recent works which address the issue of creolization and language typology from a Tibeto-Burman perspective.

We should first recall that the Tani languages constitute a "spread zone" in the sense of Nichols (1992); a set of highly similar languages spoken in contigu-

---

[26] One argument in favour of viewing MSEA language typologies as "simplified" in this sense is provided by Gil (2008).

ous areas throughout their geographic range. These and other facts[27] suggest a recent expansion in the area. One can presume language contact and language shift were part of this process.

Burling (2007b) and DeLancey (2010a; 2012; 2013), following MacWhorter (2007) among others, have suggested that such conditions – in which a newly-expanding language spreads "over" pre-existing populations as a micro-regional lingua franca – have repeatedly led to the emergence of creoloid types in Tibeto-Burman. In essence, this creoloid type *is* the MSEA-type typology we find in Sinospheric TB languages such as Lolo-Burmese and Jingpho.[28] In fact, one can even find relatively *more* simplified varieties of the same languages in high-contact circumstances throughout the region – a paradigm example being the simplified Jingpho variety Singpho, spoken in North East India, which has lost the agreement pattern so characteristic of Jingpho sentence-final predicators (41) (compare (40)). DeLancey suggests in particular that creolization might in part explain the loss of complex agreement patterns which he reconstructs to Proto-Tibeto-Burman on the basis of "archaic" TB languages (DeLancey 2010b). To the extent that any of these arguments are tenable, they seem to characterize the situation in Proto-Tani almost perfectly.

(41) Turung Singpho (Morey 2010: 440)
      ŋai³   sii³   ŋaa¹   haʔ¹
      1SG   die   be>FUT   DECL
      'I will die.'

In both North East India and in Mainland Southeast Asia, we find ideal population-contact conditions for the formation of creoloid languages. We find exceptional linguistic diversity within an area lacking a single overwhelmingly "dominant" population or cultural force, populations coming in and out of close contacts over time, multilingualism and the spread of lingua francas on a local scale, population exchanges and local migrations. A comprehensive substantiation of these observations lies well outside the scope of this chapter; our goal here has been simply to suggest that sociolinguistic dynamics which are com-

---

[27] For example, Tani oral histories almost uniformly point to a historical migration to and spread within the region, and often recount the existence of pre-existing populations whose languages are supposed to have influenced their own (Blackburn 2003/2004).
[28] Virtually the only non-creole-like feature of MSEA languages as conceived by McWhorter (2005) is a well-developed lexical tone system. It is also worth recalling, however, that lexical tone systems are reconstructible innovations among most if not all tonal MSEA languages, as well as, seemingly, in Sino-Tibetan languages more generally (Matisoff 1973b; Matisoff 1999).

patible with the evolution of creoloid typologies do appear to exist in both regions.

To summarize this section, much recent literature has argued for the emergence of an MSEA-like typological profile by means of systemic simplification under high-contact conditions. The historical circumstances of Tani languages, to the extent that they can be determined, seem compatible with a simplification-through-contact scenario. Thus, it would seem that, if claims in the literature to the effect that the characteristically MSEA typological profile is in essence a creoloid typology can be sustained by historical evidence, this hypothesis might account for the similar typological profiles of Proto-Tani and MSEA languages quite well.

6 Conclusion

The North East Indian region is an especially interesting area in the Asian ethnolinguistic context, because it constitutes a crossroads in which representatives of most major cultural and linguistic areas of mainland Asia suddenly come into contact. This has led to the emergence of a considerable overall ethnolinguistic complexity; many of the dozens or even hundreds of relatively distinct ethnolinguistic groups within the area remain little known to this day, their languages in many cases only provisionally classified if at all.

An understanding of the present ethnolinguistic distribution in North East India goes hand in hand with an understanding of its history – or how North East India came to be the way it is. In the absence of written records pertaining to the vast majority of ethnolinguistic groups in this region (or even in spite of them), prehistorical reconstruction necessarily involves the correlation of data from multiple sources and of many kinds.

The present chapter has reviewed evidence suggesting that one relatively large ethnolinguistic group of the Eastern Himalayan and Brahmaputra Plains region – the Tani – most likely descend from speakers of a proto-language whose morphological typology aligned closely with languages of the Mainland Southeast Asian linguistic area; in particular, languages of Northern Burma such as Lahu and, especially, Jingpho. By contrast, the modern Tani languages are more closely aligned to the languages of South Asia in this and other respects. The question then becomes, what sort of historical circumstances are most likely to have led to this distribution.

We considered four possible sets of circumstances: (1) descent from an ancestor held in common with MSEA languages (2) migration outward from the

MSEA region (3) contact with the MSEA region and (4) similar formative circumstances, i.e. development of a creoloid profile due to extensive language contact and imperfect adult language learning. This chapter does not take a strong position on any one of these hypotheses, which are not in most cases mutually exclusive in any case. However, from the present standpoint it would appear that hypothesis (4) may be the most likely. The Tani languages have clearly spread relatively recently – and would almost certainly have spread "over" pre-existing populations who would have learned early Tani language(s) imperfectly; as discussed above, this view is in fact echoed by Tani cultural memories in several cases. If this is so, it might imply that the appearance of a possible early connection between at least one major North East Indian ethnolinguistic group and the languages of Mainland Southeast Asia is simply that; an appearance, with no major implications for the reconstruction of a broader regional pre-history.

Even if this is so, however, some questions remain. If the canonical MSEA typology can indeed be understood as a creoloid typology, then why does it persist for so long in MSEA, while it seems to develop in different directions much more quickly in other parts of the world?

Abbreviations

ACC	accusative	IND	individuative	PRED	predicate
ADD	additive	INF	infinitive	PRO	Pronoun
ADVS	adverbializer	INFR	inferential	PSiang	Proto-Siangic
		INFL	inflection	PT	Proto-Tani
ANTR	anterior	IPFV	imperfective	QUOT	quotative
ART	article	IRR	irrealis	RDUP	reduplicant
ASM	Assamese	LOC	locative	REFL	reflexive
ATTN	attainment	N	noun	REP	reportative
AUX	auxiliary	NAGT	non-agentive	S	intransitive subject
CLF	classifier	NEG	negative	SEMB	semblative
CLFR	classifier root	NF	non-final	SFP	sentence-final particle
		NP	noun phrase		
COP	copula	NUM	numeral	SG	singular
COS	change-of-state	NUMR	numeral root	SLEV	same-level
		NZR	nominalizer	SPRX	speaker-proximate
DAT	dative	OBL	oblique	STAT	stative
DCOL	dual	PDER	predicate	SUB	subject

	collective		derivation	SVC	serial verb construc-
DECL	declarative	PERS	persistent		tion
DL	dual	PF	perfect	TAG	question tag
DST	distal	PFV	perfective	TAM	tense, aspect,
EMPH	emphatic	PFX	prefix		modality
EPF	experiential	PINFL	predicate	TB	Tibeto-Burman
	perfect		inflection	TOP	topic
ERG	ergative	PL	plural	V	verb *or* vowel
ET	Eastern Tani	POS	postposition	WT	Western Tani
F	feminine	POSD	possessed		
FUT	future	POSR	possessor		
GEN	genitive				

References

Bhatt, Rajesh. 2005. Long-distance agreement in Hindi-Urdu. *Natural Language and Linguistic Theory* 23. 757–804.

Bickel, Balthasar. 2000. Introduction: Person and evidence in Himalayan languages. *Linguistics of the Tibeto-Burman Area* 23(2). 1–11.

Bisang, Walter. 1995. Verb serialization and converbs - differences and similarities. In Martin Haspelmath & Ekkehard König (eds.), *Converbs in cross-linguistic perspective: Structure and meaning of adverbial verb forms - adverbial participles, gerunds -* (Empirical Approaches to Language Typology 13), 137–188. Berlin: Walter de Gruyter.

Blackburn, Stuart. 2003/2004. Memories of migration: Notes on legends and beads in Arunachal Pradesh, India. *European Bulletin of Himalayan Research* 25/26. 15–60.

Blench, Roger. in press. Was there once an arc of vegeculture linking Melanesia with Northeast India? In Glenn Summerhayes & David Addison (eds.), *Selected papers from the 2011 Lapita Pacific Archaeology Conference: Pacific archaeology: Documenting the past 50,000 years to the present*. Auckland: University of Auckland Press.

Blench, Roger & Mark W. Post. 2012. Declassifying Eastern Himalayan languages: Reconsidering the evidence. Cambridge, UK & Armidale, AU, Kay Williamson Educational Foundation & University of New England. Manuscript.

Blench, Roger & Mark W. Post. 2013. Re-thinking Sino-Tibetan phylogeny from the perspective of North East Indian languages. In Nathan Hill & Tom Owen-Smith (eds.), *Trans-Himalayan linguistics*, 71–104. Berlin: Mouton de Gruyter.

Bradley, David. 1997. Tibeto-Burman languages and classification. In David Bradley (ed.), *Tibeto-Burman languages of the Himalayas*, 1–72. Canberra: Pacific Linguistics.

Bradley, David, Randy J. LaPolla, Boyd Michailovsky & Graham Thurgood (eds.). 2003. *Language variation: Papers on variation and change in the Sinosphere and in the Indosphere in honour of James A. Matisoff*. Canberra: Pacific Linguistics.

Burling, Robbins. 1965. *Hill farms and padi fields: Life in mainland Southeast Asia*. Englewood Cliffs, NJ: Prentice-Hall.

Burling, Robbins. 2003. The Tibeto-Burman languages of Northeastern India. In Graham Thurgood & Randy J. LaPolla (eds.), *The Sino-Tibetan languages*, 167–192. London & New York: Routledge.

Burling, Robbins. 2007a. Language, ethnicity and identity in Northeastern India. South Asia: *Journal of South Asian Studies* 30(3). 391–404.

Burling, Robbins. 2007b. The lingua franca cycle: Implications for language shift, language change, and language classification. *Anthropological Linguistics* 49(3–4). 207–236.

Burling, Robbins. 2012. Where did the question 'Where did my tribe come from?' come from? In Toni Huber & Stuart Blackburn (eds.), *Origins and migrations in the extended Eastern Himalaya*, 49–62. Leiden: Brill.

Campbell, Lyle. 2001 [1998]. *Historical linguistics: An introduction*. Cambridge, MA: MIT Press.

Campbell, Lyle. 2006. Areal linguistics: A closer scrutiny. In Yaron Matras, April McMahon & Nigel Vincent (eds.), *Linguistic areas: Convergence in historical and typological perspective*, 1–30. Basingstoke: Palgrave Macmillan.

Cardona, George & Dhanesh Jain. (eds.). 2003. *The Indo-Aryan languages*. London: Routledge.

Chappell, Hilary. 1999. The double unaccusative construction in Sinitic languages. In Doris L. Payne & Immanuel Barshi (eds.), *External possession* (Typological Studies in Language 39), 195–228. Amsterdam: John Benjamins.

Chowdhary, Runima. 2012. On classifiers in Asamiya. In Gwendolyn Hyslop, Stephen Morey & Mark W. Post (eds.), *North East Indian linguistics* (Volume 4), 269–291. New Delhi: Cambridge University Press.

Clark, Marybeth. 1996. Where do you feel? Stative verbs and body-part terms in Mainland Southeast Asia. In Hilary Chappell & William B. McGregor (eds.), *The grammar of inalienability: A typological perspective on body part terms and the part-whole relation*, 529–564. Berlin: Mouton de Gruyter.

Comrie, Bernard. 2007. Areal typology of Mainland Southeast Asia: What we learn from the WALS maps. *Manusya* 13. 18–47.

Coupe, Alec. 2011. On core case-marking patterns in two Tibeto-Burman languages of Nagaland. *Linguistics of the Tibeto-Burman Area* 34(2). 21–47.

Dai, Qing-Xia & Lon Diehl. 2003. Jingpho. In Randy J. LaPolla, David Bradley & Graham Thurgood (eds.), *The Sino-Tibetan Languages*, 401–408. London: Routledge.

DeLancey, Scott. 2010a. Language replacement and the spread of Tibeto-Burman. *Journal of the South East Asian Linguistics Society* 3(1). 40–55.

DeLancey, Scott. 2010b. Towards a history of verb agreement in Tibeto-Burman. *Himalayan Linguistics* 9(1). 1–39.

DeLancey, Scott. 2012. On the origins of Bodo-Garo. In Gwendolyn Hyslop, Stephen Morey & Mark Post (eds.), *North East Indian linguistics* (Volume 4), 3–20. New Delhi: Cambridge University Press India.

DeLancey, Scott. 2013. Creolization in the divergence of Tibeto-Burman. In Nathan Hill & Tom Owen-Smith (eds.), *Trans-Himalayan linguistics*, 41–70. Berlin: Mouton de Gruyter.

Donegan, Patricia J. & David Stampe. 1983. Rhythm and the holistic organization of linguistic structure. In J. Richardson, M. Marks, and A. Chukerman (eds.), *Chicago Linguistic Society 19* (2: Papers from the Parasession on the Interplay of Phonology, Morphology and Syntax): 337–353.

Donegan, Patricia J. & David Stampe. 2004. Rhythm and the synthetic drift of Munda. In Rajendra Singh (ed.), *The yearbook of South Asian languages and linguistics*, 3–36. Berlin & New York: Mouton de Gruyter.

Driem, George van. 2013. Trans-Himalayan. In Nathan Hill & Tom Owen-Smith (eds.), *Trans-Himalayan linguistics*. Berlin: Mouton de Gruyter.

Dryer, Matthew S. 2008. Word order in Tibeto-Burman languages. *Linguistics of the Tibeto-Burman Area* 31(1). 1–83.

Elwin, Verrier. 2005 [1957]. *A Philosophy for NEFA*. Itanagar, Arunachal Pradesh, India: Directorate of Research, Government of Arunachal Pradesh.

Emeneau, Murray. 1956. India as a linguistic area. *Language* 32(1). 3–16.

Enfield, N. J. 2001. On genetic and areal linguistics in Mainland Southeast Asia: Parallel polyfunctionality of 'acquire'. In Alexandra Y. Aikhenvald & R. M. W. Dixon (eds.), *Areal diffusion and genetic inheritance: Case studies in language change*, 255–290. Oxford: Oxford University Press.

Enfield, N. J. 2003. *Linguistic epidemiology: Semantics and grammar of language contact in Mainland Southeast Asia*. London: Routledge.

Enfield, N. J. 2005. Areal linguistics and Mainland Southeast Asia. *Annual Review of Anthropology* 34. 181–206.

Enfield, N. J. 2007. *A grammar of Lao*. Berlin & New York: Mouton de Gruyter.

Genetti, Carol. 2007. *A grammar of Dolokha Newar*. Berlin: Mouton de Gruyter.

Gil, David. 2008. How complex are isolating languages? In Matti Miestamo, Kaius Sinnemäki & Fred Karlsson (eds.), *Language complexity: Typology, contact, change*, 109–131. Amsterdam: John Benjamins.

Gohain, B. K. 1999. *Origin of the Tai and Chao Lung Hsukapha: A historical perspective*. New Delhi: Omsons.

Huber, Toni. 2012. Micro-migrations of hill peoples in Northern Arunachal Pradesh: Rethinking methodologies and claims of origin in Tibet. In Toni Huber & Stuart Blackburn (eds.), *Origins and migrations in the extended Eastern Himalaya*. Leiden: Brill.

Iwasaki, Shoichi. 2002. Proprioceptive-state expressions in Thai. *Studies in Language* 26(1). 33–66.

Kanittanan, Wilaiwan. 1986. Kamti Tai: from an SVO to an SOV language. In B.H. Krishnamurti (ed.), *South Asian linguistics - Structure, convergence and diglossia*, 174–178. Delhi: Motilal Banarsidass.

Kiryu, Kazuyuki. 2009. On the rise of the classifier system in Newar. *Senri Ethnological Studies* 75. 51–69.

Masica, Colin P. 1976. *Defining a linguistic Area: South Asia*. Chicago: University of Chicago Press.

Matisoff, James A. 1973a. *The grammar of Lahu*. Berkeley: University of California Press.

Matisoff, James A. 1973b. Tonogenesis in Southeast Asia. In Larry M. Hyman (ed.), *Consonant types & tone* (Southern California Occasional Papers in Linguistics), 73–95. Los Angeles: UCLA.

Matisoff, James A. 1985. God and the Sino-Tibetan copula, with some good news concerning selected Tibeto-Burman rhymes. *Journal of Asian and African Studies* 29. 1–81.

Matisoff, James A. 1986. Hearts and minds in South-East Asian languages and English: An essay in the comparative lexical semantics of psycho-collocations. *Cahiers de Linguistique - Asie Orientale* 15(1). 5–57.

Matisoff, James A. 1990. On megalocomparison. *Language* 66(1). 106–120.

Matisoff, James A. 1991a. Areal and universal dimensions of grammatization in Lahu. In Elizabeth Closs Traugott & Bernd Heine (eds.), *Approaches to grammaticalization (Volume*

1): *Focus on theoretical and methodological issues,* 383–453. Amsterdam: John Benjamins.

Matisoff, James A. 1991b. Sino-Tibetan linguistics: Present state and future prospects. *Annual Review of Anthropology* 20. 469–504.

Matisoff, James A. 1999. Tibeto-Burman tonology in an areal context. In Shigeki Kaji (ed.), *Proceedings of the Symposium 'Cross-Linguistic Studies of Tonal Phenomena: Tonogenesis, Typology, and Related Topics'*, 3–32. Tokyo: Institute for the Study of Languages and Cultures of Asia and Africa, Tokyo University of Foreign Studies.

Matisoff, James A. 2001. Genetic versus contact relationship: Prosodic diffusability in South-East Asian languages. In Alexandra Y. Aikhenvald & R. M. W. Dixon (eds.), *Areal diffusion and genetic Inheritance: Problems in comparative linguistics,* 291–327. Oxford: Oxford University Press.

McWhorter, John H. 2005. *Defining creole.* Oxford: Oxford University Press.

McWhorter, John H. 2007. *Language Interrupted: Signs of non-native acquisition in standard language grammars.* Oxford: Oxford University Press.

Modi, Yankee. 2005. Emergence and impact of Hindi as a lingua franca in Arunachal Pradesh. New Delhi: Jawaharlal Nehru University MA Thesis.

Modi, Yankee. 2013. The nearest relatives of the Tani group. Paper presented at the 19th Himalayan Languages Symposium. Canberra: Australian National University.

Moral, Dipankar. 1997. North East India as a linguistic area. *Mon-Khmer Studies* 27. 43–53.

Morey, Stephen. 2006. Constituent order change in the Tai languages of Assam. *Linguistic Typology* 10. 327–367.

Morey, Stephen. 2010. *Turung: A variety of Singpho language spoken in Assam.* Canberra: Pacific Linguistics.

Morey, Stephen. 2013. The marking of noun phrases: Some observations on the languages of North East India. In Gwendolyn Hyslop, Stephen Morey & Mark W. Post (eds.), *North East Indian linguistics* (Volume 5), 171–191. New Delhi: Cambridge University Press India.

Nagaraja, K. S. 1993. Khasi dialects: A typological consideration. *Mon-Khmer Studies* 23. 1–10.

Nichols, Johanna. 1992. *Linguistic diversity in space and time.* Chicago: Chicago University Press.

Okell, John. 1969. *A reference grammar of colloquial Burmese* (2 Volumes). Oxford: Oxford University Press.

Peyraube, Alain. 1996. Recent issues in Chinese historical syntax. In C.-T. James Huang & Y.-H. Audrey Li (eds.), *New horizons in Chinese linguistics.* Dordrecht: Kluwer.

Post, Mark W. 2005a. Assamese verb serialization in functional, areal-typological and diachronic perspective. In Marc Ettlinger, Nicholas Fleischer & Mischa Park-Doob (eds.), *Proceedings of the 30th Annual Meeting of the Berkeley Linguistics Society* (February 13-16, 2004), 377–390. Berkeley: Berkeley Linguistics Society.

Post, Mark W. 2005b. Synchronic and diachronic dimensions of the tone system of Galo. Paper presented at the 36th Annual Meeting of the Australian Linguistics Society, Melbourne: Monash University, 28–30 September.

Post, Mark W. 2006. Compounding and the structure of the Tani lexicon. *Linguistics of the Tibeto-Burman Area* 29(1). 41–60.

Post, Mark W. 2009. The semantics of clause linking in Galo. In R. M. W. Dixon & Alexandra Y. Aikhenvald (eds.), *The semantics of clause linking: A cross-linguistic typology,* 75–91. Oxford: Oxford University Press.

Post, Mark W. 2010. Predicate derivations in the Tani languages: Root, suffix, both or neither? In Stephen Morey & Mark Post (eds.), *North East Indian linguistics* (Volume 2), 175–197. New Delhi: Cambridge University Press India.

Post, Mark W. 2011a. Agency-and-intention and/or knowledge-and-experience: The functional bases of egophoric marking in Tibeto-Burman. Paper presented at the Workshop on Conjunct/Disjunct Alignment. Linguistic Society of America Summer Linguistics Institute, University of Colorado at Boulder, 13 July.

Post, Mark W. 2011b. Nominalization and nominalization-based constructions in Galo. In Foong Ha Yap, Karen Grunow-Hårsta and Janick Wrona (eds.), *Nominalization in Asian languages: Diachronic and typological perspectives* (Typological Studies in Language 96), 255–287. Amsterdam: John Benjamins.

Post, Mark W. 2011c. Prosody and typological drift in Austroasiatic and Tibeto-Burman: Against "Sinosphere" and "Indosphere". In Sophana Srichampa, Paul Sidwell & Kenneth J. Gregerson (eds.), *Austroasiatic studies: Papers from ICAAL4. Mon-Khmer Studies Special Issue No. 3*, 198–221. Canberra: Pacific Linguistics.

Post, Mark W. 2012. The language, culture, environment and origins of Proto-Tani speakers: What is knowable, and what is not (yet). In Toni Huber & Stuart Blackburn (eds.), *Origins and migrations in the extended Eastern Himalaya*. (Tribal Cultures in the Eastern Himalayas), 153–186. Leiden: Brill.

Post, Mark W. 2013a. Defoliating the Tani Stammbaum: An exercise in areal linguistics. Paper presented at the 19th Himalayan Languages Symposium. Canberra: Australian National University.

Post, Mark W. 2013b. Person-sensitive TAME marking in Galo: Historical origins and functional motivation. In Tim Thornes, Joana Jansen, Gwendolyn Hyslop & Erik Andvik (eds.), *Functional-historical approaches to explanation: In honor of Scott DeLancey*, 107–130. Amsterdam: John Benjamins.

Post, Mark W. 2013c. The Siyom River Valley: An essay on intra-subgroup convergence in Tibeto-Burman. In Gwendolyn Hyslop, Stephen Morey & Mark W. Post (eds.), *North East Indian Linguistics* (Volume 5), 60–90. New Delhi: Cambridge University Press India.

Post, Mark W. (in press 2014). Galo negation and the reconstruction of Proto-Tani predicate syntax. *Language and Linguistics* 16(3).

Post, Mark W. & Roger Blench. 2011. Siangic: A new language phylum in North East India. Paper presented at the 6th International Conference of the North East Indian Linguistics Society. Tezpur, Assam, India: Tezpur University, January 31 – February 2.

Post, Mark W. & Yankee Modi. 2011. Language contact and the genetic position of Milang (Eastern Himalaya). *Anthropological Linguistics* 53(3). 215–258.

Post, Mark W. & Kanno Tage. 2013. Apatani phonology and lexicon, with a special focus on tone. *Himalayan Linguistics* 12(1). 17–75.

Prasad, Bal Ram, G. Devi Prasada Sastry & P. T. Abraham. 1991. *Mising grammar*. Mysore: Central Institute of Indian Languages.

Shafer, Robert. 1955. Classification of the Sino-Tibetan languages. *Word* 11. 94–111.

Shakespear, L.W. 1914. *History of Upper Assam, Upper Burmah, and North-Eastern Frontier*. London: Macmillan.

Sherzer, Joel. 1976. *An areal-typological study of American Indian languages north of Mexico*. Amsterdam: North Holland.

Stolz, Thomas. 2006. All or nothing. In Yaron Matras, April McMahon & Nigel Vincent (eds.), *Linguistic areas: convergence in historical and typological perspective*, 32–50. Houndmills, UK: Palgrave Macmillan.
Sun, Tian-Shin Jackson. 1993. *A historical-comparative study of the Tani (Mirish) branch of Tibeto-Burman*. Berkeley: University of California dissertation.
Sun, Tian-Shin Jackson. 2003. Tani languages. In Graham Thurgood & Randy J. LaPolla (eds.), *The Sino-Tibetan languages* (Routledge Language Family Series), 456–466. London & New York: Routledge.
Sun, Tianshin Jackson & Mark W. Post. 2014. *Proto-Tani: A Tibeto-Burman mesolanguage*. Taipei & Armidale, AU: Academica Sinica & University of New England.
Tayeng, Aduk. 1990. *Nishi phrase book*. Itanagar: Director of Research, Government of Arunachal Pradesh.
Tayu, Toku Stephen. 2010. *Nyishi grammatical sketch and dictionary*. Itanagar: All Purpose Editions.
Trudgill, Peter. 2009. Sociolinguistic typology and complexification. In Geoffrey Sampson, David Gil & Peter Trudgill (eds.), *Language Complexity as an Evolving Variable*, 98–109. Oxford: Oxford University Press.
Walker, Andrew. 2006. Beyond hills and plains: Rethinking trade, state and society in the upper Mekong borderlands. *IIAS Newsletter* 42(5). 5.
Watters, David E. 2002. *A grammar of Kham*. Cambridge: Cambridge University Press.
Wolfenden, Stuart N. 1929. *Outlines of Tibeto-Burman linguistic morphology: With special reference to the prefixes, infixes and suffixes of Classical Tibetan and the languages of the Kachin, Bodo, Nâgâ, Kuki-Chin and Burma groups*. London: The Royal Asiatic Society.

David Gil
The Mekong-Mamberamo linguistic area

1 Introduction

Mainland Southeast Asia is well-known as one of the prime examples of a linguistic area or Sprachbund, a geographical region containing a variety of languages of different families nevertheless exhibiting a significant number of shared linguistic properties due to historical processes of language contact and convergence, see for example Matisoff (1973, 2001), Clark (1992), Enfield (2005, 2011), Comrie (2007), and Dahl (2008).[1]

Linguistic areas are typically flanked by other linguistic areas, but the boundaries are seldom sharp and clearly demarcated. Instead, one linguistic area shades into another with various degrees of gradualness, resulting in transitional zones, in which languages tend to exhibit a mixture of properties, some associated with one linguistic area, others with another.

Mainland Southeast Asia is commonly thought of as being flanked by three such transitional zones, radiating out to the west, to the north, and to the east and southeast respectively. To the west, Mainland Southeast Asia shades into the equally well-known South Asia linguistic area (Masica 1976, Emeneau 1980), with a transitional zone encompassing much of Burma, north-east India and the Himalayas (Jenny this volume; Post this volume). To the north, Mainland Southeast Asia blends into a Northeast Asia linguistic area (Janhunen 1998; Anderson 2004, 2006), with a transitional zone covering much of China (Hashimoto 1976, 1978; De Sousa this volume). However, to the east and southeast, a rather different picture presents itself, one that forms the focus of this paper.

To the east and southeast of Mainland Southeast Asia, three other linguistic areas may be discerned. First, Australia, sometimes viewed as a linguistic area, even though some scholars consider all of its languages to belong to a single genealogical family (Dixon 1997, 2001). Secondly, New Guinea, a more commonly accepted example of a linguistic area, one that contains some 15% of the

---

1 Some scholars, such as Stolz (2002), have called into question the usefulness of establishing linguistic areas. Without denying the many conceptual and practical problems inherent in the notion, this paper proceeds under the assumption that the establishment of such areas remains an activity of inherent interest as well as a prerequisite for an adequate understanding of the linguistic history of a region and the processes of language contact and convergence that form part of that history.

world's languages and an extraordinarily large amount of genealogical diversity, while still exhibiting a substantial number of shared linguistic properties (Foley 1986, 2000). And thirdly, the Philippines and Taiwan, whose languages all belong to the Austronesian family, but do not form a distinct genealogical subgroup within Austronesian: nevertheless, they display an array of common properties not shared by Austronesian languages outside of the region, and therefore justify, at least to some extent, the characterization of the Philippines and Taiwan as constituting a linguistic area.

Between the Mainland Southeast Asia linguistic area on the one hand, and the Australia, New Guinea and Philippine-Taiwan linguistic areas on the other, lies the *Nusantara* archipelago, consisting of four major islands, Sumatra, Java, Borneo, and Sulawesi, two large islands groups, Maluku and Nusa Tenggara, to their east, as well as numerous other smaller island groups and individual islands.[2] The languages of Nusantara are commonly thought of as representing a progressive attenuation, dissipation, or shading out of the prototypical Mainland Southeast Asia linguistic profile. The more western parts of Nusantara are often viewed as an extension of the Mainland Southeast Asia linguistic area; as shown by Comrie (2007), the languages of Western Nusantara tend to bear a closer resemblance to those of Mainland Southeast Asia than do languages on the "other sides" of Mainland Southeast Asia, namely those of South and Northeast Asia. However, as one moves further down the Nusantara archipelago and away from Mainland Southeast Asia, the languages are generally seen to be shedding their Mainland Southeast Asia characteristics and taking on those of neighbouring linguistic areas. To the north, the languages of northern Borneo and Sulawesi have been noted to bear a closer typological resemblance to those of the Philippines. And to the east, in Nusa Tenggara, Sulawesi and Maluku, the languages are said to take on various characteristics attributable to the increasing proximity to New Guinea and/or a prior non-Austronesian substrate in the region (Klamer, Reesink and van Staden 2008).

This paper presents an alternative perspective on the languages of the Nusantara archipelago. Rather than viewing them as marginal or non-prototypical Mainland Southeast Asian languages occupying a transitional zone between linguistic areas, this paper proposes that the languages of Nusantara

---

2 The term Nusantara has a number of alternative usages differing from that adopted here. Occasionally, it is taken to refer to a larger region including also the Philippines. Alternatively, in current Indonesian parlance, it is used to refer to the territory that is now part of the Indonesian state, thus excluding parts of Borneo belonging to Malaysia and Brunei, and part of the island of Timor that forms the state of Timor Lorosae, while including the western half of New Guinea.

actually lie at the heartland of a larger linguistic area, consisting of Mainland Southeast Asia, the Nusantara archipelago, and, in addition, western parts of New Guinea. The main goal of this paper is to present evidence in support of the existence of this area: the *Mekong-Mamberamo linguistic area*.

A rough representation of the Mekong-Mamberamo linguistic area is provided in Map 1. The Mekong-Mamberamo area is delimited by two major rivers, the well-known Mekong and the somewhat lesser-known but still major Mamberamo, which flows from the central New-Guinea highlands through some of the least explored regions of the world before reaching the north coast, at a point to the east of the Cenderawasih Bay. At its north-western end, the Mekong-Mamberamo area wholly contains the Mainland Southeast Asia area; the zones that are transitional between Mainland Southeast Asia and the South and Northwest Asian linguistic areas are, ipso facto, also transitional between the Mekong-Mamberamo and these other areas. The mid-section of the Mekong-Mamberamo linguistic area is made up by the Nusantara archipelago, with the exception of the northern parts of Borneo and Sulawesi, which are transitional between the Mekong-Mamberamo area and the Philippines, which lie outside the Mekong-Mamberamo area. At its eastern end, the Mekong-Mamberamo area contains the western parts of New Guinea: the Bird's Head and Bomberai peninsulas, the Bird's Neck region, and the Cenderawasih Bay area. To the east of these is a transitional zone shading into the heartland of New Guinea, which constitutes a separate linguistic area not part of the Mekong-Mamberamo area.

The Mekong-Mamberamo linguistic area may be considered as a macro-area, in the sense that it wholly contains other linguistic areas such as Mainland Southeast Asia or East Nusantara (Klamer, Reesink and van Staden 2008). The positing of such a macro-area does not detract in any way from the validity of the smaller linguistic areas within it. For example, arguments in favour of Europe as a linguistic area do not impact on the viability of, say, the Balkans or the Circum-Baltic region as valid linguistic areas within Europe. Similarly, the existence of a Mekong-Mamberamo linguistic area does not detract from the validity of Mainland Southeast Asia or East Nusantara as linguistic areas within it. Thus, while this paper shows that some of the characteristic properties of the Mainland Southeast Asia linguistic area may in fact be associated with the broader Mekong-Mamberamo linguistic area, other characteristic properties of the Mainland Southeast Asia linguistic area do not extend into the remainder of the Mekong-Mamberamo area; such properties, then, maintain the viability of the Mainland Southeast Asia area within the larger Mekong-Mamberamo area.³

The Mekong-Mamberamo linguistic area contains languages belonging to some twenty or more distinct genealogies, as members of larger families or as isolates (following the classification provided in Nordhoff et al 2013). However, the genealogical profile of the Mekong-Mamberamo area differs in nature from west to east. To the west, almost all of the languages of Mainland Southeast Asia belong to four language families, Sino-Tibetan, Austroasiatic, Tai-Kadai and Hmong-Mien, all of which contain additional languages either outside the Mainland Southeast Asia area and hence also the Mekong-Mamberamo area, or else in transitional zones to the west or north. To the east, many of the languages of eastern Nusantara and western New Guinea are either isolates, or else belong to a relatively large number of smallish families, the relationships between which have not yet been firmly established. On the island of Sumbawa, in Nusa Tenggara, was the now extinct Tambora, not known to be related to any other language. A little further to the east are the twenty or more languages of the Timor-Alor-Pantar family, considered by some to be part of the very large Trans-New-Guinea family, but by most people currently working on them to constitute an independent family with no clearly demonstrable affinity with languages further afield. In Halmahera and some surrounding islands of north Maluku is the North Halmahera language family, which some take to be part of a larger West Papuan family, but others consider to be a family of its own, with no demonstrable relationship to languages outside the region. In the New Guinea Bird's Head are the East Bird's Head, West Bird's Head, South Bird's Head, and Konda-Yahadian families, and four isolates: Maybrat, Abun, Mpur, and Inanwatan. While some scholars consider some of these to belong to a larger West Papuan family, such claims are not generally considered to have been satisfactorily demonstrated. In the Bomberai peninsula are the West Bomberai family and two isolates, Mor and Tanahmerah. In the Bird's Neck is the Mairasi family. And in the Cenderawasih Bay region are the Geelvink Bay and Yawa-

---

3 In turn, the Mekong-Mamberamo linguistic area is wholly contained within the Pacific Rim linguistic area posited by Nichols (1998). Notably, both the Mekong-Mamberamo and the much larger Pacific Rim areas include western parts of New Guinea while excluding much or all of the remainder of the island, thereby counter-indicating the view of New Guinea as constituting a single homogeneous area. However, in a later publication, Bickel and Nichols (2006) propose a rather different delimitation of the Pacific Rim area, drawing its western boundary along the Wallace line (also the western boundary of Klamer, Reesink and van Staden's [2008] East Nusantara area), and thereby excluding western Nusantara and Mainland Southeast Asia from their Pacific Rim area.

Saweru families as well as the isolate Kehu. Finally, on the eastern fringes of the Mekong-Mamberamo area are numerous languages belonging to the Trans-New-Guinea, Greater Kwerba, Lakes Plain and other families, as well as additional isolates.

Whereas the western and eastern parts of the Mekong-Mamberamo linguistic area exhibit great genealogical diversity, the central part of the Mekong-Mamberamo area, comprising western and central Nusantara, is genealogically homogenous, consisting entirely of languages belonging to a single language family, Austronesian. In addition, within the Mekong-Mamberamo area, Austronesian languages are also present in large numbers to the east, in eastern Nusantara and western New Guinea, where they are spoken alongside other non-Austronesian languages, as well as in much smaller numbers also to the west, in Mainland Southeast Asia. Outside the Mekong-Mamberamo area, Austronesian languages are also found in Taiwan and the Philippines, Madagascar and Sri Lanka (where at least the lexifier of Sri Lankan Malay is of Austronesian provenance), and throughout the Pacific. Austronesian is by far the largest language family of the Mekong-Mamberamo linguistic area; however, it is a relative newcomer into the region. There is now general agreement that the Austronesian homeland is situated in Taiwan, from where languages belonging to the Malayo-Polynesian branch spread south into the Philippines and from there into Nusantara, arriving in the Mekong-Mamberamo area at around 2000 BC or thereabouts, before embarking on further dispersals into the Indian and Pacific Oceans.

With its origin outside the Mekong-Mamberamo linguistic area, the spread of Austronesian into the area brought an injection of non-Mekong-Mamberamo properties into the heartland of the Mekong-Mamberamo area. As a result, several Mekong-Mamberamo properties exhibit a saddle-like pattern, occurring with greater frequency and salience in the largely non-Austronesian extremities, Mainland Southeast Asia and western New Guinea, but in more attenuated fashion in the mostly Austronesian centre. However, several other Mekong-Mamberamo properties appear to be just as salient in the Austronesian centre as in the non-Austronesian extremities; for these properties, then, the incoming Austronesian languages would seem to have shed their prior non-Mekong-Mamberamo properties and assimilated to an already existing Mekong-Mamberamo profile of the non-Austronesian languages that were there before them.

2 Seventeen Mekong-Mamberamo properties

This paper proposes 17 linguistic properties as characteristic of the Mekong-Mamberamo linguistic area:

(1) *17 Mekong-Mamberamo Properties*

1. passing gesture
2. repeated dental clicks expressing amazement
3. conventionalized greeting with 'where'
4. 'eye day' > 'sun' lexicalization
5. d/t place-of-articulation asymmetry
6. numeral classifiers
7. verby adjectives
8. basic SVO word order
9. iamitive perfects
10. 'give' causatives
11. low differentiation of adnominal attributive constructions
12. weakly developed grammatical voice
13. isolating word structure
14. short words
15. low grammatical-morpheme density
16. optional thematic-role flagging
17. optional TAM marking

The above 17 properties present a potpourri ranging from gestural and paralinguistic (1,2) through idiomatic and lexical (3,4) and phonological (5) to grammatical (6-17). For the most part they are logically and empirically independent of one another; however, properties (13-17) are interrelated in ways that are discussed in the appropriate sections.

The above properties are also a rather mixed bag in terms of their quality as diagnostics of the Mekong-Mamberamo linguistic area. This is due in part to the actual facts on the ground, but is also a reflection of the amount of evidence that I have had the opportunity to muster in support of each property: while a majority of the properties are supported by ample data from published work by myself or other scholars, a few properties still represent work in progress containing elements that may be of a more conjectural or programmatic nature. A comparative evaluation of the 17 proposed Mekong-Mamberamo properties is presented in Table 1:

Table 1: Evaluation of 17 Mekong-Mamberamo Properties

property	quirkiness	internal consistency	boundary distinctiveness					internal pattern	coverage
			South Asia	North-West Asia	Philippines & Taiwan	Central & Eastern New Guinea	Australia		
1	hi	hi	hi	hi	lo	mid	hi	w<E	hi
2	hi	mid	hi	hi	hi	lo	mid	w<E	mid
3	low	hi	mid	mid	lo	mid	lo	=	hi
4	hi	mid	hi	hi	hi	mid	hi	W>e	hi
5	hi	lo	lo	hi	lo	lo	hi	=	hi
6	mid	hi	mid	lo	hi	hi	hi	W>c<E	hi
7	lo	hi	hi	mid	lo	hi	hi	=	hi
8	lo	mid	hi	hi	hi	hi	hi	W>c<E	hi
9	hi	mid	hi	hi	hi	lo	hi	=	mid
10	mid	mid	hi	hi	hi	mid	hi	W>e	lo
11	hi	lo	hi	hi	hi	hi	hi	=	mid
12	mid	hi	hi	hi	mid	lo	mid	W>c<E	lo
13	mid	mid	hi	hi	hi	hi	hi	W>c<E	hi
14	hi	lo	mid	hi	hi	lo	hi	W>c<E	hi
15	hi	hi	hi	hi	hi	hi	hi	=	hi
16	mid	hi	hi	hi	mid	lo	mid	=	hi
17	lo	hi	hi	mid	high	mid	high	=	hi

In Table 1, the first column presents the number of the property as listed in (1). The second column ranks the property for quirkiness, or cross-linguistic scarcity. Whereas some properties are of high quirkiness, rare or unattested outside the Mekong-Mamberamo area, other properties are of lower quirkiness, occurring frequently outside the Mekong-Mamberamo area as well as in it; all else being equal, properties of high quirkiness provide stronger evidence for the Mekong-Mamberamo area than their counterparts of lower quirkiness. The third column ranks the properties for internal consistency within the Mekong-Mamberamo area, distinguishing between properties of high consistency, exhibited by most or all languages within the Mekong-Mamberamo area, and others of lower consistency, exhibited by a smaller proportion of such languages; again, all else being equal, properties of higher consistency will provide stronger support for the Mekong-Mamberamo area than those of lower consistency.

The next five columns provide measures for how distinctively the property in question demarcates the boundary between the Mekong-Mamberamo area and each of the five neighbouring linguistic areas. Ideally, a given property would provide a distinctive demarcation of the Mekong-Mamberamo in all five directions, that is to say, it would be completely absent from all five neighbouring linguistic areas; however, the facts are rarely so neat, and in many cases the property in question may only demarcate the Mekong-Mamberamo area in a subset of the five relevant directions, while exhibiting "leakage" in the remaining directions, with languages outside the area also exhibiting the property in question. Once again, all else being equal, the more directions strongly demarcated by the property, the better it is as a diagnostic for the Mekong-Mamberamo linguistic area. The next and penultimate column presents a rough characterization of the internal geographical pattern exhibited by the property in question, making reference to three sub-regions: W(est), encompassing Mainland Southeast Asia, C(entral), covering western Nusantara, and E(ast), including eastern Nusantara and western New Guinea. While a "=" sign suggests that the property in question is distributed more or less equally across the area, the ">" symbol represents a cline; for example, "W>e" indicates that a property occurs more frequently in western parts of the area than in eastern parts. Similarly, the saddle-like pattern discussed at the end of Section 1 above is indicated as "W>c<E". Finally, the last column provides an indication of how extensive the empirical coverage is. Whereas in many cases, the property in question is based on an extensive cross-linguistic survey examining a large number of languages in the Mekong-Mamberamo area and worldwide, in some instances, for various mostly practical reasons, the property is posited on the basis of a smaller and possibly insufficient sample of languages, in which case the attribution of the feature to the Mekong-Mamberamo linguistic area must remain partly conjectural and in need of further empirical examination.[4]

---

[4] The areal claims made in this paper rely on the impressionistic "eyeballing" of maps, while making no use of statistical tests to determine whether the purportedly observed geographical patterns are statistically significant. In part, at least, this is because I remain unconvinced that many of the statistical methods currently on offer provide solutions to problems arising from the unique one-off nature of geographical areas and associated language-contact scenarios, which call into question some of the assumptions on which many such tests are based. For example, in the case at hand, that of a region stretching from Southeast Asia through Nusantara and into western New Guinea, there is no other part of the world with a comparable array of ecological and historical characteristics that can serve as a "control case" in order to test the statistical significance of the observed clustering of linguistic properties that constitutes the Mekong-Mamberamo area. However, the sceptical statistically-minded reader is invited to view

In the remainder of Section 2, which comprises the bulk of this paper, we examine, in turn, each of the 17 properties, showing how they join forces in order to define and delineate the Mekong-Mamberamo linguistic area.[5]

2.1 The passing gesture

The first Mekong-Mamberamo property is non-verbal in nature, the *passing gesture*, discussed in more detail in Gil (in preparation b). The passing gesture is made by a person while walking through what is perceived of as the personal space of one or more persons to whom the gesture is addressed. While walking, the gesturer bends the top half of the body forward, and—in the prototypical variant of the gesture—extends the right forearm forward, with the hand oriented vertically, palm facing inward, as though forging a path through an imaginary thicket. The performance of the gesture may range from highly theatrical to so subtle as to be almost imperceptible to an outside observer unfamiliar with it.

One typical situation in which the gesture is performed is when the gesturer is forced to pass through a group of people who are standing together and possibly talking to one another. Another typical context involves the gesturer entering a room and passing in front of a number of people who are sitting on the floor with their backs against the wall and facing inwards. As a gesture of politeness, the passing gesture often involves an expression of deference by a

---

the results of this paper as hypotheses in need of confirmation or refutation via appropriate statistical methods.

5 A sceptic might suggest that, given the potential infinitude of linguistic properties, any arbitrarily-delineated geographical region may be associated with its own tailor-made set of 17 distinctive properties, thereby rendering the proposed Mekong-Mamberamo area vacuous. However, the burden of proof is on the sceptic, and there is good reason to believe that such a quest would be unlikely to succeed. Whereas some of the 17 properties are of a marginal and idiosyncratic nature, others, such as basic word order, isolating word structure and low grammatical-morpheme density pertain to core aspects of grammar and correlate with additional properties, thereby governing much of the overall architecture of the language. I propose the following thought experiment to assuage the sceptic's concern. Present a linguist with three randomly selected languages, one from the New Guinea Bird's Head, one from Mainland Southeast Asia, and one from South Asia, and ask the linguist which two of the three languages bear a closer resemblance to each other. My prediction is that if the experiment is repeated sufficiently many times, with different languages and different linguists presumably using different criteria, a significant tendency will emerge for the New Guinea Bird's Head and Mainland Southeast Asian languages to be judged as more similar to each other than to the South Asian languages.

socially inferior gesturer towards addressees of higher social status; however, it is also commonly performed amongst equals in more egalitarian societies.

The distribution of the passing gesture, based on an interim sample of 252 languages, is shown in Maps 2 and 3, which make reference to the following feature values and associated colour-coded dots:

(2) *Feature values for passing gesture, Maps 2,3*

a) red: one-handed passing gesture
b) pink: one-handed or similar passing gesture
c) yellow: similar passing gesture
d) grey: no passing gesture

While feature value (2a) refers to the prototypical one-handed passing gesture described above, feature values (2b) and (2c) define variations on the theme. In some cases, the bending forward is accompanied by a different hand gesture, often a clasping together of both hands held pressed against the lower abdomen; such cases are characterized as involving a "similar" passing gesture. While feature value (2b) allows for the passing gesture to be either one-handed or similar, feature value (2c) rules out the one-handed version of the passing gesture, allowing only for other similar versions. Finally, feature value (2d) represents the case in which the passing gesture is absent.

Maps 2 and 3 reveal a remarkable areal distribution. The passing gesture is overwhelmingly present throughout the Mekong-Mamberamo area but totally unattested elsewhere, except for five extensions of the Mekong-Mamberamo area: one east into New Guinea, another north through the Philippines up to Japan, yet another into eastern parts of South Asia, and the remaining two associated with migrations of Austronesian-speaking populations east into Oceania and west to Madagascar.

Within the Mekong-Mamberamo area, the passing gesture is almost universally present in the Nusantara and western New Guinea regions, where the one-handed version is the rule. The only exceptions in my current sample are Waijewa (an Austronesian language of the island of Sumba in Nusa Tenggara) and Ujir (an Austronesian language of the Aru islands off the south coast of New Guinea), which lack the passing gesture. Mainland Southeast Asia presents a somewhat more mixed picture, with the one-handed version often occurring alongside other versions, as well as some languages apparently lacking a passing gesture, including Maniq and Jahai (Aslian, Austroasiatic) in the Malay peninsula, Bisu and Lahu (Burmese-Lolo, Sino-Tibetan) in the Mainland Southeast Asia heartland, and Hlai (Tai-Kadai) in Hainan.

In the Nusantara region, the one-handed passing gesture is sometimes perceived as being originally or prototypically Javanese, in acknowledgement of the highly stratified nature of Javanese society, their reputed refinedness, and the influence that they have exerted across the archipelago over many centuries. However, there is good reason to believe that the passing gesture predates the rise and spread of Javanese culture. Significantly, the passing gesture is widespread amongst populations of eastern Nusantara and New Guinea who are culturally Melanesian and in some cases also speakers of non-Austronesian languages. To be sure, Javanese and now also modern Indonesian culture have exerted an ever-increasing influence across all the areas now under Indonesian political control, and indeed, in some of the languages of western New Guinea, the passing gesture would seem to be a recent innovation associated with the spread of Javanese/Indonesian culture. Thus, Lourens de Vries (pc) notes that in the course of his many years of field work amongst the Korowai (of the Awju-Dumut branch of the Trans-New-Guinea family) in the southern lowlands of central New Guinea, he has observed the passing gesture being introduced by Indonesian officials and migrants and subsequently adopted by the local population. Similarly, Alpius and Niko Kobepa (pc) suggest that the passing gesture was only recently introduced into Mee (of the Wissel Lakes-Kemandoga branch of the Trans-New-Guinea family, spoken in the Paniai lakes region on the fringes of the Mekong-Mamberamo region). However, in other parts of western New Guinea, the passing gesture would seem to be of greater antiquity. At my own field site, on the island of Roon in the Cenderawasih Bay, the one-handed passing gesture is ubiquitous amongst speakers, old and young, of the eponymous language Roon (Austronesian), who from a cultural point of view appear to be solidly Melanesian, a world apart from Javanese and other Nusantara civilizations. Similarly, amongst the Yali (of the Dani branch of the Trans-New-Guinea family), in the central highlands, whose first contact with the outside world was only in the 1940s, I have also observed the passing gesture being used; and a member of the Yali community, Kristian Walianggen (pc) claims that it is an "old custom", not a product of modern Indonesian influences. These observations suggest that the one-handed passing gesture has been around in at least parts of western New Guinea for centuries at least. But the strongest support for the indigenous nature of the passing gesture in western New Guinea, predating recent Javanese and Indonesian influences, derives from its presence further to the east, in several languages of Papua New Guinea, such as Kómnzo (a language of the Morehead and Upper Maro Rivers branch of the Trans-New-Guinea family spoken in the southwestern lowlands), Tabare (of the Chimbu branch of the Trans-New-Guinea family, spoken in the highlands region), and Bargam (of the Madang branch of the Trans-New-Guinea family, spoken in the north coastal region). Thus, it may be concluded that the passing gesture was present in at least parts of the eastern Mekong-Mamberamo area prior to the spread of Javanese and Indonesian cultures.

Outside the Mekong-Mamberamo area, the passing gesture extends east into New Guinea (as noted above), northwest somewhat sporadically into eastern parts of South Asia, as well as north into the Philippines and thence into Japan. In view of the quirkiness of the passing gesture and its absence from other parts of the world, these extensions are unlikely to be due to chance; instead they would seem to be a result of presumably ancient contact and diffusion. Further to the east, various similar versions of the passing gesture extend into the Pacific. The most likely explanation for its presence in the Pacific is that it was brought by the original Austronesian settlers, though its occurrence in the non-Austronesian language Kuot spoken on the Papua New Guinea island of New Ireland may be more ancient. If indeed the passing gesture was brought into the Pacific by the original Austronesian settlers, this would suggest that it was present in western New Guinea at a time prior to the beginning of the expansion into the Pacific, that is to say, some 3,500 years ago. Finally, to the west, the one-handed passing gesture is found across the Indian Ocean in Madagascar. Its presence in Malagasy suggests that the one-handed passing gesture must have been present in Borneo when the original settlers left for Madagascar, around 1,500 years ago (Dahl 1977), though subsequent work by Adelaar (1995) raises the possibility of later contacts. In summary, the occurrence of the passing gesture in geographical outliers in the Pacific and Indian Oceans settled by speakers of Austronesian languages tells us that its presence in the core Mekong-Mamberamo area must be ancient.

2.2 Repeated dental clicks expressing amazement

The second property is also of a para-linguistic nature, involving the usage of click sounds. Whereas in English, dental clicks, spelled either *tut tut* (in the UK) or *tsk tsk* (in the USA), are typically used to express negative feelings such as impatience, regret, or disapproval, in Mekong-Mamberamo languages, repeated dental clicks are commonly used to express amazement, frequently associated with a positive affective state.

Gil (2005d) presents a worldwide survey of paralinguistic click sounds, distinguishing between two main kinds of usages: *logical*, expressing meanings such as 'yes' and 'no', typically in response to a yes/no question, and *affective*, expressing mental states such as impatience, regret, disapproval, amazement, and others. Gil (in preparation a) provides a more fine-grained picture, with separate maps for logical and affective clicks, focusing in on particularly important form-usage pairs, including repeated dental clicks expressing amazement. The map for affective clicks, based on an interim sample of 174 languages, is reproduced here in Maps 4 and 5, making reference to the following feature values and associated colour-coded dots:

(3) *Feature values for Repeated Dental Clicks Expressing Amazement, Maps 4,5*

a) red: repeated dental clicks expressing amazement
b) yellow: other clicks with other affective usages
c) grey: no clicks with affective usages

As evident in Maps 4 and 5, the distribution of repeated dental clicks expressing amazement reveals a striking areal distribution. Within the Mekong-Mamberamo area, repeated dental clicks expressing amazement are almost universally present in western New Guinea, for example Meyah (East-Bird's Head family) and Roon (of the South-Halmahera-West-New-Guinea branch of Austronesian) and in the Nusantara archipelago, for example Uab Meto (an Austronesian language of Timor) and Sundanese. However, they are rather less common in Mainland Southeast Asia, where they occur in some languages, such as Oi (of the Bahnaric branch of Austroasiatic), Kammu (Palaung-Khmuic, Austroasiatic) and Pnar (Khasian, Austroasiatic) but are absent in many others. Thus, within the Mekong-Mamberamo area, repeated dental clicks expressing amazement would appear to present an east-to-west cline similar to that observed in the preceding subsection for the passing gesture.

Following are examples of repeated dental clicks expressing amazement in naturalistic speech from two dialects of Malay/Indonesian spoken in east-central Sumatra and North Maluku respectively:[6]

---

[6] Most of the examples of naturalistic speech cited in this paper are taken from the Max Planck Institute for Evolutionary Anthropology Jakarta Field Station corpus; for such examples, the unique ID number of the utterance is cited as a reference.

(4) Tanjung Raden Malay
Ais kau, tıkʊs bsa? nian, ampʊne ck ck ck ck.
EXCL 2SG mouse big very forgive:ASSOC AMAZEMENT
'Wow, what a big rat, oh my God!'
(JFS: 135826153701201105)

(5) Ternate Malay
Orang kalo lia kita tu dong bilang
person TOP see 1SG DEM.DIST 3PL say
"hmm, ck ck ck, sambiki, sambiki bajalang."
EXCL AMAZEMENT pumpkin pumpkin NON.PAT: walk
'When people see me they say "Wow, a pumpkin, a pumpkin walking"'
(JFS: 125366131843220603, 737937132011220603)

In the above examples, the surrounding context provides a good feel for the kind of contexts in which repeated dental clicks typically occur. The use of *ck* to represent a dental click follows the conventionalized Indonesian spelling, as evidenced in written examples such as the following, from an online blog providing tips for web designers:[7]

(6) Colloquial Indonesian
HeBaT..Mirip banGet dg AsLinya....ck ck ck !!!
Hebat, mirip banget dengan aslinya, ck ck ck
great resemble very with original:ASSOC AMAZEMENT
'Great. it really resembles the original!'
(http://ecaknyo.blogspot.de/2009/09/hebatmirip-banget-dg-aslinyack-ck-ck.html (accessed 24 July 2013))

As evident in Maps 4 and 5, the distribution of repeated dental clicks spills over into central and eastern New Guinea and to a lesser extent also into Aus-

---

[7] Examples of naturalistic written-language cited in this paper—the above example, plus examples (32) and (33) below—are presented with the observed spelling in the first line, and a more normalized orthography in the second line. In example (6) above, the actual spelling reflects the loose orthographic conventions of so-called *Bahasa Alay*, commonly used in blogs, Facebook, texting, and so forth, which involves the use of various abbreviations, and also "camel case", a seemingly random alternation of lower and upper case letters.

tralia and parts of nearer Oceania. However, in other directions, namely South Asia, Northeast Asia, and Taiwan and the Philippines, repeated dental clicks expressing amazement are unattested. Indeed, repeated dental clicks expressing amazement are unattested anywhere else in the world, with the exception of a small pocket in parts of Eastern Europe.[8] Thus, repeated dental clicks provide a fine reflection of the Mekong-Mamberamo linguistic area.

2.3 Conventionalized greeting with 'Where'

First-time visitors to the region are often puzzled and bemused when people continually ask "Where are you going?" What new visitors may fail to appreciate is that such questions are merely a conventionalized greeting, not to be taken any more literally than the English *How do you do?*

The 'Where Are You Going' conventionalized greeting is discussed in more detail in Gil (in preparation c). The geographical distribution of the 'Where Are You Going' and related greetings, based on an interim sample of 363 languages, is presented in Maps 6 and 7, which make reference to the following feature values and associated colour-coded dots:

(7) *Feature values for 'Where Are You Going', Maps 6,7*

a) red: directional conventionalized greeting with 'where'
b) yellow: non-directional conventionalized greeting with 'where'
c) grey: no conventionalized greeting with 'where'

Feature value (7a) refers to the 'Where Are You Going?' greeting and a common variant, 'Where are you coming from?': languages exhibiting this fea-

---

8 Some speakers of American English also report the use of repeated dental clicks expressing amazement, though a majority of speakers who I have consulted are not familiar with such a usage, and would only associate repeated dental clicks with negative affective states. The use of repeated dental clicks to express amazement may have entered American English from Yiddish, which is one of the eastern European languages shown in Map 4 to have such clicks. Some speakers of European languages that have repeated dental clicks to express amazement feel that this usage is derived, through irony, from a more basic usage expressing negative affect, not unlike the way in which words such as *bad* may be used, in current slang, as exclamations expressing positive affective states. However, there is no evidence to suggest that the much more widespread usage of repeated dental clicks to express amazement in Mekong-Mamberamo languages involves any such irony.

ture value make use of either or both of these questions as a conventionalized greeting, with the expectation of a vague and uninformative response. Feature value (7b) refers to a less-common variant, where the conventionalized greeting is a simple 'Where Are You?', with no expression or implication of any directionality. And feature value (7c) refers to the absence of any conventionalized greeting containing a question word 'where'.

As evident in Maps 6 and 7, directional conventionalized greetings with 'where' are characteristic of the Mekong-Mamberamo linguistic area, as in the following examples:

(8) Vietnamese
     Đi   đâu?
     go   where
     'Where are you going?'

(9) Jakarta Indonesian
     Mau   ke   mana?
     want to   where
     'Where are you going?'

(10) Iha
     topon-na   whe-angge
     where-ALL   go-IRR
     'Where are you going?'
     (Mark Donohue pc)

For the most part, use of these greetings is restricted to outdoor contexts where there is at least a perceived potential for the interlocutor to be going somewhere, though in some cases such greetings can also be heard indoors. The expected response to the greeting is non-committal and uninformative. For example, in Jakarta Indonesian, one might answer with *main-main* (DISTR~play 'playing around' or 'nothing much'), *jalan-jalan* (DISTR~walk 'going for a walk'), and other similar responses.

Within the Mekong-Mamberamo area, directional conventionalized greetings with 'where' are the rule, with only isolated exceptions. Perhaps the most notable of these is a cluster of languages of the Alor-Pantar group, including Kamang, Kaera and Wersing, which have no such greetings; however, conventionalized greetings with 'where' are present in the related Timor languages of the Timor-Alor-Pantar family, including Bunaq, Fataluku and Makasae, as well as in nearby Austronesian languages such as Lamalera, Waima'a and Leti.

Outside the Mekong-Mamberamo area, languages with and without directional conventionalized greetings with 'where' are both widespread. Worldwide, of the 363 languages in the interim sample, 237, or 65%, have directional conventionalized greetings with 'where'.

It must be acknowledged that none of the boundaries of the Mekong-Mamberamo region are clearly demarcated by the 'Where are you going?' greeting. In South Asia, directional conventionalized greetings with 'where' extend into the Himalayas, while in North Asia, they also occur in some languages. An interesting pattern is in evidence in the East Asian Pacific rim, where directional conventionalized greetings with 'where' are the rule throughout the Philippines, occurring also in some of the languages of Taiwan as well as the southwesternmost islands of the Ryukyu archipelago of Japan.[9] In central and eastern New Guinea, directional conventionalized greetings with 'where' occur interspersed with languages lacking such greetings, while in Australia such greetings are the rule—as is also the case for the Austronesian languages of the Pacific. In summary, then, although the 'Where are you going?' greeting occurs outside the Mekong-Mamberamo area as well as within it, its frequency drops off noticeably in at least three directions: west into South Asia, north into Northeast Asia, and east into New Guinea. Accordingly, the directional conventionalized greeting with 'where' may be said to provide further support, albeit of a somewhat less striking nature, for the Mekong-Mamberamo linguistic area.

2.4 'Eye Day' > 'Sun' lexicalization

Mata Hari will be familiar to readers versed in early 20th century European history as the stage name of the renowned Dutch dancer and courtesan executed by the French during World War I on charges of being a German spy. Her name comes from Indonesian, where *mata hari* 'sun' is actually a left-headed compound, formed from *mata* 'eye' and *hari* 'day'.

---

[9] The Grammar Atlas of Japanese Dialects (National Institute for Japanese Language 2006) maps the distribution of the 'Where are you going?' conventionalized greeting across the islands of Japan; essentially it occurs in the southwesternmost islands of the Ryukyu archipelago and nowhere else. The Japanese version of this map thus provides a fine example of how an isogloss large enough to demarcate an entire linguistic macro-area can nevertheless cross-cut a closely-related set of language varieties.

But the *mata hari* compound is not unique to Indonesian. Urban (2010) presents a cross-linguistic study of lexicalizations in which the word for 'sun' is formed from the words for 'eye' and 'day', or from clearly related combinations such as Vietnamese *mặt trời* (face sky 'face of the sky'). From a worldwide sample of 214 languages, augmented with an additional sample from Southeast Asia and Oceania, he finds that such lexicalizations occur across Mainland Southeast Asia and the Nusantara archipelago, as well as in areas to which the Austronesians migrated out of Nusantara, namely Madagascar and the Pacific. In contrast, such lexicalizations are completely unattested in the rest of the world. Thus, the distribution of 'eye day' > 'sun' lexicalizations presents a very clear Mekong-Mamberamo pattern.

In Mainland Southeast Asia, Urban adduces examples of 'eye day' > 'sun' lexicalizations from Austroasiatic and Tai-Kadai languages, but does not find any examples in the Sino-Tibetan and Hmong-Mien families. In the Nusantara region, 'eye day' > 'sun' lexicalizations occur primarily in Austronesian languages, though one non-Austronesian language is also cited as displaying this lexicalization pattern, the North Halmaheran language Sahu. Whereas the passing gesture and repeated dental clicks expressing amazement exhibit an east-to-west cline, diminishing in frequency from western New Guinea through Nusantara to Mainland Southeast Asia, 'eye day' > 'sun' lexicalizations display a mirror-image pattern, diminishing in frequency from west to east. Within the Nusantara region, Urban shows that such "west-east skewing" is statistically significant. The west-to-east cline for 'eye day' > 'sun' lexicalizations culminates in the absence, so far, of any attestations from the western New Guinea mainland.

Perhaps the most striking support for the areal Mekong-Mamberamo character of 'eye day' > 'sun' lexicalizations derives from their complete absence from the languages of Taiwan, the Austronesian homeland, and those of the Philippines, into which Austronesian languages first spread, and from which they continued to spread into the Nusantara archipelago. As argued by Urban, this makes it unlikely that 'eye day' > 'sun' lexicalizations can be reconstructed for proto-Austronesian, and thus unlikely also that their presence in both Austronesian and Austroasiatic may be due either to a potential deep genealogical relation between Austronesian and Austroasiatic, or, alternatively, to ancient contact, on the Asian mainland, between possible precursors of proto-Austronesian and proto-Austroasiatic. In order to account for the geographical distribution of 'eye day' > 'sun' lexicalizations, Urban proposes two possible contact scenarios. The first involves borrowing from one or more Western-Malayo-Polynesian languages into Austroasiatic ones. The second involves the adoption of such lexicalizations by incoming speakers of Western-Malayo-

Polynesian languages from a now-extinct Austroasiatic substrate in western Nusantara. In Section 3 below it is suggested that a version of the latter, substrate scenario might be able to account for the presence of Mekong-Mamberamo properties such as 'eye day' > 'sun' lexicalizations in the languages of Nusantara, with the qualification that the now-extinct substrate languages need not necessarily have been Austroasiatic—many probably belonged to other, now completely extinct, linguistic families.

2.5 d/t Place-of-articulation asymmetry

The phonemic inventory of Malay/Indonesian has what seems for the most part to be a fairly straightforward system of oral stops, distinguishing four places of articulation (labial, coronal, palatal and velar) and two manners of articulation (unvoiced and voiced). However, there is one irregularity to the otherwise neat and symmetric pattern. Whereas the unvoiced coronal stop is dental, the voiced coronal stop is alveolar:

(11) *Malay/Indonesian oral stops*

```
p  t̪      c  k
t      d  j  g
```

The above asymmetry is not unique to Malay/Indonesian. Donohue (2009) presents a detailed survey of what he calls "dental discrepancies" in a sample of 1691 languages of the Austronesian world plus Mainland Southeast Asia, New Guinea and Australia, while the Donohue, Hetherington and McElvenny (2012) database maps dental discrepancies worldwide. A phonemic inventory is said to exhibit a dental discrepancy if there is a distinction between manner of articulation of stops in at least some places of articulation, and if, in addition, coronal stops of different manner of articulation differ also with respect to place of articulation. For the purposes of the survey, it does not matter whether the distinction is purely phonetic or bears phonological consequences and may thus be said to be phonemic. A further distinction is made between "prototypical" discrepancies, in which the stop with greater VOT (Voice Onset Time) is articulated more to the front than the other coronal stop, and "non-prototypical" discrepancies in which the stop with smaller VOT has the more anterior articulation. As evident in (11) above, Malay/Indonesian exhibits a prototypical dental discrepancy.

Sprouse, Solé and Ohala (2008) propose an articulatory-phonetic motivation for the development of prototypical dental discrepancies. Nevertheless, such asymmetries occur in a mere 1% or so of the world languages in the database of Maddieson (1984), though it is likely that this figure is smaller than the actual one due to under-reporting.

As shown in the Donohue, Hetherington and McElvenny map, prototypical dental discrepancies occur almost exclusively in two large regions, one encompassing much of equatorial Africa, the second consisting of the Mekong-Mamberamo area plus spillover into eastern parts of South Asia, Taiwan, and Papua New Guinea, Solomon Islands and Vanuatu. Some of the Mekong-Mamberamo languages exhibiting prototypical dental discrepancies include Palaung, Khmer, Sundanese, Palu'e (a Central-Eastern Malayo-Polynesian language of Nusa Tenggara), Kesui (a Central-Eastern Malayo-Polynesian language of Maluku) and Bauzi (an East Geelvink Bay language spoken near the mouth of the Mamberamo river). Although only a small minority of Mekong-Mamberamo languages have prototypical dental discrepancies, their complete absence from large expanses of the rest of the world makes it possible to characterize them as a Mekong-Mamberamo property.

Within the Austronesian family, the diachrony of dental discrepancies is disputed. While Haudricourt (1965) and Ross (1992) reconstruct a prototypical dental discrepancy for proto-Austronesian, Donohue (2009) considers it to be an areal feature adopted by Austronesian languages as they moved south into Nusantara, attributing it to influence from Australian languages, which typically possess phonemically distinct dental and laminal stops. However, Donohue's scenario fails to account for the presence of dental discrepancies in the Formosan language Pazeh, as well as two other languages in the straits separating Taiwan from the Philippines, Yami and Ivatan. Regardless of whether a d/t place-of-articulation asymmetry is reconstructible for proto-Austronesian, its presence in contemporary non-Austronesian languages ranging from Palaung to Bauzi would seem to suggest that it was an areal feature present in at least some of the pre-Austronesian languages of the Nusantara archipelago into which Austronesian languages spread.

2.6 Numeral classifiers

While the preceding five properties are associated with diverse linguistic domains, the remaining twelve Mekong-Mamberamo properties all involve grammar proper, that is to say, morphology and syntax.

Numeral classifiers are commonly cited as one of the most characteristic properties of Mainland Southeast Asian languages (Nichols 1992: 132-133; Bisang 1999; Aikhenvald 2000: 121-124; Comrie 2007; Enfield 2011 and others). In many Mainland Southeast Asian languages, a numeral cannot occur in direct construction with a noun, even when the noun is of high semantic individuation, e.g. Cantonese *$saam^{55}$ $piŋ^{11}$-guo^{35} (three apple); instead, the presence of a sortal numeral classifier is required, e.g. $saam^{55}$ go^{33} $piŋ^{11}$-guo^{35} (three CLF apple). In contrast, in many of the languages of Nusantara, in a numeral-noun construction, a sortal classifier is available, but its presence is optional, e.g. Minangkabau *tigo (buah) cubadak* (three (CLF) jackfruit). Gil (2005c) maps the distribution of numeral classifiers worldwide, distinguishing between three feature values, depending on whether, in a numeral-noun construction in which the noun is highly individuated, a sortal numeral classifier is (a) absent, as in English; (b) optional, as in Minangkabau; or (c) obligatory, as in Cantonese.

As evident from the map in Gil (2005c), numeral classifiers show a clear Mekong-Mamberamo distribution. While within the Mekong-Mamberamo area numeral classifiers are the rule, elsewhere they occur in just a handful of smaller regions. As is the case for some of the other properties considered here, the distribution of numeral classifiers leaks out of the Mekong-Mamberamo area into several adjacent regions. Into the Himalayas, the leakage resembles that seen above for conventionalized greetings with 'where'. Another leakage is north into coastal Northwest Asia. Finally, like many of the other Mekong-Mamberamo properties, numeral classifiers are brought into the Pacific by the expansion of Austronesian languages.

The distinction between optional and obligatory numeral classifiers made in Gil (2005c) highlights a saddle effect attributable to the intrusion of Austronesian languages into Nusantara. The obligatoriness of numeral classifiers in most of Mainland Southeast Asia is mirrored by a corresponding obligatoriness in the eastern reaches of the Mekong-Mamberamo area, including languages such as Sawu and Kambera from Nusa Tenggara, Alune and Taba from Maluku, and Tehit and Abun from the New Guinea Bird's Head; this latter area of obligatory numeral classifiers extends out into Micronesia. However, in between these two peaks of obligatoriness is a relative trough, encompassing most of western Nusantara, in which a majority of the languages have optional numeral classifiers, as is the case for Minangkabau above. Key to understanding this pattern is the observation that numeral classifiers are unattested in the Austronesian languages of Taiwan and the Philippines. What this suggests, then, is that the spread of Austronesian from the Philippines into Nusantara involved Austronesian languages without numeral classifiers coming into contact with now-extinct non-Austronesian languages with numeral classifiers, as a result of which the Austronesian languages assimilated to the Mekong-Mamberamo profile but in an often incomplete fashion, resulting in the typically optional use of numeral classifiers.

2.7 Verby adjectives

Stassen (2005) maps the ways in which predicative adjectives are encoded, distinguishing between two types: verbal, in which predicative adjectives are encoded similarly to predicative verbs, and nonverbal, in which they are not. For example, whereas in Minangkabau *Ali baiak* (Ali kind) and *Ali pai* (Ali go) exhibit identical morphosyntax, involving the simple juxtaposition of a bare adjectival or verbal predicate to a subject noun, the corresponding English sentences *Ali is kind* and *Ali has gone* instantiate quite different construction types. This distinction gives rise to a three-way language typology, represented in Stassen's map with three feature values, distinguishing between languages in which the coding of predicative adjectives is (a) verbal; (b) nonverbal; or (c) mixed, that is to say, combining elements of verbal and nonverbal coding.

Stassen's map shows that within the Mekong-Mamberamo area, an overwhelming majority of languages have verby adjectives, with just a sprinkling of the mixed type in eastern Nusantara. In contrast, outside the Mekong-Mamberamo area, all three types are widespread. Noticeably, languages with verby adjectives are absent from South Asia, central and eastern New Guinea, and Australia; in these three directions, then, the boundaries of the Mekong-Mamberamo area are clearly demarcated. However, to the north, verby adjectives are the rule in the Philippines, and are also found in some Northeast Asian languages, while to the east, there is the usual Austronesian leakage of verby adjectives into the Pacific. In sum though, verby adjectives can be considered characteristic of the Mekong-Mamberamo linguistic area.

2.8 Basic SVO word order

Dryer (2005a) maps basic word order across the world's languages, distinguishing between the six logically possible orderings of S(ubject), V(erb) and O(bject), with a seventh feature value for languages lacking a readily-identifiable dominant order.

Inspection of Dryer's map reveals that within the Mekong-Mamberamo area, SVO word order is predominant. What is perhaps most striking is that although

SVO word order is widespread cross-linguistically, all of the neighbouring linguistic areas are associated with other word orders. Thus, South Asia, Northwest Asia, and mainland central and eastern New Guinea are predominantly SOV, while the Philippines is largely verb-initial. Only in Australia is there a significant number of SVO languages, though even here, SVO is a minority alongside SOV and languages with no dominant order. Thus, basic SVO order is one of the properties providing the most faithful delineation of the boundaries of the Mekong-Mamberamo linguistic area.

A somewhat more fine-grained examination of Dryer's map reveals a number of intrusions of other word orders, from outside, into the Mekong-Mamberamo area. In Mainland Southeast Asia, SOV word order, associated primarily with Tibeto-Burman languages, makes inroads into northern and western parts of the region; this is clearly associated with the migration of Tibeto-Burman speakers into the area.

A somewhat more complex picture is in evidence in eastern Nusantara, which contains two pockets of SOV languages, associated exclusively with non-Austronesian languages. One, represented in Dryer's map by Tobelo, is constituted by languages of the North Halmahera family. A second, not represented in Dryer's sample, is made up by languages of the Timor-Alor-Pantar family. In contrast to the Tibeto-Burman case, here it is less clear whether these two pockets of SOV word order are genealogically connected to the solidly SOV mainland of central and eastern New Guinea. Although some scholars have attempted to include the North Halmahera family within a larger West Papuan family, and others have suggested that the Timor-Alor-Pantar family forms part of the larger Trans-New-Guinea family, neither of these proposals have gained general acceptance. Moreover, a putative West Papuan family containing North Halmaheran languages would link these languages to others in the New Guinea Bird's Head that are SVO.

Moving east to New Guinea, the southern Bird's Head, Bomberai peninsula and Bird's Neck and Cenderawasih Bay regions contain a mix of SVO and SOV languages. Amongst the latter are some, such as Inanwatan, Iha and Mairasi, which have been assigned by some scholars to the Trans-New-Guinea family and which therefore might plausibly be considered as intrusive, though more conservative classifications would have these languages belonging to smaller families located entirely within the region. However, the remainder of the Bird's Head is occupied by languages that are non-Austronesian, belonging to a half dozen or so families not demonstrably related to one another, and which are solidly SVO. Some of the SVO languages of the Bird's Head included in Dryer's sample are Abun, Maybrat, Hatam and Meyah.

The fact that most of the languages of New Guinea are SOV has led several scholars to suggest that the SVO languages of the Bird's Head must have undergone shift from an earlier SOV word order, presumably under the influence of Austronesian; see, for example Foley (2000: 364, 2010: 805-806) and Klamer, Reesink and van Staden (2008: 113-115). However, as argued here, the Bird's Head is part of the Mekong-Mamberamo area, that is to say, Bird's Head languages share many linguistic properties with the languages of Nusantara and Mainland Southeast Asia, and SVO word order is just one of these properties. Thus, from an areal perspective, there is nothing out of the ordinary in the presence of SVO languages in the New Guinea Bird's Head. Indeed, in making this same point, Donohue (2005b) notes the presence of other SVO languages further into central New Guinea, and suggests that there might have been more such languages prior to the expansion of the large SOV Trans-New-Guinea family. Moreover, as pointed out by Donohue, there is no evidence that the incoming Austronesian languages themselves were SVO; they were more likely to have exhibited their original verb-initial word order still observable in Taiwan and the Philippines.[10]

More generally, as suggested by Dryer's map, it is the Austronesian languages that changed to SVO as they spread southwards from the Philippines into the Mekong-Mamberamo area. The Philippines, as mentioned above, is solidly verb-initial, and in many parts of western Nusantara, verb-initial languages can also be found interspersed amongst the SVO languages of the region. For example, in Sumatra, SVO word order is found to the south, in languages such as Lampung and Enggano, while verb-initial word order is found further to the north, in languages such as Toba Batak and Nias; in yet other languages, SVO and verb-initial orders coexist with neither one being dominant, as is the case for Minangkabau and Acehnese. Similarly, in the southeast arm of Sulawesi, SVO, verb-initial and mixed word orders occur side by side, in Muna, Tukang Besi and Bajau respectively. However, in other parts of Nusantara, SVO word order is the norm. The emerging picture is one in which verb-

---

10 The scenario being described here does not rule out the possibility that some or all Bird's Head languages might have been SOV in the past; it merely suggests that one argument commonly offered in support of this claim does not hold water. If future work were to establish that some or all of the Bird's Head languages are related to those of North Halmahera within a larger West Papuan family, then some form of word order change will have had to have taken place. For example, an SOV Proto-West-Papuan might have changed to SVO in the languages of the Bird's Head; alternatively, an SVO Proto-West-Papuan might have changed to SOV in the languages of North Halmahera; or various other more complex scenarios involving word order change might have played out.

initial Austronesian languages moving south out of the Philippines gradually assimilated to a previously existing SVO word order; while in some regions the assimilation was complete, in other regions it was only partially effected. Resulting from this is a saddle-like pattern resembling that observed previously for numeral classifiers, with the Mekong-Mamberamo property of SVO word order most clearly evident in the Mainland Southeast Asia and Bird's Head extremities, but in somewhat more attenuated fashion in some central parts of the Mekong-Mamberamo area.

2.9 Iamitive perfects

The perfect is a grammatical category associated with events that take place before a temporal reference point but are still relevant at that point. Closely related to the perfect is the *iamitive* category (from the Latin *iam* 'already'), introduced by Dahl and Wälchli (2013). As described in Olsson (2013: 43), the iamitive combines two different features, "the notion of a 'new situation' that holds after a transition", which it shares with words such as *already*, and "the consequences that this situation has at reference time for the participants in the speech event", which it has in common with the perfect.

Examples (12) -14) below show iamitives in three languages spanning the Mekong-Mamberamo area, Vietnamese *rồi*, Minangkabau *alah* and Roon *kwar*:

(12)　Vietnamese

　　a.　*Sự　ăn　rồi*
　　　　su　eat　PFCT
　　　　'Su has eaten'

　　b.　*Sự　no　rồi*
　　　　su　full　PFCT
　　　　'Su is already full'

(13)　Minangkabau

　　a.　*Ujang　alah　pai*
　　　　Ujang　PFCT　go
　　　　'Ujang has gone'

    b. *Ujang alah gaek*
       Ujang PFCT old
       'Ujang is already old'

(14) Roon

    a. *Wefur ibur kwar*
       wefur 3SG.ANIM: go.home PFCT
       'Wefur has returned home'

    b. *Wefur ibwa kwar*
       wefur 3SG.ANIM: big PFCT
       'Wefur is already big'

In the (a) sentences in each pair, the iamitive marker occurs in construction with an activity word, and the construction is appropriately translated into English with the present perfect. In contrast, in the (b) sentences, the iamitive marker occurs with a property word, and here, a present-perfect translation into English is impossible; instead, the most appropriate translation is with a present-tense copula plus, optionally, 'already'. Note that for the (b) constructions to be felicitous, the property word must be one that is characteristic of a new situation representing the outcome of a transition over time; if 'full', 'old' and 'big' are replaced by their antonyms 'hungry', 'young' and 'small', the resulting constructions are often strange, anomalous, or require an unusual licensing context. In general, iamitives are distinguished from other perfects by their availability in constructions such as the (b) sentences above, where their meaning is most readily translated with 'already'.

Iamitives are widespread throughout the Mekong-Mamberamo linguistic area. Dahl and Velupillai (2005) provide a map of perfects, in which one of the subtypes is of forms related to 'already' or 'finish', thus overlapping considerably with iamitives. In their 222 language sample, 21 languages have perfects with 'already' or 'finish', of which 11 are in the Mekong-Mamberamo area, and 3 others in a spill-over region extending through New Guinea and into the Pacific. Among the Mekong-Mamberamo languages that they cite with 'already' or 'finish' perfects are Khmer, Sundanese and Buli (a language of the South Halmahera West New Guinea subgroup of Austronesian spoken in Maluku).[11] Dahl and Wälchli (2013) adopt a somewhat different bottom-up approach, proposing a subclassification of perfect markers by means of Multi-Dimensional-Scaling based on a corpus of approximately 950 translations of the New Testament. The first dimension to emerge from their analysis, correlating well with the functional range of the iamitive, presents a striking Mekong-Mamberamo distribution, from Mainland Southeast Asia through Nusantara and into western New Guinea, with no leakage into neighbouring regions with the exception of central and eastern parts of New Guinea. Thus, the iamitive perfect presents a robust characteristic marker of the Mekong-Mamberamo linguistic area.

2.10 'Give' causatives

Another characteristic property of Mekong-Mamberamo languages is the formation of causative constructions by means of a word or affix, one of whose meanings is 'give' or whose etymological source is in a form, one of whose meanings is 'give'. Some examples are given below:

(15) Lao
 man2 haj5 nòòj4 paj3 talaat5
 3BARE give Noi go market
 'He made Noi go to the market'
 (Enfield 2007: 423)

(16) Muarasiberut Mentawai
 Bela akek ngangam
 go.out give sound: CN: POSS.2SG
 'Make your voice come out'
 (JFS 892955143841060208)

---

[11] Donohue, Hetherington and McElvenny (2012) map a larger sample of languages according to the same criteria as Dahl and Velupillai (2005); their 739 language sample contains 92 languages with 'already' or 'finish' perfects, of which 85 are in the Mekong-Mamberamo area or closely adjacent regions.

(17) Roon
Bimbo bye arriya fa rikwan
BIMBO <3SG.ANIM>give fence: 3SG.INAN: DEF for 3SG.INAN: long
'Bimbo lengthened the fence'

Often, the word meaning 'give' is but one of several strategies available within the same language for the formation of causative constructions, of similar or different kinds. Thus, in Lao, in addition to *haj5* 'give' illustrated above, causatives can be formed with *hêt1* 'make', or with a combination of the two, *hêt1-haj5*; similarly, in Roon, in addition to *-be* 'give', causatives can be formed with a frozen causative prefix *fa-*, or, perhaps most commonly, by "zero-conversion" from a non-causative predicate. In addition, the word meaning 'give' may have additional functions, other than that of causativization (and the expression of giving). Thus, in Muarasiberut Mentawai, *akek* 'give' is frequently used also to form applicative constructions, or simply to express high transitivity (as is the case in example (27) below); similarly, in Roon, *-be* 'give' also means 'make' or 'do', and has a variety of other functions, including nominalizer, relativizer, and goal marker.

A number of recent cross-linguistic studies deal with various properties of causative constructions, however, to the best of my knowledge, none offers a systematic comparison of the words or affixes used to form causative constructions, and the other functions associated with such words, or their etymologies. The best source that I am aware of is Heine and Kuteva's (2002) *World Lexicon of Grammaticalization*, which offers three diachronic sources for causative markers, 'do', 'take' and (p.152) 'give'. Examples of causatives with 'give' are provided from six languages, of which three, Vietnamese, Khmer and Thai, are from Mainland Southeast Asia, another, Siroi, from Madang Province in Papua New Guinea, and the remaining two, Luo and Somali, from East Africa. Although suggestive, their sample is insufficient for the drawing of any firm conclusions regarding the worldwide distribution of causatives with 'give'. Thus, in the absence of the requisite systematic cross linguistic survey, the present observations are of a tentative and impressionistic nature, in need of further empirical support.

A rough and ready overview of the languages in the area suggests that causatives with 'give' are common in Mainland Southeast Asia, and can also be found, albeit with apparent decreasing frequency, in Nusantara and into western New Guinea. In Mainland Southeast Asia, in addition to Thai, Khmer and Vietnamese, cited by Heine and Kuteva, causatives with 'give' are attested, among others, in Lahu with *pî* 'give' (Matisoff 1976: 429-430), in Maonan (a language of the Kam-Sui branch of Tai-Kadai spoken in Guizhou province of southern China) with *ʔna: k7* 'give' (Lu 2008: 254), and in several other languages (Jenny this volume). However, in many other languages, particularly those of the Austroasiatic family, causatives with 'give' are infrequent or absent. Moving into Nusantara, the examples are somewhat more sporadic. In Madurese, the causative suffix *-agi* is presumably related to the verb *bagi* 'give'; similarly, in Central Javanese, the causative suffix *-ake* is possibly derived from the verb *kei* 'give'.[12] In Ternate (of the North Halmahera family), *haka* 'give' preceding a verb may impart a causative interpretation, as in *haka hita* 'give see', or 'show' (Hayami-Allen 2001: 190). Further east, in Saweru (which together with Yawa forms a two-language family on the island of Yapen in the Cenderawasih Bay), *awe* 'give' may be used to form causative constructions (Donohue 2001: 329). And in Warembori (of contentious genealogical affiliation,[13] spoken near the mouth of the Mamberamo river), *ore* 'give' may form causative constructions, as in *ore tire* 'give see' or 'show' (Donohue 1999: 38). Finally, it is worth noting that in many dialects of Malay and Indonesian, typically those functioning as contact varieties, a word meaning 'give' is used to form periphrastic causatives; these include *bagi* in Kuala Lumpur Malay, and *kasi* in, among others, Singaporean Bazaar Malay, Kupang Malay and Papuan Malay.

Thus, causatives with 'give' are attested, albeit in a somewhat intermittent fashion, throughout the Mekong-Mamberamo area, with apparently decreasing frequency from west to east. Outside the Mekong-Mamberamo area, however, it is hard to form a clear picture in the absence of a systematic survey. Impressionistically, however, the two most common types of causatives are morphological causatives, in which the causative affix is of unknown provenance, and periphrastic causatives formed from a word meaning 'do' or 'make'. In particular, some combination of these two types would seem to constitute the most common types in South and Northeast Asia, Taiwan and the Philippines, Australia,

---

12 Although Javanese is not particularly closely related to Mentawai within the Malayo-Polynesian branch of Austronesian, the similarity in form and function of their respective causative markers (cf. example (16) above) seems too close to be a coincidence. In addition, the Javanese and Mentawai forms may also be related to the corresponding affix or enclitic in several languages of the Malayic subgroup, such as *-kan* in Siak Malay, *-kah* in Besemah, *-kɛ* in Sarang Lang. Note that in Javanese and Malayic, as in Mentawai, the forms in question function also as applicatives.

13 While Donohue (1999) characterizes Warembori and the nearby Yoke language as constituting their own stand-alone family, Malcolm Ross (pc) considers it to be an Austronesian language that has undergone extensive non-Austronesian influence, along similar lines to the better-known Takia; this latter position is represented also in Nordhoff et al. (2013).

and possibly also New Guinea, though for the latter, Foley (1986) cites causatives formed from a word meaning 'say' as being widespread, providing examples from Barai, Enga, Kiwai and Yimas. In summary, then, it would seem to be the case that causatives with 'give' are more common within the Mekong-Mamberamo area than outside it; to the extent that such an impression can be supported by future work, causatives with 'give' would qualify as another property characteristic of the Mekong-Mamberamo area.

2.11 Low differentiation of adnominal attributive constructions

Gil (2005a) surveys the extent to which languages differentiate between various kinds of adnominal attributive constructions, comparing the coding of three specific types of attributive expressions, involving alienable possessors, property words, and activity expressions in which the head noun bears the semantic role of patient. In many languages, these three types of attributive expressions enter into three formally distinct constructions, commonly referred to as genitival, adjectival and relative-clause attribution respectively. For example, in English, *John's book*, *red book*, and *book that John bought* exemplify distinct constructions, which differ with respect to the position of the attribute (prenominal, prenominal and postnominal respectively), the coding of the attributive relationship (with *'s*, zero marking, and *that* respectively), and, arguably, other more abstract behavioural syntactic properties. Thus, English distinguishes maximally between genitival, adjectival and relative-clause adnominal attributive constructions.

In other languages, however, the distinction between these three types of adnominal attributive constructions is partially or completely collapsed. The following examples, from across the Mekong-Mamberamo area, show languages which employ the same construction to express adnominal attribution involving, respectively, alienable possessors, property words, and activity expressions in which the head noun bears the semantic role of patient:

(18) Cantonese

    a. *a^{33}-faay^{55} ge^{33} piŋ^{11}-guo^{35}*
        Ah Fai   ASSOC   apple
        'Ah Fai's apple'

    b. *hooŋ^{11} ge^{33} piŋ^{11}-guo^{35}*
        red   ASSOC   apple
        'red apple'

    c. *a^{33}-faay^{55} maai^{13} ge^{33} piŋ^{11}-guo^{35}*
        Ah Fai   buy   ASSOC   apple
        'apple that Ah Fai bought'

(19) Minangkabau

    a. *rumah   Fajar*
        house   Fajar
        'Fajar's house'

    b. *rumah   ketek*
        house   small
        'small house'

    c. *rumah   Fajar   bali*
        house   Fajar   buy
        'house that Fajar bought'

(20) Maybrat

    a. *fane   ro   Yan*
        pig   ASSOC   Yan
        'Yan's pig'

b. *fane   ro   m-api*
   pig   ASSOC   3-big
   'big pig'

c. *fane   ro   Yan   m-kai*
   pig   ASSOC   Yan   3-find
   'pig that Yan found'

In Cantonese, all three semantic types of adnominal attributives occur prenominally, with the associative marker *ge*[33]. In Minangkabau, all three types of attributives occur postnominally, with no additional construction marker. And in Maybrat, all three types occur postnominally, with the associative marker *ro*. Thus, these three languages exhibit the case of minimal differentiation of adnominal attribution, with a single construction type expressing all three semantic types of adnominal attribution.[14]

In Gil (2005a), 15 out of 138 languages surveyed worldwide exhibit minimal differentiation of adnominal attributive constructions, as in examples (18) - (20) above. Of these 15 languages, 12 occur within the Mekong-Mamberamo area and only 3 outside of it (Ngizim, Lango and Mosetén). Admittedly, within the Mekong-Mamberamo area, minimal differentiation of adnominal attributive constructions is a minority option; a majority of languages in the area exhibit at least some differentiation of such constructions. For example, languages such as Vietnamese, Balinese and Hatam make use of the same construction for attributive expressions involving property words and activity expressions in which the head noun bears the semantic role of patient, but use a different construction for attributive expressions involving alienable possessors; such languages may thus be said to distinguish between a genitive and an adjectival/relative clause construction. However, languages exhibiting minimal differentiation of adnominal attribution constructions, such as Cantonese, Minangkabau and Maybrat, are substantially more common within the Mekong-Mamberamo area than outside it, thereby justifying the claim that this property

---

14 Languages with a maximally general adnominal attribution construction such as those illustrated in (18) - (20) above may also have additional constructions that are of lesser generality. For example, in Minangkabau, adnominal attribution of alienable possessors, as in (19a), may also be expressed with the associative enclitic *-nyo*, ie, *rumahnyo Fajar*, while adnominal attribution of property words and activity expressions, as in (19b) and (19c), may also be expressed with the participant marker (or relativizer) *nan*, ie. *rumah nan ketek* and *rumah nan Fajar bali*.

is, in a quantitative sense, a characteristic feature of the Mekong-Mamberamo linguistic area.

2.12 Weakly developed grammatical voice

A language may be said to have a strongly-developed grammatical voice system to the extent that (a) the relevant semantic and pragmatic functions are expressed by means of formal voice markers as opposed to just word-order alternations; (b) the voice markers are morphological rather than periphrastic; (c) the voice markers are dedicated as opposed to expressing a range of other functions; (d) a privileged argument selected by the voice (or "subject") is assigned a wide range of morphosyntactic, semantic and pragmatic features (or "subjecthood properties").

Mekong-Mamberamo languages tend to have weakly-developed voice systems. Some completely lack formal voice markers; others have just periphrastic markers as opposed to morphological ones; often the expression of voice is just one of a wider range of functions associated with the marker in question; and in many cases the privileged argument selected by the voice in question is associated with but a restricted set of distinctive properties. At present, there is no single cross-linguistic study that ranks the voice systems of the world's languages in accordance with the above criteria.[15] However, grammatical voice usually features prominently in linguistic descriptions of individual languages, and in addition there is an extensive literature on voice in the Austronesian languages that lie at the heart of the Mekong-Mamberamo area. Thus, sufficient data is available to facilitate an informed and empirically grounded characterization of voice systems within the Mekong-Mamberamo area.

Broadly speaking, and with some over-simplification, one may distinguish between four main types of voice or voice-like phenomena within the Mekong-Mamberamo linguistic area: (a) word-order-based alternations; (b) periphrastic undergoer constructions; (c) Indonesian-type voice systems; and (d) Sundic-type voice systems. These four types exhibit overlapping distributions across the languages of the Mekong-Mamberamo area, with many languages displaying coexisting voice or voice-like phenomena belonging to more than one type. We shall examine each of these four types in turn.

---

[15] In particular, the WALS map of passive constructions by Siewierska (2005) makes use of somewhat different criteria, which render it inapplicable to the present study.

2.12.1 Word-order-based alternations

Although typically exhibiting a basic SVO word order, languages of the Mekong-Mamberamo area commonly exhibit a substantial degree of flexibility with regard to word order; see, for example, Enfield (2007: 272-277) for Lao, Conners (2008: 69-87) for Tengger Javanese, Gravelle (2010: 208-209) for Meyah, among many others. In languages such as these, a patient-initial word-order variant may assume the pragmatic functions typically associated with passive constructions, namely, highlighting of the patient and concomitant downplaying of the agent. However, in the absence of any grammatical subjecthood properties associated with the patient, or of additional morphosyntactic markings signalling the word-order alternation, such variant word orders fail to meet most definitions of a passive construction.

In some cases, however, variation in word order may be associated with additional grammatical properties, in which case the construction in question begins to bear a closer resemblance to a passive. For example, in Manggarai (an Austronesian language of Flores), PVA word order requires the post-verbal agent to be marked with a preposition (Arka and Kosmas 2005); similarly, in nearby Palu'e, patient-initial word order associates the patient with certain grammatical subjecthood properties such as quantifier float and conjunction reduction (Donohue 2005a). The most well-known case of this type is the so-called "second passive" construction of some varieties of Malay/Indonesian, which involves PAV word order with the agent cliticized to the verb; see, for example Yanti (2010: 37-40) for Tanjung Raden Malay and Cole, Hermon and Tjung (2006) for a mesolectal variety of Jakarta Indonesian. An extensive debate with regard to whether this is a "real" passive construction as opposed to a mere topicalization highlights the similarities and differences between this construction and more prototypical instances of passive.

In terms of their geographical distribution, word-order-based alternations are widespread throughout the Mekong-Mamberamo area. However, whereas in Mainland Southeast Asia and western Nusantara such alternations typically occur alongside other types of voice or voice-like constructions, in eastern Nusantara and western New Guinea there are generally no other voice or voice-like phenomena. The boundary between these two regions, as defined by the presence or absence of morphological voice marking, is shown in the map provided in Donohue and Denham (2010: 233). Thus, most languages in eastern parts of the Mekong-Mamberamo area are either completely lacking in grammatical voice or have, at best, an extremely rudimentary voice system.

2.12.2 Periphrastic undergoer constructions

The second type of voice-like phenomenon in Mekong-Mamberamo languages is the periphrastic undergoer construction. Examples of the periphrastic undergoer construction in three languages of the Mekong-Mamberamo area are given below:

(21) Lao
    a.   khòòj5   **thùùk5**   toq2
           1SG.POL   strike   table
           'I bumped into the table'

    b.   khòòj5   **thùùk5**   ñing2
           1SG.POL   strike   shoot
           'I got shot'
           (Enfield 2007: 439, pc)

(22) Tengger Javanese
    a.   Eyang   **kenek**   watu
           1M   undergo   stone
           'I got hit by a stone' / 'I tripped over a stone'

    b.   Eyang   **kenek**   antem
           1M   undergo   hit
           'I got hit'
           (Conners to appear, pc)

(23) Papuan Malay
    a.   Sa   **dapa**   uang
           1SG   get   money
           'I got some money'

    b.   Sa   **dapa**   pukul
           1SG   get   hit
           'I got hit'

At the heart of the periphrastic undergoer construction is a bivalent word expressing an undergoer relationship between its two arguments, in which one argument, typically the first, is the undergoer or experiencer, while the other argument, usually the second, is the causer, agent, or otherwise relevant participant accountable for the undergoing. In the above examples, the word in question is indicated in bold. A crucial feature of the construction is that the second argument may denote either an object, as in the (a) sentences, or an activity, as in the (b) sentences.

The meaning of the bivalent word may vary from language to language. In Tengger Javanese, *kenek* is associated with a rather abstract meaning providing a direct expression of the undergoer relationship. In contrast, in Lao and Papuan Malay, *thùùk5* and *dapa* are associated with more basic concrete meanings, 'strike' and 'get' respectively. While in the (a) sentences such meanings are manifested directly, in the (b) sentences they assume a more abstract character, related to the notion of undergoing.[16]

The (b) sentences in (21) - (23), and their counterparts in other languages, are often said to instantiate passive constructions. In many instances, they are further characterized as *adversative* passives, in recognition of the fact that their most common usage involves some kind of adversity or misfortune, though there are exceptions to this generalization. However, as suggested by the examples in (21) - (23), the putative passive constructions in the (b) sentences are of similar or identical nature to the corresponding (a) sentences, which bear no resemblance whatsoever to passive constructions. This suggests that the (b) sentences are also something other than passive constructions—a point argued by Enfield (2007: 438-441) for Lao constructions with *thùùk5* and echoed by Conners, Bowden and Gil (to appear) for the corresponding constructions with *kena* 'undergo' in Jakarta Indonesian. Rather, the (a) and (b) sentences in examples such as (21) - (23) above should be viewed as instances of one and the same construction type, namely, the periphrastic undergoer construction.

---

16 This description intentionally leaves open the question of which, if any, of the various meanings, or shades of meaning, of forms such as *thùùk5* and *dapa* are more basic. Their glosses, as 'strike' and 'get' above, seem to imply that the concrete meanings are basic and their more abstract usages derived by means of metaphorical extension; however, such glosses are for convenience only, and should not be taken too literally. In his discussion of *thùùk5*, Enfield (2007: 438-441) glosses it as either 'strike' or 'come into contact with', and does not argue that either of the meanings is more basic than the other; rather, he considers *thùùk5* as having a "basic unitary meaning" of which 'strike' and 'come into contact with' are mere attempts at providing a convenient English gloss (Enfield pc).

In terms of their geographical distribution, periphrastic undergoer constructions exhibit a west-to-east cline within the Mekong-Mamberamo area. In Mainland Southeast Asia they are very widespread. In western Nusantara they are less frequent, but still more common than is sometimes acknowledged. In particular, in Malay/Indonesian and Javanese, they are absent from more formal registers, but present in many of the more colloquial varieties. Finally, in eastern Nusantara and western New Guinea they are rare—their presence in East Malay dialects such as Papuan Malay probably representing an inheritance from earlier Malay varieties of western Nusantara.

2.12.3 Indonesian-type voice systems

Smack in the middle of the Mekong-Mamberamo area are the Austronesian languages, which, as a family, are renowned for their rich morphologically-based voice systems, which have attracted a considerable amount of attention and controversy. Although this may seem, prima facie, to run counter to the characterization of the Mekong-Mamberamo area as having weakly developed voice systems, closer examination of the languages in question provides strong further support for this characterization.

Himmelmann (2005) introduces the notion of a *symmetric voice system*, one in which there are at least two voices neither of which is clearly more basic than the other. In this respect, symmetric voice systems differ from more familiar voice systems in which the passive is clearly derived from the active. For this and other reasons, scholars have questioned whether such systems are "really" voice systems, and whether the patient-oriented voice in a symmetric voice system is "really" a passive construction—witness the proliferation of competing terminology in the descriptions of such systems. Symmetric voice systems are found outside the Mekong-Mamberamo area, in the languages of Taiwan and the Philippines, and within it, in the languages of western Nusantara.

A subtype of the symmetric voice system is one that is sometimes referred to—see Adelaar (2005: 7-8, 2013) and others—as the Indonesian-type voice system (where the adjective "Indonesian" seems to be serving dual purpose denoting both a geographical region and the eponymous language). The Indonesian-type voice system may be represented schematically as follows: [17]

---

[17] While the schema in (24) captures the essence of Indonesian-type voice, alternative definitions may associate it with additional properties, such as the presence of applicative suffixes (such as those mentioned in footnote 12 above), and the presence of an additional "second

(24) *The Indonesian-Type Voice System*

(a) Clause Type 1: active
A ACT-V P
(b) Clause Type 2: passive
P PASS-V A

The Indonesian-type voice system consists of an active voice, in which a verb bearing an active prefix may be preceded by an agent and followed by a patient, and a passive voice, in which a verb bearing a passive prefix may be preceded by a patient and followed by an agent. In both active and passive clauses, agent and patient arguments are unmarked. However, the Indonesian-type voice system differs from its Philippine counterpart in that the number of voices is not several but just two. For this and other reasons, Indonesian-type voice systems are often considered to represent a "dissolution" or "weakening" of the original Philippine-type that took place when Austronesian languages spread into Indonesia (Starosta, Pawley and Reid 1982; Cole, Hermon and Yanti 2008; Blust 2009: 450-451, and others).

In spite of its name, the distribution of Indonesian-type voice systems is surprisingly difficult to ascertain. Standard Malay and Indonesian provide a close approximation, deviating from it in relatively minor ways.[18] But Standard Malay and Indonesian are artificial constructs, nobody's native language. Some Malayic languages have been described as exhibiting similar voice systems, including Jernih Muda Air Hitam and Sarang Lang (Cole, Hermon and Yanti 2008) and Tanjung Pauh Mudik Kerinci (McKinnon 2010), as have other languages such as Madurese (Davies 2005). To the extent that these reports are factually correct, such languages may be characterized as exhibiting a grammatical voice system that is more strongly developed than those characteristic of Mainland Southeast Asia and eastern Nusantara, albeit less developed than that of languages which have a robust and more prototypical active-passive distinction.

---

passive" such as mentioned in Section 2.12.1 above. Such differences with respect to how the Indonesian type is defined have no bearing on the points being made in this paper.

18 Three ways in which Standard Malay and Indonesian deviate from the pattern in (24) are (a) in the active, the presence of a lexical class of verbs (e.g. *tidur* 'sleep', *pergi* 'go') which do not take an active prefix; (b) in the passive, a variant in which the postverbal agent is flagged with the marker *oleh*; and (c) the alternative passive construction, the so-called "second passive", described in Section 2.12.1 above.

However, in all of the languages of the region that I have had occasion to examine first-hand, a supposed Indonesian-type voice system has turned out to be a chimera. Instead, languages of the region often exhibit a rather different kind of voice system, involving yet a further weakening of the Indonesian-type voice system, namely, the *Sundic-type* voice system.

2.12.4 Sundic-type voice systems

The Sundic-type voice system is so named in recognition of its geographical focus on Sumatra and Java, the two major islands flanking the Sunda straits. The Sundic-type voice system is based on morphological markers that are looser, attenuated versions of bona-fide prototypical voice markers, and hence referred to as *generalized voice markers*. The following definition is from Gil (2002):

(25) *Generalized Voice Markers:*

> For any thematic role T, a T-oriented *generalized voice marker* is a marker M which, when applied to a form X, marks the argument of X bearing the thematic role T as having a set of properties P.

The above definition makes it possible to distinguish between stronger generalized voice markers, those that associate the argument in question with a wider range of properties, and weaker generalized voice markers, those that associate the argument in question with a more limited set of properties. In particular, prototypical voice markers represent the strongest case of generalized voice markers, where the set of properties associated with the argument in question is the full array of subject properties in the language. Some examples of generalized voice markers following the above definition are presented in Table 2. (Note that in Table 2, the terms "agent" and "patient" are used rather loosely; a more precise account would make reference to more general thematic roles of which agent and patient are special cases.)

Table 2: Some Generalized Voice Markers

Language:	English		Tagalog		Languages with Sundic Voice System	
Form M:	Ø	BE -en	-um-	-in-	GEN.ACT-	GEN.PASS-
Thematic Role T:	agent	patient	agent	patient	agent	patient
Properties P:	subject properties	subject properties	some subject properties	some subject properties	existence	existence
Strength:		strong		↔		weak

In English, the voice markers Ø and *be -en* associate agents and patients respectively with an array of subjecthood properties including pre-verbal position, nominative case (for pronouns), controlling verbal agreement, and many more; thus these markers fully meet the definition of generalized active and passive markers. Since the properties they associate with the appropriate thematic role are pretty much all that is necessary to identify the subject in English, these are thus the strongest kind of generalized active and passive markers, that is to say, prototypical active and passive markers. In contrast, in Tagalog, the infixes *-um-* and *-in-* associate agents and patients respectively with just a subset of subjecthood properties. In particular, in the case of the patient-oriented marker *-in-*, some subjecthood properties, such as relativization and quantifier float, are associated with the patient, while others, such as reflexivization and control, remain associated with the agent—see Schachter (1976, 1977) and others for discussion. Because the subjecthood properties of a patient-oriented clause are distributed across two different arguments, scholars have debated long and hard whether such clauses qualify as passives. The above definition characterizes Tagalog *-in-* as a generalized patient-oriented voice marker, albeit one that is weaker than a prototypical passive marker such as English *be -en*. To the extent that the patient-oriented voice markers of Indonesian-type voice systems engender similar splits of subjecthood properties across different arguments, they may thus also be characterized as generalized patient-oriented passive markers. Thus, the notion of generalized voice makes it possible to capture the sense in which the Philippine and Indonesian voice systems are less strongly grammaticalized than their counterparts in other languages. And even further down on the scale of grammaticalization are the voice systems referred to here as Sundic

In Sundic-type voice systems, the generalized voice markers do not associate the designated argument with any subjecthood properties whatsoever; they merely assign it the most elementary of all properties, that of existence. Thus, the generalized active marker asserts that its host has an agent in its semantic frame, while the generalized passive marker asserts that its host has a patient in its argument structure. In Sundic-type voice systems, then, the voice markers have no syntactic functions, only semantic and pragmatic ones. The Sundic-type voice system may be represented schematically as follows:

(26) *The Sundic-Type Voice System*

    a) Clause Type 1: neutral
       V
       preference for preverbal argument to be A

    b) Clause Type 2: generalized active
       GEN.ACT-V
       strong preference for preverbal argument to be A

    c) Clause Type 3: generalized passive
       GEN.PASS-V
       strong preference for preverbal argument to be P

    d) Clause Type 4 (uncommon): generalized passive-active
       GEN.PASS-GEN.ACT-V

As shown in (26), Sundic-type voice systems differ from Indonesian-type voice systems in two important respects. First, whereas in Indonesian-type voice systems a clause must be either active or passive, Sundic-type voice systems allow for two further possibilities: in addition to displaying exactly one of the two generalized voice markers (as in (26b,c)), a clause may be neutral, displaying no generalized voice marker at all (as in (26a)), or it may be doubly marked, displaying both active and passive generalized voice markers (as in (26d)). Secondly, whereas in Indonesian-type voice systems, the presence of a generalized active or passive voice marker entails that a pre-verbal argument will be unambiguously interpreted as agent or patient respectively, in Sundic-type voice systems, such interpretations are strongly preferred but alternative interpretations are also available: in a generalized active clause a pre-verbal argument may on occasion be interpreted as patient, and in a generalized passive clause a pre-verbal argument may sometimes be interpreted as agent. Thus, whereas in Indonesian-type voice systems the generalized voice markers stand in paradigmatic opposition to each other and play a significant role in the syntactic organization of the clause, in Sundic-type voice systems the generalized voice markers bear a closer resemblance to optional elements such as adjectival and adverbial modifiers, which are introduced in order to enrich the semantic structure and fulfil particular pragmatic functions, but play no role in the syntactic organization of the clause. In terms of grammatical structure, then, Sundic-type voice systems are simpler than their Indonesian-type counterparts.

Sundic-type voice systems are widespread in the languages of Sumatra and Java, though their presence often goes unreported, due to prescriptive pressure applied by Standard Indonesian on speakers offering judgments, and an associated descriptive tradition that draws from the more familiar patterns of the Indonesian-type voice system. In Malay/Indonesian, Sundic-type voice systems have been described by Gil (2002) for Riau Indonesian, Gil (to appear c) for Siak Malay, and Conners, Bowden and Gil (to appear) for Jakarta Indonesian. Other languages may exhibit voice systems that are intermediate between Sundic and Indonesian types. In Javanese, many or most verbs require an obligatory voice marker and thus lack the neutral voice characteristic of Sundic-type systems. However, in at least some dialects, the presence of a generalized voice marker does not force a particular assignment of thematic roles on a preverbal argument; for example, Conners (2008: 137,151) cites constructions in Tengger Javanese where a generalized active verb is preceded by a patient, or a generalized passive verb is preceded by an agent. Moreover, in several dialects of Javanese, verbs may be doubly marked for generalized active and passive voice. Thus, Javanese dialects typically exhibit three of the four characteristic features of Sundic-type voice systems.

A particularly illuminating case study of the under-reporting of Sundic-type voice systems in the region is provided by the Muarasiberut dialect of Mentawai. Compared to Malay/Indonesian and Javanese, Muarasiberut Mentawai displays rich verbal morphology more or less on a par with that of Philippine languages. In the only existing description of the dialect that I am familiar with, Jufrizal and Arka (2006) describe a voice system that is essentially isomorphic to that of Standard Indonesian. However, a more detailed investigation paints a rather different picture. As in Indonesian-type voice systems, a verb must be marked by exactly one voice marker: neutral and doubly marked voice are not available. However, as in Sundic-type voice systems, the presence of a generalized voice marker does not impose a particular assignment of thematic roles on a preverbal argument. For example, in (27) below, the verb *akkat* 'lift' is marked by the generalized passive marker *i-*, but preceded by the agent *ita* 'we' rather than the patient *lapek* 'mat'

(27) Muarasiberut Mentawai
Cha, *ita* iakkat akek lapek, Cha!
cha 1PL.INCL GEN.PASS: lift give mat cha
'Cha, let's lift the mat, Cha'
(JFS: 846831104744080307)

Further evidence for the existence of such interpretations is provided by the results of the Association Experiment described in Gil (2007, 2008). Table 3 below provides a measure of the availability of interpretations in which a verb is preceded by its patient: [19]

Table 3: Availability of Patient-Precedes-Verb Interpretations in Some Languages with Sundic-Type Voice Systems

Language	Availability of Patient-Precedes-Verb Interpretations
Muarasiberut Mentawai	56%
Minangkabau	57%
Sundanese	49%

Whereas in Minangkabau and Sundanese, the verb in the test sentences is bare, lacking a voice marker, in Muarasiberut Mentawai, the verb is marked with a generalized active voice marker, *masi-*, *ma-* or *mu-*. Nevertheless, the availability of interpretations in which a verb is preceded by its patient in Mentawai generalized active clauses is comparable to that for the corresponding neutral clauses in Minangkabau and Sundanese. Thus, Muarasiberut Mentawai displays properties (26b,c) characteristic of Sunda-type voice systems.

So why, then, was Muarasiberut Mentawai described so differently by Jufrizal and Arka (2006)? Arka (pc) reports that their data was obtained through elicitation from Mentawai-speaking students living in the provincial capital Padang. In contrast, the 56% availability figure for patient-precedes-verb interpretations reported in Table 3 above was obtained from subjects who were ordi-

---

[19] In the Association Experiment, speakers are presented with a sentence in the target language and two pictures, and asked to choose the picture that is appropriately described by the sentence (they also have the option of choosing both pictures or neither). Table 3 presents the percentage of responses, calculated over 8 different stimuli and 30 or more subjects per language, in which a picture was chosen representing an interpretation in which a verb would be preceded by its patient. The percentages in Table 3 thus represent the relative availability of constructions in which a verb is preceded by its patient.

nary villagers living on Mentawai and tested in their natural village environment. But when the same experiment was run on Muarasiberut Mentawai-speaking university students living in the provincial capital Padang, the availability of patient-precedes-verb interpretations plummeted to just 12%, mirroring Jufrizal and Arka's description. Prima facie, these findings could reflect a situation of diglossia, in which a migrant variety of Muarasiberut Mentawai may have developed as a result of contact with other languages spoken in Padang. However, a more likely account for the discrepancy, based on other observations, would be to say that the prescriptive pressure exerted by Standard Indonesian on the more highly-educated speakers in the big city biases their responses to the experiment and distorts their judgments in situations involving elicitation, thereby resulting in an inaccurate picture of their actual linguistic competence. The real Muarasiberut Mentawai language is that reflected by the responses of the uneducated villagers back home, with at least some features of a Sundic-type voice system. And the moral of this story is that Sundic-type voice systems are probably considerably more widespread in the western Nusantara region than is commonly supposed.

2.12.5 Weakly-developed grammatical voice: summary

With all of the details now in place, we may return to the larger picture of grammatical voice in the Mekong-Mamberamo linguistic area. Broadly speaking, three main regions may be discerned. At one end is Mainland Southeast Asia, with mostly periphrastic undergoer constructions, while at the other end is eastern Nusantara and western New Guinea with few or no voice alternations. Between the two is western Nusantara with both periphrastic undergoer constructions and some combination of Indonesian- and Sundic-type voice systems. However, even the latter morphologically-based voice systems are less strongly grammaticalized than most prototypical voice systems familiar from other parts of the world. Thus, although the details differ from one part to another, the Mekong-Mamberamo area as a whole is clearly characterized by weakly developed grammatical voice.

Again, as was the case with regard to numeral classifiers and basic SVO word order above, a saddle effect is in evidence, reflecting the historical spread of Austronesian languages into the heart of the Mekong-Mamberamo area. As this dispersal progressed, the morphologically-based voice systems followed a trajectory of successive reduction and simplification from original Philippine-type systems through Indonesian-type to Sundic-type before culminating in their complete dissipation in the Austronesian languages of eastern Nusantara and western New Guinea.

Turning to neighbouring regions, Siewierska's (2005) map of the passive construction shows it to be widespread in South and Northeast Asia, though not in Taiwan and the Philippines, Australia and New Guinea. However, as noted above, in Taiwan and the Philippines grammatical voice is still more developed than in Mekong-Mamberamo languages, while in many Australian languages there is an antipassive alternation that plays an important role in the grammar. Thus, in four out of the five relevant directions, central and eastern New Guinea being the only exception, weakly-developed grammatical voice provides a good demarcation of the Mekong-Mamberamo area in relation to surrounding regions.

2.13 Isolating word structure

One of the most commonly cited properties of Mainland Southeast Asian languages is their isolating word structure, in which words typically consist of a single morpheme and therefore lack internal complexity; see Bybee (1997), Enfield (2005, 2011) and many others. In fact, this property is shared by languages across the Mekong-Mamberamo area, as evidenced by the following examples:

(28) Thai
khon súu mǎa
person buy dog
'A person is buying a dog'

(29) Tengger Javanese
Wong tuku kirik
person buy dog
'A person is buying a dog'

(30) Meyah
Isok enk mes
man buy dog
'A man is buying a dog'

In the above examples, the Thai, Tengger Javanese and Meyah sentences exhibit a 1.00 morpheme-to-word ratio; none of the words have any internal morphological structure. Contrast these with the corresponding sentence in an Austronesian language of the Philippines, lying outside of the Mekong-Mamberamo area:

(31) Tagalog
 Binibili ng tao ang aso
 <PT.REAL>IMPF: buy DIR person TOP dog
 'A person is buying the dog'

In Tagalog, the corresponding sentence exhibits a higher morpheme-to-word ratio, 1.40, by dint of the inflections contained by the word *binibili*. Similar observations can also be made with respect to the English translations of sentences (28) - (31).

Bickel and Nichols (2005) present a map of morphological type as manifest in the expression of case and tense-aspect-mood categories. Of the 162 languages in their sample, 16 display their "exclusively isolating" type, of which six are in the Mekong-Mamberamo area: five in Mainland Southeast Asia plus Indonesian. Using the same criteria but a much larger sample of some 1500 languages worldwide, Donohue and Denham (to appear) present a map showing the largest concentration of isolating languages in Mainland Southeast Asia, a secondary cluster in eastern Nusantara and western New Guinea, and sporadic cases elsewhere in the Mekong-Mamberamo area. Donohue and Denham's map thus clearly displays a Mekong-Mamberamo distribution for isolating languages. Moreover, it evinces the same kind of relative dip in the western Nusantara region characteristic also of numeral classifiers, basic word order and weakly developed grammatical voice, attributable to the intrusion of the originally more morphologically-complex Austronesian languages into the region.[20]

As pointed out, however, by Russell (1999), Haspelmath (2011) and others, descriptions of individual languages often fail to provide adequate justification for the positing of word boundaries, sometimes unquestioningly adopting an

---

[20] In subsequent maps, Donohue and Denham (to appear) decompose the holistic notion of isolating language into more specific instances of isolating structure pertaining to particular morphosyntactic features, providing maps showing the absence of verbal agreement, tense marking, bound causatives, core case marking, and subordinating morphology. In their Map 8 they then take the intersection of these maps, and the resulting languages, those in which all of the above are absent, are almost exclusively located in the Mekong-Mamberamo area.

orthographic representation proposed by an early preliminary description, adapted from a related language, or arrived at in otherwise uncritical fashion.[21] Just a little tweak in the writing system and an isolating language can suddenly seem polysynthetic, or vice versa. A related problem, noted by DiSciullo and Williams (1987), Russell (1999) and others, is that different descriptions make reference to different "kinds" of wordhood: prosodic, grammatical, and so forth. In principle, such analytic uncertainties should come out in the statistical wash of a 1500-strong language sample such as Donohue and Denham's. However, it is not inconceivable that orthographic conventions themselves may pattern areally, with different writing traditions being associated with different countries and regions.

In order to avoid such problems, we shall therefore consider some typological properties that are related in various ways to the notion of isolating word structure, but which are perhaps more readily evaluated for a large language sample in a theory neutral fashion. These are the remaining Mekong-Mamberamo properties, numbers 14-17 in (1) above.

2.14 Short words

All else being equal, isolating languages are likely to have shorter words, simply because there are fewer options for piling on multiple affixes within a single word. Of course all else is not always equal, and there can be long monomorphemic words and short multimorphemic ones; still, the general tendency should nevertheless be maintained. Measuring the length of words by counting segments or syllables is relatively straightforward, and examining wordlists based on the citation form of words provides a partial albeit imperfect solution to the problem of identifying word boundaries discussed in the preceding section.

One of the ways in which a language may have short words is by means of canonically *sesquisyllabic* words, consisting of a full syllable preceded by some additional segmental material of lesser weight: half a syllable, as it were. Mainland Southeast Asia languages are renowned for sesquisyllabic word structure; see, for example Matisoff (1973) and Diffloth and Zide (1992)—though a somewhat different perspective is offered by Pittayaporn (this volume) and Butler

---

[21] For example, as suggested in Gil (1996), the Tagalog case markers *ng* and *ang* in (31), although traditionally written as separate words, might be more appropriately analysed as proclitics; doing so would thus increase the morpheme-to-word ratio of sentence (31) to 2.33.

(this volume). Donohue, Hetherington and McElvenny (2012) map the distribution of "sesquisyllabic epenthesis" worldwide, showing it to be widespread in Mainland Southeast Asia, in languages such as Kayah Li and Khmer, and present also in some languages of Nusantara, including Gayo and Manggarai, and also western New Guinea, in Maybrat and Iha Pidgin. Outside the Mekong-Mamberamo area there is some overflow of sesquisyllabicity into the Himalayas and central and eastern New Guinea; beyond this area it is vanishingly rare. Thus, sesquisyllabicity provides a fine reflection of the Mekong-Mamberamo linguistic area.

Moving beyond sesquisyllabicity, the most extensive cross-linguistic survey of word-length to date is that of Wichmann, Rama, and Holman (2011), measuring the number of segments in the citation form of words that appear in the 40-item lists of over 3000 languages, based on the Automatic Similarity Judgment Program (ASJP) database. However, the results only partially support the claim that words tend to be shorter across the Mekong-Mamberamo area. Worldwide, they find an average of 4.019 segments per word. Compared to this, words do tend to be shorter in languages of Mainland Southeast Asia: in a breakdown by families, they find averages of 2.765 for Tai-Kadai (encompassing 35 languages), 2.932 for Hmong-Mien (9 languages), 3.197 for Sino-Tibetan (123 languages) and 3.555 for Austroasiatic (77 languages). In contrast, though, languages of Nusantara and western New Guinea are not systematically shorter than the word-wide average.

A window into relative word length within the Mekong-Mamberamo region can be found by consideration of cognate sets in languages of the Austronesian family, which spans the Mekong-Mamberamo linguistic area. Table 4 presents three such cognate sets, showing two languages each from Mainland Southeast Asia, western Nusantara, and eastern Nusantara plus western New Guinea.[22] (The inclusion of Thai in Table 4 is predicated on the proposal by Sagart (2004) to the effect that Tai-Kadai languages constitute a branch within Austronesian; however, the point remains valid even if the Thai forms are considered to be loans or accidental resemblances rather than true cognates.)

---

[22] The Hainan Cham data is from Greenhill, Blust and Gray (2008) citing Thurgood, Li and Thurgood (to appear). The Taba data is from Bowden (2001).

Table 4: Word Length in Three Austronesian Cognate Sets

	Thai	Hainan Cham	Muarasiberut Mentawai	Tengger Javanese	Taba	Roon
'eye'	taa	ta33	mata	mata	mto	maka
'bird'	nók	nuʔ24	umaʔ	manuʔ	manik	man
'die'	taay	ta:yʔ32	matey	mateʔ	-mot	-mar

In the two western Nusantara languages, Muarasiberut Mentawai and Tengger Javanese, the cognate forms are all disyllabic, reflecting the general disyllabic nature of Austronesian word bases as described by Blust (2009: 224-226). In contrast, in the two Mainland Southeast Asia languages, Thai and Hainan Cham, the corresponding forms are monosyllabic, reflecting the general tendency for shorter words in the Mainland Southeast Asia area evident in the Wichmann et al survey. Interestingly, the two languages from eastern Nusantara and western New Guinea also show evidence of shortening, though less systematically than in the languages of Mainland Southeast Asia. Thus, word length in the Austronesian languages of the Mekong-Mamberamo also exhibits a saddle effect, with shorter words at both ends, and somewhat longer ones in the middle.[23]

Focusing on the western Nusantara region, where the Mekong-Mamberamo shortness of words is least in evidence, a contrastive analysis of Malay/Indonesian and Tagalog may provide some useful insights. According to Wichmann et al, both languages have similar average word lengths: 4.725 for Malay vs. 4.525 for Tagalog. But this calculation, based on the citation form of words, fails to reflect the observation that, when fully-inflected forms are taken into consideration, Tagalog appears to be much more tolerant of longer words than Malay/Indonesian. For example, quadrisyllabic words such as *binibili* in example (31), commonplace in Tagalog and other Philippine languages, are quite the exception in Malay/Indonesian, as for that matter in most other Mekong-Mamberamo languages. While the notion of minimal word has been much discussed in recent phonological theory, an adequate characterization of word shape in Mekong-Mamberamo languages would seem to require recourse to a mirror-image notion of *maximal word*, along the lines of recent suggestions by

---

[23] Blust (2009: 224-226) cites a number of languages "that have developed a high degree of monosyllabism in relation to the [Austronesian] norm", including Chamic, Sa'ban (northern Sarawak), Modang (Northeast Kalimantan), some languages of the Aru islands, and some languages of the Raja Ampat islands. In contrast, he cites but a single language that has developed polysyllabicity, namely Enggano (spoken off the Southwest coast of Sumatra).

de Lacy (2003). Specifically, it would seem to be the case that most or all languages of the Mekong-Mamberamo region exhibit a preference, perhaps even a strong preference, for words to be not more than two syllables long.

While an empirically adequate justification of the disyllabic maximal-word hypothesis for Mekong-Mamberamo languages is still far off, some preliminary observations can be made here. In particular, Malay/Indonesian varieties provide a number of arguments in support of a disyllabic maximal-word preference. First and most obviously, longer words are rare. Secondly, they tend to undergo fast-speech reduction resulting in disyllabic forms. Thirdly, longer words are sometimes broken up in spelling to create two smaller words satisfying the maximal-word preference. Following are some examples from a corpus of SMS (text) messages from two geographically distant varieties of colloquial Malay/Indonesian. The relevant forms are in bold:

(32) Riau Indonesian
 a. *Udah sampai **mano kuari** belum pit?.bls*
    Udah sampai **Manokwari** belum   Pit?   Balas.
    PFCT   arrive   Manokwari NEG.PFCT FAM\David reply
    'Have you arrived in Manokwari yet, David? Reply.

 b. *Piiiiit tlp aku skrng pit aku **berang kat** berdua boleh tak?.bls*
    Pit   telepon   aku   sekarang pit,
    FAM\David   telephone   1SG   now   FAM\David
    aku   **berangkat**   berdua   boleh   tak?   Balas.
    1SG   depart   NON.PAT-two   can   NEG   reply
    'David, phone me now, David, can the two of us go? Reply.'

c. *Aku lg duduk2 di rumah pian.vid bang ely mau ke **beng kalis** cari unil*

Aku	lagi	duduk-duduk	di	rumah	Pian.	Vid
1SG	PROG	DISTR~sit	LOC	house	Pian	FAM\David

bang		Ely	mau	ke	**Bengkalis**	cari	Unil
FAM\elder.brother		Ely	want	to	Bengkalis	look.for	Unil

'I'm just sitting around in Pian's house. David, Ely wants to go to Bengkalis to look for Unil.'

(33) Papuan Malay

a. *Piiiiiiit krm aku plz kah,,,aku **keha bisan** plz nih*

Pit	kirim	aku	pulsa	ka,	aku
Pit	send	1SG	phone.credit	Q	1SG

kehabisan	pulsa	ni
GEN.PASS: finish: CIRC	phone.credit	DEM.PROX

'David, send me some phone credit, please, my phone credit is all gone.'

b. *epen tdi sore tong baku potong sma **manda can** dong jdi lampu semua mti*

Epen	tadi	sore	tong	baku	potong
really.important	PST.PROX	afternoon	1PL	RECIP	cut

sama	**Mandacan**	dong	jadi,	lampu	semua	mati
with	Mandacan	3PL	become	light	all	die

'Yeah, this afternoon we were fighting the Mandacan mountain people with knives, then all the lights went out.'

c. *z **sen diri** trapa2 to*

Sa	**sendiri**	trapapa	to
1SG	alone	NEG;DISTR~what	Q

'Just me on my own would be okay, right?'

In the (a) sentences, a quadrisyllabic word is broken up into two disyllabic words; in the (b) sentences a trisyllabic word is split up into a disyllabic word followed by a monosyllabic one, while in the (c) sentences a trisyllabic word is partitioned into a monosyllabic word followed by a disyllabic one. Examples such as these thus provide further evidence for a disyllabic maximal-word preference in Malay/Indonesian.[24]

Impressionistically, a similar disyllabic maximal-word preference would seem to hold across many or most languages in the Mekong-Mamberamo area. Coupled with the widespread presence of canonic sesquisyllabicity, this would then provide a further reflection for the tendency for Mekong-Mamberamo languages to favour shorter words.[25]

2.15 Low grammatical-morpheme density

While the preceding section relates isolating word structure to word length, an alternative approach to the notion of isolating languages pertains to grammatical structure. In general, many or most isolating languages exhibit a strong tendency towards sentences consisting largely of "contentives", with a relative paucity of "grammatical" or "functional" markers of various kinds. This property may be referred to as *low grammatical-morpheme density*. Syntagmatically, low grammatical-morpheme density is evident in a low ratio of grammatical as opposed to contentive morphemes in texts. Paradigmatically, low grammatical-morpheme density manifests itself in the predominance of grammatical markers that are optional as opposed to obligatory.[26]

---

24 The broken-up spellings illustrated in (32) and (33) above would seem to reflect a constraint on phonological as opposed to grammatical words. Similar mismatches in which phonological words may be shorter than grammatical words have been proposed for some polysynthetic languages of North America and Australia by McDonough (1990), Dyck (1994), Rice (1994) and Evans, Fletcher and Ross (2008).
25 An apparent exception to the tendency for Mekong-Mamberamo languages to favour short words is provided by ideophones, commonly occurring in Mainland Southeast Asian languages (though less so in the languages of Nusantara and western New Guinea), and typically consisting of two or even four syllables. By definition, however, ideophones are forms that deviate from the regular phonological and morphosyntactic patterns of the language, so their greater length may accordingly be viewed as another aspect of their special nature, the exception that proves the rule with respect to shortness of words in Mainland Southeast Asian languages.
26 It must be acknowledged that the distinction between contentives and grammatical markers is itself somewhat problematical, not least because it conflates two orthogonal dimensions, formal and semantic. In part, the distinction is of a formal nature: whereas contentives are typically independent words or word stems belonging to open word classes, grammatical markers are usually either words or word stems belonging to closed classes or else bound morphemes, often exhibiting idiosyncratic morphosyntactic behaviour. Nevertheless, the formal distinction exhibits a strong empirical correlation to a logically-independent semantic

Low grammatical-morpheme density is one of the most striking characteristics of Mekong-Mamberamo languages. Compare, once again, the Thai, Tengger Javanese and Meyah sentences in (28) - (30) above with the Tagalog sentence in (31) and the English translations of these sentences. In Thai, Tengger Javanese and Meyah, content words alone suffice to constitute a complete, non-elliptical and non-telegraphic sentence. In contrast, in Tagalog and in English, content words alone are not enough; for the sentence to be well-formed, additional grammatical formatives must be added. Thus, in Tagalog, *-bili* 'buy' is marked for voice, tense, aspect and mood by means of initial CV- reduplication and infixation of *-in-*, while *tao* 'person' and *aso* 'dog' are marked for case and for the latter also definiteness by the articles *ng* and *ang* respectively; similarly the English translation contains markings of a variety of verbal and nominal grammatical categories. In general, Mekong-Mamberamo languages typically possess little or no obligatory marking of grammatical categories; accordingly, texts in these languages typically contain a high proportion of contentives, and some individual sentences will be completely lacking in grammatical markers of any kind.[27]

---

distinction, between different kinds of concepts. For example, within the domain of time, days of the week are the kind of concept expressed by contentives such as English *Tuesday*, whereas past is the kind of concept typically expressed by grammatical morphemes such as English *-ed*, though exceptions do exist (e.g. the Riau Indonesian proximate past expression *tadi*, a separate word belonging to the single open word-class of the language and exhibiting no idiosyncratic grammatical properties whatsoever). These two kinds of concepts may be characterized with reference to *encyclopaedic knowledge*, that is to say, our structured and highly detailed understanding of the way things are in the world around us. Particular concepts may be said to be encyclopaedic to the extent that they draw upon such encyclopaedic knowledge, resulting in a classification of concepts as either *encyclopaedically-rich* or *encyclopaedically-poor*. Examples of encyclopaedically-rich concepts are 'Tuesday', 'dog', and 'buy', which make reference to complex and detailed knowledge in various domains of human activity and experience. In contrast, encyclopaedically-poor concepts are ones like past, plural and locative, typically of a more abstract, logical and relational nature, with little or no reference to such detailed real-world knowledge. For the most part, encyclopaedically-rich concepts are expressed by words and larger phrases, while encyclopaedically-poor concepts are encoded by grammatical markers, but there are exceptions (e.g. the non-grammatical but encyclopaedically-poor Riau Indonesian *tadi* above). This points towards a possible alternative semantically-based characterization of Mekong-Mamberamo languages as displaying *low encyclopaedically-poor-concept articulation*, in that the expression of encyclopaedically-poor concepts by means of overt morphemes is impoverished, that is to say, paradigmatically optional and syntagmatically infrequent.

27 The low grammatical-morpheme density of Mekong-Mamberamo languages is reflected in several impressionistic yet insightful attempts to "capture the essence" of such languages, such as, for example, Clark's (1992: 145) description of Mainland Southeast Asian languages

Although most or all languages of the Mekong-Mamberamo area are of low grammatical-morpheme density, some variation may be observed from one part to the next. In Mainland Southeast Asia and to a somewhat lesser extent also Nusantara, sentence-final particles are frequently used to express a wide range of concepts involving modality, focus, illocutionary force, speakers' attitude and so forth; to the extent that at least some of these particles are grammatical rather than contentive, their occurrence would increase the grammatical-morpheme density of the languages in question. In western Nusantara, in some languages, as discussed in Sections 2.12.3-4 above, generalized voice markers are obligatory for some or all verbs; the presence of these prefixes thus also raises the grammatical-morpheme density of the languages that employ them. Finally, in eastern Nusantara and western New Guinea, subject-verb agreement is widespread (Klamer, Reesink and van Staden 2008); in such constructions, the pronominal agreement markers also add to the grammatical-morpheme density of the languages in question. However, the above three phenomena constitute pretty much the only cases of frequent or obligatory grammatical morphemes that are widely attested throughout large parts of the Mekong-Mamberamo region; other than these, Mekong-Mamberamo languages generally follow the pattern exemplified by the constructions in (28) - (30) above. In contrast, languages in the neighbouring areas typically exhibit higher grammatical-morpheme density, with a significant amount of obligatory expression of various grammatical categories: this is true of the languages of South Asia, Northeast Asia, Taiwan and the Philippines (cf. the discussion of Tagalog above), central and eastern New Guinea, and Australia. Indeed, there is no other part of the world that exhibits a similarly broad pattern of low grammatical-morpheme density comparable to that of the Mekong-Mamberamo area; in this respect, the Mekong-Mamberamo area is truly exceptional.

As defined above, grammatical-morpheme density is a holistic property characteristic of entire languages. One may ask, however, whether grammatical-morpheme density in one grammatical domain necessarily correlates with grammatical morpheme density in other domains. There is at least some evidence of a typological split between languages that are more grammatically elaborate in nominal domains as opposed to others that are more grammatically elaborate in verbal domains. In his survey of the languages of New Guinea, Capell (1969) introduces the notion of pattern domination, distinguishing be-

---

that "spin ideas ... from a reel, with a minimum of interruptive elements", or Burgess' (1975: 183) experience with Malay as "diving into a bath of pure logic" where "[e]verything is pared to a minimum".

tween object-dominated languages, with a richness of grammaticalized nominal categories, and event-dominated languages, with a plethora of grammaticalized verbal categories, though he also allows for a class of neutral languages in which neither of the two domains is significantly more developed than the other. More generally, Nichols (1986) differentiates between dependent-marking and head-marking languages, which, at the level of the clause, results in a similar distinction between languages with more developed nominal markings and languages with more developed verbal markings, though she also acknowledges the existence of languages in which both domains are equally developed. Still, whatever the range of variation worldwide, Mekong-Mamberamo languages clearly instantiate the neutral case in which both the nominal and the verbal domains are of low grammatical-morpheme density.

The low grammatical morpheme density characteristic of Mekong-Mamberamo languages across both nominal and verbal domains is manifest in the final two Mekong-Mamberamo properties, to which we now turn.

2.16 Optional thematic-role flagging

A major manifestation of low grammatical-morpheme density in the nominal domain is the optional flagging of thematic roles, that is to say, the possible absence of any overt expression, within an NP, of its semantic relationship to its governing verb. Several different studies offer alternative perspectives on the ways in which the absence of thematic-role flagging is characteristic of languages of the Mekong-Mamberamo linguistic area.

Cross-linguistically, there is an implicational hierarchy whereby overt flagging is more likely to occur on oblique than on core arguments; equivalently, the absence of flagging is more likely to characterize core arguments than oblique ones (see, for example, Greenberg's 1963 Universal 38). The effects of this hierarchy are readily visible in an English sentence such as *The man is eating by the tree*, in which the core subject has no flagging while the locative expression is obligatorily flagged by the preposition *by*, or, alternatively, by some other, more semantically-specific preposition such as *under*, *behind*, and so on.

Whereas English and many other languages typically exhibit obligatory flagging for oblique arguments, Mekong-Mamberamo languages often exhibit optional flagging, as in the following examples:

(34) Vietnamese
 Người   đàn ông   ăn   cây
 person   CLF grandfather eat tree
 a.   'The man is eating the tree'
 b.   'The man is eating by the tree'

(35) Sundanese
 Jelema dahar tangkal
 person eat   tree
 a.   'The person is eating the tree'
 b.   'The man is eating by the tree'

(36) Meyah
 Isok et mega
 man eat tree
 a.   'The man is eating the tree'
 b.   'The man is eating by the tree'

In each of the above examples, the semantically incongruous interpretation (a), in which the post-verbal argument is associated with the thematic role of patient, is the preferred interpretation; however, the alternative interpretation indicated in (b) is available, for at least some speakers, as a dispreferred option. Under the latter interpretations, examples (34) - (36) may be said to instantiate the *bare-oblique* construction, in which an oblique argument occurs without any flagging of its thematic role.

For various reasons, bare-oblique constructions seem to fall under the radar of many grammatical descriptions of Mekong-Mamberamo languages in which they are present. For example, in Malay/Indonesian, bare-oblique constructions are sometimes rejected by native speakers in elicitation; however, they occur regularly in corpora of spontaneous speech; see for example Conners, Bowden and Gil (to appear) for Jakarta Indonesian. A measure of the availability of bare-oblique constructions of various kinds, including sentences such as those in (34) - (36), across a selection of languages of the Mekong-Mamberamo area, is provided by the Association Experiment described in Gil (2007, 2008) and mentioned in Section 2.12.4 above: [28]

Table 5: Availability of Bare-Oblique Constructions in Some Mekong-Mamberamo Languages

Language	Availability of Bare Oblique Constructions
Cantonese	42%
Vietnamese	67%
Lao	54%
Muarasiberut Mentawai	75%
Sundanese	76%
Jakarta Indonesian	68%
Nage	79%
Roon	59%
Meyah	66%

The above figures, while showing the less-than-complete availability of bare-oblique constructions within the Mekong-Mamberamo area, nevertheless contrast significantly with the corresponding figures for many languages outside the Mekong-Mamberamo area, for example 11% for the Philippine language Kapampangan, and 7% for English.

A rather different perspective on optional thematic-role flagging is provided by two broad cross-linguistic surveys of case marking. By definition, case marking involves the flagging of a noun or NP by means of morphological devices, most commonly through affixation. As such, surveys of case-marking do not take into account flagging by means of periphrastic strategies such as adpositions; more problematically, they are prey to the issues discussed in Section 2.13 above concerning the determination of word boundaries and whether a given form is most appropriately analysed as a case-marking affix or as an adposition. Nevertheless, such surveys may still provide a relatively reliable indication of areal patterns involving thematic-role flagging.

Dryer (2005b) surveys the position of case affixes in a worldwide sample of 934 languages. As is clearly evident from this map, Mekong-Mamberamo languages are largely lacking in case affixes or adpositional clitics of any kind. Outside the Mekong-Mamberamo area, the absence of case affixes and adposi-

---

[28] Table 5 presents the percentage of responses, calculated over 8 different stimuli and 30 or more subjects per language, in which a stimulus representing a bare-oblique construction was judged to be acceptable. While 4 of the 8 stimuli involved post-verbal bare obliques, such as in the (b) interpretations of examples (34) - (36), the remaining 4 stimuli involved bare obliques in preverbal position.

tional clitics is also characteristic of a wide swathe of equatorial Africa, whereas elsewhere its distribution is spotty. In the regions adjacent to the Mekong-Mamberamo area, absence of case affixes and adpositional clitics is mostly unattested in South Asia and Northeast Asia.[29] It is also unattested in most of Australia, with the exception of a small concentration of languages in the northwest corner of the Northern Territory. However, the absence of case affixes and adpositional clitics is observed in a significant proportion of the languages of central and eastern New Guinea, as well as the languages of the Pacific; it is also the predominant pattern in the languages of Taiwan and the Philippines.[30]

Donohue and Denham (to appear: Map 6) survey the worldwide distribution of "no core case marking"; their map, containing a sample of 1167 languages, is based on the criteria in Comrie (2005), and shows the distribution of languages that exhibit "neutral" alignment for both pronouns and full noun phrases. Donohue and Denham's map shows an even more striking Mekong-Mamberamo pattern, in which the Mekong-Mamberamo area, again with some leakage into Taiwan and the Philippines, central and eastern New Guinea, the Pacific, and the northwestern corner of the Northern Territory, are now the only area in the world with a predominance of no core case marking.

In conclusion, then, the observations on bare oblique constructions, Dryer's map showing the absence of case affixes and adpositional clitics, and Donohue and Denham's map showing the absence of core case marking, join forces to characterize the Mekong-Mamberamo linguistic area as exceptional with respect to the optional flagging of thematic roles, a major manifestation of low grammatical-morpheme density in the nominal domain.

---

29 Whereas in Dryer (2005b) Japanese is listed as lacking case affixes, Matthew Dryer (pc) notes that he has since become aware of evidence that the case markers of Japanese are enclitics rather than separate words, in view of which he would reclassify Japanese as having adpositional clitics. (Instances such as this underscore the difficulty of basing broad typological studies on subtle decisions with regard to wordhood.)

30 Again, the overflow of no case affixes and adpositional clitics into the languages of the Philippines suggested by Dryer's (2005b) map is more apparent than real, as it is based on a borderline coding decision. Most languages of the Philippines have a set of forms that are of intermediate nature between case markers and articles (e.g. the forms *ang* and *ng* in Tagalog example (31) above), and it was thus a near-arbitrary decision to code such forms as articles rather than case markers (Matthew Dryer pc).

2.17 Optional tense-aspect-mood marking

Turning now to the verbal domain, a central manifestation of low grammatical-morpheme density involves the distribution of markers expressing the categories of tense, aspect and mood (TAM).

Donohue and Denham (to appear, Map 4) show the worldwide distribution of "no tense marking"; this map, containing a sample of 804 languages, is based on the criteria in Dahl and Velupillai (2011a,b), and shows the distribution of languages that lack both past and future tenses. Again, this map shows a dramatic Mekong-Mamberamo pattern, in which the overwhelming majority of the languages with neither past nor future tenses are located in the Mekong-Mamberamo area plus spillover regions extending into Taiwan, the Philippines, and parts of the Pacific.

In accordance with Dahl and Velupillai's criteria, a language is said to have a past or future tense regardless of whether its expression is optional or obligatory in the appropriate contexts. Also, whereas their past-tense map includes both morphological and periphrastic expressions, their future-tense map includes only morphologically-based markers while excluding expressions of the future that are of a periphrastic nature. Yet another issue that arises when conducting and then subsequently analysing such large-scale typological surveys is that it is often quite tricky to decide, on the basis of given descriptions, whether a particular marking expresses tense or aspect, or, in other instances, tense or mood.

A different approach to the cross-linguistic comparison of the expression of TAM categories is provided in Gil (to appear b) and Maps 8-9, which make use of the following feature values and associated coded-coded dots:

(37) *Feature values for TAM marking, Maps 8-9*

a) red: optional TAM marking
b) grey: obligatory TAM marking

These maps show a binary distinction between optional TAM marking languages, in which there are some basic declarative affirmative main clauses with no expression of any TAM categories, and obligatory TAM marking languages, in which all basic declarative affirmative main causes contain an expression of at least one of the three TAM categories—tense, aspect or mood. The grammatical marking of TAM may be either bound or free. Moreover, it may be either dedicated, expressing nothing but TAM concepts, or portmanteau, combining the expression of TAM with that of other concepts. For example, in many Philippine languages, TAM is combined with voice, by means of distinct voice affixes associated with different aspects; similarly, in many European languages, TAM is combined with agreement features such as person, number and gender, via subject-verb agreement paradigms which vary in accordance with tense and/or aspect. In some languages, clauses with no overt TAM marking are constrained in their range of possible meanings; for example, in many West African languages and Atlantic creoles such clauses are interpreted as expressing either present or past time, depending on the aktionsart of the verb. If one considers TAM marking as constituting a single unitary paradigm, one might analyse such cases as involving a "zero morpheme" expressing some particular TAM value. However, the present survey takes the alternative what-you-see-is-what-you-get approach of characterizing such languages as possessing optional TAM marking.

Of the 868 languages in the Gil (to appear b) sample, 377, or 43%, exhibit optional TAM marking, while 491, or 57%, have obligatory TAM Marking. However, as evident in Maps 8 and 9, languages of the Mekong-Mamberamo linguistic area are almost exclusively characterized by optional TAM marking (as can be seen in the many examples cited in previous sections of this paper, including (15) - (17), (21) - (23), (28) - (30), (34) - (36) and others). The only exceptions in the present sample are Tukang Besi in southeast Sulawesi and Inanwatan, Mbaham and Iha in western New Guinea (note the irrealis mood marker in example (10) in Iha), with obligatory TAM marking. In contrast, in areas bordering on the Mekong-Mamberamo region, obligatory TAM marking is the rule in South Asia, common in Northeast Asia, the majority case in Taiwan and the Philippines (see example (31) in Tagalog), common in central and eastern New Guinea, and the large majority case in Australia. Thus, optional TAM marking provides a clear-cut reflection of the Mekong-Mamberamo linguistic area.

Of particular interest is the story of TAM marking within the Austronesian language family. Of the 222 Austronesian languages in the sample, 161, or 73%, have optional TAM marking, while 61, or 27%, have obligatory TAM marking. The widespread occurrence of obligatory TAM marking in Taiwan and the Philippines, extending also to northern Borneo and Sulawesi, suggests that obligatory TAM marking is an ancient feature within Austronesian, likely to have been characteristic of the first Malayo-Polynesian languages that spread south into the Mekong-Mamberamo area.[31] However, once these languages entered Nusan-

---

[31] It is not clear whether obligatory TAM marking can be reconstructed to proto-Austronesian; Laurie Reid (pc) suggests that it cannot. What is clear is that many contemporary TAM markers

tara, they shed their obligatory TAM marking and adopted instead the optional TAM marking characteristic of the Mekong-Mamberamo linguistic area.

In conclusion, then, the Donohue and Denham (to appear) and Gil (to appear b) surveys characterize Mekong-Mamberamo languages as being of low grammatical-morpheme density with respect to a major component of the verbal domain. These two surveys, together with their counterparts in the preceding section pertaining to the flagging of thematic roles, thus provide particular instantiations of the more general property of low grammatical-morpheme density, argued in Section 2.15 to be characteristic of Mekong-Mamberamo languages.

3 Historical inferences

The preceding pages have laid out the case for a Mekong-Mamberamo linguistic area extending from Mainland Southeast Asia through Nusantara and into western New Guinea, characterized by 17 distinctive linguistic properties.

While the existence of the Mekong-Mamberamo linguistic area is predicated on linguistic patterns observed in contemporary languages, it is obviously the product of myriad historical processes that have played out over time. Section 2 provided a few indications of what these processes might have been, in the context of some of the individual linguistic properties under discussion. The present section addresses the more general question of how the Mekong-Mamberamo linguistic area might have evolved over the course of time.

Languages do not exist in isolation; they are spoken by people, and they form part of larger cultural configurations or "packages". Nevertheless, the description of the Mekong-Mamberamo linguistic area in Section 2 is based on

---

are not reconstructible as such to proto-Austronesian. For example, in Tagalog, obligatory TAM marking manifests itself in paradigms such as, for the actor-oriented voice of 'buy', *bumili* (<AT.REAL>buy) / *bumibili* (<AT.REAL>IMPF~buy) / *bibili* (IMPF~buy), in which realis is marked by infixation of *-um-* while imperfective is marked by initial CV- reduplication. However, the infix *-um-* is a portmanteau form also expressing actor-oriented voice; and indeed, the latter was its original function as reconstructed for proto-Austronesian, and until relatively recently its only function in Tagalog. Still, the etymological question of whether specific TAM markers can be reconstructed for proto-Austronesian does not necessarily answer the grammatical question of whether proto-Austronesian had obligatory or optional TAM marking. What is important for present purposes is that the widespread occurrence of obligatory TAM marking in the contemporary languages of the Philippines suggests that it is likely that the Austronesian languages that first spread into the Mekong-Mamberamo linguistic area also had obligatory TAM marking.

the premise that it is a useful and important goal to describe languages, and the linguistic properties that constitute them, on their own terms, as autonomous entities, without reference to the people that speak them and the cultures within which they are embedded. Austronesian, for example, is the designation of a linguistic genealogical clade: there are Austronesian languages, but no Austronesian artefacts or Austronesian people—just artefacts used by people speaking Austronesian languages. Thus, Bellwood (2000: 12) comments that "pots don't speak or carry genes". Oppenheimer (1998: 66) further observes that "[b]ecause pots cannot talk and language splits are difficult to place and date, much of the argument relating to Austronesian origins depends on mutual underpinning by linguistics and archaeology. It is very important, therefore, that each piece of evidence in the structure be independent and not reciprocally linked to the other discipline…" In other words, only when the distributions of linguistic, cultural and genetic features are properly understood within their own individual frames of reference can they be brought together to show where they coincide and where they diverge, in order to form the basis for an integrated history of the region.[32]

From the outset, it must be acknowledged that the 17 Mekong-Mamberamo linguistic properties need not necessarily share a single common history; rather, it is eminently possible that different individual properties may have their own distinct histories and thus be associated with variable degrees of antiquity. This can be seen most readily by comparison of two individual words, also character-

---

[32] In contrast to the abundance of ongoing work exploring the linguistic, archaeological and genetic landscapes of the region, there are significantly fewer recent studies concerned with mapping out the distribution of elements of contemporary material and social culture—a notable exception being the works of Roger Blench (Blench 2007, 2013, to appear, and elsewhere). Still, it is almost certainly the case that alongside the 17 linguistic properties characteristic of the Mekong-Mamberamo area are numerous others of a more general cultural nature. One such property that I am currently engaged in mapping is a very specific superstition or taboo related to photography. Point your camera at a group of three people and they will tell you not to take the picture, because if you do the person in the middle will die. If they want to have their picture taken, they will either call somebody else to make it four, or else one will move aside to make it two. This superstition is found across the Mekong-Mamberamo area, from Cambodia through Sumatra, Sulawesi and Timor to western New Guinea. Outside the Mekong-Mamberamo region the superstition is also present in a contiguous spillover region encompassing the Philippines, China and Japan, but, to the best of my knowledge, nowhere else in the world. Although photography itself is a recent technological innovation, it is hard to imagine how such a superstition might have achieved its current distribution in the modern era; more likely, it draws from more ancient cultural beliefs that were prevalent throughout the Mekong-Mamberamo area, though what these beliefs might have been remains unclear. Cultural elements such as this should be central to any integrated history of the region.

istic, very roughly, of the Mekong-Mamberamo area, but associated with very different time depths. One such word is a term for 'banana', instantiated, among others, by Thai *klûay*, Khmer *taloi*, Toba Batak (an Austronesian language of Sumatra) *gaol*, Muna (an Austronesian language of Sulawesi) *kalei*, Saweru *karei* and Damal (a possible isolate spoken in the western highlands of Papua) *kelo*. As argued by Donohue and Denham (2009), these forms are associated with the spread of bananas across the region, over 5,000 years ago.[33] At the other end of the time scale is a term for 'mobile phone', that was first introduced in Malaysian and Singaporean English as *handphone*, and then subsequently spread across the languages of Indonesia as *henpon* and then *hape* (the Indonesian-language pronunciation of the acronym *HP*). Like the object to which it refers, this form is little more than one decade old. These two contrasting word stories show how a linguistic area may persist over long periods of time, underpinned by a historical sequence of partially coextensive cultural, economic and political spheres ultimately deriving from a relatively fixed and immutable physical ecology.

Nevertheless, it would appear that for the most part, a linguistic area stretching from the Mekong to the Mamberamo must be of substantial antiquity. Recent history, from the onset of the colonial era through to television, airplanes and mobile phones, is qualitatively different from just about everything that preceded it. Most linguistic properties are not like words for mobile phones; it is hard to see how the 17 linguistic properties of the Mekong-Mamberamo area could have spread throughout the entire region, to the remotest of villages from Mainland Southeast Asia to western New Guinea, in less than a period of a few millennia. As is suggested in Section 2 above and argued in more detail below, most if not all of the Mekong-Mamberamo properties were probably in place at least a few thousand years ago; in particular, they were probably present in Nusantara prior to the expansion into the region of the Austronesian language family.

Within the Mekong-Mamberamo linguistic area, the Austronesian family is a major protagonist, accounting for over one half of the languages in the area. With its clear cut and relatively well-known time line, the dispersal of the Austronesian languages from their Taiwan homeland into the Mekong-Mamberamo area and subsequently out of it into the Indian and Pacific oceans provides a

---

[33] While Donohue and Denham (2009) reconstruct a proto-Austronesian form **qaRutay*, Blench (to appear) argues that the forms were borrowed from non-Austronesian languages into Austronesian languages that had already begun to spread into the Nusantara archipelago. But whatever the history of the word within Austronesian, its distribution across the region is clearly ancient.

useful window into the history of the region. These two movements, into and then out of the Nusantara archipelago, are examined in reverse chronological order in the next two subsections.

3.1 The Austronesian dispersals out of Nusantara

The dispersal of Austronesian languages out of the Mekong-Mamberamo area, exporting Mekong-Mamberamo properties into new parts of the world, provides a possible tool for gauging the antiquity of specific Mekong-Mamberamo properties, suggesting that such properties might have been present at the Mekong-Mamberamo point of origin at the time when the languages embarked on their dispersal.

One particularly interesting case is provided by Malagasy. As pointed out in Section 2.1, Malagasy has the passing gesture, which, in view of its near complete absence from other parts of the world, suggests that it must have been present in the Nusantara region when the settlers first departed from Borneo some 1500 years ago. On the other hand, Malagasy fails to exhibit a number of other Mekong-Mamberamo properties. In particular, with respect to several grammatical properties, Malagasy bears a closer resemblance to Philippine languages; these include verb-initial word order, a Philippine-type voice system, relatively rich morphological structure, and long words (in particular, the apparent absence of a disyllabic maximal-word constraint). Moreover, with regard to its verb-initial word order and Philippine-type voice system, at least, the relative scarcity of these properties across the world's languages strongly suggests that Malagasy inherited them from the Malayo-Polynesian languages that first spread into Borneo. This in turn entails that there was at least one East-Barito language spoken in Borneo some 1500 years ago, an immediate ancestor of Malagasy, which also had verb-initial word order, a Philippine-type voice system, relatively rich morphological structure, and long words. So does this mean that the Mekong-Mamberamo distribution of these properties was not yet in place some 1500 years ago? Not necessarily. Given the presence of contemporary non-Austronesian languages in Mainland Southeast Asia and eastern Nusantara and western New Guinea with SVO word order, weakly grammaticalized voice systems, isolating word structure and short words, a perhaps more likely scenario would be that around 1500 years ago, the region in which the East-Barito language ancestral to Malagasy was spoken also contained other languages with a more typical Mekong-Mamberamo profile—either non-Austronesian languages belonging to families that may have since become extinct, or Austronesian languages that had already assimilated to the Mekong-

Mamberamo mould. And that in the time that passed since the ancestors of today's Malagasy speakers left the region, the remaining East-Barito languages adopted the Mekong-Mamberamo properties of the surrounding languages.

In the other direction, Austronesian languages brought many Mekong-Mamberamo properties into the Pacific, including, as shown in Section 2 the passing gesture (in various more attenuated versions), repeated dental clicks expressing amazement, conventionalized greetings with 'where', *d/t* place of assimilation asymmetries, numeral classifiers, verby adjectives, basic SVO order, isolating word structure, optional thematic-role flagging, and optional TAM marking. The Austronesian languages of the Pacific are generally assumed to descend from a common proto-Oceanic language spoken in the Bismarck archipelago around 3,500 - 4,000 years ago; presumably an immediate ancestor of proto-Oceanic would have spread relatively shortly before then from the Cenderawasih Bay region. Thus, it is likely that some 4,000 years ago, many if not all of the Mekong-Mamberamo properties observable in contemporary languages of the Pacific were already in place in the Cenderawasih Bay region and other parts of the eastern Mekong-Mamberamo area, amongst their pre-Oceanic ancestors as well as other languages, Austronesian and non-Austronesian.[34]

---

[34] While the Austronesian language family accounts for the lion's share of cases of language dispersal out of the Mekong-Mamberamo area, at least one other partially similar case is worthy of note, involving the Austroasiatic language family. While the homeland of the Austroasiatic family is subject to debate, all of the current proposals locate it either within Mainland Southeast Asia (Diffloth 2005, Sagart 2011, Sidwell and Blench 2011) or on its periphery, be it central or southern China (Norman and Mei 1976) or northeastern India and the Bay of Bengal (van Driem 2007). However, while most of the contemporary Austroasiatic languages are spoken within Mainland Southeast Asia, those of one group, Munda, are spoken in South Asia, and hence presumably also represent an instance of spread out of the Mekong-Mamberamo area. In many respects, Munda languages seem to have assimilated to the South Asian typological profile (Donegan and Stampe 1983, 2004); however, some residual Mekong-Mamberamo properties from the original homeland may have been retained. Two possible examples, exhibited by some Munda languages, are numeral classifiers and optional thematic-role flagging, but further investigation is needed before any clear conclusions can be drawn. (Another Austroasiatic group, Khasian, lies on or near the transitional zone between Mainland Southeast Asia and South Asia, and would seem to exhibit more Mekong-Mamberamo properties than its neighbours, including, notably, basic SVO word order.)

3.2 The Austronesian intrusion into Nusantara

The spread of Austronesian languages from their Taiwan homeland, through the Philippines and into Nusantara, that began some 4,000 years ago, give or take, was one of the most important events in the linguistic history of the region, and one whose effects are clearly visible in the contemporary distribution of linguistic properties. Inspection of Table 1 shows that of the 17 Mekong-Mamberamo properties, 11 exhibit a high degree of differentiation between the Mekong-Mamberamo area and the Philippines and Taiwan to the north, while an additional two properties exhibit a more moderate degree of differentiation. With respect to these 13 properties, then, Austronesian languages started out differently from the Mekong-Mamberamo norm, but then adapted to it as they spread into the area. However, their adaptation was not always complete. As is also shown in Table 1, for five of the Mekong-Mamberamo properties, namely numeral classifiers, basic SVO word order, weakly developed grammatical voice, isolating word structure, and short words, a saddle-like pattern is visible, with Austronesian languages in the centre of the Mekong-Mamberamo area tending to exhibit the properties in question to a somewhat lesser degree than their non-Austronesian counterparts in Mainland Southeast Asia and in eastern Nusantara and western New Guinea. With respect to these five properties, then, the Austronesian languages of the Mekong-Mamberamo area still betray characteristics of their Taiwan and Philippine ancestry.

For these five properties, the presence of a saddle effect provides strong additional evidence that their Mekong-Mamberamo distribution is ancient, specifically that it predates the Austronesian spread into Nusantara some 4,000 years ago. If, contrary to hypothesis, the distribution of these properties across the Mekong-Mamberamo area were more recent, dating to a period when the Austronesian languages were already present in the area, then in the course of their spreading from the non-Austronesian languages at one end of the Mekong-Mamberamo area to the non-Austronesian languages at the other end, these properties would have had, somehow, to be able to identify the Austronesian languages in their midst and—at least in part—skip over them, on their way across the Mekong-Mamberamo area. While not entirely impossible, this is a much less plausible scenario than the much simpler assumption that the five properties in question, numeral classifiers, basic SVO word order, weakly developed grammatical voice, isolating word structure, and short words, were already distributed throughout the Mekong-Mamberamo area when the Austronesian languages first arrived, and that it was their partial adoption by the incoming Austronesian languages that created the observed saddle-like pattern.

The presence of a saddle effect in five of the 17 Mekong-Mamberamo properties raises the further possibility that additional erstwhile Mekong-Mamberamo properties may have been overridden by the Austronesian intrusion not partially, as is the case for the above five, but rather completely, wiping out any remnants of an original Mekong-Mamberamo property in regions into which the Austronesian languages spread. The signature pattern for such a scenario would be a property present in Mainland Southeast Asia and eastern Nusantara and western New Guinea while totally absent from western Nusantara. The phonotactic database of Donohue, Hetherington and McElvenny (2012) provides three examples of such properties: lexical tone, prenasalized plosives, and the absence of a *g* phoneme in an otherwise symmetrical inventory of stops. Another example of such a property, from the realm of the lexicon, is the expression of 'give' as a combination of 'take' plus a locative expression, present in Sinitic languages such as Gan and Dabu Hakka (Güldemann 2013), White Hmong (Ratliff 2009), and a number of unrelated languages of the New Guinea Bird's Head (Reesink 2002: 29). The contemporary distributions of these properties may thus be remnants of an earlier distribution that spanned the entire Mekong-Mamberamo area, though of course it is equally possible that the occurrence of these properties at the two ends of the Mekong-Mamberamo area represents an accidental similarity between what in this case would be two distinct areal patterns.

While the adoption of Mekong-Mamberamo properties by the incoming Austronesian languages is obviously due to language contact, a number of different and sometimes competing models are available to capture the mechanisms of such contact-induced changes. One such model was proposed by Weinreich (1953) and others, and further developed by Ross (1996), who introduced the term *metatypy*, in his account of the presence of non-Austronesian morphosyntactic patterns in the Austronesian language Takia spoken on an island off the coast of northern New Guinea. A range of other models may be subsumed under the notion of *creolization*, which, in accordance with alternative theoretical perspectives, might involve feature pools, superstrate inheritance, relexification, and/or adoption of an innate bioprogram. As argued by Donohue and Denham (to appear), no single model can be assumed to be valid across the entire region; what is conveniently labelled as the Austronesian dispersal (in the singular) into the Nusantara archipelago actually played out as a myriad of independent and variegated instances of contact between an intrusive Austronesian language and an indigenous non-Austronesian one across the numerous islands of the archipelago and across an era spanning thousands of years—from the very first intrusion to the present day. The only way to adjudicate definitively between such alternative scenarios is by means of detailed individual case studies of particular instances of language contact.

Still, the broad perspective adopted in the present paper can offer some valuable insights. To begin with, it imposes a boundary condition on the speed in which, in accordance with the so-called "fast-train" model (Gray, Drummond and Greenhill 2009, and others), the Austronesian languages could have spread from Taiwan and the Philippines through the Mekong-Mamberamo area and then out into the Indian and Pacific oceans. Specifically, they would have had to have remained long enough within the Mekong-Mamberamo area and to have entered into situations of sufficiently intense contact to enable them to acquire those properties that they did not bring with them from Taiwan and the Philippines but ended up carrying with them—as discussed in the previous section—on their subsequent voyages out into the Indian and Pacific oceans. In the case of Malagasy, the relevant properties include the passing gesture, 'eye day' > 'sun' lexicalizations, verby adjectives and optional TAM marking, while in the case of Oceanic languages, the properties include the passing gesture, repeated dental clicks expressing amazement, conventionalized greetings with 'where', 'eye day' > 'sun' lexicalizations, *d/t* place-of-articulation asymmetry, numeral classifiers, verby adjectives, isolating word structure, optional thematic-role flagging and optional TAM marking.

An important insight into the nature of the Austronesian intrusion into the Mekong-Mamberamo linguistic area comes from an examination of the 17 Mekong-Mamberamo properties in terms of the notion of *complexity*. Of these 17 properties, the last seven, namely low differentiation of adnominal attributive constructions, weakly developed grammatical voice, isolating word structure, short words, low grammatical-morpheme density, optional thematic-role flagging and optional TAM marking all represent cases of lesser complexity than their complementary properties.[35] With respect to these seven properties, then, Mekong-Mamberamo languages are thus simpler than their non-Mekong-Mamberamo counterparts. Of the remaining ten properties, most are neither simpler nor more complex than their complementary properties, the one exception being numeral classifiers, which is associated with greater complexity than its complementary property. In balance, though, Mekong-Mamberamo lan-

---

[35] The claim that these seven properties are all instantiations of lesser complexity is based on criteria for the evaluation of linguistic complexity that are invoked in recent discussions of the issue; see, for example, several of the chapters in Sampson, Gil and Trudgill eds. (2009). Some of these criteria include: more material is more complex than less material; more structure is more complex than less structure; more distinctions is more complex than fewer distinctions; and so forth.

guages emerge as significantly simpler than their non-Mekong-Mamberamo counterparts.

The simplicity of Mekong-Mamberamo languages with respect to these seven properties might possibly be attributable to simplification resulting from imperfect second-language acquisition. The most renowned case of imperfect second-language acquisition is that which gives rise to creole languages, which, according to McWhorter (2001, 2005), Gil (2001, 2007, to appear a), and Parkvall (2008) and others are characterized by simple grammatical structures, of lesser complexity than some or all older languages.[36] And indeed, Donohue and Denham (to appear) argue that some of the scenarios associated with the intrusion of Austronesian languages into the Nusantara archipelago involved creolization, citing languages of eastern Nusantara such as Bima, Kei, Sika and Rote as being possible descendants of such creole languages.

However, creoles are not the only possible outcome of simplification due to imperfect second-language acquisition; McWhorter (2007) argues that in many cases, the result of such processes is what he calls a *Nonhybrid Conventionalized Second-Language (NCSL)* variety, among the ranks of which he includes Malay. In subsequent work, McWhorter (to appear) also characterizes many of the languages of Flores and Timor as NCSLs. Although describing some of the same languages, McWhorter's approach differs from that of Donohue and Denham in two respects: first in that it invokes a somewhat less radical process of simplification, resulting in NCSLs rather than creoles, and secondly in that it is argued to apply at a later date, and involve contact amongst Austronesian languages, rather than between Austronesian languages and their prior non-Austronesian substrates. Nevertheless, both approaches attempt to account for the observed simplicity of contemporary languages in terms of past language contact and imperfect second-language acquisition, and since they are posited for different eras, there is no reason why both of the processes—creolization and the formation of NCSLs—could not be part of the region's linguistic history.[37]

---

36 While McWhorter (2001, 2005) argues for a bidirectional implication whereby all creoles are simpler than all older languages, Gil (2001, 2007 to appear a) argues for a weaker unidirectional implication in accordance with which all creoles are simpler than some older languages, while allowing for some other older languages to be as simple as creoles. For present purposes, though, all that matters is the shared claim that creolization entails simplification.

37 Such claims bring to mind Solheim's (1984-1985: 81) positing of an earlier "Nusantao" (or 'island people') community of traders who spoke an Austronesian "barter language"; however, they differ from it in one crucial respect. Whereas Donohue and Denham (to appear) and McWhorter (to appear) view contact-induced simplification as something that happened to earlier, more complex, varieties of Austronesian, Solheim (1984-1985) identifies this trade

Thus, it is more than likely that in many parts of Nusantara, simplification due to imperfect second-language acquisition was part of the story of the dispersal of Austronesian languages. But there are good reasons why it cannot be the whole story of how and why Austronesian languages took on Mekong-Mamberamo properties, even for those languages which went the furthest in their adoption of Mekong-Mamberamo characteristics. To begin with, many Austronesian Mekong-Mamberamo languages retain at least some conservative Austronesian morphology, which one would not expect to find if these were creole languages (though a possible alternative account of such morphology in the case of Malayic languages is suggested in Gil to appear c). But more cogently, simplification through imperfect second-language acquisition cannot explain why the intrusive Austronesian languages adopted the remaining ten Mekong-Mamberamo properties, those that do not involve any kind of simplification. In order to account for these properties, alternative mechanisms of language contact must be sought. However, if one needs recourse to such alternative mechanisms to account for the first ten Mekong-Mamberamo properties, then the same mechanisms may in principle also be invoked for the remaining seven properties, thereby obviating any need for positing simplification due to imperfect second-language acquisition.[38]

Whatever the mechanisms of language contact that were involved, the picture that emerges is one of an Austronesian intrusion into a Mekong-Mamberamo linguistic area that was already largely or entirely in place some 4,000 years ago. The antiquity of the Mekong-Mamberamo linguistic area is consistent with evidence from archaeology and genetics revealing the existence of a network of trading relationships prior to the Austronesian intrusion. Blench (to appear) describes an array of cultural artefacts common to many or all parts of the Mekong-Mamberamo area, including string bags and slit gongs, and also

---

language with proto-Austronesian itself. As pointed out by Blench (2012: 132), Solheim's position is untenable, since "[t]rade languages are dispersed, and have simplified lexicon and grammar, as well as poorly developed ethnoscience lexicon and a lack of poetic and hierarchical registers. Austronesian looks nothing like this". But while proto-Austronesian and many of its descendants most certainly do not resemble trade languages, the point being made by Donohue and Denham and by McWhorter is that, pace Blench, many other Austronesian languages spoken in Nusantara do indeed look like the possible descendants of trade languages or of other kinds of languages having undergone contact-induced simplification.

38 Note that such alternative mechanisms may themselves potentially involve creolization: a hypothetical creole language with an incoming Austronesian lexifier might exhibit the simpler Mekong-Mamberamo properties not as the result of simplification due to imperfect second-language acquisition but rather as a reflection of the same properties that were present in the non-Austronesian substrate language.

an "arc of vegeculture" involving sago, taro, and other crops. Donohue and Denham (2010) point to the many domesticated plants and animals that made their way from one end of the Mekong-Mamberamo region to the other in pre-Austronesian times. Originating in Mainland Southeast Asia, pigs (Larson et al 2007, Dobney, Cucchi and Larson 2008) and chickens (Liu, Zhu and Yao 2006, Larson et al 2007) were brought across Nusantara all the way to New Guinea, while sugarcane (Grivet et al 2004) and bananas (Kennedy 2008, Denham and Donohue 2009), originating in New Guinea, crossed the archipelago in the opposite direction, to Mainland Southeast Asia and beyond. In addition, Denham and Donohue (2012) note the presence of Dong Song drums, originally from Vietnam, in places as far afield as the north-central coast of New Guinea. These and other patterns are what led Solheim (2000) to posit the existence of a pre-Austronesian "Nusantao Maritime Trading Network" encompassing the Mekong-Mamberamo area plus the Philippine archipelago. Each and every one of the above items would have been part of a scenario involving language contact, thereby playing a role in the maintenance of the Mekong-Mamberamo linguistic area.

As emphasized by Donohue and Denham (to appear), the details of the Austronesian intrusion differ from one location to another; different scenarios will have played out in different parts of the Nusantara archipelago. Nevertheless, when coupled with the archaeological evidence surveyed above, the existence of an ancient Mekong-Mamberamo linguistic area would seem to lend further support to a characterization of a significant proportion of the Austronesian spread into Nusantara in terms of scenarios of language shift involving particular linguistic properties, along the lines envisaged by Blench (2012) and Donohue and Denham (to appear), as opposed to the unitary across-the-board "classical" model that speaks of language replacement and the wholesale introduction of an integrated linguistic, cultural and genetic package. But to reiterate, it's not an "either/or" choice; different models of language contact and dispersal will be of greater appropriateness in different locations and at different times.

3.3 The mists of time

If the Mekong-Mamberamo area was in existence in a form similar if not identical to its present form at least 4,000 years ago, it is tempting to wonder what might have been the factors that brought it into existence and enabled it to survive for such a long period of time. Importantly, with respect to a majority of the relevant properties, the Mekong-Mamberamo area represents, in some cases by quite a large margin, the largest contiguous concentration of these particular properties across the languages of the world: these properties include the passing gesture, repeated dental clicks expressing amazement, conventionalized greetings with 'where', 'eye day' > 'sun' lexicalizations, d/t place-of-articulation asymmetry, numeral classifiers, iamitive perfects, low differentiation of adnominal attributive constructions, isolating word structure, low grammatical-morpheme density, optional thematic-role flagging, and optional TAM marking. It is not obvious that such a general question is at all answerable, or at least answerable in terms of a small number of general factors or principles. Still, it is worth trying, even if any such attempts are necessarily of a highly speculative nature.

With regard to the seven Mekong-Mamberamo properties that instantiate lesser complexity than their complementary properties, a logical possibility, albeit an unlikely one, is that these properties represent a direct inheritance from an earlier stage in the evolution of language, associated with simpler structures of the kind still observable in most contemporary Mekong-Mamberamo languages. Obviously, since speakers of Mekong-Mamberamo languages share more or less the same linguistically-relevant genes as people everywhere else in the world, the earlier evolutionary stage being posited would not be a stage in the development of cognitive linguistic abilities but rather a stage in the externalization of such abilities in the form of actual real languages. In other words, the seven properties in question might represent archaisms, traceable back, in a contiguous albeit probably tortured path, to an earlier era in which all languages shared these same properties, an era before distinct parts of speech, complex morphological structures, and grammatical morphemes had arisen. Such an earlier era would be one in which all human languages followed the ground plans characteristic of *protolanguage* (Bickerton 1990) or a somewhat more developed *Isolating-Monocategorial-Associational (IMA) Language* (Gil 2005b). In accordance with such a scenario, the Mekong-Mamberamo area would represent a default or residual zone, one into which the developments that swept throughout most of the world's languages had simply failed, for whatever historical reasons, to make significant inroads. But be that as it may, the above evolutionary scenario says nothing about the other ten Mekong-Mamberamo properties, those that are not associated with lesser complexity.

An alternative and somewhat less far-reaching hypothesis pertaining to the same seven Mekong-Mamberamo properties is that they are the product of ancient simplification due to imperfect second-language acquisition. The contemporary Mekong-Mamberamo area is characterized by high genealogical diversity in its western and eastern ends, and—as argued by Donohue and Denham (to appear)—the same would have been true also of its central parts, prior to the

Austronesian expansion. Such diversity would provide a fruitful breeding ground for contact and ensuing simplification. And indeed, with respect to Mainland Southeast Asia, at least, the "creole-like" appearance of its languages has been noted by LaPolla (2001), Enfield (2011), and Post (this volume). The problem is that there are many other parts of the world with comparable genealogical diversity, for example Equatorial Africa, Mesoamerica and the Amazon, and languages of those regions do not exhibit a similar array of linguistic properties associated with lesser complexity. Of course, different contact situations lead to different linguistic outcomes, so it could be that, of the aforementioned regions, it was only the Mekong-Mamberamo area that was host to the kind of contact that brings about simplification. But once again, the contact scenario fails to account for the other ten Mekong-Mamberamo properties that do not appear to be connected in any way to processes of simplification.

In order to understand the forces that might have shaped the Mekong-Mamberamo linguistic area, it is necessary to ask: What is different about the Mekong-Mamberamo area that might account for why its languages are, with respect to properties such as the 17 discussed in this paper, different from many or all of the languages spoken in other parts of the world? Unfortunately, our world is simply too small for systematic correlations between the linguistic and extra-linguistic properties of such areas to be supported. With space for no more than, say, a dozen or so regions the size of the Mekong-Mamberamo area, every one of them will happen to have at least some distinctive extra-linguistic features of an ecological, historical or cultural nature. What is necessary, then, is to find distinctive features of the Mekong-Mamberamo area that come with a plausible story about the effect that they might have exerted on the distribution of linguistic properties. In this context, two distinctive features of the Mekong-Mamberamo area come to mind.

The first and rather obvious feature is *islands*: much of the Mekong-Mamberamo area encompasses the world's largest archipelago, consisting of perhaps 18,000 different islands. However, it is not clear why the archipelagic nature of the region should make a difference. As pointed out by Donohue and Denham (to appear), population movements across an archipelago differ crucially from those across a land mass; in the case of islands, people can travel directly to a distant island while avoiding contact with islands that lie in the middle, a pattern that is not readily available in the context of land travel. However, it is not obvious what ramifications this might have with respect to the Mekong-Mamberamo area. Perhaps it is simply the distinctive subsistence patterns and seafaring technologies associated with an archipelago that gave rise to a cultural unity that is subsequently reflected in the shared linguistic properties of the Mekong-Mamberamo linguistic area. However, it should be acknowledged that the Mekong-Mamberamo area is not coextensive with islands; on the one hand it excludes the archipelagic Philippines, while on the other hand it includes Mainland Southeast Asia, not to mention substantial interior tracts of larger islands such as Borneo and New Guinea, whose contemporary populations have little or nothing to do with the distant ocean. In addition, the potential antiquity of the Mekong-Mamberamo area suggests that it might have already been at least partly in place when Sumatra, Java, Borneo and surrounding islands were still part of a single "Sundaland" land-mass connected to the Asian mainland.

The second distinctive feature of the area is *hominins*: the Mekong-Mamberamo and adjacent regions are exceptional as being home to the most recent attestations of hominin species closely related to our own, and of contacts between such hominins and modern humans. One possible such group is the *Red Deer Cave People*, known to have been present in Yunnan some 14,500-11,500 years ago (Curnoe et al 2012). Another species is *Homo Floresiensis*, a divergent population descended from *Homo Erectus*, who were present on the eponymous island of Flores up to possibly 12,000 years ago (Morwood et al 2004). Yet another species are the *Denisovans*, known from a DNA sample extracted from a bone fragment found in the Altai mountains of Central Asia (Reich et al 2010), dated back to some 41,000 years ago. Denisovan DNA has subsequently been found in human populations from the Philippines, New Guinea and Australia, pointing towards interbreeding that most probably took place in Southeast Asia (Reich et al 2011). Recently, Dediu and Levinson (2013) have speculated that Neanderthals and Denisovans may have had language, and that in view of the genetic evidence for interbreeding with modern humans, it might be possible to identify traces of Neanderthal and Denisovan languages in modern human languages, based on geographical correlations between modern linguistic properties and locations where interbreeding might have occurred. And indeed, they cite a preliminary orally-presented version of this paper, focusing on the distribution of optional TAM marking, as possibly providing an example of a linguistic property that might have spread from Denisovans to humans.[39] The relatively shallow time-depth at which several hom-

---

39 Admittedly, the contemporary distributions of Denisovan genetic admixture and of Mekong-Mamberamo linguistic properties are largely disjoint. However, the present situation could have arisen in accordance with the following scenario requiring a minimal number of further assumptions: (a) interbreeding with Denisovans (as per Reich et al 2011) and transfer of linguistic properties in the Mekong-Mamberamo area (as per Dediu and Levinson 2013); (b) migration of humans bearing Denisovan genes into New Guinea and Australia (as per Reich et al 2011); (c) replacement of humans bearing Denisovan genes in the Mekong-Mamberamo area inin species were alive in the area and, in at least one case, interacting with humans, suggests that it is not unreasonable to search for linguistic signatures of their presence in the region. More specifically, it is tempting to speculate that they might have had a role in the formation of the Mekong-Mamberamo area, through the transmission of specific linguistic properties from their languages to human ones.[40]

4 Conclusion

The results of this paper offer an alternative perspective on the linguistic geography of Mainland Southeast Asia. Traditionally, Mainland Southeast Asia, in part or in whole, is referred to as "Indochina", in recognition of its bearing host to a confluence of cultural traits associated with the two major civilizations to its west and north respectively. However, as argued in this paper, with respect to a significant array of linguistic properties, those constituting the Mekong-Mamberamo linguistic area, Mainland Southeast Asia is actually less Indian or Chinese than it is Papuan.

Acknowledgements

It was Mark Donohue who invited me on my first steps along the line of inquiry that resulted in this paper; my indebtedness is such that I find it difficult to reconstruct which of the ideas represented here originated in some comment or other by Mark, however I'm sure that quite a lot did. The ideas developed in this paper have also benefitted from discussions with Roger Blench, Tom Conners,

---

by later migrations of humans not bearing Denisovan genes out of Mainland Southeast Asia (as per Lipson et al 2013); and (d) loss of the Mekong-Mamberamo linguistic properties through later drift in the languages of central and eastern New Guinea and Australia. The resulting picture, in which once-linked linguistic and genetic signatures end up in separate albeit adjacent locations is one that has been described for the same region, though in a somewhat different context, by Reesink, Singer and Dunn (2009: 2), who write that "linguistic boundaries in this area can persist much longer than separated populations, thus retaining a signal of distinct populations after the biological signal has been obscured through interbreeding."

40 In addition, one might speculate that they may have contributed to the formation of contact language varieties; see, for example, McWhorter's (to appear) conjecture that contact with *Homo Floresiensis* might have played a role in the morphological simplification characteristic of the languages of central Flores.

Nick Enfield, Martin Haspelmath, Tim McKinnon, John McWhorter, Laura Robinson, Malcolm Ross, and Antoinette Schapper. Helpful comments on an earlier draft of this paper were provided by Bernard Comrie and Nick Enfield. The rather copious amounts of data on which this paper is based were provided by more colleagues and friends than I have the space to acknowledge individually, so thank you all. Bits and pieces of the material in this paper were presented at several conferences and seminars, at which many colleagues, again too numerous to thank individually, provided lots of helpful comments, suggestions and criticism.

Abbreviations

ASSOC	associative	NEG	negative
ALL	allative	NON.PAT	non-patientive
ANIM	animate	PAT	patientive
CIRC	circumfix	PFCT	perfect
CLF	classifier	PL	plural
CN	construct state	POL	polite
DEF	definite	POSS	possessive
DEM	demonstrative	PROG	progressive
DIR	direct case	PROX	proximate
DIST	distal	PST	past
DISTR	distributive	PT	patient-topic voice
EXCL	exclamation	Q	question
FAM	familiar	REAL	realis
GEN.PASS	generalized passive	RECIP	reciprocal
IMPF	imperfective	SG	singular
INAN	inanimate	TOP	topic
INCL	inclusive	1	first person
IRR	irrealis	2	second person
LOC	locative	3	third person
M	masculine		

References

Adelaar, K. Alexander. 1995. Borneo as a crossroads for comparative Austronesian linguistics. In P. Bellwood, J.J. Fox & D. Tryon (eds.), *The Austronesians*, 75–95. Canberra: Australian National University.

Adelaar, K. Alexander. 2005. The Austronesian languages of Asia and Madagascar: A historical perspective. In K.A. Adelaar & N.P. Himmelmann (eds.), *The Austronesian languages of Asia and Madagascar*, 1–42. London: Routledge.

Adelaar, K. Alexander. 2013. Voice variation in Austronesian languages of Indonesia: Introduction. *NUSA, Linguistic studies of languages in and around Indonesia* 54. 1–3.

Aikhenvald, Alexandra Y. 2000. *Classifiers, a typology of noun classification devices*. Oxford: Oxford University Press.

Anderson, Gregory D. S. 2004. The languages of Central Siberia: Introduction and overview. In E. J. Vajda (ed.), *Languages and prehistory of Central Siberia*, 1–119. Amsterdam & Philadelphia: John Benjamins.

Anderson, Gregory D. S. 2006. Towards a typology of the Siberian linguistic area. In Y. Matras, A. McMahon & N. Vincent (eds.), *Linguistic areas: Convergence in historical and typological perspective*, 266–300. New York: Palgrave Macmillan.

Arka, I Wayan & Jeladu Kosmas. 2005. Passive without passive morphology. In I W. Arka & M. Ross (eds.), *The many faces of Austronesian voice systems: Some new empirical studies*, 87–117. Canberra: Pacific Linguistics.

Bellwood, Peter. 2000. Some thoughts on understanding the human colonisation of the Pacific. *People and Culture in Oceania* 16. 5–17.

Bickel, Balthasar & Johanna Nichols. 2005. Fusion of selected inflectional formatives. In M. Haspelmath, M. Dryer, D. Gil & B. Comrie (eds.), *The World Atlas of Language Structures*, 86–89. Oxford: Oxford University Press

Bickel, Balthasar & Johanna Nichols. 2006. Oceania, the Pacific Rim, and the theory of linguistic areas. *Proceedings of the 32nd Annual Meeting of the Berkeley Linguistic Society* 32S. 3–15.

Bickerton, Derek. 1990. *Language and species*. Chicago: University of Chicago Press.

Bisang, Walter. 1999. Classifiers in East and Southeast Asian languages: Counting and beyond. In J. Gvozdanovic (ed.), *Numeral types and changes worldwide*, 113–185. Berlin: Mouton de Gruyter.

Blench, Roger. 2007. Using ethnography to reconstruct the culture of early modern humans. Manuscript.

Blench, Roger. 2012. Almost everything you believed about the Austronesians isn't true. In M.L. Tjoa-Bonatz, A. Reinecke & D. Bonatz (eds.), *Crossing borders: Selected papers from the 13th International Conference of the European Association of Southeast Asian Archaeologists* (Volume 1), 128–148. Singapore: NUS Press.

Blench, Roger. 2013. Ethnographic and archaeological correlates for a Mainland Southeast Asia linguistic area. Manuscript.

Blench, Roger. to appear. Was there once a zone of vegeculture linking Melanesia with Northeast India? In G. Summerhayes & David Addison (eds.), *Selected papers from the 2011 Lapita Pacific Archaeology Conference: Pacific Archaeology: Documenting the Past 50,000 Years to the Present*. Auckland: Auckland University Press.

Blust, Robert. 2009. *The Austronesian languages*. Canberra: Pacific Linguistics.

Bowden, John. 2001. *Taba: Description of a South Halmahera language*. Canberra: Pacific Linguistics.

Burgess, Anthony. 1975. *Language made plain* (Revised Edition). Glasgow: Fontana/Collins.

Bybee, Joan. 1997. Semantic aspects of morphological typology. In J. Bybee, J. Haiman & S. A. Thompson (eds.), *Essays on language function and language type, dedicated to T. Givón*, 25–37. Amsterdam: John Benjamins.

Capell, Arthur. 1969. *A survey of New Guinea languages*. Sydney: Sydney University Press.

Clark, Marybeth. 1992. Serialization in Mainland Southeast Asia. In S. Luksaneeyanawin (ed.), *Pan-Asiatic linguistics, proceedings of the Third International Symposium on Language and Linguistics* (Volume 1), 145–168. Bangkok: Chulalongkorn University.

Cole, Peter, Gabriella Hermon & Yassir Nasanius Tjung. 2006. Is there *pasif semu* in Jakarta Indonesian? *Oceanic Linguistics* 45. 64–90.

Cole, Peter, Gabriella Hermon & Yanti. 2008. Voice in Malay/Indonesian. *Lingua* 118. 1500–1553.

Comrie, Bernard. 2005. Alignment of case marking. In M. Haspelmath, M. Dryer, D. Gil & B. Comrie (eds.), *The World Atlas of Language Structures*, 398–405. Oxford: Oxford University Press.

Comrie, Bernard. 2007. Areal typology of Mainland Southeast Asia: What we learn from the WALS maps. *Manusya* 13. 18–47.

Conners, Thomas. 2008. *Tengger Javanese*. New Haven: Yale University dissertation.

Conners, Thomas. to appear. Javanese undressed: Isolating phenomena in 'Peripheral' dialects. In David Gil & J. McWhorter (eds.), *Austronesian undressed: How and why languages become isolating*. Berlin: DeGruyter.

Conners, Thomas, John Bowden & David Gil. to appear. Valency classes in Jakarta Indonesian. In B. Comrie & A. Malchukov (eds.), *Valency classes: A comparative handbook*. Berlin: Mouton De Gruyter.

Curnoe, Darren, Ji Xueping, Andy I.R. Herries, Bai Kanning, Paul S.C. Taçon, Bao Zhende, David Fink, Zhu Yunsheng, John Hellstrom, Luo Yun, Gerasimos Cassis, Su Bung, Stephen Wroe, Hong Shi, William C.H. Parr, Huang Shengmin & Natalie Rogers. 2012. Human remains from the Pleistocene-Holocene transition of Southwest China suggest a complex evolutionary history for East Asians. *PLoS One* 7(3). e31918.

Dahl, Otto Christian. 1977. La subdivision de la famille Barito et la place du Malgache. *Acta Orientalia (Copenhagen)* 38. 77–134.

Dahl, Östen. 2008. An exercise in 'A Posteriori' language sampling. *Sprachtypologie und Universalienrorschung* 61. 208–220.

Dahl, Östen & Viveka Velupillai. 2005. Tense and aspect. In M. Haspelmath, M. Dryer, D. Gil & B. Comrie (eds.), *The World Atlas of Language Structures*, 266–281. Oxford: Oxford University Press.

Dahl, Östen & Viveka Velupillai. 2011a. The past tense. In M. S. Dryer & M. Haspelmath (eds.), *The World Atlas of Language Structures Online*. Munich: Max Planck Digital Library. Available online at http://wals.info/.

Dahl, Östen & Viveka Velupillai. 2011b. The future tense. In M. S. Dryer & M. Haspelmath. (eds.), *The World Atlas of Language Structures Online*. Munich: Max Planck Digital Library. Available online at http://wals.info/.

Dahl, Östen & Bernhard Wälchli. 2013. Disentangling the variability of the perfect gram type. Paper presented at the Association for Linguistic Typology 10th Biennial Conference, Leipzig, 17 August 2013.

Davies, William D. 2005. The richness of Madurese voice. In I W. Arka & M. Ross (eds.), *The many faces of Austronesian voice systems: Some new empirical studies*, 197–220. Canberra. Pacific Linguistics.

De Lacy, Paul. 2003. Maximal words and the Maori passive. *MIT Working Papers in Linguistics* 44. 20–39.

Dediu, Dan & Stephen C. Levinson. 2013. On the antiquity of language: The reinterpretation of Neanderthal linguistic capacities and its consequences. *Frontiers in Psychology* 4, doi: 10.3389/fpsyg.2013.00397.

Denham, Tim & Mark Donohue. 2009. Pre-Austronesian dispersal of banana cultivars west from New Guinea: Linguistic relics from Eastern Indonesia. *Archaeology in Oceania* 44. 18–28.

Denham, Tim & Mark Donohue. 2012. Lack of correspondence between Asian-Papuan genetic admixture and Austronesian language dispersal in Eastern Indonesia. *PNAS* 109(39): E2577.

Diffloth, Gerard. 2005. The contribution of linguistic palaeontology to the homeland of Austroasiatic. In L. Sagart, R. Blench & A. Sanchez-Mazas (eds.), *The peopling of East Asia: Putting together archaeology, linguistics and genetics*, 79–82 London & New York: Routledge/Curzon.

Diffloth, Gerard & Norman Zide. 1992. Austro-Asiatic languages. In W. Bright (ed.), *International Encyclopaedia of Linguistics* (Volume 1), 137–142. New York: Barnes and Noble.

DiSciullo, Anna-Maria & Edwin Williams. 1987. *On the definition of word*. Cambridge: MIT Press.

Dixon, Robert M.W. 1997. *The rise and fall of languages*. Cambridge: Cambridge University Press.

Dixon, Robert M.W. 2001. The Australian linguistic area. In A. Y. Aikhenvald & R. M. W. Dixon (eds.), *Areal diffusion and genetic inheritance: Problems in comparative linguistics*, 64–104. Oxford: Oxford University Press.

Dobney, Keith, Thomas Cucchi & Gregor Larson. 2008. The pigs of Island Southeast Asia and the Pacific: New evidence for taxonomic status and human-mediated dispersal. *Asian Perspectives* 47. 59–74.

Donegan, Patricia J. & David Stampe. 1983. Rhythm and holistic organization of language structure. In J.F. Richardson, M. Marks & A. Chukerman (eds.), *Papers from the parasession on the interplay of phonology, morphology and syntax*, 337–353. Chicago: Chicago Linguistic Society.

Donegan, Patricia J. & David Stampe. 2004. Rhythm and the synthetic drift of Muṇḍā. In R. Singh (ed.), *The Yearbook of South Asian languages and Linguistics* (2004), 3–36. Berlin: Mouton De Gruyter.

Donohue, Mark. 1999. *Warembori* (Languages of the World/Materials 341). Munich: Lincom Europa.

Donohue, Mark. 2001. Split intransitivity and Saweru. *Oceanic Linguistics* 40. 321–336.

Donohue. 2005a. The Palu'e passive: From pragmatic construction to grammatical device. In I. W. Arka & M. Ross (eds.), *The many faces of Austronesian voice systems: Some new empirical studies*, 59–85. Canberra: Pacific Linguistics.

Donohue, Mark. 2005b. Word order in New Guinea: Dispelling a myth. *Oceanic Linguistics* 44: 527–536.

Donohue, Mark. 2009. Dental discrepancies and the sound of Proto Austronesian. In B. Evans (ed.), *Discovering history through language: Papers in honour of Malcolm Ross,* 271–287. Canberra: Pacific Linguistics.

Donohue, Mark & Tim Denham. 2009. Banana (Musa spp.) domestication in the Asia-Pacific region: Linguistic and archaeobotanical perspectives. *Ethnobotany Research and Applications* 7. 293–332.

Donohue, Mark & Tim Denham. 2010. Farming and language in Island Southeast Asia: Reframing Austronesian history. *Current Anthropology* 51. 223–256.

Donohue, Mark & Tim Denham. to appear. Becoming Austronesian: Mechanisms of language dispersal across Indo-Malaysia. In D. Gil & J. McWhorter (eds.), *Austronesian undressed, how and why languages become isolating.* Berlin: DeGruyter.

Donohue, Mark, Rebecca Hetherington & James McElvenny. 2012. *World Phonotactics Database.* Canberra: Australian National University. http://phonotactics.anu.edu.au. (accessed 8 August 2013).

Dyck, Carrie. 1994. The definition of 'Word' in polysynthetic languages. In C. Dyck (ed.), *Proceedings of the 1993 Annual Conference of the Canadian Linguistic Association* (Toronto Working Papers in Linguistics), 187–203. Toronto: University of Toronto.

Driem, George van. 2007. Austroasiatic phylogeny and the Austroasiatic homeland in light of recent population genetic studies. *Mon-Khmer Studies* 37. 1–14.

Dryer, Matthew. 2005a. Order of subject, object, and verb. In M. Haspelmath, M. Dryer, D. Gil & B. Comrie (eds.), *The World Atlas of Language Structures,* 330–333. Oxford:Oxford University Press.

Dryer, Matthew. 2005b. Position of case affixes. In M. Haspelmath, M. Dryer, D. Gil & B. Comrie (eds.), *The World Atlas of Language Structures,* 210–211. Oxford: Oxford University Press.

Emeneau, Murray B. 1980. *Language and linguistic area.* Stanford: Stanford University Press.

Enfield, N. J. 2005. Areal linguistics and Mainland Southeast Asia. *Annual Review of Anthropology* 34. 181–206.

Enfield, N. J. 2007. *A grammar of Lao.* Berlin & New York: Mouton de Gruyter.

Enfield, N. J. 2011. Linguistic diversity in Mainland Southeast Asia. In N.J. Enfield (ed.), *Dynamics of human diversity: The case of Mainland Southeast Asia,* 63–79. Canberra: Pacific Linguistics.

Evans, Nicholas, Janet Fletcher & Belinda Ross. 2008. Big words, small phrases: Mismatches between pause units and the polysynthetic word in Dalabon. *Linguistics* 46. 89–129.

Foley, William A. 1986. *The Papuan languages of New Guinea.* Cambridge: Cambridge University Press.

Foley, William A. 2000. The languages of New Guinea. *Annual Review of Anthropology* 29. 357–404.

Foley, William A. 2010. Language contact in the New Guinea Region. In R. Hickey (ed.), *The handbook of language contact,* 795–813. Riley-Blackwell, Chichester.

Gil, David. 1996. How to speak backwards in Tagalog. In *Pan-Asiatic linguistics, proceedings of the Fourth International Symposium on Language and Linguistics* (January 8–10, 1996) (Volume 1), 297–306. Salaya: Mahidol University.

Gil, David. 2001. Creoles, complexity and Riau Indonesian, *Linguistic Typology* 5. 325–371.

Gil, David. 2002. The prefixes *di-* and *N-* in Malay / Indonesian dialects. In F. Wouk & M. Ross (eds.), *The History and Typology of Western Austronesian Voice Systems,* 241–283. Canberra: Pacific Linguistics.

Gil, David. 2005a. Genitives, adjectives and relative clauses. In M. Haspelmath, M. Dryer, D. Gil & B. Comrie (eds.), *The World Atlas of Language Structures*, 246–249. Oxford: Oxford University Press.

Gil, David. 2005b. Isolating-monocategorial-associational language. In H. Cohen & C. Lefebvre (eds.), *Categorization in cognitive science*, 347–379. Oxford: Elsevier.

Gil, David. 2005c. Numeral classifiers. In M. Haspelmath, M. Dryer, D. Gil & B. Comrie (eds.), *The World Atlas of Language Structures*, 226–229. Oxford: Oxford University Press.

Gil, David. 2005d. Para-linguistic usages of clicks. In M. Haspelmath, M. Dryer, D. Gil & B. Comrie (eds.), *The World Atlas of Language Structures*, 572–575. Oxford: Oxford University Press.

Gil, David. 2007. Creoles, complexity and associational semantics. In U. Ansaldo & S.J. Matthews (eds.), *Deconstructing Creole: New horizons in language creation*, 67–108. Amsterdam: John Benjamins.

Gil, David. 2008. How complex are isolating languages? In F. Karlsson, M. Miestamo & K. Sinnemäki (eds.), *Language complexity: Typology, contact, change*, 109–131. Amsterdam: John Benjamins.

Gil, David. to appear a. Sign languages, Creoles, and the development of predication. In F. J. Newmayer & L. Preston (eds.), *Formal linguistics and the measurement of grammatical complexity*. New York: Oxford University Press.

Gil, David. to appear b. Tense, aspect and mood marking. In M. Dryer & M. Haspelmath (eds.), *World Atlas of Language Structures Online*. Max Planck Digital Library: Munich. Available online at http://www.wals.info/.

Gil, David. to appear c. What happened to Riau Indonesian. In D. Gil & J. McWhorter (eds.), *Austronesian undressed, How and why languages become isolating*. Berlin: DeGruyter.

Gil, David. in preparation a. Para-linguistic usages of clicks. In M. Dryer & M. Haspelmath (eds.), *World Atlas of Language Structures Online*. Munich: Max Planck Digital Library. Available online at http://www.wals.info/.

Gil, David. in preparation b. The passing gesture. In M. Dryer & M. Haspelmath (eds.), *World Atlas of Language Structures Online*. Munich: Max Planck Digital Library. Available online at http://www.wals.info/.

Gil, David. in preparation c. Where are you going? In M. Dryer & M. Haspelmath (eds.), *World Atlas of Language Structures Online*. Munich: Max Planck Digital Library. Available online at http://www.wals.info/.

Gravelle, Gilles. 2010. *Meyah, a language of West Papua, Indonesia*. Canberra: Pacific Linguistics.

Gray, Russell D., Alexei J. Drummond & Simon J. Greenhill. 2009. Language phylogenies reveal expansion pulses and pauses in Pacific Settlement. *Science* 23(5913). 479–483.

Greenberg, Joseph H. 1963. Some universals of grammar with particular reference to the order of meaningful elements. In J.H. Greenberg (ed.), *Universals of grammar*, 73–113. Cambridge: MIT Press.

Greenhill, Simon J., Robert Blust & Russell D. Gray. 2008. The Austronesian basic vocabulary database: From bioinformatics to lexomics. *Evolutionary Bioinformatics* 4. 271–283.

Grivet, Laurent, Christian Daniels, Jean-Christophe Glaszmann & Angelique D'Hont. 2004. A review of recent molecular genetics evidence for sugarcane evolution and domestication. *Ethnobotany Research and Applications* 2. 9–17.

Güldemann, Tom. 2013. Using minority languages to inform the historical analysis of major written languages: A Tuu perspective on the 'give' - object marker polysemy in Sinitic. *Journal of Asian and African Studies* 85. 41–59.

Hashimoto, Mantaro. 1976. Language diffusion on the Asian continent: Problems of typological diversity in Sino-Tibetan. *Computational Analysis of Asian and African Languages* 3. 49–63.

Hashimoto, Mantaro. 1978. *Linguistic typogeography*. Tokyo: Kobundo.

Haspelmath, Martin. 2011. The indeterminacy of word segmentation and the nature of morphology and syntax. *Folia Linguistica* 45. 31–80.

Haudricourt, André G. 1965. Problems of Austronesian comparative philology. *Lingua* 14. 315–329.

Hayami-Allen, Rika. 2001. *A descriptive study of the language of Ternate, the Northern Moluccas, Indonesia*. Pittsburgh: University of Pittsburgh dissertation.

Heine, Bernd & Tania Kuteva. 2002. *World lexicon of grammaticalization*. Cambridge: Cambridge University Press.

Himmelmann, Nikolaus P. 2005. The Austronesian languages of Asia and Madagascar: Typological characteristics. In K.A. Adelaar & N.P. Himmelmann (eds.), *The Austronesian languages of Asia and Madagascar*, 110–181. London: Routledge.

Janhunen, Juha. 1998. Ethnicity and language in prehistoric Northeast Asia. In R. Blench & M. Spriggs (eds.), *Archaeology and language II, archaeological data and linguistic hypotheses*, 195–208. London & New York: Routledge.

Jufrizal & I Wayan Arka. 2006. Voice in Mentawai: A note on its typological position in the Austronesian languages of Indonesia. Paper presented at the 16th Annual Meeting of the Southeast Asian Linguistics Society, Jakarta, Indonesia, 21 September 2006.

Kennedy, Jean. 2008. Pacific bananas: Complex origins, multiple dispersals? *Asian Perspectives* 47(1). 75–94.

Klamer, Marian A.F., Ger P. Reesink & Miriam van Staden. 2008. East nusantara as a linguistic area. In P. Muysken (ed.), *From linguistic areas to areal linguistics*, 95–149. Amsterdam: John Benjamins.

LaPolla, Randy J. 2001. The role of migration and language contact in the development of the Sino-Tibetan language family. In A.Y. Aikhenvald & R.M.W. Dixon (eds.), *Areal diffusion and genetic inheritance: Problems in comparative linguistics*, 225–254. Oxford: Oxford University Press.

Larson, Greger, Thomas Cucchi, Masakatsu Fujita, Elizabeth Matisoo-Smith, Judith Robins, Atholl Anderson, Barry Rolett, Matthew Spriggs, Gaynor Dolman, Tae-Hun Kim, Nguyen Thi Dieu Thuy, Ettore Randi, Moira Doherty, Rokus Awe Due, Robert Bollt, Tony Djubiantono, Bion Griffin, Michiko Intoh, Emile Keane, Patrick Kirch, Kuang-Ti Li, Michael Morwood, Lolita M. Pedriña, Philip J. Piper, Ryan J. Rabett, Peter Shooter, Gert Van den Bergh, Eric West, Stephen Wickler, Jing Yuan, Alan Cooper & Keith Dobney. 2007. Phylogeny and ancient DNA of Sus provides insights into Neolithic expansion in Island Southeast Asia and Oceania. *Proceedings of the National Academy of Sciences of the USA* 104(12). 4834–4839.

Lipson, Mark, Po-Ru Loh, Nick Patterson, Priya Moorjani, Yin-Chin Ko, Mark Stoneking, Bonnie Berger & David Reich. 2013. Reconstructing the ancestry of Austronesian-speaking populations. Manuscript.

Liu, Yi-Ping Liu, Qing Zhu & Yong-Gang Yao. 2006. Genetic relationship of Chinese and Japanese gamecocks revealed by mtDNA sequence variation. *Biochemical Genetics* 44(1–2). 18–28.
Lu, Tian Qiao. 2008. *A grammar of Maonan*. Boca Raton: Universal Publishers.
Maddieson, Ian. 1984. *Patterns of sounds*. Cambridge: Cambridge University Press.
Masica, Charles P. 1976. *Defining a linguistic area*. Chicago: University of Chicago Press.
Matisoff, James A. 1973. Tonogenesis in Southeast Asia. In L. M. Hyman (ed.), *Southern California Occasional Papers in Linguistics* (No 1.), 72–95. Los Angeles: University of Southern California.
Matisoff, James A. 1976. Lahu causative constructions: Case hierarchies and the morphology/syntax cycle in a Tibeto-Burman perspective. In M. Shibatani (ed.), *Syntax and Semantics, Volume 6, The grammar of causative constructions*, 413–442. New York: Academic Press.
Matisoff, James A. 2001. Genetic versus contact relationship: Prosodic diffusability in South-East Asian languages. In A.Y. Aikhenvald & R.M.W. Dixon (eds.), *Areal diffusion and genetic inheritance: Problems in comparative linguistics*, 291–327. Oxford: Oxford University Press.
McDonough, Joyce. 1990. *Topics in the phonology and morphology of Navajo verbs*. Amherst: University of Massachusetts dissertation.
McKinnon, Timothy. 2010. *Morphophonology and morphosyntax of Kerinci word-shape alternations*. Newark, DE: University of Delaware dissertation.
McWhorter, John. 2001. The world's simplest grammars are Creole grammars. *Linguistic Typology* 5. 125–166.
McWhorter, John. 2005. *Defining Creole*. Oxford and New York: Oxford University Press.
McWhorter, John. 2007. *Language interrupted: Signs of non-native acquisition in standard language grammars*. New York: Oxford University Press.
McWhorter, John. to appear. Affixless in Austronesian: Why Flores is a puzzle and what to do about It. In D. Gil & J. McWhorter (eds.), *Austronesian undressed, how and why languages become isolating*. Berlin: DeGruyter.
Morwood, M.J., R.P. Soejono, R.G Roberts, T. Sutikna, C.S.M. Turney, K.E. Westaway, W.J. Rink, J.-x. Zhao, G.D. van den Bergh, Rokus Awe Due, D.R. Hobbs, M.W. Moore, M.I. Bird & L.K. Fifield. 2004. Archaeology and age of a new Homonin from Flores in Eastern Indonesia. *Nature* 431(7012). 1087–1091.
National Institute for Japanese Language. 2006. *Grammar Atlas of Japanese Dialects* (Volume 6, Map 349). Tokyo: The National Language Research Institute.
Nichols, Johanna. 1986. Head-marking and dependent-marking grammar. *Language* 62. 475–521.
Nichols, Johanna. 1992. *Linguistic diversity in space and time*. Chicago: University of Chicago Press.
Nichols, Johanna. 1998. The origin and dispersal of languages: Linguistic evidence. In N.G. Jablonski & I.C. Aiello (eds.), *The origin and diversification of language* (Memoirs of the California Academy of Sciences, Number 24), 127–170. San Francisco: California Academy of Sciences.
Nordhoff, Sebastian, Harald Hammarström, Robert Forkel & Martin Haspelmath (eds.). 2013. *Glottolog 2.0*. Leipzig: Max Planck Institute for Evolutionary Anthropology. http://glottolog.org (accessed 10 August 2013).

Norman, Jerry & Mei Tsu-lin. 1976. The Austroasiatics in ancient South China: Some lexical evidence. *Monumenta Serica* 22. 274–301.

Olsson, Bruno. 2013. *Iamitives, perfects in Southeast Asia and beyond*. Stockholm: Stockholm University, Department of Linguistics MA Thesis.

Oppenheimer, Stephen. 1998. *Eden in the East, the drowned continent of Southeast Asia*. London: Weidenfleld and Nicolson.

Parkvall, Mikael. 2008. The simplicity of Creoles in a typological perspective. In F. Karlsson, M. Miestamo & K. Sinnemäki (eds.), *Language complexity: Typology, contact, change*, 265–285. Amsterdam: John Benjamins.

Ratliff, Martha. 2009. Loanwords in White Hmong. In M. Haspelmath & U. Tadmor (eds.), *World Loanword Database* (WOLD), Max Planck Digital Library. http://wold.livingsources.org/ (accessed 10 August 2013).

Reesink, Ger P. 2002. The Eastern Bird's Head languages compared. In G.P. Reesink (ed.), *Languages of the Eastern Bird's Head*, 1–44. Canberra: Pacific Linguistics.

Reesink, Ger, Ruth Singer & Michael Dunn. 2009. Explaining the linguistic diversity of Sahul using population models. *PLoS Biology* 7(11). e1000241. doi: 10.1371/journal.pbio.1000241.

Reich, David, Richard E. Green, Martin Kircher, Johannes Krause, Nick Patterson, Eric Y. Durand, Bence Viola, Adrian W. Briggs, Udo Stenzel, Philip L. F. Johnson, Tomislav Maricic, Jeffrey M. Good, Tomas Marques-Bonet, Can Alkan, Qiaomei Fu, Swapan Mallick, Heng Li, Matthias Meyer, Evan E. Eichler, Mark Stoneking, Michael Richards, Sahra Talamo, Michael V. Shunkov, Anatoli P. Derevianko, Jean-Jacques Hublin, Janet Kelso, Montgomery Slatkin & Svante Pääbo. 2010. Genetic history of an archaic Hominin group from Denisova cave in Siberia. *Nature* 468(7327). 1053–1060.

Reich, David, Nick Patterson, Martin Kircher, Frederick Delfin, Madhusudan R. Nandineni, Irina Pugach, Albert Min-Shan Ko, Ying-Chin Ko, Timothy A. Jinam, Maude E. Phipps, Naruya Saitou, Andreas Wollstein, Manfred Kayser, Svante Pääbo & Mark Stoneking. 2011. Denisova admixture and the first modern human dispersals into Southeast Asia and Oceania. *American Journal of Human Genetics* 89(4). 516–528.

Rice, Keren. 1994. The structure of the Slave (Northern Athapaskan) verb. In S. Hargus & E. Kaisse (eds.), *Phonetics and Phonology 4, Studies in Lexical Phonology*, 145–171. New York: Academic Press.

Ross, Malcolm D. 1992. The sound of Proto-Austronesian: An outsider's view of the Formosan evidence. *Oceanic Linguistics* 31. 23–64.

Ross, Malcolm D. 1996. Contact-induced change and the comparative method: Cases from Papua New Guinea. In M. Durie & M.D. Ross (eds.), *The comparative method reviewed: Regularity and irregularity in language change*, 180–217. New York: Oxford University Press.

Russell, Kevin. 1999. What's with all these long words anyway? *MIT Working Papers in Linguistics* 17. 119–130.

Sagart, Laurent. 2004. The higher phylogeny of Austronesian and the position of Tai–Kadai. *Oceanic Linguistics* 43. 411–440.

Sagart, Laurent. 2011. The Austroasiatics: East to west or west to east? In N.J. Enfield (ed.), *Dynamics of human diversity: The case of Mainland Southeast Asia*, 345–359. Canberra: Pacific Linguistics.

Sampson, Geoffrey, David Gil & Peter Trudgill (eds.). 2009. *Language complexity as an evolving variable*. Oxford: Oxford University Press.

Schachter, Paul. 1976. The subject in Philippine languages: Topic, actor, actor-topic, or none of thea. In C.N. Li (ed.), *Subject and Topic*, 491–518. New York: Academic Press.
Schachter, Paul. 1977. Reference-related and role-related properties of subjects. In P. Cole & J.M. Sadock (eds.), *Syntax and Semantics, Volume 8: Grammatical relations*, 279–306. New York: Academic Press.
Sidwell, Paul & Roger Blench. 2011. The Austroasiatic urheimat: The Southeastern Riverine hypothesis. In N.J. Enfield (ed.), *Dynamics of human diversity: The case of Mainland Southeast Asia*, 315–343. Canberra: Pacific Linguistics.
Siewierska, Anna. 2005. Passive constructions. In M. Haspelmath, M. Dryer, D. Gil & B. Comrie (eds.), *The World Atlas of Language Structures*, 434–437. Oxford: Oxford University Press.
Solheim, Wilhelm G. II. 1984–1985. The Nusantao hypothesis: The origin and spread of Austronesian speakers. *Asian Perspectives* 26. 77–88.
Solheim, Wilhelm G. II. 2000. Taiwan, coastal South China and northern Viet Nam and the Nusantao maritime trading network. *Journal of East Asian Archaeology* 2. 273–284.
Sprouse, Ronald L., Maria-Josep Solé & John J. Ohala. 2008. Oral cavity enlargement in retroflex stops. In R. Sock, S. Fuchs & Y. Laprie (eds.), *8th International Seminar on Speech Production (2008)* (Proceedings), 429–432. Strasbourg.
Starosta, Stanley, Andrew K. Pawley & Laurie Reid. 1982. The evolution of focus in Austronesian. In A. Halim, L. Carrington & S.A. Wurm (eds.), *Papers from the Third International Conference on Austronesian Linguistics*, (Volume 2), 201–216 Canberra: Pacific Linguistics.
Stassen, Leon. 2005. Predicative adjectives. In M. Haspelmath, M. Dryer, D. Gil & B. Comrie (eds.), *The World Atlas of Language Structures*, 478–481. Oxford: Oxford University Press.
Stolz, Thomas. 2002. No Sprachbund beyond this line! On the age-old discussion of how to define a linguistic area. In P. Ramat & T. Stolz (eds.), *Mediterranean languages, Papers from the MEDTYP Workshop, Tirrenia, June 2000*, 259–281. Bochum: Brockmeyer.
Thurgood, Graham, Fengxiang Li & Ela Thurgood. to appear. *The Cham of Hainan: A study of linguistic restructuring and change under intense contact, based on the work of Zheng Yiqing and Ouyang Jueya*.
Urban, Matthias. 2010. 'Sun' = 'Eye of the Day': A linguistic pattern of Southeast Asia and Oceania. *Oceanic Linguistics* 49. 568–579.
Weinreich, Uriel. 1953. *Languages in contact*. New York: Linguistic Circle of New York.
Wichmann, Søren, Taraka Rama & Eric W. Holman. 2011. Phonological diversity, word length, and population sizes across languages: The ASJP evidence. *Linguistic Typology* 15. 177–197.
Yanti. 2010. *A reference grammar of Jambi Malay*. Newark, DE: University of Delaware dissertation.

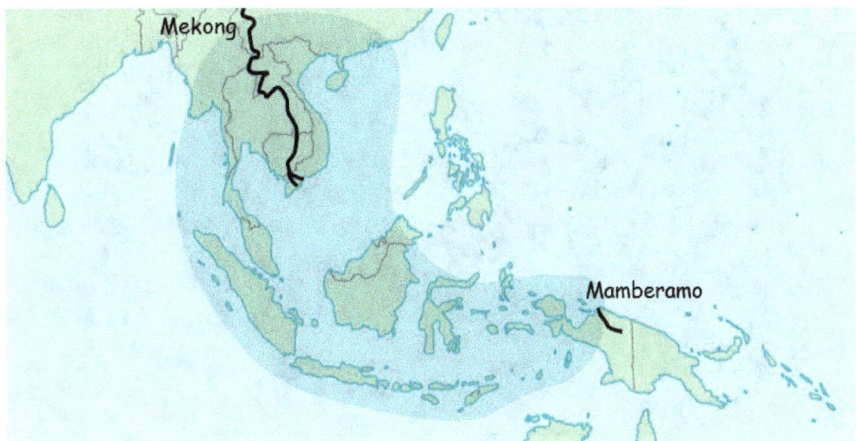

Map 1: The Mekong-Mamberamo Linguistic Area

352 — David Gil

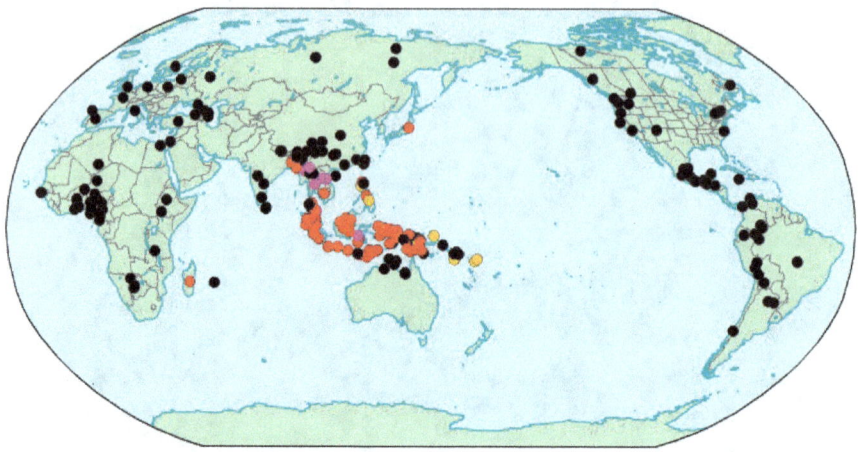

Map 2: Passing Gesture, Worldwide

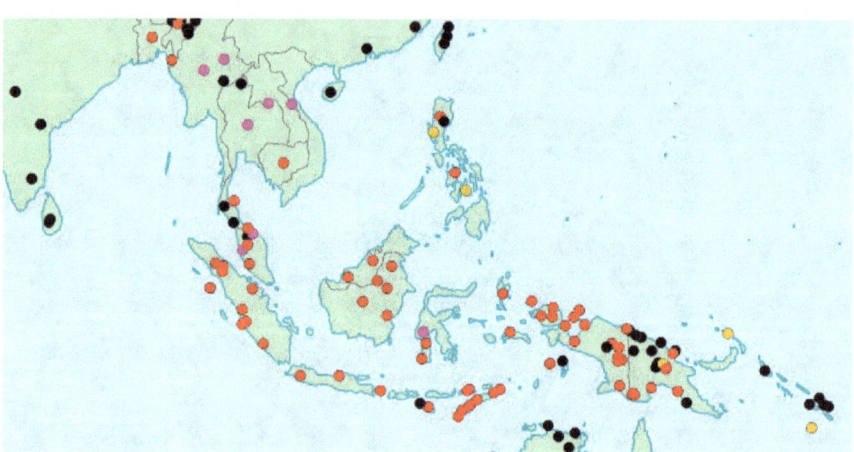

Map 3: Passing Gesture, Mekong-Mamberamo

Red: one-handed passing gesture
Pink: one-handed or similar passing gesture
Yellow: similar passing gesture
Grey: no passing gesture

The Mekong-Mamberamo linguistic area —— 353

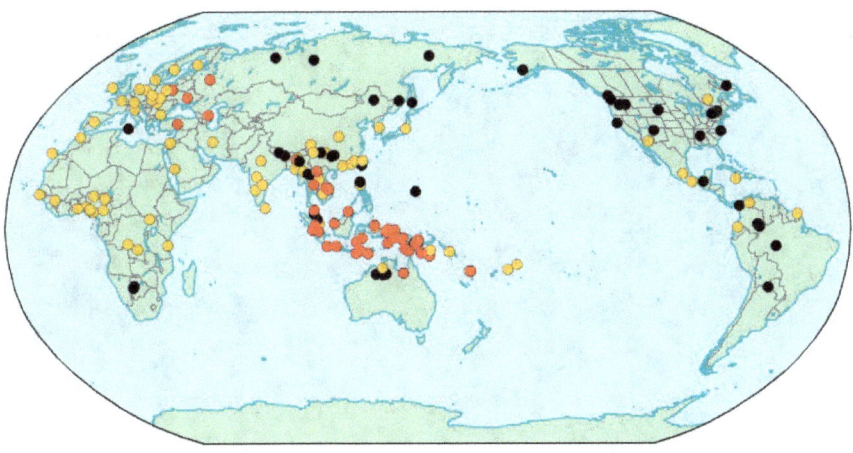

Map 4: Repeated Dental Clicks Expressing Amazement, Worldwide

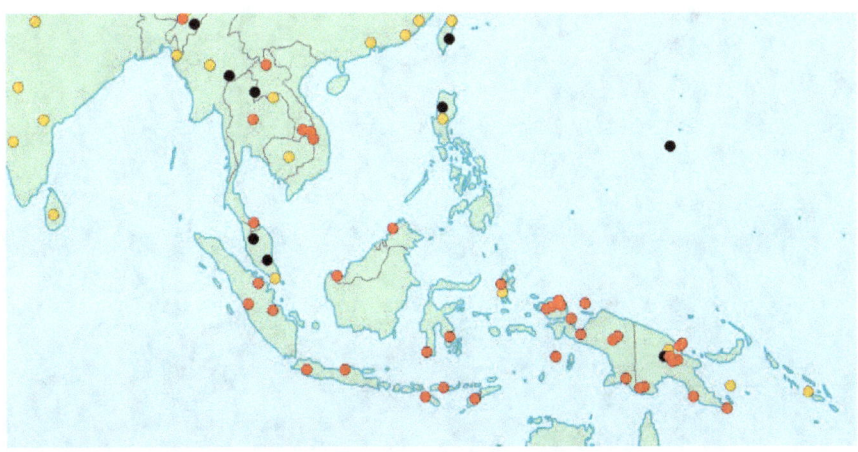

Map 5: Repeated Dental Clicks Expressing Amazement, Mekong-Mamberamo

Red: repeated dental clicks expressing amazement
Yellow: other clicks with other affective usages
Grey: no clicks with affective usages

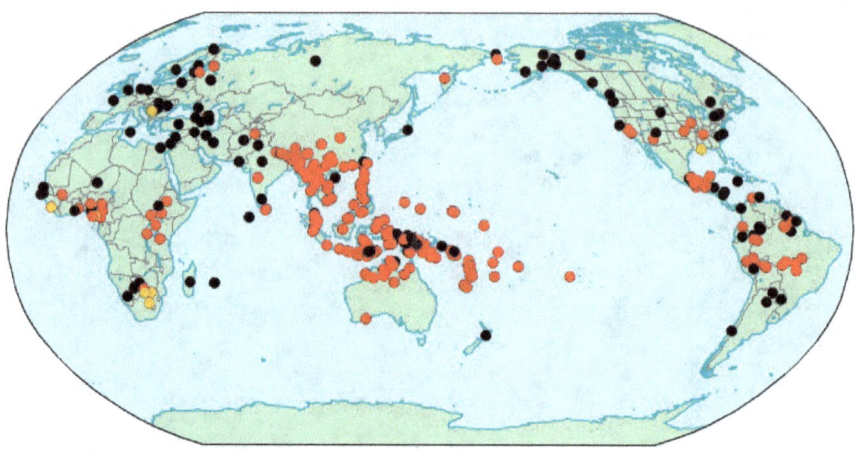

Map 6: Conventionalized Greetings with 'Where', Worldwide

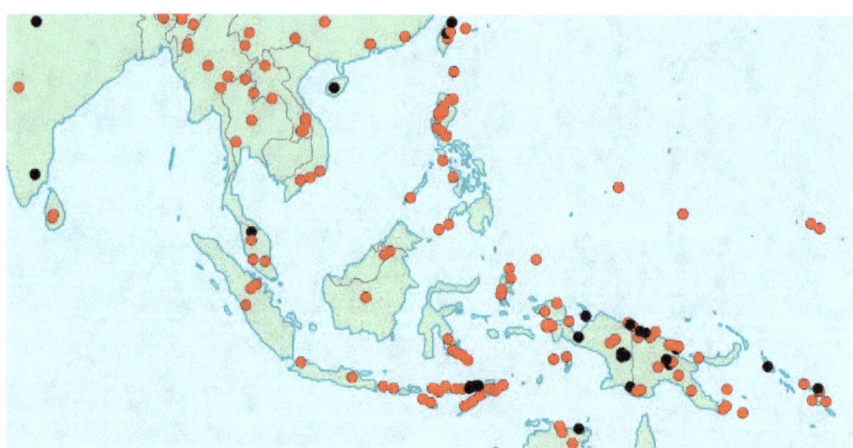

Map 7: Conventionalized Greetings with 'Where', Mekong-Mamberamo

Red: directional conventionalized greeting with 'where'
Yellow: non-directional conventionalized greeting with 'where'
Grey: no conventionalized greeting with 'where'

The Mekong-Mamberamo linguistic area —— 355

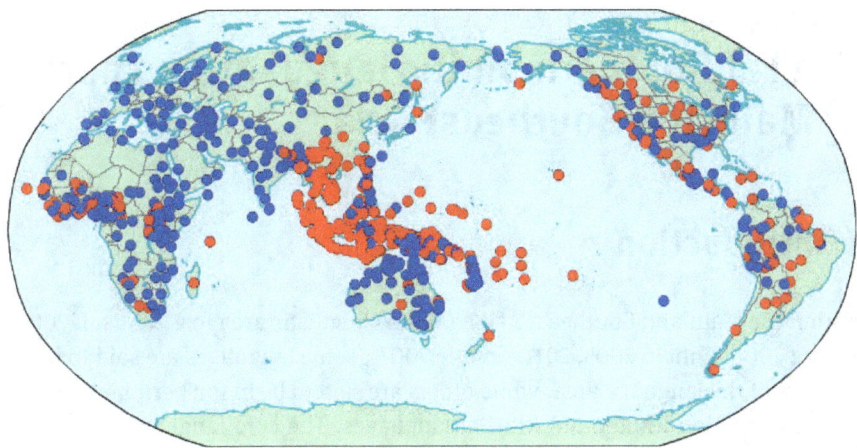

Map 8: Tense-Aspect-Mood Marking, Worldwide

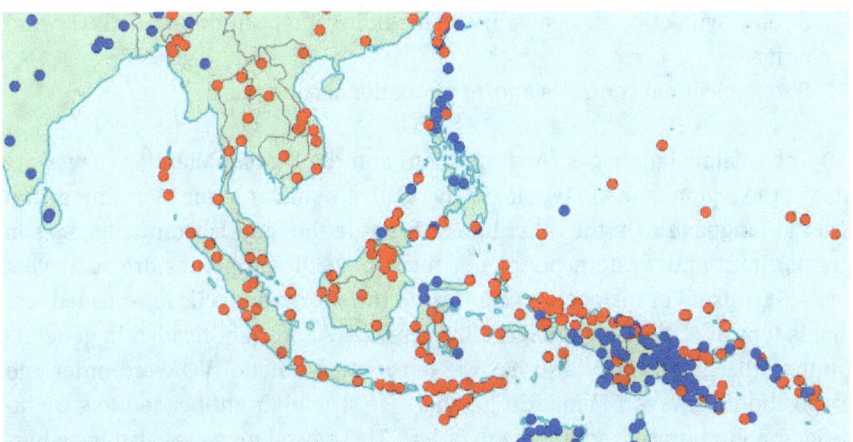

Map 9: Tense-Aspect-Mood Marking, Mekong-Mamberano.

Red: optional TAM marking
Blue: obligatory TAM marking

Hilário de Sousa
The Far Southern Sinitic languages as part of Mainland Southeast Asia

1 Introduction

Within the Mainland Southeast Asian (MSEA) linguistic area (e.g. Matisoff 2003; Bisang 2006; Enfield 2005, 2011, Comrie 2007), some languages are said to be in the core of the language area, while others are said to be in the periphery. In the core are the Mon-Khmer and Kra-Dai languages. The core languages generally have:

– Analytic morphological profile with many sesquisyllabic or monosyllabic words
– Strong syntactic left-headedness, including prepositions and SVO word order
– Phonemic tonal contrasts and/or phonational contrasts

The Chamic languages (Austronesian) and the Hmong-Mien languages are also in the region, and are typologically relatively similar to the Mon-Khmer and Kra-Dai languages. On the other hand, there are the Sino-Tibetan languages in the northern and western periphery; their linguistic properties are somewhat less MSEA-like. For instance, in contrast to the strong syntactic left-headedness that is typical of MSEA languages, Burmese is OV and right-headed in general.[1] On the other hand, Mandarin has the left-headed traits of VO word order and preposition. However, Mandarin is otherwise strongly right-headed (e.g. right-headed noun phrases, adjunct-verb order). These two languages also have fewer lexical tones than most tonal languages in MSEA.

The aim of this paper is to discuss some of the phonological and word order typological traits amongst the Sinitic languages, and to compare them with the typological profiles of some MSEA languages. While none of the Sinitic languages could be considered to be in the core of the MSEA language area, the Far

---

[1] Nonetheless, Burmese still has some left-headed traits like post-nominal adjectives ('stative verbs') and numerals. In fact, it is more common for OV languages to have NAdj order (e.g. Dryer 2013). The North Asian type of consistent right-headedness for the OV and AdjN word orders is actually cross-linguistically slightly rarer.

Southern Sinitic languages, namely Yuè, Pínghuà, and the Sinitic dialects in Hăinán Island and Léizhōu Peninsula (largely corresponding to Chappell's (2012, 2013) 'Southern Zone') are typologically closer to the non-Sinitic MSEA languages to the south and west than the other Sinitic languages. Studies on the MSEA linguistic area would benefit from taking a closer look in a wider range of Sinitic languages, and include at least the Far Southern Sinitic languages as part of the MSEA linguistic area.

The rest of the paper is structured as follows. In Section 2, I present a brief overview of the Sinitic languages; I outline the history of the Sinitic languages, and also the genealogical relationships within and beyond the Sinitic language family. In Section 3, I discuss the typological features that are canonical of MSEA, and Comrie's (2007, 2008a) discussions on this based on the data from WALS. In Section 4, I discuss some of the MSEA-like phonological traits in the Sinitic languages. In Section 5, I discuss the variation in word order amongst the Sinitic languages. A conclusion is presented in Section 6.

2 The Sinitic languages

The Sinitic languages are the descendants of the historically attested Chinese language. The periodization of the Chinese language differs amongst linguists, with historical syntacticians usually favouring terms like 'Archaic Chinese' and 'Medieval Chinese', and historical phonologists usually favouring terms like 'Old Chinese' and 'Middle Chinese'.[2] The earliest attested stage of the Chinese language is 'Pre-Archaic Chinese', as exemplified by the fourteenth to eleventh century BCE oracle bone scripts (Shāng Dynasty). The earliest phonologically reconstructible form of Chinese is 'Old Chinese', which is reconstructed with the help of the Book of Odes/ *Shījīng*, the earliest collection of rhyming texts, composed between tenth to seventh century BCE (Western Zhōu and early Eastern Zhōu Dynasties). The diversity and time depth of the modern Sinitic language is comparable to that of the Romance languages (e.g. Norman 2003: 82). Around the same time that Vulgar Latin was spread by Roman conquests, spoken Chinese was spread by the expansions of the Qín (221 BCE – 206 BCE) and Hàn

---

[2] Historical syntacticians and phonologists of Archaic/Old Chinese deal with morphology in different ways. Historical phonologists of Old Chinese often reconstruct single-consonant affixes that are not necessarily indicated in the writing system, e.g. 王 *$*_{G}{^w}aŋ$ 'king', 王 *$*_{G}{^w}aŋ\text{-}s$ 'be king' (Baxter and Sagart 2014). On the other hand, historical syntacticians usually only look at the syntax and morphology of the strings of characters in texts.

Empires (206 BCE – 220 CE) from the Yellow River Region. Based on lexical and phonological innovations, Sagart (2011) dates the most recent common ancestor of the modern Sinitic languages to about the third or second century BCE,[3] with Xiānghuà 鄉話 (also known as Wǎxiāng(huà) 瓦鄉(話)) being the earliest branch. The Sinitic languages are often called 'Chinese dialects'. The term 'dialect' is a (mis)translation of the Chinese term 方言 (Mandarin *fāngyán*), which literally means 'regional speech'. The Chinese term *fāngyán* is semantically wider than the notion of 'dialect' in English, and readily includes what would be considered separate languages of the same language family in Western linguistics.

The Language Atlas of China (Zhāng et al. in press; Wurm & Li et al. 1987) classifies the Sinitic languages into ten major dialect groups, plus other unclassified smaller varieties, based primarily on phonological criteria. Each major dialect group includes a number of dialects that are not mutually intelligible. The ten major dialects groups are (Xióng and Zhāng 2008):

- Jìn 晉
- Mandarin 官話
- Wú 吳
- Huī 徽
- Gàn 贛
- Xiāng 湘
- Mǐn 閩
- Hakka (or Kèjiā) 客家
- Yuè 粵
- Pínghuà 平話

The smaller Sinitic languages which fall outside of the ten-group classification are:

- The 'patois' (*tǔhuà* 土話 in Chinese) of Southern Húnán (*Xiāngnán Tǔhuà* 湘南土話), Northern Guǎngdōng (*Yuèběi Tǔhuà* 粵北土話) and Eastern Guǎngxī (*Guìdōng Tǔhuà* 桂東土話)[4]

---

[3] More specifically, a time that is later than 330 BCE, the year that Alexander III of Macedon invaded Central Asia, and during or before the earlier stages of the Hàn Dynasty (202 BCE – 220 CE). See Sagart (2011) for details.

[4] In the first edition of the Language Atlas of China (Wurm & Lǐ et al. 1987), the Northern Guǎngdōng Patois are called Sháozhōu Patois. Nowadays, this term only refers to the patois in Mid-Northern Guǎngdōng near Sháoguān 韶關. The term 'Eastern Guǎngxī Patois' is not actual-

- The Dānzhōu 儋州 language in Northeastern Hǎinán (somewhat Yuè-like, with influence from other Sinitic and non-Sinitic languages in lowland Hǎinán)
- The Xiānghuà 鄉話 (a.k.a. Wǎxiāng(huà) 瓦鄉(話)) language in western Húnán (e.g. Wǔ and Shén 2010, Chappell forthcoming)
- The Sinitic first language of Blue Dress Miáo people in Southwestern Húnán and neighbouring Northern Guǎngxī (Qīngyī Miáo Rénhuà 青衣苗人話; Lǐ 2004)
- The Sinitic first language of the Shē 畲 people (somewhat Hakka-like) (Yóu 2002)

Externally, the Sinitic language family is a member of the larger Sino-Tibetan language family. There are two groups of languages that are thought to be very close to the Sinitic languages in some ways. Firstly, there are the Bái 白 languages in Yúnnán. Some argue that Proto-Bái is a sister of Old Chinese (e.g. Starostin 1995; Zhèngzhāng 1999; Wāng 2006, 2012), while others argue that Bái is a family of Tibeto-Burman languages that has been heavily influenced by Chinese (e.g. Matisoff 2001b, Lee and Sagart 2008). Also in Southwestern China is the recently discovered Càijiā 蔡家 language (Bó 2004) on the Yúnnán–Guìzhōu border. Zhèngzhāng (2010) argues that Càijiā is a sister of Bái (and hence also genealogically related to Sinitic, according to his theory). Sagart (2011) considers Càijiā a sister of Xiānghuà (or at least the Sinitic layer in Càijiā is related to Xiānghuà if Càijiā turns out not to be a Sinitic language). Wǔ and Shěn (2010: 30–42) point out the lexical similarities between Xiānghuà, Old Chinese, Càijiā and Bái.

A number of factors contributed towards the distribution and diversity of the Sinitic languages. Firstly, there are the usual political and geographical factors which influence the distribution of languages in general. With the Sinitic family, the boundaries amongst the Sinitic languages follow the boundaries of the historical prefectures or counties to some degree.[5] For instance, although nowadays the language area of Huī 徽 Chinese is split amongst the three modern provinces of Ānhuī, Zhèjiāng, and Jiāngxī, it largely corresponds to the his-

---

ly used in the Language Atlas of China; this term is increasingly popular in referring to the Patois in Eastern Guǎngxī in the Hèzhōu 賀州 area (e.g. Chén and Liú 2009). These patois are considered a type of Northern Pínghuà in the Atlas. However, they are better viewed as a geographical continuation of the neighbouring Patois of Southern Húnán.

5 County is one level below prefecture, and prefecture is one level below province. Unlike India, China has an informal policy of not allowing provincial boundaries and linguistic boundaries to coincide.

torical prefectures of Huīzhōu 徽州 (plus a small portion of neighbouring areas). Waterways facilitate the migration of people and linguistic features along them, and mountains between drainage basins impede the migration of people and diffusion of features across them. For instance, Xiāng 湘 Chinese is largely confined within the drainage basin of the Xiāng 湘 and Zī 資 rivers (both tributaries of the Yangtze). Unusual amongst the world's languages is the fact that the language diversity in Northern China, where the Chinese language originated, is low, whereas the language diversity in Southern China, where Chinese people migrated to, is high. This has to do with terrain: Southern China is mountainous, whereas in Northern China, there is the North China Plain, where one language, Mandarin, is spoken. In Northern China, there is also the Jìn dialect area which is linguistically diverse; correlating with this fact is the unevenness of the terrain of this area, which is not part of the North China Plain. On top of the historical political boundaries and physical geography, there is also the complicated migration history of the Chinese people. For instance, in the case of Mandarin, Mandarin expanded outward from the North China Plain area rapidly within the last few centuries towards the northeast, northwest, and southwest. Towards Manchuria (northeast), the ban on Hàn Chinese people settling in Manchuria began to relax in 1860. Towards Dzungaria (northwest), Northern Xīnjiāng Mandarin formed in about 1780 (Liú 1993:4). Towards the Yúnnán-Guìzhōu Plateau (southwest), Mandarin speakers arrived during the Míng Dynasty (1368–1644). Due to the relatively late outward expansion, Mandarin dialects cover a huge area, and the mutual intelligibility amongst the Mandarin dialects, even for the far-flung ones, is relatively high (in comparison with other Sinitic groups).

The Sinitic languages are also notable in that most of the speakers have been under unified single regimes for most of their history. Chinese people in general recognize the hegemony of the Common Chinese language, of which the latest stage is Standard Mandarin. Even when China was not unified, people from the various Chinese states used varieties of the same (written and spoken) Common Chinese language as a lingua franca. The concept of there being a Common Chinese language began as early as the Western Zhou dynasty (11th century BCE – 771 BCE). Common Chinese is based on the language of the contemporary or preceding political centre of China, which is usually in the North China Plain, neighbouring Wèi River Valley, or Lower Yangtze Region. One factor which contributed to the diversity amongst the modern Sinitic languages is the influence of prestigious varieties, with Common Chinese being overwhelmingly influential. The various Sinitic languages preserved linguistic material from different historical stages of Common Chinese. For instance, out of the major branches of Sinitic, only Mǐn retained a phonological layer from Old Chinese. Early Middle Chinese, the stage of Common Chinese represented by the language of the rime dictionary *Qièyùn* 切韻 (published in 601 CE during Suí Dynasty), has basically wiped out all phonological diversity amongst the Sinitic languages other than Mǐn. (However, the lexical and grammatical diversity amongst the Sinitic languages predates Early Middle Chinese.) The tree model is ill-fitted to the Sinitic family, as the Sinitic languages have preserved multiple layers of phonological material from Common Chinese (see Wáng 2009). Not only with phonology, the Sinitic languages have accumulated various layers of lexicon and grammar from various historical stages of Common Chinese ('stratification' in Chappell 2012). To complicate the matter even further, the non-standard Sinitic languages often create hybrid constructions from native material and material from Common Chinese ('hybridisation' in Chappell 2012). Other than influence from Common Chinese, there is also diffusion amongst the various non-standard Sinitic languages (e.g. the influence of Cantonese on Hakka and Mǐn in Guǎngdōng Province), making the classification of the Sinitic languages a notoriously difficult task.

The last major factor that contributes to the diversity of the Sinitic languages is the variation in areal influence from neighbouring non-Sinitic languages. This is where MSEA linguistics comes into Sinitic linguistics, the primary concern in this paper. Hashimoto (1978) and (1986) are the first major works that discuss Altaic influence on Northern Chinese, and Tai and Hmong-Mien influence on Southern Chinese. The historical interactions between Chinese people and their northern versus southern neighbours were drastically different. Northern China was dominated by various North Asian peoples, and sometimes Tibeto-Burman peoples, intermittently for more than one thousand years during the last two thousand years. The most influential dynasties were Mongolic (e.g. the Khitan Liáo Dynasty, 907–1125 CE) or Tungusic (e.g. the Jurchen Jīn Dynasty, 1115–1234 CE). There have been two dynasties where North Asians governed China as a whole rather than just Northern China: the Mongol Yuán Dynasty (1279–1368 CE) and the Manchu Qīng Dynasty (1644–1912 CE). There were also dynasties headed by Turkic people (e.g. the various Shato Turk Dynasties during the Five Dynasty period, 907–979 CE), Qiangic people (e.g. the Tangut Xīxià Dynasty, 1038–1227 CE), and people of other Northern or Western ethnicities.[6] Northern Chinese was influenced greatly by the North Asian lan-

---

6 During the Sixteen Kingdoms period (304–439 CE), there were various polities headed by the Dī 氐 people, whose descendants might be the modern Baima Tibetans (but see counterarguments in Chirkova (2008)), who speak a Bodic language (e.g. Sun 2003). There were also the Jié (<*kiat) 羯 people, the leaders of the Later Zhào state (319–351 CE), who were probably Yeneseian (Pulleyblank 1963: 264; Vovin 2000). There were also kings of other ethnicities. King

guages, Mongolian and Manchu in particular, due to the North Asian languages being politically powerful, and also to the fact that many of the North Asian people shifted into speaking Chinese.[7] For instance, under Altaic influence, in Mandarin and Jìn there are fewer tones, fewer classifiers, and many syntactic environments where clauses are verb final (Sinitic languages are normally verb-medial). In northwestern China, under the influence of neighbouring Turkic, Mongolic and Tibetan languages, there are even varieties of Mandarin with postpositional case markers and usually verb-final constituent order, for instance the Far-Western Central Plains Mandarin dialects in Línxià 臨夏 (a.k.a. Hézhōu 河州) and Xīníng 西寧 areas (e.g. Dede 2007), and the Tángwàng 唐汪 language (Djamouri forthcoming). The following is an example: the verb 'eat' is clause-final, and the object 'meat' is marked by an object case postposition 哈 xa.[8]

(1) Huàngshuǐ Mandarin (Xīníng area)
狗 肉 哈 吃 了
dog meat [OBJ] eat PRF
'The dog ate the meat.'
(Dede 2007: 867)[9]

Gāo Yún 高雲/ Ko Un 고운 (reign 407–409) of Later Yān (384–409) or Northern Yān (407–436) was a descendent of the Goguryeo royal family (≈ Korean) adopted into the Yān royal family. The Táng Dynasty General Ān Lùshān 安祿山, who founded the short-lived Yān 燕 Kingdom (756–763 CE), had a father who was perhaps of Sogdian origin, and a mother who was a Turkic Zoroastrian priestess.

7 This is particularly the case with the Manchus: there are currently more than 10 million ethnic Manchus, but only a handful of native Manchu speakers left. The rest have shifted into speaking Mandarin or other Sinitic languages. Even when Xibe, an offshoot of Manchu, is included, there are fewer than 30,000 speakers.

8 Nearby there is also the mixed language Wǔtún 五屯 (e.g. Janhunen, Peltomaa, Sandman and Dongzhou 2008) of which the vocabulary is over 50% Mandarin, and the grammar is mostly Tibetan. The phonology and lexicon in Wǔtún is not as obviously Sinitic-like as Tángwàng. See Zhōng (2007) on the language contact situation in this area.

9 Linguistic publications in the Chinese world often have examples with only Chinese characters and no phonological transcription of the characters. In this paper I try to include examples with phonological transcription as much as possible. With no phonological transcriptions, it is not always easy to determine whether a particular Chinese character is used for a morpheme because the morpheme: a) is a reflex of the same character in older stages of Chinese; b) is homophonous with that character but etymologically different; or c) is synonymous with the character, but etymologically and phonetically not related.

The situation with Southern China was the opposite: Chinese people cause disturbance to the Southern non-Sinitic people more often than the opposite. Before the arrival of Han Chinese people, in Southern China there were Kra-Dai,[10] Hmong-Mien, Austronesian and Austroasiatic-speaking people.[11] China first set up administrative bases in the Pearl River region and in the lower Red River regions during the Qín Dynasty (221–207 BCE). From then onwards, the primary migration routes for Chinese people have been from Northern China to Southern China. The migration of Chinese people to Southern China intensified whenever Northern China was ravaged by natural disaster or war (Chinese people had many wars with North Asians). The southward migration of Chinese people caused the southward migration of some of the Southern indigenous people deeper into Southeast Asia. Some of the indigenous populations of Southern China were assimilated by the migrant Chinese population. Genetically, it is known that the patrilineage of many Southern Chinese males is of Northern Chinese origin, while the matrilineage of most Southern Chinese people is of Southeast Asian origin (Wen et al. 2004). There is also a study which concluded that Northern Pínghuà speakers are genetically primarily Southeast Asian in both their patrilineage and matrilineage (Gan et al. 2008).[12] Linguistically, many Southern Sinitic languages are claimed to have Southeast Asian substrata. For instance, Cantonese has an obvious Tai substratum (e.g. Ōuyáng 1989, Bauer 1996). Nearly all Southern Sinitic languages have been argued to have at least some Kra-Dai vocabulary (see Lǐ 2002: 94–149). Hakka is often said to be a Gàn-like Sinitic language that was influenced by the Hmong-Mien language originally spoken by the Shē 畲 people (e.g. Sagart 2002).[13] Mǐn is argued

---

10 'Kra-Dai' is a name propagated by, e.g. Ostapirat (2000, 2005); Pittayaporn (2009), for the language family which is also known as Tai-Kadai.
11 Ostapirat (2005) argues for the close relationship between Kra-Dai and Austronesian, and Sagart (2004) argues that Kra-Dai people were Austronesian who migrated from Taiwan back to the Mainland. That some conservative Kra languages have segments in their sesquisyllabic words matching the segments in the disyllabic words in Austronesian languages is a strong support for the link between Kra-Dai and Austronesian families. Many Kra groups have legends of their ancestors coming from the east and having crossed the sea in big boats (Lǐ 1999: 2). If Sagart's viewpoint is correct, this 'sea' could well be the Taiwan Strait. If not, perhaps this 'sea' refers to a larger water crossing like the Mouth of the Pearl River.
12 Gan et al. (2008) make their claim for Pínghuà people in general. However, all but one of their sampling groups are Northern Pínghuà-speaking.
13 Shē people these days speak Sinitic dialects closely related to Hakka, with layers of Hmong-Mien and Kra-Dai vocabularies, and influences from their current Mǐn- and/or Wú-speaking neighbours (Yóu 2002). The Ho Ne people in Southern Guǎngdōng, who speak a Hmongic language (Ratliff 1998), are considered by the government to be the last remaining people who

by Norman and Mei (1976) to have an Austroasiatic substratum (but this theory is criticized by Sagart (2008)). Historically, corresponding roughly to the modern day Wú-speaking area (around and south of the mouth of the Yangtze) was the Yuè 越 kingdom (? – 222 BCE), of which the commoners were probably Kra-Dai-speaking. There are bilingual Chinese-Yuè 越 texts like the sixth century BCE Song of the Yuè (*Yuèréngé* 越人歌; Wěi 1981, Zhengzhang 1991),[14] and the Record of Yuè (*Yuèjuéshū* 越絕書; Zhengzhang 1998), which was compiled in the first century CE. Currently there are still islands of non-Sinitic languages in Southern China that have not (yet) been totally engulfed by the surrounding Sinitic languages. There are two such languages in Guǎngdōng: the Kam-Sui language of Biāo (Liáng 2002) which is surrounded by Yuè, and the Hmongic language of Ho Ne (Ratliff 1998), which is surrounded by Hakka. Given that many non-Sinitic MSEA people were absorbed into the Chinese community, it is not surprising that the Southern Sinitic languages bear similarities with languages in the core of MSEA.

In the rest of this paper, I will outline the typological features of the Sinitic languages in reference to the surrounding typological zones, and concentrate on the linguistic features in the Southern Sinitic languages that are typical of MSEA but atypical of Sinitic languages as a whole.

3 The typology of the MSEA linguistic area and the Sinitic languages

The MSEA linguistic area is commonly understood to include the following groups of languages (e.g. Matisoff 2003; Bisang 2006; Enfield 2005, 2011; Comrie 2007):

- "Mon-Khmer" languages (i.e. Austroasiatic family minus the Munda branch)
- Kra-Dai languages

---

still speak the original Hmong-Mien language of the Shē people (Máo and Méng 1986). However, there are doubts that the Ho Ne people are actually Shē, based on the many cultural differences between Ho Ne and Shē Proper. Culturally, Ho Ne most closely resembles Yáo (≈ Mien) in Northern Guǎngdōng, and Ho Ne people do in fact consider themselves Yáo (according to Yóu 2002: 8–10).

14 There are competing theories in Vietnam that the language in *Yuèréngé* (*Việt Nhân Ca* in Vietnamese) is Vietic.

- Hmong-Mien languages
- Chamic languages
- Some of the surrounding Sino-Tibetan languages, e.g. Karen, Lolo-Burmese, some nearby Sinitic languages

Towards the north, the Sino-Tibetan languages and the strongly Chinese-influenced varieties of Kra-Dai and Hmong-Mien languages can be said to be on the periphery of the MSEA linguistic area.

We will start by discussing Comrie (2007, 2008a), which present a measurable framework in comparing the typological profiles of languages (albeit with pitfalls, as Comrie admits). Most studies on language areas begin by having preconceptions about what linguistic features are common in a linguistic area, and then the geographical extent of the said features are determined. Comrie (2007) takes a different approach. Instead of having a preconceived list of typological features, all the linguistic features in the World Atlas of Language Structures (WALS; Haspelmath, Dryer, Gil, and Comrie 2005) are examined to see whether there are typological features that distinguish MSEA from other areas. (See also Dahl (2008) on this approach.) The results of Comrie (2007) are largely congruent with the conclusions in other research on the MSEA linguistic area: there is a 'core' to the MSEA linguistic area with languages like Thai, Khmer, and Vietnamese which possess more canonical MSEA typological features, and a 'periphery', including languages like Indonesian, Burmese, and Mandarin which possess fewer canonical MSEA features. Comrie (2008a) follows similar methods, but concentrates on the Sinitic languages, comparing them with both MSEA and North Asia. There are twenty features that are said to be canonical of MSEA, and another set of twenty features that are said to be canonical of North Asia. Mandarin achieves a score of 8 out of 20 for MSEA features (the lowest scored language out of the surveyed languages),[15] and 11 out of 20 for North Asian features (the lowest scored language out of the surveyed languages, together with Nivkh). The conclusion is that Mandarin is typologically between MSEA and North Asia.[16]

---

15 Comrie (2007) has an extra MSEA feature that is not featured in Comrie (2008a): feature 45A 'Politeness Distinctions in Pronouns'.
16 Instead of saying that Mandarin is 'half-MSEA-like' and 'half-North-Asian-like', one could also say that the MSEA and North Asian languages are typologically 'half-Mandarin-like'. However, MSEA and North Asia serve as better typological standards of comparison due to their word order typological profiles being relatively normal: the MSEA languages are rather consistently left-headed, while the North Asian languages are very strongly right-headed.

The following are the twenty features that are said to be canonical in the MSEA linguistic area (Comrie 2008; see also introduction to this volume, pp7-8):

- Having implosives
- Velar nasal used as onsets
- No front rounded vowels
- Complex tone systems
- Little affixation
- Having plural words
- No distributive numerals
- Obligatory use of numeral classifiers
- The perfect marker is synchronically a word meaning 'finish'
- A number of left-headed traits
    - Verb-Object order
    - Preposition-NP order
    - Noun-Genitive order
    - Noun-Adjective order
    - Noun-Demonstrative order
    - Noun-Numeral order
    - Noun-Relative clause order
    - Adjective-Degree word order
- 'Topic' predicative possession construction ("possessor-TOPIC exist possessum")
- Verbal encoding for predicative adjectives
- Different markings for nominal and locative predication

For this section, I have repeated the exercise using the twenty MSEA features in Comrie (2008a), with data from the 2011 online edition of WALS (Dryer and Haspelmath 2011), and added the following languages: Cantonese, Hakka, Eastern Kayah Li, Hmong, and Mien. Having more data from the Sinitic languages would be preferable (since this paper focuses on the Sinitic languages), but Cantonese and Hakka are the only non-Mandarin Sinitic languages with a reasonable amount of data in WALS. Eastern Kayah Li is chosen as a representative of the Karen languages. The Karen languages are interesting from a Sinitic point of view, as both the Sinitic and Karen families are SVO with mixed left-headed and right-headed typological profiles. Gaps in the WALS data are filled

---

These contrast with the Sinitic languages, which have the very unusual typological profiles of being SVO, but otherwise strongly right-headed, as discussed in the rest of this paper.

with the help of Matthews and Yip (2011) for Cantonese, Lo (1988) for Hakka, Solnit (1997) for Eastern Kayah Li, Wáng (1985) and Jarkey (1991) for Hmong,[17] and Máo, Méng, and Zhèng (1982) for Mien. Based on the set of criteria used in Comrie (2007, 2008a), Cantonese, Hakka, and Mien (which score 9, 10, and 11 respectively) are comparable to Burmese (which scores 10) in terms of the distance between their typological profile and the MSEA typological canon. Eastern Kayah Li and Hmong score 14 and 13 respectively, which are closer to the score of 16 achieved by Khmer in the core of MSEA.[18]

---

17 Data from various dialects of Hmong proper are used in this paper: Mong Njua (Green Hmong) data from WALS, Hmong Daw (White Hmong) data from Jarkey (1991), and Dànánshān Hmong data from Wáng (1985). Dànánshān Hmong is the standard variety of Western Hmongic (Chuānqiándiàn Miáo) chosen by the China government. These three dialects of Western Hmongic are very closely related to each other, and for the linguistic features discussed in this paper, the three dialects behave in the same way, unless specified. In the feature tables, 'Hmong' refers to Green Hmong and White Hmong, the varieties spoken by all Hmong speakers outside of China.
18 Amongst the Hmong-Mien languages, the Hmongic languages are generally less influenced by Chinese than the Mienic languages. The Hmongic languages are thus typologically more like the core MSEA languages than the Mienic languages (e.g. Ratliff 2010: 239–240).

Table 1: Some typological features in Sinitic and MSEA languages (based on Comrie 2008a; added information is put in parentheses)

Map	Feature	Thai	Khmer	Vietnamese	Indonesian	(EKayahLi)	Burmese	(Hmong)	(Mien)	(Cantonese)	(Hakka)	Mandarin
7A	C?	No	Implosives	Implosives	No	No	No	No	No	No	No	No
9A	ŋ	Initial	No initial	Initial	Initial	Initial	Initial	No initial	(Initial)	Initial	(Initial)	No initial
11A	y ø œ	None	None	None	None	None	None	None	None	/y œ/	None	/y/
13A	Tone	Complex	No	Complex	No	Complex	Complex	Complex	Complex	Complex	Complex	Complex
26A	-fix in inflc. morph.	Little af-	Little af-	Little af-	Strong suf-	Little af-	Strong suf-	Little af-	Little af-	Little af-	(Little af-)	Strong suf-
33A	Noml Pl.	?	Pl. word	Pl. word	Plural redup	No plural	Pl. word	(No plural)	No plural	No plural	(No plural)	Plural suf-
54A	Distrib. Num	No	?	No	No	?	suffix	?	?	No	No	No
55A	Num. Clf	Obligatory	Optional	Obligatory	Optional	Obligatory	Obligatory	(Obligatory)	(Obligatory)	Obligatory	(Obligatory)	Obligatory
68A	Perfect	'Finish'	'Finish'	Other	'Finish'	('Finish')	'Finish'	No perfect	(Other)	Other	(Other)	Other
83A	Obj & Verb	VO	VO	VO	VO	VO	OV	VO	VO	VO	VO	VO
85A	Adpos & NP	Prepos.	Prepos.	Prepos.	Prepos.	No dom. order	Postpos.	Prepos.	No Adpos.	No dom. order	(No dom. order)	No dom. order
86A	Gen & N	N-Gen	N-Gen	N-Gen	N-Gen	N-Gen	Gen-N	Gen-N	Gen-N	Gen-N	(Gen-N)	Gen-N
87A	Adj & N	N-Adj	N-Adj	N-Adj	N-Adj	N-Adj	N-Adj	N-Adj	N-Adj	Adj-N	(Adj-N)	Adj-N
88A	Dem & N	N-Dem	N-Dem	N-Dem	N-Dem	N-Dem	Dem-N	N-Dem	Dem-N	Dem-N	Dem-N	Dem-N
89A	Num & N	N-Num	N-Num	N-Num	N-Num	N-Num	N-Num	Num-N	Num-N	Num-N	Num-N	Num-N

The far southern Sinitic languages as part of MSEA — 369

Map	Feature	Thai	Khmer	Vietnamese	Indonesian	(EKayahLi)	Burmese	(Hmong)	(Mien)	(Cantonese)	(Hakka)	Mandarin
90A	Rel & N	N-Rel	N-Rel	N-Rel	N-Rel	(Rel-N)[19]	Rel-N	N-Rel	(Rel-N)	Rel-N	Rel-N	Rel-N
91A	Deg & Adj	Adj-Deg	Adj-Deg	(Deg-Adj)	Dem-Adj	(Adj-Deg)	Deg-Adj	Adj-Deg	Adj-Deg	Deg-Adj	No dom. order	Deg-Adj
117A	Predicative Possession	Topic	Topic	Topic	Topic	(Topic)	Locational	(Topic)	(Topic)	(Topic)	(Topic)	Topic
118A	Predicative Adjectives	Verbal	Verbal	Verbal	Verbal	(Verbal)	Verbal	(Verbal)	Verbal	(Verbal)	(Verbal)	Verbal
119A	Noml and Loc Pred.	Different	Different	Different	Different	(Different)	Different	(Different)	Different	(Different)	(Different)	Different
	Total +:	18	16	17	13	(14)	10	(13)	11	(9)	(10)	7

In the rest of this paper, I shall discuss further some of the phonological and word order issues discussed in Comrie (2007, 2008a), and some other related issues.

I shall also take this opportunity to introduce Chappell's (2012, 2013) classification of the Sinitic languages into four macro-areas (Chappell 2012: 5–6), with my own minor alterations, due to differences in linguistic criteria used.

- Northern zone:
  Běijīng Mandarin, Northern (Jìlǔ) Mandarin, Peninsular (Jiāoliáo) Mandarin, Northeastern Mandarin, Northwestern (Lányín) Mandarin, Central Plains (Zhōngyuán) Mandarin (portion), and Jìn.

- Central zone (≈ Chappell's "Transitional Area"):
  Central Plains (Zhōngyuán) Mandarin (portion), Southeastern (Jiānghuái) Mandarin, Southwestern Mandarin, Xiāng, Xiānghuà (a.k.a. Wǎxiāng), Gàn, Mǐn-Gàn (i.e. Western Mǐn, which is strongly Gàn-influenced), and Hakka.

- Southeastern zone:
  Wú, Huī, Mǐn.

- Far-Southern zone (≈ Chappell's "Southern Area"):
  Yuè, Pínghuà, Sinitic languages in Léizhōu Peninsula and Hǎinán Island.[20]

---

20 Some of the differences between the four typological zones in this paper and Chappell's (2012) four macro-areas are:

- the term 'Far-Southern zone' is used here instead of Chappell's 'Southern area'. The term 'Southern Sinitic' is ambiguous: it typically refers to the non-Mandarin Sinitic languages in Southern China, sometimes it also includes Southwestern Mandarin, and sometimes also Southeastern (Jiānghuái) Mandarin
- Northern Wú and Huī are included here in the same Southeastern zone as Mǐn and Southern Wú. Northern Wú and Huī are more strongly influenced by Mandarin, and are hence sometimes treated differently from Southern Wú
- the Mǐn exclaves in Léizhōu Peninsula and Hǎinán, which are spoken to the south of Yuè, are grouped together with Yuè in the Far-Southern zone. The Mǐn dialect of Hǎinán Island (a.k.a. Hainanese) is strongly influenced by the Kra-Dai language Ong-Be (i.e. the lowland indigenous language of Hǎinán), and the Mǐn dialect of Léizhōu Peninsula is closely related to that of Hǎinán. Yuè and Pínghuà have also been strongly influenced by Kra-Dai languages

In terms of word order, amongst the four zones, the languages with the most verb-medial traits are unsurprisingly in the Far-Southern zone; the Far-Southern Sinitic zone borders the Kra-Dai and Mien speaking areas, and many Kra-Dai and Mien speakers in China also speak Far-Southern Sinitic languages. As is to be expected, the languages in the Northern zone have a number of verb-final traits, being in contact with the North Asian languages. However, putting the aforementioned Far-Western Central Plains Mandarin dialects aside (which can be said to be actual SOV languages), the languages with the most verb-final traits are, surprisingly, in the Southeastern zone. This will be discussed in Section 5.

In the rest of this paper, unless specified, Sinitic data are provided by the seven members of the ERC Sinotype project,[21] based on their fieldnotes, their first-language knowledge, or their heritage-language knowledge. The following are the list of the team members and the data they contributed:

- Hilary Chappell: Gǔzhàng Xiānghuà (fieldnotes)
- Wěiróng Chén: Huì'ān Southern Mǐn (first language and field notes)
- Yùjié Chén: Zhōukǒu Central Plains Mandarin (first lg and field notes)
- Xūpíng Lǐ: Yíchūn Gàn (fieldnotes)
                     Fùyáng Wú (first language)

--
– Western Mǐn is a Mǐn dialect that is strongly influenced by Gàn, and is here included in the same Transition zone as Gàn, rather than being in the Southeastern Zone together with other Mǐn dialects
– Chappell (2012) has the Hakka in Guǎngdōng in her 'Southern area', whereas other Hakka dialects to the north in the 'Transitional area'

Chappell's (2012) division of the Sinitic languages into four macro-areas is a refinement on Norman's (1988: Section 8.1) division of the Sinitic languages into the typological zones of North (Mandarin), South (Yuè, Hakka, Mǐn), and Central (Xiāng, Gàn, and Wú). The four macro-areas in Chappell (2012) were based on the distribution of the various grammaticalization pathways of the passive and object marking constructions. However, it is noted (2012: 6) that the boundaries amongst the four macro-areas are approximate, and the boundaries would change slightly depending on the typological criteria used. The boundaries between the four typological zones proposed in this paper are also approximate, due to the paucity of data.

21 The Sinotype research project, funded by the European Research Council, was headed by Hilary Chappell, and hosted at École des hautes études en sciences sociales, from 2009 to 2013. See the acknowledgement section for more details.

- Sing Sing Ngai: Shàowǔ Mǐn-Gàn, (a.k.a. Western Mǐn; fieldnotes)
  Fúqīng Eastern Mǐn (heritage language)
  Standard Cantonese (first language)
- Hilário de Sousa: Nánníng Southern Pínghuà (fieldnotes)
  Standard Cantonese (first language)
- Jiàn Wáng: Jīxī Huī (fieldnotes)
  Suīníng Central Mandarin (first language)

4 Phonology

In this section, I shall discuss the following phonological phenomena in the Sinitic languages and the MSEA languages to the south:

- Tones and onsets (Section 4.1)
- Codas (Section 4.2)
- Implosives (Section 4.3)
- Front rounded vowels (Section 4.4)
- 'Apical' vowels (Section 4.5)

We shall see that the Sinitic dialects in the Far-Southern zone and surrounding areas often have phonological traits that are typical of MSEA, but atypical for Sinitic languages. A summary of the phonological features is presented in Section 4.6.

Maps from the 'Phonetics' volume of the Linguistic Atlas of Chinese Dialects (LACD; Cáo et al. 2008) are shown. The maps are referred to by abbreviations like 'Map P117', where P stands for the Phonetics volume of LACD, and 117 for map 117 therein.

4.1 Tones and onsets

Most MSEA languages have phonemic use of pitch and/or phonational differences. Pitch and phonation are two closely related phenomena; both are primarily produced by configurations of the glottis. In this paper, 'tone' refers to systems where at least pitch contrasts have been phonemicized. Many of these phonemicized pitch systems also include phonational contrasts. (Languages where only phonational contrasts have been phonemicized are not considered to be 'tonal' in this paper. See also Brunelle and Kirby (this volume).)

Many language families in this area with tones had an earlier stage where there were three tones for sonorant-ending syllables, and no tonal contrasts (or 'one' tone) for obstruent-ending syllables. This set of tonal contrasts is notated here as '3/1' tones. The proto languages with 3/1 tones include:

– Proto Kra-Dai
– Proto Hmong-Mien
– Middle Chinese
– Proto Mĭn
– Proto Việt-Mường
– Proto Bái
– Proto Lolo-Burmese
– Proto Karen

The development of the three tones for sonorant-ending syllables is clear in some cases: one tone is related to an earlier *-h (<*-s), another to an earlier *-ʔ, while the third is related to the lack of an obstruent at the end of a syllable. Haudricourt made this observation when comparing the tones in Vietnamese with the codas in cognates in other Mon-Khmer languages (Haudricourt 1954). The Sino-Tibetan languages have Written Tibetan as a reference. (Classical Tibetan was non-tonal; while many Tibetan varieties have developed tones, there are many Tibetan dialects in the periphery which remain non-tonal.) Written Burmese in fact still often marks the high tone with ◌ः, which is related to the Indic sign *visarga* ◌ः (*-h*), suggesting the high tone came from an earlier *-h. There is also the case of Utsat, which, when compared with the other Chamic languages, developed tones in similar ways: normally a high tone developed out of *-h, mid and low tones developed out of syllables with no obstruent ending, and rising and falling tones developed out of the plosive codas including *-ʔ (Thurgood 1993).

Most languages in MSEA and East Asia have moved beyond this 3/1 tone system. The voicing of an onset influences the pitch value of a tone. Initially, the difference in pitch of a tone with different onsets might not be noticeable to speakers, but what typically happens is that the difference in pitch becomes more noticeably different. (The process of developing noticeable allotones are commonly referred to as 'tone-splitting'.) If the voicing contrast of the onsets is lost, the allotones become separate tonemes. Theoretically a language with 3/1 tones would thus end up with 6/2 tones. However, most languages do not have 6/2 tones, as the tones have gone through other splits and mergers. For instance, while Northern Vietnamese has 6/2 tones, Southern Vietnamese has 5/2 tones as it has merged the *hỏi* and *ngã* tones. Standard Lao has 5/4 tones, and

Central Thai has 5/3 tones; both have experienced different splits and mergers of the tones. Amongst the Sinitic languages, the Far-Southern languages, being closest to the core of MSEA, have the most tones on average. The Southeastern languages have slightly fewer tones,[22] the Central languages have even fewer tones, and the Northern languages, being closest to the non- or less-tonal languages of North Asia, have the least tones on average. For example, prototypically (there are variations within each group):

- Yuè and Southern Pínghuà dialects have 6/3 tones
- Mǐn and Wú dialects have 6/2 or 5/2 tones
- Hakka dialects have 4/2 tones
- Xiāng dialects have 5/1 tones
- Southeastern Mandarin dialects have 5/1 or 4/1 tones
- Jìn dialects have 4/1 tones
- Other Mandarin dialects have 4/0 or 3/0 tones
  (Many Mandarin dialects have '/0' tones as they have lost all plosive codas)

LACD Map P001 (Figure 1) shows the number of 'tone categories' amongst the Sinitic languages. ('Tone categories' in traditional Chinese linguistics refers to all the allotones in a language counted separately, including the tones for sonorant-ending syllables and tones for obstruent-ending syllables. For instance, Standard Cantonese has '9 tone categories' according to traditional Chinese linguistics; in my notation, Cantonese has '6/3' tones, i.e. 6 tonemes.) The Sinitic dialects with the highest number of tone categories are clearly concentrated in Far-Southern China, the area closest to the core of MSEA. Mandarin has the smallest number of tone categories, especially Northwestern Mandarin.

One prominent non-Sinitic historical tonal trait in Yuè and many Southern Pínghuà dialects is the split of tone D (the tone for obstruent-ending syllables) based on vowel length. This is a hallmark of Kra-Dai languages.[23] The only other non-Kra-Dai language that I know of with this trait is Kim Mun (Mienic) in Hǎinán (Lǐ 2003: 694–697). This trait in Kim Mun is perhaps due to influence from Hlai, the dominant Kra-Dai language in central Hǎinán.

---

22 In terms of tonal behaviour, one major difference between the Far Southern and the Southeastern zone is that languages in the Far Southern zone tend to be poor in tone sandhi, whereas languages in the Southeastern zone tend to have complex tone sandhi.
23 Unlike other Southern Pínghuà dialects, Southern Pínghuà dialects in Nánníng and areas to the west split the tone D not by vowel length, but by the sonority of the initial consonant in Middle Chinese, e.g. Nánníng Wèizǐlù Pínghuà /wət^{23}/ 域 'region' (< *wik), /wət^2/ 活 'live' (< *ywat). See de Sousa (forthcoming).

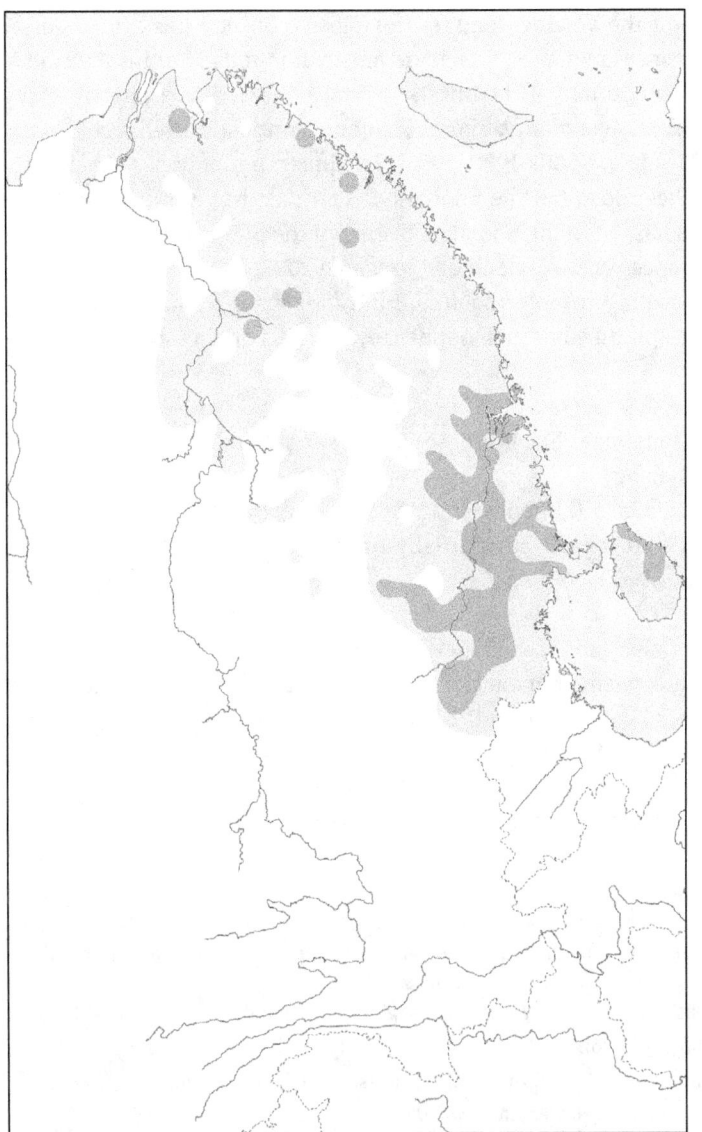

Fig. 1: Areas with nine or more allotones are highlighted in dark gray, areas with six to eight allotones in light gray. Other Sinitic languages have two to five allotones. (Data derived from LACD Map P001).

The loss of the voicing contrast (for plosive onsets) has also occurred in many Mon-Khmer languages, which are mostly non-tonal. For instance, in Mon, the old voicing contrast of the onsets is now expressed as a phonational contrast of modal versus breathy. The phonational contrast caused a change in the vowel qualities (e.g. Ferlus 1980, 1984). In Khmer, not only has the onset voicing contrast been lost, but the phonational contrast has also been lost in most dialects. This has led to the phonemicization of the previously allophonic vowel quality differences (e.g. Wayland and Jongman 2002).[24]

It is interesting to note that there are languages in MSEA where (onset-related) tone-splitting has not happened, i.e. still at the stage of having 3/1 tones:

- Burmish languages like Burmese, Achang and Xiāndǎo
- Nusu (Loloish)[25]
- A-Hmyo dialects (Luóbóhé 羅泊河 Miáo, at, e.g. Fúquán 福泉; Western Hmongic; but tone D has partially or totally merged with tone A) (Ratliff 2010: 185; Lǐ 2003: 686–688)

There are also languages where tone-splitting has occurred, but the allotones have not been phonemicized, as the original contrast between modal voice and modal voiceless onsets is still intact (i.e. the difference in pitch is still predictable by the phonemic voicing contrast of the onsets).[26] These languages include:

---

24 There are also some tonal languages in China where the tones are divided into two categories, and the vowels have allophones conditioned by the category of tone. This 'vowel-splitting' occurred presumably through an intermediary stage with phonational difference which has since been lost or become not very noticeable:
- Mang (Máshān 麻山 Miáo, Western Hmongic; tones B2 and C2 versus others) (Wáng 1985: 107; Ratliff 2010: 196);
- The southern half of the Eastern Mǐn dialects, e.g. Fúzhōu, Fúqīng (tones C2, C1 and D1 versus others; D1 has lower pitch than D2).

The commonality is that tone C developed out of -*h*, which 'encourages' breathy phonation, and tone 2, which correlates with voiced onset and lower pitch, which also 'encourages' breathy phonation.

25 Other Burmish languages have shown signs of tone-splitting: Zaiwa/Atsi, Maru/Langsu and Lashi. As for Loloish languages, most have departed from the ancestral 3+1 tone system (e.g. Lǐ 2010: 56).

26 The original modal voicing for the onsets may have changed into something like breathy voice, but these onsets are still distinct from the modal voiceless onsets. Dialects of Wú, e.g. Shanghainese, are mostly like this.

- Wú dialects, including some neighbouring Wú-influenced Mǐn varieties as in:
    - Eastern Mǐn in Cāngnán, Zhèjiāng
    - Southern Mǐn in Guǎngfēng, Jiāngxī
    - Northern Mǐn in Pǔchēng, Fújiàn (Zhèngzhāng 1995)[27]
- Southern Xiāng dialects ('Old Xiāng')
- Xiānghuà and some nearby Mandarin dialects in western Húnán
- A few Northern Gàn dialects, e.g. Wǔníng (Zhū et al. 2009)
- A few Northern Yuè dialects, e.g. Liánshān, Yángshān (Zhèngzhāng 1995)
- A-Hmao dialects ("Northeastern Yunnan" Miao, at, e.g. Shíménkǎn 石門坎 in Wēiníng 威寧; Western Hmongic; it has also developed noun versus non-noun contrasts with tones B2 and C2/D2) (Ratliff 2010: 185; Lǐ 2003: 708)

The phonemicizing of suprasegmental features based on the loss of the original contrast between modal voiced and modal voiceless onsets is the norm in MSEA. This is summarized in Table 2 in Section 4.6.

4.2 Consonantal codas

Many proto languages in East and MSEA are reconstructed with at least six consonantal (i.e. non-glide) codas. For example:

- Pre-Angkorian Khmer (Jacob 1993): *-p -t -c -k -m -n -ñ -ṅ -r -l -v -s -h*
- Proto Hmong–Mien (Ratliff 2010): *-p -t -k -m -n -ŋ*
- Proto Tai (Pittayaporn 2009): *-p -t -c -k -m -n (-ɲ) -ŋ -l*
- Middle Chinese (Baxter 1992): *-p -t -k -ʷk -m -n -ŋ -ʷŋ*

In some languages there is a dramatic loss of coda distinctions. For instance, while Mien has preserved *-p -t -k -m -n -ŋ* (Máo, Méng and Zhèng 1982: 16), Hmong has lost all the plosive codas, and all nasal codas have collapsed into an *-ŋ* or vowel nasalization (Wáng 1985: 18). Most Kra-Dai, Mienic and Mon-

---

[27] One important feature that distinguishes Wú and Huī, which are otherwise very similar to each other, is that Huī dialects have phonemicized the splitting of tones. The inventory of onsets in Huī is similar to Gàn to the west; amongst many similarities, they have both lost the voicing distinction of the Middle Chinese onsets.

Khmer languages have at least three plosive codas and three nasal codas. In table 2 (Section 4.6), the sampled East and MSEA languages are classified based on two criteria: a) having more than one contrastive plosive coda; and b) having more than one contrastive nasal coda.[28] It is the norm in MSEA to have at least two plosive codas and two nasal codas (usually there are at least three each). With the Sinitic languages, LACD Map P121 (Figure 2) shows the distribution of -m -n -ŋ, and LACD Map P124 (Figure 3) shows the distribution of -p -t -k -ʔ -l in the Sinitic languages.

The norm for Sinitic languages is to have just -n and/or -ŋ, and to have just -ʔ or no plosive codas at all. Nonetheless, there are many Sinitic languages in or near Far-Southern China which are relatively conservative with their codas, similar to the core of MSEA. Sinitic dialects with two or more plosive codas, and -m plus at least one other nasal coda, are largely confined to the following Sinitic languages in or near Far-Southern China:

- Southern Mǐn (including Mǐn in Hǎinán Island and Léizhōu Peninsula)
- Yuè
- Southern Pínghuà
- Hakka in Guǎngdōng
- Some Gàn dialects

The number of contrastive codas is summarized in Table 2 in Section 4.6.

4.3 Implosives

Many MSEA languages have the implosive consonants ɓ and ɗ (but not ɠ).[29] Examples of languages with ɓ and ɗ include Khmer, Vietnamese and Sgaw Karen. Some MSEA languages, e.g. Eastern Kayah Li (Solnit 1997), are said to have non-implosive b and d (but no g, analogous to nearby languages which have ɓ and ɗ but no ɠ). As for the Sinitic languages, neither Middle Chinese nor Old Chinese were reconstructed with implosive consonants. However, some

---

28 The syllabic nasals that exist in many Southern Sinitic languages are not included in the criterion of having more than one nasal coda.

29 Implosive ɠ is cross-linguistically rare. For the velar ɠ, the voicing that is common for implosives is more difficult to maintain because the distance between the glottis and the oral closure at the velar position is short. Similarly, the plumonic g is also cross-linguistically rarer than b and d (Maddieson 2013a).

modern Sinitic languages have implosives. LACD Map P044 (Figure 4) shows the distribution of implosive onsets in the Sinitic languages.

According to this map, implosives are found in:

– Mǐn in Hǎinán Island and Léizhōu Peninsula
– Dānzhōu dialect (the Yuè-like language in Northeastern Hǎinán)
– Some of the Gōulòu Yuè dialects near the Guǎngxī–Guǎngdōng border
– Some Southern Wú dialects
– Some Northern Wú dialects around Shànghǎi

The most famous example is Hainanese (i.e. Hǎinán Mǐn), which was very strongly influenced by Ong Be, the lowland Kra-Dai language in northern Hǎinán, which also has ɓ and ɗ. Across the Hǎinán Strait, some of the Gōulòu Yuè dialects also have implosive ɓ and ɗ. (However, in some localities they are becoming p and t respectively.) Further away to the northeast, there are implosives in some of the Wú dialects.

Their origins differ. In Hǎinán and Léizhōu Mǐn, ɓ and ɗ developed out of *p and *t after *b and *d lost their voicing and merged into *p and *t, whereas in the other Sinitic languages (including the Yuè-like Dānzhōu dialect in Hǎinán) ɓ and ɗ developed out of *p and *t when *b and *d were still distinct from *p and *t. In areas surrounding Shanghai, a new ɠ has developed out of voiced *g (unlike ɓ and ɗ which developed out of voiceless *p and *t).

See Zhū (e.g. 2006b, et al. 2009) on implosives in Sinitic languages, including some newly developed implosives in Northern Gàn dialects and Cháoshàn Mǐn dialects (e.g. Shàntóu/ Swatow). The existence or non-existence of ɓ ɗ ~ b d is summarized in Table 2 in Section 4.6.

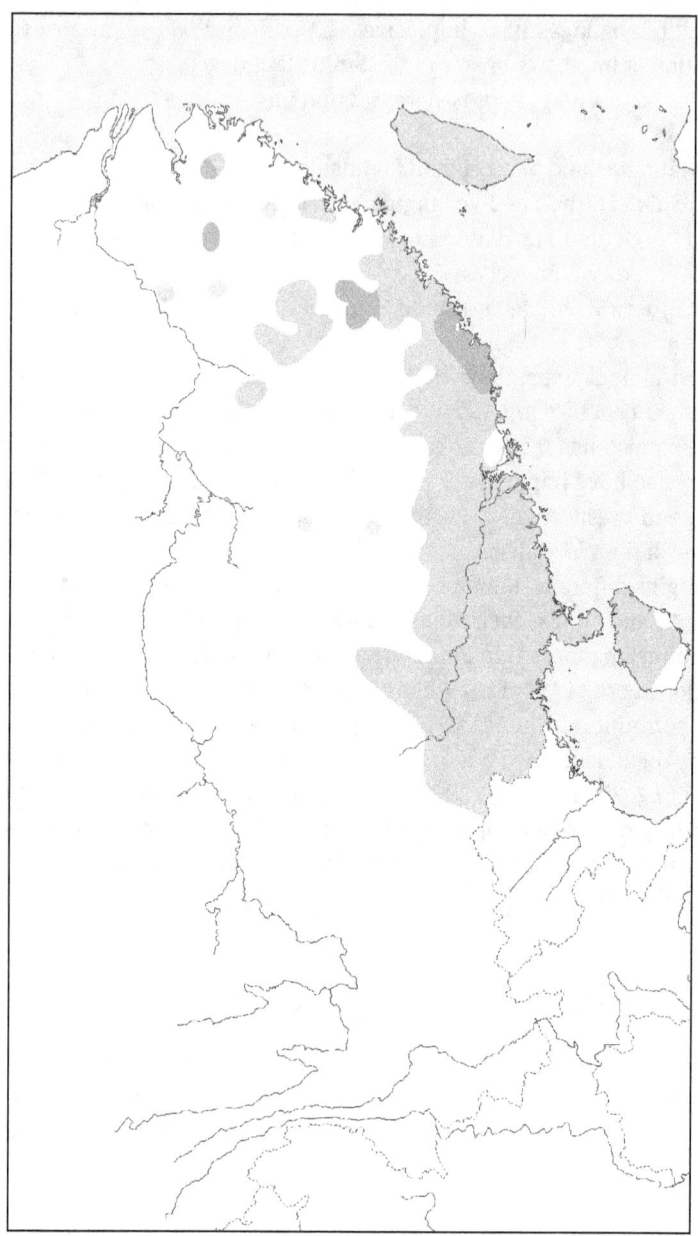

Fig. 2: Areas with -m -n -ŋ highlighted in light gray, and areas with -m -ŋ or -m -n in dark gray. Other Sinitic languages have -n -ŋ, just one of them, or in rare cases, no nasal codas. (Data derived from LACD Map P121).

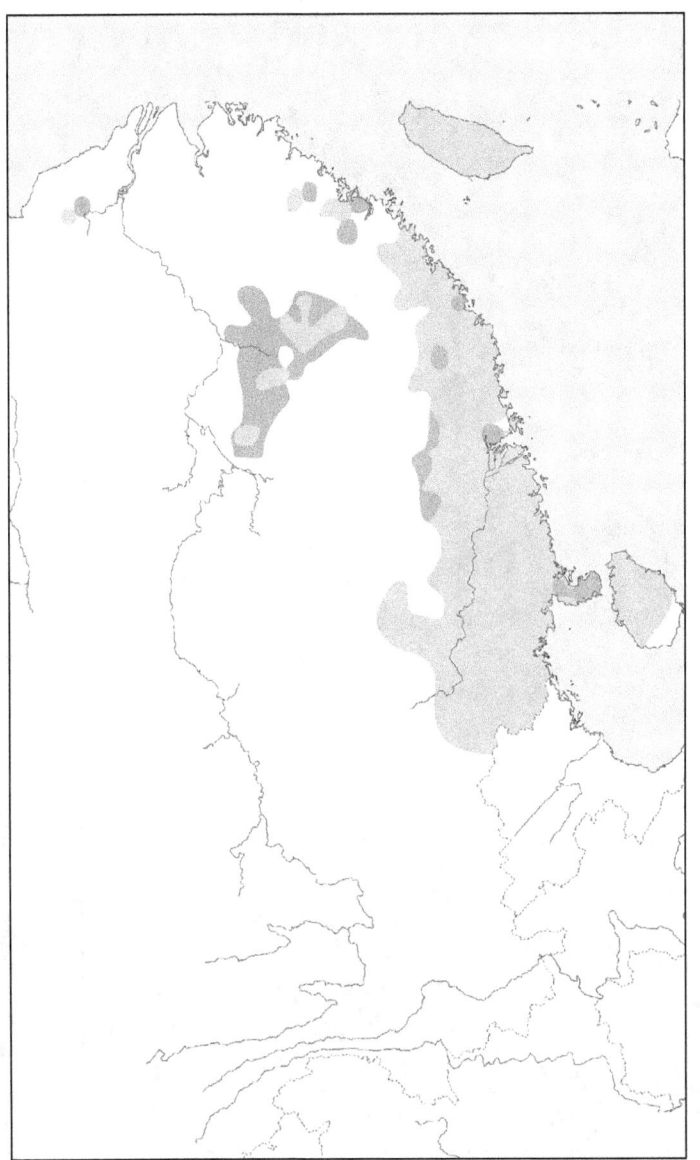

Fig. 3: Areas with three or four non-nasal codas are highlighted in light gray, areas with two non-nasal codas in dark gray. Other Sinitic languages have no non-nasal codas, a single -*ʔ*, or in rare cases a single -*t* or -*l*. (Data derived from LACD Map P124).

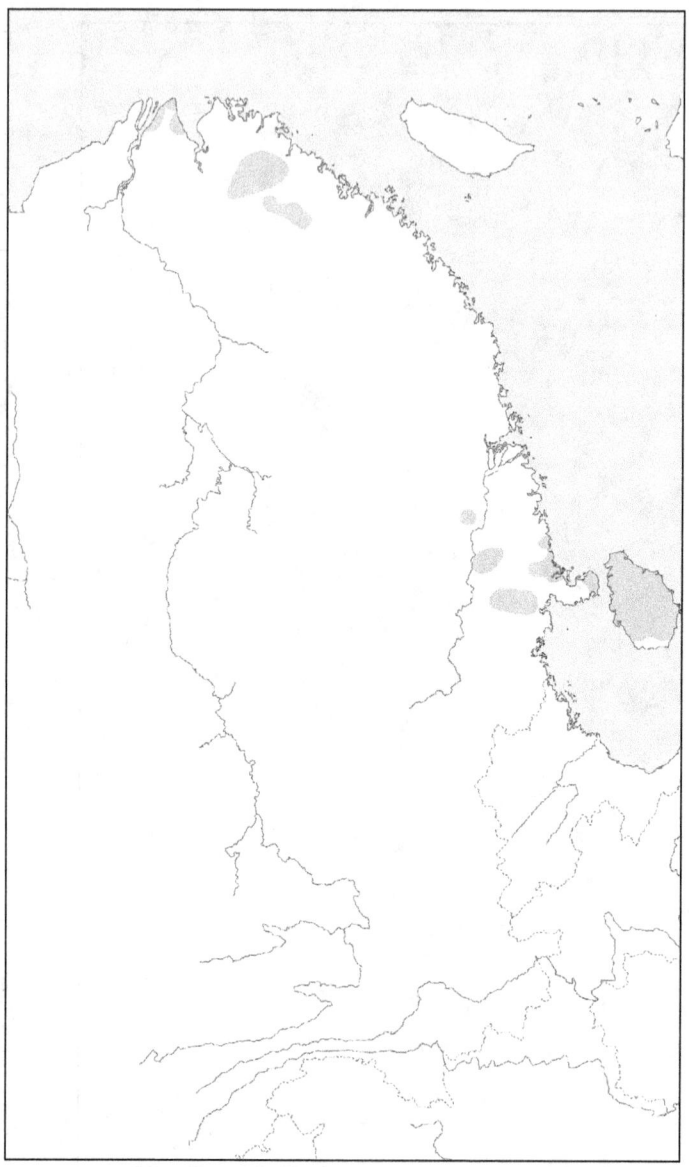

Fig. 4: Areas with implosive consonants are highlighted. Other Sinitic languages have no implosives. (Data derived from LACD Map P044).

4.4 Front rounded vowels

The vast majority of the world's languages lack front rounded vowels (Maddieson 2013b). Most MSEA languages also lack front rounded vowels. Many Sinitic languages in Southern China also lack front rounded vowels. Otherwise, the norm for Sinitic languages is to have front rounded vowels. The following are the main examples of Sinitic languages in Southern China without front rounded vowels:

– Southern Mǐn, including Mǐn of Hǎinán Island and Léizhōu Peninsula
– most Hakka dialects and some neighbouring Southern Gàn dialects
– most Yuè dialects not in the drainage basin of the Pearl River (which entails being somewhat less influenced by Standard Cantonese)

– Most Southern Pínghuà dialects
– Some Southern Mandarin dialects, especially in Yúnnán and Guìzhōu

Map P117 in LACD (Figure 5) shows the distribution of /y/ (including medial glide /ɥ/) in Sinitic dialects.

4.5 'Apical' vowels

Sinitic languages are well known for their 'apical vowels', which are basically syllabic sibilants.[30] There are the alveolar [z̩] and the retroflex [ʐ̩]; the Sinologist symbols for these are <ɿ> and <ʅ> respectively. There are also the lip-rounded versions of these; the Sinologist symbols for these are <ʮ> and <ʯ>, respectively.

Unlike most Sinitic languages, but like languages in MSEA, many Sinitic languages in or near the Far-Southern zone lack apical vowels. These include most Yuè and Pínghuà dialects, most Mǐn dialects, and some Gàn dialects. Map P118 of LACD (Figure 6) shows the distribution of apical vowels in Sinitic dialects.

---

[30] Phonetically, the amount of friction in the oral cavity varies between speakers when they produce the apical vowels. Stereotypically, Northerners produce apical vowels with prominent friction, and the friction lasts nearly throughout the duration of the rime. On the other hand, Far-Southerners stereotypically produce the apical vowels in Mandarin with a corresponding approximant or vowel. Most Chinese people pronounce the apical vowels somewhere between these two extremes: starting off with prominent friction, and then the friction weakens towards the end of the rime and becomes a phonetic vowel.

The existence or non-existence of apical vowels is summarized in Table 2 in Section 4.6.

4.6 Summary of phonological traits

Table 2 summarizes the phonological points raised in Section 4.1 to Section 4.5. The Sinitic dialects in or near the Far-Southern zone (represented by Cantonese and Nánníng Pínghuà here) and Southern Mǐn show many more phonological traits that are more akin to the core of MSEA than to the other Sinitic languages.

Table 2: Some phonological features in Sinitic and MSEA languages

	Non Sinitic							FS Sin.		SE Sinitic				C Sinitic			N
	Thai	Khmer	Vietnamese	E Kayah Li	Burmese	Hmong	Mien	Cantonese	Nánníng Pínghuà	Huī'ān S Mǐn	Fúqīng E Mǐn	Fúyáng Wú	Jīxī Huī	Shàowǔ Mǐn-Gàn	Yíchūn Gàn	Gǔzhàng Xiānghuà	Suīníng C Mandarin
Having "Complex tones" (WALS)																	
	+	−	+	+	+	+	+	+	+	+	+	+	+	+	+	+	+
Phonemicized tonal or phonational contrast from devoicing of onsets																	
	+	(+)[31]	+	+	−	+	+	+	+	+	−	+	+	+	+	−	+
More than one contrastive plosive coda																	
	+	+	+	−	−	−	+	+	+	+	−	−	−	−	−	−	−
More than one contrastive nasal coda																	
	+	+	+	−	−	−	+	+	+	+	−	−	−	+	+	−	+
ɓ ɗ ~ b d (but no ɠ ~ g)																	
	+	+	+	+	−	−	−	−	−	−	−	−	−	−	−	−	−
No rounded front vowels (+ = no)																	
	+	+	+	+	+	+	+	−	+	+	−	−	−	−	−	−	−
No 'apical vowels' (+ = no)																	
	+	+	+	+	+	+[32]	+	+	+	+	+	+	−	−	−	+	−
Total:	7	6	7	5	3	4	6	5	6	6	3	2	2	3	3	2	3

---

31 Except for some conservative Khmer dialects which have preserved the phonational contrast (e.g. Thung Kabin Khmer in Chanthaburi, Thailand; Wayland and Jongman 2003), all Khmer dialects have lost the original phonational contrast.

32 However, apical vowels exist in Dànánshān Hmong (Wáng 1985: 18), the standard variety of Western Hmongic in China.

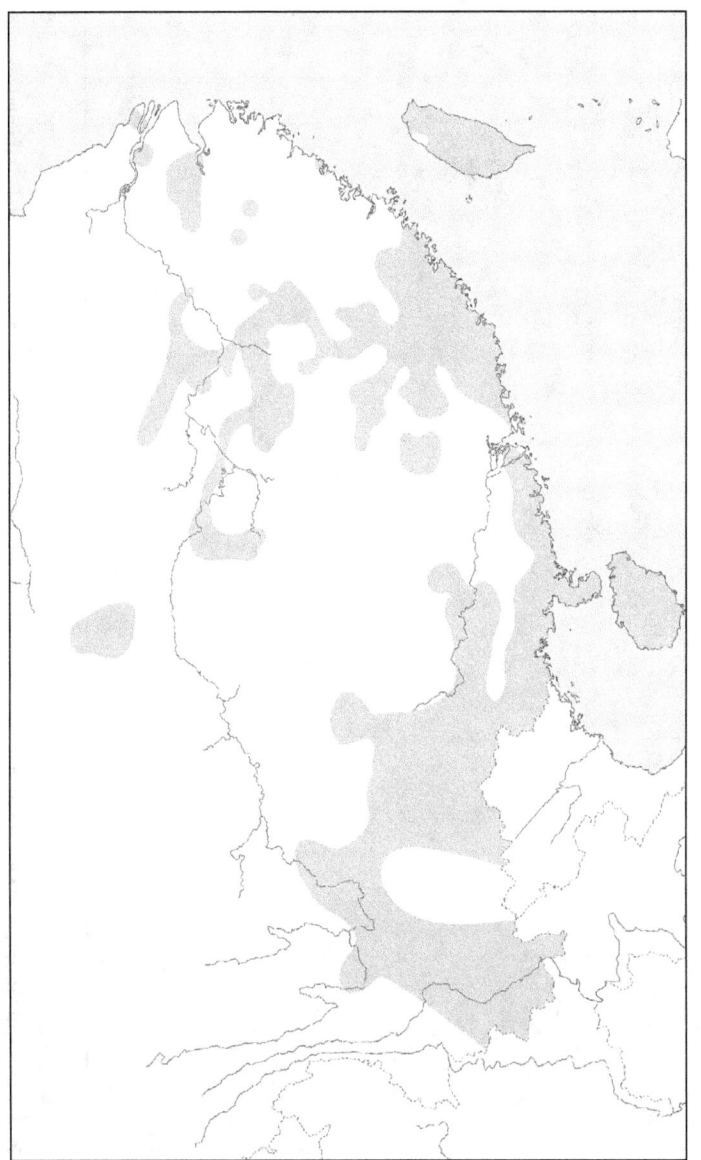

Fig. 5: Areas with neither medial glide *y* nor vowel *y* are highlighted. Other Sinitic languages have both *y* and *y*, or in rare cases, just one of them. (Data derived from LACD Map P117).

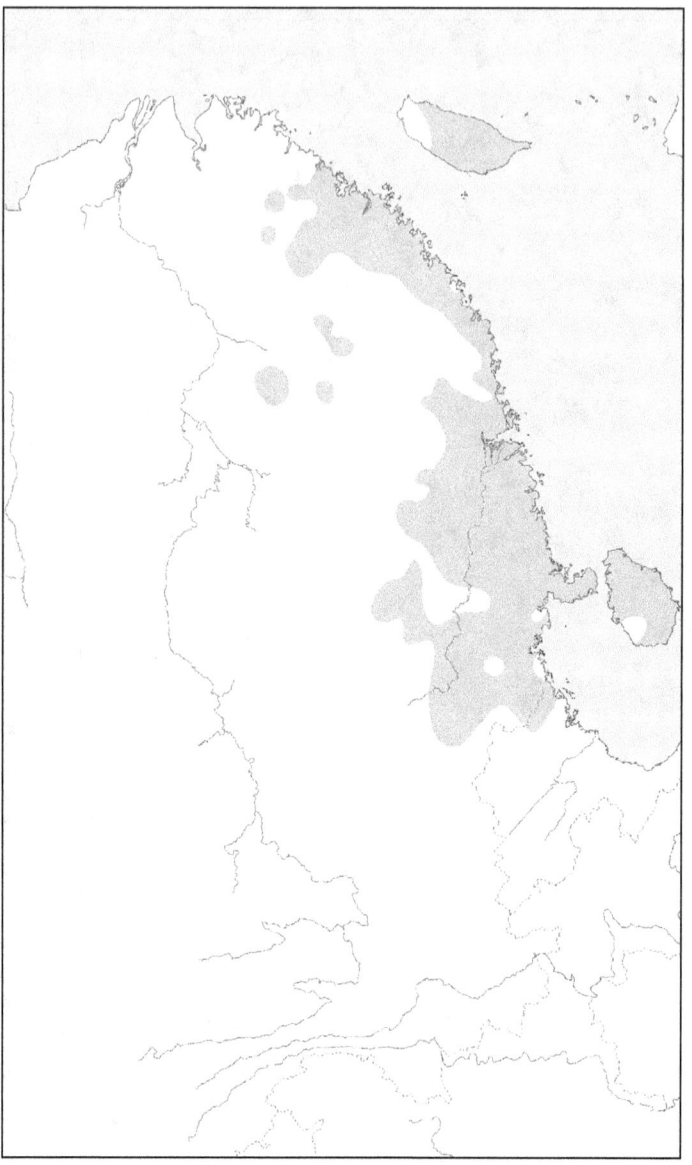

Fig. 6: Areas with no apical vowels are highlighted. Other Sinitic languages have at least one apical vowel. (Data derived from LACD Map P118).

5 Word order

The 'basic' word order in the core of MSEA is SVO. The core MSEA languages are also more strongly left-headed than the usual SVO language (see, e.g. Dryer 2001 on Mon-Khmer word order). The Sinitic languages are also primarily SVO. However, the Sinitic languages are otherwise strongly right headed: noun phrases are strongly right headed, and most adjuncts are placed before the verb. Contrast the word order in the following sentences from Northern Zhuang (Tai) and Cantonese (Sinitic).

(2) Northern Zhuang (SVO order)
de gai byaek youhcaiq gai noh
3SG sell vegetable as:well sell meat
'S/he sells vegetables and sells meat.'
(Wéi and Qín 2006: 198)

(3) Head noun left of most modifiers
go oij [duz vaiz gou caij laemx
CLF sugar_cane CLF buffalo 1SG step fall
henz roen] haenx raek lo
side road that break FP
'The sugar cane that my buffalo trampled on the side of the road snapped.'
(Wéi and Qín 2006: 251)

(4) Standard Cantonese (SVO order)
佢 賣 菜 又 賣 肉
kʰɵy¹³ mai²² tʃʰɔi³³ jɐu²² mai²² jʊk²
3SG sell vegetable as:well sell meat
'S/he sells vegetable and sells meat.'

(5) Head noun right of modifiers
 我   隻   牛   喺   路   邊   踩   冧
 [ŋɔ¹³ tsɛk³ ŋeu¹¹ hei²⁵ lou²² pin⁵⁵ tsʰai²⁵ lem³³]
 1SG CLF bovine at   road side step   fall
 嗰   碌   蔗   斷咗
 kɔ²⁵ lʊk⁵ tsɛ³³ tʰyn²⁴-tsɔ²⁵
 DEM   CLF   cane break-PFV
 'The sugar cane that my buffalo trampled on the side of the road snapped.'

This mix of SVO word order and strong right-headedness has created some extraordinarily rare co-occurrences of word order traits in the Sinitic languages. For instance, the co-occurrence of VO and Relative clause–Noun is nearly unique to the Sinitic languages (WALS feature 96A).[33] The Sinitic languages are the only VO languages with obliques predominantly placed in front of the verb in WALS (feature 84A).[34] Having the Adjective–Noun word order (feature 81A) for SVO languages (feature 87A) is also very rare in the region.[35]

Looking at the word order typological profiles of the languages in the vicinity of the Sinitic languages provides hints as to why the Sinitic languages devel-

---

33 Of the 879 languages sampled in WALS feature 96A, five have the co-occurrence of VO and Rel–N. Cantonese, Hakka and Mandarin are Sinitic. Bai is strongly influenced by Sinitic languages. Amis is also geographically close-by, but this co-occurrence in Amis is probably independent of Chinese (Comrie 2008b). As Comrie (2008b: 729–730) points out, having Rel–N order in SVO languages might aid processing when the object is relativized, as having a SV relative clause in front of the relativized object head resembles the normal SVO word order (Yip and Matthews 2007). There are indeed cases like Pwo Karen where relativized objects can have a prenominal relative clause, and relativized subjects must have a postnominal relative clause (Kato 2003: 641), resembling normal SVO word order in both cases (with the relative clauses considered externally headed in both cases).
34 Of the 500 languages sampled in WALS feature 84A, only the three Sinitic languages sampled have the word order of XVO (where X is an oblique).
35 Based on WALS feature 81A (SVO) and 87A (Adjective–Noun), there are 347 SVO languages with the Noun–Adjective order, and 66 SVO languages (including the Sinitic and Bai) with Adjective–Noun word order. This latter co-existence is mostly concentrated in Europe (20 languages) and Central Africa (15 languages). On the other hand, in Asia, including Western Austronesia, there are only two languages other than Sinitic and Bái which are marked as SVO and Adjective–Noun in WALS: Kashmiri and Palauan. However, the status of both being SVO is questionable. Kashmiri is verb-second (e.g. Wali and Koul 1996, Koul and Wali 2006). With Palauan, the slot in front of the verb can only be occupied by a subject agreement marker; subject nominals are placed after the object (i.e., VOS; Georgopoulos 1986). This leaves the Sinitic languages and Bai as the only SVO and Adjective–Noun languages in Asia.

oped such an unusual mixture of VO order and strong right-headed traits. The Sinitic languages had the most interactions with the following three neighbouring word order areas:

Area A

Area A is the verb-medial core-MSEA zone to the south. The prototypical MSEA languages are SVO and more left-headed than the average SVO languages. Included in this zone are the Hmong-Mien, Kra-Dai, Mon-Khmer and Chamic languages. In the following examples, the clauses are verb-medial, and the modified constituents are generally to the left of the modifiers.

(6)　Utsat (Chamic; Chinese influenced)
　　　ʔa¹¹thai¹¹　se¹¹　phai³³siaŋ¹¹　ho¹¹lien¹¹　ʔa¹¹kai³³　sa³³　ta¹¹　se⁵⁵,
　　　litl.sister CLF very　　　feel:sorry　old.man MOD one CLF
　　　kian³³　ʔa¹¹kai³³　ni³³　sa³³　ta¹¹　se⁵⁵　ten³²　pa³³,
　　　know old.man this MOD one CLF stomach hungry
　　　'The little sister was very sorry for the old man, and knew that the old man was hungry,' (Zhèng 1997: 238)
　　　(*phai³³siaŋ¹¹　ho¹¹lien¹¹* 非常可憐 are Chinese loanwords in Chinese word order.)

(7)　Green Hmong (Hmong-Mien)
　　　kuv　nyam　tug　　txivneej　kws　ncaws pob
　　　1SG　like　　CLF　　man　　　　REL　　kick　　ball
　　　hab　tug　txivneej　kws　moog　rua　Fresno
　　　and　CLF　man　　　REL　　go　　to　　Fresno
　　　'I like the man who plays soccer and the man who went to Fresno.'
　　　(Li 1989: 120)

Area B (and Area A~B)

Area B is the verb-final Tibeto-Burman zone to the west. These languages are SOV, they are generally right-headed, but they also have some left-headed traits (e.g. Tibetan and Burmese are SOV and have N–Num and N–Adj word order). Having N–Adj is in fact the norm for SOV languages cross-linguistically (Dryer 2013). In the following examples, clauses are verb-final, adpositions are placed at the right edge, and the modified constituents are to the right of some modifiers, and to the left of some modifiers.

(8) Burmese
 thu di hsei: thau' me
 3 this medicine drink IRR
 'He's going to take this medicine.'
 (Soe 1999: 132)

(9) *thu. le' nyi'=pa' ne. nga. ḵou la tou. te*
 3GEN hand dirty with 1 OBJ come touch RLS
 '(He) touched me with his dirty hands.'
 (Soe 1999: 256)

There are also languages which are transitional between area A and area B. Some Tibeto-Burman languages are exceptionally SVO. They, like the Sinitic languages, exhibit interesting mixtures of properties associated with VO and OV orders. These SVO Tibeto-Burman languages include the Karen languages, Bái languages, and Mru (Peterson 2005).[36]

(10) Eastern Kayah Li (Karenic)
 phremɔ̀ méthʌ phrekhū sí nā̄
 woman look:see man CLF two
 'Some women saw two men.'
 (Solnit 1997: 181)

(11) *ʔa khē təlwá sɔklā̄ né sɔkhō*
 3 paddle pass boat PREP snag
 'He paddled the boat past the snag (fallen log).'
 (Solnit 1997: 159)

Area C

Area C is the verb-final North Asia zone to the north. These languages are SOV and strongly right-headed. In and near China are the following families of SOV languages: Turkic, Mongolic, Tungusic, Korean and Japanese-Ryūkyūan.

---

[36] Tibeto-Burman languages that have SVO word order are often assumed to have acquired SVO word order under the influence of neighbouring SVO languages. Mru is an interesting case because it is totally surrounded by verb-final languages (Chittagonian, Rakhine, and Kuki-Chin languages). It is also spoken very far away from verb-medial languages like the Khasic or Palaungic languages, and there seems to be no Mon-Khmer lexical borrowings in Mru (Löffler 1966). See more discussions in Djamouri, Paul and Whitman (2007).

The historical Tokharian languages also fit this typological profile.[37] In the following examples, clauses are verb-final, and modified constituents are always to the right of the modifiers.

(12) Uyghur (Turkic)
 sɛn bu kino-ni kør
 2SG this film-ACC see[IMP]
 'You watch this film!'
 (Abulimit 2006: 239)

(13) top ojna-watqan bala bizniŋ sinip-ta oqu-jdu
 ball play-CONT boy 1PL:GEN class-LOC study-3.NPST
 'The boy who is playing with a ball studies in our class.'
 (Abulimit 2006: 324)

The SVO word order in the Sinitic languages resembles that of the verbmedial MSEA zone to the south (Area A), while the strong right-headedness in the Sinitic languages resembles that of the verb-final North Asian zone to the north (Area C). In fact, the strong right-headedness of the Sinitic languages makes them typologically more similar to the North Asian languages than their relatives—the Tibeto-Burman languages—to the west (Area B). This suggests that the Sinitic family, as a whole, had strong interactions with the North Asian languages to the north and the non-Sinitic MSEA languages to the south, and relatively less so with their relatives, the Tibeto-Burman languages, to the west.

We shall discuss noun phrase level syntax in Section 5.1, and then clause level syntax in Section 5.2.

---

37 Other than the three typological areas discussed here, there are also the following typological areas in and around China that the Sinitic languages have less contact with: a) languages of the Formosan–Philippine area, which are mostly verb initial; b) languages of the Indic area, which are verb final and strongly-right headed, except Kashmiri and several other Dardic languages which are verb-second; and c) languages of the Iranian area, with Sarikoli and Wakhi represented in China (Gawarjon 1985). These two Pamiri languages are verb final and more strongly right-headed than the other Iranian languages, but they still have the Iranian trait of having prepositions (although they also have some Uyghur-like postpositions).

5.1 Word order in noun phrases

In or close to the core of MSEA, most modifiers follow the head noun (e.g. Simpson 2005).

(14) Lao
 khon2 suung3
 person tall
 'tall person'
 (Enfield 2007: 93)

(15) *khaw5 niaw3*
 rice sticky
 'sticky rice'
 (Enfield 2007: 93)

(16) Khmer
 civeut ti: pi: rabawh knjom
 life place two of me
 'my second life'
 (Haiman 2011: 168)

(17) Eastern Kayah Li
 ʔiswí nā bēlɔ̄ du
 curry two bowl big
 'two big bowls of curry'
 (Solnit 1997: 180)

In the periphery of MSEA, Burmese, which is verb final, has some postverbal modifiers, like the nominalized stative verb *a-thi'* 'new' and stative verb *hklei:* 'small' in the following example. (Attributive nouns like *thi'tha:* 'wood' precede the head noun.)

(18) Burmese
 thi'tha: ein a-thi' hkalei:
 wooden house new small
 'small new wooden house'
 (Myint Soe 1999: 44)

Looking into the history of Chinese, noun phrases were already mostly right headed in Pre-Archaic and Archaic periods.

(19) Pre-Archaic Chinese (14th to 11th century BCE)[38]
上甲 惠 王 報 　 用 五 伐
shàngjiǎ huì wáng bào　yòng wǔ fá
shangjia FOC king bao:sacrifice use five human:victim
土 小 牢
shí xiǎo láo
ten little sacrificial:sheep
'As for (the ancestor) Shangjia, it must be the king who addresses (him) with a *bao* sacrifice by using five human victims and ten little sacrificial sheep.'
(Djamouri 2001: 162; Jiágǔwén Héjí 924)

(20) Early Archaic Chinese
天 不 庸 釋 　 于 文 王 受 命
tiān bū yóng shì　yú [[wén wáng shòu] mìng]
heaven not then relinquish to [[wen king receive] destiny]
'Then Heaven will not relinquish [the destiny which King Wen received].'
(Aldridge, 2013: 47; Shàngshū, Jūnshì 君奭; approx 8th century BCE)

(21) 非 時 伯夷 播 　 刑 之 迪？
fēi [[shí bóyí bō]　xíng] zhī dí?
not.be [[then boyi promulgate] law] GEN guide
'Is it not the laws promulgated by Boyi which guide (you)?'
(Aldridge, 2013: 47; Shàngshū, Lǚxíng 呂刑; approx 8th century BCE)

However, there were some post-nominal modifiers in the earliest stages of Chinese. SVO languages typically have some pre-nominal and some post-nominal modifiers, and the earlier stages of Chinese had more post-nominal modifiers than the modern Sinitic languages.

---

38 As is the convention in the West and most of China, historical Chinese texts are transcribed and pronounced in modern Mandarin pronunciation. The pronunciation of the characters in Pre-Archaic Chinese (fourteenth to eleventh century BCE) is earlier than the earliest reconstructable phonological form of Chinese (Old Chinese: tenth to seventh century BCE) anyway.

(22) Pre-Archaic Chinese (14th to 11th century BCE)
子 央 歲 于 丁
zǐ *yāng* *suì* *yú dīng*
prince yang immolate to Ding
'The prince Yang [will] immolate something for the ancestor Ding.'
(Djamouri 2001: 146; Jiágǔwén Héjí 3018)

Numerals, in particular, were placed variously in front of or after the head noun.

(23) 獲 唯 鳥 七
huò *wéi* *niǎo* *qī*
capture COP bird seven
'The catch is seven birds.'
(Djamouri 2001: 151; Jīnzhāng suǒ cáng Jiágǔ Búcí 742)
(Numerals were more often prenominal than postnominal in Pre-Archaic Chinese.)

The earliest classifier-like words more often follow, rather than precede, the head noun.

(24) Pre-Medieval Chinese
分 與 文君 僮 百 人
fēn *yǔ* *wénjūn* *tóng* *bǎi* *rén*
distribute give wenjun slave hundred people
'(He) distributed a hundred slaves to Wenjun.'
(Chappell and Peyraube 2007; Shǐjì, Sīmǎ Xiāngrú Lièzhuǎn 司馬相如列傳, approx 1st century BCE)

(25) Early Medieval Chinese
時 跋跋提 國 送 獅子兒 兩 頭 與
shí *bá bátí* *guó* *sòng* *shīzi ér* *liǎng* *tóu* *yǔ*
time ? Bactria country offer lion child two CLF'head' give
乾陀羅 王
gāntuóluó *wáng*
Gandhāra king
'At that time, the kingdom of Bactria offered two lion cubs to the king of Gandhāra.'
(Chappell and Peyraube 2007; Luòyáng Qiélánjì 5 洛陽伽藍記 5; 6th century CE)

These post-nominal classifier-like words in earlier stages of Chinese were argued to be not part of the noun phrase of the preceding noun (e.g. Peyraube 1988). Indeed, it can also be argued that the post-nominal classifiers do not form a phrase with the preceding noun in some MSEA languages. For example, in Lao, a phrase can often intervene between a [num + clf] phrase and the preceding noun which it attributes semantically.

(26) Lao
 kuu3 sùù4 paa3 sòòng3 too3
 1SG buy fish two   CLF
 'I bought two fish.'
 (Enfield 2007: 120)

(27) kuu3 sùù4 paa3 juu1 talaat5 sòòng3 too3
 1SG buy fish be.at market two   CLF
 'I bought fish at the market, two (of them).' (= 'I bought two fish at the market')
 (Enfield 2007: 120)

Looking at the modern Sinitic languages, their noun phrases are even more strongly right-headed than the ones in older stages of Chinese.

(28) Nánníng Pínghuà
 我   個   對   舊   皮   鞋
 ŋa¹³ kə⁵⁵ tɔi⁵⁵ kəu²² pəi¹¹ hai¹¹
 1SG DEM pair old   leather shoe
 'My pair of old leather shoes.'

Nevertheless, there are typically some non-productive left-headed compounds in the Southern Sinitic languages, e.g. Cantonese 魚生 jy¹¹ saŋ⁵⁵ (fish raw) 'raw fish', 菜乾 tsʰɔi³³ kɔn⁵⁵ (vegetable dry) 'dried vegetable', 人客 jen¹¹ hak³³ (person guest) 'guest', 熊人 huŋ¹¹ jen¹¹⁻²⁵ (bear person) 'brown bear (child's word)'. (See also, for example, the many left headed compounds in Wēnzhōu Wú (Zhèngzhāng 2008: 232).) More productive than these fixed compounds are the sex affixes for animals. The general trend is for the Northern Sinitic languages to have sex prefixes, resembling the right-headed word order in North Asia, and the Southern Sinitic languages to have sex suffixes, resembling the left-headed word order in MSEA. (Nánníng Pínghuà is a major exception for being in the Far-Southern zone, but having sex prefixes predominantly.) Some Sinitic dialects in the centre are somewhat mixed; for instance, some dialects have a prefix for one sex and a suffix for the other sex, or a prefix for one animal and a suffix for another animal.

    Standard Mandarin (prefixes)
(29) 公豬 gōng-zhū (male-pig) 'boar'
(30) 母豬 mǔ-zhū (female-pig) 'sow'

    Xiānghuà (prefixes and suffixes)
(31) ○豬 ɕiaŋ²⁵-tiəɯ⁵⁵ (male-pig) 'boar'
(32) 豬娘 tiəɯ⁵⁵-n̠iẽ⁵⁵ (pig-female) 'sow'

    Fùyáng Wú (prefixes and suffixes)
(33) 雄雞 'ɦioŋ-'tɕi (male-fowl) 'rooster'
(34) 雞娘 'tɕi-'niã (fowl-female) 'hen'

    Shàowǔ Mǐn-Gàn (suffixes)
(35) 雞公 kɛi²¹-kuŋ²¹ (fowl-male) 'rooster'
(36) 雞嬤 kɛi²¹-ma²² (fowl-female) 'hen'

    Fūqīng Eastern Mǐn (suffixes)
(37) 雞公 kiɛ³²-kuŋ⁵³ (fowl-male) 'rooster'
(38) 雞母 kiɛ³²-mɔ⁵³ (fowl-female) 'hen'

    Cantonese (suffixes)
(39) 雞公 kei⁵⁵-kʊŋ⁵⁵ (fowl-male) 'rooster'
(40) 雞嫲 kei⁵⁵-na²⁵ (fowl-female) 'hen'

    Nánníng Pínghuà (prefixes)[39]
(41) 公雞 kʊŋ⁵³-kɐi⁵³ (male-fowl) 'rooster'
(42) 母雞 mu¹³-kɐi⁵³ (female-fowl) 'hen'

The following table summarizes the noun phrase features discussed in Section 5.1. In general, the languages in the core of MSEA have rather strongly left-headed noun phrases, whereas the modern Sinitic languages have strongly right-headed noun phrases. The Southern Sinitic languages have marginally more nominal left-headedness in having some morphologically left-headed words.

---

39 Pínghuà dialects to the west also have gender prefixes, e.g. Chóngzuǒ (Lǐ and Zhū 2009: 177).

Table 3: Left-headedness on the noun phrase level in some Sinitic and MSEA languages

	Non Sinitic							FS Sin.		SE Sinitic				C Sinitic			N
	Thai	Khmer	Vietnamese	E Kayah Li	Burmese	Hmong	Mien	Cantonese	Nánníng Pínghuà	Huī'ān S Mǐn	Fúqīng E Mǐn	Fúyáng Wú	Jìxī Huī	Shàowǔ Mǐn-Gàn	Yìchūn Gàn	Gǔzhàng Xiānghuà	Suīníng C Mandarin
N – Genitive	+	+	+	−	−	−	−	−	−	−	−	−	−	−	−	−	−
N – "Adjective" (e.g. chicken – big)	+	+	+	+	+	+	+	−	−	−	−	−	−	−	−	−	−
N – Noun (e.g. egg – chicken)	+	+	+	−	−	+	−	−	−	−	−	−	−	−	−	−	−
N – Sex (e.g. chicken – male)	+	+	+	+	+	+	+	+	−	+	+	±	±	+	+	±	−
N – Demonstrative	+	+	+	−	+	−	−	−	−	−	−	−	−	−	−	−	−
N – Relative clause	+	+	+	−	−	+	−	−	−	−	−	−	−	−	−	−	−
Total:	6	6	6	3	2	5	2	1	0	1	1	½	½	1	1	½	0

5.2 Word order in clauses

The core MSEA languages are SVO, and modifiers usually follow the head. The Sinitic languages are also said to be primarily SVO. However, these languages require the preposing of objects to a pre-verbal position in some situations. In addition, other than the VO word order, the Sinitic languages are strongly right-headed.

This rare combination of SVO word order and strong right-headedness in the modern Sinitic languages, and the fact that the vast majority of Tibeto-Burman languages, i.e., the relatives of the Sinitic languages, are verb-final, has led to the common assumption of Chinese having more verb-final traits the further one goes back into the history of Chinese (Li and Thompson 1974: 208, LaPolla 1994). However, looking at the written records of Chinese up till fourteenth century BCE, the opposite was true: the further one goes back into the history of written Chinese, the more verb-medial traits there were (Peyraube 1997; Djamouri, Paul, and Whitman 2007). In other words, the exceptionally rare combination of SVO and right-headedness in Chinese has been stable for at least thirty-four centuries (from fourteenth century BCE to twentieth century CE), and Chinese developed from a strange SVO language into a group of even stranger SVO languages, typologically speaking.

First of all, Pre-Archaic Chinese was clearly a SVO language: looking at Pre-Archaic Chinese texts (Shang Dynasty oracle bone script), 93.8% of clauses with two place predicates were (S)VO in Djamouri's corpus (2001: 146); OV order only occurred in specific syntactic environments.[40] Pre-Archaic and Archaic Chinese also had wh-movement, which is a trait not uncommon for VO languages, but rare for OV languages (e.g. Dryer 1991). Modern Sinitic languages have most obliques placed in front of the verb, which is extremely rare for VO languages. (In WALS, the modern Sinitic languages are the only VO languages that predominantly place oblique phrases before the verb (WALS feature 84A).) However, Pre-Archaic Chinese is a relatively normal VO language, in that it usually places obliques after the object (i.e. VOX word order).[41]

(43) Pre-Archaic Chinese
呼　　多　　　犬　　　　网　　鹿　　于　　辳
hū　　duō　　quǎn　　wǎng　lù　　yú　nóng
order numerous dog.officer net　deer at Nong
'Call upon the many dog-officers to net deer at Nong.'
(Djamouri, Paul, and Whitman 2007: 3; *Jiǎgǔwén Héjí* 10976 recto.)

The same VOX word order is also the norm in the core of MSEA. The following are some examples.

(44) Lao
phen1 lin5 phaj4 juu1 talaat5
3POL play cards be.at market
'She is playing cards at the market.'
(Enfield 2007: 390)

---

40 In Pre-Archaic Chinese and Archaic Chinese, OV order only occurred in: a) cleft constructions: {COP ... O V} (the copula was obligatory in Pre-Archaic Chinese, but became optional in the Early Archaic period); b) negative sentences with an accusative pronoun: {NEG O V} (in Pre-Archaic Chinese this was restricted to the negator 不 *bù* (Djamouri, Paul and Whitman 2007: 4), but in Archaic Chinese this applies to other negators as well); and c) wh-questions; the non-subject question word is placed between the subject and the verb: {S Q V?}. See Aldridge (2013).
41 Other than the post-object position, another common position for locative phrases, for temporal phrases in particular, is the pre-subject position (Djamouri 2001: 147–148).

(45) Khmer
knjom tradaw: sra:j krama: pi: cangkeh
I struggle untie scarf from waist
'I struggle to untie the scarf from my waist.'
(Haiman 2011: 204)

In contrast to Pre-Archaic Chinese, which is a relatively normal SVO language, two related tendencies developed amongst the modern Sinitic languages (e.g. Zhāng 2010, Liú 2012, Bisang 2012):

– the Sinitic languages accept postverbal constituents less readily
– in many Sinitic languages, the association of postverbal constituents with new information became stronger[42]

This created many more verb-final sentences in the modern Sinitic languages than older stages of Chinese. These traits are relatively weak in the Far-Southern Sinitic languages, Cantonese for instance; the Far-Southern Sinitic languages are relatively close to the core of MSEA, in both a geographical sense, and also in a typological sense, in that the Far-Southern Sinitic languages have the most verb-medial traits amongst the Sinitic languages. The Northern Sinitic languages have many verb-final traits; the Far-Western Central Plains Mandarin dialects even have postpositions and are predominately SOV. The Northern Sinitic languages have been under the influence of verb-final Altaic languages. Nevertheless, putting the aforementioned SOV Mandarin dialects aside, the Sinitic languages with most verb-final sentences are not the Northern Sinitic languages, but the Southeastern Sinitic languages, which are not known to have significant contacts with verb-final languages.[43] It is rare for more than one

---

[42] For Mandarin, Li (2011) characterizes postverbal constituents as primarily conveying new information. There are also accounts which characterize postverbal constituents in Mandarin as focused (LaPolla 1995) or indefinite (Li and Thompson 1975). While the information status account seems to model the situation in Mandarin well, in other Sinitic languages definiteness may be the primary motivating factor. More studies are needed on the variation in word order amongst the Sinitic languages.

[43] The reason for this is unknown to me. Perhaps this is an independent development. It is known that in SVO languages, there is a correlation between the preverbal position and definiteness (see Section 5.2.3), and perhaps the Southeastern Sinitic languages further grammaticalized this on their own accord.
Before Southeastern China was Sinicized, the indigenous people in the area spoke Kra-Dai, Hmong-Mien, and perhaps also Austroasiatic languages, none of which are known to have SOV word order. Whether there were SOV-speaking indigenous people in the area or not is not

constituent to occur after the verb. As an example of an often-verb-final South-eastern Sinitic language, M. Qián (2008) summarizes the following syntactic environments where sentences have to be verb final in Níngbō Wú (with my reinterpretation and with the help of the description of the tense and aspect system of Níngbō Wú in N.R. Qián 2008):

- Sentences with a post-verbal tense-aspect marker (e.g. present perfective, past perfective, durative, simultaneous, experiential; these markers are often grammaticalized from locative words)
- Some Irrealis sentences, e.g.:
    - Negative sentences (S – O – neg – V)
    - Yes-no questions (S – O – V – Q)
    - Rhetorical questions (S – O – V – Q)
    - Imperative sentences (except that [num–clf] phrase and verbal complements can occur post-verbally)
- Emphatic possessive sentences (S – O – possess – emph)
- 'To' (e.g. I place go) and 'from' (e.g. I place from go)
- Transitive sentences with an object which is definite

Contrast this with a Far-Southern Sinitic language like Cantonese, where all of these sentences above would normally be in SVO order, similar to a canonical MSEA language.

In the following subsections, I will discuss the situations in which non-subject constituents have to be preverbal in Sinitic languages. I will show that the Northern and Southeastern Sinitic languages have more instances of verb-final sentences, whereas the Far-Southern Sinitic languages have far fewer instances of verb-final sentences, being closer to the core of MSEA. The following word order traits will be discussed:

- Position of adverbials and adpositions (Section 5.2.1)
- Position of modifiers of verbs (Section 5.2.2)
- Position of objects (Section 5.2.3)
    - The object marking construction (Section 5.2.3.1)

---

known to me. There had been some, typologically speaking, relatively insignificant contacts with SOV languages from the east across the sea: the colonization of Southern-Mǐn- and Hakka-speaking Taiwan by Japan, and the historical link between the Eastern-Mǐn-speaking Fúzhōu and the Ryūkyūan Kingdom.

- Preverbal and Postverbal definite objects (Section 5.2.3.2)
- Word order in clauses with three place predicates (Section 5.2.3.3)

A summary of Section 5.2 is presented in Section 5.2.4.

5.2.1 Position of adverbials and adpositions

Modern Sinitic languages allow post-verbal constituents less readily than Archaic Chinese and MSEA languages. To my knowledge, the only modern Sinitic language that, like Archaic Chinese, commonly has adverbials after the object is Jīxī Huī.

(46) Jīxī Huī
我 看 電影 是 電影園 (裏)
a^{55} $kʰã^{324>35}$ $tʰẽ^{223}iã^{55}$ se^{55} $tʰẽ^{223}ia^{55>53}yẽ^{223}$ (ni)
1SG see film at cinema (in)
'I watched a film in the cinema.'[44]

(47) 爾 ○ 柴 (是) 哪○ 啊?
$õ^{55}$ $tsoʔ^{32>35}$ sa^{32} (se^{55}) $na^{55>53}xa^{324}$ a?
2SG chop firewood at where Q
'Where do/did you chop firewood?'

Otherwise, it is probably universal amongst modern Sinitic languages that most adverbials are placed in front of the main verb, especially for temporal phrases. The following are some examples.

(48) Nánníng Pínghuà
我 大早 住 屋頭 看了 一 出 戲
$ŋa^{13}$ $tai^{22}tʃau^{33}$ $tʃət^{22}$ $uk^3təu^{11}$ han^{25}-$lə^{33}$ et^3 $tʃʰət^3$ $hət^{25}$
1SG just:now at home watch-PFV one CLF film
'I watched a film at home just now.'

---

44 是 se^{55} is a locative preposition in Jīxī Huī. The copula is also 是 se^{55}.

(49) Xiānghuà
 我 朝頭 ○ 三 個 鉴
 u²⁵ tiau⁵⁵ta ziəɯ¹³ so⁵⁵ kəɯ³³ tɕi¹³
 1SG morning eat   three CLF bun
 'I ate three buns this morning.'

(50) Standard Mandarin
 我 明天 在 站台 上 等 你
 wǒ míngtiān zài zhàntái shàng děng nǐ
 1SG tomorrow at platform on wait 2SG
 'I will wait for you at the platform tomorrow.'

MSEA languages, on the other hand, usually have many adverbials which can be placed after the object.

(51) Vietnamese
 bố cháu đã từng dạy học ở Ha-oai
 father 1SG ANT EXP teach study in Hawaii
 'My dad has taught in Hawaii.'
 (Nguyễn 1997: 158)

(52) Thai
 sûa kàw ca aw pay bɔricàak phrûŋníi
 clothes old will take go donate tomorrow
 'I'll give away the old clothes tomorrow.'
 (Smyth 2002: 117)

While most adverbials are placed in front of the verb, most Sinitic languages have some location phrases that are placed after the verb (as arguments or adjuncts, depending on the verb). This is especially the case with destinations.

(53) Cantonese
 我 今日 去 台北
 ŋɔ²⁵ kɐm⁵⁵jɐt² hɵy³³ tʰɔi¹¹pɐk⁵
 1SG today go Taipei
 'I am going to Taipei today.'

(54) Fúqīng Eastern Mǐn
 我　　今晏　　　去　　　北京
 ŋua³² kiŋ⁵³naŋ²¹ kʰyɔ²¹ peʔ³kiŋ⁵³
 1SG today go Beijing
 'I am going to Beijing today.'

However, some Sinitic languages require even destinations to be placed before the main verb. This is the norm in Wú and Huī in the Southeastern Zone, the Sinitic dialects in the Northern Zone, and some in the Central zone. The destination precedes the verb, and the destination is at least preceded by a preposition.[45]

(55) Jīxī Huī
 到　　績溪　　　　去
 tə³²⁴ tseʔ³²⁾³⁵tɕʰi²¹ kʰe³²⁴
 to Jīxī go
 'Going to Jīxī.'

(56) Xiānghuà
 你　　到　何○　　去？
 ni²⁵ tau³³ uo¹³ni⁴¹ kʰəu³³?
 2SG to where go
 'Where are you going?'

(57) Pínglì Central Mandarin
 你　　到　　哪兒　　去　耶？我　　到　城　　　裏頭　　　去
 ni⁴⁴ tau²³ lar⁴⁴⁵ tɕʰi²³ iɛ? ŋo⁴⁴ tau²³ tʂʰən⁵² li⁴⁴⁵tʰou tɕʰi²⁴
 2SG to where go Q 1SG to city in go
 'Where are you going? I am going to the city.' (Zhōu 2009: 408)

(58) Wēnzhōu Wú (Southern Wú)
 我　　走　　　　溫州　　　　去
 ŋ³⁴ tsau⁴⁵⁾⁰ ʔjy³³⁾¹¹tɕau³³ kʰei⁴²⁾⁰
 1SG to Wenzhou go
 'I am going to Wenzhou.' (Zhèngzhāng 2008: 340)

---

45 The constituents translated as 'to' are grammaticalized from verbs; as main verbs, 到 is 'arrive', and 走 in Wēnzhōu is 'go'. However, the 'to' in these examples are no longer verbs. For instance, they cannot take any verbal morphology.

In Northern Wú dialects, the preposition is usually elided (discussed below), resulting in what appears to be a SOV sentence.

(59)　Fùyáng Wú (Northern Wú)[46]
　　　我　今朝　（到）　上海　　去
　　　ŋɤ　'kintsɔ　('tɔ)　zɔŋhɛ　tɕʰi
　　　1SG today　to　　Shanghai go
　　　'I am going to Shanghai today.' (It is more common to omit 'tɔ 'to'.)

The Sinitic languages have both prepositions and postpositions. SVO languages usually have prepositions. Postpositions are rarer for SVO languages. However, having postpositions in a SVO language is itself not too surprising, if the postposition is grammaticalized from a noun, and when genitives occur in front of the noun. So, to indicate location, instead of having a left headed structure like the following from Northern Zhuang:

(60)　Northern Zhuang
　　　[youq [gwnz [taiz]]]
　　　at　　above table
　　　'on the table'

Sinitic languages would have a general locative preposition, and a postposition which signifies a semantically narrower locative relation. In Sinitic languages, the locative postposition, which is grammaticalized from a noun, is usually no longer a free noun. For instance, in the following example, 上 ɬeŋ²² 'above' is not a noun meaning 'top'.

(61)　Nánníng Pínghuà
　　　住　　檯　　上
　　　[tsəi²² [[tai¹¹] ɬeŋ²²]]
　　　at　　table　above
　　　'on the table'

Similar structures exist in Karenic languages, which also have mixed VO-associated and OV-associated typological profiles like the Sinitic languages.

---

46 A proper analysis of the tonal system in Fùyáng Wú is yet to be done. There are two or three contrastive word melodies (and various allo-melodies).

However, in Eastern Kayah Li at least, the postnominal locative word is still a noun.

(62) Eastern Kayah Li
 dý lē kū
 at ravine interior
 'in the ravine'
 (Solnit 2007: 209)

(63) dý pjā kū
 at bag interior
 'in the bag'
 (Solnit 2007: 209)

(64) dý hi lē
 at house bottom
 'under the house'
 (Solnit 2007: 211)

(65) dý dɔ́ lē
 at village bottom
 'below (downhill from) the village'
 (Solnit 2007: 211)

What is surprising is that the (newer) locative postposition has become obligatory in some Sinitic dialects. This is especially the case in Wú dialects (e.g. Liú 2003; 2012: 11–12). Looking at some less-unusual SVO languages first, the locative postposition is usually optional in Cantonese and Mandarin.

(66) Cantonese
 掛 喺 客廳 (道)
 k^wa^{33} $hɐi^{25}$ $hak^3tɛŋ^{55}$ (tou^{22})
 hang at living.room at
 'hung up in the living room'

(67) Mandarin
 掛 在 客廳 (裏)
 guà zài kètīng (lǐ)
 hang at living.room in
 'hung up in the living room'

On the other hand, the postposition is compulsory in most Wú dialects (Liú 2012: 12).

(68) Sūzhōu Wú
 掛 勒 客廳 *(裏)
 ko⁵² ləʔ⁵⁵ kʰaʔ⁵⁵tʰin²³ *(li⁴⁴)
 hang at living.room in
 'hung up in the living room'
 (Lǐ 1998: 164)

Whereas the preposition is often optional in Northern Wú dialects.

(69) Níngbō Wú (Preposition usually omitted for preverbal adverbials)
 賊骨頭 (來) 屙坑間 裏 幽 該
 thief (at) toilet in hide FP
 'The thief hid in the toilet'
 (Liú 2003: 272)

(70) 老師 (來該) 黑板 上 寫 字
 teacher (at) black:board on write word
 'The teacher wrote on the blackboard'
 (Liú 2003: 272)

In fact the preposition is often optional, or even used as a postposition in some Northern Wú dialects.

(71) 圖書館 裏 來該
 library in at
 'at the library'
 (Liú 2003: 272)

In Níngbō Wú (and most other Northern Wú dialects), 'go to' is usually expressed with no adposition, whereas 'come from' is usually expressed with a postposition 'from'. The Northern Wú dialects (especially the ones spoken outside of Shanghai) in general show many verb-final typological traits, while SVO word order is still commonly used.

(72) Níngbō Wú
囡囡 幼兒班 去
baby kindergarten go
'Baby goes to kindergarten.'
(M. Qián 2008: 136)

(73) 我 學校 介 來
1SG school from come
'I came from the school.'
(M. Qián 2008: 136)[47]

5.2.2 Position of adverbials

Adverbials are usually placed in front of the verb.

(74) Shanghainese (Wú)
挌個 人 討飯 能介個 樣子 立辣 依答
geq-geq njin thaovae nenkaxeq xiangtsir liq-laq iitaq
this-CLF person beggar like appearance stand-PROG there
'The man stood there like a beggar.'
(Zhu 2006a: 155)[48]

(75) Standard Cantonese
佢 慢慢 行
$k^h\theta y^{13}$ $man^{22}man^{25}$ $haŋ^{11}$
3SG slowly walk
'S/he walks slowly.'

---

[47] M. Qían (2008: 136) describes 介 as a postposition meaning 'from'. However, Zhū et al. (1996), the Níngbō dictionary, only lists 介 /ka^{44}/ as being a demonstrative meaning 'like this' or a particle meaning '-like' (Zhū et al. 1996: 40–41). I would like to thank my colleague Xūpíng Lǐ for questioning the status of 介 as a postposition.

[48] Wú languages have tonal domains that are longer than a syllable. In Shanghainese, except for toneless syllables, there are two contrastive tonal melodies. Zhu (2006a) notates the 'marked' melody with a grave accent.

(76) Xiānghuà
 你 快 ○手
 ni²⁵ kʰua³³ tsau²⁵ɕiəɯ²⁵
 2SG quick move:hand
 'Hurry up and get moving,'

(77) Standard Mandarin
 你 先 吃 吧 多 吃 一點
 nǐ xiān chī ba duō chī yīdiǎn
 2SG first eat FP more eat a:bit
 Eat first. Eat a bit more.'

However, many Southern Sinitic dialects (primarily Wú, Gàn, Hakka, Yuè, Pínghuà, Hǎinán Mǐn) have a few adverbs which are placed after the verb (either immediately after the verb, or at the end of the clause).

(78) Fùyáng Wú
 杭州 到 快 嘚。
 ɦãtsɤ 'tɔ 'kʰua diɛ
 Hángzhōu arrive soon COS
 'We are arriving in Hángzhōu soon.'
 (This 快 'kʰua may be a prospective marker. 快 'kʰua meaning 'fast' is placed in front of the verb.)

(79) Yíchūn Gàn
 (再) 去 幾 個 湊
 (tsæ⁴⁴) tɕʰiɛ⁴⁴ tɕi⁵³ kɔ⁴⁴ tsʰɛu⁴⁴
 again go few CLF more
 'Send a few more people.'

(80) 食 多 發積
 tɕʰiʔ⁵ to³⁴ faʔ⁵-tɕiʔ⁵
 eat more bit-DIM
 'Eat a bit more.'

(81) 你 食 飯 先
 ni³⁴ tɕiaʔ⁵ fan²¹³ siɛn³⁴
 2SG eat rice first
 'You eat your meal first.'

(82) Hakka
坐 一 下 添
tsʰo²⁴ it² ha⁵⁵ tʰiam²⁴
sit one CLF more
'Sit a bit more.'
(Lo 1988: 301–302)

(83) 著 少 一 領 衫
tsok² seu³¹ it² liaŋ¹¹ sam¹³
wear less one CLF clothes
'Wear one piece of clothing less.'
(Lo 1988: 303)

(84) Standard Cantonese
食 埋 雪糕 添 啦
sɪk² mai¹¹ syt³kou⁵⁵ tim⁵⁵ la⁵⁵
eat as_well ice:cream in_addition FP
'Have ice cream too!'

(85) 打 多 兩 行 字
ta²⁵ tɔ⁵⁵ lœŋ¹³ hɔŋ¹¹ tsi²²
hit more two line word
'Type two more lines.'

(86) 我 行 先 啦。
ŋɔ¹³ haŋ¹¹ sin⁵⁵ la³³
1SG go first COS
'I am going now.'
(See, e.g., Peyraube 1996, who discusses the post-verbal adverbs in Cantonese.)

MSEA languages usually have adverbials after the verb.

(87) Northern Zhuang
gou bae gonq
1SG go first
'I am going now.'

(88) *gou gwn vanj haeux dem*
      1SG eat bowl rice in_addition
      'I eat another bowl of rice.'
      (Wéi and Qín 2006: 208)

(The word *dem* itself is perhaps a Chinese loan, c.f. Cantonese 添 *t*^{h}*im*[55] 'add'.)

(89) Thai
      raw pay thîaw mɯaŋ thay bɔ̀ybɔ̀y.
      1PL go trip country Thai often
      'We visit Thailand often.'
      (Smyth 2002: 104)

(90) Green Hmong
      tuam moog rua suavteb hab
      Tuam go to China too
      'Tuam went to China too.' (Li 1989: 121)

(91) Khmer
      knjom kampung raut lee:ng ja:ng sa'ba:j
      I engage.in run play kind happy
      'I was running along happily.'
      (Haiman 2011: 216)

(92) *knjom skoal koat cbah nah*
      I recognize 3 clear very
      'I recognized him very clearly.'
      (Haiman 2011: 216)

5.2.3 Position of objects

Not only are adverbials mostly placed in front of the verb, objects are also sometimes placed in front of the verb in the Sinitic languages. Although the Sinitic languages could be said to be SVO in general, constituents that can occur postverbally are restricted. With relatively few restrictions are the Far-Southern Sinitic languages like Cantonese; Far-Southern Sinitic languages are relatively free to have two or more constituents after the main verb. At the other extreme are the Southeastern Sinitic languages, where it is rare to have more than one constituent after the verb. Other Sinitic languages, like Mandarin, are somewhat in between these two extremes.

In addition, some Sinitic languages require old information to be placed in front of the verb. This causes even more objects to be preposed to a preverbal position. This is strongly the case in the Southeastern Sinitic languages. Having old information in preverbal position is also strongly preferred in the Northern Sinitic languages, Standard Mandarin for instance,[49] but the requirement is not as strong as in the Southeastern Sinitic languages. At the other extreme are the Far-Southern Sinitic languages, where there is no grammatical requirement for old information to occur pre-verbally. Closely correlating with old information is definiteness. Although it is known that in SVO languages there are correlations between the pre-verbal position and definiteness, and the post-verbal positions and indefiniteness (Keenan and Comrie 1977), it is rare for the correlation to be as strong as in the Southeastern Sinitic languages, where definite noun phrases (which usually express old information) are grammatically required to appear pre-verbally.

There are three types of constructions that can be used to prepose an object to a pre-verbal position:

– topicalization (the surface order could, grammatically speaking, freely alternate between SOV and OSV)
– passivization (both the undergoer and actor phrases are pre-verbal)
– object marking (OM) construction

The syntax of these construction varies amongst the Sinitic languages. I will discuss briefly the object marking construction first in Section 5.2.3.1. The interaction between old information status and the preverbal position is discussed in Section 5.2.3.2, and word order in clauses with three place predicates is discussed in Section 5.2.3.3. Discussions on topicalization and passivization are interspersed among other discussions in Section 5.2.3.2 and Section 5.2.3.3.

5.2.3.1 The object marking construction

The object marking construction (OM) is also known as the 'disposal' construction or pre-transitive construction. The object marker is most commonly gram-

---

49 Li (2011) characterizes the post-verbal position in Mandarin as new information. Others have characterized the postverbal position in Mandarin as indefinite (Li and Thompson 1974b) or 'focal' (LaPolla 1995).

maticalized from a verb meaning 'to take' or 'to grab hold of', and the most common syntactic configuration is {subject – OM – object – verb}. (There are other grammatical pathways, and other configurations, see Chappell (2006, in press).) The object marking construction in Mandarin is well discussed (Li and Thompson 1981: Section 15, Sybesma 1992, Ding 2007, Iemmolo & Arcodia 2014, amongst many others). In Mandarin, the object marking construction is used primarily to highlight the change of state or change of location of the undergoer. Sometimes an object-marked sentence and its SVO counterpart are both grammatical. Internet search results indicate that with the following two examples, the object-marked construction is more prevalent than the SVO counterpart, but both are frequently used.

(93) Standard Mandarin
關上　　門　了
guān-shàng mén le
close-up　door COS
'(Someone) locked the door'
("關上門了" on Google: 1,690,000 results; accessed 3 Nov 2012)

(94) 把　門　關上　　了
bǎ mén guān-shàng le.
OM door close-up　COS
'(Someone) locked the door.'
("把門關上了" on Google: 1,970,000 results; accessed 3 Nov 2012)

In Mandarin, the *bǎ*-marked object is usually definite, but not necessarily. Old information objects are usually preposed by the object marking construction, or topicalization. An innovation in Mandarin is that the object marking construction can be used with intransitive predicates, in which case the S argument is marked by the 'object' marker (see Chappell 2013).

The Far-Southern Sinitic languages require the preposing of objects far less often. The object marking construction is absent in many Far-Southern Sinitic dialects, for instance Chōngzuǒ Pínghuà (Lǐ and Zhū 2009: 193, Liáng and Lín 2009: 322) and Nánníng Cantonese (Lín and Qín 2008: 346–348). Some other Far-Southern Sinitic dialects have object marking constructions, but their usage is restricted and infrequent (e.g. Cheung 1992 on Standard Cantonese). In the case of Hainanese, the object marking construction is restricted to inanimates (Lee 2009). (However, they have the non-grammaticalized 'take' serial verb construction; see below.) The following is a demonstration of how the OM construction is basically not used in Cantonese for sentences comparable to the Mandarin examples above.

(95) Standard Cantonese
閂咗　　門
san^{55}-*tsɔ*^{25} *mun*^{11}
close-PFV door
'(Someone) closed the door(s).' or 'They (shops etc.) are closed.'
(Google search of the string "閂咗門": 11,000 results; 3 Nov 2012)

(96) 閂咗　　[度/　道]　門
san^{55}-*tsɔ*^{25} [*tou*^{22}/ *tou*^{22}] *mun*^{11}
close-PFV CLF　　CLF　door
'(Someone) closed the door.'
(Google search of the string "閂咗度門": 1,410 results; "閂咗道門": 277 results; 3 Nov 2012)

(97) ?　將　　(度/　道)　門　　閂
　　　tsœŋ^{55} (*tou*^{22}/ *tou*^{22}) *mun*^{11} *san*^{55}
　　　OM　　CLF　CLF　door　close
(Google search of the string "將門閂": 0 results; "將度門閂": 9 results, "將道門閂": 3 results; 3 Nov 2012)[50]

The syntax of the object marking constructions varies greatly amongst the Sinitic languages. Mandarin dialects towards the northwest (Western Central Plains Mandarin, Northwestern Mandarin) and the Southeastern Sinitic languages in general have fewer constraints with their object marking constructions than Standard Mandarin. For instance, Standard Mandarin and Cantonese do not allow the object marking construction to be used with negative predicates. However, this construction is commonly found in Mandarin spoken towards the northwest.

---

50 Using other classifiers like 對 *tøy*^{33} and 隻 *tsɛk*^{3} yielded negligible numbers of search results (less than 10).

(98) Dungan (Western Central Plains Mandarin in Kyrgyzstan/ Kazakhstan)
ба гу кан бу жян ли,
pa²⁴ kou⁵¹ kʰæ̃⁴⁴+ pu²⁴+ tɕiæ̃⁴⁴ li
OM dog look+ NEG+ achieve COS
'[He] could not see the dog anymore,' (Lín 2003: 312)

(99) ба та бу кэщин сы ли ма?
pa²⁴ tʰa⁵¹ pu²⁴ kʰɛ²⁴ɕiŋ²⁴ sz⁵¹ li ma
OM 3SG NEG happy die COS Q
'Wouldn't it be so unhappy?' (*lit.* 'unhappy to death') (Lín 2003: 313)
(Similar structures exist in Western Central Mandarin dialects in China as well; see, e.g., Bié 2005.)

Similarly, Standard Mandarin and Cantonese do not allow the object marking construction to be used with monosyllabic predicates. However, such constructions are commonly found in the Southeastern Sinitic languages.

(100) Fùyáng Wú
伊 ○ 我 打
ɦi kʰəʔ ŋʏ 'tæ̃
3SG OM 1SG hit
'S/he hit me.'

(101) Taiwanese Southern Mǐn
goan² kia ⁿ² ka⁷ goa² chim¹
1SG:GEN son OM 1SG kiss
'My son kissed me.'
(Lee 2009: 480)

On the other hand, Hǎinán Mǐn, a Far-Southern Sinitic language, would use a normal SVO sentence in this situation, as the object marking construction cannot be used with animates:

(102) Hǎinán Mǐn, a.k.a. Hainạnese
i⁴⁴ soi²¹ gua²¹
3SG kiss 1SG
'He kissed me.'
(Lee 2009: 480)

Similar object marking constructions also exist in many Hmong-Mien languages. Unlike Sinitic languages like Mandarin and Cantonese where the object markers are no longer used as lexical verbs, in White Hmong the object marker is synchronically still used as a main verb meaning 'take'. Nonetheless, as shown in the example below, the protagonist is clearly not physically handling the undergoer marked by *muab* 'take', testifying that *muab* 'take' has acquired a grammatical function.

(103) White Hmong
nws <u>muab</u> pojniam nrauj   lawm
3SG <u>take</u> woman divorce PRF
'He has divorced his wife.'
(Jarkey 1991: 249; quoting Heimbach 1979:174)

The object marking construction in most Sinitic languages, including Mandarin and Cantonese, came from the Medieval Chinese 'take' serial verb construction, where the verb 'take' has not yet been grammaticalized. (The grammaticalization of the 'take' verb began when the coreferential pronoun, e.g. the pronoun 之 *zhī* 3SG in the example below, became optional (Peyraube 1996: 169–170).)

(104) Medieval Chinese
船者   乃   將   此   蟾   以   油   熬   之
chuánzhě nǎi   jiāng cǐ   chán yǐ   yóu   áo   zhī
boat:person then take this toad with oil   fry   3SG
'Then the boatman took the toad and fried it.'
(Chappell 2006; quoting Peyraube 1988, 1996)

Similar 'take' serial verb constructions exist in the MSEA languages. The choice between the 'take' and 'non-take' construction in the MSEA languages, including the Far-Southern Sinitic languages, is usually a stylistic choice in how the event is presented, rather than a grammatical preference or requirement as the other Sinitic languages to the north have with their object marking constructions. (The object of 'take' is usually old information, but it is not that old information must occur in a 'take' construction, unlike many non-Far-Southern Sinitic languages where old information is strongly preferred to be expressed preverbally).

(105) Lao
  man2 thim5   ngen2
  3   discard money
  'She discarded (the) money.'

(106) man2 qaw3 ngen2 thim5
  3   take money discard
  'She took the money (and) discarded (it).'
  (Enfield 2007: 381)

(107) Vietnamese
  tôi tặng cho bạn   một miếng gà   rán
  1   gift DAT friend one CLF   chicken fried
  'I gave you a piece of fried chicken.'

(108) tôi lấy một miếng gà   rán   tặng cho bạn
  1   take one CLF   chicken fried gift DAT friend
  'I took a piece of fried chicken (and) gave it to you.'
  (John Phan p.c.)

The Far-Southern Sinitic languages also often employ the MSEA-type of ungrammaticalized 'take' constrcution.

(109) Nánníng Pínghuà
  'Non-take' construction:
  佢   一   拋   個   隻   煎餅   呢
  kəi¹³ ɐt³ pʰau⁵³   ə⁵⁵   tʃət³ tʃin⁵³pən³³   nɛ⁵⁵
  3   once throw   DEM   CLF   pan:cake   TOP
  就   跌落   大象   隻   煎鍋
  tʃəu²² tit³+lek²³   tai²²tʃɛŋ²² tʃət³ tʃin⁵³ku⁵³
  then   fall+descend   elephant   CLF   frying:pan
  'He [the mouse] threw the pancake, and it fell on the elephant's frying pan.'

(110) 'Take' construction:
佢　抓　燒餅　　來　　一　　拋
kəi¹³ ɲa⁵³ ɬiu⁵³pən³³ lɐi¹¹ et³ pʰau⁵³
3　　take pan:cake come once throw
燒餅　　　就　　跌落　　　地下
ɬiu⁵³pən³³ tʃəu²² tit³+lɐk²³ təi²²ja²²
pan:cake then fall+descend ground
'He [the mouse] took the pancake and threw it, and the pancake fell on the ground.'

5.2.3.2 Preverbal and Postverbal objects

The Southeastern languages strongly require old information to appear before the main verb. New information noun phrases are usually, but not necessarily, placed after the main verb. In the following example, definiteness corresponds with old information and indefiniteness corresponds with new information. It is ungrammatical for the definite object to occur post-verbally, and very strange for the indefinite object to occur pre-verbally.

(111)　Fúqīng Eastern Mǐn
老板　　　買〇　　　蜀　架　車
lɔ³²peŋ⁵³ mɛ³²-lau²¹ θoʔ² ka²¹ tɕʰia⁵³
boss　　 buy-PFV　one CLF car
'The boss bought a car.'

(112)　許　蜀　架　車　　老板　　　買〇
hy³² θoʔ² ka²¹ tɕʰia⁵³ lɔ³²peŋ⁵³ mɛ³²-lau²¹
that one CLF car　 boss　　 buy-PFV
'The boss bought the car.'

(113)　Fùyáng Wú
個　老板　買得　　部　車子
kɤ 'lɔpæ̃ ma-lə bu 'tsʰotsz
CLF boss buy-PFV CLF car
'The boss bought a (/*the) car.'
(Li and Bisang 2012: 336)

(114) 個　老板　部　車子　　買得回來　　　　　喋
     kɤ　'lɔpæ̃　bu　'tsʰotsz　ma-lə-'uɛ-lɛ　　diɛ
     CLF boss CLF car　buy-pfv-return-hither COS
     'The boss bought the car.'

(115) 我　去　放　兩　　件　衣裳　得　大　衣櫃　裏
     ŋɤ　tɕʰi　fã　'niã　dʑi izã　lə　da　idʑy　ni
     1SG go put several CLF clothes to big closet inside
     'I put several items of clothing into the big closet.'

(116) 我　兩　　件　衣裳　去　放　放　得　大　衣櫃　裏
     ŋɤ　'niã　dʑi izã　tɕʰi　fã　fã　lə　da　idʑy　ni
     1SG several CLF clothes go put put to big closet inside
     'I put the several items of clothing into the big closet.'

    The following data from Jīxī Huī show that new information need not occur in post-verbal position. Here we have to make a distinction between two different and independent types of givenness (i.e. old information) versus newness (i.e. new information): *referential* givenness/newness, which relates to the old and new information status of objects in the external world or preceding discourse, and *relational* givenness/newness, which relates to the information structure within a sentence (Gundel 1988, 1998). It seems that in Jīxī Huī at least, and perhaps in all Southeastern Sinitic languages, it is *referential* givenness, and not *relational* givenness, that governs the syntactic position of object phrases. As an example, the following three sentences describe three different scenarios of buying a book. In all cases, the book referred to is both specific and definite. The *relational* givenness and newness of a noun phrase is expressed by the optionality versus obligatoriness of a pre-classifier modifier (the demonstrative in this case), respectively. The *referential* givenness and newness of an object noun phrase determines whether it is placed before or after the main verb. In example (117) below, where the book is mentioned in preceding discourse, the book is both relationally and referentially old, and so the demonstrative is optional (relationally old), and it has to be in a preverbal position (referentially old). In example (118) below, where the speaker points at a book, the *relational* newness of the book is indicated by the obligatory demonstrative. However, the book is *referentially* old: it is used to refer to something already known to the speaker, and it is immediately identifiable by the addressee, in the sense that the speaker is pointing to an exemplar of the book that the speaker already owns. Due to the *relational* newness of the object, the demonstrative is obligatory; due to the *referential* givenness of the object, the object is placed pre-verbally. Example (119) where the speaker is telling the shop assistant that s/he intends to buy a book, involves new information in both senses, and hence the demonstrative is obligatory, and the object is post-verbal.

(117) Jīxī Huī
Old information
(爾)　　　本　　書　我　今朝　　　　買仂
(õ²¹⁻²²)　pã⁵⁵　ɕy²¹　a⁵⁵　tɕiã²¹⁻²²tɕiə²¹　ma⁵⁵-nə
this　　　CLF　book　1SG　this:morning　buy-PFV
'I bought the book.' (referring to an aforementioned book)

(118) Relational new information, referential old information
*(爾)　　　本　書　我　已經　　　　買　哩
*(õ²¹⁻²²)　pã⁵⁵　ɕy²¹　a⁵⁵　tɕiã²¹⁻²²tɕiə²¹　ma⁵⁵　ni
this　　　CLF　book　1SG　this:morning　buy　COS
'I have already bought this book.' (e.g. pointing to a book at bookstore)

(119) Relational new information, referential new information
我　買　*(爾)　　　本　書
a⁵⁵　ma⁵⁵　*(õ²¹⁻²²)　pã⁵⁵　ɕy²¹
1SG　buy　this　　　CLF　book
'I will buy this book.' (e.g. buying a book at a bookstore)

Outside of the Southeastern zone, old information/ definite noun phrases are usually not grammatically required to occur pre-verbally. Nevertheless, the pre-posing of old information/ definite noun phrases is still fairly common in the Northern zone, Standard Mandarin for instance.

(120) Standard Mandarin
把　車子　買　了
bǎ　chēzi　mǎi　le
OM　car　buy　COS
'Bought the car.'
("把車子買了" on Google: 247,000 results; accessed 12 Nov 2012)
(The marked object is definite by default.)

(121) 買 了 這 輛 車子
      mǎi le zhē liàng chēzi
      buy PFV this CLF car
      'Bought this car.'
      ("買了這輛車子" on Google: 278,000 results; accessed 12 Nov 2012)

On the other hand, in the Far-Southern zone, there is no grammatical correlation between the syntactic position of an object noun phrase and givenness/definiteness. Far-Southern Sinitic languages, Cantonese for instance, readily accept post-verbal definite noun phrases. In fact, it is often strange to prepose an object using an object marking construction. As for the Central Transitional zone, it is transitional between the Far-Southern and the Northern zones in terms of how much they dis-prefer having post-verbal definite noun phrases. The Shàowǔ Mǐn-Gàn examples below are from the Central Transitional zone.

(122) Shàowǔ Mǐn-Gàn
      老板 買了 蜀 架 車
      lau^{55}pan^{21} miɛ^{53}-ə ɕi^5 ka^{35} tɕʰia^{21}
      boss buy-PFV one CLF car
      'The boss bought a car.'

(123) 老板 買了 ○ 蜀 架 車
      lau^{55}pan^{21} miɛ^{53}-ə tɕioŋ^{53} ɕi^5 ka^{35} tɕʰia^{21}
      boss buy-PFV this one CLF car
      'The boss bought this car.'

(124) Very Strange:
      ?? 老板 拿 ○ 蜀 架 車 買了
      ?? *lau^{55}pan^{21} na^{22} tɕioŋ^{53} ɕi^5 ka^{35} tɕʰia^{21} miɛ^{53}-ə*
      boss OM this one CLF car bought-PFV
      'The boss bought this car.'

(125) Cantonese
      個 老板 買咗 架 車
      kɔ^{33} lou^{13}pan^{25} mai^{13}-tsɔ^{25} ka^{33} tsʰɛ^{55}
      CLF boss buy-PFV CLF car
      'The boss bought the/a car.'
      (Li and Bisang 2012: 336)
      ("買咗架車" on Google: 43,900 results; 13 Nov 2012)

(126) Very strange:
　　?? 個　老板　　將　　架　車　　買咗
　　?? kɔ³³ lou¹³pan²⁵ tsœŋ⁵⁵ ka³³ tsʰɛ⁵⁵ mai¹³-tsɔ²⁵
　　　CLF boss　　om　CLF car　buy-PFV
　　'The boss bought the car.'
　　("將架車買" on Google: 4 results; accessed 13 Nov 2012)[51]

The Far-Southern Sinitic languages are like the other MSEA languages in not having grammaticalized the correlation between the givenness/definiteness and the syntactic position of an object. Below are examples of definite noun phrases existing in preverbal and postverbal positions in Green Hmong and Ong Be (Kra-Tai).

(127) Green Hmong
　　khi tug dlev ces　　　tug miv lug
　　tie CLF dog [and.then] CLF cat come
　　'Tie up the dog and subsequently the cat will come!'
　　(Li 1989: 122)

(128) Ong Be
　　lai³³ vən⁵⁵ hə³³ sai⁵⁵tsu³³ biaŋ³³ tuaŋ⁵⁵ hu⁵⁵ uk⁵ mia⁵⁵,
　　exist day one rich:man release goat CLF out come
　　ma¹³ hu⁵⁵ [...] huk³ tuaŋ⁵⁵ hu⁵⁵ dai¹³ vɔi³³.
　　dog CLF　　make goat CLF die FP
　　'[There was a rich man who kept a goat...] One day the rich man released the goat, the dog [...] caused the goat to die.'
　　(Liú 2009: 97)

5.2.3.3 Word order in clauses with three place predicates

MSEA languages in general have fewer instances of double object constructions. For example, Enfield (e.g. 2007: 355–382) argues that there are no real double object constructions in Lao. Some ways to avoid having two unmarked 'normal' objects after the main verb in Lao are eliding an object, topicalizing an object, putting them in a serial verb construction (e.g. the 'take' serial verb construc-

---

[51] In both Cantonese and Shàowǔ Mǐn-Gàn, the 'acquiring' meaning of 'buy' conflicts with the 'disposal' meaning of the object marking construction. Replacing these sentences with 'sell' would make the object marking construction more acceptable.

tion), incorporating the patient into the verb, or making one of the objects an oblique object. The main point is that the prohibition is only towards having two unmarked objects after the verb; it is not a prohibition towards having more than one constituent, as having an oblique object after an unmarked object is often an option.

(129) Lao
Noun incorporation (not 'real' double object construction)
laaw2 [thaa2 sii3] hùan2 lang3 nii4
3SG.FAM apply paint house CLF DEM
'She painted (i.e., 'applied paint (to)') this house.'
(Enfield 2007: 357)

(130) * laaw2 [thaa2 [sii3 lùam5]] hùan2 lang3 nii4
3SG.FAM apply paint shiny house CLF DEM
(intended meaning: 'She applied shiny paint to this house.'; Enfield 2007: 357)

(131) Topicalization
hùan2 lang3 nii4 laaw2 thaa2 sii3 lùam5
house CLF DEM 3SG.FAM apply paint shiny
'This house, she applied shiny paint (to).'
(Enfield 2007: 358)

(132) sii3 lùam5 laaw2 thaa2 hùan2 lang3 nii4
paint shiny 3SG.FAM apply house CLF DEM
'Shiny paint, she applied (to) this house.'
(Enfield 2007: 358)

(133) Serial verb construction
laaw2 qaw3 sii3 lùam5 thaa2 hùan2 lang3 nii4
3SG.FAM take paint shiny apply house CLF DEM
'She took shiny paint (and) applied (it to) this house.'
(Enfield 2007: 358)

(134) Oblique strategy
laaw2 thaa2 hùan2 lang3 nii4 duaj4 sii3 lùam5
3SG.FAM apply house CLF DEM with paint shiny
'She applied this house with shiny paint.'
(Enfield 2007: 358)

Khmer also has restrictions towards having two unmarked objects after the verb. The following is an example of this being resolved by a 'take' serial verb construction.

(135) Khmer
  * kɔ̀ət ha:l   khaoʔa:v thŋay
   he expose clothes sun

(136) kɔ̀ət yɔ̀:k khaoʔa:v tr̆u ha:l   thŋay
   he take clothes go expose sun
   'He put the clothes out in the sun.'
   (Bisang 2012: 12)

The syntax of three-place constructions varies considerably across Sinitic languages. The Southeastern Sinitic languages have a dis-preference of having two phrases after the verb; one of the objects has to be placed in front of the verb somehow.

(137) Huì'ān Southern Mǐn
   Theme topicalized
   伊   一   叢   筆   與   我
   i¹ tsit⁸⁾⁴ tsaŋ²⁾⁴ pet⁷ kʰɔ⁵ ua
   3SG one   CLF   pen give 1SG
   'S/he gave me a/one pen.'

(This is the most preferred word order; S – V – IO – DO order is also possible, but not often used. The agent is often omitted.)

In fact, Southern Mǐn's preference for having definite objects in front of the main verb is so strong that the definite object is often expressed twice in front of the main verb: the definite object is topicalized, and then it is (optionally) repeated by a resumptive pronoun supported by an object marker, as shown in the following example.

(138) 我   冊   共   伊 ○   咧   桌   咧
   ua³ tsʰeʔ⁷ ka⁵⁾⁴ i¹ hio⁵⁾⁴ leʔ⁷⁾⁸ tɔʔ⁷ leʔ
   1SG book OM   3SG put at   table LOC
   'I put the book on the table.'

The following are examples from another Southeastern Sinitic language.

(139) Fùyáng Wú
　*　伊　親得　　我　一　口
　* ɦi　'tɕʰin-lə　ŋɤ　iəʔ　kʰiu
　　3SG kiss-PFV 1SG one CLF_mouth
　(親 'tɕʰin 'kiss' is a three-place predicate in Fùyáng Wú)

(140) Passivized
　　我　撥　伊　親得　　一　口
　　ŋɤ　pəʔ　ɦi　'tɕʰin-lə　iəʔ　kʰiu
　　1SG PASS 3SG kiss-PFV one CLF_mouth
　　'I was kissed by him/her once.'

(141) Object marking construction
　　伊　○　我　親得　　一　口
　　ɦi　kʰəʔ　ŋɤ　'tɕʰin-lə　iəʔ　kʰiu
　　3SG OM 1SG kiss-PFV one CLF_mouth
　　'S/he kissed me once.'

In Xiānghuà, which is spoken in the Central Transitional zone, the most commonly used ditransitive construction involves a preposition-marked indirect object placed in front of the main verb.

(142) Xiānghuà[52]
　　就　　跟　　它　　放　　到　　○　　裏
　　tɕiəu²⁵　kai⁵⁵　tʰa⁵⁵　fɤŋ³³　tau³³　pi¹³　la²⁵
　　then　OM　3SG　place　to　　jar　in
　　'[...] then put it in the jar.'

(143) 　○　　跟　　我　　得　　件　　衣
　　zɤ³³　kai⁵⁵　u²⁵　tɤ³³　tɕʰia²⁵　i⁵⁵
　　3SG DAT 1SG give CLF　clothes
　　'He gave me a shirt.'

On the other hand, the Far-Southern Sinitic languages, similar to the non-Sinitic MSEA languages to the south, are relatively freer in having two constituents (of any sort) after the main verb. (Although these Sinitic and non-Sinitic

---

[52] The word 跟 kai⁵⁵ has many functions in Xiānghuà, amongst them object marker and dative marker. See, e.g., Chappell, Peyraube, and Wu (2011), Chappell (forthcoming).

MSEA languages are still not totally free in having two constituents after the main verb, as seen in the case of Lao discussed earlier in this section.)

(144) Cantonese[53]
阿華　錫咗　我　一　啖
$a^{33}wa^{11}$　$sɛk^3$-$tsɔ^{25}$　$ŋɔ^{13}$　jet^5　tam^{22}
Ah.Wah kiss-PFV 1SG one CLF
'Ah Wah kissed me once.'

(145) 佢　畀咗　啲　藥　我
$k^hɵy^{13}$　pei^{25}-$tsɔ^{25}$　ti^{55}　$jœk^3$　$ŋɔ^{13}$
3SG give-PFV CLF:MASS medicine 1SG
'S/he gave me the/some medicine.'

---

53 Since Hashimoto (1976), the variation in the order of the (non-topicalized) T and R arguments in double object constructions is often cited as an example of the 'north–south' divide within the Sinitic family. Mandarin has the cross-linguistically more common V R T word order, whereas Cantonese has the cross-linguistically rarer V T R order. The rarer word order in Cantonese is attributed to 'Taicization'; Thai also has (or appears to have) the rarer V T R order. In reality, the variation in ditransitive constructions amongst Sinitic languages is much more complex than Hashimoto's (1976) generalization. Firstly, Cantonese only uses the V T R order for 'give'-type verbs; other double-object verbs use the V R T word order, e.g. kau^{33} 'teach', p^hun^{33} 'sentence' (i.e. sentence [convict] [penalty]). Secondly, it is not the case that all Southern Sinitic languages use the V T R word order. For instance, Southern Mǐn only uses the V R T word order like Mandarin. Nánníng Pínghuà also only uses the V R T word order (although some speakers accept the V T R word order, under the influence of Nánníng Cantonese). Thirdly, the V T R word order in Cantonese has probably nothing to do with influences from nearby non-Sinitic languages. In Northern Zhuàng, the V R T construction is the default order, whereas the V T R order can only be used when the R phrase is very short. In Vietnamese, only the V R T construction is used. In fact, the V T R word order in Cantonese is a relatively recent development; the V T R word order is developed from a serial verb construction with the second verb elided: 'give' T 'pass' R > 'give' T R (Chin 2011). In fact, the serial verb 'give-pass' construction is still commonly heard in Cantonese films from the 'black-and-white' era. Somewhat similarly, the V T R 'give' construction in Thai can be thought of as having the R-marking preposition kɛ̀ɛ omitted: 'give' T (kɛ̀ɛ) R (see Thepkanjana 2008). See Zhāng (2011) for a very-thorough diachronic and synchronic account of the development of ditransitives amongst Sinitic languages.

(146) 個　　阿婆　　　收埋咗　　　　　嗰　　五百萬　　　喺
　　　 kɔ³³　a³³pʰɔ¹¹　sɐu⁵⁵mai¹¹-tsɔ²⁵　kɔ²⁵　ŋ¹³pak³man²²　hei²⁵
　　　 CLF　o.woman　hide-PFV　　　　that　five.mil　　at
　　　 櫃桶　　　　底
　　　 kʷei²²tʰʊŋ²⁵　tei²⁵
　　　 drawer　　　under
　　　 'The old woman hid the five million [units of currency] under the table.'

(147) Hainanese (Hǎinán Mǐn)
　　　 我　　分　　　蜀　　○　　冊　　　(至)　伊
　　　 gua²¹　ɓun⁴⁴　dziak³³　ɓui²¹　seʔ⁵⁵　(ti¹¹)　i⁴⁴
　　　 1SG　give　one　CLF　book　to　3SG
　　　 'I gave a book to him.'
　　　 (Lee 2011: 502-503)

The following are examples showing other MSEA languages readily allowing two constituents (either bare or full) after the main verb.

(148) Ong Be
　　　 ɓeu³³　jua³³　nə²¹　hiu⁵⁵　(jɔu³³)　hau⁵⁵
　　　 deliver　clothes　that　CLF　to　1SG
　　　 'Pass me that shirt/ Pass that shirt to me.' (Liú 2009: 35)

(149) Khmer
　　　 aoj　cee:k　cru:k muaj camnuan
　　　 give banana pig　one　amount
　　　 '[G]ive the pig some bananas.'
　　　 (Haiman 2011: 207)

(150) aoj　cee:k　muaj camnuan dawl　cru:k
　　　 give banana one　bunch　towards pig
　　　 '[G]ive a bunch of bananas to the pig.'
　　　 (Haiman 2011: 207)

5.2.4 Summary of word order in clauses

The following table summarizes the clause-level word order traits discussed in this Section 5.2.

Table 4: Left headedness on the clause level (for the most-common construction in each category). (± adpositions: both preposition and postposition. other ±: both orders are prevalent)

	Non Sinitic							FS Sin.		SE Sinitic				C Sinitic			N
	Thai	Khmer	Vietnamese	E Kayah Li	Burmese	Hmong	Mien	Cantonese	Nánníng Pínghuà	Huì'ān S Mǐn	Fúqīng E Mǐn	Fúyáng Wú	Jīxī Huī	Shàowǔ Mǐn-Gàn	Yíchūn Gàn	Gùzhàng Xiānghuà	Suíníng C Mandarin
VO: bought the car	+	+	+	+	−	+	+	+	+	−	−	−	−	+	+	+	±
VO: bought a car	+	+	+	+	−	+	+	+	+	+	+	+	+	+	+	+	+
VO: hit me	+	+	+	+	−	+	+	+	+	±	+	−	+	+	+	+	+
VO(P)O: give me the book	+	+	+	+	−	+	+	+	+	−	+	−	−	+	+	−	−
VO(P)O: give me a book	+	+	+	+	−	+	+	+	+	−	+	+	+	+	+	+	+
VOPO(P): put the book on table	+	+	+	+	−	+	+	+	+	−	−	−	−	−	−	−	−
go destination	+	+	+	+	−	+	+	+	+	+	+	−	−	+	+	−	−
at inside location	+	+	+	±	−	+	±	±	±	±	±	±	±	±	±	±	±
VOX: play ball location	+	+	+	+	−	−	−	−	−	−	−	−	−	−	−	−	−
go first	+	+	+	+	−	+	+	+	−	−	−	−[54]	−	+	−	−	−
eat more	+	+	+	+	+	+	?	+	+	−	−	±	±	−	+	−	−
Total:	11	11	11	10½	1	10	8½	9½	8½	3	5½	3	4	6½	8½	4½	4

In Table 4 (and all the feature tables above), the absolute values of the total score have little significance, as the criteria are hand-picked to demonstrate some of the word order differences amongst the Sinitic languages. Nevertheless, the relative scores amongst the Sinitic languages do show the relative difference in left-headedness on the clause level amongst the Sinitic languages. The Far-

---

[54] However, for very old speakers, the word order is 'go first' (+) rather than 'first go' (−).

Southern Sinitic languages (represented by Cantonese and Pínghuà here) have relatively more left-headed traits, as they are close to the core of MSEA. The Northern Sinitic languages (represented by Mandarin here) have more right-headed traits, as they are influenced by North Asia. However, the Southeastern Sinitic languages (represented by Southern Mǐn, Eastern Mǐn, Wú and Huī here) are also have many right-headed traits; this is probably an independent development (see also footnote 43).

6 Conclusions and discussion

In this paper I have discussed some of the phonological and word order traits in the Sinitic languages. The Far-Southern Sinitic languages are the most similar to the core of MSEA: highly tonal, conservative with codas, and relatively normal SVO languages. In terms of word order, some left-headed word order traits in the Far-Southern Sinitic languages arise from influence from the core of MSEA. However, not all left-headed traits are influences from the core of MSEA. For instance, having less restrictions on having multiple constituents after the main verb in the Far-Southern Sinitic languages could simply mean that they are relatively normal SVO languages, and that they are less influenced by the other Sinitic languages to the north, where this restriction exists. We have also seen that other than the Mandarin dialects that are SOV, the Sinitic languages with the most OV-associated traits are not the Northern Sinitic languages, but the Southeastern Sinitic languages. The strong prevalence of verb-final clauses in the Southeastern Sinitic languages is probably an internal development. It cannot be a direct influence from North Asia, as North Asia is so far away, and the Central and Northern Sinitic languages in between are in general not as strongly right-headed as the Southeastern Sinitic languages. Also, there have not been any large scale migrations of North Asians into Southeastern China.

The summary tables (Tables 2 to 4 above) sometimes show the Far-Southern Sinitic languages as having higher scores of 'MSEA-ness' than other Sino-Tibetan languages like Burmese and Southern Mǐn. Their high scores do not indicate that the Far-Southern Sinitic languages are more MSEA-like than these other Sino-Tibetan languages: the scores only indicate that the Far-Southern Sintic languages have some traits that are more MSEA-like than Burmese and Southern Mǐn. There are many other typological traits, for instance lexical patterns and grammaticalization pathways, which would better illustrate the strong link between the core of MSEA and languages like Burmese and Southern Mǐn (see, e.g., Matisoff 1991, 2001a). What this paper is trying to argue is that, just as there are linguistic criteria which firmly place Burmese in the MSEA linguistic area, there are also many criteria which firmly place the Far-Southern Sinitic languages in the MSEA linguistic area. The Burmish languages and the Far-Southern Sinitic languages are both at the periphery of the MSEA linguistic area, but neither are as 'fringe' as, e.g., Mandarin. Some studies on the MSEA linguistic area leave out the languages in China. This is unwise, as the centres of diversity for the Kra-Dai and Hmong-Mien families are still in Southern China, and the Southern Sinitic languages also have many MSEA linguistic traits. Studies of the MSEA linguistic area would benefit immensely if the Southern Sinitic languages, the Far-Southern Sinitic languages in particular, are included in the MSEA linguistic area.

Abbreviations

1	first person	LOC	locative
2	second person	MASS	mass (i.e. part or more than one)
3	third person	MOD	modifier marker
ACC	accusative	N	non-
ANT	anterior	NEG	negative
CLF	classifier	OBJ	object
CONT	continuous	OM	object marker (in object-marking construction)
COP	copula	PASS	passive
COS	change of state	PFV	perfective
DAT	dative	PL	plural
DEM	demonstrative	POL	polite
DIM	diminutive	PREP	preposition
EXP	experiential	PRF	perfect
FAM	familiar	PROG	progressive
FOC	focus	PST	past
FP	final particle	Q	question
GEN	genitive	REL	relative clause
IMP	imperative	RLS	realis
IRR	irrealis	SG	singular

Acknowledgements

I would like to thank the team members of the ERC Sinotype project and their language consultants for providing some of the Sinitic data. I would also like to thank John Phan for providing data from Vietnamese, Martha Ratliff and Lisa Ginsburg for providing data from Hmong, and other participants at the 'Mainland Southeast Asian Languages: The State of the Art in 2012' Workshop at the Max Planck Institute for Evolutionary Anthropology, Leipzig for their comments. The research leading to these results has received funding from the European Research Council under the European Community's Seventh Framework Programme (FP7/2007-2013): ERC Advanced Grant agreement No. 230388: 'The hybrid syntactic typology of Sinitic languages' (2009-2013), and partial funding from the Netherlands Organization for Scientific Research grant 'Human olfaction at the intersection of language, culture and biology'.

References

Abulimit, Azgül. 2006. 阿孜古丽阿布力米提 Àzīgǔlĭ Ābùlìmĭtí. *Wéiwúěryǔ Jīchǔ Jiàochéng* 维吾尔语基础教程 [Uyghur Basic Course]. Běijīng: The Central University of Nationalities Press.

Aldridge, Edith. 2013. Survey of Chinese Historical Syntax Part I: Pre-Archaic and Archaic Chinese. *Language and Linguistic Compass* 7(1). 39–57.

Bauer, Robert S. 1996. Identifying the Tai Substratum in Cantonese. In *Pan-Asiatic Linguistics. Proceedings of the Fourth International Symposium on Languages and Linguistics* V, 1806-1844. Bangkok: Mahidol University.

Baxter, William H. 1992. *A Handbook of Old Chinese Phonology*. Berlin: Mouton de Gruyter.

Baxter, William H. & Laurent Sagart. 2014. *Old Chinese: A new reconstruction*. Oxford: Oxford University Press.

Bié, Mǐn'gē 别敏鸽. 2005. Guānzhōng fāngyán tèshū "bǎ"zìjù tànyuán 关中方言特殊"把"字句探源 [Searching the origins of the special Bǎ construction in Guānzhōng dialect]. *Journal of Huainan Normal University* 2005(1). 127–128.

Bisang, Walter. 2006. Southeast Asia as a linguistic area. In Keith Brown (Editor in Chief), *Encyclopedia of Languages & Linguistics* (Volume 11, 2nd edition), 587–595. Oxford: Elsevier.

Bisang, Walter. 2012. Chinese from a typological perspective. Paper presented at the Fourth International Conference on Sinology. Taipei: Academia Sinica.

Bó, Wénzé 薄文泽. 2004. Càijiāhuà Gàikuàng 蔡家话概况 [Sketches of the Càijiā Language]. *Mínzú Yǔwén* 2004(2). 68–81.

Cáo, Zhìyún 曹志耘 et al. (eds.). 2008. *Hànyǔ Fāngyán Dìtújí* 汉语方言地图集 *Linguistic Atlas of the Chinese Dialects*. Běijīng: The Commercial Press.

Chappell, Hilary. 2006. From Eurocentrism to Sinocentrism: The case of disposal constructions in Sinitic languages. In Felix Ameka, Alan Dench & Nicholas Evans (eds.), *Catching Language: the Standing Challenge of Grammar Writing*. 441–486. Berlin: Mouton de Gruyter.
Chappell, Hilary. 2012. The role of language contact and hybridization in Sinitic languages. Paper presented at the Fourth International Conference on Sinology. Taipei: Academia Sinica.
Chappell, Hilary. 2013. Pan-Sinitic object marking: Morphology and syntax. In Guangshun Cao, Hilary Chappell, Redouane Djamouri & Thekla Wiebusch (eds.), *Breaking down the barriers: Interdisciplinary studies in Chinese linguistics and beyond*. (Language and Linguistics Monograph Series 50), 785–816. Taipei: Academia Sinica.
Chappell, Hilary. forthcoming. *A Grammar of Waxiang, a Sinitic language of Northwestern Hunan*. Berlin: De Gruyter Mouton.
Chappell, Hilary & Alain Peyraube. 2007. The diachronic syntax of the dative construction from Medieval Chinese to early Southern Min (Sinitic). Talk presented at Conference on Ditransitive Constructions. Leipzig: Max Planck Institute for Evolutionary Anthropology.
Chappell, Hilary, Alain Peyraube & Yunji Wu. 2011. A comitative source for object markers in Sinitic languages: 跟 kai^{55} in Waxiang and 共 $kang^{7}$ in Southern Min. *Journal of East Asian Linguistics* 20(4). 291–338.
Chén, Hǎilún 陈海伦 & Cūnhàn Liú 刘村汉. 2009. *Yuèyǔ Pínghuà Tǔhuà Fāngyīn Zìhuì — Dìèrbiān: Guìběi Guìdōng jí Zhōubiān Pínghuà Tǔhuà Bùfèn* 粤语平话土话方音字汇－第二编: 桂北桂东及周边平话土话部分 [Dialectal Pronunciation of Characters in Yuè, Pínghuà and Patois — 2nd Volume: Pínghuà and Patois in Northern Guǎngxī, Eastern Guǎngxī and Surrounding Areas]. Shànghǎi: Shanghai Education Publishing House.
Cheung, Samuel Hung-nin. 1992. The pretransitive in Cantonese. In 中國境内語言暨語言學 *Chinese Languages and Linguistics* 1. 241–303.
Chin, Andy Chi-on. 2011. Grammaticalization of the Cantonese double object verb [pei^{35}] 畀 in typological and areal perspectives. *Language and Linguistics* 12(3). 529–563.
Chirkova, Katia 齊卡佳 Qí Kājiā. 2008. *Báimǎ Zàngyǔ wéi Dīzú shuō zhīyí* 白馬藏族為氐族說質疑 The Baima Tibetans and the Di people of Chinese historical records: Challenging the link. *Bulletin of Chinese Linguistics* 3(1). 167–180.
Comrie, Bernard. 2007. Areal typology of Mainland Southeast Asia: what we learn from the WALS maps [Special issue]. *Manusya* 13. 18–47.
Comrie, Bernard. 2008a. The areal typology of Chinese: between North and Southeast Asia. In Redouane Djamouri, Barbara Meisterernst & Rint Sybesma (eds.), *Chinese Linguistics in Leipzig, Chinese Linguistics in Europe* 2, 1–21. Paris: Centre de recherches linguistiques sur l'Asie Oriental, École des hautes études en sciences sociales.
Comrie, Bernard. 2008b. Prenominal relative clauses in verb-object languages. *Language and Linguistics* 9(4). 723–733.
Dahl, Östen. 2008. An exercise in *a posteriori* language sampling. *Sprachtypologie und Universalienforschung* 61(3). 208–220.
Dede, Keith. 2007. The origin of the anti-ergative [xa] in Huangshui Chinese. *Language and Linguistics* 8(4). 863–881.
Ding, Picus Sizhi. 2007. *Studies on Bǎ Resultative Construction: A Comprehensive Approach to Mandarin Bǎ Sentences* (Lincom Studies in Asian Linguistics 62). Munich: Lincom.
Djamouri, Redouane. 2001. Markers of predication in Shang bone inscriptions. In Hilary Chappell (ed.), *Sinitic Grammar: Synchronic and Diachronic Perspectives*, 143–171. Oxford: Oxford University Press.

Djamouri, Redouane. forthcoming. Tángwàng Language.
Djamouri, Redouane, Waltraud Paul & John Whitman. 2007. Reconstructing VO constituent order for Proto-Sino-Tibetan. Paper presented at The 18th International Conference on Historical Linguistics. Montréal: Université du Québec à Montréal.
Dryer, Matthew S. 1991. SVO languages and the OV/VO typology. Journal of Linguistics 27. 443–482.
Dryer, Matthew S. 2001. Mon-Khmer Word Order from a Crosslinguistic Perspective. In Karen L. Adams & Thomas John Hudak (eds.), *Papers from the Sixth Annual Meeting of the Southeast Asian Linguistics Society 1996*, 83–99. Tempe: Arizona State University
Dryer, Matthew S. 2013. Relationship between the Order of Object and Verb and the Order of Adjective and Noun. In Matthew S. Dryer & Martin Haspelmath (eds.), *The World Atlas of Language Structures Online*. Leipzig: Max Planck Institute for Evolutionary Anthropology. http://wals.info/chapter/97 (accessed 24 March 2014).
Dryer, Matthew & Martin Haspelmath (eds.). 2011. *The World Atlas of Language Structures Online*. Munich: Max Planck Digital Library. http://wals.info/
Enfield, N. J. 2005. Areal linguistics and Mainland Southeast Asia. Annual Review of Anthropology 34. 181–206.
Enfield, N. J. 2007. *A Grammar of Lao*. Berlin & New York: Mouton de Gruyter.
Enfield, N. J. 2011. Linguistic diversity in Mainland Southeast Asia. In N. J. Enfield (ed.), *Dynamics of Human Diversity*, 63–79. Canberra: Pacific Linguistics.
Ferlus, Michel. 1980. Formation des registres et mutations consonantiques dans les langues Mon-Khmer. Mon-Khmer Studies 8. 1–76.
Ferlus, Michel. 1984. Essai de phonétique historique de môn. Mon-Khmer Studies 12. 1–90.
Gan, Rui-Jing, Shang-Ling Pan, Laura F. Mustavich, Zhen-Dong Qin, Xiao-Yun Cai, Ji Qian, Cheng-Wu Liu, Jun-Hua Peng, Shi-Lin Li, Jie-Shun Xu, Li Jin, Hui Li & The Genographic Consortium. 2008. Pinghua Population as an Exception of Han Chinese's Coherent Genetic Structure. Journal of Human Genetics 53. 303–313.
Gawarjon 高尔锵 Gāo Ěrqiāng. 1985. *Tǎjíkèyǔ Jiǎnzhì* 塔吉克语简志 [Sketch of the Tajik Language]. Běijīng: The Ethnic Publishing House.
Georgopoulos, Carol. 1986. Palauan as a VOS language. In Paul Geraghty, Lois Carrington & Stephen A. Wurm (eds.), *FOCAL I: Papers from the Fourth International Conference on Austronesian Linguistics* (Pacific Linguistics C-93), 187–198. Canberra: Australian National University.
Gundel, Jeanette K. 1988. Universals of topic-comment structure. In Michael Hammond, Edith A. Moravcsik & Jessica Wirth. *Studies in Syntactic Typology*. Amsterdam; Philadelphia: John Benjamins.
Gundel, Jeanette K. 1998. Centering theory and the givenness hierarchy: a proposed synthesis. In Marilyn A. Walker, Aravind K. Joshi & Ellen F. Prince (eds.). *Centering Theory in Discourse*. Oxford: Oxford University Press.
Haiman, John. 2011. *Cambodian: Khmer* (London Oriental and African Language Library 16). Amsterdam, Philadelphia: John Benjamins.
Hashimoto, Mantaro. 1976. Language diffusion on the Asian continent: problems of typological diversity in Sino-Tibetan. Computational Analyses of Asian and African Languages 3. 49–65.
Hashimoto, Mantarō 橋本萬太郎. 1978. *Gengo Ruikei Chili Ron* 言語類型地理論 [Thesis on Geography of Language Typology]. Tōkyō: Koubundou 弘文堂.

Hashimoto, Mantaro. 1986. The Altaicization of Northern Chinese. In McCoy, John & Timothy Light (eds.), *Contributions to Sino-Tibetan Studies* (Cornell Linguistic Contributions V), 76–97. Leiden: Brill.
Haspelmath, Martin, Matthew Dryer, David Gil & Bernard Comrie (eds.). 2005. *The World Atlas of Language Structures*. Oxford: Oxford University Press.
Haudricourt, André-Georges. 1954. De l'origine des tons en Vietnamien. *Journal Asiatique* 242. 69–82.
Heimbach, Ernest E. 1979. *White Hmong – English Dictionary* (1979 revised edition) (Linguistic Series IV, Data Paper 75). Ithaca & New York: Cornell University.
Iemmolo, Giorgio & Giorgio Francesco Arcodia. 2014. Differential object marking and identifiability of the referent: a study of Mandarin Chinese. *Linguistics* 52(2): 315–334. doi 10.1515/ling-2013-0064.
Jacob, Judith M. 1993. An examination of the vowels and final consonants in correspondences between Pre-Angkor and Modern Khmer. In David A. Smyth (ed.), *Cambodian Linguistics, Literature and History*, 87–102. London: University of London.
Janhunen, Juha, Marja Peltomaa, Erika Sandman & Xiawu Dongzhou. 2008. *Wutun*. Munich: Lincom.
Jarkey, Nerida. 1991. Serial verbs in White Hmong: a functional approach. Sydney: University of Sydney dissertation.
Kato, Atsuhiko. 2003. Pwo Karen. In Graham Thurgood & Randy J. LaPolla (eds.), *The Sino-Tibetan Languages*, 632–648. London & New York: Routledge.
Keenan Edward L. & Bernard Comrie. 1977. Noun phrase accessibility and universal grammar. *Linguistic Inquiry* 8. 63–99.
Koul, Omkar N. & Kashi Wali. 2006. *Modern Kashmiri Grammar*. Springfield, VA: Dunwoody Press.
Lee, Yeon-Ju & Sagart, Laurent. 2008. No limits to borrowing: the case of Bai and Chinese. *Diachronica* 25(3). 357–389.
LaPolla, Randy J. 1994. On the change to verb-medial order in Proto-Chinese: evidence from Tibeto-Burman. In Hajime Kitamura, Tatsuo Nishida & Yasuhiko Nagano (eds.), *Current Issues in Sino-Tibetan Linguistics*, 98–104. Ōsaka: Organizing Committee of the 26th International Conference on Sino-Tibetan Languages and Linguistics.
LaPolla, Randy J. 1995. Pragmatic relations and word order in Chinese. In Pamela Downing & Michael Noonan (eds.), *Word Order in Discourse*, 297–329. Amsterdam & Philadelphia: John Benjamins.
Lee, Hui-chi. 2009. On the object marker *BUE* in Hainan Min. *Language and Linguistics* 10(3). 471–487.
Lee, Hui-chi. 2011. Double object construction in Hainan Min. *Language and Linguistics* 12(3). 501–527.
Lee, Yoen-Ju & Laurent Sagart. 2008. No limits to borrowing: the case of Bai and Chinese. *Diachronica* 25(3). 357–385.
Li, Chao. 2011. Postverbal constituents in Mandarin Chinese. In Zhuo Jing-Schmidt (ed.), *Proceedings of the 23rd North American Conference on Chinese Linguistics* (Volume 2), 30–37. Eugene: University of Oregon.
Li, Charles N. 1989. The origin and function of switch reference in Green Hmong. In Leiv Egil Breivik & Ernst Håkon Jahr (eds.), *Language Change: Contributions to the study of its causes*. (Trends in Linguistics Studies and Monographs 43), 115–129. Berlin & New York: Mouton de Gruyter.

Li, Charles N. & Sandy Thompson. 1974. An explanation of word order change SVO → SOV. *Foundations of Language* 12. 201–214.

Li, Charles N. & Sandy Thompson. 1975. The semantic function of word order: a case study in Mandarin. In Charles N. Li (ed.), *Word Order and Word Order Change*, 164–195. Austin: University of Texas Press.

Li, Charles N. & Sandy Thompson. 1981. *Mandarin Chinese: A Functional Reference Grammar*. Berkeley, Los Angeles & London: University of California Press.

Lǐ, Jǐnfāng 李锦芳. 1999. *Bùyāngyǔ Yánjiū* 布央语研究 [Studies of the Bùyāng Language]. Běijīng: The Central University of Nationalities Press.

Lǐ, Jǐnfāng 李锦芳. 2002. *Dòng-Tái Yǔyán yǔ Wénhuà* 侗台语言与文化 [Kam-Tai Language and Culture]. Běijīng: The Ethnic Publishing House.

Lǐ, Lán 李蓝. 2004. *Húnán Chéngbù Qīngyī Miáo Rénhuà* 湖南城步青衣苗人话 [The People's Speech of Blue Dress Miáo in Chéngbù, Húnán]. Běijīng: China Social Sciences Press.

Lǐ, Liánjìn 李连进 & Yàn'é Zhū 朱艳娥. 2009. *Guǎngxī Chóngzuǒ Jiāngzhōu Zhèyuánhuà Bǐjiào Yánjiū* 广西崇左江州蔗园话比较研究 [Comparative Studies of the Sugarcane Field Dialect in Jiāngzhōu, Chóngzhǒ, Guangxi]. Guìlín: Guangxi Normal University Press.

Lǐ, Yǒngsuì 李永燧. 2010. Miǎn-Yíyǔ: yīzhǒng shēngdiào zúyǔ 缅彝语：一种声调语言 [Lolo-Burmese: a type of tonal proto language]. In Zhāomíng Dài 戴昭铭 & Mǎtísōfū 马提索夫 (James Matisoff) (eds.), *Hànzàngyǔ Yánjiū Sìshínián: Dì Sìshíjiè Guójì Hànzàng Yǔyán jì Yǔyánxué Huìyì Lùnwénjí* 第40届国际汉藏语言暨语言学会议论文集 [Forty years of Sino-Tibetan Research: Proceedings of the 40th International Conference on Sino-Tibetan Languages and Linguistics], 47–57. Harbin: Heilongjiang University Press.

Lǐ, Xiǎofán 李小凡. 1998. *Sūzhōu Fāngyán Yǔfǎ Yánjiū* 苏州方言语法研究 [Research on the Syntax of the Sūzhōu Dialect]. Běijīng: Peking University Press.

Li, Xuping & Walter Bisang. 2012. Classifiers in Sinitic languages: from individuation to definiteness marking. *Lingua* 112. 335–355.

Lǐ, Yúnbīng 李霎兵. 2003. Miáo-Yáoyǔ shēngdiào wèntí 苗瑤語聲調問題 [The question of tones in Miáo-Yáo languages]. *Language and Linguistics* 4(4). 683–712.

Liáng, Mǐn 梁敏. 2002. *Biāohuà Yánjiū* 标话研究 [Studies on the Biāo Language]. Běijīng: The Central University of Nationalities Press.

Liáng, Wěihuá 梁伟华 & Yì Lín 林亦. 2009. *Guǎngxī Chóngzuǒ Xīnhé Zhèyuánhuà Yánjiū* 广西崇左新和蔗园话研究 [Studies of the Sugarcane Field Dialect in Xīnhé, Chóngzhǒ, Guangxi]. Guìlín: Guangxi Normal University Press.

Lín, Tāo 林涛. 2003. *Zhōngyà Dōnggānyǔ Yánjiū* 中亚东干语研究 Жуня Дунганйу Янҗю [Studies of the Dungan Language of Central Asia]. Hong Kong: Hong Kong Educational Press.

Lín, Yì 林亦 & Fèngyǔ Qín 覃凤余. 2008. *Guǎngxī Nánníng Báihuà Yánjiū* 广西南宁白话研究 [Studies of Nánníng Cantonese of Guangxi]. Guìlín: Guangxi Normal University Press.

Liú, Dānqīng 刘丹青. 2003. *Yǔxù Lèixíngxué yǔ Jiècí Lǐlùn* 语序类型学与介词理论 [Typology of Word Order and Theories on Adpositions]. Běijīng: The Commercial Press.

Liú, Dānqīng 刘丹青. 2012. Gǔjīn Hànyǔ de jùfǎ lèixíng yǎnbiàn: kuā-fāngyán de kùcáng lèixíngxué shìjiǎo 古今汉语的句法类型演变：跨方言的库藏类型学视角 [Changes in the syntactic typology in diachronic and synchronic Chinese: viewpoints from pan-dialectal inventory typology]. Paper presented at the Fourth International Conference on Sinology. Taipei: Academia Sinica.

Liú, Jiànsān 刘剑三. 2009. *Lín'gāoyǔ Huàyǔ Cáiliàojí* 临高语话语材料集 [Corpus Material Collection of the Lín'gāo Language]. Běijīng: The Central University of Nationalities Press.

Liú, Lìlǐ 刘俐李. 1993. Xīnjiāng Hànyǔ fāngyán de xíngchéng 新疆汉语方言的形成 [The formation of Chinese dialects in Xīngjiāng]. *Fāngyán* 1993(4). 265–274.

Lo, Seo-Gim 羅肇錦. 1988. *Kèyǔ Yǔfǎ* 客語語法 [Grammar of the Hakka Language]. Taipei: Taiwan Student Book Co.

Löffler, Lorenz G. 1966. The contribution of Mru to Sino-Tibetan linguistics. *Zeitschrift der Morgenländischen Gesellschaft* 116(1). 118–159.

Ian Maddieson. 2013a. Voicing and Gaps in Plosive Systems. In Matthew S. Dryer & Martin Haspelmath (eds.), *The World Atlas of Language Structures Online*. Leipzig: Max Planck Institute for Evolutionary Anthropology. http://wals.info/chapter/5 (accessed 31 March 2014).

Ian Maddieson. 2013b. Front Rounded Vowels. In Matthew S. Dryer & Martin Haspelmath (eds.), *The World Atlas of Language Structures Online*. Leipzig: Max Planck Institute for Evolutionary Anthropology. http://wals.info/chapter/11 (accessed 31 March 2014).

Máo, Zōngwǔ 毛宗武 & Cháojí Méng 蒙朝吉. 1986. *Shēyǔ Jiǎnzhì* 畬语简志 [Sketch of the Shē Language]. Běijīng: The Ethnic Publishing House.

Máo, Zōngwǔ 毛宗武, Cháojí Méng 蒙朝吉 & Zōngzé Zhèng 郑宗泽. 1982. *Yáozú Yǔyán Jiǎnzhì* 瑶族语言简志 [Sketch of the Language of the Yáo Nationality]. Běijīng: The Ethnic Publishing House.

Matisoff, James. 1991. Areal and universal dimensions of grammatization in Lahu. In Elizabeth C. Traugott & Bernd Heine (eds.), *Approaches to Grammaticalization* (Volume 2), 383–453. Amsterdam, Philadelphia: John Benjamins.

Matisoff, James. 2001a. Genetic vs. contact relationship: prosodic diffusibility in South-East Asian languages. In Alexandra Y. Aikhenvald & R. M. W. Dixon (eds.), *Areal Diffusion and Genetic Inheritance: Problems in Comparative Linguistics*, 291–327. Oxford: Oxford University Press.

Matisoff, James. 2001b. On the genetic position of Bai within Tibeto-Burman. Paper presented at the 34th International Conference on Sino-Tibetan Languages and Linguistics. Kūnmíng: Yunnan Nationalities Institute.

Matisoff, James. 2003. Southeast Asian languages. In William Frawley & Bernard Comrie (eds.), *International Encyclopedia of Linguistics* (2nd edition, Volume IV), 126–130. New York & Oxford: Oxford University Press.

Matthews, Stephen & Virginia Yip. 2011. *Cantonese – A Comprehensive Grammar* (2nd edition). Abingdon[-on-Thames] & New York: Routledge.

Nguyễn, Đình-Hoà. 1997. *Vietnamese: Tiếng Việt Không Son Phấn* (London Oriental and African Language Library 9). Amsterdam; Philadelphia: John Benjamins.

Norman, Jerry. 1988. *Chinese*. Cambridge: Cambridge University Press.

Norman, Jerry. 2003. The Chinese dialects: phonology. In Graham Thurgood & Randy J. LaPolla (eds.), *The Sino-Tibetan Languages*. (Routledge Language Family Series), 72–83. London & New York: Routledge.

Norman, Jerry & Tsu-lin Mei. 1976. The Austroasiatics in Ancient South China: some lexical evidence. *Monumenta Serica* 32. 274–301.

Ostapirat, Weera. 2000. Proto-Kra. *Linguistics of the Tibeto-Burman Area* 23(1). 1–251.

Ostapirat, Weera. 2005. Kra-Dai and Austronesian: notes on phonological correspondences and vocabulary distribution. In Laurent Sagart, Roger Blench & Alicia Sanchez-Mazas (eds.), *The Peopling of East Asia: Putting Together Archaeology, Linguistics and Genetics*, 107–131. London & New York: Routledge-Curzon.

Ōuyáng, Juéyà 欧阳觉亚. 1989. Hànyǔ Yuèfāngyán lǐ de Gǔ Yuèyǔ chéngfèn 汉语粤方言里的古越语成分 [Elements of the Ancient Yuè Language in the Yuè Dialect of Chinese]. In Shūxiāng Lǚ 吕叔湘 (ed.), *Yǔyán Wénzì Xuéshù Lùnwénjí — Qìngzhú Wáng Lì Xiānshēng Xuéshù Huódòng Wǔshí Zhōunián* 语言文字学术论文集— 庆祝王力先生学术活动五十周年 [Academic Proceedings of Language and Writing — Celebrating the Fiftieth Anniversary of Professor Wáng Lì's Academic Activities]. Běijīng: Knowledge Publishing House.

Peterson, David A. 2005. Initial observations on Bangladesh Mru morphosyntax. Paper presented at the 38th International Conference on Sino-Tibetan Language and Linguistics. Xiàmén: Xiamen University.

Peyraube, Alain. 1988. *Syntaxe Diachronique du Chinois: Évolution des Constructions Datives du XIVe Siècle av. J.-C. au XVIIIe Siècle*. Paris: Collège de France, Institut des Hautes Études Chinoises.

Peyraube, Alain. 1996. Le Cantonais est-il du chinois? *Perspectives Chinoises* 34. 26–29.

Peyraube, Alain. 1997. On word order in Archaic Chinese. *Cahiers de Linguistique - Asie Orientale* 26(1). 3–20.

Pittayaporn, Pittayawat. 2009. The phonology of Proto-Tai. PhD dissertaion. Cornell University.

Pulleyblank, Edwin George. 1963. The consonantal system of Old Chinese (Part II). *Asia Major* 9. 206–265.

Qián, Méng 钱萌. 2008. Níngbō fāngyán zhōng de SOV jù 宁波方言中的SOV句 [SOV sentences in Níngbō dialect]. In Linguistic Association of Shanghai and Chinese Linguistic Association of Hong Kong (eds.), *Wúyǔ Yánjiū: Dìsìjiè Guójì Wúfāngyán Xuéshù Yántǎohuì Lùnwénjí* 吴语研究：第四届国际吴方言学术研讨会论文集 [Studies of Wú Language: Proceedings of the Fourth International Conference on Wú Dialects], 134–140. Shànghǎi: Shanghai Education Publishing House.

Qián, Nǎiróng 钱乃荣. 2008. Níngbō fāngyán de shítài 宁波方言的时态 [Tense and aspect in Níngbō dialect]. In Linguistic Association of Shanghai and Chinese Linguistic Association of Hong Kong (eds.), *Wúyǔ Yánjiū: Dìsìjiè Guójì Wúfāngyán Xuéshù Yántǎohuì Lùnwénjí* 吴语研究：第四届国际吴方言学术研讨会论文集 [Studies of Wú Language: Proceedings of the Fourth International Conference on Wú Dialects], 121–126. Shànghǎi: Shanghai Education Publishing House.

Ratliff, Martha. 1998. Ho Ne (She) is Hmongic: one final argument. *Linguistics of the Tibeto-Burman Area* 21(2). 97–109.

Ratliff, Martha. 2010. *Hmong-Mien Language History* (Pacific Linguistics 613). Canberra: Australian National University.

Sagart, Laurent. 2002. Gan, Hakka and the formation of Chinese dialects. In Dah-an Ho (ed.), *Dialect Variations in Chinese, Papers from the Third International Conference on Sinology, Linguistics Section*, 129–153. Taipei: Academia Sinica.

Sagart, Laurent. 2004. The higher phylogeny of Austronesian and the position of Tai-Kadai. *Oceanic Linguistics* 43(2). 411–444.

Sagart, Laurent. 2008. The expansion of *Setaria* farmers in East Asia: a linguistic and archaeological model. In Alicia Sanchez-Mazas, Roger Blench, Malcolm D. Ross, Ilia Peiros & Marie Lin (eds.), *Past Human Migrations in East Asia: Matching Archaeology, Linguistics and Genetics*, 133–157. London & New York: Routledge.

Sagart, Laurent. 2011. Classifying Chinese dialects/Sinitic languages on shared innovations. Talk given at Centre de recherches linguistiques sur l'Asie orientale, Norgent sur Marne.

Shěn, Míng 沈明. 2006. Jìnyǔ de fēnqū (gǎo) 晋语的分区（稿）[The classification of Jìn (draft)]. *Fāngyán* 2006(4). 343–356.

Simpson, Andrew. 2005. Classifiers and DP Structure in Southeast Asia. In Guglielmo Cinque & Richard S. Kayne (eds.), *The Oxford Handbook of Comparative Syntax*, 806–838. Oxford & New York: Oxford University Press.

Smyth, David. 2002. *Thai: An Essential Grammar*. London & New York: Routledge.

Soe, Myint. 1999. A grammar of Burmese. Eugene, OR: University of Oregon dissertation.

Solnit, David B. 1997. *Eastern Kayah Li: Grammar, Texts, Glossary*. Honolulu: University of Hawai'i Press.

Sousa, Hilário de. forthcoming. *A Grammar of Nanning Pinghua*.

Starostin, Sergej. 1995. The historical position of Bai. *Moskovskiy Lingvisticheskiy Zhurnal Московский Лингвистический Журнал* [Moscow Journal of Linguistics] 1. 174–190.

Sun, Hongkai. 2003. Is Baima a dialect or vernacular of Tibetan. *Cahiers de Linguistique – Asie Orientale* 32(1). 61–81.

Sybesma, Rint P. E. 1992. Causatives and accomplishments: the case of Chinese ba. Leiden: Leiden University dissertation.

Thepkanjana, Kingkarn. 2008. Ditransitive Constructions in Thai. In Andrej Malchukov, Martin Haspelmath & Bernard Comrie (eds.), *Studies in Ditransitive Constructions: A Comparative Handbook*, 409–426. Berlin & New York: De Gruyter Mouton.

Thurgood, Graham. 1993. Phan Rang Cham and Utsat: tonogenetic themes and variants. In Jerold A. Edmondson & Kenneth J. Gregerson (eds.), *Tonality in Austronesian Languages* (Oceanic Linguistics Special Publication 24), 91–106. Honolulu: University of Hawai'i Press.

Vovin, Alexander. 2000. Did the Xiongnu speak a Yeniseian language? *Central Asiatic Journal* 44(1). 87–104.

Wali, Kashi & Omkar N. Koul. 1996. *Kashimiri: A Cognitive-Descriptive Grammar*. London, New York: Routledge.

Wang, Feng. 2006. *Comparison of languages in contact: the distillation method and the case of Bai* (Language and Linguistics Monograph Series B: Frontiers in Linguistics III). Taipei: Institute of Linguistics, Academia Sinica.

Wāng, Fēng 汪锋. 2012. *Yǔyán Jiēchù yǔ Yǔyán Bǐjiào: yǐ Báiyǔ wéi Lì 语言接触与语言比较：以白语为例* [Language Contact and Language Comparison: using Bái as an example]. Běijīng: The Commercial Press.

Wáng, Fùshì 王辅世. 1985. *Miáoyǔ Jiǎnzhì 苗语简志* [Sketch of the Miáo Language]. Běijīng: The Ethnic Publishing House.

Wáng, Hóngjūn 王洪君. 2009. Jiāngù yǎnbiàn, tuīpíng hé céngcì de Hànyǔ fāngyán lìshǐ guānxì móxíng 兼顾演变、推平和层次的汉语方言历史关系模型 [A historical relationship model of Chinese dialects which encompasses change, leveling and stratification]. *Fāngyán* 2009 (4). 204–218.

Wayland, Ratree P. & Allard Jongman. 2002. Registrogenesis in Khmer: a phonetic account. *Mon-Khmer Studies* 32: 101–115.

Wayland, Ratree P. & Allard Jongman. 2003. Acoustic correlates of breathy and clear vowels: the case of Khmer. *Journal of Phonetics* 31. 181–201.

Wéi, Jǐngyún 韦景云 & Xiǎoháng Qín 覃晓航. 2006. *Zhuàngyǔ Tōnglùn 壮语通论* [Common Theories on the Zhuàng Language]. Běijīng: The Central University of Nationalities Press.

Wéi, Qìngwěn 韦庆稳. 1981. Yuèréngē yǔ Zhuàngyǔ de guānxì chūtàn 越人歌与壮语的关系初探 [First discussions on the relationship between Yuèréngē and the Zhuàng language]. In Editorial board of Mínzú Yǔwén 民族语文编辑部 (eds.), *Mínzú Yǔwén Lùnjí* 民族语文论集 [Essays in Ethnic Languages]. Běijīng: China Social Sciences Press.

Wen, Bo, Hui Li, Daru Lu, Xiufeng Song, Feng Zhang, Yungang He, Feng Li, Yang Gao, Xianyun Mao, Liang Zhang, Ji Qian, Jingze Tan, Jianzhong Jin, Wwei Huang, Ranjan Deka, Bing Su, Ranajit Chakraborty & Li Jin. 2004. Genetic Evidence Supports Demic Diffusion of Han Culture. *Nature* 431: 302–305.

Wǔ, Yúnjī 伍云姬 & Ruìqīng Shěn 沈瑞清. 2010. *Xiāngxī Gǔzhàng Wǎxiānghuà Diàochá Bàogào* 瓦乡话调查报告 [Survey Report on the Wǎxiāng Language in Gǔzhàng, Western Húnán]. Shànghǎi: Shanghai Educational Publishing House.

Wurm, Stephan Adolphe, Rong Li, Theo Baumann & Mei W. Lee (eds.), 1987. *Language Atlas of China*. Hong Kong: Longman.

Xióng, Zhènghuī 熊正辉 & Zhènxīng Zhāng 张振兴. 2008. Hànyǔ fāngyán de fēnqū 汉语方言的分区 [Classification of the Chinese dialects]. *Fāngyán* 2008(2). 97–108.

Yip, Virginia & Stephen Matthews. 2007. Relative clauses in Cantonese-English bilingual children: typological challenges and processing motivations. *Studies in Second Language Acquisition* 29(2). 277–300.

Yóu, Wénliáng 游文良. 2002. *Shēzú Yǔyán* 畲族语言 [The language of the Shē Nationality]. Fúzhōu: Fujian People's Publishing House.

Zhāng, Mǐn 張敏. 2010. "Dònghòu xiànzhì" de qūyù tuīyí jí qí shízhí "動後限制"的區域推移及其實質 The postverbal constraint as a geographical continuum. Talk presented at the International Symposium for Comparative and Typological Research on Languages of China, The Hong Kong University of Science and Technology.

Zhāng, Mǐn 張敏. 2011. Hànyǔ fāngyán shuāngjíwù jiégòu nánběi chāyì de chéngyīn: lèixíngxué yánjiū yǐnfā de xīn wèntí 漢語方言雙及物結構南北差異的成因：類型學研究引發的新問題 Revisiting the alignment typology of ditransitive constructions in Chinese dialects. *Bulletin of Chinese Linguistics* 4(2). 87–270.

Zhāng, Zhènxīng 张振兴 & Zhènghuī Xióng 熊正辉 et al. (eds.). in press. *Zhōngguó Yǔyán Dìtújí* 中国语言地图集 [Atlas of Languages of China], new edition. Běijīng: The Commercial Press.

Zhèng, Yíqīng 郑贻青. 1997. *Huíhuīhuà* 回辉话 [The Huíhuī Language]. Shànghǎi: Shanghai Far East Publishers.

Zhengzhang, Shangfang. 1991. Decipherment of Yue-Ren-Ge (song of the Yue boatman). *Cahiers de Linguistique — Asie Orientale* 20(2). 159–168.

Zhèngzhāng, Shàngfāng 郑张尚芳. 1995. Gàn, Mǐn, Yuèyǔ lǐ gǔquánzhuó shēngmǔ jīndú zhuóyīn de fāngyán 赣、闽、粤语里古全浊声母今读浊音的方言 [The Gàn, Mǐn and Yuè dialects where Middle Chinese voiced obstruent onsets remained voiced]. In Tsu-Lin Mei 梅祖麟 (ed.), *Wúyǔ hé Mǐnyǔ de Bǐjiào Yánjiū* 吴语和闽语的比较研究 *Comparative Studies among Wu and Min Dialects*: 13–17. Shànghǎi: Shanghai Education Publishing House.

Zhèngzhāng, Shàngfāng 郑张尚芳. 1998. Gǔ Yuèyǔ zhāng 古越语章 [Section on the Ancient Yuè language]. In Dǒng, Chǔpíng 董楚平 & Yǒngpíng Jīn 金永平 (eds.), *Wǔ–Yuè Wénhuà Tōngzhì* 吴越文化通志 [Annals of Wǔ and Yuè Cultures]. Shànghǎi: Shanghai People Publishing House.

Zhèngzhāng, Shàngfāng 郑张尚芳. 1999. Báiyǔ shì Hàn–Bái Yǔzú de yīzhī dúlì yǔyán 白语是汉白语族的一支独立语言 [Bái is an independent language in the Sinitic–Bái language family]. In Shí, Fēng 石锋 & Wǔyún Pān 潘悟云 (eds.), *Zhōngguó Yǔyánxué de Xīn Tuòzhǎn* 中国语言学的新拓展 [New Expansions in Linguistics in China], 19–73. Hong Kong: City University of Hong Kong Press.

Zhèngzhāng, Shàngfāng 郑张尚芳. 2008. *Wēnzhōu Fāngyán Zhì* 温州方言志 [Records of the Wēnzhōu Dialect]. Běijīng: Zhonghua Book Company.

Zhèngzhāng, Shàngfāng 郑张尚芳. 2010. Càijiāhuà Báiyǔ kuānxì jí cígēn bǐjiào 蔡家话白语关系及词根比较 [The relationship between Càijiā language and Bái language, and comparison of word roots]. In Wǔyún Pān 潘悟云 & Zhōngwěi Shěn 沈钟伟 (eds.), *Yánjiū zhī Lè* 研究之乐 *The Joy of Research II*: 389–400. Shànghǎi: Shanghai Educational Publishing House.

Zhōng, Jìnwén 钟进文. 2007. Gān-Qīng Dìqū Tèyǒu Mínzú Yǔyán Wénhuà de Qūyù Tèzhēng 甘青地区特有民族语言文化的区域特征 Area Features of Minorities Language and Culture Unique to Gansu and Qinghai Provinces. Běijīng: The Central University of Nationalities Press.

Zhōu, Zhèng 周政. 2009. Pínglì Fāngyán Diàochá Yánjiū 平利方言调查研究 [Investigative Study on the Pínglì Dialect]. Běijīng: Zhonghua Book Company.

Zhu, Xiaonong. 2006a. A Grammar of Shanghai Wu. Munich: Lincom Europa.

Zhū, Xiǎonóng 朱晓农. 2006b. Nèibàoyīn 内爆音 On Implosives. Fāngyán 2006(1). 16–21.

Zhū, Xiǎonóng 朱晓农, Zémín Liú 刘泽民 & Fùqióng Xú 徐馥琼. 2009. Zìfā xīnshēng de nèibàoyīn — láizì Gànyǔ, Mǐnyǔ, Hāníyǔ, Wúyǔ de dìyīshǒu cáiliào 自发新生的内爆音 — 来自赣语、闽语、哈尼语、吴语的第一手材料 [Recently developed implosives: new findings from Gàn, Mǐn, Hani and Wú]. Fāngyán 2009(1). 10–17.

Zhū, Zhāngnián 朱彰年, Gōngmù Xuē 薛恭穆, Wéihuī Wāng 汪维辉, Zhìfēng Zhōu 周志锋 (eds.), 1996. Níngbō Fāngyán Cídiǎn 宁波方言词典 [Dictionary of the Níngbō Dialect]. Shànghǎi: Chinese Dictionary Publishing House.

Part 3: **Defining the sesquisyllable**

Becky Butler
Approaching a phonological understanding of the sesquisyllable with phonetic evidence from Khmer and Bunong

1 Introduction

The sesquisyllable is generally considered to be a word type consisting of a final heavy syllable preceded by a light and phonologically reduced first syllable. It is usually thought to be an areal feature of Southeast Asia, particularly mainland Southeast Asia, including Myanmar, Laos, Thailand, Cambodia and Vietnam (Diffloth and Zide 1992; Enfield 2005). Despite the pervasive use of the sesquisyllable as a diagnostic for Southeast Asian type languages, there is little agreement as to what the sesquisyllable actually is. The goals of this paper are to lay out a more explicit phonological proposal for what the term *sesquisyllable* means and to phonetically test this proposal by investigating two purportedly sesquisyllabic languages.

The paper is organized as follows. In the remainder of this section, I review the properties of the sesquisyllable and the minor syllable, and I propose a new definition for the word type as a maximally disyllabic iamb, which is couched in articulatory terms.[1] In Section 2, I present the results of an acoustic investigation of a set of words in Khmer and show that due to their lack of a phonological nucleus, they should not be considered sesquisyllables but monosyllables with word-initial consonant clusters that have intervening *phonetic* material. In Section 3, I argue that, in contrast, Bunong, an Austroasiatic (henceforth AA) language of Cambodia, has a set of words with two *phonological* nuclei which should indeed be considered sesquisyllables.

---

[1] While a number of studies have considered the sesquisyllable from a diachronic perspective (cf. Matisoff 1990, 2003; Brunelle and Pittayaporn 2012, *inter alia*), the analysis presented here is not diachronic.

1.1 An overview of descriptions of the sesquisyllable

The sesquisyllable was first defined by Matisoff (1973: 86) in a discussion of the tonal features of Austroasiatic languages. He states, "Proto-[AA] had what one might call a 'sesquisyllabic' structure, with morphemes that were 'a syllable and a half' in length. That is, the prevocalic consonant was often preceded by a 'pre-initial' consonant... It is perhaps no accident that these 'halfway tonal' [AA] languages also have a syllabic structure intermediate between the truly monosyllabic [Sino-Tibetan] and truly polysyllabic [Austronesian] types." Although this was the first explicit use of *sesquisyllable*, the component parts of the sesquisyllable – the major syllable and the minor syllable – were discussed twenty years earlier by Henderson (1952) in her work on Khmer.

Henderson (1952) described Khmer as having four types of syllables: simple monosyllables, extended monosyllables, minor disyllables and major disyllables (1a-d). The disyllables are named after their non-final syllables, which Henderson refers to as *minor* and *major*, respectively. She notes, "Disyllables of this type [i.e. minor disyllables] are intermediate structurally between the extended monosyllable and the full, or major disyllable" (p. 150).

(1) Khmer
    a) Simple monosyllable: [kaɨt] 'to wake up'
    b) Extended monosyllable: [pʰdek] 'to put to bed'
    c) Minor disyllable: [sɔm.naɨm] 'humidity
    d) Major disyllable: [kaɨt.laɨŋ] 'to grow'
    (Henderson 1952, transcription mine)

Over time, the sesquisyllable has come to be understood as a word-final "major" syllable, which in all respects is a canonical and phonotactically well-formed syllable, and which is preceded by a "minor" syllable, sometimes called a pre-syllable. Michaud (2012: 2) provides a typical contemporary definition of the minor syllable, stating that the minor syllable consists of "a simple consonant... plus an optional nucleus, V: either a vowel, or a sonorant (nasal or liquid) serving as nucleus. In the Austroasiatic domain, the most frequently encountered situation is one in which there can be no vowel contrast in the presyllable: the nucleus consists simply in a *schwa*, a noncontrastive, optional vowel." Similarly, Diffloth and Zide (1992: 3) state that in contrast to the major syllable in which final-syllable stress and lack of suffixation converge to make it the "richest and most stable part of the word," the minor syllable has a poor consonant inventory as well as a "vocalism", which they suggest reduces to a single possible vowel, i.e. [ə], in most cases. Two instantiations of this structure are given in Figure 1. Although we will see that this characterization does not capture the complexity of how sesquisyllables have been described, I take this as a starting point.

Fig. 1: Component parts of the sesquisyllable, where σ$_{min}$ = minor syllable and σ$_{maj}$ = major syllable

1.2 The essential properties of the sesquisyllable

Based on the above descriptions of the sesquisyllable, what stands out are the differences between the minor and major syllables. I propose that the cross-linguistic descriptive properties that are common to all sesquisyllables can be expressed as a small set of characteristics, which can then be used as the basis for a structural model of the sesquisyllable. As a starting point for this analysis, we can look to a similar scenario, in which Hyman (2009) addresses the issue of the validity of so-called pitch-accent languages. Just like sesquisyllables are claimed to fall between monosyllables and disyllables, pitch-accent languages are often understood to lie on a continuum between stress and tone languages. In deconstructing the notion of pitch-accent languages, Hyman (2009) poses two questions: Are there any characteristics which apply to all pitch-accent languages, and are any of these characteristics unique to pitch-accent languages? Similarly, in determining whether the sesquisyllable is a category of word unto itself, these two questions must be addressed. Is there a set of properties common to all sesquisyllabic languages? Are any of these properties exclusive to sesquisyllabic languages? Yet I suggest that before we can determine which properties are shared among sesquisyllables cross-linguistically, we must first take a step back and determine which are not.

1.2.1 Minor syllables

While descriptions of the major syllable are generally consistent, much of the definitional variation in previous work on sesquisyllables relates to the minor syllable. As Brunelle and Pittayaporn (2012: 414) note, "While many authors take sesquisyllables to be any disyllabic words with a reduced number of contrasts in initial syllables (Larish 1999; Thurgood 1999), others take the more restrictive position that the syllabicity of the minor syllable is carried by a neutral vowel or a syllabic consonant (Diffloth 1976: 232; Svantesson 1983: 27)". The examples in (2) display the wide array of minor syllables in words which have been described as sesquisyllabic: (2a) and (2c) have schwa vowels, while (2b) has a non-schwa vowel, and (2d) is a syllabic nasal. (2c) also contains a coda while the other examples do not.

(2) a) [rə.bɨŋ] 'gourd' Bunong (Butler 2014)
    b) [ti.jɔ̃k] 'to point' Jahai (Burenhult 2001)
    c) [tər.pah] 'to slap each other' Pacoh (Watson 1964)
    d) [m̩.ləm] 'one' Stieng (Haupers 1969)

These examples suggest a number of ways minor syllables cannot be categorized. First, many languages allow codas in the minor syllable, although some allow only nasals while others include other liquids as well. In the examples below, we note that standard Burmese does not allow any codas in minor syllables (3a). However, in So, an AA language of Thailand (3b), nasal codas are allowed in minor syllables.

(3) a) No codas: Burmese (Green 2005)
    [tɕə.bó]   <   [tɕáN + pó]   'bed-bug'
    [n̥ə.la̰]   <   [n̥ḭʔ + la̰]   'two months'

    b) Codas: So (Migliazza 2003)
    [baŋ.pɛ̣c]   'to work sorcery'
    [sam.loːŋ]   'slipknot'

In addition, cross-language descriptions of minor syllables vary in the types of vowels allowed. These might include [ə] exclusively, responses to vowel harmony or a small set of peripheral vowels. There can even be variability in the phonetic realization of a minor syllable within one language. For example in

Turung (a Tibeto-Burman language spoken in India) the word /ljung/ 'finger' can be realized in three different ways, i.e. with no intervening vowel (4a), with a schwa (4b) or with a vowel that is either harmonized with that of the main syllable or the C2 glide, if applicable (4c).

(4) Turung (Morey 2005, Example 6)
    a) [ljung] 'finger'
    b) [ləjung] 'finger'
    c) [lijung] 'finger'

1.2.2 Language properties

There are two additional properties that do not address the minor syllable in particular which must be taken into account of a description of the sesquisyllable. These are the type of prosodic prominence found in a language, whether stress or tone, and the notion of a "sesquisyllabic language" itself. In the first place, sesquisyllables are found in both stress and tone languages (5), indicating that neither system is required for, or excludes the presence of, sesquisyllables. The examples below are from Cua, an AA language spoken in Vietnam, and Thai. This finding is not surprising given the somewhat arbitrary division of languages into stress systems and tone systems since many languages, like Thai, have both.

(5) a) Stress: Cua (Maier 1969)
       [ka.ˈlaat] 'hunk of meat'
       [ta.ˈrʌk] 'unison call'
   b) Tone: Thai (Bennett 1995)
       [la.mút] 'sp. fruit'
       [sa.nùk] 'fun'

Finally, there is no language-wide maximality requirement for sesquisyllables to be present. In other words, there is a notion of a "sesquisyllabic language" (Diffloth and Zide 1992) in which the sesquisyllables are the largest possible words. However, sesquisyllables can be found in languages in which they are the maximal word shape, i.e. languages which contain no (or almost no) words larger than sesquisyllables, as well as in languages that have words far larger than sesquisyllables. Examples of the latter are given in (6).

(6) a) Thai (Bennett 1995)
    [ma.nút.sa.ja.chon]   'human'
    [săa.thāa.ra.ná?]   'public, common'
   b) Khmer (Henderson 1952, transcription mine)
    [bɔ.raw.hit]   'family priest'
    [kɔ.ru.na]   'pity'

1.2.3 Shared properties

Despite these differences, however, there is a set of phonological properties shared cross-linguistically by all so-called sesquisyllables. Bennett (1995) suggests minor and major syllables should be understood as a convergence of four properties. These include a more restricted inventory in minor syllables than in major syllables, lighter minor syllables than major syllables, tonal contrasts on major syllables but not minor syllables, and the necessity of major (but not minor) syllables for the phonotactic well-formedness of a word. I review these properties here, with some slight modifications, as presented in (7).

(7) *Properties of sesquisyllables*

a) Prosodic prominence is word-final
b) Non-final syllables are phonologically reduced

   i) Non-final syllables have a reduced segmental inventory
   ii) Non-final syllables have a reduced syllable shape
   iii) Non-final syllables are light
   iv) Non-final syllables do not constitute well-formed words on their own

First, prosodic prominence (i.e. stress or tone) must be word-final. Although some alternative definitions of the sesquisyllable suggest this may not be the case (cf. Bennett 1995 on Chinese), I take the position that if this property does not hold, a word cannot be considered a sesquisyllable. One potential counter example to this property is found in Northern Kammu, an AA language spoken in Laos, in which tonal contrasts are present on penultimate syllables. However, this contrast is a marginal one (Butler 2014).

The second property of sesquisyllables is that non-final syllables are phonologically reduced. This includes segmental properties, syllable shape and weight. Bennett (1995) separates these into distinct characteristics, but because these are all a type of reduction, I group them together as one property. Although the types of reduction vary across languages, sesquisyllables always display a smaller inventory of possible segments in the minor syllable than in the major syllable. For example, in Bunong, implosives are allowed in major syllables but not in minor syllables. In addition, the shape of the minor syllable is always reduced. Even if codas are allowed, for example, their inventory is restricted.

Finally, the minor syllable is always light, which leads to Bennett's (1995) final criterion that the minor syllable on its own is insufficient for the minimality requirements on words. A major syllable is always necessary for phonological well-formedness while a minor syllable is not. Because this is both implied by the property of phonological reduction and is dependent on language specific requirements on word minimality, I do not list it as a property unto itself.

1.3 The sesquisyllable as a maximally disyllabic iamb

Having laid out the cross-linguistic descriptive properties by which sesquisyllables can be characterized, we are now in a position to address the second question posed in Section 1.2.2, i.e. are any of the definitional properties of sesquisyllables exclusive to sesquisyllables? Given that the properties I established are word-final prosodic prominence and phonological reduction of the penultimate syllable, the answer is clearly *no*. There is nothing about the properties laid out here which differentiates sesquisyllables from words that are maximally disyllabic iambs that exhibit a weak-strong pattern. In other words, sesquisyllables can be described as words which are at most two syllables (i.e. maximally disyllabic), the first syllable of which is unstressed and the second of which is stressed (i.e. iambic). This is not to say that every iamb is a sesquisyllable since heavy monosyllables may be well-formed iambs and even light monosyllables may be considered iambs, albeit degenerate iambs (Hayes 1995). In other words, all sesquisyllables are iambs (i.e. exhibit a weak-strong pattern) but not all iambs are sesquisyllables. This is because sesquisyllables must be disyllabic, but iambs can be either disyllables or monosyllables.

Indeed, it is quite clearly the case that the terms *disyllabic iamb* and *sesquisyllable* do not refer to identical sets of word types. A priori, disyllabic iambs can be iterative (i.e. one word can have multiple disyllabic iambs, e.g. CV.CVV.CV.CVV), and so the uniqueness of the sesquisyllable is that it characterizes a word which is maximally a disyllabic iamb. This raises a potential problem for my analysis in that the basis for the distinction between trochees and iambs is iterativity, or the repetition of stress patterns, i.e. feet, within prosodic words. However, in shorter words, like disyllables and monosyllables, diagnosing stress patterns is far more difficult. And when a language is maximally di- or monosyllabic, assigning a foot type to the language in its entirety becomes even more difficult. In other words, without any sort of prosodic iterativity, we really cannot say whether a language is trochaic or iambic. This is particularly problematic for many so-called sesquisyllabic languages in which words are maximally disyllabic.

What is striking then, is the (near) exclusivity of iambicity in languages that are maximally disyllabic. They are characterized by the descriptive properties given above, in which initial syllables are more phonologically reduced in terms of segmental inventory, syllable shape and weight than are final syllables. Initial syllables are also durationally shorter than final syllables, which suggests that these systems are iambic. Indeed this pervasive tendency is what has in part motivated the use of the sesquisyllable as a word type. In other words, it connotes the strong correlation between disyllabic maximality and the placement of prosodic prominence at the word level.

1.4 An articulatory model of the minor syllable

I have thus far defined the sesquisyllable as a maximally disyllabic iamb. In addition, have noted that the least marked (i.e. less common and/or more difficult) and most variable part of the word is the minor syllable. Yet if the definition of the minor syllable is so clear, we must wonder why the sesquisyllable has often been conceived of as lying vaguely between the monosyllable and the disyllable. I suggest that the answer to this question is found in the issue of the dividing line between phonetics and phonology, and more particularly, in the difference between excrescent or phonetic transitions and phonological vowels, especially epenthetic vowels. In this section, I discuss the difference between these two, first in descriptive terms and then within the framework of Articulatory Phonology, subsequently proposing an articulatory model for the minor syllable.

1.4.1 Descriptive properties of epenthetic and excrescent "schwa"

The vowel(s) generally referred to as *schwa* stand out from other vowels in a number of ways. In English, for example, schwa is usually used to refer to a reduced variant of some other vowel. Schwa tends to be shorter than other vowels and more co-articulated (Silverman 2011). The term *schwa* is particularly confusing when we consider the number of linguistic entities to which it can refer. Two of the more common referents of the term which are particularly relevant for the classification of minor syllables are what arises from epenthesis and what arises from excrescence.

Epenthesis is a well-studied *phonological* process (Itô 1989, Fleischhacker 2001, *inter alia*). As used here, epenthesis refers to a phonological process by which a sound is inserted to prevent the violation of some constraint on a language. These restrictions which require vowel epenthesis can be one of two types. First, a language may not tolerate sonority violations (cf. Clements and Keyser 1981, 1983; Clements 1990). Second, a language may not allow strings of consonants in certain positions, like onsets or codas, e.g. Arabic (Mascaró 2004; McCarthy 2007), Japanese (Itô and Mester 2004) and Finnish (Keyser and Kiparsky 1984; Prince 1984), *inter alia*.

On the other hand, excrescence refers to a *phonetic* process by which a short, vowel-like sound is produced when the tongue is in a transition state between two other sounds. Hall (2011) provides a number of properties regarding excrescent schwa-like transitions, including that they are often phonetically weaker than other vowels and do not always appear in the phonemic vowel inventory of a language. In addition, they tend to be short, do not bear stress and have no effect on the satisfaction of phonotactic constraints of a language. Hall (2011) notes that they occur in a number of languages including Piro (Matteson and Pike 1958), Finnish (Harms 1976), Sanskrit (Allen 1953) and South Hamburg German (Jannedy 1994).

In order to disambiguate the notation of excrescent transitions and epenthetic vowels from one another and from underlying mid central vowels (where "underlying" means present in the phonological representation of the word and in no way inserted), the following notation will be used throughout the remainder of the chapter. Excrescent vowel-like elements will be represented by [ᴲ]. Epenthetic mid central vowels will be notated by [ə] and referred to as 'schwa', and underlying mid central vowels will be given as /ʌ/ or [ʌ] as appropriate, even if they are lexically underspecified, and referred to as 'wedge'. A summary of these is provided in Table 1.

Table 1: Notational conventions for mid central vocalic elements

Symbol	Name	Description
ᴲ	excrescent vocoid	Phonetic transition; not phonological
ə	schwa	Epenthetic; phonological but not underlying
ʌ	wedge	Underlying; may be fully specified or not

Given my definition of the sesquisyllable as a disyllabic iamb, it follows that minor syllable nuclei must be phonologically real, i.e. epenthetic or underlying but not excrescent. This is because if there is no nucleus present phonologically, then the purported sesquisyllable should be considered a monosyllable with a word-initial consonant cluster instead. As noted in Table 2, in various grammars all of the words with an unstressed phonological vowel or with schwa-like transitional material have been considered sesquisyllabic.

Table 2: Scale of possible word types

	Phonological Structure	Example		
	Monosyllable with simplex onset	/tak/	→	[tak]
	Monosyllable with consonant cluster (no excrescence)	/trak/	→	[trak]
Has been considered a sesquisyllable	Monosyllable with consonant cluster and optional excrescent vocoid	/rtak/	→	[rtak] [rᵊtak]
	Disyllabic iamb (epenthetic vowel)	/rtak/	→	[rə.'tak]
	Disyllabic iamb (underlying vowel)	/rʌtak/	→	[rʌ.'tak]
	Disyllabic trochee (epenthetic vowel)	/rtak/	→	['rə.tak]
	Disyllabic trochee (underlying vowel)	/rʌtak/	→	['rʌ.tak]

The most ambiguous point on this scale is the line between the monosyllable with an excrescent vocoid and the disyllable with epenthetic schwa.
I suggest that much of the confusion between these categories is due to (i) the fact that grammars are based on impressionistic transcriptions and (ii) the lack of both a phonological model which could adequately account for this difference as well as the instrumentation necessary to verify such a model. Despite the impressive level of language descriptions by Southeast Asian field linguists, the acoustic differences between a phonological vowel and an excrescent vocoid can be both difficult to hear and concurrently easy to misinterpret because of L1 bias.

A likely example of mistranscription comes from Svantesson's (1983) work on Northern Kammu (See Section 1.2.3 above), which has been widely cited and used to argue for various phonological positions (e.g. Shaw 1994). Kammu minor syllables were described as consisting of one or two consonants but no vowel, so that the nucleus of the minor syllable was consonantal and tone bearing in those minor syllables with tonal contrasts (8).

(8) Northern Kammu
    a)   [sm̩.kàr]   'straight'
          [l̩.màːc]   'get stuck (expressive)'
    b)   [s.kár]   'cause to be straight'
          [p.káːy]   'cause to return'

However, in more recent work, Svantesson and Karlsson (2004: 1) state, "The phonological representation of a Kammu minor syllable consists of either one or two consonants, and in addition *there is a vowel nucleus* which is not phonemic, but can be regarded as an epenthetic schwa vowel" (emphasis mine). Indeed, all tone-bearing minor syllables have a nuclear schwa, which, although not underlying, is phonological. Therefore, the minor syllable consonants are not moraic and do not bear tone.

Furthermore, even the small set of non-sonorant consonant minor syllables which are claimed to lack tone by Shaw (1994) and Svantesson (1983) are reanalysed by Svantesson and Karlsson (2004) as both having an epenthetic schwa and being tone-bearing, although their tone is always identical to that of the major syllable. Some examples are given in (9a), and suggested reanalysed structures of (8b) are given in (9b).

(9)   a)   [kə́.múːl]   'silver' (Svantesson and Karlsson 2004)
         [cə̀.mə̀ʔ]   'rope'
         [sə́.cáːŋ]   'elephant'
    b)   [sə́.kár]   'cause to be straight' (adapted from Svantesson 1983)
         [pə́.káːy]   'cause to return'

In summary, the conceptualization of the sesquisyllable as a disyllabic iamb necessitates that the minor syllable nucleus be phonologically present and not just a transitional state. The potential for confusion in descriptions of sesquisyllabic languages underlies the need for a more descriptively accurate model. Articulatory Phonology, or AP, (Browman and Goldstein 1986, 1989, 1990, 1992; Saltzman and Kelso 1987; *inter alia*) offers such a framework. It provides a mechanism for understanding the difference between various types of inserted vocalic material – in particular, whether a vocalic tongue gesture is present or not. We now turn to this model, which will shed some light on why phonological vowels and transitional vocoids are so easily confused.

1.4.2 Mid central vocalic elements in articulatory phonology

Traditional theories often divide speech into two different components – the physical/phonetic component and the cognitive/phonological component. In such theories, a mapping between the two is required. In contrast, Articulatory Phonology assumes that these components belong to the same system, in which speech is composed of gestures, or goal-oriented articulatory actions, that are related to each other both spatially and temporally. Because the primitives are actions, they are crucially dynamic, not static. In addition, utterances are conceived of as a set of gestural units which simultaneously involve a number of articulators. Relevant for our purposes here is the fact that utterances can contrast with one another through the presence or absence of a gesture. For example, [ɪd] and [kɪd] differ from one another in that the latter has an additional velar tongue body gesture that the former does not.

This difference in the presence or absence of a gesture has a direct bearing on the discussion of phonological epenthesis and phonetic excrescence. Within the AP framework, the minor syllable mid central vocalic element (henceforth MCVE), can be defined as *phonological* in the case of the presence of a gesture and *phonetic* in the absence of a gesture. In addition, I suggest that the differences in acoustic correlates between a phonologically present vowel, whether epenthetic schwa or underlying wedge, and an excrescent vocoid directly result from their gestural configurations.

Because AP differs from segment-based frameworks in that it can encode temporal information, speech sounds can be understood as overlapping, and acoustic outputs can be understood as the result of varying degrees of target attainment. In addition to overlapping, gestures can also underlap, whereby the first gesture is released before the next begins, which often creates the appearance of schwa-like material between consonant gestures. While overlap and underlap are specified or planned before gestures take place, the extent to which they occur can be affected by speech rate. As a result, there can potentially be a large range of possible durations for phonological and excrescent sounds, which can make them appear to lie on a continuum instead of being discrete categories. However, defining the difference between these two types of sounds in terms of the presence or absence of a gesture supports the strict differentiation I have made between monosyllables with word-initial consonant clusters, which are not sesquisyllables, and disyllabic iambs, which properly include the class of sesquisyllables.

As can be seen in Table 3, there are three possible types of articulatory specifications for what is often referred to as schwa and which I refer to as MCVEs. Although there is undoubtedly variability within these categories due to rate of speech and gesture type, they are distinct, and I refer to them here as A, B and C. First, the Type A "vowel" does not have an associated gesture and is, in fact, just a transition state between two other gestures. Second, in Type B, the vowel has a gestural target but does not have enough time to reach that target. Third, in Type C, the vowel has an associated gesture, and its gestural target is attained.

Aside from the three types of inserted MCVEs, there is another possibility for gestural configuration, given in the first row of Table 3. There are strings of segments which not only do not require phonological epenthesis but also do not exhibit an excrescent vocoid either. For example, the /kl/ sequence in the English word /klæp/ 'clap' has no intervening excrescent material because the sounds do not underlap. In addition, two of the three MCVE types overlap in their gestural configurations with underlying ʌ, which is not inserted by either a phonological or phonetic process. For example, in the English words /kʌ.ˈpʊt/ *kaput* and /kʌp/ *cup*, there is no doubt that each sound has an associated gesture and that all else being equal the latter has a greater likelihood of fully attaining its target because of stress placement and word size.

Table 3: Possible gestural representations of mid central vocalic elements (MCVEs)

	MCVE Type	Gesture	Target Attainment	Gestural Representation	Phonetic Properties
	No MCVE	✗	N/A		N/A
A	Excrescent ɘ (gestural underlap)	✗	N/A		Shorter Duration Lower F1
B	Partial ə ʌ with undershoot	✓	✗		Shorter Duration Equal or higher F1
C	Full ə Underlying ʌ	✓	✓		Longer Duration

Each of these gestural representations tends to have different phonetic properties. First, after controlling for speech rate, consonant type, etc., the stressed Type C MCVE is the longest of the three. Type B MCVEs are vowels with a gesture that do not have enough time to reach their targets, often because they are unstressed. Unstressed vowels are demonstrably shorter than their stressed counterparts (barring higher level prosodic differences, of course). Just as with Type C MCVEs, the gestural configuration for Type B MCVEs can represent an underlying or epenthetic vowel. Type A MCVEs will be the shortest of all and can be thought of as transition states with the tongue in a neutral position as it is effectively interpolating between other gestures. In addition, Type A MCVEs tend to have lower first formant (F1) values, while for Type B MCVEs, the tongue is expected either to be in an equivalent position to an underlying vowel with full target attainment or to be slightly lower, resulting in an equal or slightly higher F1 (Davidson 2006).

We are now in a position to compare these types of MCVEs to the word types presented in Table 2, and through configurations of gestures we can better understand where the ambiguity in the classification of sesquisyllables arises. As stated earlier, I reject the notion that monosyllables with word-initial consonant clusters are sesquisyllables and propose instead that sesquisyllables are non-iterative disyllabic iambs, or words with maximally two syllables in a weak-strong pattern. This difference between monosyllables and disyllables is exhibited in Table 4 (based on Table 2) in which monosyllables contain Type A MCVEs and disyllables contain either Type B or Type C MCVEs, such that they can be either iambs or trochees. Note that in previous accounts of sesquisyllables both Type B MCVEs and Type A MCVEs were considered to be the nuclei of minor syllables. However, in Table 4 only disyllabic iambs are associated with Type B MCVEs, indicating that only vowels which are reduced but still have a gestural target can potentially be minor syllable nuclei.

Table 4: Word types and their associated MCVE types

Word Type	MCVE Type
Monosyllable with simplex onset	None
Monosyllable with consonant cluster (no excrescence)	
Monosyllable with consonant cluster and optional excrescent vocoid	Type A
Disyllabic iamb (epenthetic vowel)	Type B
Disyllabic iamb (underlying vowel)	
Disyllabic trochee (epenthetic vowel)	Type C
Disyllabic trochee (underlying vowel)	

(Has been considered a Sesquisyllable: Monosyllable with consonant cluster and optional excrescent vocoid; Disyllabic iamb (epenthetic vowel); Disyllabic iamb (underlying vowel))

1.4.3 Summary

The model presented here is both prosodic and articulatory in nature. The sesquisyllable is conceptualized as a word which is a maximally disyllabic iamb.

This requires that the minor syllable nucleus be a phonological vowel that is most likely phonetically reduced, i.e. a Type B MCVE. As a working model, Figure 2 shows each of the possible MCVE types (including None) as what can be thought of as schematized spectrograms, in which the dark bars represent relative F1 and F2 values. We can take the schematic with no MCVE in its word-initial consonant cluster in (i) as a baseline, assuming that the F1 of the stressed vowel is that of an underlying /ʌ/ of 500Hz.

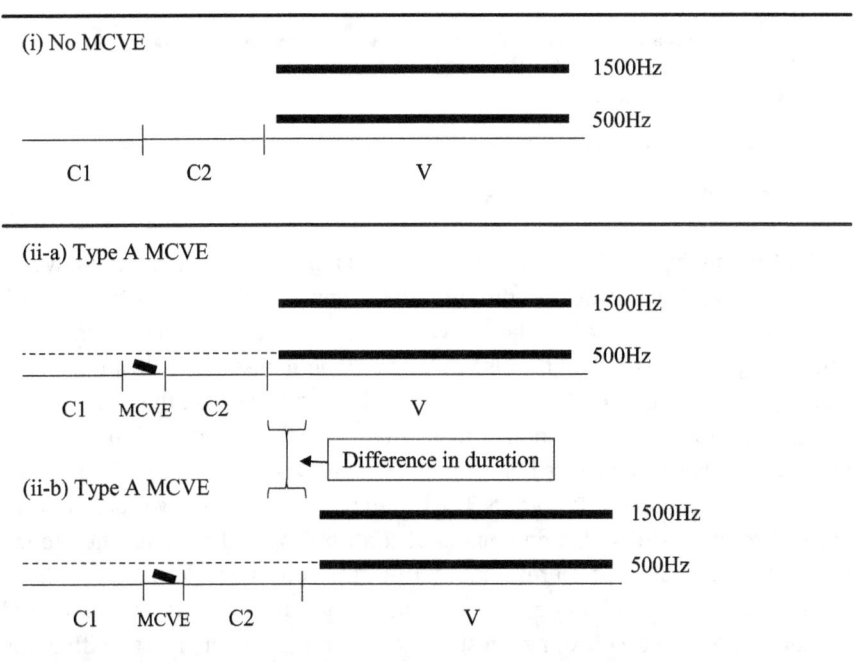

Fig. 2 (continues overleaf): Schematized spectrographic predictions of MCVE types

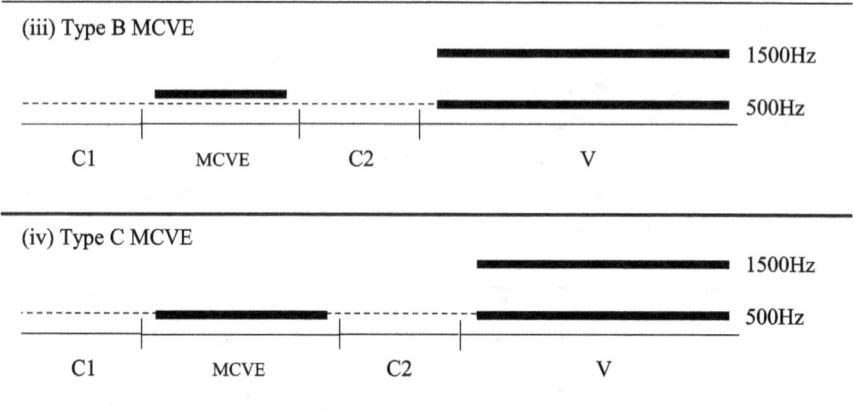

Fig. 2 (continued): Schematized spectrographic predictions of MCVE types

In (ii), the Type A MCVE has two possible realizations. First, note that word-final full vowel is equivalent in duration to the vowel in the word with no MCVE in (i). Since each is a monosyllable, we do not expect any noticeable effects of shortening due to word length. Also note that in both possible realizations, F1 is sloping. This is because F1 of a Type A MCVE is contingent on the formant values of its surrounding consonants. Also note that it is lower than that of underlying wedge, because all else being equal, F1 of a Type A MCVE should be lower than that of an underlying wedge. The difference between the two possibilities is whether or not the transitional material contributes additional duration to the CC sequence. In the first representation (ii-i), the consonant gestures are shortened so that the MCVE does not contribute any duration, and in the second sequence (ii-ii), the consonant gestures are simply farther apart so that the MCVE does contribute additional duration.

Type B MCVEs in (iii) differ from Type A MCVEs in that they are both longer and their F1s are higher. Indeed, their F1s should be either a similar value as or higher than the F1 of underlying wedge. The Type C MCVEs in (iv) are longer still than Type B MCVEs, and their F1s are equal to or lower than Type B MCVEs. Note that the words represented here are assumed to be said either in isolation or focused, so although disyllables with Type C schwas are taken to be trochees, the MCVE is actually not longer than the vowel in the final syllable.

We now turn to two phonetic experiments in which these ideas are explored with primary language data from two AA languages spoken in Cambodia – Khmer and Bunong. Although the model I present is largely one of articulation and gestural configurations, the experiments themselves are acoustic in nature. To date no articulatory data have been collected for these languages. While collecting such data would be a useful further study, as is widely discussed in the literature, many articulatory events can be interpreted from the acoustic record (cf. Davidson 2006). Thus this acoustic study is able to shed some light on the structure of sesquisyllables and minor syllables.

Finally, as noted in Section 1.2 above, sesquisyllables in a number of languages have been described as having a small but restricted set of vowels in the minor syllable; however the following experiments focus exclusively on MCVEs. Further – and ideally articulatory – experiments are needed to determine whether or not those vowels have gestural targets and should be considered phonological.

2 The minor syllable in Khmer

Henderson (1952) divides word types in Khmer into four categories: simple monosyllables, extended monosyllables, minor disyllables and major disyllables (Table 5). Simple monosyllables have simplex onsets, and extended monosyllables have word-initial consonant clusters which often include a transition state. Minor disyllables are composed of a minor syllable followed by an unreduced major syllable and are "intermediate structurally between the extended monosyllable and the full, or major disyllable" (p. 150). Major disyllables are composed of two major syllables.

Table 5: Khmer word types (adapted from Henderson 1952)

Simple Monosyllables		Extended Monosyllables	
[kæʌt]	'to be born, grow'	[khnæʌt]	'waxing of moon'
[t͡ʃam]	'to await, keep watch'	[prʌt͡ʃam]	'to watch another one'
[sæʌm]	'wet'	[psæʌm]	'to wet'
Minor Disyllables		**Major Disyllables**	
[bɔŋkæʌt]	'to produce, give birth'	[kæʌtlæʌn]	'to grow'
[bɔɲt͡ʃam]	'to pledge'	[t͡ʃammʌl]	'to wait to see'
[sɔnsæʌm]	'dew'		

In Henderson's (1952) view, extended monosyllables and minor disyllables are differentiated in two important ways. First, the minor syllable vowel in minor disyllables can have a different register than the following major syllable. In contrast, when mid central vocalic elements (MCVEs) appear in extended monosyllables, they always match the register of the major syllable. Second, extended monosyllables are more permissive in their consonantal inventory than are minor disyllables, but they are more restrictive in their vowel inventory. In minor disyllables, C1 cannot be nasal, and a nasal coda must always be present, whereas there are no restrictions on the consonantal inventory of extended monosyllable onsets, aside from the phonotactic constraints that apply to all onsets in the language. In terms of vowels, however, extended monosyllables allow only an MCVE (in addition to [h] or nothing), whereas minor disyllables may contain an [ʌ], [u] or [ɔ].

On the other hand, there are many similarities between extended monosyllables and minor disyllables. For example, in slow speech, Henderson (1952) suggests that the vocalic portion of the extended monosyllable can be identical in quality to the minor syllable vowel of minor disyllables, assuming the registers are the same. In addition, both the MCVE of extended monosyllables and the nucleus of minor syllables are unstressed. Finally, differences are further obscured in fast speech, when minor syllable codas are dropped, as in (10). Note, however, that the orthographic forms represent the slower pronunciations, i.e. those including the coda.

(10) a) /kɔnlaːt/ → [kʌlaːt] 'type of insect'
 b) /bɔŋkoːl/ → [pʌkoːl] 'stake'
 c) /tʃɔŋkiʌŋ/ → [tʃʌkiʌŋ] 'lamp'

Henderson (1952: 170) notes there is a "gradual progression from simple monosyllable, through extended monosyllable and minor disyllable, to major disyllable. Between the stages there is only a relatively small structural difference. There is no sharp boundary between monosyllable and disyllable". Nonetheless, some important difference must remain because as she states, speakers do differentiate between forms like those in (11), which reflect a fairly prevalent morphological process.

(11) a) [khlah] ឃ្លាះ 'bolt (v)'
 b) [kʌlah](< [kɔnlah]) កន្លាះ 'bolt (n)'

Subsequently, Huffman (1972) builds on and reinterprets Henderson's analysis, further emphasizing the lack of a clear dividing line between monosyllables and disyllables. However, in his analysis, the focus of ambiguity is on Henderson's (1952) extended monosyllables, not the minor disyllables. In fact, Huffman (1972) groups minor disyllables with major disyllables and does not address the differences between minor and major disyllables at all. However, he does discuss at length the extensive reduction of disyllables, including both major and minor disyllables.

Huffman (1972) suggests that monosyllables with word-initial consonant clusters have predictable transition states depending on which consonants are involved. These are grouped into three classes: Class 1 has no transition, Class 2 has a voiceless aspirated transition, and Class 3 has an MCVE transition (Table 6).

Table 6: Classes of word-initial consonant clusters in Khmer, according to Huffman (1972)

Class 1		Class 2				Class 3	
C1	C2	C1	C2			C1	C2
p	s	pʰ	p	m	w	p	b
t	r	tʰ	t	n	j	t	d
tʃ	h	tʃʰ	tʃ	ɲ	l	tʃ	ʔ
k		kʰ	k	ŋ		k	

These class types are further exemplified in Table 7 below. C1s are listed along the y-axis, and C2s are listed along the x-axis. Each degree of shading represents a different class of word-initial consonant clusters. First, Class 1 sequences, which are the most darkly shaded, are not claimed to have any material intervening between the consonants. They are described by Huffman (1972: 55) as having "a relatively close transition" from C1 to C2. Next, Class 2 consonant sequences, which are lightly shaded, are claimed to have "slight aspiration" between C1 and C2 (represented here by [ɜ̥]). Finally, Class 3 sequences, which have no shading, are described as having a "weak intruded vocalism of a mid-central quality" (represented here by [ɜ]). Only a subset of possible clusters are reported on in this study; those are found in the double-outline boxes.

Classes 1 and 2 remain phonetically separate from reduced disyllables because disyllables will always have some sort of vocalism in the unstressed syllable, as in (12).

(12) a) Class 1: [slaː] /slaː/ 'to make stew'
         Reduced Disyllable: [sʌlaː] /sʌlaː/ 'stew'
     b) Class 2: [pɜ̥teah] /pteah/ 'house'
         Reduced Disyllable: [pʌteah] /pʌteah/ 'to meet'

However, this is not true for Class 3 monosyllables, as can be seen in (13). Given these differences, Huffman (1972) concludes that there are three, not four, word types in Khmer. These are simple monosyllables, i.e. those with simplex onsets; complex monosyllables, i.e. those with word-initial consonant clusters; and disyllables, which includes both of Henderson's minor and major disyllables.

Table 7: Khmer word-initial consonant clusters based on Huffman (1972)

C1 \ C2	s	h	r	l	p	t	tʃ	k	m	n	ɲ	ŋ	ʔ	b	d
p	ps	ph	pr	pl		pt	ptʃ	pk		pn	pɲ	pŋ	pʔ		d
t		th	tr	tl	tp			tk	tm	tn		tŋ	tʔ	tb	
tʃ		tʃh	tʃr	tʃl	tʃp			tʃk	tʃm	tʃn		tʃŋ	tʃʔ	tʃb	tʃd
k	ks	kh	kr	kl	kp	kt	ktʃ		km	kn	kɲ	kŋ			
s			sr	sl	sp	st		sk	sm	sn	sɲ	sŋ	sʔ	sb	sd
m	ms	mh	mr	ml		mt	mtʃ			mn	mɲ		mʔ		
l		lh			lp			lk	lm			lŋ	lʔ	lb	

(13) a) Class 3:   [lƎbaːŋ] /lbaːŋ/ 'to test'
      b) Reduced Disyllable: [lʌbaːŋ] /lʌbaːŋ/ 'fence'

By the time the term *sesquisyllable* was introduced by Matisoff (1973), monosyllables with word-initial consonant clusters had begun to be considered a type of sesquisyllable. This is further apparent in Thomas' (1992) description of Khmer sesquisyllables; he characterizes them by the equivalence of word-initial CƎC- sequences with word-initial CC- sequences. I suggest this is indeed the case in Khmer, in which there is variability in the realization of monosyllables with word-initial consonant clusters, i.e. sometimes there is intervening material between C1 and C2 and sometimes there is not, as seen in (14).

(14) a-1) [mteh]
      a-2) [mƎ'teh]   'pepper'   ម្ទេស
      b-1) [pt͡ʃoap]
      b-2) [pƎ't͡ʃoap]   'attach'   ភ្ជាប់

Generally, only the voiced variants like those in (14a) are considered sesquisyllables. In other words, there are no accounts of any language in which a voiceless vocalism between two consonants is considered a minor syllable vowel. Therefore, only words with Class 3 word-initial consonant clusters could be considered sesquisyllables, while words with Classes 1 and 2 word-initial consonant clusters could not.

Following Huffman's (1972) assessment, I treat minor disyllables and major disyllables as being structurally identical in their phonological forms. As such, in what follows, I consider these both as mid central nuclei of unstressed syllables in disyllables and transcribe them as [ʌ]. However, when a mid central vocalism appears in monosyllables with word-initial consonant clusters, it will be transcribed as [ɘ] when voiced and as [ɘ̥] when voiceless.

2.1 Goals and hypotheses

In order to determine the phonetic and phonological nature of MCVEs intervening in word-initial consonant clusters, i.e. transitional or intrusive vocoids, in Khmer, I investigate the duration of word-initial consonant sequences and the duration and formant values of their vocalic transitions. Based on previous descriptions of Khmer consonant clusters, the presence of a transitional MCVE is likely to be predictable. Although this suggests that it is not lexical, it does not tell us whether the MCVE is epenthetic with an associated gesture or excrescent with no gestural target. However, because sesquisyllables have traditionally been described as different from disyllabic words, in the sense that they do not comprise two full syllables, transitional vocoids are likely to be substantively different from underlying unstressed wedges (Figure 3). This means that they are probably the result of gestural underlap – in which the release of one consonantal gesture occurs before the achievement of the target of a following one – and therefore word-initial consonant sequences with MCVEs should be durationally identical to or only slightly longer than word-initial consonant sequences without MCVEs but shorter than unstressed syllables in disyllabic words, as exemplified in Figure 2, and their formant values should differ in predictable ways, as well.

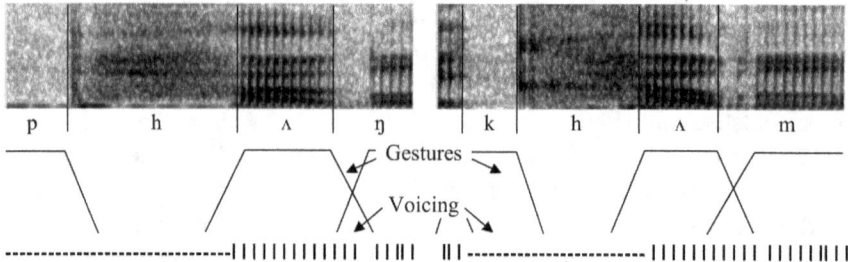

Fig. 3: [Khmer] Underlying stressed wedge in [phʌŋ] (left) and underlying unstressed wedge in [khʌm.'khat] (right). Duration = 500ms.

There are three possible realizations of the word-initial consonant clusters in Khmer. First, they may be produced with an intrusive vocoid, i.e. [ɨ], between C1 and C2 (Figure 4, left). This is characterized by a voiced period with formant structure between the two consonants. I will refer to this as voiced underlap. Second, they may be realized with non-harmonic material, i.e. [ɨ̥], between C1 and C2 (Figure 4, right). This is likely what Huffman (1972) refers to as aspiration and what I will call voiceless underlap. Finally, they could be produced such that no underlap is discernible (Figure 5). In this latter case, which is particularly relevant for sibilant-initial clusters, an absence of visible underlap may indicate either that there is no separation between consonants, i.e. no underlap, or that underlap *is* present but is being obscured by frication noise from C1.

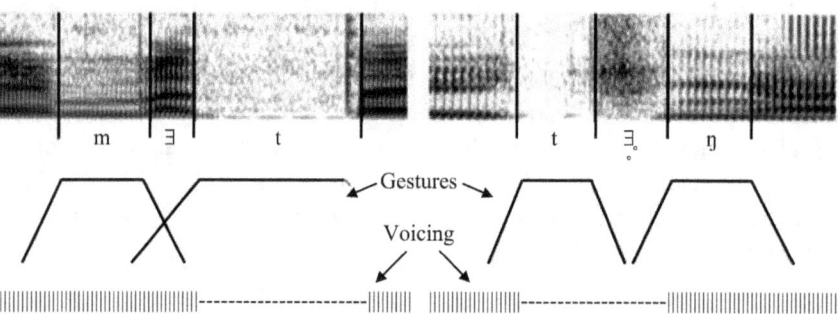

Fig. 4: [Khmer] Voiced and voiceless underlap

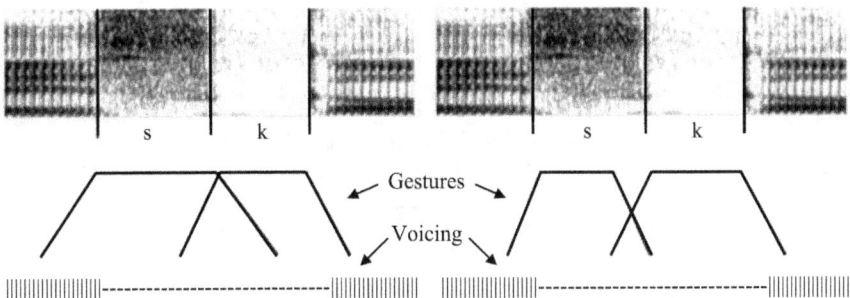

Fig. 5: [Khmer] Possible gestural configurations for sibilant-initial clusters

These possibilities lead to several other questions. First, is there a phonological difference between [ə] and [ə̯] in Khmer? In addition, are words with intrusive [ə] or [ə̯] different from words without visible underlap? What are the conditioning factors for their realizations and distributions, and what role do manner and place of articulation play? Next, how does underlap, i.e. the transitional vocoid, compare with unstressed lexical wedge in disyllabic words?

Differences between transition states and phonological vowels should be apparent not only in durational differences but also in an analysis of formant values. Transitions are not predicted to have formant targets. Therefore, if the MCVE is a transition, we expect its formants to differ from formants of underlying wedge or epenthetic schwa. There are at least two ways in which this could manifest. First, intrusive vocoids could be more strongly influenced by their consonantal context than lexical wedges. Second, all else being equal, intrusive vocoids are likely to have a lower F1 than underlying wedges. This is because the tongue will not lower completely between consonant gestures since there is no vocalic target. A schematic representation of what these possibilities might look like is given in Figure 6.

With these predictions in mind, we now turn to the experiment itself, particularly how the hypotheses are tested and how the acoustic results bear on our understanding of the sesquisyllable. The main goals are to determine what the nature of the MCVE in purported sesquisyllables actually is, how it patterns and how it compares to other types of MCVEs. Each of these goals is addressed in terms of articulation.

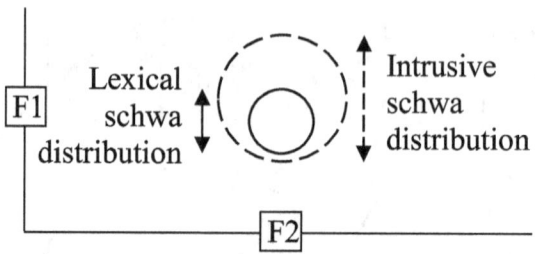

Fig. 6: Predictions about lexical wedge and the intrusive vocoid

2.2 Methods

2.2.1 Participants

Participants included eighteen native speakers of Khmer between the ages of 18 and 44 (μ = 27). Although all recordings were made in Phnom Penh, many participants were from other provinces of Cambodia, including Pursat, Siem Riep, Kampot, Kampong Speu, Preah Vihear, Kompong Chhnang, Takeo, Kandal, Battambang and Kompong Cham. Seven of the participants were females and eleven were males.

2.2.2 Stimuli

Stimuli were randomized and presented to the participants one word at a time. Participants were instructed to read each aloud three times in the frame sentence [nijij ___ mdɔŋ tiʌt] ('Say ___ one more time.'). Twenty words of type C(∃/ᴣ)CVC were recorded, along with 4 disyllabic CʌC.'CVC words and 13 monosyllabic CʌC words, as controls. In monosyllabic words and in the unstressed syllables of disyllabic words, all vowels were phonologically short lexical wedges.

2.2.3 Measurements

Stimuli were recorded on a Dell laptop with a Sennheiser headset microphone at a sampling rate of 44,100Hz, and all measurements were done in PRAAT (Boersma and Weenink 2012). Segmentation was completed by hand using spectrograms and waveforms. Three types of measurements were made: duration, formant values and spectral energy.

To obtain durations, the onset and offset of the second formant were considered to be the beginning and ending of vowels, where possible. Nasal-to-vowel and vowel-to-nasal transitions were demarcated at clear transitions in the amplitude of the second formant.

To calculate formant values, all sound files were downsampled to 10,000Hz and transformed into formant objects via a short-term spectral analysis with a window length of 25ms and a pre-emphasis of 50Hz. For males, the maximum value for three formants was set at 3,400Hz, and for females, 4,000Hz. Formant measurements were taken at vowel midpoints.

To obtain quantitative results, two different methods were used. For statistical analyses, only the second repetition of each word was used. However, to calculate distributional results, the second and third repetitions were both counted in order to make clear the general tendencies in the data, yielding 716 tokens.

2.3 Results

In general the results show that voiced underlap and voiceless underlap, as seen in Figure 4 above, are not significantly different in duration, although sonority is shown to have an important effect on the duration of CC sequences. In addition, the voicing of the underlap is found to be predictably dependent on the voicing of C1. These results suggest that both voiced and voiceless underlap are a result of the same type of gestural configuration. In contrast, their durations are much shorter than both unstressed and stressed lexical wedge, supporting the hypothesis that they are in fact transition states. This is further confirmed by formant measurements, which show that vowel qualities differ significantly between voiced underlap and unstressed lexical wedge, suggesting that the latter have associated gestures while the former do not.

Throughout this section, box plots are presented to show the range of various results. The horizontal line in each figure represents the overall mean of all the data presented in that figure. For each category of data presented, the boxes contain the range of data which constitutes the 25th percentile through the 75th

percentile. The horizontal line in each box represents the mean value for that category, and the whiskers on the boxes are calculated by the formulae *(1ˢᵗ quartile – (1.5 * interquartile range))* and *(3ʳᵈ quartile + (1.5 * interquartile range))*.

2.3.1 Token distribution

Two measures are important for the evaluation of consonant sequences: the percentage of consonant sequences that have underlap and the percentage of those instances of underlap which are voiced versus voiceless. First, of 716 C(ə/ɨ)CVC words (5 were omitted due to error), 442 tokens (62%) have some form of underlap, and 274 tokens (38%) do not. The percentage of instances of underlap in those sequences are given in Table 8. Again, the sequences tested in the present experiment are double-outlined. The percentages range from 0%, i.e. there is no underlap, whether voiced or voiceless, to 100%, i.e. every repetition has some amount of underlap.

Table 8: [Khmer] Word-initial C1C2 combinations – Percentage of sequences with underlap

C1 \ C2	s	h	r	l	p	t	tʃ	k	m	n	ɲ	ŋ	ʔ	b	d
p	ps	ph	100	pl		pt	92	100		94	pɲ	94	pʔ		pd
t		th	tr	tl	tp			tk	tm	tn		94	tʔ	tb	
tʃ		6	tʃr	tʃl	tʃp			6	tʃm	tʃn		31	tʃʔ	56	tʃd
k	ks	kh	kr	kl	kp	kt	ktʃ		km	kn	kɲ	kŋ			
s			sr	sl	sp	0		0	6	sn	sɲ	0	sʔ	sb	sd
m	ms	mh	mr	ml		77	mtʃ			86	mɲ		mʔ		
l		lh			lp		97	97				97	lʔ	100	

Next, with respect to voicing, of the tokens with underlap, 123 (55%) have voiced underlap, and 99 (45%) have voiceless underlap, as represented in Figure 4. The percentage of repetitions with voiced underlap is given in the double-outlined boxes in Table 9. Sequences which show no underlap, i.e. those represented by 0% in Table 8, are labelled with an X here since they obviously have neither voiced nor voiceless underlap. While the percentage of voicing also ranges from 0% to 100%, the voicing results are much more categorical. That is, with only two exceptions ([pn] and [tʃb]), underlap for a given sequence is either always voiced or always voiceless.

Table 9: [Khmer] Word-initial C1C2 combinations – Percentage of underlap tokens with voiced underlap

C1\C2	s	h	r	l	p	t	tʃ	k	m	n	ɲ	ŋ	ʔ	b	d
p	ps	ph	100	pl		pt	0	0			3	pɲ	0	pʔ		pd
t		th	tr	tl	tp			tk	tm	tn		0	tʔ	tb	
tʃ		0	tʃr	tʃl	tʃp			0	tʃm	tʃn		0	tʃʔ	75	tʃd
k	ks	kh	kr	kl	kp	kt	ktʃ		km	kn	kɲ	kŋ			
s			sr	sl	sp	X		X	0	sn	sɲ	X	sʔ	sb	sd
m	ms	mh	mr	ml		100	mtʃ			100	mɲ		mʔ		
l		lh			lp			100	100			100	lʔ	100	

With the exception of [pr] sequences, for sequences in which C1 is a non-sibilant obstruent, i.e. [p] or [t], 95% have some form of underlap. Of those 95% of sequences, 99% have voiceless underlap. Overall, when C1 is voiceless, 94% of sequences have voiceless underlap, and <1% have voiced underlap, which results from one repetition of [pn]. The voiced material in [pr] sequences is likely a result of the articulation of [r] which is realized as a tap or trill.[2] Complementarily, for sequences in which C1 is voiced, i.e. [m] or [l], 93% have underlap. Of that 93%, 100% are voiced. In other words, voiceless underlap never occurs when C1 is voiced. These results indicate that the presence and type of underlap is highly contingent on the voicing and manner of C1.

Finally, of sequences with sibilant C1s, i.e. [s] or [tʃ], only 10% appear to have underlap. Of those 10%, 58% have voiced underlap and 42% have voiceless underlap. Overall, of sequences in which C1 is a sibilant, 4% show voiceless underlap and 6% have voiced underlap. However, more than three quarters of these sequences with underlap – 77% – are [tʃb] sequences, suggesting that not only the voicing but also the manner of C2 affects underlap. Butler (2014) shows that centre of gravity measurements suggest that underlap is probably present

---

[2] Kirby (2014) finds that C2 [r] is devoiced in some utterances. Whether or not [ɹ] is still present in these cases requires further investigation.

in many more affricate-initial tokens than these cursory results suggest, but not in [s]-initial tokens.

2.3.2 Underlap analysis

Voiced underlap and voiceless underlap vary not only by their context but also by their durational distributions. Figure 7 shows that voiceless underlap has a wider range of possible durations than does voiced underlap.

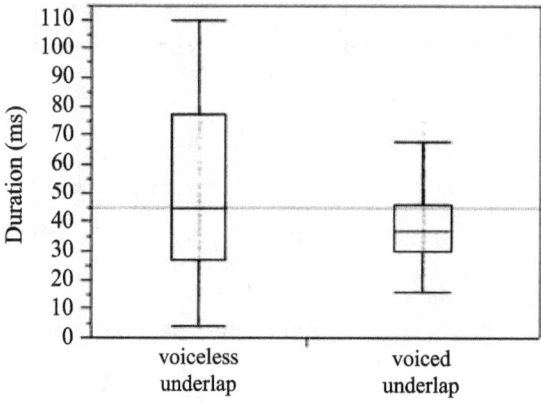

Fig. 7: [Khmer] Distributions of underlap durations (voiceless and voiced)

To further explore this distributional difference in duration, comparisons between the durations of CC sequences with voiced underlap and voiceless underlap are necessary. However, because of the near-complementary relationship of the C1 contexts of voiced underlap and voiceless underlap, making meaningful comparisons across types, i.e. CƷCVC and C̬ƷCVC, is not possible. Because of inherent durational differences between voiceless stops ([p] and [t]) and sonorants ([l] and [m]), there are two possible sources of durational variation in CC sequences. In other words, there are both durational differences between consonant types and possible durational differences between underlap types. Therefore, the variation of C1 and C2 types was removed by calculating the residuals of a regression of the total duration (or the underlap duration) with C1 and C2 types and Speaker as a random variable (15). Subsequently, those residuals were used to make interpretable comparisons.

(15) a) Total Duration = C1 Type + C2 Type + [Speaker] + $\varepsilon_{TotalDur}$
  b) Underlap Duration = C1 Type + C2 Type + [Speaker] + $\varepsilon_{UnderlapDur}$

Results show that once the variation in C1 and C2 type is removed via the residuals, underlap type, i.e. voiced underlap versus voiceless underlap, is not significantly correlated with the total duration ($p = 0.9934$) or with underlap duration ($p = 0.7565$). This indicates that neither the total duration of the CC sequences nor the duration of underlap alone (whether voiced or voiceless) is correlated with underlap type, suggesting that voiced underlap and voiceless underlap are not intrinsically distinct. Nonetheless, the total duration is correlated with the underlap duration ($p < 0.0001$), suggesting that the duration of the underlap contributes to the entire duration of the CC sequence.

2.3.3 Formant analysis

As we expect place of articulation to have a greater effect on the vowel formants than manner or voicing, all C1s and C2s were grouped according to their place of articulation to perform the formant analysis. Again because not all of the consonant environments were recorded for all the word types, just as for the duration measurements, the consonantal differences were accounted for by means of residuals, as seen in (16).

(16) a-1) F1 = C1 Type + C2 Type + [Speaker] + ε_{F1}
  a-2) F2 = C1 Type + C2 Type + [Speaker] + ε_{F2}
  b-1) ε_{F1} = Word Type + [Speaker]
  b-2) ε_{F2} = Word Type + [Speaker]

Results show that F1 and F2 of the intrusive vocoid pattern differently than underlying stressed and unstressed wedge. This is demonstrated in the vowel plot in Figure 8, which shows the values for [ɜ], stressed [ʌ] and unstressed [ʌ] following alveolar and labial C1s. Indeed, these results match the predicted MCVE patterns almost exactly as predicted. F1 for unstressed [ʌ], which I interpret as a Type B MCVE, is both equivalent to and higher than F1 of stressed [ʌ], for alveolar and labial C1s respectively. Moreover, F1 of [ɜ] is largely dependent on the place of the preceding consonant. When following alveolars, it is pulled higher and more forward in the mouth. When following labials, however, it is pulled downward. Its backness is less easily explained, and more data are needed to confirm these results.

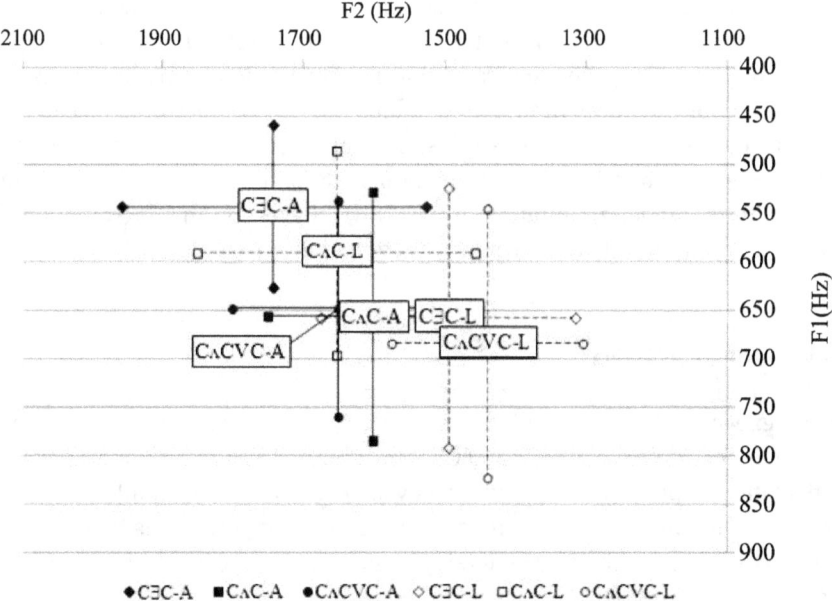

Fig. 8: [Khmer] Vowel plot of average values and standard deviations for the intrusive vocoid (◊), stressed wedge (□) and unstressed wedge (O) following alveolar (A) and labial (L) consonants

An investigation of a subset of consonant types shows that for alveolar-velar CC pairs (chosen because they are present in all word types), the differences between the intrusive vocoid and underlying wedge are significant ($p \leq 0.0009$). The formant values in Table 10 suggest that [ɜ] is produced significantly higher and more forward in the mouth than both underlying unstressed and stressed wedge for both males and females (Statistical significance is represented by double solid lines). In addition, for males, F2 for underlying unstressed wedge is also significantly higher than stressed wedge.

Table 10: [Khmer] Median formant values (Hz) for female and male productions of CƎCVC, CʌC.'CVC and CʌC, where C1 is alveolar and C2 is velar. Significant differences are represented by double solid lines.

	Female			Male		
	CƎCVC	CʌC.'CVC	CʌC	CƎCVC	CʌC.'CVC	CʌC
Median F1 (Hz)	562 ‖	771 ‖	821	477 ‖	651 ‖	639
Median F2 (Hz)	1976 ‖	1673 ‖	1714	1825 ‖	1588 ‖	1505

These formant results accord with our predictions about the differences between the excrescent vocoid and underlying wedge laid out in Table 3 above. The F1 results suggest that the tongue does not lower between consonants, which I take to be evidence that it lacks a gestural target. This is further supported by F2 measurements, which indicate that the intrusive vocoid is more susceptible to influence from surrounding consonants, which I again attribute to its lack of an associated gesture and target.

Finally, before moving on to discussion of the data, I suggest that all of these results are also applicable to the consonant sequences that were not tested. As indicated above, only a small subset of word-initial consonant sequences was investigated. These particular sequences were selected because the consonant combinations were also found in CVCVC and CVC words which could be used to make comparisons. Because the patterns found here are so robust, I propose that if the remaining consonant sequences are investigated in future work, these results would be supported. In other words, sequences with C2 [r] are likely to show some voiced underlap, along with sequences with C1 [m] and [l]. Still other sequences that begin with voiceless stops will most likely display voiceless underlap.

2.4 Discussion

Although its presence is variable, the contexts in which the Khmer intrusive vocoid appears are highly predictable. In particular, when C1 is voiced, only [Ǝ] may appear, and when C1 is voiceless, only [Ǝ̥] may appear. While the above results have shown that voiced underlap and voiceless underlap are durationally indistinguishable from each other, they are significantly shorter than unstressed syllables with lexical wedge. Formant values also suggest underlap is more variable and qualitatively different than lexical unstressed wedge. These results together indicate that Khmer "sesquisyllables" are better understood as monosyllables with word-initial consonant clusters that have gestural underlap, instead of a separate word type, as I have suggested throughout.

Only those forms with voiced underlap (not voiceless underlap) have previously been considered sesquisyllables. Consonant sequences with voiceless underlap or without audible underlap would not have been interpreted as minor syllables since they have no vowel-like material. In other words, what I have classed together as monosyllables with Type A MCVEs, i.e. [CƷCVC] and [ÇƷCVC], are considered distinct in older accounts of sesquisyllables and would not have been categorized as one entity, the former being considered a sesquisyllable and the latter a monosyllable because excrescent [Ʒ] was identified as being equivalent with epenthetic [ə] and even unstressed /ʌ/, while excrescent [Ʒ̥] was only considered aspiration, distinct from [Ʒ]. However, duration measurements and the predictability of the voicing context suggest that voiced underlap and voiceless underlap are both the result of gestural separation.

In conclusion, this study has shown that the distinction between monosyllables and disyllables in Khmer is more clear-cut than previously thought. Although the issue of reduction in Henderson's (1952) minor disyllables still needs to be addressed, I have demonstrated that "extended" or "complex" monosyllables, i.e. monosyllables with word-initial consonant clusters, are indeed monosyllables. Given that our definition of the sesquisyllable states that sesquisyllables are maximally disyllabic iambs, then we must conclude that Khmer "sesquisyllables", and by extension all sesquisyllables with Type A MCVEs, do not fit our criteria of sesquisyllabicity. Next, we turn to another AA language – Bunong – which is also claimed to be sesquisyllabic, although descriptions of sesquisyllables in Bunong suggest they are distinct from Khmer monosyllables in that they are more similar to disyllables with Type B MCVEs, which are phonological and have an associated gesture.

3 The minor syllable in Bunong

Bunong (also called Phnong or Mnong) is a South Bahnaric AA language spoken in eastern Cambodia and in the Central Highlands of Vietnam. It is spoken by about 52,000 people worldwide (Lewis et al. 2013) and is considered vulnerable. Like many AA languages, Bunong has been claimed to have sesquisyllables, most recently by Phaen et al. (2012). Unlike the set of words addressed in Khmer, descriptions of minor syllables in Bunong suggest they contain Type B MCVEs (/ʌ/ or [ə]) instead of Type A MCVEs.

Most sources say very little about word shape in Bunong. Phillips (1973) notes that the vowel and consonant inventories he provides are for the "main stressed syllable," suggesting that the inventory for the minor syllable is distinct from the inventory for the major syllable. Vogel and Filippi (2006) provide slightly more detail, stating that Bunong has "pre-syllables" or "minor syllables" which consist of a consonant followed by an epenthetic schwa vowel. They suggest that the pre-syllable often derives from a prefix in which the vowel is neutralized due to lack of stress. However, there are two sources which provide a comprehensive analysis of word shapes in Bunong, including sesquisyllables. These are Phaen et al. (2012) and Bequette (2008), and I take them as the starting point for this discussion.

Bunong has a limited number of word shapes, including monosyllables, putative sesquisyllables and a very small number of disyllables. First, monosyllables must be heavy, either with a long vowel or a final consonant or both. The nucleus may be preceded by either one or two consonants (17).

(17) Bunong Monosyllables
    a) /briː/ 'forest'
    b) /plaj/ 'fruit'
    c) /cuaj/ 'offend'
    d) /khʌt/ 'die'
    e) /kuʔ/ 'sit'
    f) /koːɲ/ 'uncle'

Bunong minor syllables, i.e. the word-initial syllables in sesquisyllabic words, are claimed to be realized as Cʌ, CʌN or N̩ (Bequette 2008, Phaen et al. 2012). However, although Bunong does have an underlying /ʌ/ vowel and an orthographic symbol to represent it, minor syllable vowels are always written as ‹a›.³ In an effort to avoid ambiguity, I have chosen to transcribe the minor syllable vowels as /ʌ/ (Differences among stressed [ʌ], unstressed [ʌ] and [a] are investigated below). Examples are given in (18).

---

3 As is the case in many abugidas (i.e. segmental writing systems in which consonants and vowels are written as a consonant-based unit in which the vowel notation is secondary), the orthographic symbol for Bunong [a] is not written independently but must be attached to a consonant symbol, as in ‹ᝣᝊᝑ› ‹kanar› [kʌnar] 'well-worn path'.

(18) Purported Bunong Sesquisyllables
    a) /rʌ.laːw/ 'more than'
    b) /lʌ.hat/ 'tightly fitting'
    c) /tʌm.tɔl/ 'to fight'
    d) /kʌ.tojç/ 'hatchet'
    e) /m̩.lam/ CLASSIFIER

Finally, Bunong has a very small set of disyllabic words (19). Unstressed syllables in truly disyllabic words allow a greater variety of vowels than do minor syllables.

(19) Bunong Disyllables
    a) /ko.raɲ/ 'lord'
    b) /ka.mɔk/ 'knee'
    c) /tʃa.lot/ 'fall over'

As presented by Bequette (2008) and Phaen et al. (2012), Bunong sesquisyllables ($C_{1ʌ}.C_2VC$) can be distinguished from monosyllables with complex onsets (C_1C_2VC) by systematic differences in their consonant distributions. In particular, C1 in complex onsets may be any consonant in the inventory of the language, but in minor syllables with vowel nuclei, i.e. excluding those formed by a syllabic nasal, C1 must be one of /p pʰ cʰ k r l/. In addition, C2 in complex onsets is limited to /r l w j/. A schema of the possibilities is given in Table 11.

Table 11: Word-initial C_1C_2VC and $C_{1ʌ}.C_2VC$ sequences in Bunong

C_1C_2VC		$C_{1ʌ}.C_2VC$		
C1	C2	C1	V	C2
any consonant	r l w j	p pʰ cʰ k r l	ə	any consonant, except liquids or glides

This suggests that word-initial consonant sequences may be divided into two non-overlapping groups – (i) onsets of monosyllables or (ii) onsets of minor syllables – as seen in Figure 9.[4]

Onsets of Monosyllables include:

- Monosyllables with word-initial consonant clusters, in which C2 is either [r] or [l]. These include /pr, pl, tr, cr, kr, kl, khl, sr, sl, rl/. They are represented by the darkest shading and the structure CCVC.

- CC- sequences, which include a C1 nasal followed by a homorganic stop, i.e /mp, nt, ɲc, ŋk/. These should actually be considered unary prenasalized stops. They are represented by the lightest shading and the structure ^{N}CVC.

Onsets of Minor Syllables include:

- Any C1 which is /p pʰ cʰ k r l/ that does not precede an /r/ or /l/ C2, such as the C1s in /kp, kt, kc, km, kn, rp, rt, rc, rk, rs, rh, rm, rn, rɲ, rŋ, lh/. These are represented by the second darkest shading and the structure Cʌ.CVC.

- Nasals preceding any consonant which is neither a homorganic stop nor /r/ nor /l/. In this case, nasals may be realized as syllabic – [n̩] – or with an intervening vowel – [nə]. These include /mh, ns, nh, ɲh/. They are represented by the second lightest shading and the structures N̩.CVC and Nə.CVC.

In addition, some C1s are ambiguous. When nasals precede glides, /r/ and /l/, Phaen et al. (2012) report ambiguity in syllabification judgments across speakers. Some speakers consider the nasals as minor syllables while other speakers produce them as C1s in word-initial consonant clusters. These ambiguous sequences, i.e. /mr, ml, ŋr, ŋl/, are highlighted with diagonal stripes in Figure 9.

---

4 Shading includes all consonant sequences predicted to exist by descriptions found in Bequette (2008) and Phaen et al. (2012). Consonant sequences for which the author has evidence are only those written in the table.

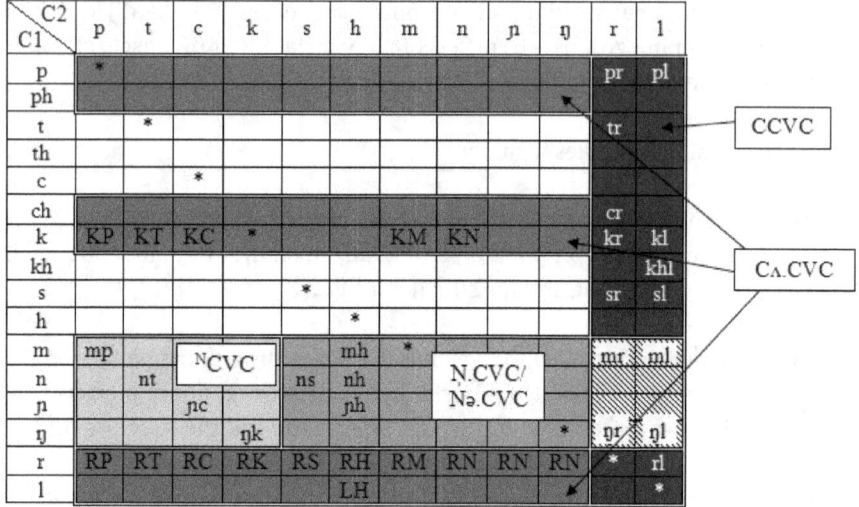

Fig. 9: Word-initial consonant sequences in Bunong

3.1 Goals and hypotheses

Descriptions of sesquisyllables in Bunong differ from descriptions of Khmer "sesquisyllables", i.e. monosyllables with word-initial consonant clusters, in an important way. In particular, in Khmer they have been defined as a set of words distinct from disyllables (and indeed, the analysis above showed them to be monosyllabic). Bunong, however, is not claimed to have disyllabic words, save for a few exceptions. Therefore, there is no meaningful way in which Bunong sesquisyllables can differ from non-existent Bunong disyllabic words. This leaves two possibilities as to the phonological structure of sesquisyllables in Bunong. First, if there is transitional vocalic material present between consonants in CCVC sequences as there is in Khmer, then minor syllable vowels in Bunong, i.e. CᴀCVC vowels, might be durationally and qualitatively similar to that transitional vocalic material, in which case Bunong would essentially be a strictly monosyllabic language. Alternatively, unstressed minor syllable vowels in Bunong might be more similar to stressed vowels in CVC monosyllables, in which case Bunong sesquisyllables should be considered disyllables. Regarding the latter comparison, because Bunong minor syllable nuclei are written with an ‹a› and are suggested to be reduced to [ʌ] in their phonetic realization (Phaen et al. 2012), they should be compared to both /a/ and /ʌ/ in monosyllables.

Figure 10 provides a schema of what the Bunong minor syllable vowel might look like as compared to the underlying vowel in monosyllables. Figure 10a provides gestural representations of CVC monosyllables and Figure 10b provides an example of a monosyllable with a word-initial consonant cluster. These represent two ends of a continuum, regarding possible vocalic material intervening between [k] and [l]: In (a) there is a vowel with full target attainment, whereas in (b) two consonants, i.e. [kl], are directly adjacent with no intervening material. We might expect Bunong minor syllables to fall somewhere in between these two. Possible gestural representations of the putative minor syllable [mʌ] are given in (Figure 10c-1) and (Figure 10c-2).

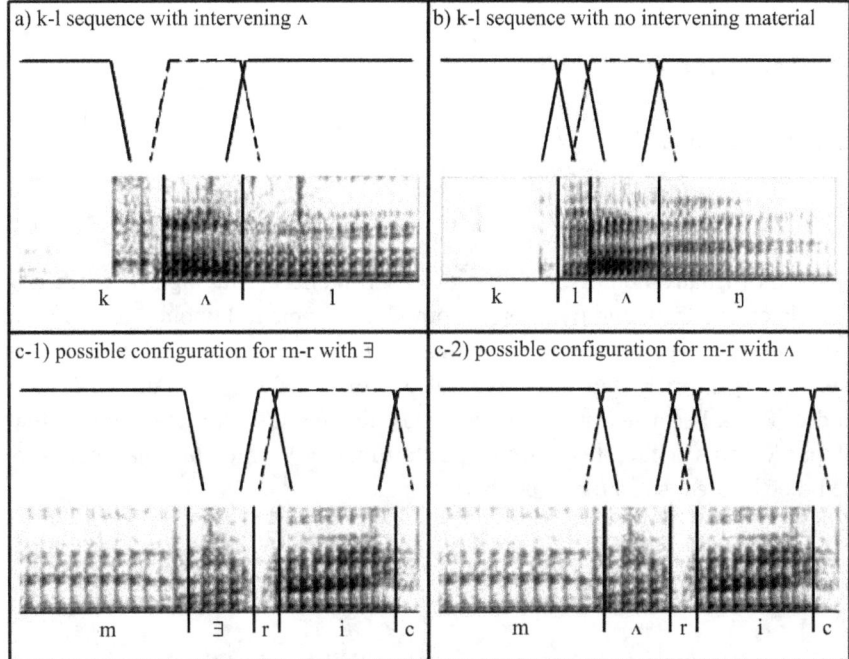

Fig. 10: Bunong words and their proposed gestural representations: (a) [kʌl] CVC, (b) [klʌŋ] CCVC, (c-1) [mɜric] CCVC, (c-2) [mʌric] CvCVC. Consonant gestures are solid; vowel gestures are dashed.

In order to determine which gestural representation is more accurate, two main comparisons are made. First, CCVC word-initial sequences (given in Table 11) are analysed to confirm the presence of intervening harmonic or non-harmonic material which may be the result of underlap, similar to what was found for Khmer "sesquisyllables". Next, underlap in CCVC sequences is compared to the minor syllable vowel CʌCVC. If they are durationally and/or qualitatively different, this might suggest differences in their phonological statuses. In particular, I hypothesize that CʌCVC vowels will be longer and their vowel quality will be less variable or reduced than vowel-like material found in CCVC sequences. Second, minor syllable vowels are compared to underlying vowels in monosyllables. Because minor syllable vowels are always unstressed, they will undoubtedly be shorter than CVC vowels. However, a comparison with both underlying /a/ and stressed /ʌ/ might suggest whether the minor syllable vowel has a gestural target.

3.2 Methods

3.2.1 Participants

Twelve native Bunong speakers from Bou Sra village in Mondulkiri province, Cambodia, participated in the study. Ten participants were recorded in quiet locations (usually homes) in Bou Sra or Sen Monorom (a slightly larger city outside of Bou Sra), and two were recorded in a home in Phnom Penh. Participants were between the ages of 22 and 36 years old (μ = 28). All participants were bilingual in Khmer, and some also spoke English, Vietnamese, French and/or Rade. Because the experiment was a reading task, it was necessary that all participants be literate in Bunong. Unfortunately, no literate female speakers could be located, so all participants were male.

3.2.2 Stimuli and Task

The wordlist consists of 21 tokens of type CVC, 7 of type CCVC, and 11 of type CʌCVC. Because speech rate can affect the realization of underlap as well as the target attainment of shorter vowels (Davidson 2006) each word was recorded in two blocks, which differed by speed. Speakers were instructed to read at a slow, comfortable pace during the first block and then quickly during the second. Other than the speech rate differentiated trials, the Bunong experiment followed the same methodology as the Khmer experiment in Section 2.2, i.e. stimuli were randomized and presented to the participants one word at a time, and three repetitions of each word were recorded. The frame sentence was [lah nau ____] ('Say the word ____.'). Like the Khmer experiment, both the 2nd and 3rd repetitions were used to determine distributional results, i.e. the percentage of repetitions that have underlap and the percentage type of underlap. For all other results presented, including all statistical analyses regarding duration, formant values and spectral energy, only the second repetition was used.

3.3 Results

The results are organized in order to highlight comparisons between sesquisyllables and other word types in Bunong. First, purported minor syllable vowels are compared with transition states in word-initial consonant sequences in monosyllables. In order to make this comparison, CCVC sequences are analysed for underlap in the context of both non-sibilant C1s and sibilant C1s. Next, C_ACVC vowels are compared to CVC vowels in monosyllables.

Finally, because rate of speech was not found to have a significant effect for any of the statistical tests in the analysis, the results presented below are for fast speech, unless otherwise indicated. In addition to the raw fast and slow speech data, both speeds were also normalized relative to the duration of the frame sentence for each utterance. Statistical tests run on the normalized data yielded the same results as for the raw data. Results of tests run on normalized data are presented in lieu of fast speech data in Section 3.3.1 (CCVC vs. C_ACVC) because there were too few tokens for the tests run on fast speech alone to be reliable.

3.3.1 C_ACVC and CCVC

The goal of the first part of this experiment is to compare minor syllable [ʌ] with word-initial CCVC sequences. In order to do so, the latter were investigated to determine if they have any harmonic mid central vocalic material or any non-harmonic material intervening between Cs and, if so, to investigate the durational and qualitative properties of that material. Distributional results are presented first. As in Khmer, because frication noise may obscure visibility of voiceless underlap, results for CCVC sequences with non-sibilant C1s and CCVC sequences with sibilant C1s are presented separately. This is followed by a comparison of CCVC transitions with C_ACVC vowels.

3.3.1.1 CCVC distributional results

Figure 11 shows the distribution of underlap found in word-initial consonant clusters of monosyllables. These include /kl, sr, mr, ɲr, ŋl/, as well as the prenasalized stops /mp/ and /nt/ (double outlined) for which we do not expect any underlap. Two repetitions of each cluster were measured for each speaker at two rates of speech, for a total of 45 to 48 tokens for each form, once pronunciation errors were removed. Speech rates and repetitions are combined here for increased statistical accuracy. There is no effect of speaker or repetition. In terms of speech rate, the largest discrepancy is for /mr/, in which the faster rate has two more instances of underlap than the slow rate.

C1 \ C2	p	t	r	l
k				98 / 0
s			80 / 100	
m	0 / X		89 / 100	
n		6 / 100		
ŋ			98 / 100	13 / 0

Fig. 11: [Bunong] Percentage underlap (top) and percentage voiced underlap (bottom)

The top number in the boxes in Figure 11 shows the percent of tokens with some form of intervening material. The bottom number represents the percentage of those underlap tokens in which that material is voiced [ɜ] as opposed to voiceless [ɜ̥]. For example, 98% (or 47 of 48) /ɲr/ tokens have some intervening material, and of those tokens, in 100% of them it is voiced. Note that in all sequences, intervening material is either voiced (100%) or voiceless (0%), but none have both types.

These distributions show several tendencies within the data. First, the prenasalized stops /mp/ and /nt/ usually do not have any material intervening between C1 and C2, which supports the hypothesis that they are unary segments, as has been proposed in previous literature (cf. Phaen et al. 2012).[5] Second, in contrast, sequences with C2 /r/, i.e. /sr/, /mr/, /ŋr/, generally do have some intervening material, and that material is always voiced. Given that /r/ in Bunong is usually realized as a tap or trill with some pre-voicing, this is not surprising (Ladefoged and Maddieson 1996). Third, there is almost always a period of non-harmonic voiceless material between the consonants of the /kl/ sequence, indicating that /l/ voicing does not contribute to transition voicing.

In addition, a small percentage of /ŋl/ tokens (6 of 45) are recorded as having a transition period. It is important to note that when a transition does occur in these, it is voiceless. This is due to a small burst of air released simultaneously with the nasal closure, suggesting that there is a short but complete oral closure as well. Although this burst of air is counted as intervening material, it is shorter than the intervening material found in /kl/ sequences (Figure 12 and Figure 13).

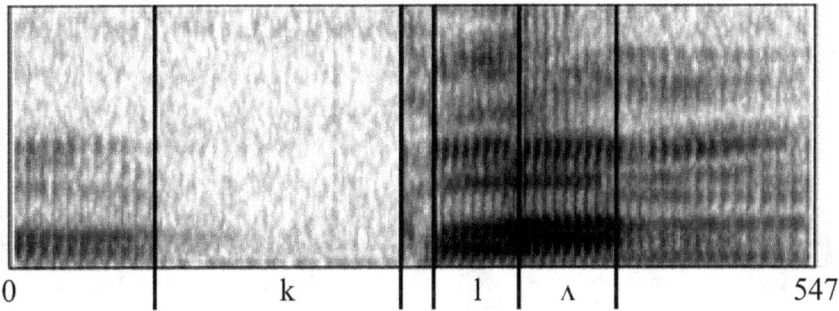

Fig. 12: [Bunong] Underlap in /kl/ cluster. Duration in ms.

Finally, the most variation in the presence of underlap is found in the /sr/ clusters, in which 37 of 46 have voiced underlap. This likely derives from the anticipatory voicing of [r]. However, as in the Khmer data, there is a possibility that voiceless underlap is also present in the remaining tokens but is being obscured by frication noise. However, only non-sibilant C1s are discussed here; for an analysis of sibilant C1s in Bunong, see Butler (2014).

---

5 Unexpectedly, 3 of 47 repetitions did have some intervening material. These three may be speech errors or may be the result of hyperarticulation due to the experimental setup; however, it is highly doubtful that these intervening MCVEs are simply transition states since both consonants have the same place of articulation.

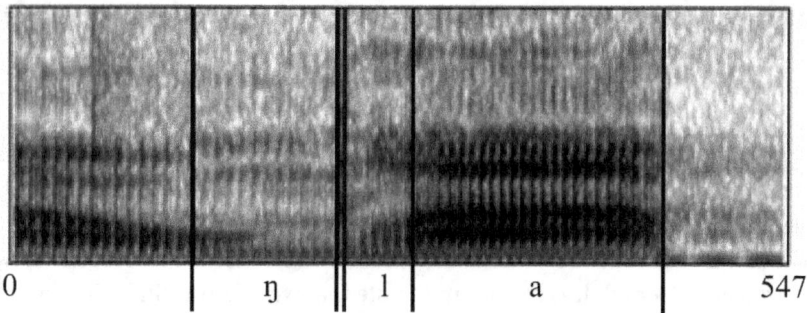

Fig. 13: [Bunong] Underlap in /ŋl/ cluster. Duration in ms.

3.3.1.2 CCVC underlap analysis

Having noted the general tendencies of the distributions of voiced and voiceless transition periods in word-initial CC sequences, I now take a more systematic approach to determine if there are meaningful differences in their durations. First, just as in the Khmer data, a linear regression shows that the voicing of the transitions, i.e. [ɘ] vs. [ɘ̥], is significantly correlated with the total duration of CC sequences ($p < 0.0001$), which indicates that either (i) duration of the sequence depends on the voicing of the transition or (ii) duration of the sequence depends on the consonants present, with which the voicing of the transitions is correlated. Indeed, just as in Khmer, C1 and C2 types are correlated with the total duration of the CC sequences ($p = 0.0408$ and $p = 0.0001$, respectively), making it impossible to distinguish which of these analyses is correct.

In addition, different consonant types have inherent durational differences that should be accounted for. Therefore, a linear regression was run in which total duration of the CC sequence was regressed by C1 and C2 types (20). Subsequently, the residuals of this regression were regressed by transition voicing, i.e. [ɘ], [ɘ̥] or no apparent transition (21), the results of which show that the total duration of CC sequences is not correlated with the voicing of the transition ($p = 0.1402$).

(20) Total Duration = C1 Type + C2 Type + [Speaker] + $\varepsilon_{TotalDur}$

(21) $\varepsilon_{TotalDur}$ = Transition Voicing + [Speaker] + ε

Figure 14 shows distributions of the total durations by transition voicing and distributions of the residuals of the total duration by transition voicing, respectively. Here and throughout, box plots are presented to show the range of the results and should be interpreted as explained in Section 2.3 above. A post-hoc Tukey HSD test shows that both CƎC and CꟻC sequences are significantly longer than CC sequences ($p = 0.0046$ and $p = 0.0388$, respectively). There is no significant difference among the residuals; however, Figure 14 (left) shows that CƎC and CꟻC sequences are still on average longer than CC sequences, although the distribution of the CC sequences is also noticeably larger than the distribution of either the CƎC or CꟻC sequences.

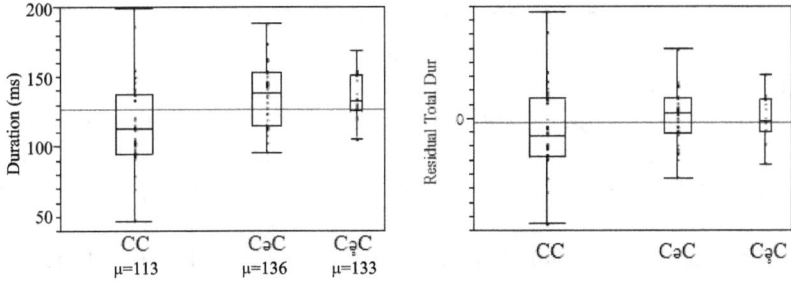

Fig. 14: [Bunong] Total duration (left) and residual total duration (right) for consonant sequences with no transition, voiced transition and voiceless transition

In addition to comparing durations of the total sequences, durations of the transitions can be compared directly between CƎC and CꟻC types to determine if there are qualitative differences between them. A linear regression shows that the duration of the transition is significantly correlated with its voicing specification ($p < 0.0001$). Just as for the total duration, the duration of the transition is also significantly correlated with C1 and C2 types ($p = 0.0113$ and $p = 0.0001$, respectively). Therefore, the same procedure to calculate residuals for total duration above was followed for transition duration.

Figure 15 shows the distributions of transition duration by transition voicing and the distributions of residuals of transition duration by transition voicing, respectively. A post-hoc Tukey HSD test shows that [Ǝ] is significantly longer than [ꟻ] ($p < 0.0001$); however, there is no significant durational difference between the residuals of voiced and voiceless underlap, meaning that consonantal context has an important effect on underlap duration.

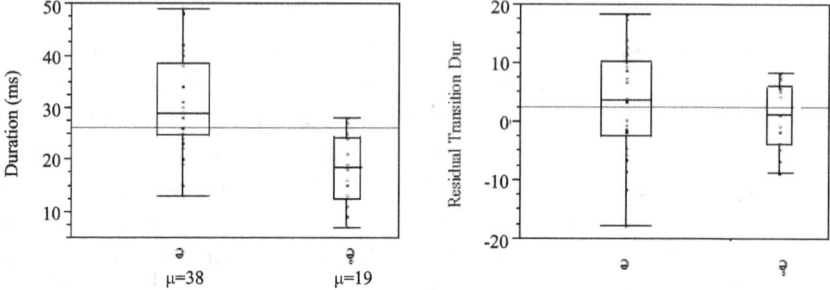

Fig. 15: [Bunong] Transition duration (left) and residual transition duration (right) for consonant sequences with voiced and voiceless transitions

In sum, comparisons of the total duration of CC sequences and of transition durations indicate that transition voicing and its duration are highly correlated with consonant type. Indeed, transition duration is dependent on voicing specification, and voicing specification is dependent on consonant type. In general, consonant sequences can be classed into one of three categories: (i) prenasalized stops/no transition sequences, (ii) C-r/voiced transition sequences and (iii) C-l/voiceless transition sequences. Although a larger sample of sequences will shed more light on the total picture, these results suggest that (i) C2 [r] requires a longer transition period than C2 [l] and that (ii) the voicing of the transition is conditioned by anticipatory voicing of the [r].

3.3.1.3 Comparison of CCVC transitions with C$_A$CVC vowels

Thus far, I have established that a voiced transition period is usually present in consonant sequences with C2 [r], whether C1 is a sibilant or not. Other consonant sequences are either prenasalized stops without underlap or have C2 [l], in which case voiceless underlap occurs but only rarely. We are now in a position to compare these transitions with purported minor syllable vowels in C$_A$CVC sequences. This comparison comprises two parts: duration and formant values. Such a comparison allows us to evaluate whether voiced transition periods are significantly different from what have been described as minor syllable vowels. If these transition sequences are equivalent to purported minor syllable vowels, we can conclude that just as in Khmer, Bunong minor syllables are not syllables at all. In contrast, if differences are found, this would suggest that purported minor syllables in Bunong are in fact syllables. Examples of CCVC transitions and C<u>A</u>CVC vowels are given in Figure 16 and Figure 17, respectively.

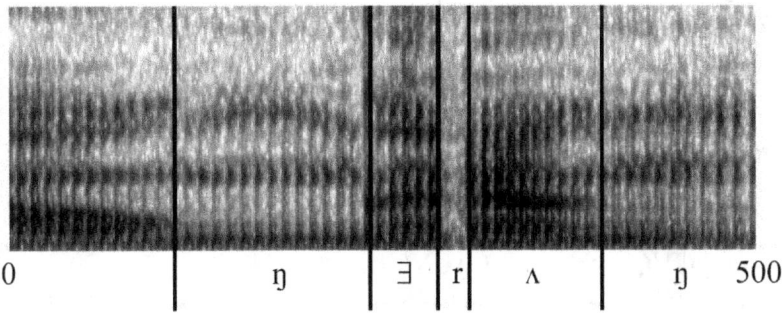

Fig. 16: [Bunong] Vocalic transition in [ŋɜrʌŋ] 'hammock'. Duration in ms.

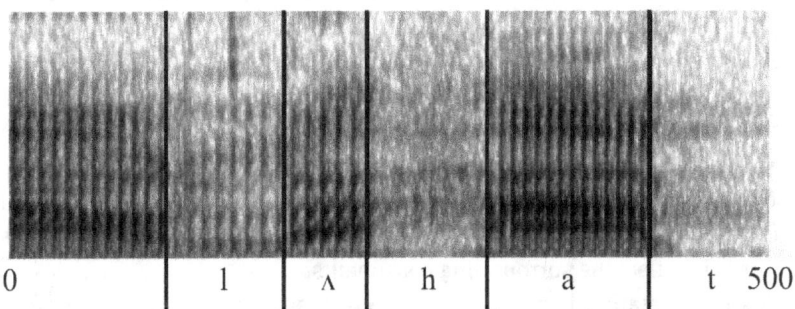

Fig. 17: [Bunong] Purported minor syllable vowel in [lʌ.hat] 'tightly fitting'. Duration in ms.

To compare the durations of these CCVC transitions and C<u>A</u>CVC vowels, a linear regression of transition and vowel durations normalized by the frame sentence was performed. Normalized values were obtained by dividing the duration of the transitions and vowels by the duration of the frame sentence. Results reveal that vowels (n = 248) in C<u>A</u>CVC sequences have a normalized mean of 145ms with a range from 20ms to 318ms. Vocalic transition periods (n = 57) in CCVC sequences have a mean normalized duration of 62ms, with a range from 12ms to 183ms. C<u>A</u>CVC vowels are significantly longer than transition periods in CCVC sequences ($p < 0.0001$), as seen in Figure 18.

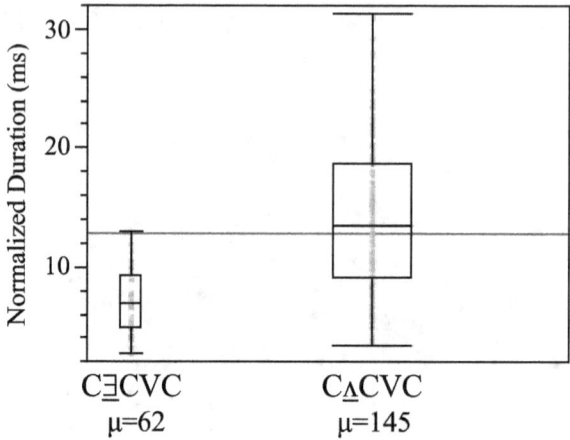

Fig. 18: [Bunong] Normalized durations for CCVC transitions and CᴧCVC vowels

With regard to vowel quality, F2 values are not significantly different between CCVC vocalic transitions and CᴧCVC vowels ($p = 0.9540$), indicating that both have approximately the same amount of backness. F1 values, however, are higher for CᴧCVC vowels than for CCVC vocalic transitions ($p < 0.0001$), as can be seen in Figure 19. Just as in the Khmer data, F1 is lower for the vocalic transition than for the minor syllable vowel. These acoustic results suggest that this is because in the former, the tongue does not lower between consonants since it lacks a gestural target, i.e. the tongue position for CCVC vocalic transitions should directly reflect the surrounding consonants.

If this interpretation is accurate, we might then wonder why in Figure 19 there is a noticeable amount of overlap between the CCVC transitions and the CᴧCVC vowels at lower values of F1. Why are these categories not more separated? In fact, the most overlap between these groups is found in shorter CᴧCVC tokens. As seen in Figure 20, there is a significant correlation between the duration of the CᴧCVC vowel and the value of F1 ($p = 0.0013$, $R^2 = 0.18$). In particular, the longer the vowel, the higher the F1. This suggests that lower F1 values for CᴧCVC are due to insufficient time for complete target attainment. This fact, along with the formant measurements above, suggests that the vocalic transition period present in CCVC sequences is excrescent and should be interpreted as underlap between consonant gestures.

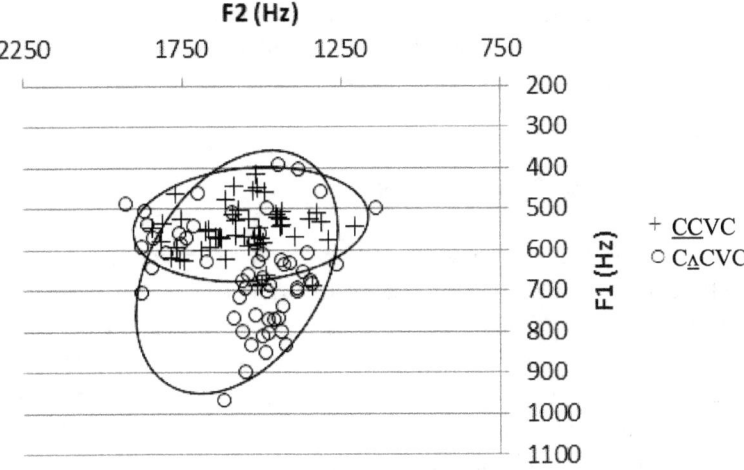

Fig. 19: [Bunong] Formant values for word-initial C̲C̲VC vocalic transitions and CᴀCVC vowels

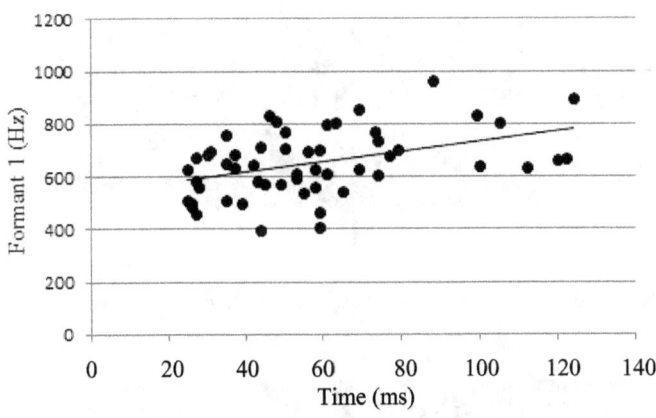

Fig. 20: [Bunong] Correlation between the duration of the CᴀCVC vowel and F1

In summary, Bunong clusters have transition states which should be interpreted as underlap although the environments in which underlap is found are far fewer than in Khmer, in turn because Khmer contains far more consonant clusters than does Bunong. In addition, duration and formant measurements suggest that underlap in Bunong is both quantitatively and qualitatively different from the purported minor syllable vowel nucleus, i.e. C̬ACVC.

3.3.2 Comparison of C̬ACVC vowels with CV̬C vowels

Having established that unstressed C̬ACVC vowels are durationally and qualitatively different from CC̬VC transitions, we can now evaluate them in light of underlying vowels in CVC monosyllables. In Bunong, C̬ACVC vowels have been claimed to be underlyingly /a/, and are written as such in the orthography (Phaen et al. 2012). However, impressionistically, they are in most cases pronounced in a more centralized way. Therefore, in the following analysis, they are compared to the vowels of both CʌC and CaC monosyllables. Examples of C̬ACVC, CʌC and CaC are given in Figure 21, Figure 22 and Figure 23, respectively.

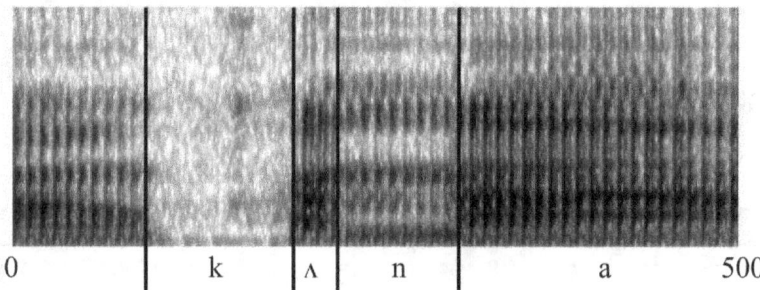

Fig. 21: [Bunong] Purported minor syllable vowel in [kʌna:r] 'wing'. Duration in ms.

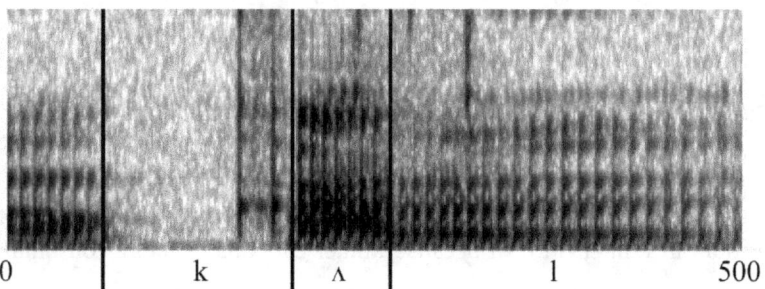

Fig. 22: [Bunong] Underlying /ʌ/ in [kʌl] 'big turtle'. Duration in ms.

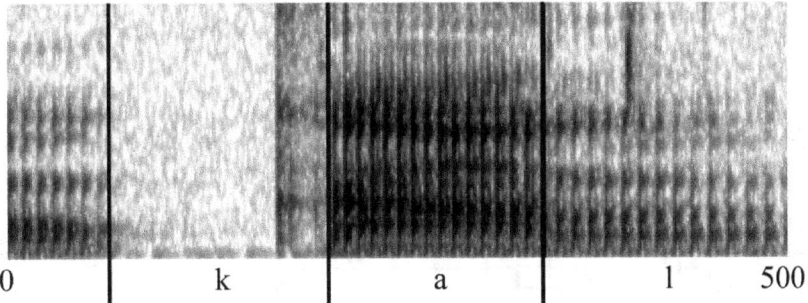

Fig. 23: [Bunong] Underlying /a/ in [kal̪] 'chop'. Duration in ms.

Because C₄CVC vowels are unstressed and are found in disyllabic words while CVC vowels are stressed, we expect the latter to be longer than the former, and indeed they are. Both CaC and CʌC vowels are significantly longer than C₄CVC vowels ($p < 0.0001$), and CaC vowels are actually significantly longer still than CʌC vowels ($p < 0.0001$), as seen in Figure 24, which is not unexpected given the correlation between duration and vowel height. However, duration alone does not allow us to draw conclusions about the status of these vowels since many factors are known to greatly influence vowel duration (Klatt 1973, 1976).

Formant values, however, are more telling. Just as was the case for unstressed C₄CVC vowels and CCVC transitions, there is no significant difference in F2 among any of the categories tested here. As Figure 25 shows, the C₄CVC vowel as well as /a/ and stressed /ʌ/ are central. However, the distribution of C₄CVC is noticeably wider than either /a/ or stressed /ʌ/. This is likely a result of its short duration, which prevents it from being able to fully reach its gestural target and which also makes it more susceptible to influence from neighbouring sounds. Indeed, Figure 26 shows that all the more peripheral C₄CVC vowels, i.e. those that lie outside the F2 range of stressed /ʌ/, which is approximately 1350Hz – 1800Hz, have a duration less than 56ms, with one exception.

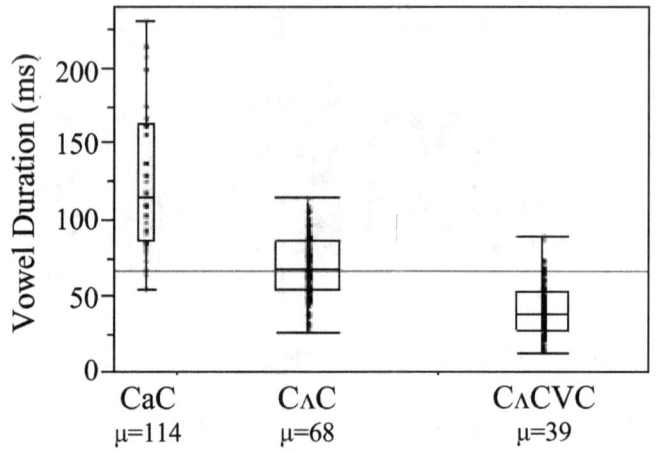

Fig. 24: [Bunong] Vowel durations for CaC, CᴧC and CᴧCVC vowels

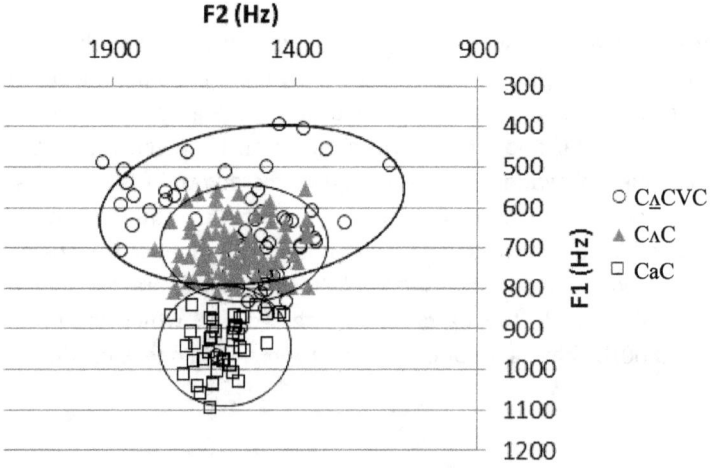

Fig. 25: [Bunong] Formant values for CᴧCVC, CᴧC and CaC vowels

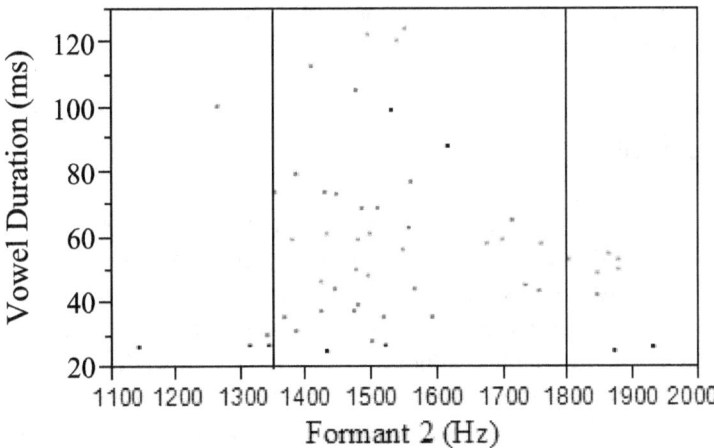

Fig. 26: [Bunong] F2 by Vowel Duration for CᴀCVC vowels

F1 differs significantly between each of the three types. As expected, /a/ has a higher F1 than stressed /ʌ/ ($p < 0.0001$). In addition, despite the substantial amount of overlap seen in Figure 25, the CᴀCVC vowel has a significantly lower F1 than stressed /ʌ/ ($p = 0.0036$). Therefore, the phonetic realization of this unstressed vowel is certainly not [a], and although it may be /a/ underlyingly, it is realized as something much closer to stressed [ʌ]. Still, the difference in F1 between stressed /ʌ/ and CᴀCVC is unexpected if both unstressed and stressed /ʌ/ have the same gestural target. However, this difference is actually neutralized in slow speech, suggesting that the longer speakers take to produce unstressed /ʌ/, the more similar to stressed /ʌ/ it becomes, and as was demonstrated in Figure 20, F1 is inversely correlated with speech rate. Indeed, the average duration for CᴀCVC vowels whose F1 is equal to or less than 550Hz is 42ms, while the average duration for CᴀCVC vowels whose F1 is greater than 550Hz is 62ms.

In sum, results suggest that the unstressed CᴀCVC vowel is quantitatively distinct from the stressed nuclei of monosyllables but qualitatively quite similar. First, CᴀCVC is durationally shorter than CaC and CᴀC, which is expected given the effects of stress on duration (cf. Lehiste and Peterson 1959, Liberman 1960). Next, although it has a more widely distributed F2 and a lower F1 than either /a/ or stressed /ʌ/, these differences are speculatively due to a shortened duration, which prevents the tongue from fully reaching its gestural target. These results suggest that what have been considered minor syllable vowels in

Bunong have an associated gesture, as opposed to the underlap in word-initial consonant clusters, which does not.

3.4 Discussion

The results indicate several properties of purported minor syllables in Bunong. First, Bunong C$_\Delta$CVC vowels are distinct from underlap. In this way, Bunong minor syllables differ from Khmer "minor syllables", which, as I have established previously, should not actually be considered syllables. When compared to nuclei of CVC monosyllables, Bunong C$_\Delta$CVC vowels are yet again distinct. Not only are they shorter than monosyllabic nuclei, they often have a greater distribution in their acoustic realizations, which is likely due to their shorter duration, which in turn correlates with their lack of stress. These results, considered together, suggest that Bunong minor syllables are indeed syllables that are unstressed.

This conclusion supports the hypothesis that word types which are commonly called sesquisyllables are in fact disyllabic iambs. Under this interpretation, the reduced segmental inventory as well as the weight restrictions on minor syllables are expected properties of the weak initial syllables that are characteristic of iambs (Hayes 1995). Therefore, I conclude that purported minor syllables in Bunong indeed have phonological nuclei and therefore Bunong has a set of words which are maximally disyllabic iambs, i.e. sesquisyllables

4 Conclusion

The phonetic experiments in Sections 2 and 3 have demonstrated that the term *sesquisyllable* has been interpreted broadly and has been used to describe a number of structurally distinct word types including both monosyllables with voiced excrescent transitions and iambic disyllables. I have proposed that the scope of the term be narrowed to describe only non-iterative disyllabic iambs like those found in Bunong. And while the gestural representations of these two types of words – monosyllables and disyllables – distinctly differ, a comparison of the two provides a partial explanation as to why so many different types of words have been called sesquisyllables.

Because minor syllables are noted for their supposed instability (Sidwell 2000; Brunelle and Pittayaporn 2012, *inter alia*), it is useful to understand how their phonological representations as gestures can change over time. For example, based on data from related South Bahnaric languages, it is fairly well accepted that at least some Bunong minor syllables were formed as part of a reduction of prefixed derivational morphology (Sidwell 2000). This may explain in part the somewhat skewed inventory of consonants that occur in the onset position of minor syllables, i.e. /p, p^h, c^h, k, r, l/. If these are remnants of morphemes, the lack of other consonants in this position, e.g. /t/, is less surprising than if motivated purely on phonological grounds.

If the change from disyllables to monosyllables (with an assumed intermediate step of sesquisyllables) is due to a process of deletion, it is important to understand what that process looks like in terms of articulation. Browman and Goldstein (1990; 360) suggest that what are often thought of as categorical deletions in fast speech are actually not deletions at all: "In faster, casual speech, we expect gestures to show decreased magnitudes (in both space and time) and to show increasing temporal overlap. We hypothesize that the types of casual speech alternations observed (segment insertions, deletions, assimilations and weakenings) are consequences of these two kinds of variation in the gestural score." In other words, it is quite often the case that "deletions" are not actually deletions but are just a matter of a particular gesture being obscured by gestures on other tiers. For example, Browman and Goldstein (1989, 1990) show that the /t/ in 'perfect memory' can be deleted in the sense that it is neither visible on a waveform nor audible in the speech stream, while remaining present in the articulation.

More relevant to the deletion of minor syllables, Davidson (2006) suggests that pre-tonic wedge, which is often thought to be deleted in fast speech in English, is actually not deleted entirely. Although her experiment is not articulatory, the results suggest that "acoustic residue," e.g. longer consonant durations or aspiration of stops in fricative-stop clusters, indicates that the wedge gesture is not deleted entirely. Instead, some effects of the wedge gesture are still observable. Davidson concludes that this type of "deletion" is more consistent with an overlap account than an account in which rules only apply in fast speech. Nonetheless, Browman and Goldstein (1989) do acknowledge that it is possible for gestures to be deleted entirely. Indeed, we assume this is often the case when sesquisyllables become monosyllables. In particular, one generation of speakers may hide a gesture to such an extent that subsequent generations re-interpret the utterance omitting the hidden gesture altogether.

To summarize, I have presented a concrete definition of the sesquisyllable as a disyllabic word and proposed that monosyllables with excrescent vocoids are not sesquisyllables. However, the perceptual distance between an excrescent transition state and a reduced vowel with an underlying and partially obscured gesture is not nearly so unambiguous. I suggest that this perceptual grey area is what has contributed to the wide variation in the definition of the sesquisyllable. In addition, Pittayaporn (this volume) further explores the cross-linguistic variation in the conceptualization of sesquisyllables, especially regarding sonority and syllabification. As a consequence of these many ambiguities, the role of the sesquisyllable as a characteristic feature of Southeast Asian languages should be thoughtfully reconsidered.

References

Allen, S. 1953. *Phonetics in ancient India*. London: Oxford University Press.
Bennett, J. F. 1995. *Metrical foot structure in Thai and Kayah Li: Optimality-theoretic studies in the prosody of two Southeast Asian languages*. Urbana-Champaign: University of Illinois dissertation.
Boersma, P. & D. Weenink. 2012. *Praat: doing phonetics by computer*. www.praat.org (accessed 20 June 2012).
Bequette, R. 2008. *Participant reference, deixis, and anaphora in Bunong narrative discourse*. Duncanville, TX: Graduate Institute of Applied Linguistics MA Thesis.
Browman, C. & L. Goldstein. 1986. Towards an articulatory phonology. In C. Ewen & J. Anderson (eds.), *Phonology Yearbook 3*, 219–252.
Browman, C. & L. Goldstein. 1989. Articulatory gestures as phonological units. *Phonology 6*. 201–251.
Browman, C. & L. Goldstein. 1990. Tiers in articulatory phonology, with some implications for casual speech. In J. Kingston & M. Beckman (eds.), *Papers in laboratory phonology I: Between the grammar and physics of speech*, 341–376. Cambridge: Cambridge University Press.
Browman, C. & Goldstein, L. 1992. Articulatory phonology: An overview. *Haskins Laboratories Status Report on Speech Research*.
Brunelle, M. & P. Pittayaporn. 2012. Phonologically-constrained change: The role of the foot in monosyllabization and rhythmic shifts in Mainland Southeast Asia. *Diachronica* 29(4). 411–433.
Burenhult, N. 2001. Jahai phonology: A preliminary survey. *Mon-Khmer Studies* 31. 29–45.
Butler, B. 2014. *Deconstructing the Southeast Asian sesquisyllable: A gestural account*. Ithaca, NY: Cornell University dissertation.
Clements, G. N. 1990. The role of the sonority cycle in core syllabification. In J. Kingston & M. Beckman (eds.), *Papers in laboratory phonology 1: Between the grammar and the physics of speech*, 283–333. Cambridge: Cambridge University Press.
Clements, G. N. & S. J. Keyser. 1981. *A three-tiered theory of the syllable* (Occasional Paper No. 19). Cambridge, MA: MIT, Center for Cognitive Science.
Clements, G. N. & S. J. Keyser. 1983. *CV phonology: A generative theory of the syllable*. Cambridge: MIT Press.
Davidson, L. 2006. Schwa elision in fast speech: segmental deletion or gestural overlap? *Phonetica* 63. 79–112.

Diffloth, G. 1976. Minor-syllable vocalism in Senoic languages. In Philip N. Jenner, Laurence C. Thompson & Stanley Starosta (eds.), *Austroasiatic Studies, Part 1* (Oceanic Linguistics Special Publications No. 13), 229–247. Honolulu: University of Hawai'i Press.

Diffloth, G. & N. Zide. 1992. Austro-Asiatic languages. In W. Bright (ed.), *International encyclopedia of linguistics* (vol. 1), 137–142 New York: Oxford University Press.

Enfield, N. J. 2005. Areal linguistics and mainland Southeast Asia. *Annual Review of Anthropology* 34, 181–206.

Fleischhacker, H. 2001. Cluster-dependent epenthesis asymmetries. In A. Albright & T. Cho (eds.), *Papers in phonology* 5 (UCLA Working Papers in Linguistics 7), 71–116. Los Angeles, CA: UCLA.

Green, A. 2005. Word, foot, and syllable structure in Burmese. In J. Watkins (ed.), *Studies in Burmese Linguistics*, 1–25. Canberra: Pacific Linguistics.

Hall, N. 2011. Vowel epenthesis. In M. van Oostendorp, C. Ewen, E. Hume & K. Rice (eds.), *The Blackwell companion to phonology*, 1576–1596. Chichester: Wiley-Blackwell.

Harms, R. T. 1976. The segmentalization of Finnish "nonrules". In R. Harms & F. Karttunen (eds.), *Papers from the transatlantic Finnish conference* (Texas Linguistics Forum 5), 73–88. Austin: University of Texas.

Haupers, R. 1969. Stieng phonemes. *Mon-Khmer Studies* 3. 131–137.

Hayes, B. 1995. *Metrical stress theory: Principles and case studies*. Chicago: University of Chicago Press.

Henderson, E. J. A. 1952. The main features of Cambodian pronunciation. *Bulletin of the School of Oriental and African Studies* 14(1). 149–174.

Huffman, F. 1972. The boundary between the monosyllable and the disyllable in Cambodian. *Lingua* 29. 54–66.

Hyman, L. 2009. How (not) to do phonological typology: The case of pitch-accent. *Language Sciences* 31(2-3). 213–238.

Itô, J. 1989. A prosodic theory of epenthesis. *Natural Language & Linguistic Theory* 7(2). 217–260.

Itô, J. & A. Mester. 2004. The phonological lexicon. In J. J. McCarthy (ed.), *Optimality theory in phonology: A reader*, 552–568. Malden, MA: Blackwell.

Jannedy, S. 1994. Rate effects on German unstressed syllables. *Ohio State University Working Papers in Linguistics* 44, 105–124.

Keyser, S. J. & P. Kiparsky. 1984. Syllable structure in Finnish phonology. In M. Aronoff & R. Oehrle (eds.), *Language sound structures*, 7–31. Cambridge, MA: MIT Press.

Kirby, J. 2014. Incipient tonogenesis in Phnom Penh Khmer: Acoustic and perceptual studies. *Journal of Phonetics* 43. 69–85.

Klatt, D. H. 1973. Interaction between two factors that influence vowel duration. *Journal of the Acoustical Society of America* 54(4). 1102–1104.

Klatt, D. H. 1976. Linguistic uses of segmental duration in English: Acoustic and perceptual evidence. *Journal of the Acoustical Society of America* 59(5). 1208–1221.

Ladefoged, P. & I. Maddieson. 1996. *The sounds of the world's Languages*. Malden, MA: Blackwell.

Larish, M. 1999. *The position of Moken and Moklen within the Austronesian language family*. Manoa: University of Hawai'i dissertation.

Lehiste, I. & G. E. Peterson. 1959. Vowel amplitudes and phonemic stress in American English. *Journal of the Acoustical Society of America* 31(4). 428–435.

Lewis, M. P., G. Simons & C. Fennig (eds.). 2013. *Ethnologue: Languages of the world* (17th ed.). Dallas, TX: SIL International. Retrieved from http://www.ethnologue.com/ (accessed 14 February 2013).

Liberman, P. 1960. Some acoustic correlates of word stress in American English. *Journal of the Acoustical Society of America* 32(4). 451–454.

Maier, J. 1969. Cua phonemes. *Mon-Khmer Studies* 3. 9–19.

Mascaró, J. 2004. External allomorphy as emergence of the unmarked. In J. McCarthy (ed.), *Optimality theory in phonology: A reader*. Malden, MA: Blackwell.

Matisoff, J. 1973. Tonogenesis in Southeast Asia. In L. M. Hyman, (ed.), *Consonant types and tone* (Southern California Occasional Papers in Linguistics 1), 71–96. Los Angeles: University of Southern California.

Matisoff, J. 1990. Bulging monosyllables: Areal tendencies in Southeast Asian diachrony. In K. Hall (ed.), *Proceedings of the 16th Annual Meeting of the Berkeley Linguistics Society*, 543–559.

Matisoff, J. 2003. *Handbook of Proto-Tibeto-Burman: System and philosophy of Sino-Tibetan Reconstruction* (University of California Publications in Linguistics, 135). Berkeley: University of California Press.

Matteson, E. & K. Pike. 1958. Non-phonemic transition vocoids in Piro (Arawak). *Miscellanea Phonetica* 3. 22–30.

McCarthy, J. 2007. Derivations and levels of representation. In P. de Lacy (ed.), *the Cambridge handbook of phonology*, 99–117. Cambridge: Cambridge University Press.

Michaud, A. 2012. Monosyllabicization: Patterns of evolution in Asian languages. In N. Nau, T. Stolz, & C. Stroh (eds.), *Monosyllables: From phonology to typology*, 115–130. Berlin: Akademie Verlag.

Migliazza, B. 2003. So stories: A preliminary analysis of texts in a Mon-Khmer language. *Mon-Khmer Studies* 33. 67–158.

Morey, S. 2005. The tone and syllable structure of Turung. In P. Sidwell (ed.), *Papers from the 15th Annual Meeting of the Southeast Asian Linguistics Society* (Vol. XV), 149–168. Canberra: Pacific Linguistics.

Phaen, T., M. Sok & T. Bequette. 2012. *Bunong-Khmer bilingual dictionary*. Mondulkiri Province, Cambodia: International Cooperation Cambodia, READ Project.

Phillips, R. 1973. Mnong vowel variations with initial stops. *Mon-Khmer Studies* 4. 119–127.

Prince, A. 1984. Phonology with tiers. In M. Aronoff & R. Oehrle (eds.), *Language sound structures*, 234–244. Cambridge: MIT Press.

Ridouane, R. & C. Fougeron. 2011. Schwa elements in Tashlhiyt word-initial clusters. *Laboratory Phonology* 2(2). 275–300.

Saltzman, E. & J. A. S. Kelso. 1987. Skilled actions: A task dynamic approach. *Psychological Review* 94. 84–106.

Shaw, P. 1994. The prosodic constituency of minor syllables. In E. Duncan, D. Farkas & P. Spaelti (eds.), *The Proceedings of the 12th West Coast Conference on Formal Linguistics*, 117–132.

Sidwell, P. 2000. *Proto South Bahnaric: A reconstruction of a Mon-Khmer language of Indo-China*. Canberra: Pacific Linguistics.

Silverman, D. 2011. Schwa. In M. van Oostendorp, C. Ewen, E. Hume & K. Rice (eds.), *The Blackwell Companion to Phonology*, 628–642. Malden, MA: Blackwell.

Svantesson, J. O. 1983. *Kammu phonology and morphology*. Lund: CWK Gleerup.

Svantesson, J. O. & A. M. Karlsson 2004. Minor syllable tones in Kammu. In Bernard Bel & Isabelle Marlien (eds.), *International Symposium on Tonal Aspects of Languages: With Emphasis on Tone Languages*, 177–180. Lund: Lund University.
Thomas, D. 1992. On sesquisyllabic structure. *Mon-Khmer Studies* 21. 206–210.
Thurgood, G. 1999. *From Ancient Cham to modern dialects: Two thousand years of language contact and change.* Honolulu: University of Hawai'i Press.
Vogel, S. & J. M. Filippi. 2006. *Elements de langue Phnong.* Phnom Penh: Editions Funan.
Watson, R. 1964. Pacoh phonemes. *Mon-Khmer Studies* 1. 135–148.

Pittayawat Pittayaporn
Typologizing sesquisyllabicity

The role of structural analysis in the study of linguistic diversity in Mainland Southeast Asia

1 Introduction

Mainland Southeast Asia (MSEA), roughly comprising Laos, Vietnam, Cambodia, Thailand, Myanmar, northeast India, southern China, and peninsular Malaysia, has long been recognized as a linguistic area. In terms of linguistic diversity, it is an area with high phylogenetic diversity but very low structural diversity (Enfield 2011). With respect to phonology, structural traits often cited as common across language families include complex vowel systems, a restricted set of final consonants, contrastive tones and registers, among others (Comrie 2007; Enfield 2011; Matisoff 2001). Despite the tremendous amount of fieldwork that has been carried out, the areality of these traits is still poorly understood.

A pertinent example is sesquisyllabicity. The type of prosodic words commonly known in the literature on MSEA today as sesquisyllables have been recognized as deserving special attention at least since the 1950's. Henderson (1952) describes a class of Khmer monosyllables as having extended onsets, e.g. [pʰdeːk] 'to put to bed' and [psaɣm] 'to wet', and a class of disyllables as consisting of a "minor syllable" followed by a "major syllable," e.g. [bɔŋkaɣt] 'to produce' and [tùmlɛ̀ək] 'to fell'.[1] Note that Henderson (1952: 170) marks the vowel of the minor syllable with an underline perhaps to indicate that its qualities are not contrastive but predictable from the onset and the register.[2] Similarly, Shorto (1960: 545) describes Palaung disyllables as consisting of a minor syllable followed by a major syllable, e.g. [kᵊrtaʔ] 'tongue' and [rᵊnpo] 'to dream'. Crucially, he states that the minor syllable has "no vowel other than an anaptyc-

---

[1] Henderson (1952) does not consider the first consonant of an extended onset a minor syllable. Butler (this volume: 1-11) provides a comprehensive summary of the evolution and variation of the term of "minor syllable."
[2] Henderson (1952) marks nucleus of syllables with second register with a grave accent (`).

tic one."[3] However, it was Matisoff (1973: 86) in a paper on tonogenesis, who coined the term "sesquisyllable" to refer to words that were "a syllable and a half" long. He also cited as examples Khmer words that Henderson would call monosyllables with extended onsets, e.g. [psaː] 'market' and [kŋaok] 'peacock'.

Since its coinage, sesquisyllabicity has played an important role in the study of linguistic diversity in MSEA. In synchronic studies, an abundant number of languages from the major language families of the area have been described as having the sesquisyllable as a predominant word type. In addition, sesquisyllables behave differently from their monosyllabic and disyllabic counterparts in many languages of the area, e.g. Kammu (Svantesson 1983) and Jahai (Burenhult 2005). Diachronically, the sesquisyllable has often been claimed to be the intermediate stage in the evolution from disyllables to monosyllables (Brunelle 2008; Brunelle and Pittayaporn 2012; Matisoff 2001; Thurgood 1999). Proto-languages of various language groups have also been reconstructed with sesquisyllabic words, e.g. Proto-Tai (Ferlus 1990; Pittayaporn 2009), Proto-Tibeto-Burman (Matisoff 2003), Old Chinese (Baxter and Sagart, 2014; Handel, 1998). However, it is unclear how this structure differs from disyllables and more crucially monosyllables, and how it came to be a common feature in MSEA. An implicit assumption commonly shared among these studies is that sesquisyllabicity is a unified phenomenon that characterizes MSEA as a linguistic area. In other words, the sesquisyllable is thought to be sufficiently similar structurally across the different languages. However, a survey of languages that are thought to have sesquisyllables reveals a great diversity not detected without theoretically informed structural analysis.

The focus of the study of the MSEA linguistic area has been on documenting and describing the tremendous numbers of languages found in the area while trying to make sense of the typological homogeneity among those languages. In the last few decades the emphasis has thus been on fieldwork, areal typology, and historical linguistics. Taking sesquisyllabicity as a case study, this paper illustrates how a theoretically informed structural analysis can further advance our understanding of linguistic diversity in MSEA. In the broadest sense, a structural analysis is an account of a linguistic phenomenon that pays explicit attention to how units are interrelated within the system, cf. Crystal (1997). In phonology, it addresses how sound elements are organized into sound systems of languages, and how they interact with each other, contrasting with surface description of the inventory cf. Hyman (2007). Even though structural analysis

---

[3] Vowels that are described as anaptyctic or excrescent in the original sources are (re)transcribed as superscripted.

is not necessarily tied to a particular framework, linguistic theory is essential in understanding the structures being analysed.

Crucially, the current paper shows that languages which have been described as sesquisyllabic in the literature in fact differ from each other with respect to at least two crucial aspects. The first is the presence or absence of a complex onset. In other words, different sesquisyllabic languages may or may not allow two consonants in the onsets of their syllables. The second aspect is the contrastivity of sesquisyllabicity, i.e. whether there is a phonological contrast between sesquisyllables and monosyllables with complex onsets in a given language. In other words, languages differ in whether sesquisyllabicity is predictable from the segmental make-up of prosodic words. In phonological theory, these two structural differences are manifestations of cross-linguistic variation in syllabification. According to this proposal, sesquisyllabicity can be viewed as a strategy that MSEA languages use to avoid violating constraints on syllabification. Thus these languages highlight the importance of theoretically informed structural analysis in understanding the linguistic diversity of MSEA.

2 Terminology and transcription

Most studies of Southeast Asian languages that use the term sesquisyllable typically describe the structure as consisting of a reduced first syllable followed by a stressed full syllable. The first syllable is typically called the "minor syllable", and the second one is referred to as the "major syllable." This characterization of prosodic words of this type is too general as it only says that the second syllable is more prominent than the first. What distinguishes sesquisyllables from disyllables and monosyllables is rarely discussed. As noted by Brunelle and Pittayaporn (2012), many authors consider any disyllabic words with a reduced number of phonemic contrasts in initial syllables as sesquisyllables while others only include those whose initial syllables are headed by a neutral vowel or a syllabic consonant. This brief section establishes a working definition of the term "sesquisyllable" as well as the transcription convention to be used in this paper, before proceeding to discuss the structural diversity among sesquisyllabic languages.

At least three definitions of sesquisyllables are found in the literature. The first one considers any disyllabic words with a reduced number of contrasts in initial syllables to be sesquisyllables. For example, Thurgood (1999: 61-62) equates sesquisyllables to disyllables with an iambic stress pattern, thus by implication considering Northern Roglai words such as [uraʔ] 'vein', and [iku] 'tail' as sesquisyllables. Similarly, Solnit (1997: 24-25) considers Kayah Li words beginning with unstressed syllables [ʔi-] and [Cə-] as sesquisyllables, e.g. [ʔícʰē] 'to sell', [ʔipiə] 'narrow', [kədā] 'door', and [təmɔ́] 'sun'. This is in contrast with the second definition, which reserves the term for those words whose initial syllables are headed by a neutral vowel or a syllabic consonant only. For instance, Rischel (1995: 77) describes sesquisyllables in Mlabri as words with a full syllable preceded by a syllable without a full vowel, e.g. [dəkat] 'cold', [rəʔɤk] 'chest', and [kr̩nap] 'song'. Similarly, Svantesson (1983: 27) describes the vowel in Kammu minor syllables as "non-phonemic", e.g. [cəlɔ̀ːŋ] 'boat' and [cʰə́kb̥ɨk] 'expressive for black'. Most restrictive is the third definition, which considers as sesquisyllables only those words whose penultimate syllables consist of one and only one consonant. For example, Burenhult (2005: 30) views [Cə.CVC] words such as [kənɛc] 'comb' and [ɟəlɔʔ] 'hole' as sesquisyllabic, contrasting with [CəC.CVC] words such as [təmkal] 'male' and [ʔəntɛŋ] 'ear', which are considered disyllables phonologically.

Given the terminological confusion, it is necessary to establish a precise working definition of "sesquisyllable." In the current paper, the sesquisyllable is defined as a prosodic word consisting of a full stressed syllable preceded by a consonant or a sequence of consonants. The consonant or consonant sequence must not contain a phonemically contrastive vowel. This definition excludes words whose initial syllables have phonemic non-central vowels such as /i/ and /u/ as well as words with central vowels /ə/ or /ʌ/ that contrast phonologically with other vowels. Therefore, /kawip/ 'sun bear' and /timɔʔ/ 'hard surface' in Jahai (Burenhult, 2005) are not considered sesquisyllables but prototypical disyllables. Similarly, Thai words such as /sapʰaːp³/ 'state' and /supʰaːp³/ 'polite' are not considered sesquisyllables because the vowels in their first syllables are phonologically contrastive.[4]

Note that this working definition is agnostic in two respects. Firstly, it leaves open the possibility that the so-called minor syllables in some languages do not structurally form their own syllables, cf. Henderson's "monosyllables with extended onsets". They may in fact be part of the major syllable. This highlights one crucial difference between this definition and the one adopted by Butler (2014; this volume), who excludes words that are structurally monosylla-

---

[4] Bennett (1995) refers to the initial unstressed syllables in words like /sanuk²/ 'fun' and /kathi²⁴/ 'coconut milk' as minor syllables. However, disyllabic words containing these light syllables are not considered sesquisyllables according to this working definition because the vowels of their initial syllables are phonemically contrastive, e.g. /sapʰaːp³/ 'state' vs. /supʰaːp³/ 'polite', and /nalaːt³/ 'forehead' vs. /niraːt³/ 'poems of separation'. Note that Bennett himself treats these syllables identically to other light syllables in his metrical analysis of Thai.

bles. Secondly, the definition does not claim whether the minor syllable contains a non-contrastive vowel or not. It may contain a phonetic vowel-like transition, or a phonological epenthetic vowel. It may also lack any vocalic element altogether. The nature of the vocalic elements in the minor syllables is studied experimentally in (Butler 2014; this volume).

Given this definition, all minor syllables are (re-)transcribed without a vowel for ease of comparison. In addition, the boundary between the minor syllable and the onset of the major syllable is marked with a stress symbol (') to clearly distinguish monosyllables from sesquisyllables. For example, Thavung [tʰaluaŋ] 'hollow' and [ʔapoː] 'to dream' are transcribed with [a] in the original source (Premsrirat 2004) but would be re-transcribed in this paper as [tʰ'luaŋ] 'hollow' and [ʔ'poː] 'to dream' respectively. Similarly, the Jeh words [tərah] 'squawk' and [trah] 'to chop out' cited in Thomas (1992) would be transcribed here as [t'rah] and [trah], respectively.

3 Sonority-based syllabification

The prosodic word is the phonological domain that roughly corresponds to the morphological word, and is thus the smallest prosodic constituent that can stand alone (Dixon and Aikhenvald 2002; Inkelas 1989; Inkelas and Zec 1988; McCarthy and Prince 1986; Nespor and Vogel 1986). This kind of prosodic constituent is made up of one or more syllables, which serve as the most basic units in the organization of phonological segments. In phonological theory, the grouping of segments into syllables is not prespecified in the underlying representation of the word but derived from a process called syllabification (Clements 1990; Levin 1985; Selkirk 1984; Zec 2007). This general view means that syllabification is not phonologically contrastive but predictable from the segmental make-up of the prosodic words. There are, however, known exceptional cases of unpredictable parsing, e.g. English [ʔáj.da] 'Ida' vs. [ʔa.íj.da] 'Aïda', in which information regarding syllabification must be considered part of the underlying representations of the individual words (Levin 1985).

From this perspective on syllabification, the number of syllables within a given prosodic word is largely determined by the segmental profile of the word. This generalization is believed to be true cross-linguistically and should also apply to sesquisyllables. The observation that sesquisyllabicity is predictable from segment-based principles is not new. Svantesson (1983: 46) states that Kammu sesquisyllabic words are syllabified so that a syllable break is found as close to the left edge of the word as possible and so that the major syllable has one single consonant or one permissible cluster as onset. Similarly, Kruspe (2004: 40) explicitly states that syllable structure is not prespecified in underlying representations but is determined by a syllabification process driven by principles of syllable formation.

Perhaps the most important factor in syllabification is sonority, which can be roughly understood as either relative resonance or prominence of segments. Although its definition is an issue of much debate, sonority seems to be linked at least partly to intensity or loudness (Clements 1990; Parker 2002). Sonority is generally characterized in terms of a hierarchy or scale that arranges segments from less sonorous to more sonorous classes. The sonority hierarchy is crucial with respect to the well-formedness of prosodic words as strings of segments are generally syllabified into syllables according to constraints on the relative sonority of the segments. Many versions of this hierarchy have been proposed (e.g. Hooper 1976; Selkirk 1984; Steriade 1982), but this paper adopts Clements's (1990) proposal given in Figure 1. In this version of the sonority hierarchy, obstruents are the least sonorous and thus have the sonority value of 0. On the opposite end of the scale, glides are the most sonorous among non-syllabic segments and have the sonority value of 3. Being intermediate between the two ends of the scale, nasal and liquid consonants have the sonority values of 1 and 2, respectively.

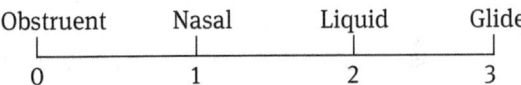

Fig. 1: Sonority scale (based on Clements 1990: 292)

Most relevant to syllabification is the role of relative sonority in determining whether a consonant sequence forms a well-formed complex onset of a syllable or not. Generally speaking, consonant sequences are syllabified according to universal and language-specific principles. Cross-linguistically, permissible consonant clusters are subject to an important constraint, generally known as the Sonority Sequencing Principle (SSP), which states that "in any syllable, there is a segment constituting a sonority peak that is preceded and/or followed by a sequence of segments with progressively decreasing sonority values (Selkirk 1984: 116)." In other words, a given syllable has the lowest sonority at the edges and the highest sonority at the syllabic nucleus.

The importance of SSP is illustrated by the case of Spanish initial clusters in Table 1. Spanish strictly obeys SSP so that all permissible complex onsets consist of a stop followed by a liquid or a glide. For instance, [kl-], [kr-] and [kw-] are well-formed initial clusters as in [klaβe] 'key', [krisis] 'crisis', and [kwota] 'quota'. This is because [k-] has lower sonority than [-l-], [-r-] and [-w-], which are closer to the syllabic nucleus. In contrast, *[lk-], *[rk-], *[wk-], are not allowed because [k-] is less sonorous than [-l-], [-r-], and [-w-], thus violating SSP (Harris 1983; Hualde 1991).

Table 1. Examples of clusters in Spanish

Allowed	Not allowed
[kl-] as in *clave* 'key'	*[lk-]
[kr-] as in *crisis* 'crisis'	*[rk-]
[kw-] as in *cuota* 'quota'	*[wk-]

In addition to SSP, languages may also impose a language-specific minimal sonority distance (MSD) on complex onsets (Levin 1985; Selkirk 1984; Venneman 1972; Zec 2007). The MSD constraint requires that members of complex onsets meet a certain difference in sonority values. As illustrated in Table 2, [kl-] and [kr-] are well-formed onsets in Spanish because the sonority distance between the obstruent [k-] and the following liquids is exactly 2. Similarly, the difference in sonority values between the initial obstruent [k-] and the glide [w-] is 3, exceeding the required minimal sonority distance. On the other hand, *[kt-], *[kn-], and [nl-] are banned even though they do not violate SSP, because the sonority distance within each of the consonant sequences is below 2 (Harris 1983). Note that complex onsets that violate neither SSP nor MSD like [kl-], [kr-] and [kw-] are considered unmarked, contrasting with typologically marked clusters like [kt-], [kn-] and [nl-].

Table 2. Sonority profiles of Spanish clusters

Allowed	Not allowed
[kl-]: $|k(0) - l(2)| = 2$	*[kt-]: $|k(0) - t(0)| = 0$
[kr-]: $|k(0) - r(2)| = 2$	*[kn-]: $|k(0) - n(1)| = 1$
[kw-]: $|k(0) - w(3)| = 3$	*[nl-]: $|n(1) - l(2)| = 1$

The central role of sonority and syllabification in understanding the diversity among sesquisyllabic languages is illustrated by differences in the syllabification of initial consonant sequences in different languages. The following section shows that a sonority-based analysis of initial consonant sequences in MSEA languages helps reveal a great deal of structural diversity among the so-called sesquisyllabic languages of the area.

4 Structural diversity among sesquisyllabic languages

The first attempt at typologizing the structural diversity of sesquisyllables is perhaps Thomas's (1992) classification of sesquisyllabic languages into four types. The most straightforward are type III and type IV. Languages belonging to these two types have phonemically contrastive vowels in their minor syllables. The crucial difference between the two types is the range of vowels that can occur in their minor syllables. Type-III languages allow only a restricted subset of the phonemes from their vowel inventory. For instance, Pacoh may have either /a/, /i/, or /u/ as nuclei of the minor syllables, e.g. /pa.pi/ 'to converse' vs. /ti.nol/ 'post' vs. /ku.cet/ 'die'. In contrast, in type-IV languages nearly all vowels are permitted in the minor syllables. For instance, Kensiw minor syllables can take any vowel except for /ū/ and /ī/.[5] Because their initial syllables contain contrastive vowels, these two types are not considered sesquisyllables according to the working definition adopted. Therefore, they will not be discussed in this paper.

Of vital importance given our working definition of sesquisyllables are type-I and type-II languages. Type I consists of those in which minor syllables do not have contrastive vowels. For instance, Stieng [bᵊnaŋ] '24 hours' phonemically starts with a consonant sequence /bn-/. The short [ᵊ] in the minor syllable is considered a phonetic transition between the two consonants only. In this type of language, there is no phonological contrast between sesquisyllables and monosyllables with complex onsets, i.e. [bᵊnaŋ] does not contrast with [bnaŋ] phonologically. As for type II, sesquisyllables also do not contain contrastive vowels but show a phonological contrast between sesquisyllables and complex monosyllables. For example, Jeh phonologically contrasts [tərah] 'squawk' and [trah] 'to chop out'. Although structural differences among sesquisyllabic languages are recognized in Thomas's classification, this first study of the diversity of sesquisyllabicity does not examine what structural properties or principles underlie the typological differences observed.

This section examines four languages of MSEA representing the diversity among sesquisyllabic languages. It focuses on two structural aspects of sesqui-

---

[5] Thomas (1992), following his source (Duangchan 1984), distinguishes between the presyllable and the minor syllable (see Section 2). He states that the presyllable can only take /ə/ but the minor syllable may take any vowel except /ə, ū, ī/. In the current paper, the two types of non-major syllables are tentatively grouped as one category.

syllabicity, namely onset complexity, and contrastivity of sesquisyllabicity. With respect to onset complexity, Kammu, Khmer, and Turung represent languages that allow complex onsets at the phonological level. In contrast, Jahai represents those that do not. With respect to the contrastivity of sesquisyllabicity, Khmer, Jahai, and Turung represent languages in which sesquisyllabicity is predictable from the make-up of the initial consonant sequences.[6] In contrast, Kammu represents languages that have a phonological contrast between sesquisyllables and monosyllables with complex onsets.

4.1 Jahai

Jahai belongs to the Aslian branch of the Austroasiatic family. It is spoken by approximately 9,000 people in the north of peninsular Malaysia (Burenhult 2005: 4-6). The following discussion is based on the description by Burenhult (2005). It is an example of a sesquisyllabic language in which sesquisyllabicity is not contrastive and complex onsets are not allowed. In other words, a word beginning with an underlying consonant sequence is always realized as a sesquisyllable in Jahai.

In terms of word size, a Jahai prosodic word may be monosyllabic, sesquisyllabic, disyllabic or trisyllabic. Most crucial is the fact that monosyllables and sesquisyllables behave differently in morphological processes. For example, the causative affix is realized as a prefix [pr-] or an infix [-ri-] depending on the shape of the stem. It occurs as [pr-][7] when the stem is monosyllabic, e.g. [pr'lɔj] 'to cause to run' from [lɔj] 'to run' and [pr'gej] 'to feed' from [gej] 'to eat'. In contrast, it appears as an infix [-ri-] when added to sesquisyllables, e.g. [kˌri'bis] 'to kill' from [k'bis] 'die' and [bˌri'kɨt] 'to heat' from [b'kɨt] 'hot'. Another example is the reciprocal formation, which occurs either as a prefix [Ca-][8] or an infix [-a-]. The prefixal variant [Ca-] is attached to monosyllabic bases yielding disyllabic derived words, e.g. [ca'cɔl] 'to tell each other' from [cɔl] 'to tell', and [gagej] 'to eat together' from [gej] 'to eat'. In contrast, the infix variant [-a-] occurs when the base is sesquisyllabic, e.g. [ba'dil] 'to shoot each other' from [b'dil] 'to

---

6 While sesquisyllabicity in these three languages seems to be merely a phonetic phenomenon, in languages like Bunong and Burmese it seems to be phonological. Whether sesquisyllabicity in a given language is phonetic or phonological seems to depend on the status of the vocalic element in the minor syllables. See Butler (2014; this volume) for a detailed and explicit discussion.
7 The sonorant [r] is the nucleus of the syllable.
8 The C- here represents a reduplicated consonant.

shoot', and [ʔaˈnaj] 'to bathe each other' from [ʔˈnaj] 'to bathe'. These morphological alternations clearly show that the phonological structures of sesquisyllables and monosyllables in Jahai are different.

Unlike in the majority of languages in other branches of the Austroasiatic family, Jahai syllables only allow simple onsets. All initial CC- sequences are thus syllabified into minor syllables followed by simple onsets of major syllables such as those shown in Table 3.

Table 3. Examples of minor syllables plus major syllable onsets in Jahai

Not allowed	Allowed	Examples
*[bl-]	[bˈl-]	[bˈləh] 'to enter'
*[pr-]	[pˈr-]	[pˈraʔ] 'to reside'
*[kw-]	[kˈw-]	[kˈwal] 'white-rumped shama'
*[lg-]	[lˈg-]	[lˈget] 'mountain pass'
*[kt-]	[kˈt-]	[kˈtit] 'egg'

That no complex onsets are allowed in this language indicates that SSP and MSD do not play a role in the phonotactics of Jahai. Not only are clusters that violate SSP like *[lg-] and *[kt-] banned, even typologically unmarked clusters like *[bl-] and *[pr-] that do not violate SSP are also disallowed. Similarly, the total absence of clusters including those with the greatest possible sonority distance like *[kw-] means that MSD is irrelevant to the well-formedness of the prosodic word. Not only does the fact that complex onsets are disallowed in Jahai indicate the irrelevance of the sonority constraints, it also shows that sesquisyllabicity is not a contrastive property used to distinguish lexical items but is completely predictable from the combination of consonants in the initial consonant clusters.

In summary, CC- sequences in Jahai are always treated as sesquisyllabic regardless of their sonority profiles. Word size is predictable simply from the number of consonants in the word-initial position. This indicates that sesquisyllables and monosyllables are not underlyingly contrastive, although paradoxically they are phonologically distinguished with respect to morphological processes. This apparent discrepancy is in fact explainable by the idea that derivational processes may manipulate prosodic constituents rather than unsyllabified strings of segments (McCarthy and Prince 1986).

4.2 Khmer

Khmer, or Cambodian, is another MSEA language whose sesquisyllabicity is not contrastive. However, unlike Jahai, it allows monosyllabic words with complex onsets. The language belongs to the Khmeric branch of the Austroasiatic family. It is spoken in Cambodia as well as adjacent areas in Thailand and Vietnam. The current account is based on the description by Huffman (1972) and also by Henderson (1952).

According to Huffman (1972), Khmer monosyllables and disyllables are difficult to distinguish because the phonetic juncture between the two consonants of a complex onset is so "loose" that it approaches the reduced vowels in disyllables. At one end of the continuum are simple monosyllables, which begin with a single consonant, e.g. [tuːk] 'boat', [kou] 'to stir', and [kon] 'film'. At the other end are true disyllables whose first-syllable vowels can be pronounced full or reduced, e.g. [kɑkaːj]~[kəkaːj] 'to scratch', [prɑkan]~[prəkan] 'to maintain', and [bɑŋkaət]~[bəŋkaət] 'to originate'. In between these two classes are what Huffman calls "complex monosyllables." This class is characterized by words beginning with any sequence of two consonants, e.g. [pʰliən] 'rain', [pʰtĕəh] 'door', and [psaː] 'market'. It is words belonging to this intermediate category that are considered sesquisyllables in the areal literature. Crucially, Matisoff (1973) cites Khmer complex monosyllables [psaː] 'market' and [kŋaok] 'peacock' as examples when he first introduces the concept of "sesquisyllables."

Despite their phonetic similarity, true disyllables and these so-called complex monosyllables behave phonologically quite differently. While the vowel of the initial syllable of a disyllabic word is expandable in careful speech, the transition between the two consonants in the onset of a complex monosyllable is always phonetically weak. For example, the Khmer disyllabic word for 'to make a stew' is pronounced as [səlɑː] in rapid speech but [sɑmlɑː] or [səmlɑː] in careful speech, contrasting with its monosyllabic counterpart 'stew', which is always pronounced as [sᵊlɑː]. The disyllable and the complex monosyllable can be phonemically transcribed as /sɑmlɑː/ and / sᵊlɑː/ respectively. The minimal pairs illustrate the contrast in Table 4.

Table 4. Khmer disyllables and complex monosyllables in careful and rapid speech

	Phonemic representation	Careful speech	Rapid speech
disyllables	/ʔamnaoj/ 'gift'	[ʔamnaoj]~[ʔəmnaoj]	[mənaoj]
	/samlaː/ 'to make a stew'	[samlaː]~[səmlaː]	[səlaː]
	/pratĕəh/ 'to meet'	[pratĕəh]~[prətĕəh]	[pətĕəh]
complex monosyl-	/mnŏəh/ 'pineapple'		[mᵊnŏəh]
lables	/slaː/ 'stew'		[sᵊlaː]
	/ptĕəh/ 'house'		[pʰtĕəh]

The most important question is whether Huffman's complex monosyllables are indeed structurally monosyllabic. A closer examination reveals that prosodic words starting with CC- sequences cannot be meaningfully divided into monosyllables and sesquisyllables. Rather, they are best classified according to the type of transition that comes between their two elements as summarized in Table 5. Note that many surface aspirated stops are in fact phonologically clusters, e.g., /kh/, /ch-/, /ph-/. This analysis is supported by infixation patterns like /kamhɤŋ/ 'anger' from /khɤŋ/ 'angry' (Huffmann 1972; Jacob 1993; Minegishi 2006; Schiller 1994). Crucially, the /-h-/ is phonetically different from the aspirated transition [ʰ], cf. Kirby (2013).

Table 5. Transitions in CC- sequences in Khmer (based on Huffmann, 1972)

		-C₂-																
		p	t	c	k	ʔ	b	d	m	n	ɲ	ŋ	w	j	l	r	s	h
C₁-	p		h	h	h	ə		ə	h	h	h		h	h		Ø	Ø	Ø
	t	h			h	ə		ə	h	h	h		h	h	h	Ø		Ø
	c	h			h	ə	ə	ə	h	h			h	h		Ø		Ø
	k	h	h	h		ə	ə	ə	h	h	h	ə		h	h	Ø	Ø	Ø
	ʔ												ə					
	s	h	h		h	ə	ə	ə	h	h	h	h			h	h		
	m		ə	ə		ə			ə			ə			ə	ə	ə	ə
	l	ə		ə	ə	ə			ə		ə	ə						ə

The first type of CC- sequence is characterized by a voiceless stop [p], [t], [c], or [k] followed by [r], [s], and [h] linked by a relatively close juncture between the two consonants, e.g. [khəŋ] 'angry', [trəj] 'fish' and [psaː] 'market'. In contrast, CC- sequences in the second type consist of a voiceless stop followed by either another voiceless stop or a sonorant other than [r], with the exception of

[k]+[ŋ]. The transition between the two consonants is best described as a slight aspiration, e.g. [pʰliən] 'rain', [kʰmæe] 'Khmer' and [pʰtĕəh:] 'door'. The last type of CC- sequence in Khmer consists of any sequence other than those in the first two groups. They are characterized by having a weak vocalic transition between the two consonants, e.g. [kᵊba:l] 'head', [sᵊdaəŋ] 'thin', [lᵊbæeŋ] 'game', and [kᵊŋa:n] 'goose'.

This distribution of Khmer CC- sequences is hard to reconcile with the monosyllable/sesquisyllable distinction. Both the first and second types consist of both prosodic words that are canonical monosyllables, e.g. [trəj] 'fish' and [pʰliən] 'rain', and those that have been considered sesquisyllables by other linguists, [psa:] 'market' and [pʰtĕəh:] 'door'. Although the presence of a vocalic element between the consonants in words of the third type makes them impressionistically like (half-)syllables with a distinct vowel, Butler (2014; this volume; to appear), however, argues based on an acoustical study that the vocalic transition found between the two is best characterized as a result of gestural underlap between two consonants. These distributional facts thus indicate that the distinction between monosyllables and sesquisyllables is not a phonological property of Khmer, but a mere phonetic phenomenon. Therefore, all prosodic words with initial CC- sequences are syllabified as monosyllables, albeit with typologically marked clusters e.g. [pt-]. In other words, Khmer monosyllables with complex onsets and sesquisyllables are structurally indistinguishable, in contrast to the case of Jahai.

In any case, it is clear that sesquisyllabicity is not contrastive in Khmer but predictable from the composition of the consonant sequences. A question remains, however, whether sonority plays a role in syllabification in Khmer. If prosodic words showing the three types of initial consonant sequences are all structurally monosyllabic as Henderson (1952) and Huffman (1972) claim, sonority must also be considered irrelevant to Khmer syllabification. More importantly, this claim entails that the units typically referred to as minor syllables, in fact, are not syllables structurally. In summary, Khmer is a good example of a sesquisyllabic language that does not contrast between monosyllables with complex onsets and sesquisyllables phonologically, but allows initial clusters as onset of monosyllabic words.

4.3 Turung

Spoken in northeast India, the Turung language belongs to the Northern Naga branch of the Sino-Tibetan family. This variety of Singpho is another example of languages that allow monosyllabic words with complex onsets but do not have a phonological contrast between such monosyllables and sesquisyllables. Unlike Khmer, however, its sesquisyllabicity is subject to the sonority constraints, i.e. SSP and MSD. Whether a prosodic word with an initial CC- sequence is syllabified as monosyllabic or sesquisyllabic depends on the sonority profile of the sequence. The following discussion is based on the description by Morey (2010).

In Turung, monosyllables and sesquisyllables co-exist. Monosyllabic prosodic words can be either simple or complex. Complex monosyllables can only occur with medial [-r-]. In other words, complex onsets must have a rising sonority profile and show a sonority distance of 2. This means that Turung strictly respects the SSP and imposes an MSD requirement on its complex onsets. It is important to note that non-sonority constraints are also active in this language. For example, clusters with [-l-] and [-w-] are not allowed even though they do not violate the constraints. Attested complex onsets in Turung are given in Table 6.

Table 6. Complex onsets in Turung monosyllables

	voiceless	aspirated	velar
labial	pru:³ 'to come out'	pʰro:ŋ² 'white'	braʔ³ 'to divorce'
	prat³ 'time'	pʰraŋ² 'to wake'	brep³ 'to kill'
velar	kra:¹ 'hair'	kʰriŋ² 'to stay'	grai³ 'very'
		kʰrat¹ 'to fall'	grum³ 'to help'

In contrast to monosyllables, CC- sequences that make up sesquisyllabic structures are characterized by violations of SSP or MSD. In addition, sequences with [-l-], [-w-], and [-j-] as second members are also syllabified as sesquisyllabic even though they do not violate the sonority constraints. The presence of these sequences and the absence of their monosyllabic counterparts reinforce the conclusion that sesquisyllabicity is not phonologically contrastive in Turung. This view is further supported by the phonetic realization of sesquisyllables. In this language, words classified as sesquisyllables may be phonetically realized 1) as a single syllable with an initial cluster, 2) with a schwa in the minor syllable, or 3) with the vowel of the minor syllable identical to that of the major syllable. It thus seems that, similar to the case of Khmer, the distinctive realization of these monosyllabic and sesquisyllabic forms is articulatorily mandated rather than structurally encoded. Examples of sesquisyllables in Turung are given in Table 7. Note that only minor syllables consisting of one consonant are attested.

Table 7. Examples of sesquisyllables in Turung

	Sonority distance < 2	Sonority distance ≥ 2
SSP violated	[sˈban²] 'flower'	[lˈtaʔ²] 'arm'
	[dˈgaː¹] 'seed'	[lˈsiː²] 'lean'
	[gˈɲet³] 'to grind'	
SSP respected	[mˈreːŋ³] 'village'	*[Cˈr-] not allowed[9]
	[sˈŋoːn³] 'to discuss'	[kˈlau²] 'come'
	[gˈmuŋ²] 'matter'	[gˈwun²] 'temple (skull)'

In summary, Turung is a language with both complex monosyllables and sesquisyllables. However, its sesquisyllabicity is not phonologically contrastive but completely predictable. Whether CC- sequences are treated as complex onsets or minor syllables plus onsets depends mainly on the sonority profiles of the sequences. Only those that do not violate SSP or MSD are allowed to form complex onsets. Those that do, in contrast, are predictably sesquisyllabic. In addition, non-sonority constraints also play a role in Turung syllabification. As clusters with [-l-], [-w-], and [-j-] are not allowed, consonantal sequences that contain any of these sounds are predictably syllabified as minor syllables followed by major syllable onset. This fact strongly suggests that Turung sesquisyllables are, like Khmer complex monosyllables, phonotactically derived.

4.4 Kammu

Spoken in Laos, Thailand, China, Vietnam, and Myanmar, the Kammu language belongs to the Northern-Mon-Khmer branch of the Austroasiatic family. The language is also known by other names including "Kmhmu'" (e.g. Miller 2013) and "Khmu" (e.g. Premsrirat 2001). The following discussion is based on the Yuan dialect described by Svantesson (1983). Kammu is a sesquisyllabic language in which complex onsets are allowed. In other words, the onset of a monosyllable can consist of either one or two consonants. In addition, sesquisyllabicity is a phonologically contrastive characteristic in this language. Although

---

[9] According to Morey (2010), examples of sesquisyllables starting with [gˈr-] are also found, in addition to monosyllables with initial [gr-]. However, Morey (personal communication) himself suggests that cases of surface [gˈr-] might in fact be from the cluster /gr-/ underlyingly. This means that there is probably no phonological contrast between the two. In other words, [gˈr-] and [gr-] most likely represent stylistically- and/or socially-conditioned variation. Anecdotally, the orthography developed by Turung speakers themselves does not distinguish monosyllables from sesquisyllables.

syllabification of CC- is largely predictable, words with initial CC- sequences that do not violate sonority constraints can be syllabified either as monosyllables or as sesquisyllables.

Both monosyllabic and sesquisyllabic words are commonly found in Kammu. The first and most important question to be addressed is whether Kammu sesquisyllables are in fact monosyllables with typologically unmarked complex onsets, cf. complex monosyllables in Khmer. From a structural point of view, monosyllables with complex onsets and sesquisyllables display different behaviors with regard to certain phonological processes. For example, the causative affix is realized as a prefix [pn] when the stem is monosyllabic, e.g. [pn̍'tè?] 'to cause to get' from [tè?] 'to get' and [pn̍'kruàl] 'to spare somebody's life' from [kruàl] 'alive'. However, it becomes an infix when the stem is sesquisyllabic, e.g. [cm̍'ŋàːr] 'to make green' from [c'ŋáːr] 'green', and [sm̍'kàr] 'to straighten' from [s'kár] 'straight'. Another example of a process that treats monosyllables and sesquisyllables differently is a word play called [kàm pŕ'?èːn], in which the onset of the stressed syllable is copied, e.g. [kɔ́? kɔ́ːn kʌ́ːn] from [kɔ́ːn] 'child'. If the base is a monosyllable with a complex onset, both consonants are copied, e.g. [klɔ́? klè? klʌ̀ːn] from [klè?] 'husband'. In contrast, if the base is a sesquisyllable, only the onset of the major syllable is copied, e.g. [s'?ɔ́? ?ɔ́ːŋ ?ʌ́ːn] from [s'?ɔ́ːŋ] 'tree' and [lm̀'pɔ́? pɔ̀ːn pʌ̀ːn] from [lm̀pɔ̀ːn] 'to talk'. These phonological processes indicate that sesquisyllables are indeed structurally different from complex monosyllables. This distinction in turn suggests that derivational processes apply to prosodic constituents rather than linear strings of segments (McCarthy and Prince 1986).

Among the monosyllables, a large number have a sequence of two consonants as their onset. The first member of these complex onsets must be a stop, while the second must be a liquid or a glide as illustrated in Table 8. Other types of CC- sequences such as *[pt-], *[rp-], and *[lr-] are not allowed in this language. The generalization is that from the first to the second consonant there must be an increase in sonority of at least 2 on the sonority scale. This means that Kammu strictly respects the SSP and imposes an MSD requirement on its complex onsets.

Table 8. Complex onsets in Kammu monosyllables (based on Svantesson 1983: 18)

	-l-	-r-	-w-
p-	plĭam 'landleech' plìa 'beautiful'	prím 'old' prì? 'forest'	-
t-	-	trá:k 'buffalo' trù:ɲ 'termite'	-
c-	-	crɔ́? 'weir' crĭas 'comb'	-
k-	klɛ́h 'bald' klè? 'to smile'	krá:s 'to laugh' krɔ̀:ŋ 'stalk'	[kwá:ŋ] 'red cotton tree' [kwà:c] 'to beckon'
kʰ-			[kʰwá:ŋ] 'across'

In addition to monosyllables, sesquisyllabic words also abound in this language. Kammu sesquisyllables can be further divided into two types according to the shape of their minor syllables. The first type consists of those whose minor syllables are made up of two consonants, e.g. [pr̆'lòn] 'door' and [sń'lù?] 'lake'. The second type comprises those whose minor syllables consist of one single consonant. It is this latter type that is relevant to the phonological contrast between monosyllabic and sesquisyllabic words beginning with CC- sequences. Sesquisyllabic words of this type may violate either or both of the two sonority constraints, namely SSP and MSD. Examples of sesquisyllables with monoconsonantal minor syllables are given in Table 9.

Table 9. Examples of sesquisyllables with monoconsonantal minor syllables in Kammu

	Sonority distance < 2	Sonority distance ≥ 2
SSP violated	[r̆'mà:ŋ] 'rich' [p'té?] 'earth' [s'?ɔ́:ŋ] 'tree' [k'?áːɲ] 'wasp'	[r̆'kèŋ] 'stretched'
SSP respected	[t'ma?] 'flea' [k'né?] 'rat' [p'nùm] 'termite hill' [c'mɔ̀:l] 'to sow'	[k'rúk] 'to fall' [k'lóːk] 'slit drum' [h'yĭər] 'fowl' [k'rùən] 'neck eczema of sambar deer'

With respect to the contrastivity of sesquisyllabicity in Kammu, comparing complex monosyllables and sesquisyllables with monoconsonantal minor syllables reveals that word shape is largely but not always predictable from the sonority profile of the initial CC- sequences. More specifically, sequences that violate SSP or MSD must be realized as sesquisyllabic, while those that violate neither are attested with both syllabification options. To put it differently, the phonological contrast between sesquisyllables and complex monosyllables in

Kammu is neutralized when the sonority constraints are violated. The contrast is maintained only in CC- sequences that can be legally syllabified as complex onsets of monosyllables. This underlying contrast is manifested by CC- sequences that violate neither of the two sonority constraints but are specified in the phonological structure as minor syllables plus onset, e.g. [kˈrúk] 'to fall' and [kˈrùən] 'neck eczema of sambar deer'. The phonological contrast is further evidenced by such minimal pairs as [klóːk] 'bamboo' vs. [kˈlóːk] 'slit drum'. In these cases, sesquisyllabification must be prespecified in the underlying representation of the prosodic words. The correlation between consonant combination and word shape is summarized in Table 10.

Table 10. Consonant combination and word shape

Initials	monosyllabic	sesquisyllabic
single C	✓	
obstruent+liquid	✓	✓
obstruent+nasal	×	✓
obstruent+obstruent	×	✓
nasal+obstruent	×	(✓)[10]
liquid+obstruent	×	✓

The fact that consonant sequences that violate SSP and MSD are treated as minor syllables plus onset suggests that sesquisyllabicity in Kammu largely results from the failure to form permissible onsets, just like in Jahai and Turung. This view is supported by the fact that CC- sequences that violate non-sonority constraints are also syllabified as sesquisyllabic structures. For example, Kammu does not allow coronal segments to be combined with [-l-], e.g. *[cl-], and *[tl-], and thus treats such sequences as sesquisyllabic, e.g. [cˈlɔ́ːŋ] 'river bank' and [tˈláː] 'bamboo'. Further support comes from causative formation. Prefixing [p-], an allomorph of the causative affix, to stems beginning with liquids results in monosyllabic words, e.g. [pláːc] 'to take away' from [láːc] 'to disappear', and [prɨ́h] 'to raise' from [rɨ̀h] 'to rise'. If the stems start with other types of consonants, the derived words are sesquisyllables, e.g. [pˈkúːt] 'to take in' from [kùːt] 'to go in', and [pˈŋɔ́ːm] 'to make something fall on something' from [ŋɔ̀ːm] 'to fall

---

[10] Sesquisyllabic structures of this type seem possible because there are plenty of words with syllabic nasals as the nucleus of biconsonantal minor syllables, e.g. [pn̩ˈtè?] 'to cause to get'. However, I have not found a minor syllable consisting of a single nasal consonant in Svantesson (1983).

on something'. These two facts offer further support for viewing sesquisyllabicity as a strategy to avoid violating syllabification constraints.

In summary, Kammu is an example of a sesquisyllabic language that allows complex onsets. These complex onsets are typologically unmarked and must respect the sonority constraints on syllabification. Moreover, the language also displays a phonological contrast between monosyllabic and sesquisyllabic words but only in cases where the initial CC- sequences do not violate the sonority constraints. This neutralization suggests that sesquisyllabicity is best viewed as a strategy that MSEA languages use to avoid violating the constraints on syllabification.

5 Typologizing the diversity of sesquisyllabicity

In contrast to the general view of sesquisyllabicity as a unified phenomenon, the cases of Jahai, Khmer, Turung and Kammu illustrate that sesquisyllabic languages are in fact quite diverse. More specifically, two simple structural characteristics, namely the onset complexity and the contrastivity of sesquisyllabicity, can be used to classify sesquisyllabic languages into three main types as summarized in Table 11. Note that a language that does not allow complex onsets logically cannot have a phonological contrast between complex monosyllables and sesquisyllables.

Table 11. Types of sesquisyllabic languages

	Sesquisyllabicity not contrastive	Sesquisyllabicity contrastive
Complex onsets not allowed	(A) Jahai	
Complex onsets allowed	(B1) Khmer	(C) Kammu
	(B2) Turung	

Represented by Jahai, type-A languages are those that neither allow complex onsets nor have a phonological contrast between sesquisyllables and complex monosyllables. In these languages, sonority does not play any role in syllabification. What seems to be at work is the cross-linguistic dispreference against complex onsets (see discussion in Zec 2007). All initial CC- sequences are thus predictably syllabified as a sesquisyllabic structure such that neither typologically unmarked clusters e.g. *[pr], nor typologically marked clusters e.g. *[pt] are allowed. Only sesquisyllabic structures, e.g. [pᵊt] and [pᵊr], are attested. Three of the 18 languages in the survey are identified as belonging to type A, as summarized in Table 12.

Table 12. Type-A sesquisyllabic languages

Languages	Family	[pt]	[pr]	[pᵊt]	[pᵊr]
Jahai (Burenhult 2005)	Austroasiatic			✓	✓
Semelai (Kruspe 2004)	Austroasiatic			✓	✓
Thavung (Premsrirat 2004)	Austroasiatic			✓	✓

At the opposite end, type-B languages are those that allow complex onsets but do not show contrastivity between sesquisyllables and monosyllables. These languages can be further divided into two subtypes according to whether syllabification is sonority-based. Languages of the B1 type treat all initial CC-sequences as complex onsets of monosyllables regardless of their sonority profile. In these languages, both typologically marked and unmarked complex onsets are possible, e.g. [pr-] and [pt-]. In contrast, B2-type languages show sonority-based syllabification of consonant sequences, allowing only unmarked complex onsets e.g. [pr-] and [pᵊt-]. While Khmer represents the B1 type, Turung represents B2. Among the 18 languages surveyed, six are classified as B-type languages as shown in Table 13. Note that Khmer is so far the only clear case of a B1-type language. This may be because distinguishing between the two subtypes must be based on adequate theoretically informed structural analyses. Most descriptions of these languages only give surface inventories but do not address structural issues such as phonological processes and phonotactic constraints.

The last type of sesquisyllabic language is the C type, represented by Kammu. These languages both allow complex onsets, and show contrast between sesquisyllables and monosyllables with complex onsets. Initial CC- sequences in these languages are predictably syllabified as minor syllables followed by major-syllable onsets e.g. [pᵊt-], if they violate SSP or MSD and are thus unqualified to form typologically unmarked complex onsets of monosyllables. In cases where neither sonority constraint is violated, it is not predictable whether the CC- sequences would be syllabified as complex onsets e.g. [pr-], or sesquisyllabic structures e.g. [pᵊr-]. In other words, sesquisyllabicity is phonologically contrastive only when the initial consonant sequences are potential complex onsets. Among the 18 languages surveyed, nine are classified as C-type languages as shown in Table 14.

Table 13. Type-B sesquisyllabic languages

Languages	Family	[pt]	[pr]	[pᵗt]	[pᵗr]
Khmer (Henderson 1952)	Austroasiatic	✓	✓		
Lawa (Ratanakul and Daoratanahong 1987)	Austroasiatic			✓	✓
Kuay (Markowski 2005)	Austroasiatic			✓	✓
Mon (Kitisarn 1986)	Austroasiatic			✓	✓
Pacoh (Alves 2006)	Austroasiatic			✓	✓
Turung (Morey 2010)	Sino-Tibetan			✓	✓

Table 14. Type-C sesquisyllabic languages

Languages	Family	[pt]	[pr]	[pᵗt]	[pᵗr]
Kammu (Svantesson 1983)	Austroasiatic		✓	✓	✓
Nyah Kur (Diffloth 1984)	Austroasiatic		✓	✓	✓
Sedang (Smith 2000)	Austroasiatic		✓	✓	✓
Chrau (Thomas 1979)	Austroasiatic		✓	✓	✓
Bruu (L-Thongkum 1980)	Austroasiatic		✓	✓	✓
Ruc (Nguyễn 1993)	Austroasiatic		✓	✓	✓
Burmese (Green 2005)	Sino-Tibetan		✓	✓	✓
Sgaw Karen (Ratanakul 1986)	Sino-Tibetan		✓	✓	✓
Jarai (Nguyễn 1975)	Austronesian		✓	✓	✓

One intriguing observation from this survey is that two logically possible types are not attested. The first type is a language that allows sesquisyllabic structures that do not violate sonority constraints but disallows those that do. In other words, a language that has [pʼr-] but not [pʼt-] is absent from the survey. The absence of this type is, however, not surprising given the current proposal. If it is true that sonority-based syllabification creates sesquisyllabic structures from CC- sequences that violate SSP and MSD, then [pʼt-] must be considered less marked than [pʼr-] which is contrastively sesquisyllabic. It is thus expected that languages that have the more marked [pʼr-] would also have the less marked [pʼt-]. Note that syllabification of the [pʼr-]-type structures must be pre-specified in the underlying representation, cf. English [ʔáj.da] 'Ida' vs. [ʔa.íj.da] 'Aïda' (Levin 1985).

Another unattested type is a language that has a phonological contrast between typologically marked clusters and sesquisyllabic structures. In other words, a language that has both [pt-] and [pʼt-] is not found in the survey. Again, this gap is not surprising given that sesquisyllabicity is a strategy that MSEA languages use to avoid violation of the constraints on syllabification. A hypothetical language that allows typologically marked clusters like [pt-] would, therefore, have no motivation to treat consonant sequences as sesquisyllabic structures to start with. Even if they existed, [pt-] and [pʼt-] would be extremely difficult to distinguish due to their phonetic similarities in languages that have no morphological process treating sesquisyllables differently from monosyllables. These two gaps point to a robust implicational hierarchy of sesquisyllabicity as given in Figure 2.

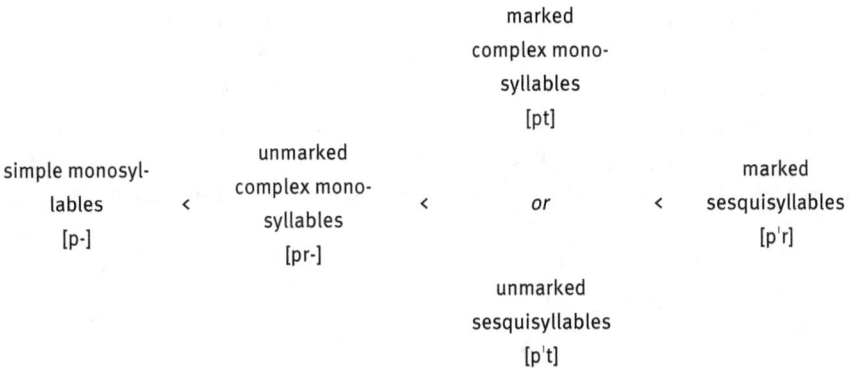

Fig. 2 Implicational hierarchy of sesquisyllabicity

The hierarchy captures the markedness ranking of CC- sequences. While marked sesquisyllables are the most marked combination [pʼr-], simple monosyllables are the least marked. The generalization is that a language that has a type of prosodic word further to the right of the scale must also have all the other types to the left. For example, if a hypothetical language has marked sesquisyllables of type [pʰr-], it must also have all the other types of prosodic words including [pt-] or [pʰt-], [pr-] and [p]. Similarly, if a language has marked complex monosyllables beginning with [pt-] or unmarked sesquisyllables beginning with [pʰt-], it must also have unmarked complex monosyllables with [pr-] as well as simple monosyllables with [p-].

This hierarchy also suggests that sesquisyllabic languages must have both monosyllabic and sesquisyllabic prosodic words. This prediction is consistent with the result of the survey as all sesquisyllabic languages, without exception, also have monosyllabic words in addition to sesquisyllables. This is in contrast with monosyllabic languages, e.g. Vietnamese, which by definition cannot have sesquisyllables or longer prosodic words. This intriguing asymmetry is, in fact, predicted by the current view that sesquisyllabicity is derived from syllabification of typologically marked CC- sequences.

Not only does the typology of sesquisyllabicity reveal the heterogeneity among so-called sesquisyllabic languages, but it also has implications for the study of convergence in MSEA. In particular, it helps refine our understanding of the monosyllabization process reported to have happened in Vietic (Ferlus 1996; Haudricourt 1954) and Chamic languages (Thurgood 1999, 2005), for example. Brunelle and Pittayaporn (2012) argue that the Iambic-Trochaic Law plays a crucial role in constraining the change from disyllabicity to sesquisyllabicity to monosyllabicity but do not discuss how exactly this gradual shift occurs. However, the typology of sesquisyllabic languages proposed here suggests that the path from sesquisyllabicity to monosyllabicity comprises a series of changes in syllabification. From this perspective, type C is the least evolved type of sesquisyllabic language, while types A and B represent intermediate steps before losing sesquisyllabicity altogether. One possible scenario is schematized in Figure 3, but full discussion will be a topic for future occasions.

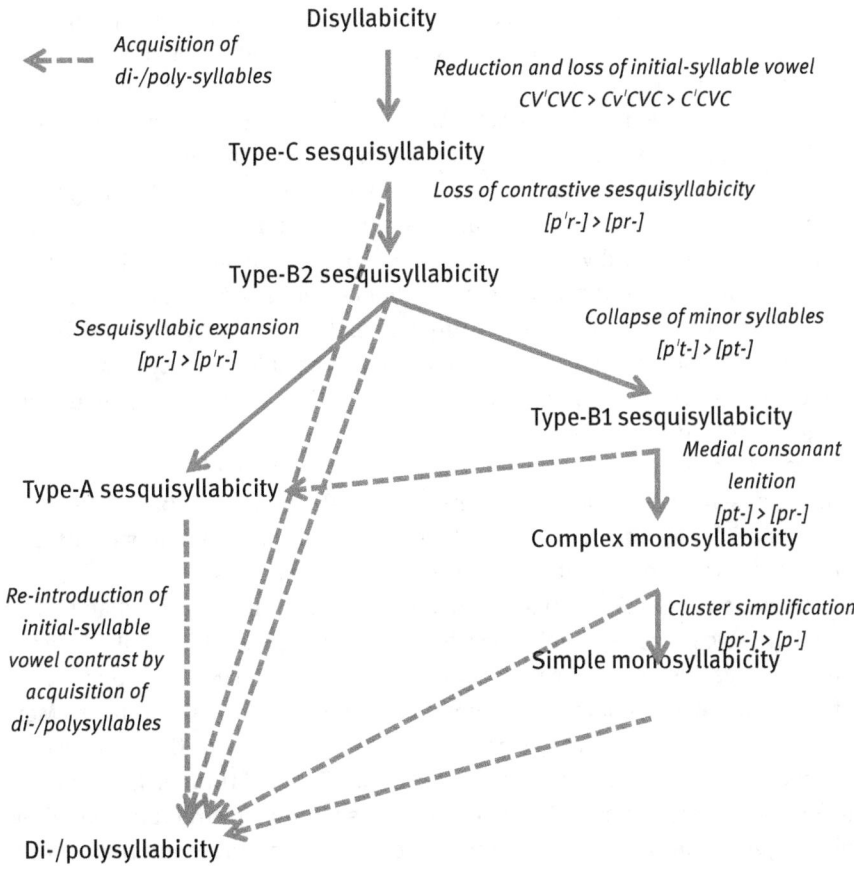

Fig. 3 Possible paths of sesquisyllabization and monosyllabization

6 Conclusion

In summary, this paper examines the structural diversity among sesquisyllabic languages in MSEA. Informed by the theory of syllabification, it attempts to typologize the sesquisyllabic languages of MSEA using onset complexity and the contrastivity of sesquisyllabicity as criteria. It shows that languages thought to be sesquisyllabic are in fact more diverse than generally believed. More importantly, it shows that the attested and unattested types of sesquisyllabic languages are explainable in terms of sonority-based syllabification. Further examination into structural properties of minor syllables, i.e. presence/absence of non-contrastive phonological vowels, prosodic status within the prosodic word, ability/inability to occur with other minor syllables within the same word, etc., would surely reveal an even greater diversity among sesquisyllabic languages. Sesquisyllabicity is an oft-cited MSEA feature but among the least understood. Having examined the diversity of sesquisyllables in languages of MSEA, it has become clear that sesquisyllabicity is not homogenous across languages. Without denying the importance of identifying similarities among sesquisyllables, this paper has shown that sesquisyllabic languages differ from each other with respect to the types of monosyllables and sesquisyllables that occur in each language. This diversity is elegantly captured using two simple structural characteristics, namely onset complexity and contrastivity of sesquisyllabicity. These traits are closely tied to sonority-based syllabification, which determines whether a CC- sequence is to be syllabified as complex onsets of monosyllables, or sequences of minor syllable plus onsets of major syllables.

In some languages, initial consonant sequences are always syllabified as sesquisyllabic because complex onsets are not allowed at all, e.g. Jahai. On the other hand, some languages may not treat all CC- sequences as complex onsets of monosyllables, rendering sesquisyllabicity irrelevant, e.g. Khmer. More common, however, are languages in which syllabification of CC- sequences is completely predictable from their sonority profile, e.g. Turung. Lastly, many languages syllabify most CC- sequences as sesquisyllabic structures but allow phonological contrast between complex monosyllables and sesquisyllables only when sonority constraints on syllabification permit, e.g. Kammu. Attested and unattested types of languages strongly suggest an implicational hierarchy of sesquisyllabicity based on word shapes explainable in terms of sonority-based syllabification. Structurally speaking, the so-called sesquisyllables may, in fact, consist of either one or two syllables depending on the language. In this sense, sesquisyllables do not distinguish themselves from more canonical types of words in terms of the number of syllables they contain. The only shared characteristic among sesquisyllables in different languages seems to be an impression of a defective prosodic element to the left of their stressed syllables. However, as demonstrated here, the minor syllables in some languages are, in fact, part of complex onsets rather than autonomous prosodic entities. Under this view, sesquisyllabicity is best considered as a strategy that MSEA languages use to avoid violating the constraints on syllabification.

Acknowledgements

This research was supported by the Higher Education Research Promotion and National Research University Project of Thailand (HS1231A), Office of the Higher Education Commission, Ministry of Education, Thailand. Special thanks go to my research assistants Jakrabhop Iamdanush, Chawadon Ketkaew, and Thanasak Sirikanerat for their help with the typological survey. I am also indebted to Marc Brunelle, Abby Cohn, Bernard Comrie, Nick Enfield, and Stephen Morey for their inputs at various stages of this paper.

References

Alves, Mark J. 2006. *A grammar of Pacoh: a Mon-Khmer language of the Central Highland of Vietnam*: Canberra: Australian National University.
Baxter, William H., & Laurent Sagart. 2014. *Old Chinese: A new reconstruction*. Oxford: Oxford University Press.
Bennett, J. Fraser. 1995. *Metrical foot structure in Thai and Kayah Li: Optimality-Theoretic studies in the prosody of two Southeast Asian languages*. Urbana-Champaign: University of Illinois dissertation.
Brunelle, Marc. 2008. Monosyllabicization in Eastern Cham. In Wilaiwan Khanittanan & Paul Sidwell (eds.), *Papers from the 14th annual meeting of the Southeast Asian Linguistics Society* (Volume 1 [2004]), 43–58. Canberra: Pacific Linguistics.
Brunelle, Marc, & Pittayawat Pittayaporn. 2012. Phonologically-constrained change: The role of the foot in monosyllabization and rhythmic shifts in Mainland Southeast Asia. *Diachronica* 29(4), 411–433.
Burenhult, Niclas. 2005. *A grammar of Jahai*. Canberra: Research School of Pacific and Asian Studies, Australian National University.
Butler, Becky. 2014. *Deconstructing the Southeast Asian sesquisyllable: a gestural account*. Ithaca, NY: Cornell University dissertation.
Butler, Becky. to appear. A gestural account of minor syllables: evidence from Khmer. *Proceedings of the 48th Annual Meeting of the Chicago Linguistic Society*.
Clements, G. N. 1990. The role of syllabification cycle in core syllabification. In John Kingston & Mary E. Beckman (eds.), *Papers in Laboratory Phonology I: Between the grammar and physics of speech*, 283–333. Cambridge; New York, Port Chester, Melbourne, Sydney: Cambridge University Press.
Comrie, Bernard. 2007. Areal typology of Mainland Southeast Asia: What we learn from the WALS maps. *Manusya: Journal of Humanities, Special issue no. 13*, 18–47.
Crystal, David. 1997. *A dictionary of linguistics and phonetics* (4th ed.). Malden, MA; Oxford: Blackwell Publishers.
Diffloth, Gérard. 1984. *The Dvaravati Old Mon language and Nyah Kur*. Bangkok: Chulalongkorn University Printing House.

Dixon, R. M. W., & Alexandra Y. Aikhenvald 2002. Word: a typological framework. In R. M. W. Dixon & Alexandra Y. Aikhenvald (eds.), *Word: A cross-linguistic typology*, 1–41. Cambridge: Cambridge University Press.

Duangchan, Paiboon. 1984. *A phonological description of the Kensiw language (a Sakai dialect)*. Nakhon Pathom: Mahidol University MA thesis.

Enfield, N. J. 2011. Linguistic diversity in mainland Southeast Asia. In N. J. Enfield (ed.), *Dynamics of human diversity: The case of mainland Southeast Asia*, 63–80. Canberra: Pacific Linguistics.

Ferlus, Michel. 1990. Remarques sur le consonantisme de proto thai-yay (révision du proto-tai de Li Fangkuei). Paper circulated at the 23rd International Conference on Sino-Tibetan Languages and Linguistics. Arlington: University of Texas.

Ferlus, Michel. 1996. Evolution vers le monosyllabisme dans quelques languages de l'Asie du Sud-Est. Paper presented at the Séance du 23 novembre 1996, la Société de Linguistique de Paris.

Green, Antony D. 2005. Word, foot, and syllable structure in Burmese. In J. Watkins (ed.), *Studies in Burmese linguistics*, 1–25. Canberra: Australian National University

Handel, Zev. 1998. *The medial systems of Old Chinese and Proto-Sino-Tibetan*. Berkeley: University of California dissertation.

Harris, James W. 1983. *Syllable structure and stress in Spanish: a nonlinear analysis*. Cambridge, MA: MIT Press.

Haudricourt, André-Georges. 1954. De l'origine des tons en vietnamien. *Journal Asiatique* 242, 69–82.

Henderson, Eugénie J.A. 1952. The main features of Cambodian pronunciation. *Bulletin of the School of Oriental and African Studies* 14, 149–174.

Hooper, Joan B. 1976. *An introduction to Natural Generative Phonology*. New York: Academic Press.

Hualde, José Ignacio. 1991. On Spanish syllabification. In Héctor Campos & Fernando Martínez-Gil (eds.), *Current studies in Spanish linguistics*, 475–494. Washington, D.C.: Georgetown University Press.

Huffmann, Franklin E. 1972. The boundary between monosyllable and disyllable in Cambodian. *Lingua* 29, 54–66.

Hyman, Larry. 2007. Where's phonology in typology? *Linguistic Typology* 11, 265–271.

Inkelas, Sharon. 1989. *Prosodic constituency in the lexicon*. Palo Alto: Stanford University dissertation.

Inkelas, Sharon, & Draga Zec. 1988. Serbo-Croatian pitch accent: the interaction of tone, stress, and intonation. *Language* 64, 227–248.

Jacob, Judith M. 1993. The structure of the word in Old Khmer. In Judith M. Jacob & David Smyth (eds.), *Cambodian Linguistics, Literature and History*, 1–17. London: University of London, School of Oriental and African Studies.

Kirby, James. 2013. Tonogenesis in Khmer: A cross-dialect comparison. Paper presented at the The 23rd Annual Meeting of the Southeast Asian Linguistics Society. Bangkok: Chulalongkorn University.

Kitisarn, Prayat. 1986. *The phonology of Mon at Ban Khlong Khru, Tambol Thasai, Amphoe Muang, Samut Sakhon province*. Nakhon Pathom: Mahidol University MA thesis.

Kruspe, Nichole. 2004. *A grammar of Semelai*. Cambridge & New York: Cambridge University Press.

Levin, Juliette. 1985. *A Metrical theory of syllabicity*. Cambridge, MA: MIT dissertation.

L-Thongkum, Theraphan. 1980. *A Bruu-Thai-English dictionary*. Bangkok: Chulalongkorn University.
Markowski, Linda M. 2005. *A comparative study of Kuy varieties in Cambodia*. Chiang Mai: Payap University MA thesis.
Matisoff, James A. 1973. Tonogenesis in Southeast Asia. In L. M. Hyman (ed.), *Consonant types & tones*, 71–95. Los Angeles: University of Southern California, The Linguistic Program.
Matisoff, James A. 2001. Genetic versus contact relationship: prosodic diffusibility in South-East Asian languages. In Alexandra Y. Aikhenvald & R. M. W Dixon (eds.), *Areal diffusion and genetic inheritance: problems in comparative linguistics*, 291–327. Oxford & New York: Oxford University Press.
Matisoff, James A. 2003. *Handbook of Proto-Tibeto-Burman: System and philosophy of Sino-Tibetan reconstruction*. Berkeley: University of California Press.
McCarthy, John, & Alan Prince . 1986. *Prosodic morphology. manuscript*. Amherst: University of Massachusetts & Waldham: Brandeis University.
Miller, Michelle. 2013. A description of Kmhmu' Lao script-based orthography. *Mon-Khmer Studies* 42, 12–25.
Minegishi, Makoto. 2006. Khmer. In Keith Brown (ed.), *Encyclopedia of language and linguistics* (2nd ed.), 4981–4984. Elsevier: Oxford.
Morey, Stephen D. 2010. *Turung – a variety of Singpho language spoken in Assam*. Canberra: Pacific Linguistics.
Nespor, Marina, & Irene Vogel. 1986. *Prosodic phonology*. Dordrecht, Holland; Riverton, USA: Foris Publications.
Nguyễn, Tong Nang. 1975. *An outline of Jarai grammar*. Huntington Beach, CA: Summer Institute of Lingusitics.
Nguyễn, Văn Lợi. 1993. *Tiếng Rục* [The Ruc language]. Hà Nội: Nhà xuất bản Khoa học xã hội.
Parker, Stephen. 2002. *Quantifying the sonority hierarchy*. Amherst: University of Massachusetts dissertation.
Pittayaporn, Pittayawat. 2009. *Phonology of Proto-Tai*. Ithaca, NY: Cornell University dissertation.
Premsrirat, Suwilai. 2001. Tonogenesis in Khmu dialects of SEA. *Mon-Khmer Studies* 31, 47–56.
Premsrirat, Suwilai. 2004. *So (Thavung) dictionary*. Nakhon Pathom: Mahidol University, Institute of Language and Culture for Rural Development and University of Melbourne: Department of Linguistics and Applied Linguistics.
Ratanakul, Suriya. 1986. *Thai-Sgaw Karen dictionary*. Nakhon Pathom: Mahidol University.
Ratanakul, Suriya & Lakhana Daoratanahong. 1987. *Thai-Lawa dictionary*. Nakhon Pathom: Mahidol University.
Rischel, Jørgen. 1995. *Minor Mlabri: a hunter-gatherer language of northern Indochina*. Copenhagen: University of Copenhagen, Museum Tusculanum Press.
Schiller, Eric. 1994. Khmer nominalizing and causativizing infixes. In Karen L Adams & Thomas J. Hudak (eds.), *Papers from the Second Annual Meeting of the Southeast Asian Linguistics Society*, 309–326. Tempe, AZ: Arizona State University, Program for Southeast Asian Studies.
Selkirk, Elizabeth. 1984. On the major class features and syllable theory. In Mark Aronoff & Richard T. Oehrle (eds.), *Language sound structure*, 107–136. Cambridge, MA: MIT Press.
Shorto, Harry. 1960. Word and syllable pattern in Palaung. *Bulletin of the School of Oriental and African Studies* 23(3), 544–557.

Smith, Kenneth D. 2000. *Sedang dictionary: with English, Vietnamese, and French glossaries.* Bangkok & Dallas: Mahidol University & Summer Institute of Linguistics.

Solnit, David B. 1997. *Eastern Kayah Li: grammar, texts, glossary.* Honolulu: Hawai'i University Press.

Steriade, Donca. 1982. *Greek prosodies and the nature of syllabification.* Cambridge, MA: MIT dissertation.

Svantesson, Jan-Olof. 1983. *Kammu phonology and morphology.* Lund: CWK Gleerup.

Thomas, David. 1979. Chrau grammar. Honolulu: University of Hawai'i Press.

Thomas, David. 1992. On sesquisyllabic structure. *Mon-Khmer Studies* 21, 206–210.

Thurgood, Graham. 1999. *From ancient Cham to modern dialects : two thousand years of language contact and change.* Honolulu: University of Hawai'i Press.

Thurgood, Graham. 2005. The tones from Proto-Chamic to Tsat (Hainan Cham): Insights from Zheng 1997 and from summer 2004 fieldwork. In Anthony Grant & Paul Sidwell (eds.), *Chamic and beyond: Studies in Mainland Austronesian languages*, 247–271. Canberra: Pacific Linguistics.

Venneman, Theo 1972. On the Theory of Syllabic Phonology. *Linguistische Berichte* 18, 1–18.

Zec, Draga. 2007. The syllable. In Paul de Lacy (ed.), *The Cambridge handbook of phonology*, 161–194. Cambridge: Cambridge University Press.

Part 4: **Explorations in MSEA morphosyntax**

Mark J. Alves
Morphological functions among Mon-Khmer languages
Beyond the basics

1 Overview

Mon-Khmer languages[1] are known for their morphologically analytic and isolating structure (Donegan and Stampe 1983). They have fossilized remnants of prefixes and infixes, often in the form of phonologically reduced sesquisyllables, of an apparently historically early productive morphological system. Grammatical functions among Mon-Khmer languages thus tend to be expressed via word order and lexemes, not affixation. Of the readily identifiable morphology, the most widespread and thus best known affixes in Mon-Khmer, including causative prefixes on verbs and nasal nominalizing infixes, are reconstructible to Proto-Austroasiatic (Sidwell 2008),[2] though these tend to be derivational morphemes with non-grammatical functions. The focus on causative *pV- prefixes, nominalizing nasal infixes, reciprocal prefixes, and reduplicants (grouped with 'expressives'; cf., Diffloth 1976a, Svantesson 1983, Section 2.7), combined with the somewhat limited research on morphology in Mon-Khmer, has created a limited picture of morphology in Mon-Khmer.[3]

This study looks beyond the most common derivational affixes to the complex range of morphological functions among Mon-Khmer languages, including aspect, mood, case-marking, and a variety of other notable, specialized and

---

[1] This study does not include the Munda languages due to the significant historical and typological distinctions. For a discussion of the typological differences between Munda languages and other Austroasiatic languages, see Donegan and Stampe (1983) and Donegan (1993). For an overview of Munda word formation, see Pinnow (1966), Zide and Anderson (2001), and Anderson (2004) and (2007).
[2] In this paper, it is assumed that Munda is one of the 13 posited sub-branches of Austroasiatic, not a sister branch equal to all Mon-Khmer languages, as per Sidwell and Blench (2011). Thus, the term 'Mon-Khmer' is essentially shorthand for all non-Munda Austroasiatic languages.
[3] In the World Atlas of Language Structures Online, no Mon-Khmer languages are shown to have prefixing and suffixing inflectional morphology or case marking (Dryer and Haspelmath 2011).

often grammatical functions (e.g., desideratives, time deictics, intensification, etc.). While some morphosyntactic categories of morphemes are specific to sub-branches or even languages, some categories are widespread geographically in the language family but still do not have reconstructible forms. The diversity of morphological functions throughout Mon-Khmer shows innovation, often without apparent external sources of influence, which highlights both the time-depth of the sub-branches' separation as well as a natural tendency for human language to generate morphosyntactic complexity. Moreover, most of the identified categories are grammatical or overlap with grammatical functions. This paper provides the sources of data, the approach for this typological study, key examples to highlight the diversity of morphological categories, and thoughts on issues surrounding the geographic spread of these categories and historical implications of the data.

2 Sources, diversity, and morphological functions

The research for this study on word-formation functions comes from a survey of 12 sub-branches and over three dozen Mon-Khmer languages. (As there are over 160 Mon-Khmer languages (Ethnologue.com), this is clearly only a sampling.) While descriptions of many of the 30 plus languages provide ample accounts of the full range of types of morphology (see the list of references grouped by sub-branch in Table 1), some are brief and incomplete or leave questions of status of affixes versus clitics unanswered.[4] The information gathered thus far is sufficient to highlight the fuller range of morphological functions among the sub-branches of Mon-Khmer.

---

[4] In instances in which there is a question of whether a morph is an affix or clitic, this is addressed in the paper. In general, the study includes clitics due to their affix-like status and their tendency to become bound morphemes over time. Also, in some cases, it is not possible, without additional investigation beyond available publications, to determine with certainty the status of such segments, thereby making exclusion of these inappropriate. When there is doubt, comments are made in the relevant sections. Finally, excluding forms based on the potential for clitic status does not seem legitimate as they are generally intermediaries to status as affixes.

Table 1: Sub-branches and languages, with references

Sub-branches	Languages and Primary Sources
Aslian (Peninsular Malaysia)	Entire branch (Matisoff 2003); Jah-Hut (Diffloth 1979); Jahai (Schebesta 1926 and 1931; Burenhult 2002 and 2011); Kentakbong (Omar 1976); Semelai (Kruspe 2004); Semai/Sengoi (Diffloth 1976a and 1976b; Means and Means 1986); Temiar (Benjamin 1976 and 2011; Means 1998)
Bahnaric (Central Vietnam, Laos, Cambodia and Thailand)	Bahnar (Banker 1964a and 1964b); Chrau (Dorothy Thomas 1969; David Thomas 1971); Halang (Cooper 1966); Jeh (Cohen 1966; Gradin 1976); Koho (Hoàng, et. al. 1984; Tạ 1998); Mnong (Dinh 2007); Rengao (Gregerson 1979); Sedang (Smith 1969); Sre (Manley 1972)
Katuic (Central Vietnam and Laos)	Entire branch (Hoàng Văn Hành 1993); Bru (Nguyễn, Trần, Hồ, and Hương 1986; Hoàng and Tạ 1998); Katu (Costello 1966, 1998, and 2001; Ngeq (Smith 1973); Nguyễn and Nguyễn 1998; Nguyễn Hữu Hoành 1998); Pacoh (S. Watson 1964 and 1966; R. Watson 1966a, 1966b, 1976, and 2011; Nguyễn, Đoàn, and Phan 1986; Alves 2000 and 2006)
Khasic (Northeastern India)	Khasi (Gurdon 1914; Nagaraja 1985 and 1993)
Khmeric (Cambodia and Vietnam)	Khmer (Nacaskul 1978; Jenner 1977; Jenner and Pou 1982; David Thomas 1987-1988; Dorothy Thomas 1990; Schiller 1994 and 1999)
Khmuic (Southern China, Thailand, Laos, and Vietnam)	Khmu (Svantesson 1983; Premsrirat 1987); Mal (Filbeck 1996); Mlabri (Rischel 1995)
Mangic/Pakanic (China, Vietnam, Laos, Thailand)	Bugan (Li 1996; Li 2005); Kemie (Chen 2005); Mang (Nguyễn, Nguyễn, and Tạ 2008)
Monic (Thailand and Burma)	Mon (Bauer 1982, 1989, and 1991; Jenny 2003 and 2005); Nyah Kur (Diffloth 1984)
Nicobarese (Nicobar Islands of India)	Nancowry Nicobarese (Man 1889; Radakhrisnan 1976 and 1981); Car Nicobarese (Braine 1961)
Palaungic (Burma, Thailand, and China)	Buxing (Gao 2004); De'ang (Chen et. al. 1986); Kemie (Chen 2005); Palaung (Milne 1921; Shorto 1963); Riang-Liang (Shorto 1963)
Pearic (Cambodia and Thailand)	Pearic (Headley 1977; Premsrirat 2011)
Vietic (Vietnam and Laos)	Kri (Enfield and Diffloth 2009); Muong (Nguyễn, Bùi, and Hoàng 2002); Muong reduplication (Hoàng Văn Hành 1998); Ruc (Nguyễn Văn Lợi 1993); Thavung (Premsrirat 1998 and 1999); Vietnamese (Thompson 1965; Nguyễn Tài Cẩn 1996; Nguyễn Đình Hoà 1966); Vietnamese reduplication (Hoàng Văn Hành 1985; Viên Ngôn Ngữ Học (Institute of Linguistics, Hanoi) 1996; Vu 2007);
General Issues in Mon-Khmer	Affixes (Bauer 1986 and 1987-88); Clark 1970; Sidwell 2008); Pronouns (Pinnow 1965); Phonological aspects of reduplication (DiCanio 2005); Typology (Donegan and Stampe 1983; Donegan 1993)

The word formation types among all the languages reviewed include compounding, affixation (prefixes and infixes, with almost no suffixation except some limited instances[5]), and reduplication, including full and alternating[6] (e.g., alliteration, rhyming, etc.) reduplication. For this study, the focus is on affixation and reduplication, both of which have several identifiable categories, including many grammatical (e.g., aspect, subject-agreement, etc.) and semi-grammatical (e.g., iteration, mood, etc.) categories. Despite sharing the common core of Mon-Khmer fossilized affixes discussed above, there is significant variety of morphological categories throughout the entire family and some distinct morphological categories within sub-branches.

To give a sense of the variety, consider the Aslian[7], Khmuic, and Katuic sub-branches, spoken in three geographic regions. Aslian languages have a morphological paradigm to indicate verb aspect. They also have subject prefixes and incopyfixation, that is, copying of coda consonants as infixes (cf. Matisoff 2003, et alia). Katuic languages exhibit 18 categories of word-formation functions, including the highly marked case-marking pronouns. Finally, reduplication in the Khmu language is not only phonologically complex but also virtually synthetic in its compacting of semantic and semi-grammatical functions. Even Vietnamese, which has no affixational morphology, only Chinese-style pseudo-compounding,[8] has utilized alternating reduplication to generate thousands of lexical items, with several semi-grammatical functions. There is a good deal

---

5 The Aslian language Semelai has borrowed suffixes, including iterative [-iʔ] and nominalizing [-an] as well as the Malay circumfix [b-...-an] (Kruspe 2004: 68). Similarly, Means (1998: 15) provides a list of about a dozen Malay affixes in Temiar, including the Malay possessive suffix '-nya', causativizing '-kan', and the nominalizing suffix 'ke-...-an' are included.

6 The term 'alternating reduplication' used here has been referred to in other ways in various publications. Functionally, the terms 'expressives', 'echo-formatives', and 'ideophones' involve alliteration, rhyming, and "chiming," among others, of both monosyllabic and polysyllabic forms and even phrases in a complex range of morpho-phonologically derived forms which are beyond the scope of this paper.

7 Many Aslian languages have borrowed Malay morphology. These Malay loans have not been included in this study in order to focus on older, native Mon-Khmer forms. Adding these to the study would show that Aslian languages have even more complex morphology, which would give a skewed picture of Mon-Khmer. Thus, while not wishing to exclude data, this large-scale borrowing was excluded from the study in order to focus on somewhat more native Mon-Khmer aspects.

8 For description of pseudo-compounding in Vietnamese, Chinese, see Thompson (1965) and Starosta (1992). One way of considering pseudo-compounds is the phonological and semantic prominence (e.g., recognition of source words) but simultaneous phonological connection and semantic generalization, such as one would expect of pure affixes.

more morphological complexity than expected in what has been considered a language family of analytical languages.

Broad semantico-syntactic categories were identified and put in a column in Table 2. For each sub-branch, when at least one language has a feature, the sub-branch is marked for that trait. A minus sign means that such a feature was not found in published sources. In this way, the total numbers of types of morphological traits for each sub-branch can be shown, indicating the amount of diversity of morphological functions in each branch. The details in the table will likely change as more information becomes available, so it is tentative but still indicative of the morphological diversity in the various sub-branches.

Table 2 shows 23 categories of semantico-syntactic functions of both affixational (16 categories) and reduplicative (seven categories) morphology. The categories are grouped into types of affixes deriving verbs, affixes deriving nouns, and reduplication. Affixes which are universal or common to the point of being reconstructible in proto-Mon-Khmer (i.e., causative, reciprocal, stativizing, and nominalizing) are marked with asterisks. One caveat is that the table omits some details, such as how productive or not a trait is in a particular sub-branch or the subtle semantic distinctions in a class such as stative verbs. Finally, the isolating Viet-Muong languages (VM) are shown in a separate column from the conservative Chut languages of Vietic (VT), which are typologically like other Mon-Khmer languages, having prefixes.

The table also lists total numbers of categories, including both affixation and reduplication, in each sub-branch. Focusing on affixation, Katuic, Aslian, and Bahnaric have the highest numbers, while the numbers in a few other sub-branches number several each. It is surprising to see that Mon and Khmer[9] have such low total numbers of morphological functions. Also worth noting is that Viet-Muong, despite its strongly isolating morphology, has several categories of reduplication. As for reduplication, there is a concentration of higher numbers of categories among the Mon-Khmer languages of Vietnam. The implications of these numbers are considered in the conclusion.

---

9 However, see Jenner and Pou (1982: xxvi - lv) for a more complete listing of semantic distinctions of prefixes and infixes in Khmer. However, while some are readily identifiable forms in other Mon-Khmer languages, many of Jenner and Pou's proposed categories are fossilized to the point that they can only be identified through consideration of Old Khmer scripts or highly nuanced, speculative semantics (e.g., for the proposed frequentive prefix /R-/, one aspect is described as 'any light or sudden, albeit non-repetitive, movement: *droma* /tróom/ 'to drop, sink' > *dadroma* /ttróom/ 'to flop down'). In many instances, they acknowledge that certain forms only appear in a few lexical items, making these forms too rare to be included in this study.

Table 2: Mon-Khmer Sub-Branches and Morphological Categories

SUB-BRANCHES / CATEGORIES	KS	MG	PL	KU	AS	NC	PR	MN	KR	BN	KT	VT	VM
# OF TOTAL	7	8	9	9	12	4	2	7	7	15	18	9	6
# OF AFFIXATION	5	4	7	6	10	4	2	4	5	9	13	5	0
# OF REDUP.	2	4	2	3	2	0	0	3	2	6	5	4	6
VERBS													
1. *Causative	+	+	+	+	+	+	+	+	+	+	+	+	-
2. *Reciprocal	-	-	+	+	+	-	-	-	+	+	+	-	-
3. *Stativizing	+	-	-	+	+	-	-	-	-	+	+	-	-
4. Aspectual/completive	-	-	-	-	+	-	-	-	-	+	+	-	-
5. Verbalizing	-	+	-	+	+	-	-	-	-	+	-	-	-
6. Involuntary	-	-	-	-	+	-	-	-	-	-	+	-	-
7. Desiderative	+	-	-	-	+	-	-	-	-	-	+	-	-
8. Negation	-	-	-	-	-	-	-	+	+	+	+	-	-
9. Pretence	-	-	+	-	-	-	-	-	-	-	+	-	-
NOUNS													
10. *Nominalizing	+	+	+	+	+	+	+	+	+	+	+	+	-
11. Pronominal affixes	+	-	+	+	-	+	-	-	-	+	+	-	-
12. Case-marking	-	+	-	-	+	+	-	-	-	-	+	+	-
13. Singular	-	-	-	-	-	-	-	-	+	+	-	+	-
14. Plural nouns	-	-	+	-	+	-	-	+	-	-	-	-	-
15. Existential/locative	-	-	-	-	-	-	-	-	-	-	+	+	-
16. Number of days/months	-	-	+	-	-	-	-	-	-	-	+	-	-
REDUPLICATION													
17. Time adverbials	+	-	+	+	-	-	-	+	-	+	+	+	+
18. Degree of intensity	+	+	+	+	+	-	-	+	-	+	-	+	+
19. Progression/iteration	-	+	-	-	+	-	-	-	-	+	+	+	+
20. Generalized	-	+	-	-	-	-	-	+	+	+	+	-	+
21. Derogatory/Dismissive	-	+	-	-	-	-	-	-	-	+	+	-	+
22. Stative verbs with plural subjects	-	-	-	+	-	-	-	-	+	-	+	-	-
23. Distributive/Plural nouns	-	-	-	-	-	-	-	-	-	+	-	-	+

Notes:

– The following abbreviations are used for the sub-branches: AS-Aslian, BN-Bahnaric, KR-Khmeric, KS-Khasic, KT-Katuic, KU-Khmuic, MG-Mangic, MN-Monic, NC-Nicobarese, PL-Palaungic, PR-Pearic, VM-Vietnamese, VT-Vietic (languages in Vietic other than Vietnamese and Muong).

– The low number for Nicobarese stems from the fact that its morphology, while complex, in many cases simply does not match the morphological types focused on in this study.

- Pearic has a low number in the chart due to the lack of morphological descriptions available.
- While Vietnamese is completely monosyllabic, with strict CVC syllable structure, a small number of prefixes and infixes is recoverable through comparative reconstruction. Original Mon-Khmer prefixes and infixes presumably merged into single initial consonants, but some lexical pairs still appear semantically and phonologically related. An example of the causative is the pair /cet^5/ 'to die' and /ziət^5/ 'to kill', while potential remnants of the nasal infix include /dæ:n^1/ 'to weave' /næ:n^1/ 'bamboo splint' and /cɔk^6/ 'to puncture' /nɔk^6/ 'stinger', of which the latter two have comparable forms in Khmu, as noted by Ferlus (1977).

3 Word-formation subcategories

The list below provides a summary of the main semantico-syntactic categories for the various functions seen in Table 2. They are grouped according to broad categories of overlapping features. Most of these categories are grammatical. While the non-grammatical, derivational categories (e.g., causative verbs, nouns derived from nouns, etc.) tend to produce the largest number of lexical items among the languages overall, grammatical functions of Mon-Khmer morphology are somewhat common.

1. *Aspect*: completive, progressive, time adverbials
2. *Indication of semantic roles*: subject agreement, case-markers, existential/locative
3. *Deriving lexical categories*: nominalizing, verbalizing, stativizing
4. *Mood functions*: involuntary, pretence, desiderative, derogatory
5. *Plurality*: plural, singular, stative verbs with plural subjects, distributive, number of days/months
6. *Other grammatical changes*: negation, reciprocity, degree of intensity
7. *Other semantic changes*: causative, semantic generalization

There is little overlap in the functions of affixes and reduplication. The iconic nature of reduplication tends towards certain semantic fields that affixation does not. For instance, reduplication can express progressive action and form time adverbs and plural nouns, all of which also occur in genealogically unrelated languages in the region. In contrast, only prefixes express involuntary actions, pretence, and desiderative mood. Derogatory/dismissive meanings are expressed solely by reduplication in four sub-branches (cf. English 'fancy-schmancy').

3.1 Aspect: Completive affixes and progressive reduplicants

Most often, Mon-Khmer languages use time words, aspectual markers, and context to encode time of actions and events. However, in several sub-branches, affixation is used to express completion, and in some, reduplication is used to express progression, or at least iteration/repeated action.

Many languages of the Aslian sub-branch have complex morphological systems to express aspect, though Khmu also has some morphology involved in expressing aspect (see in particular chapter 3 in Svantesson 1983), and even some Bahnaric and Katuic languages utilize both categories, though with much less productivity. Aslian has the most complex morphological system to express aspect, having in some languages perfective, imperfective, and progressive action expressed variously by affixes and copied segments. Matisoff (2003: 38), based on Diffloth (1976b), provides a chart of this. These aspectual systems are essentially fully inflectional morphology unlike any other non-Munda sub-branch of Mon-Khmer. However, in Bahnar of Bahnaric, aspect is expressed by a proclitic which can attach to a variety of words, including polysyllabic words.

- Bahnar (Bahnaric) : /kədah/ 'to kick' → /tə-kədah/ 'to have kicked' (Banker 1964a: 113)
- Katu (Katuic): /teŋ/ 'to do' → /ta-teŋ/ 'to have done' (Nguyễn and Nguyễn 1998: 77)
- Temiar (Aslian): /kɔ̃w / 'to call' → /ka-kɔ̃w/ 'to have called' (Matisoff 2003: 39)

Reduplication to express continuous and/or iterative action is seen in five sub-branches, though Aslian appears to be the only one in which this is fully productive. It is unclear how productive this is in the Vietic language, Ruc. Phonemically, some instances involve full reduplication, while some languages use partial reduplication, as shown below (e.g., Jah-hut, Mang, and Wa).

- Jahut (Aslian): /caʔ/ 'to eat' → /cʔ-caʔ/ 'to be eating' (Diffloth 1979: 96)
- Ruc (Vietic):[10] /pu³⁵/ 'to suckle' → /pu³⁵pu³⁵/ 'to be suckling' (Nguyễn V.L. 1993: 90)

Such morphology can also be used to create lexical items which are repetitive in nature, not grammatically progressive. These sometimes have additional semantic properties, such as emphasis of the repetition of an activity. While these secondary semantic properties are not strictly aspectual, they overlap semantically with progressive aspect. The Katuic language Bru has a prefix with iterative meaning. This appears to be a more generally semantic (i.e., referring to manner of the action) than grammatical (i.e., refers to position in time of a situation) function, and yet, it overlaps significantly with grammatical aspect.

- Bru (Katuic): /ɲiəm/ 'to weep' → /si-ɲiəm/ 'to keep on weeping' (Hoàng and Tạ 1998:77)
- Katu (Katuic): /taːp/ 'to clap' → /taːp-taːp/ 'to clap repeatedly' (Nguyễn and Nguyễn 1998: 90)
- Mang (Mangic): /ladik³⁵/ 'to shake side to side' → /dak³⁵-ladik³⁵/ 'to shake with a bobbing motion' (Nguyễn, Nguyễn, and Tạ 2008: 165)
- Vietnamese[11]: /kɔj³³/ 'to look at' → /kɔj³³-kɔj³³/ 'to keep looking' (Thompson 1965: 152)
- Wa (Palaungic): /dik/ 'to pedal' → /du-dik/ 'to pedal repeatedly and randomly' (Zhou and Yan 2006: 390)

Typically, full reduplication of entire words without alternating segments is used in the creation of time adverbials as well, as is also the case in languages belonging to other language families in the region. Time adverbials tend to have the nature of repeated, frequent, or gradual activity. While the number of words in this category is small, the common application of reduplication to express this category is associated with the iconic, iterative nature of these expressions.

---

10 Different publications mark tones in different ways. For clarity of presentation, tone contours and heights are indicated. Languages with two-way differences of high-low, such as Khmu and Sre, are marked with diacritics. For complex tonal systems, such as Vietic and Mangic languages, contour is indicated with a 5-number system. 1 is the lowest point and 5 the highest. The first number is the starting point, and the last number the ending point. Tones with dipping may have three numbers. Some languages, such as Ruc, may have neutral presyllables unmarked for tone. Glottalization is indicated where needed.
11 For ease of comparison with other languages in this study, Vietnamese is transcribed into IPA based on the official Northern Vietnamese standard for all examples in this article.

- Khasi (Khasic): /teŋ-teŋ/ 'sometimes'; /bu:n-bu:nsien/ 'most of the time' (Nagaraja 1985: 43)
- Taoih (Katuic): /kat.tro:ʔ-kat.tro:ʔ/ 'sometimes'; /ti:ʔ-mi:ʔ/ 'gradually' (Nguyễn, Đoàn, and Phan 1986: 143, 149)
- Vietnamese: /zən²¹-zən²¹/ 'gradually'; /tʰɯəŋ²¹-tʰɯəŋ²¹/ 'frequently'; /tʰin³¹-tʰwaŋ³¹/ 'occasionally'

3.2 Marking semantic roles: Prefixes on verbs, pronouns, and nouns

Despite Mon-Khmer languages' tendency towards isolating morphology, some instances of morphological case-marking and subject-agreement are seen in a few sub-branches. In Aslian and Katuic languages, there are subject-marking prefixes on verbs. In Katuic and Vietic, there are case-marking prefixes on pronouns, including accusative marking in several languages, but also dative and genitive in a few languages. Some Bahnaric and Katuic languages both have nasal prefixes on locative demonstratives, though with some different syntactic functions. Finally, in Mang there is an object marker used on nouns which is described as a prefix.

Are all of these true affixes or are some clitics? In some cases, there are associated lexical cognates, as is the case in Aslian languages, though as those full-form pronouns can co-occur with the reduced forms, the bound presyllable forms are still likely candidates for prefixes. In the Katuic language Pacoh, a persuasive argument has been made for the clitic status of case-marking forms on pronouns (Watson 2011). However, for this study, considering that in at least some cases these cannot be related to word forms, it is best to consider them to be prefixes as part of a continuum from clitic to affix or at least a process of delexicalization/morphologization.

3.2.1 Subject prefixes

Subject-marking prefixes are seen in both Aslian and Katuic, though Aslian languages have more forms. Despite the above-mentioned debate regarding their status as prefixes versus proclitics, all are bound morphemes without the ability to have other material (e.g., negation words) between them and their associated verbs. The Katuic language Pacoh has a 3rd person /ʔu-/ 'he/she' form and a generalized /ʔi-/ 'one,' neither of which has a related unbound form. In contrast, most Aslian languages have markers from 1st to 3rd person, singular to plural, all of which are obviously phonologically reduced forms of the sets of personal pronouns. Moreover, while in Pacoh verbs with these forms do not take subject nouns in their clauses, in Aslian languages, both main nouns and pronouns can co-occur with the reduced pronominal prefixes in a kind of grammatical agreement.

(1) Pacoh (Katuic)
 ʔi-taʔ   pəllo: ʔalɔːŋ
 One-make tube wood
 'One makes a wooden tube.'
 (Alves 2006: 39)

(2) Temiar (Aslian)
 yeːʔ ʔi-tɛrsəg cɛp
 1s   1s-trap   bird
 'I trapped the bird.'
 (Benjamin 1976: 175)

3.2.2 Case-marking prefixes on pronouns

Case-marking on pronouns is common among languages in the Katuic branch, though some dative pronouns also are seen in the Vietic language Ruc. In Katuic, Taoih has the largest range, with genitive, dative, and locative case-marking (Solntseva 1996), though there has not been a full description with examples of the syntactic uses of these. Pacoh, also a Katuic language, has possessive and dative pronouns (S. Watson 1964: 83-85; Alves 2006: 35). In these languages, there is no morphological distinction between the nominative and accusative case, a distinction which is marked only by word order.

– Ruc (Vietic): /mi³¹/ 'you' → /pa-mi³¹/ '(to) you' (Nguyễn V.L. 1993: 97)
– Taoih (Katuic): /hɛ/ 'we'; /ʔəŋ-hɛ/ 'our'; /ʔa-hɛ/ 'to us (dative)'; /ʔi-hɛ/ 'to us (locative/directional)' (Solntseva 1996: 34)

3.2.3 Case-marking prefixes on nouns

To date, Mangic is the only Mon-Khmer language to be shown to have apparent case-marking of nouns, marking both the accusative and dative.

(3) Mang (Mangic)
ɵɔ⁴²⁷ căp³⁵ ta-ɲo¹⁴⁷   ʔu³²³ ʔɔ²² lam⁵⁵⁷ ʔæŋ-ciəj⁵⁵⁷
dog chase ACC-cat   I   give rice DAT-chicken
(a) 'The dog chases the cat.' (b) 'I give rice to the chicken.'
(Nguyễn, Nguyễn, and Tạ 2008: 148)

3.2.4 Existential/locative marking and Impersonal predicates

The Bahnaric and Katuic sub-branches both have nasal prefixes on pronouns which have both a locative and existential function.

- Bru (Katuic): /naj/ 'here' → /ʔn-naj/ 'this here is (something)' (Hoàng et.al. 1986: 39)
- Koho (Bahnaric): /dɔ/ 'this' → /ʔn-dɔ / 'at this place'; /hə/ 'that' → /ʔn-hə/ 'at that place' (Hoàng et.al. 1986: 53-54)

Pro-drop and impersonal verbs are common in Mon-Khmer languages. In Katuic languages, these words become, in effect, impersonal predicates derived from pronouns.

(4) Bru (Katuic)
ʔn.tih tṳ:m   huk
that   stream NAME
'That there is Huk stream.'
(Hoàng et.al. 1986: 64)

(5) Pacoh (Katuic)
kɨ: vi: praʔ   ʔŋ-kɨ vi: praʔ
1s have money   1s.POSS exists money
(a) 'I have money.'   (b) 'Of that which is mine, there is money.'
                        (Alves 2006: 67)

3.3 Deriving lexical categories: Nouns, verbs, and stative verbs

Affixes to derive lexical categories are among the more common types in the language family. The nominalizing infix is shared by virtually all sub-branches in Mon-Khmer, though it is often not productive. Sidwell (2008) reconstructs several distinct nasal and sonorant infixes according to semantic features (e.g., agentive, instrumental, etc.), as discussed more below. Stativizing is somewhat less common, occurring in five sub-branches, though Sidwell (2008: 14) tentatively posits a reconstruction of *h-/*hN-. Finally, verbalizing is also seen in five sub-branches, though the morphs vary considerably in form, indicating distinct developments.

Nominalizing in Mon-Khmer involves the creation of a noun from a verb. It is most often accomplished by means of a nasal infix, though there is a large range of allomorphs among the sub-branches and even within individual languages.

– Jahai (Aslian): /tbɔh/ 'to beat' → /t-n-bɔh/ 'act of beating' (Burenhult 2002: 72)
– Kasong (Pearic): /khéːt/ 'to comb' → /kh-an-éːt/ 'comb' (Premsrirat 2011: 143)
– Nicobarese (Nicobaric): /ʔití/ 'to laugh' → /m-ití/ 'one who laughs' (Radhakrishnan 1981: 58)

Additionally, some sub-branches appear to have distinct semantic subcategories of these infixes, with potentially reconstructible forms: cf. Diffloth's (1984: 263) discussion of such reconstructed morphemes in Mon, as shown in Table 3.

Table 3: Infixes in Mon with reconstructions

AFFIX	FUNCTION	RECONSTRUCTED MON FORMS
-w- infix	nominalizer	*caaʔ 'eat' → *cwaaʔ 'flesh'
-m- infix	attributive	*jlɛɛʔ 'be short' → *jmlɛɛʔ 'short'
-m- infix	agentive	*daac 'hit, slap' → *dmaac 'smith'
-n- infix	nominalizer	*saal 'make bamboo strips' → snaal 'bamboo mat'
-n- infix	instrument	*twas 'sweep' → tnwas 'broom'
-rn- infix	instrument	*tun 'climb' → trnun 'ladder, stairs'
-r- infix	locative	*dmɔŋ 'stay' → drmɔŋ 'place'

Stativizing prefixes occur on active verbs to derive stative, adjectival verbs or verbs with passive-like semantic properties.

– Katu (Katuic): /toh/ 'to tear' → /ha-toh/ 'to be torn' (Nguyễn and Nguyễn 1998: 76)

- Khmu (Khmuic): /làk/ 'to split' → /hn-làk/ 'to be split' (Svantesson 1983: 51)
- Sre (Bahnaric): /hàl/ 'to cut' → /gə-hàl/ 'to be cut' (Manley 1972: 46)

Some languages, such as Khasi, Buxing and De'ang (Palaungic) have innovated prefixes which are not clearly related to proto-Mon-Khmer nasal infixes.

- Buxing (Khmuic (uncertain)): /kɛŋ/ 'to rest one's head' → /rəŋ-kɛŋ/ 'pillow' (Gao 2004: 62)
- Khasi (Khasic): /sa:r/ 'to broom' → /sɨn-sar:/ 'a broom' (Nagaraja 1985: 10)

Verbalizing of nouns is accomplished by a variety of morpho-phonological types. It is worth noting that these forms, while phonologically distinct, occur only in languages of the Truong Son mountain range bordering Vietnam and Laos.

- Bru (Katuic): /ra-ŋɨh/ 'breath' → /ta-ŋɨh/ 'to breathe' (Hoàng and Tạ 1998: 73)
- Koho (Bahnaric): /tɛ:/ 'the sound of one calling pigs' → /və-tɛ:/ 'to call pigs' (Hoàng et.al. 1984: 54)
- Kri (Vietic): /plaajh/ 'an arm span' → /p-a-laajh/ 'to measure something by arm spans' (Enfield and Diffloth 2009: 46)

3.4 Other grammatical categories: Involuntary, pretence, desiderative, and derogatory meanings

Modality is expressed morphologically in a relatively small number of Mon-Khmer languages. However, a notable variety of mood functions are seen, including involuntary actions (e.g., Aslian and Katuic), pretence (e.g., Katuic and Palaungic), desiderative meanings (Khasic, Aslian, and Katuic), and derogatory meaning (Mangic, Katuic, Bahnaric, and Vietnamese). The first three moods are expressed through affixes, while the latter function is expressed through reduplication.

Verbs morphologically marked with the sense of involuntary (or 'happenstance', as Kruspe 2004 describes these) action appear in different geographic regions.

- Katu (Katuic): /lum/ 'to meet (someone)' → /ta-lum/ 'to meet (someone) accidentally' (Nguyễn and Nguyễn 1998: 82)

- Semelai (Aslian): /jɔk/ 'to take' → /tr-jɔk/ 'to happen to take' (Kruspe 2004: 141)

To express pretence in Pacoh, the nasal prefix is followed by reduplication of the verb, but it requires 'to do' as part of the construction. Milne (1921:7) also mentions in passing that causative [p-] in Palaung, an apparently related morph, might also have such a general meaning.

- Palaung (Palaungic): /ravyn/ 'to be drunk' → /pən-vyn/ 'to pretend to be drunk' (Milne 1921: 74)
- Pacoh (Katuic): /cɔːm/ 'to know' → /taʔ ʔn-cɔːm-cɔːm/ (to do-know) 'to pretend to know' (S. Watson 1964: 29)

Desiderative affixes are seen only as prefixes, but they are all phonetically distinct and appear to be distinct developments in sub-branches. It is worth considering the possibility that these forms are related to or derived from semantic or modal verbs and thus may be proclitics rather than prefixes, though at this point, there is not sufficient information to determine this.

- Bru (Katuic): /beʔ/ 'to sleep' → /ʔi-beʔ/ 'want to sleep/about to sleep' (Hoàng, Nguyễn, Đoàn, and Phan 1986: 38)
- Kentakbong (Aslian): /ciʔ/ 'to eat' → /maʔ-ciʔ/ 'to want to eat' (Omar 1976: 955)
- Khasi (Khasic): /tʰjaʔ/ 'to sleep' → /sam-tʰjaʔ/ 'drowsy/feel like sleeping' (Nagaraja 1985: 26)

Considering the fact that four sub-branches have been shown to express derogatory meaning through reduplication, it appears the iconic nature of alternating reduplication, a kind of playful phonological manipulation, lends itself to a dismissive or critical tone. However, it is also worth noting that these sub-branches are in a roughly close geographic region. In both Vietnamese and Mang, copying of the initial combined with a set alternating rhyme is used to generate these.

- Mang (Mangic): /to^{323}/ 'large' → /to^{323}-tac^{55ʔ}/ 'large (dismissive)' (Nguyễn, Nguyễn, and Thông 2008: 164)
- Vietnamese: /bæn^{11ʔ}/ 'friend' → /bæn^{11ʔ}-biək^{35}/ 'friend (dismissive)' (Vu 2007: 174)

3.5 Plurality and other indication of number

While plurality in Mon-Khmer languages is often either unmarked or indicated lexically, there are ways that both affixes and reduplication are used to indicate number and plurality. Nouns can be marked singular or plural, but there are other numeric phenomena, such as ordinals, stative verbs with plural subjects, and precise time deictics for number of days or years in the past or future.

Numeral prefixes appear limited to reduced forms of the word for 'one,' generally /mV-/ attached to a classifier or measure word. In all cases, there is a full phonological free form of the word for 'one', while the singular prefixes are unstressed with neutral vowels and loss of off-glides. Furthermore, this tends to occur only with 'one' and not higher numbers. Notably, except for the apparent form [sa-] of Malay origin in Temiar, all other languages have derived the singular from the Mon-Khmer word for 'one'.

- Bugan (Mangic): /mə^{55}paw^{31}/ (unit-person) 'one person' (Li 1996: 148)
- Katu (Katuic): /panoŋ/ 'to strike' → /ma-panoŋ/ 'one stroke' (Nguyễn H.H. 1998: 239)
- Khmer (Khmeric): /mə-daəm/ (one-stick-like item) 'one (stick-like) thing' (Huffman 1970: 49)
- Pacoh (Katuic): /mu-lam/ (one-unit) 'one thing' (Alves 2006: 53)
- Ruc (Vietic): /mu-hal^{33}/ (unit-two) 'two-finger span' (Nguyễn V.L. 1993: 238)
- Temiar (Aslian): /sa-kebœ-gɔ/ (single-UNIT-bamboo cooking pot) 'a bamboo cooking pot' (Means 1998: 16)

Plural affixes appear on nouns only in Aslian languages, not other subbranches, possibly due to contact with Austronesian (Benjamin 1976 as noted in Matisoff 2003: 41). However, such instances do not always appear to have full productivity.

- Jahai (Aslian): /hali/ 'leaf' → /h-n-ali/ 'leaves' (Schebesta 1926: 811)
- Ple-Temer (Aslian): /bamug/ 'tiger' → /mən-mamug/ 'tigers' (Schebesta 1931: 646)
- Temiar (Aslian): /taaʔ/ 'sir' → /tataaʔ/ 'old man' → /tɛʔtaaʔ/ 'old men' (Benjamin 2011: 12)

In the Wa language (Palaungic), dual/plural distinctions among pronouns are expressed by forms related by distinct vowels (Zhou and Yan 2006:404), as shown in Table 4.

Table 4: Pronouns in Wa

PERSON	SINGULAR	DUAL	PLURAL
1st (incl)	ʔɤʔ	ʔaʔ	ʔeʔ
1st (excl)		ʑiɛʔ	ʑiʔ
2nd	maiʔ	paʔ	peʔ
3rd	nɔh	kɛʔ	kiʔ

Ordinal prefixes are not always described in grammars. It is difficult to determine the status of these as affixes or clitics. The Bahnaric language Sedang has ordinal prefixes, though only on one to four, which are monosyllabic in Sedang, while higher, bisyllabic numbers are made ordinals by separate words.

- Khmer (Khmeric): /tiː-pram/ (ORDINAL-five) 'fifth' (Huffman 1970: 32)
- Bru (Katuic): /ʔa-paj/ (ORDINAL-three) 'third' (Hoàng and Tạ 1998: 69)
- Sedang (Bahnaric): /mo-moːj/ (ORDINAL-one) 'first'; /mo-paj/ (ORDINAL-three) 'third' (Smith 1969: 127)

Prefixes in Katuic and Khmuic mark adjectival verbs to indicate that the subjects are plural. A related usage is seen in Khmer, in which reduplicated modifiers of nouns indicate plurality of the head noun (Headley p.c.).

- Khmer (Khmeric): /kon toc/ (person-small) 'a child' → /kon toc-toc/ 'children' (Headley p.c.)
- Khmu (Khmuic): /cŋák/ 'one being nods once' → /r̆-ŋàk/ 'many beings nod once at the same time' (Svantesson 1983: 57).
- Pacoh (Katuic): /ka-kɛt/ 'small (in regards to a plural subject)' (Alves 2006: 39)

3.6 Affixes on pronominals

Affixes on personal and demonstrative pronouns are naturally expected as such words are already grammaticalized and tend to undergo further grammaticalization, as in many languages. In Mon-Khmer, morphology on pronouns has already been discussed in Section 3.2 on case-marking with the nasal prefix, and Section 3.5 on plurality. Indeed, the Koho nasal derives a variety of pronouns and interrogative words.

- Koho (Bahnaric): /ci/ 'thing' → /ʔɲ-ci/ 'what'; /kar/ 'remaining' → /ʔŋ-kar/ 'how much remaining'; /teːŋ/ 'place' → /ʔn-teːŋ/ 'where'; /vɛ/ 'similar to' /ʔm-vɛ/ 'like what' (Hoàng, Lý, Tạ, et. al. 1986: 53)

Demonstrative pronouns have been shown to have similitive prefixes, though it is not clear whether these are potentially proclitics. Still, as there are no comparable free forms, such as prepositions, to which these are related, they would appear to be prefixes.

- Bahnar (Bahnaric): /nu/ 'this' → /nə-nu/ 'like this' (Banker 1964b: 112)
- Ruc (Vietic): /ni³³/ 'this' → /kə-ni³³/ 'like this' (Nguyễn Văn Lợi 1993: 88)

Even Vietnamese shows evidence of an earlier system of morphology in its demonstrative system, as noted by Thompson (1965: 142). While differences in rhymes correspond to speaker, the initials vary according to function (e.g., place, reference, etc.), as shown in Table 5.

Table 5: Vietnamese demonstratives

	Unspecified	Close to Speaker	Remote
Place	ɗəw³³	ɗəj³³	ɗəj³⁵
Reference	naːw²¹	naj²¹	nɔ¹¹ˀ
Proportion	ɓaːw³³	ɓəj³³	ɓəj³⁵
Manner	saːw³³	vəj²¹	vəj¹¹ˀ

Another case is Car Nicobarese, which is described as having a pronoun system distinguished by pronoun forms with categories of subject, interrogative, subordinate, possessive, and emphatic functions in addition to having demonstrative pronoun contractions involving 'to' (Braine 1961: 135), though these are clearly distinct developments from the rest of the Mon-Khmer sub-branches.

3.7 Other grammatical functions: Reciprocity, negation, and degree of intensity

Additional grammatical functions expressed morphologically in Mon-Khmer include reciprocity, negation, and degree of intensity. Reciprocity and negation are seen in prefixes, while degree of intensity is indicated through reduplication.

The reciprocal has been reconstructed for Proto-Mon-Khmer by Sidwell as *t-/*tN- (2008: 13), though considering the forms below, a tentative reconstruction of *CVr- can be suggested at this point.[12]

- Bru (Katuic): /sabaw/ 'to call' → /sa-r-baw/ 'to call each other' (Hoàng and Tạ 1998: 82)
- Chrau (Bahnaric): /pəm/ 'to hit' → /tam-pəm/ 'to fight' (Thomas 1971: 154)
- Khmer (Khmeric): /cum/ 'to surround' → /prɑ-cum/ 'to join together' (Jenner and Pou 1982: 85)
- Khmu (Khmuic): /pók/ 'to bite' → /tr̀-pók/ 'to bite each other' (Svantesson 1983: 39)
- Palaung (Palaungic): /ʔɛːh/ 'to scold' → /kər-ʔɛːh / 'to abuse each other' (Milne 1921: 52)
- Rengao (Bahnaric): /ʔwaj/ 'to reside' → /ta-ʔwaj/ 'to live together' (Gregerson 1979: 108)
- Semelai (Aslian): /tmɨɲ/ 'to smile (at s.o.) in acknowledgment on meeting' -> /b-tmɨ-tmɨɲ/ 'to smile at one another in acknowledgment on meeting' (Kruspe 2004: 121)

Negation is quite limited as a derivational function. While the negation prefix appears fairly productive in Bahnar and Mon, in Khmer and Pacoh it is strictly lexical with only a few examples.

- Bahnar (Bahnaric): /wih/ 'to go home' → /kə-wih/ 'not go home' (Banker 1964a: 116)
- Mon (Monic): /ket/ 'take' → /h-k-w-et/ 'not take' (Jenny 2003: 56)
- Khmer (Khmeric): /miən/ 'have' → /k-miən/ 'not have' (Huffman 1970: 412)
- Pacoh (Katuic): /ʔiɲ/ 'want' → /ʔa-ʔiɲ/ 'hate' (R. Watson 2011: 229)

Degree of intensity is often indicated through reduplication, a widely attested feature cross-linguistically. However, whether the degree of intensity is increased or decreased varies according to language, and in some languages, either meaning is possible. These constructions more often involve full reduplication than alternating reduplication.

---

[12] However, see Bauer (1987-1988) for an argument of an *-r- infix, with CVr- shape resulting from a reanalysis and combining of *-r- with CV prefixes, such as causative prefixes. Also, another issue is the possibility of contact with Austronesian groups, such as the Cham or the Malay (Diffloth pc). However, both of these possibilities encounter problems when faced with the data in Khmu and Palaung.

- Khasi (Khasic): /khruj/ 'many' → /khruj-ruj-ruj/ 'in many great numbers' (Nagaraja 1985: 40)
- Ruc (Vietic): /ɟal³³-ɟal³³/ 'rather long' (Nguyễn 1993: 90)
- Muong: /haw³⁵-haw³⁵/ 'to want somewhat' (Hoàng V. H. 1998: 168)
- Vietnamese: /ɗɛp¹¹²-ɗɛp¹¹²/ 'somewhat pretty' (Thompson 1965: 152)

3.8 Other Semantic Functions

The nearly universal Mon-Khmer causative prefix with a general shape of [pV-] has numerous phonetic realizations throughout the language family (Alves 2014). Adding to the morphological complexity is the wide range of syntactic constructions that apply to these verbs among the languages (Alves 2001).

- Chong (Pearic): /hoːc/ 'to die' → /ma-hoːc/ 'to kill' (Premsrirat 2011: 143)
- Khmer (Khmeric): /coːl/ 'to enter' → /bɔɲ-coːl/ 'to cause to enter' (Nacaskul 1978: 193)
- Mlabri (Khmuic): /ʔem/ 'to sleep' → /pa-ʔem/ 'to cause to sleep' (Rischel 1995: 304 and 357)
- Nicobarese (Nicobaric): /cím/ 'to cry' → /ha-cím/ 'to cause someone to cry' (Radhakrishnan 1981: 58)
- Thavung (Vietic): /jɯːn³⁵³/ 'to arise' (Premsrirat 1998: 197) → /pa-jɯːn³⁵³/ 'to wake up' (Premsrirat 1999: 107)

Another kind of word formation derives semantically more generalized concepts than their roots. This is often achieved through full, unaltered reduplication. However, in Bru, it involves a copied consonant in a [Cu-] prefix, and in Mang, alternating reduplication is involved. There can be syntactic consequences. Generalized verbs tend to be intransitive, and generalized nouns tend not to take quantifiers or modifiers.

- Bru (Katuic): /taʔ/ 'to do/make' → /tu-taʔ/ 'to do/make in general' (Nguyễn, Đoàn, Phan 1986: 40)
- Khmer (Khmeric): /srej/ 'woman' → /srej-srej/ 'women in general' (Huffman 1970: 298)
- Mang (Mangic): /əa²²/ 'to eat' → /əa²²-əac³⁵/ 'to eat (in general)' (Nguyễn, Nguyễn, and Tạ 2008: 164)

4 Conclusions

This survey, while revealing a substantial amount of diversity, also suggests the possibility of more morphological phenomena that have not yet been described in print. Morphological categories seen in just one sub-branch were not included in this paper. One example is the detransitivizing prefixes in De'ang (Chen, Wang, and Lai 1986: 974-975) and Wa (Zhou and Yan 2006: 392), a feature I did not find in other Mon-Khmer descriptions. Thus, while it is common for articles to conclude by suggesting the need for more research, in this case, the need for more research is urgent. Needed in particular is closer investigation of even previously described languages, especially those on the rapidly growing list of endangered languages.

Some typological tendencies emerge from this study with historical implications. Certain types of prefixes, such as singular nouns and forms to change parts of speech, appear to be important enough to have been innovated in various languages independently, though more highly specialized semantic functions are not as widespread and appear largely in separate sub-branches. Pronouns have, as one might expect, a tendency to undergo various kinds of additional grammaticalization. Also, reduplication appears to have a universal tendency to express concepts of an iterative nature, overlapping with progression and plurality, as well as generalizing and intensifying meanings, but it also serves to express disdain.

It is interesting that the languages with the largest number of speakers, namely Vietnamese and Khmer, which also have long literary traditions, have the smallest number of grammatical categories. It may be supposed that, while other non-literate languages change and innovate at regular rates, these codified languages have not innovated, even though they have became lingua francas of sorts, which are prone to streamlining and morphological simplification. It appears that languages such as Vietnamese via Chinese and Khmer via Thai have undergone McWhorter's interrupted transmission, while the non-mainstream varieties have developed their own complexity of non-essential grammatical features, a natural state of languages without interference (McWhorter 2007: 4). More isolated groups which have co-existed largely with speakers of related speech varieties have more original language situations. However, it is also the case that, for example, Aslian languages, speakers of which have extensive bilingualism in Malay, have adopted large numbers of Malay affixes (cf. a list of a dozen Malay affixes in Temiar (Means 1998: 15)).

On the issue of historical relatedness, the morphological categories are only in some cases possibly connected within sub-branches. An example is some of the case-marking phenomena in neighbouring Bahnaric, Katuic, and Vietic. But otherwise, the forms seen throughout the languages are generally not reconstructible to higher branch nodes. The variety of unrelated forms expressing the same semantic categories in various sub-branches shows the time depth of the separation of these related languages. And yet, the shared categories themselves are suggestive of typological similarity. While it is tempting to consider shared morphological traits to be signs of preservations of earlier forms in the languages, it is also possible that these are innovations with or without the influence of neighbouring languages. Indeed, as for the morphological diversity of Mon-Khmer languages without writing systems, this morphological complexity highlights (a) the depth of time of separation among the sub-branches and (b) the general tendency of human languages to innovate complex grammar even without a particular communicative need.

References

Alves, Mark J. 2000. *A Pacoh analytic grammar*. Honolulu: University of Hawai'i dissertation.
Alves, Mark J. 2001. Distributional properties of causative verbs in Mon-Khmer languages. *Mon-Khmer Studies* 31. 107–120.
Alves, Mark J. 2006. *A Pacoh grammar*. Canberra: Pacific Linguistics.
Alves, Mark J. 2014. A survey of derivational morphology in the Mon-Khmer Language Family. In Pavel Stekauer & Rochelle Lieber (eds.), *The Oxford handbook of derivational morphology*, 520–544. Oxford: Oxford University Press.
Anderson, Gregory D.S. 2004. Advances in Proto-Munda reconstruction. *Mon-Khmer Studies* 34. 159–184.
Anderson, Gregory D.S. 2007. *The Munda verb: typological perspectives*. Berlin: Walter de Gruyter.
Banker, Elizabeth M. 1964a. Bahnar affixation. *Mon-Khmer Studies* 1. 99–117.
Banker, Elizabeth M. 1964b. Bahnar reduplication. *Mon-Khmer Studies* 1. 119–134.
Bauer, Christian. 1986. Recovering extracted infixes in Middle Khmer. *Mon-Khmer Studies* 15. 155–164.
Bauer, Christian. 1987-1988. Reanalyzing reanalyses in Katuic and Bahnaric. *Mon-Khmer Studies* 16–17. 143–154.
Bauer, Christian. 1982. *Morphology and syntax of spoken Mon*. London: University of London dissertation.
Bauer, Christian. 1989. The verb in spoken Mon. *Mon-Khmer Studies* 15. 87–110.
Bauer, Christian. 1991. Old Mon s-. In Jeremy H.C.S. Davidson (ed.), Austroasiatic languages. Essays in honour of H. L. Shorto, 241–249. London: University of London, School of Oriental and African Studies.
Benjamin, Geoffrey. 1976. An outline of Temiar grammar. In P. N. Jenner, L. C. Thompson & S. Starosta (eds.), *Austroasiatic studies part II* (Oceanic Linguistics Special Publication No. 13), 129–188. Honolulu: University of Hawai'i Press.

Benjamin, Geoffrey. 2011. *Temiar morphology (and related features): A view from the field.* (Fifth International Conference on Austroasiatic Linguistics). Bangkok: Mahidol University.

Braine, Jean C. 1961. *Nicobarese grammar (Car dialect).* Berkeley: University of California dissertation.

Burenhult, Niclas. 2002. *A grammar of Jahai.* Lund: Lund University dissertation.

Burenhult, Niclas. 2011. The coding of reciprocal events in Jahai. In N. Evans, A. Gaby, S. C. Levinson & A. Majid (eds.), *Reciprocals and semantic typology*, 163–176. Amsterdam: Benjamins.

Chen Guoqing 陈国庆. 2005. *Kemie yu yan jiu / 克蔑语研究* [A study of the Kemie language]. Beijing: 民族出版社 / Min zu chu ban she.

Chen Xiangmu, Wang Jingliu & Lai Yongliang 陈相木, 王敬骝 & 赖永良. 1986. *De'ang yu jianzhi 德昂语简志* [An outline of the Palaung language]. Beijing: Min zu chu ban she / 民族出版社.

Clark, Marybeth. 1970. *Notes on the causative prefix in some Mon-Khmer languages* (Seminar in problems in comparative Vietnamese linguistics). Honolulu: University of Hawai'i. Manuscript.

Cohen, P.D. 1966. Presyllables and reduplication in Jeh. *Mon-Khmer Studies* 2. 31–53.

Cooper, James S. 1966. Halăng verb phrase. In David D. Thomas (ed.), *Papers on four Vietnamese languages,* 28–34. Auckland: Linguistic Society of New Zealand.

Costello, Nancy A. 1966. Affixes in Katu. *Mon-Khmer Studies* 2. 63–86.

Costello, Nancy A. 1998. Affixes in Katu of the Lao P.D.R. *Mon-Khmer Studies* 28. 31–42.

Costello, Nancy A. 2001. Aspect and Tense in Katu of the Lao P.D.R. *Mon-Khmer Studies* 31. 121–125.

DiCanio, Christian. 2005. Expressive alliteration in Mon and Khmer. *UC Berkeley Phonology Lab Annual Report (2005)*. 337–393.

Diffloth, Gérard. 1976a. Expressives in Semai. In Philip N. Lenner, Laurence C. Thompson & Stanley Starosta (eds.), *Austroasiatic Studies Part I* (Oceanic Linguistics Special Publications No. 13), 249–264. Honolulu: University of Hawai'i Press.

Diffloth, Gérard. 1976b. Minor-syllable vocalism in Senoic languages. In Philip N. Lenner, Laurence C. Thompson & Stanley Starosta (eds.), *Austroasiatic Studies Part I* (Oceanic Linguistics Special Publications, No. 13), 229–247. Honolulu: University of Hawai'i Press.

Diffloth, Gérard. 1979. Jah-Hut, an Austroasiatic language of Malaysia. In Nguyen Dang Liem (ed.), *South-east Asian linguistic studies vol. 2*, 73–118. Canberra: Pacific Linguistics.

Diffloth, Gérard. 1984. *The Dvaravati Old-Mon language and Nyah Kur.* Bangkok: Chulalongkorn University Printing House.

Dinh, Le Thu. 2007. Reduplication in the M'nong Language. In Mark Alves, Paul Sidwell & David Gil (eds.), *SEALS VII: Papers from the 8th Annual Meeting of the Southeast Asian Linguistics Society* (1998), 57–65. Canberra: Pacific Linguistics.

Donegan, Patricia Jane. 1993. Rhythm and vocalic drift in Munda and Mon-Khmer. *Linguistics of the Tibeto-Burman Area* 16(1). 1–42.

Donegan, Patricia Jane & David Stampe. 1983. Rhythym and the holistic organization of language structure. In John F. Richardson, Mitchell Marks & Amy Chukerman (eds.), *Papers from the parasession on the interplay of phonology, morphology, and syntax*, 337–353. Chicago: Chicago Linguistic Society.

Dryer, Matthew S. & Haspelmath, Martin (eds.). 2011. *The World Atlas of Language Structures Online.* Munich: Max Planck Digital Library. http://wals.info/ (accessed 19 June 2013).

Enfield N. J. & Gérard Diffloth. 2009. Phonology and sketch grammar of Kri, a Vietic language of Laos. *Cahiers de Linguistique Asie Orientale* 38(1). 3–69.

Ferlus, Michel. 1977. L'infixe instrumental rn en Khamou et sa trace en Vietnamien. *Cahiers de Linguistique Asie Orientale* 2. 51–55.

Filbeck, D. 1996. Couplet and duplication in Mal. *Mon-Khmer Studies* 26. 91–106.

Gao Yongqi. 高永奇 / 2004. *Buxing yu yan jiu* / 布兴语研究 [A study of the Buxing language]. Beijing: Min zu chu ban she / 民族出版社.

Gradin, D. 1976. Word affixation in Jeh. *Mon-Khmer Studies* 5. 25–42.

Gregerson, Kenneth. 1979. *Predicate and argument in Rengao grammar*. Dallas, TX: University of Texas at Arlington, SIL.

Gurdon, Philip R.T. 1914. *The Khasis*. London: Macmillan & Co.

Headley, Robert. 1977. A Pearic vocabulary. *Mon-Khmer Studies* 6. 69–149.

Hoang, Tuệ, Nguyễn Văn Lợi, Đoàn Văn Phúc & Phan Xuân Thành. 1986. *Sách Học Tiếng Bru Vân Kiều* [A text to study the Bru language]. Hanoi: Ủy Ban Nhân Dân.

Hoang, Tuệ, Lý Toàn Thắng, Tạ Văn Thông, K'breu & K'broh. 1986. *Ngữ Pháp Tiếng Kơho* [A Grammar of Koho]. Lam Dong, Vietnam: Sở Văn Hóa và Thông Tin Lâm Đông.

Hoàng, Văn Hành. 1985. *Từ láy trong Tiếng Việt* [Reduplication in Vietnamese]. Hanoi: Nhà Xuất Bản Khoa Học Xã Hội.

Hoàng, Văn Hành. 1993. Từ láy trong các ngôn ngữ Katuic ở Việt Nam [Reduplication in the Katuic languages in Vietnam]. *Ngôn Ngữ* 4. 8–17.

Hoàng, Văn Hành. 1998. *Từ Láy Đôi trong Tiếng Mường* [Reduplication in Muong]. In Từ Láy: Những Vấn Đề Còn Để Ngỏ [Reduplication: Remaining Issues], 165–193. Hanoi: Institute of Linguistics.

Hoàng, Văn Ma & Tạ Văn Thông. 1998. *Tiếng Bru-Vân Kiêu* (The Bru-Van Kieu language). Hà Nội: Nhà Xuất Bản Khoa Học Xã Hội.

Huffman, Franklin E. 1970. *Modern spoken Cambodian*. Ithaca, NY: Cornell University, Southeast Asia Program.

Jenner, P. 1977. Anomalous expansions in Khmer morphology. *Mon-Khmer* Studies 6. 169–189.

Jenner, P. & Pou, S. 1982. A lexicon of Khmer morphology. *Mon-Khmer Studies* 9–10. 1–517.

Jenny, Mathias. 2003. New Infixes in spoken Mon. *Mon-Khmer Studies* 33. 183–194.

Jenny, Mathias. 2005. *The verb system of Mon* (Arbeiten des Seminars für Allgemeine Sprachwissenschaft 19). Zurich: University of Zurich.

Kruspe, Nicole. 2004. *A grammar of Semelai*. Cambridge: Cambridge University Press.

Li, Jinfang. 1996. Bugan: A new Mon-Khmer language of Yunnan province, China. *Mon-Khmer Studies* 26. 135–159.

Li Yunbing 李云兵. 2005. *Bugeng yu yan jiu* / 布赓语研究 (A Study of Bugeng [Bugan]). Beijing: Min zu chu ban she / 民族出版社.

Man, Edward Horace. 1889. *A dictionary of the central Nicobarese language (English-Nicobarese and Nicobarese-English)*. London: W.H. Allen & Co.

Manley, Timothy McLemore. 1972. *Outline of Sre structure* (Oceanic Linguistics Special Publication No. 12). Honolulu: University of Hawai'i Press.

Matisoff, James. A. 2003. Aslian: Mon-Khmer of the Malay peninsula. *Mon-Khmer Studies* 33. 1–58.

McWhorter, John. 2007. *Language Interrupted: Signs of non-native acquisition in standard language grammars*. Oxford: Oxford University Press.

Means, Nathalie. 1998. *Temiar-English English-Temiar dictionary*. St. Paul, MN: Hamline University Press.

Means, Nathalie & Paul B. Means. 1986. *Sengoi-English English-Sengoi dictionary*. Toronto: The Joint Centre on Modern East Asia, University of Toronto.

Milne, Leslie. 1921. *An elementary Palaung grammar*. London: Oxford University Press.

Nacaskul, Karnchana. 1978. The syllabic and morphological structure of Cambodian words. *Mon-Khmer Studies* 7. 183–200.

Nagaraja, K. S. 1985. *Khasi: A descriptive analysis*. Pune: Deccan College Post-Graduate and Research Institute.

Nagaraja, K. S. 1993. Khasi dialects: a typological consideration. *Mon-Khmer Studies* 23. 1–10.

Nguyễn, Đình Hoà. 1966. *Vietnamese-English dictionary*. Rutland, VT: Charles E. Tuttle Co.

Nguyễn, Hữu Hoành. 1998. *Katu language word formation* (Hanoi-Leiden Series: Data papers on minority languages of Vietnam). Hanoi: Nhà Xuất Bản Khoa Học Xã Hội.

Nguyễn, Hữu Hoành & Nguyễn Văn Lợi. 1998. *Tiếng Katu* [The Katu language]. Hanoi: Nhà Xuất Bản Khoa Học Xã Hội.

Nguyễn, Tài Cẩn. 1996. *Ngữ pháp Tiếng Việt* [Vietnamese grammar]. Hà Nội:Nhà Xuất Bản Đại Học Quốc Gia Hà Nội.

Nguyễn, Văn Khang, Bùi Chỉ & Hoàng Văn Hành. 2002. *Từ điển Mường-Việt* (A Muong-Vietnamese dictionary). Hà Nội: Nhà Xuất Bản Văn Hoá Dân Tộc.

Nguyễn, Văn Lợi. 1993. *Tiếng Rục* (The Ruc language). Hà Nội: Nhà Xuất Bản Khoa Học Xã Hội.

Nguyễn, Văn Lợi, Nguyễn Hữu Hoành & Tạ Văn Thông. 2008. *Tiếng Mảng* (The Mang Language). Hà Nội: Nhà Xuất Bản Khoa Học Hà Nội.

Nguyễn, Văn Lợi, Đoàn Văn Phúc & Phan Xuân Thành. 1986. *Sách học tiếng Pakôh-Taôih* [Text for studying Pakoh-Taoih]. Hà Nội: Ủy Ban Nhân Dân, Tỉnh Bình Trị Thiên (The People's Committee, Binh Tri Thien Province).

Nguyễn Văn Tài, Trần Giang Nam, Hồ Xuân Xiếu, & Vương Hữu Lễ. 1986. *Sách học Tiếng Brũ Vân Kiều* (A text to study the Bru language). Hà Nội: Ủy Ban Nhân Dân, Tỉnh Bình Trị Thiên (The People's Committee, Binh Tri Thien Province).

Omar, Asmah Haji. 1976. The verb in Kentakbong. In P. N. Jenner, L. C. Thompson & S. Starosta (eds.), *Austroasiatic studies part II* (Oceanic Linguistics Special Publication No. 13), 951–960. Honolulu: University of Hawai'i Press.

Pinnow, Heinz Jürgen. 1965. Personal pronouns in the Austroasiatic languages: a historical study. *Lingua* 14. 3–42.

Pinnow, Heinz Jürgen. 1966. A comparative study of the verb in the Munda languages. In N.H. Zide (ed.), *Studies in Comparative Austroasiatic Linguistics*, 96–193. The Hague: Mouton.

Premsrirat, Suwilai. 1987. *Khmu, a minority language of Thailand*. Canberra: Pacific Linguistics.

Premsrirat, Suwilai. 1998. So (Thavung)-English-Thai glossary Part I. *Mon-Khmer Studies* 28. 189–218.

Premsrirat, Suwilai. 1999. So (Thavung)-English-Thai glossary Part II. *Mon-Khmer Studies* 29. 107–132.

Premsrirat, Suwilai. 2011. Pearic, a dying branch of Austroasiatic languages and its struggle for survival. In Sophana Srichampa & Paul Sidwell (eds.), *Austroasiatic studies: Papers from ICAAL 4, Mon-Khmer Studies Special Issue No. 2*. 138–153.

Radhakrishnan, R. 1976. A note on the morphology of the causative in Nancowry. In Philip N. Jenner, Laurence C. Thompson & Stanley Starosta (ed.), Austroasiatic studies. Honolulu: The University Press of Hawaii. 1035–1040.

Radhakrishnan, R. 1981. The Nancowry word: phonology, affixal morphology and roots of a Nicobarese language. *Current Inquiry into Language and Linguistics 37*. Edmonton, Alberta, Canada: Linguistic Research, Inc.

Rischel, Jørgen. 1995. *Minor Mlabri: A hunter-gatherer language of northern Indochina*. Denmark: Museum of Tusculanum Press, University of Copenhagen.

Schebesta, Pater P. 1926. Grammatical sketch of the Jahai dialect, Spoken by a Negrito tribe of the Ulu Perak and Ulu Kelantan, Malay Peninsula. *Bulletin of the School of Oriental and African Studies* 4. 803–826.

Schebesta, Pater P. 1931. Grammatical sketch of the Ple-Temer language. *Journal of the Royal Asiatic Society of Great Britain and Ireland* 63(3). 641–652.

Schiller, Eric. 1994. Khmer nominalizing and causativizing infixes. In K.L. Adams & T.J. Hudak (eds.), *Papers from the Second Annual Meeting of the Southeast Asian Linguistics Society*, 309–326. Phoenix, AZ: Arizona State University, Program for Southeast Asian Studies.

Schiller, Eric. 1999. *Reduplication in Khmer morphology*. Published on the internet at Linguistics Unlimited: http://www.ericschiller.com/pdf/Khmer_Reduplication.pdf (accessed 19 March 2014).

Shorto, Harry L. 1963. The structural patterns of Northern Mon-Khmer languages. In Harry L. Shorto (ed.), *Linguistic comparison of Southeast Asia and the Pacific*, 47–61. London: University of London, School of Oriental and African Studies.

Sidwell, Paul. 2008. Issues in the morphological reconstruction of Proto-Mon-Khmer. in Claire Bowern, Bethwyn Evans & Luisa Miceli (eds.), *Morphology and Language History: In honour of Harold Koch*, 251–265. Amsterdam: Benjamins

Sidwell, Paul & Roger Blench. 2011. The Austroasiatic Urheimat: The Southeastern Riverine hypothesis. In N. J. Enfield (ed.), *Dynamics of Human Diversity*, 317–345. Canberra: Pacific Linguistics.

Smith, Kenneth D. 1969. Sedang affixation. *Mon-Khmer Studies* 3. 108–129.

Smith, R.L. 1973. Reduplication in Ngeq. *Mon-Khmer Studies* 4. 85–111.

Solntseva, Nina. 1996. Case-marked pronouns in the Taoih language. *Mon-Khmer Studies* 26. 33–36.

Starosta, Starosta. 1992. Sora combining forms and pseudo-compounding. *Mon-Khmer Studies* 18–19. 77–105.

Svantesson, Jan-Olof. 1983. *Kammu phonology and morphology* (Travaux de L'Institut de Linguistique de Lund XVIII). Lund: Liber Förlag.

Tạ, Văn Thông. 1998. Phương thức Láy trong Tiếng Kơho [Methods of reduplication in Koho]. In Từ Láy (ed.), *Những Vấn đề còn Để Ngỏ*, 194–213. Hà Nội: Nhà Xuất Bản Khoa Học Xã Hội.

Thomas, David. 1971. *Chrau grammar* (Oceanic Linguistics Special Publication No. 7). Honolulu: University of Hawai'i Press.

Thomas, David. 1987-1988. The instrument/locative and goal affix -N- in Surin Khmer. *Mon-Khmer Studies* 16–17. 85–98.

Thomas, Dorothy M. 1969. Chrau affixes. *Mon-Khmer Studies* 3. 90–107.

Thomas, Dorothy M. 1990. The instrument/locative and goal affix -N- in Surin Khmer. *Mon-Khmer Studies* 16–17. 85–98.

Thompson, Laurence. 1965. *A Vietnamese grammar*. Seattle: University of Washington Press.

Viên Ngôn Ngữ Học [Institute of Linguistics]. 1996. *Từ Điển Từ Láy Tiếng Việt* [A dictionary of reduplication in Vietnamese]. Hà Nội: Nhà Xuất Bản Giáo Dục.

Vu, Sonny X. 2007. A Unified analysis of some Vietnamese reduplication forms. In Mark Alves, Paul Sidwell & David Gil (eds.), *SEALS VII: Papers from the 8th Annual Meeting of the Southeast Asian Linguistics Society* (1998), 165–192. Canberra: Pacific Linguistics.
Watson, Richard. 1966a. Clause to sentence gradations in Pacoh. *Lingua* 16. 166–188.
Watson, Richard. 1966b. *Reduplication in Pacoh*. Hartford CT: Hartford Seminary Foundation thesis.
Watson, Richard. 1976. Pacoh numerals. *Linguistics* 74. 81–88.
Watson, Richard. 2011. A Case for Clitics in Pacoh. In Sophana Srichampa, Paul Sidwell & Kenneth Gregerson (eds.), Austroasiatic Studies: Papers from ICAAL4: Vol. 2. [Special Issue]. *Mon-Khmer Studies* 3, 222–232.
Watson, Saundra. 1964. Personal pronouns in Pacoh. *Mon-Khmer Studies* 1. 81–97.
Watson, Saundra. 1966. Verbal affixation in Pacoh. *Mon-Khmer Studies* 2. 15–30.
Zhou Zhizhi & Yan Qixiang 周植志 颜其香. 2006. *佤语简志 Wa yu jianzhi* [An outline of the Wa language]. Beijing: Min zu chu ban she / 民族出版社.
Zide, Norman H. & Gregory D. S. Anderson. 2001. The Proto-Munda verb: Some connections with Mon-Khmer. In K. V. Subbarao & P. Bhaskararao (eds.), *Yearbook of South-Asian languages and linguistics-2001*, 517–540. Delhi: Sage Publications.

Roger Blench
The origins of nominal classification markers in MSEA languages

Convergence, contact and some African parallels

1 Introduction

The languages of the world characteristically have morphological strategies both to classify nouns and to signify to speakers and hearers alike aspects of the semantics of those nouns. These strategies can be broadly divided into two categories: noun classes and numeral classifiers. Noun classes are here treated as devices for categorizing nouns semantically. Noun classes can be expressed overtly through bound affixes or other direct marking on the noun, or indirectly, on verbs (as in Navajo) or other parts of speech such as dependent verbs, adjectives, pronouns and prepositions, as in North Caucasian. Where the class is marked with a bound affix, noun class marking can be concordial: that is, other parts of speech, typically adjectives and demonstratives, agree with the class marker. This agreement may be alliterative, where the segmental material is the same or closely related, or non-concordial, where the relationship between class and marker is regular but the segments are dissimilar[1]. A classifier is a word which accompanies a noun in certain grammatical contexts, and reflects a semantic classification of nouns. Typically, where the noun is counted or measured, the classifier is an obligatory accompaniment to the noun.

Classifiers are typical of most South and East Asian language phyla, as well as being scattered across the New World. Compared with noun class markers, classifiers in individual languages tend to be very numerous, and some languages may have several hundred. The lists given in Adams (1989) or Post (2007) are extremely long, and the classes are strongly concerned with the shape and appearance of the noun. Although this type of semantic association is also characteristic of Niger-Congo languages, noun class markers are always restricted to a small number of bound affixes.

---

1 This is typical of many Bantoid languages, where an originally alliterative system has been restructured, producing a disjunction between agreement markers.

Although noun classes are often thought to be absent in SE Asia, there is increasing evidence that they exist as a parallel system in both Daic and Hmong-Mien. Ratliff (2010: 267) treats the nominal prefixes of Hmong-Mien as 'weakly classifying'. Enfield (2007: 146) calls one system of marking nominal semantics in Lao [and also Thai] 'class-terms'[2]. These consist of obligatory accompaniments to nouns, such as Thai marking all fish with a preceding *pla*, corresponding to Lao *pa* (reduced from *paa*[3]). Lao has quite a number of these terms, which are almost always etymologically transparent, although Lao *ka-* is somewhat opaque, applied to small creatures and objects (Enfield 2007: 150). They typically define taxonomic essences, colours, roles and functions. Exactly how widespread they are in SE Asia is unclear since their description is often conflated with numeral classifiers. De Lancey (1986) argues that class-terms can be reconstructed back to proto-Tai. English has a fragmentary system of this type in that the names of birds and fish are sometimes accompanied by the term itself ('blackbird', 'mutton-bird', 'dogfish', 'catfish'). In contrast to numeral classifiers, they are unrelated to number and quantity. Reduced noun class systems, such as the four-term systems in Australian languages like Dyirbal (Dixon 1972) are quite common in the Papuan and Australian language areas (Harvey and Reid 1997).

A third system, characteristic of phyla such as Indo-European and Afroasiatic, is the sex-gender system, which classifies nouns through notional male/female oppositions. Although animates with biological gender are marked with the appropriate sex marker, their extension to non-animates rarely conveys further semantic information. In French, for example, extremely similar body parts, such as 'arm' and 'hand', are assigned different genders. Noun classes in concordial languages are often referred to as 'genders' but this is a confusing terminology as it conflates a genuine semantic categorization with sex-gender systems. Sex-gender systems are usually concordial, unless they are part of a broader system of noun classes. Dyirbal, for example, marks male/ female distinctions, but includes water, fire and violent acts with the female class (Dixon 1972).

Languages are, broadly speaking, conservative and phyla can be characterized by particular strategies. So the great majority of Niger-Congo languages have noun classes or nothing; numeral classifiers or sex-gender systems rarely develop. Afroasiatic languages exhibit sex-gender throughout the phylum and indeed the morphology used to express this is highly conservative. Austroasiat-

---

[2] A term said to have been introduced by Mary Haas (1964). See also Beckwith (1993) for further discussion of this terminology.

ic, Austronesian, Hmong-Mien and Sino-Tibetan languages all have numeral classifier systems which do not show agreement. However, at least in two phyla of SE Asia, semantically associated affixes show formal and functional similarities. This paper considers various models to account for these formal and functional similarities.

Concordial noun classes are not found in SE Asia, but they do occur sporadically in Papua and Australia, notably in the Ngarnic language Yanyuwa, which has sixteen classes (Kirton 1988). Hammarström (2013) has reviewed the occurrence of these in some detail. Astonishingly, Yanyuwa has a *ma-* prefix for fruits, which although identical to a common SE Asian class-term, is presumably just coincidence. However, concordial systems are common in Niger-Congo languages, as well as in some New World language phyla, such as Arawan and Kiowan. The evolution of these systems is not well understood, but the recent description of predicate classifiers in Nilo-Saharan (Ahland 2010) may provide a clue as to how these have developed in Niger-Congo. A secondary argument of this paper is that some of the morphological processes at work in SE Asia also help shed light on nominal classification in African languages.

2 Noun class affixes

Typical noun class morphology consists of a root and an affix. The affix can be prefixed, suffixed, infixed or appear as a circumfix. In rare cases, languages exhibit double-affixing: two separate affixes which alternate according to distinct rules. Examples of such languages in Africa are Bassari on the Togo-Ghana borderland and the Tivoid languages of SE Nigeria (Greenberg 1977). As part of the erosion of such systems, various types of fusion can occur, but the original morphemes are usually reconstructible. The affix in principle has a semantic assignation, which may or may not be opaque. Affixes frequently alternate; thus singulars can have one or two marked plurals. In Nilo-Saharan it is often considered that the 'middle' is the unmarked term and a singulative and a plurative can be formed from the root (Dimmendaal 2000). But this is not a necessary requirement of a noun class language; in Niger-Congo the *m-* class for mass nouns is always an unpaired class (Greenberg 1963; Blench 1995).

In SE Asian language phyla, word structure is often described as 'sesquisyllabic' (Matisoff 1973). That is, words have major and minor syllables, i.e. an iambic structure. The major syllables are the stem and the minor syllable a prefix, generally C or CV. Since the -V is often represented orthographically with a mid-central vowel, it may be that it is not realized phonetically. Minor syllable prefixes are either lost or optional in many languages, and they seem to change in ways that do not suggest phonological shift but affix substitution. Austroasiatic, Sino-Tibetan and Hmong-Mien all show this behaviour. In Austronesian languages, the tendency is for the prefix to have a (C)V form and to be conserved. In other words, once a prefix has been fused to a stem, it is retained, from Taiwan to New Zealand, as it were. Daic languages are typically CV(C) and except in rare cases no longer retain the minor syllable. The loss of prefixes in Daic may well explain the adoption of class-terms as a substitute strategy for semantic marking of nouns.

Minor syllables thus have the appearance of optional prefixes in many languages. Anderson (2004) observes that in Munda the final syllable is the 'stable, meaning-associated element' while the prefixed syllables are unstable and cannot be assigned a meaning. Intriguingly, Blust (1988) also identifies an apparently similar system in Austronesian, where roots seem to retain a cross-language basic meaning, but are preceded by a variety of CV prefixes which transform the meaning in individual languages. Extended examples can be seen in the 'roots' section of the online Austronesian Comparative Dictionary[3]. Blust considers this as an example of phonosemantic association, similar to phonaesthemes identified elsewhere in the world (e.g. sl/gl in English). However, as Sagart (2011) observes, this system has striking similarities to the MSEA structures identified here.

It is certainly the case that the minor or prefix syllables have no obvious semantic assignations, and in no SE Asian language do they show concord. But to assume that they have 'no meaning' suggests a curious model of language. A general postulate of morphology is surely that the elements of words either do have or formerly have had meanings. These can be obscured over time, but one task of linguistics is to tease them out. In the case of prefixes in MSEA languages, the fact that they vary dynamically from one language to another is a reflection of their significance for speakers. They cannot be simply euphonious noise. Outside SE Asia, Nilo-Saharan languages show a wide range of affixes which suggest a former nominal marking system (Bender 1996; Storch 2005), but synchronically, no Southeast Asian language shows a productive system comparable to those in Niger-Congo. Affixes certainly change to mark number, but alliterative concord is unknown. This system is stable, and Nilo-Saharan

---

3 http://www.trussel2.com/acd/. It is striking that the majority of Blust's examples focus on Western Malayo-Polynesian, especially the Philippines. It is as if the system is completely dropped in Oceanic.

shows no sign of eliminating this unproductive morphological baggage and developing in the direction of a SE Asian type system.

Austroasiatic and many branches of Sino-Tibetan[4] have a common word structure where the root is preceded by a C- prefix. Although C- prefixes may have semantic correlates, this is inconsistent between languages. The prefix may disappear or be substituted, while the root remains static. The C- prefix can sometimes be incorporated into the stem, and a new prefix added, leading to complex initial sequences (cf. examples in Matisoff 2003). Additional evidence for this is drawn from the typical pattern of pronouncing initial consonant sequences as individual segments; thus 'spr' in Austroasiatic and Sino-Tibetan is pronounced s.p.r, rather than a cluster as in Indo-European. These similarities between the two phyla are rather perplexing, as few historical linguists consider them to be related. Globally, such systems are extremely rare, and for them to have arisen independently given their direct geographical proximity is unlikely. However, clear examples of common lexemes of any time-depth are few[5], and these are often shared with other regional phyla such as Daic and Hmong-Mien. A historical scenario to account for this structural convergence is not obvious; the likely Urheimats of these two phyla are far apart.

This paper describes the features of word structure in Austroasiatic and Sino-Tibetan that appear to be convergent and suggests how they might have arisen. It argues that such features are transitional towards the evolution of true noun classes and introduces a typological parallel from West Africa. The hypothesis is that the SE Asian affix system originates from frozen numeral classifiers (and noun class terms) and that as the system is renewed, these prefixes co-exist together with productive classifiers. It will examine possible borrowing scenarios and suggest that while these can be detected, they are inadequate to explain the diachronic morphology.

---

[4] I am aware of the controversy between this term and Tibeto-Burman. See below for further discussion. Whatever the case, Sinitic languages are in consideration, as the evidence for the type of canonic form described here is well attested in Old Chinese.

[5] Benedict (1990: 4) says, 'there is little evidence of any borrowing of lexical items of 'core' type by TB/ST from AA/MK'. However, he does give some striking examples from kin terms, as also the animal names 'hawk' and 'tiger' (cf. Table 7).

3 Word structure in Austroasiatic and Sino-Tibetan

Word structure in Austroasiatic (at least for nouns) seems to consist of one or more optional C(V) prefixes, a CV(CV) or CVA stem [where A is an approximant] and a C suffix, often weakened to a glottal stop or deleted. The optional C(V) prefixes are sometimes referred to as a 'pre-syllable' in the literature. Many nouns may have had a labial or palatal approximant in final position and this has a strong tendency to be incorporated into the stem. If it represents a different prosody from the vowel of the stem, then the synchronic output may be either a diphthong or a long vowel.

There is a background murmur in the literature suggesting the existence of old affixes with semantic content which derive from frozen classifiers (e.g. Costello 1996, 1998). For example, Thomas (1969: 105) gives evidence for a *sa-* prefix in the Bahnaric language Chrau which denotes animals. She says "For the most part the first syllable is never dropped, except in direct address" which of course does mark its optionality in the minds of speakers. Although she was unable to find comparative evidence, in fact this prefix appears to be quite widespread, as Shorto (2006: 469) notes a number of cognates. Table 1 cites cognates for the Chrau term for 'bear' [the animal] which shows that the *s-* prefix occurs in Bahnaric, Katuic and Vietic, with further possible cognates for the root itself in Aslian and Pearic.

Table 1: An Austroasiatic root for 'bear' with variable prefixes

Language	Subgroup	Attestation
Jahai	Aslian	kaw.ip
proto Bahnaric	Bahnaric	*c.kaw ~ *gaw
Laven [Jru']	Bahnaric	h.kaw
Sedang	Bahnaric	rə.kɔw
Chrau	Bahnaric	si.kaw
Ngeq	Katuic	haŋ.kaw
Bru	Katuic	sa.kaw
Chong [of Kanchanaburi]	Pearic	kəw.ɣaj suːʔt
Vietnamese [Hanoi]	Vietic	gấu
Chứt [Rục]	Vietic	cə.kuː

Smith (1975) points to the widespread presence of a velar prefix for animal names both in Sedang, and more broadly in the Vietnamese languages he sampled. But this prefix is found across Austroasiatic and also, strikingly, widely in

Sino-Tibetan. Matisoff (1973) draws attention to its presence in Lolo-Burmese, but as Benedict (1990) notes, it is present on the words for 'tiger' and 'hawk' throughout the phylum.

The Sino-Tibetan language phylum has a disputed internal structure and thus debatable reconstructed forms. Van Driem (2008), Handel (2008) and Blench and Post (2013) give an overview of some of the key issues. These swirl around the position of Sinitic, formerly considered a primary branching, but now often treated as simply another branch within Sino-Tibetan, hence the rechristening by some authors of Sino-Tibetan as Tibeto-Burman. Proposals to rename the phylum in a more neutral fashion (e.g. Tibeto-Burman or Trans-Himalayan) certainly have merit. Sinitic shares far more lexically with Tibeto-Burman than some of the isolated groups of Arunachal Pradesh (Blench and Post 2013). As with Austroasiatic, Sino-Tibetan words tend to have a core segmental structure, very often CV(N), and then one or more affixes, both prefixed and suffixed. Affixes can shift right or left into root medial position, inducing consonant and vowel changes, and prosodies affecting C_1. Change in the segmental character of C_1, such as n→ɲ or ŋ, is deemed to be driven by a shift of palatalization or velarization into the core. The perceived incorporation of a consonant within the stem leads to affix renewal, and thus stacking of unproductive morphemes.

In some languages of the region, the use of the fricative to mark animal names is notable. Table 2 gives an example from Western Miji, an only doubtfully Sino-Tibetan language spoken around Nafra in Arunachal Pradesh[6]. The palatal fricative /ʃ/ is the most common prefix, but I am assuming s~ts are probably its allomorphs.

The neighbouring Hruso language also shows an S- prefix for animals, although it shares almost no lexical cognates with Miji, except probably 'ant' ʃn (Table 3).

These dissimilarities suggest strongly that what has been transferred is the idea of the semantics of a prefix rather than actual lexical items. By contrast, the neighbouring Koro language, which is structurally very similar to Hruso and Miji, shows no trace of S- prefixes.

---

[6] All data from NE Indian languages is based on my own fieldwork in 2010 and 2011, and I would like to take the opportunity to thank the many people who helped me, as well as Jummar Koyu and Jiken Bomjen, who arranged my field trips.

Table 2: Animal names in Nafra Miji

Gloss	ʃ	s/ts
'animal'		stɕõ
'horse'	ʃgrɔ	
'stallion'	ʃgrɔ mbŭ	
'mare'	ʃgrɔ mněʔ	
'colt'	ʃgrɔ i	
'sheep'	ʃgθɔʔ	
'goat'	ʃprn	
'dog'	ʃazi	
'barking deer'		tstshũ
'deer'		tstsə
'flying squirrel'	ʃbiã	
'leopard'	ʃnmu	
'monkey'	ʃbŏ	
'musk deer'		tstsɲãw
'pangolin, anteater'	ʃgdʒɔ	
'wild cat'	ʃgrĕ	
'wild dog'	ʃkʃə	
'sparrow'		slĩʔ
'ant'	ʃɲi	
'fish sp. I'		sθŭ
'fish sp. II'		sviaʔ
'fish sp. III'		sgiɔʔ

Table 3: Hruso animal names with S- prefix

Gloss	Hruso
'wild animal'	sm tʃi
'dog'	ʃʎuɔ
'bear'	stʃɔ
'otter'	sʒɛ
'rat'	ʒmɔ
'ant'	ʃn
'caterpillar'	ʃblu
'flea'	sgzə
'bloodsucking fly'	sdʒm
'cobra'	ʒtɔ̃
'python'	ʒʃaba
'snake sp. I'	ʒmə
'frog I'	ʃdʑa
'snail'	svankɔ̃

Miji and the related Bangru also have a very marked *m-* prefix related to body parts, both for humans and animals. Table 4 shows a comparative list of Western and Eastern Miji as well as Bangru. The Bangru citations are orthographic, and on comparative grounds, it is assumed the vowel following the *m-* prefix is epenthetic. Forms in square brackets are cited for completeness, where one branch has an *m-* prefix and the other lacks it.

Table 4: Miji and Bangru body parts with an m- prefix

Gloss	W. Miji	E. Miji	Bangru	Comment
'arm, hand'	(m)gĭ	(m)gĭ	m(e)gey	No Tibeto-Burman cognates
'beard'	mɔmyuʔ	mmɯʔ	m(a)maŋ	Widespread Tibeto-Burman root, though not with m- prefix
'bone'	mrian	mrian	mnii	Possibly cf. Northern Naga *raŋ
'brain'	mɲɔʔ	mɲɔʔ		No certain external cognates, though cf. Bodic, e.g. Tshangla n̻oktaŋ
'breast'	mɲu	mnɯʔ		m- 'body part prefix' plus widespread Tibeto-Burman etymon *nu(w)
'chest'	mθm kʸu	mlɔŋ kə̌ʔ		The kV- element has widespread Tibeto-Burman cognates. Note Puroik tə kɯ
'chin'	mugudza	mgutɕǎ		No Tibeto-Burman cognates
'ear'	mʒɔʔ	mzɔʔ	m(i)bwa	No certain external cognates, but cf. Memba namdʒo
'eye'	mmreʔ	mreʔ		No Tibeto-Burman cognates
'face'	mgmiaʔ	mkmiaʔ	m(e)kwii/mekuyi	Matisoff (2003) proposes #s.myal for PTB. The best cognates are in Maraic, e.g. Lakher h.mia, but the velar preceding the Miji stem is of unknown origin.
'finger'	mgi tso		m(e)gey tʃowa	cf. 'arm'
'flesh'	mzaʔ	mʒaʔ		#sa is widespread in Tibeto-Burman, but this may be coincidence
'heart'	luŋ, [θɔm vʸu]		mloŋ	#luŋ is widespread in Naga complex languages
'kidney'	mkbɔ̌		mpega	Neither root has a Tibeto-Burman cognate
'liver'	mtn		m(a)tayiŋ	cf. Chin roots such as Thado tʰin, and possibly proto-Tani *zin.
'lungs'			mloŋ wasayi	cf. 'heart'
'mouth'	mugɔ̌		m(i)niŋ	STEDT relates the gɔ element to proposed PTB #ku(w). Some Tani languages have apparently similar forms, e.g. Apatani a.gū but this is not apparently proto-Tani. The Bangru form has no obvious cognates.
'navel'	mʃmay			No Tibeto-Burman cognates. The ʃ- appears to be an earlier prefix.

Gloss	W. Miji	E. Miji	Bangru	Comment
'neck'	[dmuzɔ̃]		m(i)niŋri	Scattered attestations in Kuki and Chin, e.g. Lushai #riŋ. Possibly related to much more widespread #luŋ
'nose'	[ɲubyuŋ]		m(i)niiko	Miji has ɲi 'blow nose'. Chin languages have common *niit* for 'blow nose'
'rib'			mpelowa	No Tibeto-Burman cognates.
'shoulder'	'mfa		mpotʃ	Miji has very scattered Tibeto-Burman cognates, e.g. Chinbon *pá*, though forms with a back high vowel are widespread. No obvious cognates for Bangru.
'stomach'	mrõ		mulgu	No Tibeto-Burman cognates.
'thigh'	mləʔ		murʰ	No clear Tibeto-Burman cognates. Isolated Thado *mʌ́l*, also possibly metathesis of Bodic *lum* (e.g. Tshangla).
'throat'	mryɔnza			No Tibeto-Burman cognates.
'tooth'	mtĩ		m(e)tʰu	No clear Tibeto-Burman cognates, except possible Puroik *kətuŋ*
'vein'	mdtʔ			No clear Tibeto-Burman cognates.
'wrist'	gi mvθɛ			No clear Tibeto-Burman cognates.
Animals				
'horn'	mʃɔ̃		m(e)ws	No clear Tibeto-Burman cognates.
'tail'	mdmray		m(u)lwe	Tibeto-Burman has widespread *may or similar. If this is cognate then it is an example of multiple re-affixing
'hump'	mkbʸu			Isolated possible cognate Bokar (Tani) *gur buɯŋ*
'tusk'	mtũ			No Tibeto-Burman cognates. In many Sino-Tibetan languages, the same word as 'tooth' but not here.
'udder'	mɲŭʔ			Possibly cf. Tangkhulic Huishu ʔa-nə-nuk
'fur, feather'	mɔmyŭʔ			Widespread Tibeto-Burman *mu(l)* but no other language shows palatalization
'wing'	mktɕi			No clear Tibeto-Burman cognates.

Table 4 shows that Mijiic has a strong preference for an *m-* prefix for human and animal body parts, even where this is not attested in external cognates. There is limited comparative evidence for a Tibeto-Burman *m-* prefix, see for example Matisoff (2008: 183) on *m-ley~*m-li for 'penis'.

A language spoken nearby, Mey [=Sherdukpen] of Rupa, also has the *m-* prefix but marking fruits (Table 5), which parallels the widespread *ma(k)* class-term, found in Tai languages.

Table 5: m- prefix for fruits in Mey of Rupa

Gloss	Rupa
'fruit'	m.laŋ
'banana'	m.suŋ
'lemon'	m.kẽ
'sugar-cane'	m.ʧi
'walnut'	m.ku

Forrest (1962), in an article not often cited, points out that Lepcha (Rong) has the same *kV-* prefix for animals noted for Palaungic and Khmer. Rong also shares other prefixes with Austroasiatic, for example, the *sV-* prefix mentioned above, which is also attested in Khasian and Palaungic. Rong uses a *ma-* prefix for trees and fruits, similar to the examples above. The nominalizer which forms abstracts in Rong, *nun/num-*, is also widely attested in Austroasiatic.

As an example of how the *kV-* animal affix is realized synchronically, Table 6 shows a widespread root for 'buffalo' attested in most branches of Austroasiatic[7]. The term is borrowed into Austronesian and gives us the common English name carabao. The attestations in different languages provide an example of the complex build-up of prefixes that characterizes this type of morphology. Shorto (2006) reconstructs *krpiʔ* for PMK[8], but the evidence seems to better support either a back or central vowel and a final palatal, thus the suggestion *k.r.pu.y*. I have analysed the synchronic forms as a combination of a root, plus segmental affixes, each separated by a full stop. The proposal for the leftwards movement of the final palatal to the interior of the root is shown with a raised ^{y}, thus $p^y u$. The front vowels arise from the final -y being incorporated into the stem. Sometimes this is merely lost and the back vowel is retained or lengthened. Whether the earliest form had a three consonant cluster in initial position is debatable. The original could have been *r.pu* as in Khmuic, which subsequently gained a *k-* animal prefix. Proto-Khmuic must have had something like *g.r.pu* to explain the synchronic forms. In Vietic, the b/p of the root was lost and r→l, generating *k.l.Vw* structures. The final nasal in Mon is mysterious unless it arose under the influence of the *k-* prefix.

---

[7] Munda has *bɔŋtel* throughout, which may be the same root with the *-tel* an old compound. Mangic languages have *vɔ*, which again could well be cognate but a lack of morphology makes this speculative.

[8] I use proto-Mon-Khmer when citing previous literature, but in general this terminology should be discouraged, as perpetuating an outmoded classification (Sidwell and Blench 2011).

Table 6: 'Buffalo' #k.r.pu.y in Austroasiatic

Phylum	Branch	Language	Attestation	Formula	Comment
Austroasiatic		PMK (Shorto)	*krpiʔ	k.r.pi.ʔ	
Austroasiatic		PAAS (RMB)		k.r.*pu*.y	
Austroasiatic	Monic	Mon	preaŋ	r.*pʸu*.ŋ	
Austroasiatic	Monic	Nyah Kur	chəlọw	k.r.(p)*u*	? < Vietic
Austroasiatic	Vietic	proto Vietic	*c-lu	k.r.(p)*u*	
Austroasiatic	Vietic	Thavung	khuay¹	k.r.(p)*u*.y	
Austroasiatic	Vietic	Pong	klow	k.r.(p)*u*	
Austroasiatic	Khmeric	Khmer	krəbɤy	k.r.*pu*.y	? < Stieng
Austroasiatic	Pearic	Pear	krəpa:w	k.r.*pu*.y	
Austroasiatic	Pearic	Chong	kapa:wᴬ	k.*pʸu*	
Austroasiatic	Bahnaric	PNB	*kapɔ:	k.*pu*	
Austroasiatic	Bahnaric	Sedang	kopôu	k.*puu*	
Austroasiatic	Bahnaric	Tampuon	kəpəu	k.*pʸu*	
Austroasiatic	Bahnaric	Bahnar	kəpo:	k.*pʸu*	
Austroasiatic	Bahnaric	PSB	*g~rəpu:	k.r.*pu*	
Austroasiatic	Bahnaric	Mnong	rpu	r.*pu*	
Austroasiatic	Katuic	Proto-Katuic	*krpiiw	k.r.*pʸu*	
Austroasiatic	Katuic	Pacoh	kərbɤ:	k.r.*pu*.w	alligator; dragon [!]
Austroasiatic	Katuic	Chatong	karpiiw	k.r.*pʸu*	
Austroasiatic	Khmuic	Sre	rəpu	r.*pu*	
Austroasiatic	Khmuic	Chrau	gəpu:	k.*pu*	
Austroasiatic	Khmuic	Biat	rpu:	r.*pu*	
Austroasiatic	Aslian	Kensiw	kɛˈpaw	k.*pʸu*	unless < Malay
Austroasiatic	Aslian	Temiar	kəɹbau	k.r.*pʸu*	< Malay

'Buffalo' indicates clearly the morphological path these nouns characteristically take: prefixes seem originally to have been numeral classifiers with semantic coherence. As they became semantically bleached, a new prefix was added, and the initial prefix incorporated into the stem. This creates a consonant string in initial position (i.e. k.r.p) and any one of these consonants can be deleted. This can lead to highly diverse synchronic outcomes. An Austronesian language such as the Chamic Rhade, which today has *kbao*, probably originally had a longer, more characteristically Austronesian form, and has restructured it under the influence of its Austroasiatic neighbours. A Daic language such as Nung has a synchronic form *tû vai*, i.e. classifier plus stem, which may have been borrowed from a Vietnamese Austroasiatic language. This could also explain deviant Katuic forms such as Katu *tariiq*, which would originally have resembled Chatong *karpiiw*. The *k-* prefix became a suffix, the stem consonant *p-* was deleted and a now unproductive *t-* prefix was added, perhaps on the model of the Daic nominal classifiers.

Table 7 is a second illustration of the *k-* prefix for animals in SE Asian languages, showing a common root for 'tiger', attested across phylic boundaries.

Table 7: The #kVla root for 'tiger' in SE Asian languages

Phylum	Branch	Language	Attestation
Sino-Tibetan	Sinitic	OCM	*hlâʔ
Sino-Tibetan	Burmic	Old Burmese	klya
Sino-Tibetan	Bodish	Monpa	khai-la
Austroasiatic	Khmeric	Angkorian Khmer	khlaa
Austroasiatic	Pearic	Samre	kanɔh[A]
Austroasiatic	Bahnaric	PB	*kəlaa
Austroasiatic	Bahnaric	Sedang	klá
Austroasiatic	Katuic	Pacoh	kulaa
Austroasiatic	Katuic	Ir	kalaʔ
Austroasiatic	Katuic	So	kula
Austroasiatic	Palaungic	Shinman	kaʔ[4] vai[3]
Austroasiatic	Monic	Proto-Monic	*klaaʔ
Austroasiatic	Aslian	Sakai	kla
Austroasiatic	Khasian	War Jaintia	kʰla
Austroasiatic	Muṇḍā	Muṇḍā	kula
Daic	Tai	Thai	kla

The root for 'tiger' illustrates how semantically assigned affixes are borrowed. The tiger is an animal of great symbolic importance across the region and the word has probably been borrowed extensively, including its fossil morphology. Once a semantic association of a *k-* prefix for 'animal' is set up (cf. Table 6) it is easily generalized to other animals within a particular speech community and thence to other languages in the same geographic region.

Table 8 is intended to demonstrate how this works in Tibeto-Burman with the root for 'two', not a noun, but subject to analogous processes. The starred forms are drawn from standard sources, and are not necessarily endorsed, merely cited for a convenient comparison. It is assumed there was a core *ni*, with a velar prefix and two suffixes, a fricative and a high front vowel or an approximant. The velar prefix was regularly suffixed and weakened to ʔ. The fricative suffix was either affricated or weakened to *-h* and switched to a prefix. Forms like Cho *hngih* may represent copying, so that the affix appears at both ends of the word. Other more sporadic affixes are added, such as *p-*, *t-*, *r-* and possibly *a-*.

Table 8: The root C.ni.C(C) for 'two' in Tibeto-Burman

Language	Group	Attestation	Formula
*Sino-Tibetan	Sino-Tibetan	gnyis	g.n^{y}i.s
*Tibeto-Burman	Tibeto-Burman	g-ni-s	g.ni.s
*Karen	Karenic	hni	h.ni
*Lolo-Burmese	Lolo-Burmese	ʔnit	ʔ.ni.t
*Loloish	Loloish	s-ni(k)[2]	s.ni.k
*Northern Naga	Northern Naga	ʔ-ni	ʔ.ni
Bugun	Bugun	ɲeŋ	n^{y}i.ŋ
Taraon	Mishmic	kaiŋ	k.ni
Idu	Mishmic	kaɲi	k.n^{y}i
Puroik	Puroik	ɲi	n^{y}i
Kamengic	Mey of Shergaon	ɲit	n^{y}i.t
Miji	Mijiic	gni	g.ni
Miju	Mijuish	knîn	k.ni.n
Koro	Siangic	ki-ne	k.ni
Milang	Siangic	nə	ni
Karbi	Mikir	hiní	h.ni
Meithei	Meithei	ə-nì	ə.ni
Newar (Dolakhali)	Newar	nis	ni.s
Atong	Bodo-Garo	ni	ni
Garo	Bodo-Garo	gəni	g.ni
Kokborok	Bodo-Garo	nəy	ni.y
Ao (Mongsen)	Naga	anət	a.ni.t
Rongmei	Naga	kənəi	k.ni.y
Tangkhul	Naga	³khə ³ni	k.ni
Phom	Northern Naga	ñi³¹	n^{y}i
Cho (Mindat)	Chin	hngih	h.n(g)i.h
Daai	Chin	ŋn̥iʔ	ŋ.ni.ʔ
Khumi	Chin	nue(ng)	ni.ŋ
Lai (Hakha)	Chin	pa-hniʔ	p.h.ni.ʔ
Lakher [Mara]	Chin	³sa ²nō	s.ni
Lakher [Mara]	Chin	pā-nō	p.n^{w}i
Lushai [Mizo]	Chin	hnih	h.ni.h
Matu	Chin	pan̥iʔ	p.ni
Nyhmoye	Chin	ŋn̥iʔ	ŋ.ni
Bhramu	Himalayish, Western	nis	ni.s
Kanauri	Himalayish, Western	nis	ni.s
Motuo Menba	Monpa	n̥ik tsiŋ	n^{y}i.k
Kaike	Bodic	nghyi	g.h.n^{y}i
Tshona (Mama)	Bodic	nʌi¹³	a.ni
Tibetan (Alike)	Tibetic	ɣn̥i	g.n^{y}i
Tibetan (Amdo: Bla-brang)	Tibetic	hn̥i	h.n^{y}i
Tibetan (Balti)	Tibetic	ɲis	n(g)i.s
Tibetan (Sherpa)	Tibetic	ngyi	g.n^{y}i

Language	Group	Attestation	Formula
Dirang	Tibetic	nitsiŋ	ni.ts.ŋ
Tawang	Tibetic	neⁱ	ni
Memba	Tibetic	ɲi	nʸi
Meyor	Tibetic	ni	ni
Burmese (Written)	Burmish	hnats	h.ni.ts
Marma	Burmish	hnɔi?	h.nʷi.?
PNL	Loloish	?nitᴸ	?.ni.t
Ahi	Loloish, Central	ni²¹	ni
Lalo	Loloish, Northern	ni²¹	ni
Nasu	Loloish, Northern	n̠i⁵⁵	nʸi
Nusu (Southern)	Loloish, Northern	ɦĩ³⁵	h.ni
Akha	Loloish, Southern	nyì	nʸi
Mpi	Loloish, Southern	ɲi?²	nʸi.?
Naxi	Naxi	n̠i²¹	nʸi
Chinese (Old)	Sinitic	njijs	nʸi.(y)s
Sak	Luish	níŋ-hvú	ni.ŋ
Anong	Nungic	əni	ə.ni
Dulong	Nungic	a³¹ ni⁵⁵	a.ni
Nung	Nungic	a³¹ n̠⁵⁵	a.nʸi
Ersu	Qiangic	nɛ⁵⁵	ni
Guiqiong	Qiangic	n̠i³³	nʸi
Namuyi	Qiangic	n̠i⁵³	nʸi
Qiang (Mawo)	Qiangic	ɣnə	g.ni
Tangut [Xixia]	Qiangic	nji̱	nʸi
Caodeng	rGyalrongic	ʁnes	r.ni.s
Daofu	rGyalrongic	ɣnə	g.ni
rGyalrong	rGyalrongic	kěněs	k.ni.s
Gurung (Ghachok)	Tamangic	ŋĩhq	ŋ.nʸi.h.q
Tamang (Sahu)	Tamangic	'nyi:h	nʸi.h
Thakali	Tamangic	'ngih	n(g)i.h
Kayan (Pekon)	Karenic	θanî	t.ni
Magar	Kham-Magar	nis	ni.s
Thulung	Kiranti	nək	ni.k
Limbu	Kiranti, Eastern	nɛccʰi	ni.s
Bahing	Kiranti, Western	nik-si	ni.k.s
Apatani	Tani	tá-ñe	t.nʸi
Nah	Tani	a-ɲi	a.nʸi
Tujia	Tujia	n̠ie⁵⁵	nʸi.V

The rapid switching and replacement of affixes in Tibeto-Burman illustrates the problems inherent in the usual process of reconstruction. The 'method', such as it is, involves choosing a common segmental core and then proposing the most commonly attested affixes to accompany it. But common affixes may well be evidence for lower-level nodes, or indeed diffusion. The similarities between affixes attested in both Austroasiatic and Sino-Tibetan show that these can spread from language to language and indeed across phylum boundaries.

Sinitic historical phonology allows us to see these processes as they occur. Early Zhou Chinese has many more affixes familiar from other Tibeto-Burman languages than its later descendants. Table 9 shows a set of lexemes attested in Zhou which are found either with fewer or no affixes in later forms.

Table 9: Affix movement and loss in the evolution of Chinese

Gloss	Early Zhou	Classical	Character
blood	s.wi:t	wi:t	血
fire	s.mə:yʔ	m̥ə̌:y	火
head	s.luʔ	l̥ǔ	首
black	s.mə:k	m̥ə:k	黑
see	ke:n.s	ke:n.s	見
seed	toŋ.ʔ	tŏŋ	種

To illustrate the semantic convergence of Sino-Tibetan and Austroasiatic affixes, Table 10 shows one of the principal roots for 'bear' in Tibeto-Burman. The original form may have been something like *twŏ.m*, currently attested in rGyalrong. This would account for many synchronic forms with roots such as *vom*, *wom*, *hom*, with or without affixes. However, strikingly, the common prefix for 'bear', as for some other animal names in Sino-Tibetan, is *s-*, just as in Austroasiatic.

This evidence can be taken to demonstrate;

a) that Sino-Tibetan and Austroasiatic have underlyingly similar word structures, without being genetically related
b) that the so-called 'minor syllable' is an optional affix, which can have semantic content, and which can be shifted to a different positions, or incorporated into the stem
c) that unproductive affixes can be subject to renewal, for example reprefixing, without forming consonant clusters
d) that semantic associations of affixes can be borrowed across phylic boundaries, along with the segmental material, and indeed evidently were borrowed at an early stage of the evolution of these phyla

Table 10: 'Bear' in Tibeto-Burman languages

Group	Language	Form	Formula
Central Loloish	Kucong	sa^{35} mu^{31}	s.-m
Chin	Lakher [Mara]	chā-vỳ	s.vo.m
Chin	Lushai [Mizo]	sà-váwm	s.vo.m
Kham-Magar-Chepang-Sunwar	Chepang	siŋʔ.tyamh.yom	s.t.vo.m
Meithei	Meithei	shaum	s.wom
Naga	Lotha Naga	sēváṉ	s.vo.m
Naga	Ao (Chungli)	shim	s.h^{y}om
Naga	Khoirao	chawom	tʃ.wom
Naga	Lotha Naga	seva	s.vo(m)
Naga	Maram	sahom	s.hom
Naga	Rongmei	cagüm	tʃ.g.wom
Naga	Tangkhul	¹si ¹ŋom	s.g.wom
Nungic	Rawang	ʃəwi^{53}	s.w^{y}o(m)
Sinitic	Chinese (Old/Mid)	gium/ɉiung	g.yom
Loloish, Southern	Akha	xhà-hm̀	g.hom
Loloish, Southern	Hani (Khatu)	sjhí	ʃ.h^{y}o(m)
Tani	Galo	sotum	s.tom
Tani	Padam-Mising [Abor-Miri]	si-tum	s.tom
Tani	Apatani	si-tĩ	s.t^{y}o
Tani	Bengni	šu-tum	s.tom
Tani	Bokar	šu-tum	s.tom

4 Contact, borrowing and metatypy

Describing structural similarities is one thing: accounting for them historically is quite another. A neat explanation would have Sino-Tibetan and Austroasiatic originating in neighbouring areas and these similarities would then be phenomena deriving from early contact. However, this explanation is difficult to support using current hypotheses about geographical origins. There is a long history of varied speculations about the homeland of Austroasiatic (see review in Sidwell and Blench 2011; Blench in press). Diffloth (2005) has generally argued for a southern, tropical locus on the basis of faunal reconstructions. Sidwell and Blench (2011) propose a riverine dispersal from the Central Mekong, based on their parallel array model of Austroasiatic classification. Hypotheses of the homeland of Sino-Tibetan are similarly varied, from the views of Matisoff ('somewhere on the Himalayan plateau'[9]), Van Driem (1998) arguing for Sichuan, and Blench and Post (2013) for Northeast India.

Unless these hypotheses are very misguided, proximate homelands are not the solution. Austroasiatic clearly spread far and fast, probably along the river systems of SE Asia, seeking humid valleys to grow taro while using improved boat technology. Only such a hypothesis would account for the arrival and diversification of the Munda languages in India. If the proposals in Sidwell and Blench (2011) are correct, then this would have been around four thousand years ago, when there is a rapid and sudden expansion of the Neolithic in mainland SE Asia, marked by the spread of 'incised and impressed' pottery (Rispoli 2008). So there may have been intensive contact between Austroasiatic and Sino-Tibetan in the zone between northern Vietnam, Laos and northeast Myanmar, and consequent diffusion of key structural traits. Purely chronologically, these traits are likely to originate in Sino-Tibetan, as they are clearly attested in Sinitic as well as in many of the highly diverse languages of NE India. Probably this question cannot be fully resolved until we have better mapping of the distribution of semantically significant prefixes across multiple language phyla.

Austroasiatic and Sino-Tibetan language phyla are intertwined across much of their geographical range today and we should expect considerable local borrowing. The Munda languages are cut off from the remainder of Austroasiatic by a zone of highly diverse Sino-Tibetan languages. There are evidently two distinct issues: local borrowing, and broader structural similarities between the two phyla. Studies of these issues are sparse; Benedict (1990) discusses Austroasiatic loans in Sino-Tibetan and Shafer (1952) is a study of similarities between Khasi and Sino-Tibetan, evaluated in Diffloth (2008). Forrest (1962) and Bodman (1988) both discuss the puzzling issue of apparent Austroasiatic similarities in Lepcha (Rong), a language no longer in direct contact with Austroasiatic.

Although there *are* deep-level lexical borrowings between Austroasiatic and Sino-Tibetan, they appear to be few (Benedict 1990). The similarities of word-structure and affixes are far more striking. What seems to have occurred is extensive metatypy, i.e. long-term bilingualism causing convergence of structures. The infrequency of lexical borrowing must be due to sociolinguistic factors, for example a desire for esoterogeny, marking the separateness of languages. This is probably at its most extreme in Arunachal Pradesh, where neighbouring lan-

---

[9] STEDT Website section: *Homeland and time-depth of Sino-Tibetan*. URL http://stedt.berkeley.edu/about-st (Accessed 09/05/14)

guages with extremely similar cultural concepts, such as Miji, Hruso and Koro, share no more lexical cognates than could be expected by chance.

The key to these convergent structures is the incorporation and re-analysis of numeral classifiers and class-terms. Both Austroasiatic and Sino-Tibetan may originally have had simple stems, with no affixes marking number, case, semantics or gender. Numeral classifiers, usually CV(C) syllables with semantic assignations, were associated with nouns, usually preceding them, as is still very much the situation in Daic languages. Sino-Tibetan and Austroasiatic numeral classifiers became bound to the root and reduced to C with an epenthetic vowel following, hence their transformation into affixes. Although this occurred to a greater or lesser extent in different languages, consciousness of their separateness was retained. As a consequence, they can be shifted to the end of the root, and even deleted in some languages. The marked template of affix plus stem required a new prefix to be added, either *de novo* or preceding the existing prefix. Meanwhile, distinct numeral classifiers continued to co-exist and continued to be incorporated and renewed. Figure 1 shows a highly schematic visualization of this process of renewal; the examples in the text indicate some of the complexities encountered on the way.

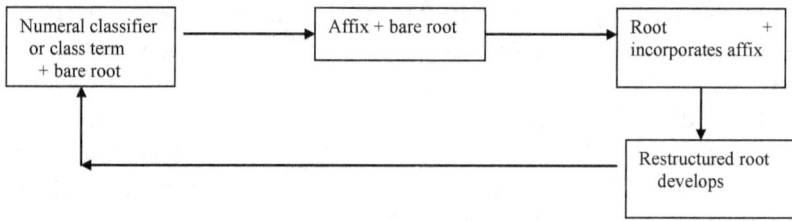

Fig. 1: Cyclical renewal of affixes in SE Asian languages

Most languages in the region also historically had suffixes; it seems likely these were also originally classifiers and indeed, the similarities of segmental material suggest that prefixes became suffixes. Harvey et al. (2006) refer to the notion that such a process is uncommon, while illustrating its operation in Northern Australia (see also Green 1995). The evolution of noun class suffixes in Gur and Adamawa languages within Niger-Congo is similarly an example of prefix-suffix shift, carrying all the segmental material and concomitant alliterative concord. Greenberg (1977) has a perceptive discussion of this issue with respect to the double-affixing languages in Niger-Congo such as Tiv. Within SE Asia, suffixes tend to weaken to glottal stops, nasals or approximants. As the final segments of a word erode, their features are incorporated into the stem, resulting in unstable vowels and vowel length. This is very similar to the sort of word shortening characteristic of languages of the Cameroon Grassfields, where final syllable erosion is responsible for complex tones (e.g. Mambiloid).

5 Parallel processes in African languages

Do these processes in SE Asian languages help model the emergence of noun classes in African languages? Apart from Afroasiatic, African languages are usually considered to characterized by noun classes, and not to have numeral classifiers at any historical time-depth. These categories are not watertight; languages can display aspects of all these, and erosion of one morphosyntactic category can lead to the partial or complete evolution of another. Krongo, one of the Kadu languages, a branch of Nilo-Saharan, appears to have nominal affixes, although these are partly fossilized and unproductive. They have no semantic assignments, but Krongo has instead adopted or developed a sex-gender system (Reh 1985, 1994; Blench 2006). However, there are some cases where numeral classifiers appear to be developing, for example Kana, a Cross River language in the Niger Delta of Nigeria (Ikoro 1996). The relatives of Kana are classic nominal affix alternation languages, but Kana seems to have pared down this system and compensated by developing numeral classifiers through grammaticalization (Williamson 1985). More surprising is the case of Mambay, an Adamawa language of northern Cameroon, which still has a quite prominent concordial nominal suffix system, but which is developing prefixed numeral classifiers (Anonby 2011). Examples given by Anonby include the 'collectives' which precede nouns, do not show concord, and have broad semantic correlations.

Nilo-Saharan nominal morphology is marked by extensive affix alternation for number, and yet there is no system of alliterative concord and no systematic association of affixes with semantic categories. However, evidence is emerging that we have been quite wrong in our understanding of Nilo-Saharan, and that its underlying morphology is a system of numeral classifiers. Various studies have noted associations between affixes and semantic themes in different branches. For example, both Stevenson (1991) and Gilley (2013) note the semantic associations of affix pairings in Kadu languages, and Storch (2005) analyses these for Western Nilotic. Carlin (1993) observes that some So number markers have broad semantic themes. But the most striking evidence comes Gumuz, a Nilo-Saharan language of the Ethio-Sudan borderland, whose Mayu dialect has been studied by Ahland (2010). Gumuz has a system of nominal incorporation, in which a series of body part nouns is incorporated into verbs and 'classifies' the object, or more rarely the subject or instrument.

Gumuz predicate classifiers mark semantic fields, typically of shape or texture. These are infixed in 'split verbs' and are copied as demonstratives. The major classifiers are -Vk^w 'head', -Vts 'body', -Vc 'eye/seed', -$k^wós$ 'tooth', and -$ts'ê$ 'ear'. Ahland (2010), adapting Mithun (1986), describes a verbal classifier whereby "a noun is incorporated into a verb to categorize an extra predicate argument...usually in S or O function." With this type of verbal classifier, there is frequently a generic-specific relationship between the incorporated NP and the external NP which accompanies it. The significance of this system is that classifiers which develop from grammaticalized body parts are governed by the semantics of nouns. For example, Ahland (2010) notes; "entities that are head-like in shape and/or function or closely associated with such objects" govern the following classes of object "fingers, toes, water, sauce, beer, lotion, soap (in a container), ears of corn, pots, pans, cans". In constructions where the classifier refers to the object of the main verb, the classifier is suffixed to the verb and thus abuts the object noun directly. It can thus become attached to the noun rather than the verb. Western Nilotic, as described by Storch (2005), has a system of nominal suffixes which appear to have semantic correlates. There are both singular and plural suffixes marking length, roundness, part of etc. And there is some evidence for a system of suffix alternation which has been overwritten by the diffusion of 'imperial' number markers *kV-* and *N-* from other branches of Nilotic. As with Gumuz, grammaticalized body parts are a major source of affixes. The T/K and N/K 'substrata' identified by Bryan in the 1950s and Greenberg's (1981) 'moveable *-k* as a Stage III article' are all reflections of this broader phenomenon.

Exactly how the Niger-Congo and Nilo-Saharan systems are related is still under discussion. Some branches of Niger-Congo, such as Mande, Dogon, Ijoid and Kaalak-Domurik, show no clear traces of any affix system. However, the remaining branches, Atlantic, Kwa, Benue-Congo and Gur-Adamawa have elaborate noun classes and alliterative concord, or traces of such systems where they have demonstrably been lost (e.g. in Volta-Niger and Kru). So this system develops *within* Niger-Congo (and is thus probably not to be reconstructed to proto-Niger-Congo, despite an extensive literature to the contrary). Other phonological evidence, such as labial-velars, ±ATR vowels etc. point to extensive contact between Nilo-Saharan and Niger-Congo, and it is not stretching credibility to propose that the noun classes of Niger-Congo represent a regularized metatypy of Nilo-Saharan affix systems. In other words, something that was implicit in the Nilo-Saharan system of numeral classifiers was borrowed as a system into part of Niger-Congo and then analogized as a rich system of nominal classes[10].

From this perspective, the similarities with SE Asian languages become clearer. Affix renewal is very common in Niger-Congo, where noun class affixes become unproductive and a new affix is added (e.g. Childs 1983). Usually, however, the unproductive affix retains its vowel, or else the conjunction of two consonants results in a complex consonant. For example, Hyamic (Plateau) has developed a complex system of alternating initial clusters due to deletion of -V in the prefix. In SE Asia, the weakening of -V does not result in consonant merger but is rather retained as a syllable sequence. Such a word structure is not typical of Niger-Congo in general, but at least one group of languages does take on this appearance synchronically. Nouns in the northwest Kainji languages (cLela, tHun, ut-Main, Gwamhi-Wuri), typically have the structure C.CVCV (the prefix is often transcribed with a schwa to ameliorate the otherwise disquieting appearance) (e.g. Hoffmann 1967). Table 11, shortened from Paterson (2012), shows the noun class prefixes of Ut-Ma'in, some of which now only have consonant prefixes, but which retain strong semantic associations. The symbol ə̄ marks the epenthetic vowel for single-consonant prefixes, which are always phonetically mid-tone in relation to the stem-tone melody.

Table 11: Ut-Ma'in noun class prefixes

Class	Prefix	Object Pronoun	Example	Gloss
1u	ū-	ú/wá	ū-mákt	'barren woman'
1ø	ø-	wá	ø-hámət	'visitor'
2	ø-	ɛ́	ø-ná	'oxen, bovines'
3u	ū-	ɔ́	ū-bù	'house'
3ø	ø-	ɔ́	ø-bò?	'dream'
4	əs-	sɛ́	əs-bò?	'dreams'
5	ər-	dɛ́	ər-kɔ́k	'calabash'
6	ət-	tɔ́	ət-kɔ́k	'calabashes'
6m	əm-	mɔ́	əm-nɔ̀:g	'oil'
7u	ū-	já	ū-ná	'ox, bovine'
7ø	ø-	já	ø-tʃámpá	'man'
aug	ā-	á	ā-kɔ́k	'huge calabashes'
dim	ī-	ɛ́	ī-kɔ́k	'tiny calabash'

---

[10] The origins of alliterative concord can be debated, but a stimulating suggestion is the proposal of Hoffmann (1967) that demonstratives which copy affixes can explain the movement from prefix to suffix. Extending this idea, if affixes became re-analysed as separable, they can easily become demonstratives or articles, and once copied, establish the principle of alliteration.

These prefixes can be said to bear tone, although as it appears to be always mid, it is no longer functional (also the case in Himalayan Sino-Tibetan, where these prefixes are uniformly low). Similarly, many Kordofanian[11] languages have C.VCV structures, where the initial C is an alternating prefix. Schadeberg (1981a, 1981b) illustrates this for both the Heiban and Talodi groups. For example, Table 12 shows the reconstructed noun class prefixes of Proto-Heiban (Schadeberg 1981a: 133).

Table 12: Proto-Heiban noun class prefixes

sg.	pl.
gu-	li-
g-	j-
d-	n-
li-	bu-
ŋ-	ɲ-
ḍ-	ḍ-

The difference with northwest Kainji is that the typical Kordofanian stem is -VCV. This suggests (perhaps) loss of C_1 of the stem, subsequent loss of -V from the prefix or assimilation of the resultant VV sequence. The overall parallels to be drawn with African languages are as follows;

a) Nilo-Saharan languages have traces of a former numeral classifier system, still realized in Gumuz, which surfaces synchronically as moveable affixes and which has sporadic semantic associations
b) A subset of Niger-Congo languages have noun class affixes with semantic associations, although these are regularly lost and re-evolve
c) These affixes can be shifted, disappear, fossilize or be incorporated into stems, leading to a process of renewal.
d) These affixes typically conserve their co-associated vowel, because it has a strongly associated segmental tone, whereas SE Asian languages weaken the vowel because there is no underlying tone.
e) However, Niger-Congo languages can occasionally lose the -V- of the affix so comprehensively that the result is a segmental affix consisting only of C, with resultant structural similarities to SE Asia

---

[11] 'Kordofanian' is a creation of Greenberg (1963) based on the assumption that the Niger-Congo languages of the Nuba Mountains must form a genetic group, although this now looks like an over-optimistic view (Blench 2013). However, these languages do share common morphological features, perhaps due to contact.

Table 13: Erosion and restructuring of CV nominal prefixes within Benue-Congo

Strategy	Languages
Complete loss of affixes	Shen
Complete loss of prefixes, vowel neutralization in stem, loss of second stem consonant, number marked by contrastive vowel length	Cara
Complete loss of prefixes, addition of generalized prefix, suffix or clitic plural marker	Lower Cross, Central Jukunoid
Complete loss of prefixes, development of nominal classifiers	Kana
Complete loss of original affixes, new affixes added on the basis of reduplication of first syllable of stem	Hasha
Loss of V of affixes leading to C- prefixes	Northwest Kainji (cLela etc.)
Loss of V of affixes leading to long C- stem initials	Kambari, Upper Cross, Jju cluster
Loss of V of affixes leading to stem initial consonant clusters and consonant alternation	Hyamic
Existing affixes become frozen to the stem and are reprefixed	Cibər [Lopa]
Reduction of all CV- prefixes to V-	Ikann, some Plateau
Reduction of all CV- prefixes to u/i- and rightwards shift into stem, leading to contrastive palatalization and labialization	Many Plateau
Reduction of RV- and NV- prefixes to R-, N-, and rightwards shift into stem, leading to sporadic nasalization and rhotacization	Many Plateau
Prefixes become suffixes	Some Mambiloid
Prefixes become suffixes, which are deleted producing complex stem tones	Mambila
Prefixes become suffixes, lose final -V, C is frozen to the stem and number marking is lost	Dakoid
Prefixes partly become suffixes, resulting in systems of double-affixing	Tivoid

For these reasons, it seems that outcomes in SE Asia, while diverse, are still less exuberant than in West Africa. Excluding Bantoid and Bantu, the principal branches of Benue-Congo are Kainji, Plateau, Jukunoid, Cross River and possibly Ikann. All of these have evidence (and usually synchronic examples) for a Bantu-like system of alternating nominal prefixes exhibiting alliterative concord on adjectives and other parts of speech. These systems are often preserved in a single branch, with other related branches exhibiting very diverse surface morphology. From this it is reasonable to conclude that nouns in the system of the proto-language had a basic (C)V.CVCV morphology, assumed by De Wolf (1971) in his now outdated study[12]. If so, the surface forms we see today are a development from this. However, those surface forms are astonishingly diverse. As an example of the complexity within Benue-Congo, Table 13 illustrates the possible outcomes from this type of restructuring.

Once the descriptive language is changed, many of these processes are also attested in Austroasiatic and Sino-Tibetan.

6 Conclusions

SE Asian languages have competing systems of noun classification, using both numeral classifiers and noun class terms. Intriguingly, not only word structure but some of the segmental morphology appears to be shared between different language phyla. In languages where these systems are residual, they may have reduced C(V) affixes with weak semantic correlations. These may be reduced classifiers or noun class terms which have become bound to the stem. It is unlikely that this is a result of genetic affiliation and thus it appears that both segmental material and the underlying concept of semantically associated affixes is borrowable. Similar classifier systems occur in some Nilo-Saharan languages, and have apparently developed into non-concordial affixes. Niger-Congo languages have taken the next step, developing strong semantic associations and alliterative concord, probably through demonstrative copying. The challenge is to see whether similar pathways can be reconstructed for noun class affix systems in other language phyla, notably Papuan, Australian and some New World languages.

Acknowledgements

This is an extensively revised version of a paper presented at the meeting *Mainland Southeast Asian Languages: The State of the Art in 2012*, 29 November - 1 December 2012 at the Max Planck Institute for Evolutionary Anthropology, Leipzig. I would like to thank the audience for the discussion, and the editors for subsequent comments. An early version of this paper was presented at the 40th Colloquium on African Languages and Linguistics, Leiden, 29th-31st August,

---

[12] De Wolf reached this view by working 'backwards' from Bantu rather than actually surveying Benue-Congo as the primary data source.

2011. I gratefully acknowledge the Kay Williamson Education Foundation for supporting my African fieldwork.

References

Adams, Karen Lee. 1989. Systems of numeral classification in the Mon-Khmer, Nicobarese and Aslian subfamilies of Austroasiatic. Canberra: Pacific Linguistics.
Ahland, Colleen A. 2010. Noun incorporation and predicate classifiers in Gumuz. *Journal of African Languages and Linguistics* 31(2). 159–203.
Aikhenvald, Alexandra Y. 2000. *Classifiers: A typology of noun categorization devices*. Oxford: Oxford University Press.
Anderson, Gregory D.S. 2004. Advances in Proto-Munda reconstruction. *Mon-Khmer Studies* 34. 159–184.
Anonby, Erik. 2011. *A grammar of Mambay*. Köln: Rüdiger Köppe.
Beckwith, C.I. 1993. Class nouns and classifiers in Thai. In Mark Alves (ed.), *Papers from the Third Annual Meeting of the Southeast Asian Linguistics Society*, 11–26. Phoenix: Arizona State University.
Bender, M.L. 1996. *The Nilo-Saharan languages: a comparative essay*. Munich: Lincom Europa.
Benedict, P. 1990. Austroasiatic loanwords in Sino-Tibetan. *Mon-Khmer Studies* 18–19. 1–13.
Blench, Roger M. 1995. Is Niger-Congo simply a branch of Nilo-Saharan? In R. Nicolai & F. Rottland (eds.), *Proceedings of the Fifth Nilo-Saharan Linguistics Colloquium, Nice, 1992*, 68–118. Köln: Rudiger Köppe.
Blench, Roger M. 2006. The Kadu languages and their affiliation: between Nilo-Saharan, Niger-Congo and Afro-Asiatic. In Al-Amin Abu-Manga, Leoma Gilley & Anne Storch (eds.), *Insights into Nilo-Saharan Language, History and Culture*, 101–127. Köln: Rüdiger Köppe.
Blench, Roger M. 2013. Splitting up Kordofanian. In Thilo Schadeberg & Roger Blench (eds.), *New research in the languages of the Nuba mountains. Nuba mountains language studies*, 571–586. Köln: Rudiger Köppe.
Blench, Roger M. in press. Reconstructing Austroasiatic prehistory. In P. Sidwell & M. Jenny (eds.), *Handbook of Austroasiatic*. Canberra: Pacific Linguistics.
Blench, Roger M. & M. Post. 2013. Rethinking Sino-Tibetan phylogeny from the perspective of Northeast Indian languages. In Thomas Owen-Smith & Nathan Hill (eds.), *Trans-Himalayan linguistics: Historical and descriptive linguistics of the Himalayan area*, 71–104. Berlin & New York: Mouton de Gruyter.
Blust, R. 1988. *Austronesian root theory: an essay on the limits of morphology*. Amsterdam & Philadelphia: John Benjamins.
Bodman, Nicholas C. 1988. On the place of Lepcha in Sino-Tibetan, a lexical comparison. *Linguistics of the Tibeto-Burman Area* 11(1). 1–26.
Carlin, Eithne. 1993. *The So language (AMO2)*. Köln: Universität zu Köln.
Childs, Tucker. 1983. Noun class affix renewal in Southern West Atlantic. In J. Kaye, H. Koopman, D. Sportiche & A. Dugas (eds.), *Current approaches to African linguistics* (Volume 2), 17–29. Dordrecht: Foris Publications.
Costello, Nancy. 1966. Affixes in Katu. *Mon-Khmer Studies* 2. 63–86.
Costello, Nancy. 1998. Affixes in Katu of the Lao P.D.R.. *Mon-Khmer Studies* 28. 31–42.

DeLancey, Scott 1986. Toward a history of Tai classifier systems. In C.G. Craig (ed.), *Noun classes and categorization*, 437–452. Amsterdam: John Benjamins.

De Wolf, P. 1971. *The noun class system of Proto-Benue-Congo*. The Hague: Mouton.

Diffloth, Gérard. 2005. The contribution of linguistic palaeontology and Austroasiatic. In Laurent Sagart, Roger Blench & Alicia Sanchez-Mazas (eds.), *The peopling of East Asia: Putting together archaeology, linguistics and genetics*, 77–80. London: Routledge Curzon.

Diffloth, Gérard. 2008. Shafer's parallels between Khasi and Sino-Tibetan. In S. Morey & M. Post (eds.), *Northeast Indian Linguistics*, 93–104. New Delhi: Cambridge University Press.

Dimmendaal, Gerrit J. 2000. Number marking and noun categorization in Nilo-Saharan languages. *Anthropological Linguistics* 42(2). 214–261.

Dixon, R.M.W. 1972. *The Dyirbal language of north Queensland*. Cambridge: Cambridge University Press.

Driem, George L. van. 1998. Neolithic correlates of ancient Tibeto-Burman migrations. In R.M. Blench & M. Spriggs (eds.), *Archaeology and language* II, 67–102. London: Routledge.

Driem, George L. van. 2008. To which language family does Chinese belong, or what's in a name. In Alicia Sanchez-Mazas, Roger Blench, Malcolm D. Ross, Ilia Peiros & Marie Lin (eds.), *Past human migrations in East Asia: Matching archaeology, linguistics and genetics*, 219–253. London & New York: Routledge.

Enfield, N.J. 2007. *A grammar of Lao*. Berlin & New York: Mouton de Gruyter.

Forrest, R.A.D. 1962. The Linguistic Position of Rong (Lepcha). *Journal of the American Oriental Society* 82(3). 331–335.

Gilley, Leoma. 2013. Katcha noun morphology. In Thilo Schadeberg & Roger Blench (eds.), *New research in the languages of the Nuba mountains. Nuba mountains language studies*, 501–521. Köln: Rudiger Köppe.

Green, Ian. 1995. The Death of 'Prefixing': contact induced typological change in Northern Australia. *Proceedings of the Annual Meeting of the Berkeley Linguistics Society* 21(1). 414–425.

Greenberg, Joseph H. 1963. *Languages of Africa* (Indiana University Research Centre in Anthropology, Folklore, and Linguistics, Publication 25). The Hague: Mouton & Co.

Greenberg, Joseph H. 1977. Niger-Congo noun class markers: prefixes, suffixes, both or neither. *Studies in African Linguistics* (Supplement 7), 97–104.

Greenberg, Joseph H. 1981. Nilo-Saharan Moveable- k as a Stage III Article (with a Penutian Typological Parallel). *Journal of African Languages and Linguistics* 3(2). 105–112.

Haas, M.R. (ed.). 1964. *Thai-English student's dictionary*. Stanford: Stanford University Press.

Hammarström, Harald. 2013. Noun class parallels in Kordofanian and Niger-Congo: evidence of genealogical inheritance? In Thilo Schadeberg & Roger Blench (eds.), *New research in the languages of the Nuba mountains. Nuba mountains language studies*, 549–570. Köln: Rudiger Köppe.

Handel, Zev. 2008. What is Sino-Tibetan? Snapshot of a Field and a Language Family in Flux. *Language and Linguistics Compass* 2/3. 422–441.

Harvey, Mark & Nicholas Reid. 1997. *Nominal Classification in Aboriginal Australia*. Philadelphia: John Benjamins.

Harvey, Mark, Rachel Nordlinger & Ian Green. 2006. From Prefixes to Suffixes: Typological Change in Northern Australia. *Diachronica* 23 (2). 289–311.

Hoffmann, Carl 1967. An outline of the Dakarkari noun class system and the relation between prefix and suffix noun-class systems. In G. Manessy. (ed.), *La Classification nominale dans les langues Négro-africaines*, 237–259. Paris: CNRS.

Ikoro, S.M. 1996. *The Kana language*. Leiden: CNWS.
Jones, Robert B. 1970. Classifier constructions in Southeast Asia. *Journal of the American Oriental Society* 90(1). 1–12.
Kirton, Jean F. 1988. Yanyuwa, a dying language. In Michael J. Ray (ed.), *Aboriginal language use in the Northern Territory: 5 reports* (Work Papers of the Summer Institute of Linguistics), 1–18. Darwin: Summer Institute of Linguistics.
Matisoff, J.A. 1973. Tonogenesis in Southeast Asia. In Larry M. Hyman, (ed.), *Consonant Types and Tone* (Southern California Occasional Papers in Linguistics, No. 1.), 71–95. Los Angeles: UCLA.
Matisoff, J.A. 2003. *Handbook of proto-Tibeto-Burman*. Berkeley: University of California Press.
Matisoff, J.A. 2008. *The Tibeto-Burman reproductive system: toward an etymological thesaurus*. Berkeley: University of California Press.
Mithun, Marianne. 1986. The convergence of noun classification systems. In Colette Craig (ed.), *Noun classes and categorization*, 379–397. Philadelphia: John Benjamins.
Paterson, Rebecca. 2012. The semantics of Ut-Ma'in noun classes. In R.M. Blench & S. McGill (eds.), *Advances in minority language research in Nigeria* (Volume I), 239–272. Köln: Rudiger Köppe.
Post, M.W. 2007. *A grammar of Galo*. Melbourne: La Trobe University PhD dissertation.
Ratliff, Martha 2010. *Hmong-Mien language history*. Canberra: Pacific Linguistics.
Reh, M. 1985. *Die Krongo-Sprache (nìino mó-dì): Beschreibung, Texte, Wörterverzeichnis*. (Kölner Beiträge zur Afrikanistik, 12). Berlin: Dietrich Reimer.
Reh, M. 1994. A grammatical sketch of Deiga. *Afrika und Übersee* 77. 197–261.
Rispoli, Fiorella 2008. The incised and impressed pottery of Mainland Southeast Asia: following the paths of Neolithization. *East and West* 57. 235–304.
Sagart, Laurent. 2011. The Austroasiatics: East to West or West to East? In N. J. Enfield (ed.), *Dynamics of human diversity in Mainland Southeast Asia*. 345–359. Canberra: Pacific Linguistics.
Schadeberg, Thilo C. 1981a. *A Survey of Kordofanian. Volume 1: The Heiban Group*. Hamburg: Helmut Buske.
Schadeberg, Thilo C. 1981b. *A Survey of Kordofanian. Volume 2: The Talodi Group*. Hamburg: Helmut Buske.
Shafer, Robert. 1952. Etudes sur l'austroasien. *Bulletin de la Société de Linguistique de Paris* 48. 111–158.
Shorto, Harry L. 2006. A Mon-Khmer comparative dictionary. (Edited by Paul Sidwell, Doug Cooper & Christian Bauer). Canberra: Pacific Linguistics.
Sidwell, Paul & Roger M. Blench. 2011. The Austroasiatic Urheimat: The Southeastern Riverine hypothesis. In N. J. Enfield (ed.), *Dynamics of Human Diversity in Mainland Southeast Asia*, 317–345. Canberra: Pacific Linguistics.
Smith, Kenneth D. 1975. The velar animal prefix in Vietnam languages. *Linguistics of the Tibeto-Burman Area* 2. 1–18.
Stevenson, Roland C. 1991. Relationship of Kadugli-Krongo to Nilo-Saharan: Morphology and lexis. In M L. Bender (ed.), *Proceedings of the Fourth Nilo-Saharan Conference (Bayreuth, 1989)*, 347–369. Hamburg: Buske.
Storch, Anne. 2005. *The noun morphology of Western Nilotic*. Köln: Köppe.
Thomas, Dorothy. 1969. Chrau affixes. *Mon-Khmer Studies* 3. 90–107.
Williamson, K. 1985. How to become a Kwa language. In A. Makkai & A.K. Melby (eds.), *Linguistics and philosophy: Essays in honor of Rulon S. Wells*, 427–443. Amsterdam: Benjamins.

Alice Vittrant
Expressing motion

The contribution of Southeast Asian languages with reference to East Asian languages

1 Introduction

This paper aims to continue and complement the cross-linguistic studies of motion event encoding initiated by Talmy's seminal work on a semantic typology of motion events (1972, 1985), given that his classification of languages based on path encoding cannot account for some constructions found in Southeast (and East) Asian languages.

After a brief review of Talmy's typology and its evolution, we will examine some Southeast Asian[1] constructions and means to encode motion and path that have been neglected by previous studies. The following section will present the elicitation material developed by the Trajectory project that helps to collect comparable data on motion.

The data collected on two Burmese dialects will then be presented, along with new data on hitherto unknown constructions, leading us to revise previous typologies of motion events. In particular we examine issues such as serialization, and also the status of the verb (satellite vs. head) in the constructions expressing motion.

2 Talmy's typology: a reminder

2.1 Original proposal

Talmy's basic typology of motion events is a semantic analysis of motion events based on four basic semantic components (1985: 61): the figure (moving or located entity), the ground (spatial reference entity for the motion), the motion

---

[1] Although this paper is devoted to Southeast Asian languages, I will nonetheless include references and examples from East Asian languages such as Japanese, or Mandarin-Chinese, when relevant for the discussion.

itself (change in position) and the path (translocation of the figure), the manner (kind of motion) being an external component that can be conflated[2] with motion. It aims to compare the encoding of the two last semantic components, i.e. path and manner— although Talmy insisted later that his typology aims to focus on path essentially (2009: 390). Looking at which component is 'incorporated' in the main verb, or where the element that delimits or 'frames' the verbal motion event is encoded, he distinguished two types of languages: *Verb*-framed languages and *Satellite*-framed languages. In the former, path, which is the framing element of a motion event, is expressed in the verb stem whereas in the Satellite-framed languages, path is expressed outside of the verb stem, in surface elements called satellites (see Talmy 2007 [1985])[3].

Romance languages and also Hebrew and Turkish (Berman and Slobin 1994) are therefore classified as Verb-framed (henceforth V-framed) languages as they encode the path component in the main verb (see examples 1a, 2a). On the other hand English, German and Polish (and most of the other Indo-European languages) are classified as Satellite-framed (henceforth S-framed) languages, path being encoded in verbal elements such as particles or preverbs (examples (1b), (2b))[4].

(1) a. *Le garçon   sortit   en courant.*   French [V-Framed]
       The boy   went.out   running
                   V_h [+ PATH]
       'The boy ran out'

    b. *The boy ran   **out***   English [S-Framed]
                 V_h [- PATH] **[+ PATH]**

---

2 'Conflation' in Talmy's terms indicates "any syntactic process – whether a long derivation involving many deletions and insertions, or just a lexical insertion – whereby a more complex construction turns into a simpler one" (Talmy 1972: 257). For instance, Romance languages such as Spanish or French typically conflate motion and path in verbs such as *entrar/ entrer* 'to go.in'.
3 Talmy (2007 [1985]: 153): "Path appears in the verb root in "verb-framed" languages such as Spanish, and it appears in the satellite in "satellite-framed" languages such as English and Atsugewi."
4 Fortis and Fagard (2010 ch.III) provide a good summary of Talmy's typology of motion, its origins and development. See also Wälchli (2001: 298-99) on semantic distinctions within the motion domain made by Tesnière (1959).

(2) a. *El hombre **entró** a la casa corriendo.*   Spanish [V-Framed]
the man entered in the house running
V_h [+ PATH]
'The man ran into the house.'

b. *kobieta **wy**-szła z*   Polish[5] [S-Framed]
woman.NOM out-walk.3SG.FEM.PST from
[+ PATH] - V_h[- PATH] [+ PATH]
kukurydzy.
corn.GEN
'The woman walked out the corn[field].'

Studies based on Talmy's (1985) framework have flourished, being extended to a larger sample of languages. Work by Berman and Slobin (1994), Shibatani and Thompson (1996), Wälchli (2001), Strömqvist and Verhoeven (2004), Bohnemeyer et al. (2007) among others, has challenged the original typology. An early challenge may be found in Aske (1989), who showed that V-framed languages like Spanish may use S-framed constructions under certain circumstances. In other words, languages are not uniform in their encoding of motion events.

Aske argued that this split-framing situation is triggered by the telicity[6] of the motion event described: the S-framed construction in Spanish is used only to describe atelic events. In other words, if the figure following a path is not passing the boundary of the ground, the event is atelic and Spanish speakers can use S-framed constructions[7] to express the motion as in (3b).

Motion event in Spanish - From Imbert (2012) (after Talmy 2000, and Aske 1989)

(3) a. *La botella entró a la cueva (flotando)*   V-framed [telic]
the bottle entered into the cave floating
figure   PATH   PATH   ground   (MANNER)
'The bottle floated into the cave'

---

[5] From A. Kopecka, p.c.
[6] Telicity in motion events has been relabelled as a "boundary-crossing constraint" by Slobin and Hoiting (1994) and Slobin (1996: 215-16).
[7] Fortis and Fagard 2010 (ch.III.3.3) show that the situation is far more complex: "the crossing of a boundary [being] neither a necessary nor a sufficient condition for the use of a V-framed construction."

b. La botella   flotó   hacia/ hasta la cueva.   S-framed [atelic]
   the bottle   <u>floated</u>   toward/to   the cave
   figure   MANNER   **PATH**   ground
   'The bottle floated toward/to the cave'

2.2 Revision and evolution: mixed and equipollent types

Further work saw Talmy's first classification of motion events modified by himself[8] and others[9], Therefore, beside languages such as Spanish[10] with "split systems", i.e. languages having both S-framed and V-framed constructions though not in the same circumstances, Talmy (2000) also adds a fourth type. It accounts for languages such as Greek, which instantiates a "parallel system", that is to say a system where V-framed and S-framed constructions may alternate without lexical or grammatical constraints (Talmy 2007 [1985]: 104).

However even this four-way typology cannot account for the rarity of pure V-framed or S-framed languages (Fortis and Vittrant 2011: 76). The typology needs to be further revised to take into account mixed-types[11], which represent the great majority of languages.

Slobin (2004) reveals also two important elements of Talmy's motion typology: first, manner has been backgrounded in the framing-types and needs more attention. Second, some languages show regular co-expressions of manner and path in verbs. This fact motivates the introduction of a third type of language[12] in the typology: the *Equipollent*-framed language, which is defined as a language "in which both manner and path are expressed by 'equipollent' elements, that is, elements that are equal in formal linguistic terms, and appear to be equal in force or significance" (Slobin, 2004: 228).

---

8 For instance, Spanish is classified as V-framed in Talmy (1985) but as a split system later (2000: 65).
9 See Beavers et al. (2010), Croft et al. (2010). See also Imbert (2012), for a summary of modified versions of Talmy's typology.
10 As for French, Kopecka (2006) and (2009) militate in favour of a mixed system. See also Iacobini and Masini (2006), and Iacobini and Fagard (2011) on Italian and other Romance languages.
11 Revisions of Talmy's typology can be found in Bohnemeyer et al. (2007), Beavers et al. (2010) and Croft et al. (2010), Fortis et al. (2011). A more complete survey of Talmy's typology and objections to it is provided by Imbert (2012).
12 See also Zlatev & Yangklang (2004: 188): " The conclusion can only be that the existence of serial-verb languages such as Thai, Ewe, and Akan entails the need to extent the Talmian binary motion-event typology *at least* into a ternary one."

This typically applies to languages with serial verb constructions (henceforth SVCs) such as Thai or Chinese. Zlatev & Yangklang (2004) demonstrate convincingly that Thai multi-verb constructions used to express motion can neither be described as V-framed nor S-framed (p. 170)[13]. One argument developed by the authors is that a path verb following a manner verb should not be treated as a deverbal adverb or preposition-like satellite verb: the Path verb *khâw* 'enter' used alone in example (4) and the 'homophonic' one following a manner verb in (5) do not show semantic differences, they have exactly the same meaning. Moreover, the analysis of the path verb of a SVC as a deverbal adverb following a main manner verb in (6) is challenged by examples such as (7), which does not contain any manner verb.

(4) Thai (Tai-Kadai)
 chán khâw hɔ̌ɔŋ
 1SG enter room
 I went into the room

(5) *chán dəən khâw paj*
 1SG walk enter go
 'I am walking in (away from Deictic Centre [DC], into some place).'

(6) Thai (Tai-Kadai)
 chán dəən won jɔ̂ɔn klàp khâw paj
 1SG **walk** [MANNER] circle reverse return enter go
 'I am walking in a circle, returning back inside.'

(7) *chán won jɔ̂ɔn klàp khâw hɔ̌ɔŋ*
 1SG circle reverse return enter room
 Zlatev & Yangklang (2004: 165-66)

Although the *Equipollent*-framed (henceforth E-framed) type has been created to handle serialization, it still remains problematic. In the E-framed type, all the verbs of a serial verb construction are clausal heads, and function as finite verbs. However, as noticed by Lambert-Brétière (2009), languages with SVCs differ from each other and cannot be uniformly described as E-framed. Indeed, verb serialization is far from being a uniform phenomenon —see Bisang

---

[13] See also Diller (2006: 161-62) for a review of the different approaches to complex multiverb constructions in Thai.

(1996: 533), Durie (1997: 292), Bril (2004: 5ff), Aikhenvald (2006: 20ff), Vittrant (2006: 310), (2012: 108), inter alia. Moreover, languages with SVCs are often grammatically complex, with a variety of constructions within a single variety of the language.

Multi-verb constructions are also central in the revision of Talmy's typology by Croft et al. (2010), who analyse SVCs and coordinated (or compounding) verbs as symmetric constructions. For instance, in Thai (and Mandarin) SVCs or Japanese converb constructions, both semantic components, i.e. Path and Manner, are expressed by forms that may occur as main predicates. On the other hand, Talmy's original two types, Satellite framing and Verb framing, are asymmetric in their encoding of the semantic components of an event: one is expressed by a dependent element that cannot function as a main predicate, whereas the other one is expressed by the main verb.

In sum, problems remain with this analysis of verb serialization languages. There is considerable disagreement on the proper way to analyse SVCs in general, and Thai and Mandarin SVCs in particular (see Xu 2008 and Beavers et al. 2010: 36-37 on Mandarin, Fortis and Fagard 2010: ch.III , p. 19 on Thai).

Other issues also remain: for instance, if path is expressed both in a verb and in a satellite, the construction does not qualify for being exclusively V-framed nor S-framed. This is the problem of "double [or multiple] framing" (Croft et al. 2010: 208).

Finally, how to account for utterances in which spatial information is not localized on particular morphemes but expressed by the syntactic organization itself (Sinha and Kuteva 1995) as shown by example (8)? And what to say when Path is specified by a morpheme that co-expresses the temporal relation of the motion event to the main event, i.e. an 'associated motion' morpheme (Koch 1984, Guillaume 2009, 2013, Vuillermet 2012a)? Thus, Fortis and Vittrant (2011, to appear) provide a summary of the unsolved problems with Talmy's typology with examples of motion event expressions the typology cannot account for.

(8) Dutch
 a. *de jongen loopt het bos in.*
    the boy walks the woods in
    'The boy walks into the woods' [path: boy enters woods]
    Sinha & Kuteva (1995: 173)

 b. *de jongen loopt in het bos.*
    the boy walks in the woods
    'The boy walks in the woods' [non-lative: activity takes place in woods]

3 Encoding motion events in Southeast Asian languages: various means

As the typology of motion event classification is based essentially on Indo-European languages, studies on motion events in Southeast Asian (henceforth SEA) languages change our view. These languages reveal other options for encoding motion events that do not fit easily into Talmy's proposal and thus force modification of the typology.

In this section, we will first discuss the new motion construction types found in Asian languages, which have been overlooked by previous motion event typologies (Section 3.1). Then, we will present the video tool developed by the Trajectory Project, by means of which we are now in a position to complement the existing cross-linguistic studies of motion events (Section 3.2).

3.1 Neglected constructions of Southeast Asian languages

Among the means of expressing motion events in languages of the world, the voice morphemes of Tagalog, the verb-less sentences of Spoken Indonesian and the Burmese 'associated motion' morpheme are good examples of constructions neglected by previous typologies. These will be described in turn.

3.1.1 Spatial Voice markers in Tagalog

Like other Austronesian languages from the Western Malayo-Polynesian branch, Tagalog (spoken in the Philippines) is famous for its voice system (cf. Lemarechal 1991, Fortis 2004, Himmelmann 2005: 363). Voice markers assign grammatical roles to the core arguments; they may also semantically interact with the verbal base, with semantic effects on the resulting construction. However, Tagalog has markers dedicated to path encoding. Tagalog expresses spatial relations either with prepositions (11), or with grammatical markers that are part of a voice system, or with both.

For instance, the voice suffix *-(h)an* commonly assigns the subject role to any landmark relevant to the motion event. However, the spatial relation is indeterminate, though inferred from the context (9).

(9) Tagalog (Austronesian)
*Ni-lakar-**an**   namin   ang tulay*
PFV-walk-Dir**VOICE** 1.PL.EXCL.GEN NOM bridge
'We walked on the bridge'
adapted from Fortis (2003: 457)

Examples (10) and (11) show another voice marker, i.e. *i-*. The bases to which *i-* is prefixed have various meanings (Fortis and Fagard 2010 ch. III: 29), but the combinations that result very frequently invoke a notion of transfer, whether concrete or metaphorical. In (10a) the Transfer Voice marker *i-* encodes the idea of a "transfer of the figure to the ground"[14]. Notice that a different spatial relation to the entity 'table' is encoded by the two voice markers *i-* and *-in*: in (10a) the argument assigned to the subject role (marked by *ang*) is the landmark; whereas in (10b) the entity corresponding to the subject argument (marked by *ang*) is the patient, and is completely or 'internally' affected by the verbal process (see Fortis 2003: 478-79 for details).

(10)   Tagalog (Austronesian)
   a. *i-   ligpit   mo   ang   mesa.*
      TVOICE- clear   2SG.GEN   NOM   table
      'Clean up the table. [lit. Put away from the table]'
      adapted from Fortis (2003: 479)

   b. *ligpit   -in   mo   ang mesa.*
      put.away -**OVOICE** 2SG.GEN NOM table
      'Put away the table.'

The transfer voice marker *i-* may also be attached to a non-verb stem to create a verb that incorporates the semantic element of the ground as in (11b).

         Tagalog (Austronesian)
(11) a. *i-   lagay mo   ang alahas sa kahon.*
         TVOICE- put 2SG.GEN NOM jewel LOC box
         'Put the jewel (in)to the box.'

---

[14] The marker *i-* is called a 'conveyance voice marker' by Fortis and Fagard (2010-III: 29) after Himmelmann (2005), and belongs to the object-focus marker category in other Tagalog grammars.

b. i-   **kahon** mo   ang mga aklat.
    Tvoice- box   2SG.GEN NOM PL book
    'Put the books in a box. [lit. Box the books]'
    Fortis (2003: 479)

3.1.2 Non verbal head

Previous motion event typologies failed also to take into account other types of motion expressions although such types are far from being rare. For instance, the clause in (12) conveys a motional meaning. However the clausal head is neither a verb nor a satellite of the verb[15]. How to classify this construction within Talmy's original framework or modified versions?

(12) Spoken Indonesian (Austronesian)
      mereka   ke   bioskop.
       3PL   towards   movies
      'They are going to the movies.'
      Hagège (2010: 247)

The Tagalog and Indonesian examples above are illuminating for more than one reason. Apart from revealing constructions not taken into account in previous studies, they pose another question: what should be considered as a verb? In other words, how to identify verbs —but also satellites— across languages? Some of these issues arise also from our Burmese data (see below).

3.1.3 Associated motion morphemes

'Associated motion' morphemes[16] are those in which motion is co-expressed (or conflates in Talmy's terms) with a temporal relation. Guillaume (2009) defined them as morphemes that associate a motion component to the event expressed by the verb stem they are attached to, whether or not this event already involves

---

[15] See also French *La voilà!* 'There she comes!'
[16] Koch (1984) coined the term to characterize a set of verbal morphemes found in Kaytej (Arandic), an Australian language. See also Wilkins (1991) on associated motion in Australian languages.

motion[17]. 'Associated motion' morphemes must also be distinguished from directional markers (Voisin 2013: 138-39). The latter are generally restricted to motion verbs and they can only specify the path of a motion that is encoded in the verb stem event, that is to say the specification of the course followed by the figure with regards to different landmarks such as deictic centre. Burmese, for instance, has a directional marker $θwa^3$ derived from the eponymic verb meaning 'to go'. The three sentences in (13) contain the form $θwa^3$, appearing as a modifier of the main verb. In (13c), it is combined with a motion verb and therefore conveys path information. However, used with other types of verbs as in (13a) and (13b), $θwa^3$ conveys an aspectual meaning.

(13)   Burmese (Tibeto-Burman)
   a.   ဒီနေ့မျက်မှန် ပျောက်သွားတယ်။
        di^2 ne^2 $myɛʔm̥aN^2$ $pyaɔʔ$ $θwa^3$ $=Tɛ^2$
        DEM day   glasses   disappear go/PFV   REAL
        'Today, (my) glasses disappeared.'

   b.   ... ဦးဖြူစင်က ကြားသွားတယ်။
        ... $ʔu^3phyu^2siN^2$ $=Ka^1$ ca^3 $θwa^3$ $=Tɛ^2$
        U Phyu Sin   S.   hear   go/PFV   REAL
        'U Phuy Sin heard [what they said].'

   c.   သူကျောင်းကို ကား မောင်းသွားတယ်။
        $θu^2$ $caɔN^3$ $=Ko^2$ ka^3 $maɔN^3$ $θwa^3$ $=Tɛ^2$
        3SG   school   OBJ   car   ride   go/DIR.CFG   REAL
        'He went by car to school. [lit. He rode a car to school (away from Deictic Centre)]'

In other words, while directionals only encode path, associated motion markers encode motion and path in addition to the temporal relationship between the path and the event denoted by the verb stem. Thus, Talmy's classifica-

---

[17] Examples of suffixes of 'associated motion' in an Amerindian language, Ese ejja (Bolivia) from Vuillermet, cited by Fortis and Vittrant (2011).
(i) ixya-**ki**-kwe!   ixya-**wa**-kwe!

eat-**CFG&DO**-IMP   eat-**CPT&DO**-IMP

(lit.) 'Go and eat!'   (lit.) 'Come and eat!'

tion of motion events expressed by motion verbs (whether or not they conflate motion with manner or with path) cannot apply to associated-motion devices.

Although the system does not seem as developed as in Amerindian languages, 'associated motion' markers may be found in SEA languages[18]. For instance, the Burmese marker *khɛ¹* fulfils this function, as it indicates that the event expressed by the preceding verb stem has taken place in another place. In other terms, the use of *khɛ¹* entails a translocation of the figure after the event described by the main verb as in (14) and (15) (see also Vittrant in press).

In (14a) the speaker is making a phone call. Speaker (S) and Hearer (H) are not located in the same place, whereas in (14b) S and H are in the same room and no change of location is expressed/implied.

(14)   Burmese (Tibeto-Burman)
   a.   စာအုပ် ယူခဲ့ပါ။
      *sa²ʔo? yu² =**Khɛ¹** =Pa² Ø*
      book take **COME&V** POL (IMP)
      'Bring(-me) a book. lit.: Come and take a book. [S and H not in the same room]'

   b.   စာအုပ် ယူလာပါ။
      sa²ʔo? yu² la² =Pa Ø
      book take come/**TOWARDS** POL (IMP)
      'Bring (-me) a book. lit.: Take towards me a book. [S and H in the same room]'

Compare also the next two sentences: (15) is uttered by a doctor talking to his patient. The use of *Khɛ¹* is needed, as the event required ('put eye-drops') has to be performed before the change of location although it is clarified by the subordinated clause. This complex event expresses motion and path and is temporally related to the action event (dropping eye-lotion). In (16) however, uttered by a daughter reminding her mother to put eye-drops in before going to meet the doctor, *Khɛ¹* is ungrammatical: the two protagonists are located in the same room. Therefore, no motional or translocational expression is required.

---

[18] Notice that 'associated motion' here has to be distinguished from its use by Jarkey (2010: 125) to refer to a sub-type of Cotemporal SVC in Hmong that expresses simultaneous motion and action.

(15) ဆေးခန်း မလာခင် ၊ မျက်စဉ်း ခပ်ခဲ့ပါ။
she³-khaN³   mə=   la²   =KhiN²   mγɛʔsiN³   khaʔ   =**Khɛ¹**   =Pa²
hospital   NEG   come before   eye-drop   put   **KHE**   POL
'Before coming to the hospital, put some [eye-lotion] drops [in your eyes].'

(16) ဆေးခန်း မသွားခင် ၊ မျက်စဉ်း ခပ် (*ခဲ့) ပါ။
she³-khaN³   mə=   θwa³ =KhiN²   mγɛʔsiN³   khaʔ   (*khɛ¹)   =Pa²
hospital   NEG   go   before   eye-drop   put   POL
'Before going to the hospital, put some [eye-lotion] drops [in your eyes].'

3.2 About the Trajectory Project

So far we have described some hitherto neglected constructions encoding motion events in Asian languages. However a more exhaustive discussion on the expression of motion events is needed. Therefore, to explore this semantic and syntactic domain further, we collected data using a video tool developed by the *Trajectory Project*.

The *Trajectory Project*[19] is a research project that aims to analyse the expression of path in dynamic events by describing the various strategies for path-encoding and by developing a typology of these strategies. It comes within the scope of a functional-typological framework adapted from Givon (2001), and could be described as a 'working typology' (Grinevald 2011). It explores the delimitation of a particular functional domain. It is then followed by (a) the identification of the strategies (morphosyntactic subsystems, constructions placed in their discourse context, etc.) used by a language to express the chosen functional domain; and (b) the description and analysis of the strategies and means identified (interaction of the subsystems with each other, their extension in other functional domains, etc.). In other words, the notion of 'working typology' is to be understood as "a systematic research of all the dimensions of a phenomenon, from semantics to morphosyntax to discourse, from categories to constructions, from a strict focus on specific items for a specific function to an

---

[19] The *Trajectory Project* ('Projet Trajectoire') (http://www.ddl.ish-lyon.cnrs.fr/trajectoire/) has been supported by CNRS - Fédération TUL (FRE 2559, Fédération Typologie et Universaux Linguistiques) from 2006 to 2011.

exploration of the place of those items in a general view of the workings of the language" (Grinevald 2011: 51). It is also to be understood as a typology leading towards the description of a language, and then in return, using the description as an input to rework the typology.

To help field linguists in this task of exploring path expression, we developed a video tool to elicit descriptions of path events (Ishibashi et al. 2006). Thus, members of the Trajectory Project collected comparable data in various languages. Using data collected from the same input (video) allows us to compare the expression of motion in different languages and to build a typology.

Inspired by the tools developed by the Max Plank Institute (Nijmegen) — see for instance the tool created for the 'Put and take' Project (Bowerman et al. 2004) —, the Trajectory video stimulus (Ishibashi et al. 2006) contains 76 short videos (roughly 10 seconds each). Most of them (55 'target' scenes) show figures involved in spontaneous motion, i.e. walking, going down, jumping, etc., in relation to a site. Some of these scenes also show a perspective on the motion event (deixis). The 'target' scenes combine the five following parameters, varying (1) the figure (man, woman, kid, groups), (2) the kind of sites (building, roads, landscape, objects, human sites), (3) the manner of motion (walk, run, jump), (4) the types of path (with boundary crossing, oriented toward the source or the goal, combining different portions of the path, etc.), and (5) the deixis or perspective on the event (toward or away from the speaker / deictic centre). Beside the 'target' scenes, the tool contains two training videos and 19 other scenes (distracters) showing various kinds of action such as eating or sleeping.

4 Motion events in SEA languages: the contribution of Burmese dialects

4.1 Burmese data

The study of motion events in Burmese dialects is based mainly on fieldwork carried out by the author in Burma in 2008 and 2010.

4.1.1 The Burmese dialects

Data from two Burmese dialects have been used in this study: Colloquial Burmese and Arakanese. They are usually considered as dialects of the same language as they are mutually intelligible. However, as is usual in such situations, speakers of the dialects with lesser social prestige understand speakers of the standard one better. In other words, Arakanese people speak and understand Standard Burmese better than Standard Burmese speakers understand Arakanese.

Colloquial or Standard Burmese (henceforth S-Burmese) is to be understood here as the language of Central Burma, spoken along the Irrawaddy valley from Mandalay to Yangon. It is the standard dialect currently used in the media and at school. Arakanese[20], on the other hand, is spoken on the western coast of Burma, up to the Bengali border. It is often considered as a conservative dialect given that Arakanese pronunciation is closer to the writing system[21].

4.1.2 Multi-verb constructions in Burmese dialects

Burmese dialects, like other SEA languages, exhibit multi-verb constructions, analysed either as serialization, verb-compounds, or clause concatenations.

Vittrant (2006, 2012) examines in detail the characteristics of multi-verb constructions in S-Burmese. These sequences of several verb roots that are not linked by any marker exhibit similar forms on the surface but have different underlying structures. Using criteria such as initial consonant realization, semantic change, syntactic behaviour as regards to negation and the insertion of a subordinating marker, four sub-types of serial verb constructions (SVC) in S-Burmese are distinguished : (1) Lexicalized (symmetrical) SVCs, (2) 'True' symmetrical SVCs, (3) 'True' Asymmetrical SVCs, and (4) Grammaticalized (asymmetrical) SVCs.

These studies confirm that multi-verb constructions have to be analysed using proper language internal criteria rather than relying on the set of common features generally applied to these constructions[22]. What also emerges from this work on serialization in S-Burmese is that the four sub-types are not clear-cut categories of SVCs, although the different sub-types could be characterized using phonological, syntactic and semantic properties. A better account of Bur-

---

20 The varieties of Arakanese studied here are mainly the ones spoken in Sittwe (Akyab) and Mrauk-U, the main towns of the Arakanese (Rakhine) State.
21 Discrepancies between the two dialects are well known, among which phonological ones are the best described. See Sprigg (1963), Okell (1995) and Vittrant (2010b) for details.
22 See Durie (1997: 290-91), Brill (2004: 3-4), Aikhenvald (2006: 1) or Vittrant (2012: 107) for a set of key characteristics.

mese multi-verb constructions analyses the different sequences of verbs found as belonging to a continuum marked out by four prototypical categories.

The next section will deal with multi-verb motion constructions in Burmese, aiming to show the evolution of motion multi-verb constructions from sequentialization to serialization on their way to producing satellites. It will rely on data from two Burmese dialects.

4.2 Multi-verb motion constructions

4.2.1 From sequentialization....

In Arakanese, and less frequently in S-Burmese, path information may be distributed throughout several clauses in a sentence. In Arakanese example (17), the verb stems (in bold) conveying motion information appear in two separate clauses, linked by the subordinator lo^1, whereas the corresponding S-Burmese verbs in (18) are part of the same clause. Compare also Arakanese (19) and S-Burmese (20). The former contains a sequential subordinator Pyi^3 / $P(r)i^3$, the latter is a single clause with serialized verbs.

Scene 045_Path_3_walk_across_bridge_back

(17) Arakanese
မာမသုံးယောက် တံတားထက်က လမ်းလျှောက်လို့ လားခရေ။ [SoSo/10, 14_045]
ma^2ma^1	$\theta oN^3=ya\mathfrak{I}?$	taN^2Tha^3	$tha?$	$=Ka^1$	laN^3
[women	3 =CLF:hum	bridge	above	=S.	road
ʃaɔʔ	=lo¹	**la³**		=kha¹=re²	
walk	=SUB]CL1	[**go**/CFG		=ACCOMP=REAL]CL2	

'Three ladies go [while] walking from above the bridge.'

(18) S-Burmese
ဟောင်းကူးတံတားလေပေါ်က ကောင်မလေးသုံးယောက် လမ်းလျှောက်သွားတယ်။
[AA/08, 44_045]
$paɔN^3.ku^2$-$təda^3$	-le^3	$pɔ^2=Ka^1$	$kaɔN^2ma^2$-le^3	$\theta oN^3=ya\mathfrak{I}?$
arch-bridge	-DIM	top.of=S.	woman-DIM	3 =CLF:hum
laN^3	**ʃaɔʔ**	**θwa³**	=$Tɛ^2$	
road	**walk**	**go**/CFG	=REAL	

'From the top of an arch bridge, three young ladies walk away.'

Scene 043_Path_F_run_behind_tree_sideRL

(19) Arakanese
မာမတယောက် အပင်တပင်နားက ဦးဦးလားခရေ။ [SoSo/10, 59_043]
*ma²ma¹ tə=yaɔʔ ʔəpoN² tə=poN² na³ =Ka¹ **bri³** =P(r)i³*
[women 1=CLF:hum tree 1=CLF:tree place=S. **run** =SUB:TPS]CL1
la³ =kha¹=re²
[**go**/CFG =ACCOMP=REAL]CL2
'A lady, from the tree's area, went away after having run.'

(20) S-Burmese
မြက်ခင်းပေါ် ကောင်မလေးတစ်ယောက် ဖြတ်ပြေးသွားပြန်ပြီ။ [AA/05, 56_043]
*myeʔ.khiN³=Pɔ² kaɔN²ma²-le³ θə = yaɔʔ **phyaʔ** **pye³***
meadow=top.of woman-DIM 1 =CLF:hum **cut/cross run**
*θwa³ **pyaN²** =Pi²*
go/CFG **return** >ITER =CRS
'A young lady crossed the meadow running away again.'

Parallel examples in (21) show that the distribution of motion information throughout a complex sentence also exists in S-Burmese. The initial section of the path indicating the place where the figure stayed before moving is expressed in the first (subordinated) clause, whereas the motion itself is expressed in the following clause. However, the most common way[23] to indicate the source of a motion event in S-Burmese is to use the syntactic organization found in (22), which contains a single clause. In this sentence, departure from the source is NOT expressed in a subordinate clause although it appears as the first constituent of the sentence similarly to the two previous examples. The source of the motion is expressed here by an adpositional phrase. In other words, the sequence *Ka¹-ne²* (S./TOP-Stay*)* is no longer transparent and functions as a complex postposition.

---

23 The *Ka¹-ne²* (*S.-stay*) sequence in (Spoken) Burmese data appeared followed by a subordinator in only 20 % of the occurrences met, however with differences among speakers. For instance, one informant used the subordinator *Pyi³Tɔ¹* after *Ka¹-ne²* only once in 18 occurrences, whereas another used it in 33 % of his sentences containing *Ka¹-ne²*.

Scene 029_Path_F_walk_outof_cave_up_stairs_back

(21) Arakanese
a. ဂူထေးကနီပြီးကေ တက်လားခရေ။ မာမတစ်ယောက်။ [SoSo/10, 44_029]
gu² the³ = *Ka¹* *nī²* =Pri³Ke² tɔʔ la³ =kha¹=re²
cave interior =s./TOP stay =SUB:TPS go.up go/CFG =ACCOMP=REAL
ma²ma¹ tə = yaɔʔ
woman 1=CLF:hum
'Given the cave, from there, (she) went up (away from DC). A lady.
(lit. The interior of the cave, after staying, she went up (away from DC).')

S-Burmese
b. ကောင်မလေးတစ်ယောက် ဂူထဲကနေ ပြီးတော့ ထွက်သွားတယ် ၊ [...]
[HNTH/08, 44_029]
kaɔN²ma²-le³ tə= yaɔʔ gu² the³ =*Ka¹-ne²* =*Pyi³Tɔ¹*
woman-DIM 1=CLF:hum cave interior =s./TOP -stay =SUB:TPS
thwɛʔ θwa³ =Tɛ²
go.out go/CFG =REAL
'A woman, then, from inside the cave, went out (away from DC).
(lit. A woman after staying in the cave, from [there] went out away.')

(22) S-Burmese
ဂူအပြင်ထွက်ဖို့ လုပ်ထားတဲ့လှေကားလေးကနေ ကောင်မလေးတစ်ယောက်
ဂူအပြင်ကို ထွက်သွားတယ်။ [AA/08, V1_029]
gu² ʔəpiN² thwɛʔ =Pho¹ loʔ tha³ =Tɛ¹ l̥e² ka³-le³
cave exterior go.out =SUB:for do RESULT REL.REAL stairs-DIM
=*Ka¹-ne²* kaɔN²ma²-le³ tə=yaɔʔ gu² ʔə.piN²= Ko²
=S.-stay (ABL) woman-DIM 1 =CLF:hum cave exterior = DIR
thwɛʔ θwa³ =Tɛ²
go.out go/CFG =REAL
'From the little stairs that have been done to go out from the cave, the young lady went out to the exterior of the cave (away from DC).'

When not distributed in different clauses, the information may be distributed across several verb stems that are combined in a single clause and constitute a single predicate.

4.2.2 .... to serialization

The use of sequences of verbs behaving like a single predicate, without any connector between them, is definitely an areal characteristic of SEA languages (Clark 1992, Bisang 1996, Matisoff 1991, Enfield 2005, Vittrant 2010a among others). As expected, these strings of verbs also exist in Burmese dialects as seen in previous examples (18), (20), (21), (22). They are referred to as serial verb constructions by Vittrant (2006), (2010a), as (i) the verbs are not separated by a connector, (ii) they share the same grammatical information (such as tense, aspect or modality) and (some) arguments, and (iii) they describe a single event. These SVCs are monoclausal (although multi-predicational[24]) and have to be distinguished from complex sentences containing several clauses (example 23).

(23)   S-Burmese: Multi-clausal sentence
... ဂူထဲကို ပြန်ပြီးတော့ ယူပြီး ဝင်သွားပါတယ်။ [TTTh/08, 27-024]
gu^2 $th\varepsilon^3 = Ko^2$ $pyaN^2$ $=Pyi^3T\jmath^1$ yu^2 $=Pyi^3$ wiN^2
[cave interior=DIR come.back =SUB:TPS] [take =SUB:TPS] [come.in
θwa^3 $=Pa^2$ $=T\varepsilon^2$
go/CFG POL REAL]
'Coming back into the cave, taking [the basket], [she] came in [away from DC].'

However, like the majority of languages with SVCs, Burmese dialects are grammatically complex, with different types of serialization. Thus, Burmese exhibits some symmetrical SVCs (i.e. co-ranking predicates) as in (24), (25), (26) and some asymmetrical SVCs (i.e. implying a head-modifier hierarchy) as in (27), both of these types of constructions containing subtypes. For instance, (24) describes consecutive events, (25) describes a single event with co-occurring elements that are causally related (i.e. resultative), while (26) refers to a single event with co-occurring elements that are NOT causally related but just happen to be true at the same time (i.e. depictive)[25].

---

24 Jarkey (2010: 110): "SVCs are monoclausal but multi-predicational. That is, they involve two or more distinct predicating morphemes, linked together in a single clause by virtue of the fact that they share one or more argument positions through coindexation."
25 See Enfield (2008: 132ff) on semantic subclasses of secondary predication constructions.

(24) S-Burmese Symmetrical SVC
ဓါး:ပြတွေ သေနတ်နဲ့ ပစ်ပြေးတယ်။ [DB-9, p.171]
də.mya¹ =Twe² θəna? =nɛ¹ **pi?** **pye³** =Tɛ²
bandit =PL gun =with **shoot, throw run** =REAL
'The bandits shot with their guns and ran.'

(25) ... ကလေးလေး ကျောက်တုံးကနေ နောက်တစ်တုံးကို ခုန်ကူးတယ်။
[AA/08, 28_075]
kəle³-le³ cɔ?-toN³ =Ka¹.ne² nɔ? tə=toN³ =Ko² **khoN²**
child-DIM stone-log =ABL next one=CLF:log =DIR **jump**
ku³ =Tɛ²
cross =REAL
'The child jumps and crosses from one rock to the next rock.'

Symmetrical SVCs are also found in Arakanese dialect as shown by (26).

(26) *Arakanese Symmetrical SVC*
မာမနိန်ယောက်ကျား ဂူထဲမှာ ငှက်ပျောသီး ထိုင်စားနီကတ်တော။
[SoSo/10, 29_011]
ma²ma¹ =neiN¹ yɔ?Ca³ gu² the³ =ma³ ŋəpyɔ³θi³
woman =WITH man cave interior =LOC banana
thaiN² sa³ ni² =ka? =te²
sit eat INACC =PL =REAL
'A woman and a man are sitting inside a cave eating bananas.'

In (27) and (28), both sentences contain the verb *ne²* 'to stay, to live', which has undergone a semantic change, as shown by the unacceptability of translations marked by (*). Following a universal grammaticalization path (Heine and Kuteva 2002: 276, Matisoff 1991: 415), *ne²* has become an aspectual marker indicating an ongoing process, i.e. unaccomplished (or imperfective) aspect. Thus, according to the definition of asymmetrical SVCs that implies a head-modifier hierarchy between the verbs and the semantic bleaching of the verb becoming modifier (see Aikhenvald 2006, Vittrant 2012), the string of verbs shown in (27) and (28) are analysed as asymmetrical SVCs, although other analyses may be proposed (see Enfield 2009 on a monosemy or heterosemy account for the grammaticalized verbs).

(27)   S-Burmese Asymmetrical SVC
   a. ရေကန်ထဲမှာ ဘဲကလေးတွေ ကူးနေတယ်။ [AA/08, 62_005]
       ye³-kaN³   thɛ³   =Ma² bɛ³-kəle³=Twe²   **ku³**   **ne²**
       water-lake inside =LOC duck-kid=PL   **cross** **stay>INACC**
       =Tɛ²
       =REAL
       'The ducklings are crossing [*cross and stay] the lake.'
   b. ကောင်မလေးတစ်ယောက် မြက်ခင်ပေါ်မှာ ပြေးနေတယ်။
       [HNTH/08, 59_043]
       kɔN²ma²-le³ tə=yaɔʔ   myɛʔ.khiN³ pɔ²=Ma² **pye³**
       woman-DIM   1=CLF:hum lawn   top.of=LOC **run**
       ne²   =Tɛ²
       stay>INACC   =REAL
       'A young lady is running [*runs and stays/ *runs while staying] on the lawn.'

(28) ဒီကောင်မလေး ဂူထဲကို ဝင်လိုက်ထွက်လိုက်လုပ်နေတယ်။ [AA/08, 064_022]
      di²   kɔN²ma²-le³ gu²   thɛ³=Ko²   **wiN²**   **laiʔ**   **thwɛʔ**
      DEM   woman-DIM   cave interior=DIR **go.in** **follow** **go.out**
      laiʔ   **loʔ** **ne²**   =Tɛ²
      follow   **do**   **stay>INACC** =REAL
      'This woman, (she) just went in and out the cave.'

Notice that in (28) above, the four first verbs follow a particular pattern that is widespread in SEA languages, and which involves the reduplication of one element, creating a sequence of the form ABCB. This 'elaborate expression'[26] depicts co-temporal actions, drawing attention to the repetitive action of the figure. Syntactically it functions as an adverbial expression modifying the verb *loʔ* 'to do'. The verbal form *ne²* also modifies the action, indicating that it is still ongoing.

---

26 Many references exist on 'Elaborate expressions', a term coined by Mary Haas (1964) talking about Thai literary four-syllables expressions. This type of construction is typical of East and Southeast Asian languages. Matisoff (1973: 81) describes them as a "compound containing four (usually monosyllabic) elements, of which either the first and third or the second and fourth are identical (A-B-A-C or A-B-C-B) [and that] characteristically convey a rather formal or elegant impression." See also Vittrant (2013) and Enfield (2007: 387ff) on elaborate expressions respectively in Burmese and Lao, and Jarkey (2012: 124ff) on Hmong elaborate expressions in SVCs.

Asymmetrical SVCs are also found in the Arakanese dialect as shown by (29), where the verb meaning originally 'to put' has become an aspectual marker, indicating the result of the action expressed by the previous main verb.

(29) Arakanese Asymmetrical SVC
ဂူရှေ့မှာ ခြင်းတစ်ခြင်း ချထားရေ။ [KZT/10, 27_024]
gu² ʃe¹ =ma² kroN³ tə = kroN³ **cha¹**
cave front =LOC basket 1 =CLF:basket **put down, fall**
tha³ =re²
put>RESULT =REAL
'A basket has been put down [and left] in front of the cave.'

How to account for this variety of constructions (multiclausal, symmetrical SVC, asymmetrical SVC) used to express motion events in S-Burmese and in Arakanese as well (although seemingly less frequently in the latter case for SVCs)? How to distinguish constructions with co-ranking predicates from those with a head-verb accompanied by verbal modifiers that could be analysed as path satellites?

Let us examine the data to investigate the status of motion verbs in SVCs, in order to (1) determine if the path satellite has developed yet in Burmese dialects, and (2) recognize head verbs in a SVC describing motion.

4.3 Are there path satellites in Burmese dialects?

4.3.1 The satellite functional category

A brief review of Talmy's work (1972, 1985, 1991, 2000, 2009) shows that he opposes adpositions to satellites (Croft et al. 2010: 205). However, a close reading reveals that the term satellite "S" has a double usage in his writing, which has led to confusion (Imbert et al. 2011: 100). He used the term to designate a type of construction (S-framed construction) but also to designate a type of surface element (such as preverbs and particles).

The first use covers any construction where path is encoded not in, but outside, the verb. See example (30) where path is encoded in an adposition. In other words, S-framed languages are simply those that are *not* V-framed. (Talmy, 2009: 389-390).

(30) *He ran **to** the house.*

In its second use, the term refers to a category that includes elements such as preverbs or verbs but NOT adpositions. Satellite is set up as a category distinct from adpositions and case-inflection, but including elements that are in a sister relation to the verb, as dependents to a head.[27]

In this paper, Satellite is to be understood as a functional super-category belonging to the verbal sphere. It is a heterogeneous category containing elements of diverse origins: adnominal, adverbial, verbal. Following Imbert et al. (2011: 103-104), the category is defined as follows:

Satellites may be in a sister relation to V, and should not introduce any syntactic arguments, unlike adpositions.

Satellites, in motion events, participate in the expression of path, indicating source, median, goal, boundary-crossing, direction, deixis.

Satellites are of lexical origin (nominal, verbal, ...) but have grammaticalized within the sphere of the verb.

It is beyond the scope of this paper to discuss in detail the category of satellites, and we limit our investigation to satellites of verbal origin given the importance of verbal constituents in SEA languages. In these languages, sentences containing a single verbal phrase with no reference to other constituents (core or outlying participants) are common if not the majority of sentences found in natural speech, as shown by examples (31) and (32)[28]. In other words, SEA languages are definitely 'verb-loving'!

(31) Vietnamese (Mon-Khmer)
 Đã làm thì phải làm cho xong
 ACCOMP do TOP must do FOR/give finish
 '(You) must finish (what) (you) undertook.'
 Adapted from Do-Hurinville (2009)

(32) Burmese (Tibeto-Burman)
 စား၊ပြီ၊ပြီလား။
 sa^3 pyi^3 $=Pi^2$ $=la^3$
 eat finish CRS =QST
 'Have (you) eaten yet?'

---

[27] The existence of a category of S distinct from adpositions, adverbs or cases, and the use of the concept of S as a cover term for everything that is not V-framed, have been discussed by Matsumoto (2003) and Beavers, Levin and Tham (2010).

[28] Diller (2006: 160) on Thai: "Informal domestic communication frequently consists of a series of verbs: 'Peel give eat.' 'Tell finish not have.' [...] ('Peel the oranges for the guests.' 'I already told you, there aren't any'.)"

4.3.2 Satellization process

Imbert et al. (2011) identify two stages in the satellization of verbal items: event sequencing and serialization.

The first stage on this grammaticalization path, called 'event sequencing'[29], refers to the special syntactic organization of a complex sentence into a pair of clauses, each of them conveying some of the path information. In some languages such as Ese Ejja (Tacanan, Bolivia), this syntactic organization is the only way to express the different parts of a path (source, goal) – see example (33). The source of the motion has to be expressed in a separate clause. A similar structure is found in Arakanese example (34)[30]. See also examples (19) to (21), p.594-95.

(33) Ese Ejja (Tacanan, Bolivia)
 eta'a=jo neki, kwaji-kwaji-jaasowa-ani[31]
 river=LOC stand run-run-go.up-PRS
 '(he) runs from the river (where he stood).
 (lit. [He] stands at the river, he goes running.')
 M. Vuillermet (2012b)

 Scene 027_Path_F_walk_outof_woods_sideRL

(34) Arakanese (Tibeto-Burman, Burma)
 ချုံကြားကနိပြီး (က) အကောင်မရေ ထွက်လာရေ။ [KZT, V3_027]
 $(k)roN^2$ Kra^3 $=Ka^1$ ni^2 $=Pri^3(Ke^2)$ $\partial?ka\partial N^2ma^1\text{-}\int e^2$ $tw\partial?$
 bush space = S./TOP stay =SUB:TPS woman-DIM go.out
 $la^2=re^2$
 come/CPT =REAL
 'From the bushes, she went out (toward DC).
 (lit. The bushes' space staying/being there, then the young lady went out (toward DC).')

---

29 See also Bohnemeyer et al. (2007) on event segmentation types, and Crowley (1987) on the sub-type of core SVC called 'ambient' serialization, where there is identity between the subject of the second verb of the string and of the sub-event described by the preceding verbal phrase.
30 It seems to also be the usual way to express the notion of Source in Kayah Li (Karen), as noted by Solnit (2006: 147).
31 Although the string of verbs looks like a SVC, Vuillermet (2012: 632ff) reports prosodic and grammatical arguments (ergative clitic marking) against this analysis.

The second stage in the satellization process is multi-verb constructions that describe a single event, in which verbs share the same grammatical information and some arguments, i.e. verb serialization. In (35) from White Hmong, the three motion verbs share a common subject. Each of them introduces a separate portion of the path (route, source and goal respectively) followed by the figure, i.e. the Hmong (*cov hmoob*). Hmong SVCs are good examples of maximally dense packaging, allowing multiple location-change-denoting verbs to occur together in a single clause (Jarkey 2010: 121).

(35) White Hmong (Hmong-Mien)
*cov   hmoob **hla**   dej   na.koom   **dim***
CLF: coll   Hmong **cross** river Mekong   **escape**
*hauv   nplog.teb **mus** thai.teb*
inside   Laos   **go**   Thailand
'The Hmong escaped from Laos to Thailand over the Mekong River.'
Jarkey (2010: 116)

When the verb stem has reached the Satellite stage, it has lost its verbal status. It has become a dependent element to the verb head and should not introduce any argument. Moreover, it is often 'bleached' or desemanticized. In other words, it has undergone grammaticalization. Thus, Jakaltek popti' 'directional' morphemes are prototypical examples of deverbal satellites. They come from motion verb stems, and, as Satellite, they convey path information only and no longer convey motional meaning. Evidence for this can be seen in their use with stative localization and verbs of speaking. For instance, in example (36), according to Grinevald (2006: 46), the two verbal morphemes *ah* and *toj* originate respectively from *ahi* 'to ascend', and *toyi* 'to go'. As path Satellites, they indicate the direction (path) of the greetings according to the position of the participants.

(36) Jakaltek popti' (Maya, Guatemala)
xtiyoxhli-ah-toj   naj   tet   ix
say.hello.PST-DIR1:up-DIR2:CFG CLF/3SG   to   CLF/her
'He said hello (up + towards) to her (from his down-position to her up-position, away from himself).'
Grinevald (2006: 54)

In Southeast (and East) Asian languages, verbal forms labelled differently such as *Coverb*, *Converb* or *Minor verb*[32] of SVCs may be considered as satellites.

A verb is considered as a *Coverb*[33] if it occurs with the function of an adposition (i.e. introducing a NP modifying the main verb) while retaining some verb characteristics, whereas a *Converb*[34] is a non-finite verb form that expresses adverbial subordination. Converbal constructions containing medial (and non-finite) verbs often followed by a linker are therefore formally different from serialized verbs, although they are functionally similar as illustrated by parallel expressions in examples (37a), (37b) and (37c) (See Shibatani 2009). See Table 1 for a summary of these terms.

(37)   Vietnamese (Mon-Khmer)
    a.   Cô ây   (đa) đi bộ
        She   (TAM) to go to walk
        'She went on foot.'
        Do-Hurinville, p.c.

        Mandarin Chinese (Sino-Tibetan)
    b.   tā   zŏu qù le
        she walk go ASP
        'She went on foot.'
        Shibatani (2009: 257)

---

32 'Minor' verb as opposed to 'major' verb refers to a verb chosen from a grammaticalized restricted class. Minor verbs in asymmetrical SVCs tend to get grammaticalized. (Aikhenvald 2006: 22)

33 According to Clark (1978), the term was coined by Chinese language teachers after the World War II to describe "a secondary verb preceding the main verb in a sentence, [a verb] followed by a NP with which it forms a constituent, [a verb that] can be translated as a preposition in English" (p.76). Li & Thomson (1981: 356ff) use it in describing Chinese multi-verb constructions containing forms that are "partly like verbs and partly like prepositions". More precisely: "A coverb and its noun form a phrase that modifies the verb of the sentence. If the Mandarin coverbs are essentially prepositions, why, then, are they called coverbs rather than prepositions? The answer is simply that the class of coverbs contains words that are partly like verbs and partly like prepositions; the traditional term coverb was coined to avoid labeling them either verbs or prepositions." (p.360)

34 *Converbs* cannot occur as the main verb of an independent clause. They lack specifications for tense (-aspect) and mood as well as for agreement with their arguments. They are verbal adverbs just like participles are verbal adjectives (Haspelmath (1995: 3-4). They are treated in the literature under different labels such as 'conjunctive' or 'adverbial participles', 'gerunds', 'free adjuncts', etc. (Bisang 1995).

Korean

c. *Kunye=nun   kel-e   ka-tta*
   she=TOP   walk-CONN   go-PST
   'She went on foot.'
   Shibatani (2009: 257)

Table 1 summarizes the functional, syntactic and semantic characteristics of Coverbs, Converbs and Minor verbs of Asymmetrical SVCs.

Table 1: Main features of Coverbs, Converbs and Minor verbs

Verb stem used as	Category	Syntactic features	Semantic features
Coverb (see Clark 1978)	similar to an adposition : introducing an NP modifying the main verb	• Generally found in analytic languages, • Often (S)VO languages • followed by a NP, with which it forms a constituent V1 in V1-NP-V2 or V2 in V1-V2 NP	Case relations such as benefactive, dative, locative
Converb (see Haspelmath 1995, Bickel 1998)	similar to a 'gerund' or 'gerundive' form : to mark adverbial subordination	• Generally found in agglutinative languages • Often verb-final languages (OV) • V1 (with a clause-linking form) • Non-finite (subordinated) verb followed by a finite verb	modifying the verbal process expressed by the main verb, adverbial meaning
Minor Verb in SVC (see Aikhenvald 2006)	similar to an auxiliary: subordinate verb	• Found in analytic languages but also in agglutinative languages • Either (S)VO, (S)OV, VO(S) languages V1 or V2 • Grammaticalized verb, grammatically restricted class of verbs	grammatical meanings such as Tense-Aspect-Modality (TAM), direction, complementation, effect, valency, etc.

Thus, the motion verbs analysed as coverbs in Thai example (38) fulfil a path satellite function despite the translation (supported by Diller's analysis)[35] suggesting they are adpositions[36]. The issue of whether or not these verbal forms introduce an argument (see the syntactic criteria postulated in our definition of Satellite in Section 4.3.1) is controversial (Enfield 2006: 13ff). Generally, however, languages where coverbs occur also possess a distinguishable adpositional category, as noticed by Aikhenvald:

> "Non-distinctness of prepositions and verbs has been considered as a typological property of serializing languages [...] In actual fact, languages with SVCs of various types have adpositions (prepositions or postpositions) as a separate class" (2006: 55).

(38) Thai (Tai-Kadai)
a. khaw^3 mo':ng **pay** tha:nh tay^2
3 stare **go** way south
'She looked intently **toward** the south'
Diller (2006: 167)

b. dek^1 wing^2 **khaw^2** ho'ng^2
child run **enter** room
'The child ran **into** the room (lit. the child ran entered the room)'

Then, the motion verb suffixed with the connector -*te* in Japanese (39), and the 'minor' verbs of asymmetrical directional SVCs[37] in (40) may also be regarded as Satellites[38].

Structurally (though not semantically), Japanese converbs are morphologically-dependent forms. Minor verbs, on the other hand, often undergo a change

---

35 Diller (2008:167) qualifies this kind of motion verbs as 'preposition-like' or 'derivative of a verb'.
36 On the status of coverb vs. adposition in Asian languages, see also Lamarre (2008) and Xu (2008) on Mandarin Chinese, Matthews on Cantonese (2006: 70), Diller (2006: 167) on Thai, and Sophana (1998) and Do-Hurinville (2010: 344) on Vietnamese.
37 On the distinction of asymmetrical and symmetrical SVCs, see Bril (2004), Aikhenvald (2006:21ff), Enfield (2009).
38 Motion verbs are well known for their propensity to develop into grammaticalized forms. Beside the directional meanings that we are interested in here, motion verbs may grammaticalize into aspectual, temporal or evaluative meanings that we will not investigate here. See Diller (2006: 165) on Thai for instance. We restrict our study to satellites with motion or directional meaning.

in meaning in addition to being functionally dependent. Thus, "motion verbs within asymmetrical SVCs often grammaticalize into directional markers indicating path, source, and trajectory of motion" (Aikhenvald, 2006: 30). The White Hmong sentence (40) illustrates this change: the motion verbs *nkag* or *mus* become directional markers, indicating respectively the endpoint of the motion and the perspective on the event.

(39) Japanese
*Zyosee-ga   dookutu-no naka-e   hait-**te**   it-ta*
woman-NOM cave-GEN   inside-DIR enter-**CONN** go-PST
'The woman entered the inside of the cave (away from me). [scene 022]'
Ishibashi, p.c.

(40) White Hmong (Hmong-Mien)
lawv nce   nkag   mus
3pl   climb enter >DIR:IN go>DIR:CFG
'They climb in (away from speaker)'
Riddle (1989: 5)

Cantonese (41) also illustrates a motion verb undergoing semantic and structural changes: the verb *lai⁴* 'to come' indicates the path followed by the figure ('clothes') towards the speaker.

Similar grammaticalization has been observed for the Mandarin Chinese verbs *lái* 'to come' and *qù* 'to go' when used in serial verb constructions (Lamarre 2008: 73). However, satellization is a gradient process, and Xu (2008: 178) shows that the loss of verbal features is correlated with the semantic role of the figure involved in the motion (i.e. agent or patient)[39]. Thus, *lái* used as a 'minor' verb keeps more verbal properties when the agent is the figure. See (42a) and compare with (42b), where the patient is a figure moved by an outside force: *lai* has lost its tone. It has become a directional suffix, i.e. a path satellite (Xu 2008: 178).

(41) Cantonese (Sino-Tibetan)
*lei⁵ lo² di¹ saam¹ **lai⁴***
2   take PL clothing **come**
'Bring some clothes. (lit. Take clothes [and] come)'
Matthews (2006: 76)

---

[39] See also Lamarre (2008: 76).

(42) Mandarin (Sino-Tibetan)
a. 他向車站跑來/去
tā xiàng chēzhàn pǎo lái
3SG toward station run **come**
'He is running **toward** the station [Speaker being at the station]'
Xu (2008: 177)

b. 別忘了把錢帶來
bié wàng le bǎ qián dài **lai**
NEG forget LE BA money bring **come(here)**
'Don't forget to bring the money'

After reviewing the satellite category, we examined the situations in which a verb becomes a dependent form (coverb, converb, gerund, or minor verb). We also identified the process by which verbs become satellites, and the stages in the satellization of verbal items.

The next section will use data from two Burmese dialects to show the evolution of motion multi-verb constructions from sequentialization to serialization on their way to producing satellites.

4.3.3 Path verb or path satellite ?

Motion event descriptions made by S-Burmese and Arakanese speakers using the Trajectory stimulus and the Frog story picture-book (Mayer 1969) usually contain two verb stems, often three (example 43), rarely four (example 20), not separated by a subordinator. However, there seem to be constraints on the order in which the components of a *verbal complex*[40] can occur together to express an elaborate motion event.

---

40 The term *verbal complex* (French 'complexe verbal') refers to a combination of bare verbs (with or without verbal morphemes) into a morphosyntactic unit that does not include any nominal phrase such as the object constituent. In that sense, it has to be distinguished from *verb phrase*, of which it could be seen as the core. It also has to be distinguished from *complex predicate*, which may contain verbs with different statuses, i.e. a head verb plus formally dependent verbs. '*Complexe verbal*' is first found in Hagège (1975).

(43) S-Burmese

... မြေလမ်းလေး အတိုင်း ပြေးတက်လာတယ်॥ [HNTH/08, 39_037]
$mye^2.laN^3\text{-}le^3$ $\text{?ə.}TaiN^3$ **pye^3 $t\varepsilon\text{?}$ la^2** $=T\varepsilon^2$
earth.road-DIM along   **run go.up come/CPT** =REAL
'(He) runs up on a little earth road [towards DC].'

Our Burmese[41] data suggests postulating five slots in the complex verb — although we have not found (yet?) a sentence with all five slots filled.

Our data reveals that manner of motion is expressed at the beginning of, but not always as the first stem of, the SVC, whereas deictic (view perspective) is the last motional component expressed. This ordering roughly matches what happens in other SEA languages (see Jarkey 2010: 121 on Hmong, Muansuwan 2001 on Thai, Son and Svenonius 2009 on Malay), with however a slight difference as for motion verbs used as 'deverbal prepositions'[42] (Enfield 2008: 129ff). A fifth slot has been added in our template to accommodate motion verbs and the like[43] that are evolving towards aspectual meaning.

Table 2 shows the constraints on the ordering of motion components in S-Burmese SVCs. The slots are filled with the most common verbs found in our data, and it is by no means an exhaustive list.

---

[41] We will restrict our analysis to S-Burmese data in what follows.
[42] This difference between Burmese and other SEA languages such as Lao is related to the syntactic type of the languages, i.e. (S) OV vs. SVO, and the position of the Site linguistic expression (source or goal) regarding the verb string.
[43] Motion has to be understood here in Talmy's sense of 'MOVE component'. It corresponds to the moving state (MOVE) **or located state** (BE$_{LOC}$) in which one object is considered to be located with respect to another object.

Table 2: Ordering of motion components in S-Burmese SVCs

1. Miscellaneous motion	2. Manner	3. Directionality		4. Deixis	5. Aspect
Position, Direction with respect to the previous path, others	Manner of motion	Directionality (telic)	Axial directionality (atelic)	Direction with respect to speech act participant	(internal, external[44])
return *pyaN²* cut~cross *pyaʔ* sit.down *thaiN³*, ...	run *pye³*, walk *ʃaɔʔ*, jump *khoN²*, shove.through *tho³*, ...	go.in *wiN²*, go.out *thwɛʔ*	go.up *thɛʔ* go.down *shiN³*, fall *cha¹*, cross.over *ku³*, climb.over *cɔ²*	go *θwa³*, come *la²*	ITER < return *pyaN²* INACC < stay *ne²/*

- As noted, the last slot in our template takes in modifying elements, i.e. dependent grammaticalized motion verbs. Given our definition of satellite, however, they cannot be considered as path satellites because they no longer convey path meaning (see example 20).

- The 3 first slots of our template contain (1) directional verbs with respect to the previous path (e.g. 'return') or position verbs (e.g. 'sit down'), (2) manner verbs and (3) telic or atelic verbs encoding a direction or an axial path[45]. They are less restricted sets than the fourth one. Semantically, the verbs all keep their original meanings, and we may consider them as head verbs rather than dependent verbs, thus as elements of an Equipollent-framed construction.

- What about the fourth slot? The set of acceptable verb stems is restricted. Only two stems may appear in this position: the non-specific motion verbs 'to go' and 'to come'. These two verbs stems have undergone semantic re-

---

44 Internal and external aspectual distinctions are from Dik (1997).
45 Slot 3 is divided into two sub-sets of verbs that cannot occur together in the same sentence: S-Burmese expresses either a telic path (e.g. 'go.in', 'go.out') or an axial or atelic path (up, down, horizontal); we have not found any sentence with both subsets 3a and 3b filled, at least in S-Burmese. But our Arakanese data shows an example of a SVC containing both 'go.in' (telic) and 'fall' (axial path). Thus, despite both referring to directionality, the two sub-sets have to be distinguished, and more research should be done on ordering of path components in Arakanese.

duction, losing the motional component to convey only path information with respect to the speaker. Hence, the verbs have clearly become path satellites. Notice also that, in our S-Burmese data describing figures involved in spontaneous motion, they are very common and appear in roughly 90% of the motion descriptions collected[46].

Compare (44) with (45) (example 22 partly repeated). In the former sentence, the verb θwa³ is used as a plain verb (motion + path) and does not locate the motion event with regard to the speaker. However in (45), θwa³ indicates the point of view of the speaker, i.e. the deictic center for this speech. The path (translocation) and motion information are given by the previous verb.

(44) S-Burmese
သစ်ပင်အောက်ကို သွားတယ်။ [TSA/08,09_032]
θiʔ.PiN² ʔaɔʔ =Ko² **θwa³** =Tɛ²
tree   under =DIR **go** =REAL
'(He) goes/went to under the tree.'

(45) ... ကောင်မလေးတစ်ယောက် ဂူအပြင်ကို ထွက်သွားတယ်။ [AA/08, V1_029]
kaɔN²ma²-le³ tə=yaɔʔ gu² ʔə.piN²= Ko² thwɛʔ **θwa³** =Tɛ²
woman-DIM 1=CLF:hum cave exterior =DIR go.out **go**/CFG =REAL
'[…], the young lady went out to the exterior of the cave (away from DC).'

Thus, when used after a verb (or sequence of verbs) conveying directionality[47], the verb stems θwa³ 'to go' and la² 'to come' have indubitably changed in function, becoming path satellites. Note, however, that these two verbs have gone further along the grammaticalization path, being also used as aspectual markers (conveying, respectively, accomplishment (46) and inchoative meanings) with other kinds of verb. This polyfunctionality[48] of the verbs 'to go' and 'to

---

46 For instance, informant AA described 56 scenes involving spontaneous motion, of which only five were described without deictic verbs. Other informants' descriptions give a similar ratio for lack of deictic verbs, i.e. 4/44, and 6/54.
47 When used in a SVC as a path satellite encoding deixis, the verb stems θwa³ 'to go' and la² 'to come' do not appear in our data without a directional verb. They never appear alone with a manner verb of motion such as 'run' or 'walk'. It looks like they lost their motional component as they became deictic markers, which entails that motion must be specified by another verb stem in the sentence.
48 On this polyfunctionality of *go/come*, see also Clark (1974), who relates their extensions of meaning (change of state, evaluative) to deixis in general.

come' exists in many other SEA languages, such as Thai (Diller 2006: 165) or Kayah Li (Solnit 2006: 155) among others.

(46) ဖန်ပုလင်းက ကွဲသွားတယ်။ [AA/05, frog-3]
phaN².pəliN³ =Ka¹ kwɛ³ **θwa³** =Tɛ²
jar =TOP be broken **ACCOMP.RESULT** =REAL
'The jar, it has been broken.'

To summarize, in this section we aimed to show that Burmese dialects (at least Standard Burmese) have path satellites that appear at the end of the verbal complex used to express a motion event. These satellites indicate the viewpoint of the speaker on the motion event she or he talked about. In other words, they express the direction of the motion event with respect to a reference point, generally the speaker himself. They are very common in Burmese.

4.4 Independent verbs in Burmese multi-verb constructions

We have seen in the previous section that deictic verbs should be considered as path satellite due to the semantic change they have undergone. We also claimed that motion verbs appearing in previous slots, before deictic verbs, should be regarded as independent verbs, participating in symmetrical SVCs similar to those verbs found in Equipollent-framed languages.

However, we need to define the criteria that allow us to consider the verbs as independent stems, and the strings of verbs as symmetrical SVCs.

Unlike what happens in other SEA languages such as Vietnamese or Lao, in S-Burmese – as well as in Arakanese –, a verbal predication requires a grammatical element to appear after the verb. This compulsory element, i.e. *Final Verb Particle (FVP)* [49], indicates the status of the event. This particle is the last element in the verbal complex, and it indicates whether the event is realized, unrealized, potential or refers to a new situation. S-Burmese[50] has a set of five

---

[49] Final Verb Particles may be followed by some Sentence Particles. Both types of markers are sometimes gathered in a single category ('Sentence markers' in Okell and Allott 2001) although they are different markers regarding their syntactic and semantic properties: the former are clausal operators, whereas the latter operate at the discourse level.

[50] Arakanese, like Spoken Burmese, possesses a realis marker (realized or present events), but it exhibits two markers for unrealized and potential events (me^2 and pho^1) where Standard Burmese has only one $mɛ^2$. Other differences exist either in the form or in the function of the final verb particles. More investigation on Arakanese FVPs remains to be done.

main particles (Vittrant 2005: 158) of which $T\varepsilon^2$ is the most used in our data. Thus, non-finite clauses are recognizable as they do not contain any Final Verb Particles (henceforth FVP) after the verb stem[51], but also as the FVP slot is filled with a subordinator as in the first clause of (47).

(47)   ... ကြောက်လို့ ငိုတယ်ပေါ့။ [Sula turtle-AA/05, 2]
       $ca\jmath\!? = lo^1$ $\eta o^2 = T\varepsilon^2$ $= P\jmath^2$
       [afraid =**SUB:causal**]$_{CL1}$ [cry =**FVP:REAL**]$_{CL2}$ =SP
       'As (she) was afraid, [the turtle] was crying, of course!'

The next examples illustrate multi-clausal versus mono-clausal sentences in S-Burmese; in (48), the sequence of verbs is followed by the FVP $T\varepsilon^2$ forming a unique clause, i.e. a SVC. In (49), on the other hand, the verb $\int a\jmath\!?$ 'to walk' is followed by the subordinator Pyi^3. It entails that the sentence contains two clauses and may be analysed as a clause chain construction (CCC). Compare also (50a) and (50b), where the verb $phya\!?$ is separated from the other verbs by Pyi^3 in (50b). The incorporated object laN^3 'road' preceding the verb $\int a\jmath\!?$ 'to walk' has been erased in (50a). This happens when the compound occurs after another verb, e.g. $phya\!?$, that is to say in a SVC.

Notice also that all these sentences are from the same informant. Thus, the variations noticed in the use of serialized verbs are not due to different speakers.

(48)   ... ကောင်မလေး လမ်းလျှောက်သွားတယ်။ [AA/08, 71_040]
       $ka\jmath N^2 ma^2$-le^3 laN^3-$\int a\jmath\!?$ θwa^3 $=T\varepsilon^2$
       woman-DIM   road- walk   go/CFG   =REAL
       'A young woman walks away [from DC].'

(49)   .... ကောင်လေး လမ်းလျှောက်ပြီး သွားတယ်။ [AA/08, 67_036]
       $ka\jmath N^2$-le^3 laN^3-$\int a\jmath\!?$ $=Pyi^3$ θwa^3 $=T\varepsilon^2$
       man-DIM   road- walk   =**SUB:TPS**   go/CFG   =REAL
       'A young man walks [going] away [from DC].'

---

51 Notice that the lack of FVP may stand for injunction when occurring with active verbs. However, in that case the FVP slot remains empty and is not filled with a subordinator.

(50) a. မြက်ခင်းပေါ် ကောင်မလေးတစ်ယောက် ဖြတ်လျှောက်သွားတယ်။
[AA/08, 49_052]
myeʔ.khiN³=Pɔ² kaɔN²ma²-le³ θə = yaɔʔ phyaʔ ʃaɔʔ
meadow =top.of woman-DIM 1 =CLF:hum cut/cross walk
θwa³ =**Tɛ²**
go/CFG =REAL
'The meadow, one young woman crosses [it] walking away.'

b. .... လူတစ်ယောက် သစ်ပင်နောက်က ဖြတ်ပြီး လမ်းလျှောက်သွားတယ်။
[AA/08, 52_039]
lu² θə = yaɔʔ θiʔ.piN² naɔʔ=Ka¹ phyaʔ =**Pyi³**
man 1 =CLF:hum tree next=S./TOP cut/cross =**SUB:TPS**
laN³-ʃaɔʔ θwa³ =**Tɛ²**
road- walk go/CFG =REAL
'One man, after crossing another tree, walks(ed) away...'

Although the picture seems clear between what should be considered as a SVC or a CCC, notice that Burmese serialized verbs cannot occur in their own right because their status is not specified but depends on that of the last verb marked by the FVP. Only the last verb in the SVC is fully autonomous and performs a predication function. In that sense, Burmese serialized verbs are functionally similar to converbs, which, as non-finite verbs, suspend their predication function. See the discussion in Shibatani (2009) on the similarities between converbs and serialized verbs.

Whether the FVP attaches only to the final verb and not to the whole string of verbs is a matter of constituent structure. Compare the position of the negative marker in (51) and (52), and recall that negation is in complementary distribution with the other FVPs. The verbal complex acts as a single constituent being encircled with and delimited by the negation morphemes in (51), while the negation intervenes between the verbs in the motion events described by (52): the FVP attaches to the whole verbal complex in (51), but only to the last item of the verb string in (52).

(51) အလုပ်ကို ဗမာတွေက သိပ်မလုပ်ချင်ကြဘူး။ [B2/21]
ʔə-loʔ =Ko² bəma²-Twe² =Ka¹ θɛiʔ **mə**= loʔ ChiN² =Ca¹ =**Phu³**
NMLZ-work OBJ Burmese-PLUR S. very NEG work wish PL **FVP:NEG**
'[This] job, Burmese people do not really wish to do (it).'

(52) ရေထဲကို ဆင်းမသွားဘူးနော်။ [TSA/08, 59_025]
   a. *ye² thɛ³ =Kɔ² shiN³* ***mə=*** *θwa³* ***=Phu³*** *=nɔ²*
      water inside OBJ/GOAL go.down NEG   go/CFG **VP:NEG** DM:CONFIRM
      '(He) did not go down into the water, did he?'

   b. ဒီအလုပ်သမားတွေက ခိုးမဝင်းဘူး။ [C/HNTH]
      di² ʔə-loʔ-θəma³-Twe²   *=Ka¹ kho³*   ***mə=*** *wiN³*   ***=Phu³***
      DEM <u>NMLZ-work-NMLZ-PL</u> S. <u>steal/secretly</u> NEG enter **FVP:NEG**
      'These workers, they did not enter in secret.'

Other Burmese constructions better correspond to what is labelled converbal constructions. Clause chain constructions (CCCs) for instance, have verbs separated by a subordinating morpheme (clause marker) and are morphologically marked as non-finite. Compare the Japanese converbal constructions in (39), (53), with the Burmese CCC in (23). In Japanese example (53), the first verbal stem *hasit-* 'run' expressing manner is a converb, i.e. a non-finite form as indicated by the morpheme *-te*. Similarly, the Burmese sentence in (23) contains several non-finite verbs as indicated by the absence of FVPs and the use of subordinating markers.

(53) Japanese
    Kare-wa ie-ni **hasit**-*te modot-te it-ta.*
    he-TOP house-DAT **run**-CONN go.back-CONN go-PST
    'He went back home running.'
    Ishibashi, p.c.

Thus, according to Shibatani (2009), both Burmese CCCs and SVCs would be analysed as multi-clausal constructions containing non-finite medial verbs. But this will not help to account for the formal and semantic differences between the two types of structure. Classifying these two types of verb sequence under a single class such as 'converbal constructions', would entail creating subtypes, one of which would be functionally similar (with identical properties) to SVCs. See Foley (2010: 91) for an analysis of multi-verb constructions in Mangap Mbula, a language characterized by "a hazy boundary between SVCs and CCCs".

We may use other criteria than the morphological one to discriminate between multi-verb constructions in Burmese. Thus analysing multi-verb constructions at a constituent level, or regarding the semantics of the event structure may give another picture of the situation.

Let us examine the example (54). Regarding the morphological structure of the string of verbs, only the last verb of the sequence (V2) is morphologically finite, i.e. specified for the event status. The verb (V2) 'to go' θwa³ is followed by a FVP, being therefore considered as the head of the clause. However, regarding the semantic structure of the event, θwa³, as a path satellite, expresses a perspective on the motion event, i.e. deictic information; it is semantically dependent, a modifier of the main verb.

On the other hand, the verb (V1) 'to go.out' thwɛʔ is morphologically not marked for status, and should be considered as a dependent or non-finite form. However, regarding the grammatical structure of the sentence, notice that thwɛʔ assigns its case to the nominal phrase indicating the ground: 'the interior of the cave' is not followed by the goal marker =Ko² as it should be if the verb 'to go' was functionally the head verb assigning cases. The NP is marked as a source (ablative), a case generated by the verb thwɛʔ 'to go.out'. Conversely in (55), the cave is marked as the goal of the motion as expected with the verb V1 'to go.in' wiN², and not favoured by the V2 'to come' la².

(54) ကောင်မလေးတစ်ယောက် ဂူထဲက ထွက်သွားတယ်။ [HNTH/08, 73_025]
kaɔN²ma²-le³ tə=yaɔʔ   gu²   thɛ³=**Ka¹**   **thwɛʔ** θwa³   =Tɛ²
woman-DIM 1=CLF:hum cave interior=s. **go.out** go/CFG =REAL
'A young woman went out of the cave [away from DC].'

(55) ကောင်မလေးတစ်ယောက် ဂူထဲကို ဝင်လာတယ်။ [HNTH/08, 70_054]
kaɔN²ma²-le³ tə=yaɔʔ   gu²   thɛ³=**Ko²**   **wiN²**   la²   =Tɛ²
woman-DIM 1=CLF:hum cave interior=DIR **go.out** come/CPT =REAL
'A young woman went into the cave [toward DC].'

To put it in other words, regarding the semantics of the event structure, V1 in Burmese serialized verbs is the head or main verb of the clause, while on a morphological level, V2, being finite, is the head of the clause[52].

---

[52] Parallel analysis in terms of semantic dependency alongside analysis in terms of morphological finiteness may be proposed for Japanese multi-verb constructions expressing motion events. See Fortis & Vittrant (2011: 94). Japanese:
(a)   ..onnanohito-ga dookutu-no naka-<u>kara</u> <u>de</u>-te iki-masi-ta.
  ..   woman-NOM cave-GEN inside-ABL go.out-CVB go-HON-PS
         'The woman went out from inside the cave [away from speaker].'

4.5 Motion events in Burmese dialects: to sum up

In this section, we investigated the expression of motion events in Burmese dialects with reference to previous work on motion in SEA languages. We compared data based on the same input in two dialects. The data shows an evolution of multi-verb constructions, from sequentialization to serialization on the way to producing satellites, S-Burmese having moved further along the grammaticalization path than Arakanese. We also discussed the serialization properties in Burmese, distinguishing between symmetrical and asymmetrical SVCs, distinguishing co-ranking predicates from dependent predicates.

Then, we looked for recurrence in the distribution of semantic components when expressing motion events, and we drew up a verb-ordering template for S-Burmese motion SVCs. After examining the properties of each verb slot, we concluded that path satellites exist in Burmese dialects—although this has only been demonstrated for S-Burmese.

The last part of this section was devoted to the verb stems of SVCs that are not satellites, questioning their status as head verbs at a morphological level (finiteness) and at a grammatical (assigning cases) and semantic level. The finite status of a Burmese verb based on a morphological criterion (presence or absence of an FVP) is easy to draw. But the morphological analysis of a SVC does not match with the semantic structure of the event. In SVCs describing motion events, the first verbs are semantically plain verbs, but they are morphologically non-finite according to the internal criteria applied.

To summarize, according to our motion event data, it seems relevant to analyse the verbs preceding the path satellite as co-ranking predicates (equipollent?) in a multi-verb construction lacking subordinators. It allows us to give an account of the differences found in Burmese multi-verb constructions (SVCs vs. CCCs), and the development noted between the two dialects.

5 Conclusion

In this chapter, we aimed to complement the cross-linguistic studies of motion event encoding initiated by Talmy, whose semantic typology of motion events has been improved several times since 1985. His classification of languages based on path encoding, i.e. Verb-framed languages and Satellite-framed languages, cannot account for some constructions found in SEA languages. These neglected constructions along with our study of motion events in Burmese dialects, lead us to revise previous analyses and typologies of motion events. Our study based on elicitation material developed by the Trajectory project, deals with the issue of satellites in the context of serialization languages. It also addresses the issue of verb status in SVCs, with special reference to Burmese serialized verbs.

What, then, is the contribution of SEA languages to the typology of motion events? What does our study of motion events in Burmese dialects teach us?

We first examined several strategies in SEA languages which are used to express motion events but which have been neglected by the typology. We noticed that adding an Equipollent-type to Talmy's dichotomy was not enough to account for this variety of expressions, although the equipollent-type deals with a widespread structure in these languages, i.e. the multi-verb construction.

Multi-verb constructions in SEA languages include varieties that are not covered by the Equipollent type, as verbs in these constructions are not always of equal status. This acknowledgement of functional differences leads us to review the satellite category, and challenges the issue of functional heads in verbal predicates. We claimed that the satellite category, as defined by Imbert et al. (2011), is a functionally relevant category. It gathers together under a single label forms that have various origins, but which function identically in the expression of a motion event. As for SEA languages, deictic verbs used to indicate the speaker's perspective on the event may be analysed as path satellites.

Then, through our presentation of Burmese data, we addressed the issue of verb status in multi-verb constructions, comparing SVCs and CCCs in both dialects. At a morphological level, Burmese dialects seem to behave more like Eurasian languages than (South)East Asian languages regarding the use of an obligatory status marker (VFP) on the last verb of the verb string. However, Burmese dialects also display resemblances to (South)East Asian languages as far as SVCs are concerned, with semantically equivalent verbs in the verb string, i.e. co-ranking predicates, and the use of another construction of the converb type.

As we examined the expression of motion events in two dialects of the same language, we first noticed the functional closeness of serial verb constructions and converbal constructions (with subordinator) — they appear in the same context (cf. (17) vs. (18)). We also noted a more pervasive use of SVCs in S-Burmese than in Arakanese. Thus, this change seems to be an innovation of S-Burmese, a language in contact with SEA languages such as Thai or Mon that lack morphology of the FVP type, and that make extensive use of SVCs. On the other hand, Arakanese uses few SVCs to express motion events, and prefers to chain predicates. Recall that Arakanese is spoken on the eastern side of Burma, near the Indian and Bangladesh borders, and is in contact with Indo-Aryan languages, which are richer in morphology and make extensive use of converbal constructions.

Finally, all our work reaffirms the idea stated by Croft et al. (2010) and Fortis and Vittrant (2011), that a typology that aims to give an account of linguistic diversity in the field of motion event encoding should classify constructions rather than languages. Thus, exploring motion events in SEA languages represents the first step towards developing the typology, i.e. it identifies the constructions, showing what does exist and is well known, but also what is rarely described[53].

The next step in our work will be to examine motion event expressions in other Burmese dialects also considered as conservative such as Intha or Tavoyen dialects. First, some new data will help (a) to better distinguish the different multi-verb constructions encoding motion events in Burmese dialects, (b) to better identify the verbs that become satellites, and (c) to explore the use of the 'sequentialization stage', i.e. the indication of the source of motion in a different clause. Then, data on motion event in other Burmese dialects will challenge the weight of contact languages in our analysis of multi-verb constructions.

Acknowledgements

An early draft of this article was presented at the Workshop "Mainland Southeast Asian Languages: The State of the Art in 2012" at the Max Planck Institute for Evolutionary Anthropology - Department of Linguistics (Leipzig, Germany) on 1 December 2012. I am grateful to Nick Enfield and Bernard Comrie for their invitation to this exciting workshop. I also wish to warmly thank Jean-Michel Fortis and Diana Lewis, whose comments substantially improved the presentation of this article. Last, I want to stress my gratitude to all my consultants in Burma, in particular Khin Hnit Thit Oo, who contributed important insights and information, in addition to providing much data presented herein, and Shwe Maong Tha and Soe Soe for their receptiveness and help during fieldwork.

---

53 See Fortis and Vittrant (2011, to appear) for a sketch of this typology of constructions.

Abbreviations

ABL	ablative	NEG	negation		
ACCOMP	accomplished aspect	NP	noun phrase		
ASP	aspect	NOM	nominative		
CCC	Clause Chain Constructions	NMZL	nominalizer		
CFG	centrifugal (away)	OBJ	object		
CLF	classifier	OVOICE	co-transitive voice		
CPT	centripetal (towards)	POL	politeness		
CONFIRM	ask for confirmation	PFV	perfective		
CONN	predicative connector	PL	plural		
CRS	Current Relevant State or new situation	PST	past		
DAT	dative	PRS	present		
DC	deictic centre	REAL	realis modality		
DEM	demonstrative	QST	interrogative		
DIM	diminutive	REL	relator		
DIR	directional	RESULT	resultative aspect		
DIRVOICE	directional voice	S	source (ablative, subject marker)		
DM	discourse marker	SG	singular		
EXCL	exclusive	SP	sentence particle (discourse marker)		
FEM	feminine	SVC	Serial Verb Construction		
FVP	final verb particle	SG	singular		
GEN	genitive	SUB	subordinator		
HUM	human	TAM	tense, aspect, modality		
IMP	imperative	TOP	topic		
INAC	unaccomplished aspect	TPS	temporal		
ITER	iterative aspect	TVOICE	Transfer voice		
LOC	locative	V	verb		

References

Aikhenvald, Alexandra Y. 2006. Serial verb constructions in typological perspective. In A.Y. Aikhenvald & R.M.W. Dixon (eds.), *Serial verb constructions: A cross-linguistic typology*, 1–68. Oxford: Oxford University Press.

Aske, J. 1989. Path predicates in English and Spanish: A closer look. *Berkeley Linguistics Society* 15. 1–14.

Beavers, J., B. Levin & S. W. Tham. 2010. The typology of motion expressions revisited. *Journal of Linguistics* 46(2). 331–377.

Berman, Ruth A. & Dan I. Slobin. 1994. *Relating events in narrative: A crosslinguistic developmental study*. Hillsdale, NJ: Lawrence Erlbaum.

Bickel, Balthazar. 1998. Review of 'Converbs in cross-linguistic perspective: Structure and meaning of adverbial verb forms— Adverbial participles, gerunds' by Martin Haspelmath & Ekkehard König. *Linguistic Typology* 2. 381–397.

Bisang, Walter. 1995, Verb serialization and converbs. Differences and similarities. In M. Haspelmath & E. König (eds.), *Converbs in cross-linguistics perspective: Structure and meaning of adverbial verb forms- Adverbial participles, gerunds*, 135–188. New York: Mouton de Gruyter.

Bisang, Walter. 1996. Areal typology and grammaticalization: Processes of grammaticalization based on nouns and verbs in East and mainland South East Asian languages. *Studies in Language* 20(3). 517–597.

Bohnemeyer, J., N.J. Enfield, J.Essegbey, I. Ibarretxe-Antunano, S. Kita, F. Luepke & F. Ameka. 2007. Principles of event segmentation in language: The case of motion events. *Language* 83(3). 495–532.

Bowerman, M., M. Gullberg, A. Majid & B. Narasimhan. 2004. Put project: The crosslinguistic encoding of placement events. In A. Majid (ed.), *Field manual* (Volume 9), 10–18. Nijmegen: Max Planck Institute for Psycholinguistics.

Bril, Isabelle. 2004. Complex nuclei in Oceanic languages: Contribution to an areal typology. In Isabelle Bril & Françoise Ozanne-Rivierre (eds.), *Complex predicates in Oceanic language: studies in the dynamics of binding and boundness*, 1–48. Berlin: Mouton de Gruyter.

Clark, Eve. 1974. Normal states and evaluative viewpoints. *Language* 50(2). 316–332.

Clark, Marybeth. 1978. *Coverbs and case in Vietnamese*. Canberra: Pacific Linguistics.

Clark, Marybeth. 1992. Serialisation in Mainland Southeast Asia. *The Third International Symposium on Language and Linguistics*, 145–159. Bangkok: Chulalongkorn University.

Croft, W., J. Barðdal, W. Hollmann, V. Sotirova & C. Taoka. 2010. Revising Talmy's typological classification of complex event constructions. In Hans Boas (ed.), *Contrastive construction grammar*, 201–235. Amsterdam: John Benjamins.

Crowley, Terry. 1987. Serial verbs in Paamese. *Studies in Language* 11. 35–84.

Dik, Simon. 1997. *The theory of functional grammar. Part 1: The structure of the clause* (Second, revised edition). Berlin: Mouton de Gruyter.

Diller, A.V.N. 2006. Thai serial verbs: cohesion and culture. In A.Y. Aikhenvald & R.M.W. Dixon (eds.), *Serial verb constructions: A cross-linguistic typology*, 160–177. Oxford: Oxford University Press

Do-Hurinville, Danh Thành. 2009. Étude du topicaliseur thì en vietnamien. *Bulletin de la Société de Linguistique de Paris* 104(1). 411–443.

Do-Hurinville, Danh Thành. 2010. Les parties du discours en vietnamien. Grammaticalisation et transcatégorialité *Bulletin de la Société de Linguistique de Paris* 105(1). 327–370.
Durie, Mark. 1997. Grammatical structures in verb serialization. In Alex Alsina, Joan Bresnan & Peter Sells (eds.), *Complex Predicates*, 289–354. Stanford: CSLI Publications.
Enfield, N. J. 2005. Areal linguistics and Mainland Southeast Asia. *Annual Review of Anthropology* 34. 181–206.
Enfield, N. J. 2006. Heterosemy and the grammar-lexicon trade-off. In F. Ameka, A. Dench, & N. Evans (eds.), *Catching Language,* 297–320. Berlin: Mouton de Gruyter.
Enfield, N. J. 2007. *A grammar of Lao*. Berlin: Mouton de Gruyter.
Enfield, N. J. 2008. Verbs and multi-verb constructions in Lao. In A. V. Diller, J. A. Edmondson & Y. Luo (eds.), *The Tai-Kadai languages*, 83–183. London: Routledge.
Enfield, N. J. 2009. Review of 'Serial verb constructions: A cross-linguistic typology' by Alexandra Y. Aikhenvald & R. M. W. Dixon (eds.). *Language* 85, 445–451.
Foley, William A. 2010. Events and serial verb constructions. In Mengistu Amberber, Brett Baker & Mark Harvey (eds.), *Complex Predicates: Cross-Linguistic Perspectives on Event Structure*, 79–109. Cambridge: Cambridge University Press.
Fortis, Jean-Michel. 2003. Voix et relations spatiales en tagalog. *Bulletin de la Société de Linguistique de Paris* 98(1). 455–484.
Fortis, Jean-Michel. 2004. Voix et rôles thématiques en tagalog. *Faits de Langues* 23/24. 231–248.
Fortis, Jean-Michel & Benjamin Fagard. 2010. Space in Language. Leipzig Summer School on Linguistic Typology (August 14-28, 2010). http://htl.linguist.univ-paris-diderot.fr/jmfortis.htm [access online 18/05/2014]
Fortis, Jean-Michel & Alice Vittrant. 2011. L'organisation syntaxique de l'expression de la trajectoire: vers une typologie des constructions. *Faits de Langues : Les Cahiers n°3*. 71–98.
Fortis, Jean-Michel & Alice Vittrant. to appear. On the morphosyntax of path-expressing constructions: Toward a typology. *STUF-Language Typology and Universals* 67.
Fortis, Jean-Michel, Colette Grinevald, Anetta Kopecka & Alice Vittrant. 2011. L'expression de la trajectoire : perspectives typologiques. *Faits de Langues: Les Cahiers n°3*. 33–42.
Givon, Talmy. 2001. *Syntax: An introduction* (Volume 1 & 2). Amsterdam: John Benjamins.
Grinevald, Colette. 2006. The expression of static location in a typological perspective. In M. Hickman & S. Robert (eds.), *Space in languages: Linguistic systems and cognitive categories*, 29–58. Amsterdam & Philadelphia: John Benjamins.
Grinevald, Colette. 2011. On constructing a working typology of the expression of path. *Faits de Langues : Les Cahiers n°3*. 43–70.
Guillaume, Antoine. 2009. Les suffixes verbaux de mouvement associé en cavineña. *Faits de Langues: Les Cahiers* 1. 181–204.
Guillaume, Antoine. 2013. Reconstructing the category of 'associated motion' in Tacanan languages (Amazonian Bolivia and Peru). In R. Kikusawa & L. Reid (eds.), *Historical Linguistics 2011. Selected papers from the 20th International Conference on Historical Linguistics, Osaka, 25-30 July 2011* (Current Issues in Linguistic Theory 326), 129–151. Amsterdam: John Benjamins Publishing Company.
Haas, Mary R. 1964. *Thai-English student's dictionary*. Stanford, CA: Stanford University Press.
Hagège, Claude. 1975. *Le problème linguistique des prépositions et la solution chinoise*. (Colletion Linguistique de la Société de linguistique de Paris, n° 71). Paris-Louvain: Peeters.
Hagège, Claude. 2010. *Adpositions*. Oxford: Oxford University Press.

Haspelmath, Martin. 1995. The converb as a cross-linguistically valid category. In Martin Haspelmath & E. König (eds.), *Converbs in cross-linguistic perspective,* 1–55. Berlin & New York: Mouton de Gruyter.

Heine, Bernd & Tania Kuteva. 2002. *World lexicon of grammaticalisation.* Cambridge: Cambridge University Press.

Himmelmann, Nikolaus. 2005. Tagalog. In Karl Alexander Adelaar & Nikolaus P. Himmelmann (eds), *The Austronesian languages of Asia and Madagascar,* 350–376. London: Routledge.

Iacobini, Claudio & F. Masini. 2006. The emergence of verb-particle constructions in Italian: locative and actional meanings. *Morphology* 16. 155–188.

Iacobini, Claudio & Benjamin Fagard. 2011. A diachronic approach to variation and change in the typology of motion event expression. *Faits de Langues Les Cahiers n°3.* 151–172.

Imbert, Caroline. 2012. Path: Ways typology has walked through it. *Language and Linguistic Compass* 6(4). 236–258.

Imbert, Caroline, Colette Grinevald & Anna Sores. 2011. Pour une catégorie de 'Satellite' de Trajectoire dans une approche fonctionnelle-typologique. *Faits de Langues: Les Cahiers* 3. 99–116.

Ishibashi, M. 2004. *Etude typologique des expressions du déplacement en français et en japonais.* (Mémoire de DEA en Sciences du Langage). Lyon: Université Lyon 2.

Ishibashi, M., A. Kopecka & M. Vuillermet. 2006. Trajectoire: matériel visuel pour élicitation des données linguistiques. Laboratoire Dynamique du Langage (CNRS/Université Lyon 2) - Projet '*Trajectoire*'. Fédération de Recherche en Typologie et Universaux Linguistiques (TUL), CNRS, France.

Jarkey, Nerida. 2010. Cotemporal serial verb constructions in White Hmong. In Mengistu Amberber, Brett Baker & Mark Harvey (eds.), *Complex Predicates: Cross-Linguistic Perspectives on Event Structure,* 110–134. Cambridge: Cambridge University Press.

Koch, Harold. 1984. The category of 'associated motion' in Kaytej. *Language in Central Australia* 1. 23–34.

Kopecka, Anetta. 2006. The semantic structure of motion verbs in French: Typological perspectives. In M. Hickmann & S. Robert (eds.), *Space in languages: Linguistic systems and cognitive categories,* 83–101. Amsterdam & Philadelphia: John Benjamins.

Kopecka, Anetta. 2009. L'expression du déplacement en français : l'interaction des facteurs sémantiques, aspectuels et pragmatiques dans la construction du sens spatial. *Langages* 173. 54–75.

Lamarre, Christine. 2008. The linguistic categorization of deictic direction in Chinese -with reference to Japanese. In Dan Xu (ed.), *Space in languages of China - Cross-linguistic synchronic and diachronic perspectives.* 69–97. Springer.

Lambert-Bretière, R. 2009 Serializing languages as satellite-framed. *Annual Review of Cognitive Linguistics* 7. 1–29.

Lemarechal, Alain. 1991. Dérivation et orientation dans les langues des Philippines. *Bulletin de la Société de Linguistique de Paris* 86(1). 317–358.

Li, Charles N. & Sandra A. Thompson. 1981. *Mandarin Chinese, a functional reference grammar.* Berkeley & Los Angeles: University of California Press.

Lin, Jo-Wang. 2012. Tenseless. In Robert I. Binnick (ed.), *The Oxford handbook of tense and aspect,* 669–695.

Matisoff, James A. 1973. *The grammar of Lahu.* Berkeley: University of California Press.

Matisoff, James A. 1991. Areal and universal dimensions of grammatization in Lahu. In Elizabeth Closs Traugott & Bernd Heine (eds.), *Approaches to grammaticalization: Focus on Theoretical and Methodological Issues* (Vol.2.), 383–453. London: John Benjamins.

Matsumoto, Y. 2003. Typologies of lexicalization patterns and event integration: Clarifications and reformulations. In Shuji Chiba (ed.), *Empirical and theoretical Investigations into Language: A Festschrift for Masaru Kajita*, 403–418. Tokyo: Kaitakusha.

Matthews, Stephen. 2006. On serial verb constructions in Cantonese. In A.Y. Aikhenvald & R.M.W. Dixon (eds.), *Serial verb constructions: A cross-linguistic typology*, 69–86. Oxford: Oxford University Press.

Mayer, Mercer. 1969 [2003]. *Frog, where are you ?*. Penguin USA.

Muansuwan, Nuttanart. 2001. Directional serial verb constructions in Thai. In Dan Flickinger & Andreas Kathol (eds.), *Proceedings of the 7th International HPSG Conference, University of California, Berkeley (22-23 July 2000)*. Stanford: CSLI Publications

Okell, John. 1995. Three Burmese dialects. In D. Bradley (ed.), *Papers in Southeast Asian Linguistics* (No.13), *Studies in Burmese languages*, 1–138. Canberra: Pacific Linguistics

Okell, John & Anna Allott. 2001. *Burmese/Myanmar: a dictionary of grammatical forms*, Richmond (Surrey): Curzon Press.

Pace, Cassandra. 2009. The typology of motion verbs in Northern Vietnamese. *Rice Working Papers in Linguistics* 1. 52–64.

Riddle, Elizabeth. 1989. Serial verbs and propositions in White Hmong. In *Linguistics of the Tibeto-Burman Area* 12(2). 1–13.

Shibatani, Masayoshi. 2009. On the form of complex predicates: toward demystifying serial verbs. In Johannes Helmbrecht, Yoko Nishina, Yong-Min Shin, Stavros Skopeteas & Elisabeth Verhoeven (eds.), *Form and Function in Language Research: Papers in Honour of Christian Lehmann*, 255–282. Berlin: Mouton de Gruyter.

Shibatani, Masayoshi & Sandra A. Thompson. 1996. *Essays in semantics and pragmatics: In honor of Charles J. Fillmore*. Amsterdam: Benjamins

Sinha, C., & T. Kuteva. 1995. Distributed spatial semantics. *Nordic Journal of Linguistics* 18. 167–199.

Slobin, Dan. I. 1996. Two ways to travel: verbs of motion in English and Spanish. In Masayoshi Shibatani & Sandra A. Thompson (eds.), *Grammatical constructions: Their form and meaning*, 195–220. Oxford: Clarendon Press.

Slobin, Dan. I. 2004. The many ways to search for a frog: Linguistic typology and the expression of motion events. In Sven Strömqvist & Ludo Verhoeven (eds.), *Relating events in narrative, Vol. 2: Typological and contextual perspectives*, 219–257. Mahwah, NJ: Lawrence Erlbaum Associates.

Slobin, Dan I. & Nini Hoiting. 1994. Reference to movement in spoken and signed languages: typological considerations. *Berkeley Linguistics Society* (BLS) 20. 487–505. Berkeley: Berkeley Linguistics Society.

Solnit, David B. 2006. Verb serialization in Eastern Kayah Li. In A.Y. Aikhenvald & R.M.W. Dixon (eds.), *Serial verb constructions: A cross-linguistic typology*, 144–159. Oxford: Oxford University Press.

Son, M. & P. Svenonius. 2009. Directed manner of motion in verb serialization: A comparative study of Indonesian/Malay and Tetun Dili. Paper presented at the 13th International Workshop on Malay/Indonesian Linguistics, Lombok, Indonesia, June 2009.

Sophana, Srichampa. 1998. Prepositional vs. directional coverbs in Vietnamese. *Mon-Khmer Studies* 28. 63–83.

Sprigg, R.K. 1963. A comparison of Arakanese and Burmese based on phonological formulae. In H.L. Shorto (ed.), *Linguistic comparison in South East Asia and the Pacific*, 109–132. London: University of London.
Strömqvist, Sven & Ludo Verhoeven (eds.). 2004. *Relating events in narratives Volume 2: typological and contextual perspectives*. Mahwah, NJ: Lawrence Erlbaum Associates.
Talmy, L. 1972. *Semantic structures in English and Atsugewi*. Berkeley: University of California dissertation.
Talmy, L. 1985 [2007]. Lexicalization patterns: Semantic structure in lexical forms. In T. Shopen (ed.), *Language typology and syntactic description III: Grammatical categories and the lexicon*, 66–168. Cambridge: Cambridge University Press.
Talmy, L. 1991. Path to realization: A typology of event conflation. *Proceedings of the Berkeley Linguistics Society* 17. 480–520.
Talmy, L. 2000. *Toward a cognitive semantics* (2 volumes). Cambridge, MA: M.I.T. Press.
Talmy, L. 2009. Main verb properties and equipollent framing. In Jiansheng Guo, Elena Lieven, Nancy Budwig, Susan Ervin-Tripp, Keiko Nakamura & Şeyda Özçalişkan (eds.), *Crosslinguistic approaches to the psychology of language: Research in the tradition of Dan Isaac Slobin*, 389–402. New York: Psychology Press.
Tesnière, Lucien. 1959. *Éléments de syntaxe structurale*. Paris: Klincksieck
Vittrant, Alice. 2005. Burmese as a modality-prominent language In J. Watkins (ed.), *Studies in Burmese linguistics*, 143–161. Canberra : Pacific Linguistics.
Vittrant, Alice. 2006. Les constructions verbales en série, une nouvelle approche du syntagme verbal birman. *Bulletin de la Société Linguistique de Paris* 101(1). 305–367.
Vittrant, Alice. 2010a. Aire linguistique Asie du Sud-Est continentale: le birman en fait-il partie? *Moussons* 16. 7–38.
Vittrant, Alice. 2010b. On Burmese and Arakanese dialects. Communication at International Burma Studies Conference (BS2010), Marseille, France, 6-9 July.
Vittrant, Alice. 2012. How typology allows for a new analysis of verb phrase in Burmese, *Lidil* 46, "*Recherches récentes en typologie fonctionnelle: Pour une 'description typologique' des langues*", Editions littéraires et linguistiques de l'Université de Grenoble. 101–126 [http://lidil.revues.org/].
Vittrant, Alice. 2013a. *Modalité et temporalité en birman vernaculaire: l'exemple du développement modal du morphème spacio-temporel /Khɛ'/*. (Cahiers CHRONOS 7). Antwerp: Rodopi.
Vittrant, Alice. 2013b. Psycho-collocational expressives in Burmese. In Jeffrey P. Williams (ed.), *The Aesthetics of Grammar*. Cambridge: Cambridge University Press.
Vittrant, Alice. to appear. Contraintes linguistiques, cognitives et culturelle dans l'expression d'événements de Trajectoire. In *Actes du colloque international Langage, discours, événements*. Paris : Lambert Lucas
Voisin, Sylvie. 2013. Expressions de trajectoire dans quelques langues atlantiques (groupe Nord). *Fait de Langue* 42. 131–152
Vuillermet, Marine. 2012a. Une typologie en cheminement: Contribution de l'ese ejja à l'étude du mouvement associé. In C.Imbert & N.Vallée (eds.), *Revue de linguistique et didactique des langues* (N.thématique 'Typologie'), 79–100.
Vuillermet, Marine. 2012b. *A grammar of Ese Ejja, a Takanan language of the Bolivian Amazon*. Lyon: Université Lumière Lyon 2 dissertation.
Wälchli, Bernhard. 2001. A typology of displacement (with special reference to Latvian). *Sprachtypologie & Universalienforschung STUF* 54(3). 298–323.

Wienold, Gotz. 1992. Lexical structures concerning movement and space in some Asian Languages. In *The Third International Symposium on Language and Linguistics*, 1222–1236. Bangkok: Chulalongkorn University.

Wilkins, David. 1991. The semantics, pragmatics, and diachronic development of 'Associated Motion' in Mparntwe Arrernte. *Buffalo Papers in Linguistics* 91. 207–257.

Xu, Dan. 2008. Asymmetry in the expression of space in Chinese – The Chinese language meets typology. In Dan Xu (ed.), *Space in languages of China - Cross-linguistic synchronic and diachronic perspectives*, 175–198. Berlin: Springer.

Zlatev, J. & Yangklang, P. 2004. A third way to travel: The place of Thai in motion-event typology. In Sven Strömqvist & Ludo Verhoeven (eds.), *Relating events in narrative: Typological and contextual perspectives*, 159–190. Mahwah, NJ: Lawrence Erlbaum Associates.

Subject index

adjectives, 224, 225, 231, 249, 295, 307, 369
- and agreement, 558, 581
- and derivation, 237
- and word order, 356, 366, 388, 397
- verb-like, 226, 241, 246, 271, 287, 333, 543, 547, 610
adverbs and adverbial expressions
adverbial subordination, 223, 610, 611
- and 'get', 187, 188, 193, 196, 198
- and 'give', 163, 184
- and word order, 400, 401-402, 406, 407-410
- borrowed, 74
- marginal, 226
- purposive, 168, 178
- temporal, 536, 537, 539
affixation, 535, 536, 537, 538; see also prefixes; suffixes; infixes
- and case marking, 322
- lack of, 366, 530, 534
- unproductive, 13
agriculture, 2, 4, 19, 24
alliteration, 74, 246, 534
alliterative concord, 558, 561, 577, 578, 579, 581, 582
ambitransitive/labile verbs; see transitivity
anaphora, 8
applicatives, 157, 161, 293, 294, 302; see also transitivity
archaeology, 2, 327, 335, 336; see also hunter-gatherers
aspect marking
- as an areal feature, 74, 212, 221, 311, 318, 325, 355, 530, 534, 536
- development from verbs, 604, 606, 612, 615, 616, 617
- egophoric, 227
- marked by affix, 537, 538-540; see also affixation
- marked by predicates, 8, 200, 237-238, 245, 247-248, 249, 595, 603
- marked by reduplication, 318, 538-539, 551; see also reduplication
- marked postverbally, 400
- pre-subject marker, 74
- telicity, 588, 616
- unmarked, 610
aspiration, 461, 495, 511, 513
- as a historical process, 54
- as voiceless underlap, 464
- pre-aspiration, 71, 72
- series of voiceless aspirated stops, 36, 38, 41, 43, 136
associated motion, 591, 592, 595, 596
Austronesian dispersal, 270, 309, 328, 329-330, 332, 336; see also migration
benefactives, 12, 157, 158, 159
- and 'give', 161-162, 166, 167, 170, 172, 178, 180, 183
bioinformatics, 11; see also statistical methods
borrowing, 77, 211, 562, 574-577; see also contact; calquing; multilingualism
- and tone, 59, 61, 83, 103, 108
- distinguishing from cognates, 313
- juncture reanalysis, 44
- lexemes, 44, 58, 72, 83, 105, 111-151, 389, 410, 534, 575
- in phonology, 37, 43, 64
- massive, 58, 123
- nativized, 218
- of adverbs, 74

634 — Subject index

- of affixes, 122, 534
- of functors, 74
- of lexemes, 117, 121, 142, 218, 283, 328, 390, 568, 569, 570

breathy voice, 7, 11, 63, 68, 86, 8; *see also* phonation type; tense/lax vowel contrast; voice quality
- historical development of, 64, 65, 67, 69, 83

calquing, 74, 115, 178, 218; *see also* borrowing

causatives
- and 'give', 159-160, 167-168, 169, 170-171, 174, 177-180, 183-184, 186-187
- as an areal feature, 311
- constructions, 157, 158
- dummy causatives, 163-164, 172, 178, 180-181
- marked by infix, 508, 515
- marked by prefix, 139, 142, 184, 293, 508, 515, 517, 530, 549-550
- marked by suffix, 534
- periphrastic, 175, 178
- permissive/jussive, 156, 173-174, 178-179, 201
- reconstructed, 535
- word formation strategy, 537

clitics, 299, 322-323, 532, 540, 547, 581, 608
- enclitics, 234, 294, 297
- proclitics, 216, 240, 250, 312, 538, 545, 548

consonant clusters
- 3-consonant clusters, 562, 467
- and geminates, 71
- and sesquisyllabicity, 505-568
- assimilation in, 64
- complex onsets, 14, 15, 44, 72, 75-77, 136, 441-499, 504-505
- development of, 72, 141, 579, 581
- reduction of, 71, 73

- rhotic/sibilant, 71
- stop-liquid clusters, 38-39
- with nasals, 32, 36, 37, 38, 39, 40

constituent order, 366, 368-369, 371, 387-418, 530, 541, 614-616
- as an areal/genetic feature, 248, 287-290, 299, 309, 329-330, 331, 356
- AVTG, 160, 165
- AVGT, 160
- change over time, 169
- flexible, 8, 74, 246
- numeral-classifier, 233
- verb-final, 212, 244, 247, 248, 362
- verb-initial, 329
- verb-medial, 47, 212, 216, 248, 271, 287-290, 309, 329-330, 331, 356

contact, 51-52, 78, 176-182, 184, 202-203, 213, 332, 546, 549, 624; *see also* borrowing; multilingualism
- ancient, 156, 283, 334
- and convergence, 52-251, 266, 371, 399, 400
- and genetic inheritance, 111, 112, 121, 250
- and language areas, 45, 142, 211, 277
- and multilingualism, 46
- and simplification, 168
- and tonogenesis, 82-110, 53, 63
- and transfer, 32
- contact chain, 122, 156, 204
- contact corridor, 210, 249, 254-258
- contact languages, 294, 309, 625
- in nominal classification, 286-287, 558-585
- in phonology, 38, 41, 46-47
- massive/prolonged, 73, 123, 217-219, 259, 333
- mechanisms of, 335
- models of, 336
- recent, 168

converbs, 591, 610-611, 612, 614, 620-621, 624
convergence, 51-81, 82-110, 200, 203-204, 212, 558-585
– convergence zones, 46, 156, 176, 213, 255, 266
– phonotactic, 444, 522
– structural, 210, 254
conversation analysis, 13
cultural diffusion, 4, 360; *see also* diffusion
deixis, 598, 607, 616, 617; *see also* demonstratives
– deictic centre, 590, 595, 598, 615, 617
– deictic verbs, 618, 624
– social deixis, 5-8, 12; *see also* pronominal systems, social deixis in; politeness; register, social
– time deixis, 532, 546
demonstratives, 407, 418, 419, 547, 548, 558, 578; *see also* deixis
– and noun order, 181-182, 366, 397
– demonstrative copying, 582, 579
– demonstrative postposition, 234
– locative demonstratives, 540
derivational morphology, 8, 14, 157, 178, 236-238, 495, 509, 530, 537, 549
– lack of, 244, 245
desideratives, 164, 178, 179, 532, 536, 537, 544-545
dialect chains, 115
diffusion, 51, 244, 254, 277, 360, 361, 572, 575, 578; *see also* cultural diffusion; contact
diphthongs, 57, 63, 64, 65, 68, 77, 245, 247, 248, 563
disyllables
– development into sesquisyllables, 46
– from monosyllables, 77
– iamb/iambic vs. trochee/trochaic, 449, 456

– into monosyllables, 56, 495, 501
– minor/major, 444, 459, 460, 461, 462, 463, 474, 500
– vs. mono/sesquisyllables, 445, 449, 478, 494, 502, 510, 511
– reduced, 461
– with unstressed syllables, 458, 476
drift, 51-81, 340
egophoric marking, 227
endangerment, 6, 12, 216, 551,
– and documentation, 10
expressives; *see* ideophones
geminates, 71, 72, 76, 77
gender; *see also* nominal classification
– marked, 212, 226-227, 229-230, 247-248, 396
– sex-based gender system, 559, 577
– unmarked, 8, 223, 244, 245, 247-248, 576
gesture, 7, 271, 274-277, 283, 329-330, 333, 337, 352; *see also* para-linguistic features
headedness, 8, 356, 388, 391, 396, 397, 398, 427
homophony, 64, 236, 362, 590
hunter-gatherers, 4; *see also* archaeology
iamb/iambic syllables, 7, 17, 44, 52, 77, 441-499, 500-528, 560
– as an areal feature, 32, 46, 212, 216, 245, 247, 560
ideophones, 225, 226, 317, 453, 503, 530, 534
– as an areal feature, 8, 246-248
idioms, 271
Indosphere, 51, 213, 216, 253
infixes
– in individual languages, 140, 305, 318, 326, 508, 535, 542, 549, 578
– infixation, 130-131, 511, 515, 534, 560
– nasal infix, 42, 530, 537, 544

inflectional morphology; see morphology, inflectional
intensity (morphological), 536, 537, 548, 549
intensity (phonological), 15, 83, 108, 505
internal development, 16, 17, 61, 78, 90, 118, 156, 176, 221, 428
isoglosses, 97, 140, 142, 220, 282
isolates, 7, 209, 215, 269, 270, 328
isolating word structure, 212, 245-247, 248, 271, 274, 310-312, 329-331, 333, 337
– as an areal feature, 158, 244, 317, 356, 530, 535, 540, 611
labile verbs; see transitivity
loan words; see borrowings
metathesis, 116, 567
metatypy, 74, 332, 574-577, 578
migration, 2, 251-254, 257-259, 288, 329-336, 338, 339-340, 360, 363, 428
– and agriculture, 4
– Austronesian, 275, 283
– local, 257
– recent, 95, 127
monophthongs, 57, 63, 64, 65, 76, 244
monosyllables, 500-528
– and short vowels, 466-480
– and tone, 98-101, 104
– areal feature, 13, 47, 52, 212, 213, 245, 314, 356
– complex, 461, 462, 463, 474, 477, 478, 479, 481, 482
– development from disyllables, 38, 56, 70-73, 495, 501
– development of, 42, 44, 46, 77, 78, 83, 107, 235, 243
– preference for short words, 317
– types of, 444, 459, 460
– vs. disyllables, 449, 452, 456
– vs. sesquisyllables, 441, 445, 454, 476, 490-495
mood
– constituent-final particle, 223
– derivational suffix, 530, 534
– derogatory, 544
– desiderative, 537, 544
– involuntary, 544
– lack of marking, 610
– optional, 324-326, 355
– potential, 200
– pretence, 544
– reduplication, 318
morphology, derivational; see derivational morphology
morphology, inflectional
– little or none, 8, 213, 223, 226-227, 530
– nominal, 212, 229, 607
– verbal, 212, 223, 236, 238-240, 241, 244, 249, 311, 538
multilingualism, 46, 58, 70, 181, 257; see also borrowing; contact
national languages, 9, 13, 14, 29, 46, 47, 82, 95, 158, 177; see also official languages; standardization
negation
– and irrealis mood, 400
– contrastive, 190
– particle, 188, 191, 192, 194, 196, 198, 244, 540
– prefix, 200, 548-549
– suffix, 238, 239, 240
– verbal, 74, 166, 168, 187, 190, 536, 537, 599, 620
nominal classification; see also gender; numeral classifiers
– as an areal feature, 8, 14
– development of, 17, 225, 558-585
– in individual languages, 15, 131, 216, 226, 231, 233, 362, 394-395, 413
numeral classifiers
– as an areal feature, 8, 13, 14, 47, 246, 271, 285-287, 311, 330-333, 366

– development of, 558-585
– lack of, 121
– reconstructed, 244
number marking, 139, 212, 226-227, 229-230, 245-248, 325, 546-547, 561, 577, 581
– dual marking, 229, 234-235, 546, 547
– lack of, 8, 223, 244, 245-248, 576, 581
– other plural marking, 537, 541, 546-547, 560, 578
– plural words/plural nouns, 229, 230, 318, 366, 368, 536
official languages, 14, 177, 181; see also national languages; standardization
para-linguistic features, 271, 277-280; see also gesture
phonaesthemes, 561
phonation type, 7; see also register
– and tone, 15, 54
– as an areal feature, 82, 83, 245, 356, 372, 384
– development of, 376
– in individual languages, 16, 61, 63, 64
pitch
– and quantity, 61
– and tone, 15, 58, 82, 83, 104, 127, 373
– and voice quality, 101-102, 106, 107
– as an areal feature, 7
– contrastive, 55, 68, 90, 106, 372
– pitch contours, 16, 56
– pitch units, 85-86, 87, 90, 92, 94, 107
– pitch-accent languages, 445
politeness, 13, 365; see also deixis, social; register, social
polysyllables, 86, 99, 213, 216, 235, 249, 314, 444, 523, 538
post-stopped nasals, 36, 37, 39, 41, 42, 43, 46
prefixes, 546, 564

– as an areal/genealogical feature, 32, 534, 561-562, 576, 577, 579
– and initial syllable prosody, 40, 42, 45, 475, 495, 508, 515, 563
– and semantic categories, 575
– and suffixes, 44, 46, 240
– causative, 139, 142, 184, 293, 508, 515, 517, 530, 549-550; see also causatives
– classifier, 559, 560, 580, 581
– compounding vs. prefixation, 138
– marking grammatical categories, 41, 224, 303, 395-396, 537, 540, 541, 546, 547, 551
– nasal prefixes, 42-43, 540, 552, 545
– productivity, 233
– similitive, 548
prenasalization, 29-50, 71, 75, 76, 332, 477, 486
presyllables, 7, 37, 41, 104, 444, 507, 540
pronominal systems, 234
– alignment in, 323
– case marking on, 229, 249, 305, 398, 534, 540, 541
– grammaticalized, 248, 250
– local/existential marking on, 542
– noun class marking on, 558, 579
– number marking in, 235, 546, 547
– resumptive, 423
– social deixis in, 12, 246, 248, 365; see also deixis, social; politeness
prosody; see word prosody
reciprocals, 508, 530, 536, 537, 581, 605
reduplication
– and 2-4 beat, 74
– semi-reduplication, 226
– CV- reduplication, 318, 326
– 'alternating reduplication', 534-535, 550
– aspect and, 318, 538-539, 551; see also aspect
– 'pretence', 545

– number, 546, 547
– intensity, 549, 551; see also intensity, morphological
register, phonological, 11, 122, 107-108, 245, 500
– and pitch, 101
– and vowel height, 61, 68-69
– articulatory correlates of, 63
– development of, 62, 70, 83-84, 90, 106
– lack of/loss of, 65, 68, 190
– register languages, 16, 54, 86, 87
– system in individual languages, 64, 86, 99, 102, 103
register, social; see deixis, social; politeness
relexification, 73, 332
restructuring, 51-81, 38, 90, 177, 558, 569, 576, 581, 582
rice farming, 1
second language, 14, 107, 334-335, 337
semantic roles, marking of
– agent, 74, 160, 299, 301, 303, 305-307, 423, 543, 613
– beneficiary, 157, 161, 166
– causee, 158, 160, 164, 169, 174, 175
– causer, 158, 175, 203, 301
– patient, 174-175, 295, 297, 299, 302-303, 305-309, 321, 422, 593, 613
– recipient, 157-161, 164, 167, 175, 180, 185, 202
– theme, 159-160, 162, 165, 167, 174, 175, 423
sentence-final particles, 8, 47, 226, 235, 244, 246, 250, 319
serial verb constructions
– and benefactives/causatives, 157, 162
– and 'get', 186, 193
– and 'give', 425
– and 'take', 412-413, 415, 421-423
– as an areal feature, 8, 47, 212, 235, 244, 246, 250

– expressing motion, 589-632
– functions of, 238
– reconstructed, 244
sesquisyllables, 14-15, 441-499, 500-528
– as a word type, 86, 99, 212
– as an areal feature, 45, 35, 312-313, 317, 356
– development of, 17, 46, 70, 73, 75-77, 107, 244, 245
– reconstructed, 42, 52
– typology of, 522
– vs. monosyllables, 42
– vs. disyllables, 363
sign languages, 7
Sinosphere, 42, 51, 52, 83, 84, 106, 213, 257
Sonority, 71-73
– in Jahai 509
– in Kammu 514-518
– in Khmer 512
– in Turung 512-514
– sonority-based syllabification 451, 504-506
– typology 518-524
Sprachbund, 153, 176, 266
standardization, 6, 167, 170, 303, 309, 360, 361; see also national languages
statistical methods, 10, 11, 52, 82, 95-103, 273-72, 283, 472-482; see also bioinformatics
stativity, 45, 241, 356, 392, 535, 536, 537, 542-544, 546, 609
stress, 444-499
– and heavy syllables, 222
– copying stressed syllables, 515
– final stressed syllables (iambic), 15, 245, 445, 502, 503
– phonemic stress, 84
– phrase-final, 190
– stress shifts, 107

Subject index — **639**

– unstressed vowels or syllables, 75, 77, 503, 546
– vs. tone languages, 445
– word final, 77, 448
SVCs; *see* serial verb constructions
suffixes
– applicative, 302-303, 368, 396, 563, 564, 570
– as an areal/genetic feature, 216, 576
– dispreference for, 46
– gender/noun class suffixes, 229, 395, 560, 576, 577, 578
– historical development, 77, 569, 576, 579, 581
– lack of, 444, 530
– marking grammatical categories, 240, 294, 592, 595, 612, 613
– universal preference for, 44
syllabic nasals, 37, 39, 75, 378, 446
syllables, major, 7, 128, 441-499, 500-528, 560
syllables, minor, 7, 42, 71, 115, 126, 128, 130, 441-499, 500-528, 560, 561, 573
syllable structure; *see* disyllables; monosyllables; polysyllables; presyllables; sesquisyllables; trisyllables
telicity; *see* aspect
tense marking, 212, 291, 311, 318, 325, 355, 400, 603, 610, 611; *see also* morphology
– and 'get', 189, 190, 192, 196
– lack of, 8, 245, 324
– optional, 324, 355
tense/lax vowel contrast, 62, 63, 64, 65, 66, 68, 69; *see also* breathy voice; phonation type; voice quality
tone
– as an areal feature, 7, 47, 245, 247, 248, 257, 332, 356, 366, 500

– in individual languages, 123, 125, 127, 128, 244, 373-377, 447, 453, 579
– lack of/loss of, 14, 108, 212, 216, 249
– phonetics of, 15-16, 55-61
– typology of, 17, 82-110
tonogenesis, 36, 54, 68, 222, 377, 445
– as a conservative feature, 222
– as an areal feature, 78
– atypical, 53, 70
– contact-induced, 82, 110
topic-comment structure, 8, 223, 244, 246-248, 249
topicalization, 299, 411, 412, 421, 422, 423, 425
transitivity
– ambitransitive/labile verbs, 8
– causative transitives, 158
– detransitive prefixes, 551
– ditransitives, 158, 160, 167, 169, 174, 175, 180, 185, 424, 425
– extended ditransitives, 180
– and 'give' constructions, 164, 166, 183, 293
– pre-transitive construction, 411
– stative/intransitive pairs, 44-45, 243
– stative/transitive pairs, 44
trisyllables, 316, 508
verbalization, 536, 537, 543, 544
voice, grammatical, 271, 298-299, 300-310, 318, 319, 329, 331, 333, 592-594
voice quality, 15, 68, 69, 82, 83, 85-88, 90, 101-102, 106-107; *see also* phonation type; register
vowel length
– and breathy voice, 67
– and tone, 55-60, 374
– development of, 65, 568, 577
– lack of contrast, 76, 77
– loss of, 53, 190
– marking number, 581

– reconstructed, 64
word order; *see* constituent order
word prosody, 13, 32, 45, 46, 216, 563
written language
– orthographic decisions, 39, 40, 127, 279, 311-312, 460, 475, 478-479, 490, 560
– practical orthographies, 126, 514
Zomia, 5

Author index

Aikhenvald, Alexandra Y., 14, 158, 286, 504, 591, 599, 604, 610-613
Benedict, P. K., 112-114, 119, 130, 137, 141, 142, 562, 564, 575
Bennett, J. Fraser, 447, 448, 449, 503
Bisang, Walter, 8, 16, 153, 157, 162, 163, 212, 286, 356, 364, 399, 417, 420, 423, 590-591, 603, 610
Blench, Roger, 4, 7, 9, 12, 17, 215-216, 219, 251, 254, 327-328, 330, 335-336, 530, 558-585
Blust, Robert, 1, 4, 9, 34, 38, 303, 313, 314, 561
Browman, C., 453, 495
Brunelle, Marc, 7, 11, 15, 16, 17, 45, 52, 67, 68, 69, 70, 82-110, 372, 441, 446, 494, 501, 502, 522
Burenhult, Niclas, 10, 11, 446, 501, 503, 508, 519, 533, 543
Burling, Robbins, 10, 111, 113, 114, 135, 214, 220, 253, 254, 257
Chan, Marjorie, 33, 34, 36, 37, 39, 41, 43, 47
Chappell, Hilary, 1, 180, 242, 357, 359, 361, 370, 371, 394, 412, 415, 424
Comrie, Bernard, 1-27, 32, 153, 158, 211, 244, 245, 246, 266, 267, 286, 323, 356, 357, 364, 365, 366, 367, 368, 370, 388, 411
DeLancey, Scott, 139, 214, 257
Diffloth, Gérard, 10, 12, 14, 15, 16, 43, 61, 90, 312, 330, 441, 444, 446, 447, 520, 530, 533, 538, 539, 543, 544, 549, 574, 575
Dixon, R. M. W., 158, 266, 504, 559
Donegan, Patricia, 45, 51, 77, 107, 213, 245, 330, 530, 533

Donohue, Mark, 11, 29, 33, 46, 106, 281, 284, 285, 289, 292, 294, 299, 311, 313, 323, 324, 326, 328, 332, 334, 335, 336, 337, 338
Dryer, Matthew S., 11, 248, 287, 288, 289, 322, 323, 356, 365, 366, 387, 389, 398, 530
Enfield, N. J., 1-27, 52, 73, 78, 82, 106, 153, 156, 159, 164, 185-190, 197, 200, 203, 211, 213, 243, 244, 245, 246, 247, 248, 254, 266, 286, 292, 299, 300, 301, 338, 356, 364, 392, 395, 398, 416, 421, 422, 441, 500, 533, 544, 559, 603, 604, 605, 612, 615
Ferlus, Michel, 10, 61, 70, 72, 104, 376, 501, 522, 537
Goldstein, L., 453, 495
Gregerson, Kenneth J., 4, 62, 63, 69, 533
Hall, E., 53, 54, 57, 58, 59, 451
Heine, Bernd, 156, 178, 293, 604
Henderson, Eugénie, 14, 15, 16, 29, 32, 33, 34, 82, 107, 153, 194, 444, 448, 459, 460, 462, 474, 500, 501, 503, 512, 520
Himmelmann, Nikolaus P., 1, 302, 592, 593
Huffman, Franklin E., 54, 55, 61, 68, 90, 460, 461, 462, 463, 464, 510, 511, 512, 546, 547, 549, 550
Huziwara, Keisuke, 114, 124-128, 130, 131, 132, 134, 136, 139, 141, 144
Hyman, Larry M., 445, 501
Kuteva, Tania, 156, 178, 293, 591, 604
La Polla, Randy J., 9, 115, 116, 117, 138, 157, 213, 338, 397, 399, 411
Maddieson, Ian, 29, 34, 68, 105, 285, 378

Masica, Colin P., 153, 211, 244, 246, 266
Matisoff, James A., 9, 10, 12, 15, 16, 17, 35, 38, 42, 43, 45, 46, 50, 51, 83, 104, 106, 111-151, 170, 183, 184, 211, 213, 214, 216, 239, 240, 249, 250, 251, 257, 266, 293, 312, 356, 359, 364, 428, 441, 444, 462, 500, 501, 510, 533, 534, 538, 546, 560, 562, 564, 567, 574, 603, 604, 605
Morey, Stephen, 1, 10, 180, 200, 201, 216, 257, 447, 513, 514, 520
Nichols, Johanna, 4, 220, 256, 269, 286, 311, 320
Pittayaporn, Pittayawat, 7, 11, 12, 15, 17, 35, 45, 107, 312, 363, 377, 441, 446, 494, 496, 500-528
Post, Mark W., 1, 4, 7, 10, 12, 17, 51, 52, 77, 209-265, 266, 338, 558, 564, 575
Ross, Malcolm D., 74, 285, 294, 332
Sagart, Laurent, 9, 11, 12, 37, 43, 44, 45, 46, 313, 330, 357, 358, 359, 363, 364, 501, 561

Sangdong, David, 114, 124, 125, 126, 130, 132, 133, 134, 136
Shibatani, Masayoshi, 610, 611, 620, 621
Shorto, H. L., 9, 15, 43, 76, 77, 500, 533, 563, 533, 568, 569
Sidwell, Paul, 4, 7, 9, 12, 15, 16, 17, 33, 51-81, 330, 494, 495, 530, 533, 542, 543, 549, 568, 574, 575
Slobin, Dan I., 587, 588, 589
Stampe, David, 45, 51, 75, 77, 107, 213, 245, 330, 530, 533
Svantesson, Jan-Olof, 10, 53, 54, 55, 56, 57, 60, 446, 452, 453, 501, 503, 504, 514, 516, 520, 530, 533, 538, 544, 547, 549
Talmy, Leonard, 586-589, 591, 592, 594, 595, 606, 615, 623, 624
Thurgood, Graham W., 9, 10, 13, 16, 35, 38, 39, 43, 61, 67, 68, 70, 105, 165, 313, 373, 446, 501, 502, 522

Place index

For languages spoken in these places please refer to the Language Index.

Africa, 29, 32, 559
– central, 388
– east, 293
– equatorial, 285, 323, 338
– noun classification in, 14
– west, 106, 562, 581
Amazon, 14, 338
Anhui, 359
Arunachal Pradesh, 6, 214-219, 252, 564, 575
Assam, 6, 112, 180, 200, 214, 217, 218, 219, 252
Australia, 1, 29, 267, 339
Bali, 2
Bangkok, 34, 97
Bird's Head, 268-269, 274, 278, 286, 288-290, 332
Bolivia, 595, 608
Bomberai Peninsula, 268, 269, 288
Borneo, 267, 268, 277, 325, 329, 339
Bou Sra village, 480
Brahmaputra River, 1, 209, 258
Brunei, 2, 267
Burma
– as a MSEA country, 84, 266
– Assam-Burma region, 112
– central, 127
– data on, 533, 598, 608
– eastern, 212
– Rakhine Province, 124
– northern, 125, 216, 251, 255, 258
Cambodia, 1, 2, 3, 6, 84, 212, 327, 466, 480, 510
Cameroon Grassfields, 577

Chaophraya River, 1
Chaukan Pass, 255
China
– as part of MSEA, 1, 6, 17, 33, 266
– Language Atlas of China, 358
– map, 2, 3
– Myanmar-China border, 180, 181
– northern China, 360, 361, 399
– southeastern China, 428
– southern China, 33, 35-36, 164, 294, 330, 360, 333-364, 370, 374, 378, 383, 500
– southwest China, 213, 214, 359
Chindwin Valley, 124, 125, 203
Ethio-Sudan borderland, 577
Fujian Province, 6, 377
Ghana, 560
Guangdong, 6, 36, 37, 358, 361, 363, 364, 371, 378, 379
Guangxi-Zhuang Autonomous region, 6, 36, 41, 358, 359, 379
Guizhou, 6, 36, 294, 359, 363
Hainan, 38, 275, 313, 314, 357, 359, 378
Hanoi, 97, 563
Himalayas, 266, 282, 286, 313
Ho Chi Minh City, 2
Hunan, 6, 358, 359, 382
India
– as part of MSEA area, 6, 500
– hiatus between India and SE Asia, 153
– Indian Ocean, 270, 277, 328, 333
– linguistic diversity in, 6, 575
– Linguistic Survey of India, 112, 114, 124
– map, 2

- northeast, 1, 5, 156, 266, 330, 512, 533
- provinces in, 359

Indochina, 1, 340
Indonesia, 1, 276, 277, 328
Insular SE Asia, 1, 2, 17, 38, 39, 82
Irawaddy Delta, 194
Irrawaddy River, 1, 194, 599
Japan, 275, 277, 282, 327, 400
Jiangxi, 6, 359, 377
Kazakhstan, 414
Kolkata, 252
Kuala Lumpur, 2
Kyrgyzstan, 414
Laos
- as part of MSEA, 1, 6, 84, 212, 441, 500
- contact zone, 575
- map, 2, 3
- northern Laos, 57
- people of, 73
- southern Laos, 70

Léizhōu Peninsula, 357, 370, 378, 379, 383
Lohit River/Lohit Valley, 255
Madagascar, 270, 275, 277, 283
Malay Peninsula, 1, 2, 4, 6, 88
Malaysia, 3, 84, 267
Maluku, 267, 269, 278, 285, 286, 292
Mamberamo River, 268, 285, 294, 266-355
Mandalay, 167, 599
Manipur, 6, 39, 112, 124, 214, 215
Meghalaya, 6, 39, 214
Mekong River, 1, 268, 574, 266-355
Mesoamerica, 29, 106, 338
Micronesia, 286
Mizoram, 6, 214, 215
Mondulkiri Province (Cambodia), 480
Mrauk-U, 599
Muhse, 181, 182, 202, 204
Myanmar, 1, 2, 3, 6, 17, 153-208, 441, 500, 514
Nagaland, 6, 39, 214, 215

Nepal, 139, 156, 182, 201, 213
New Guinea, 29, 32, 33, 39, 46, 266-355
New Ireland, 277
Nicobar Islands, 533
Nigeria, 560, 577
Nusa Tenggara, 267, 269, 275, 285, 286
Nusantara, 266-355
Pacific Ocean, 270, 277, 283, 328, 330, 333
Pacific Rim, 269, 282
Pakistan, 124, 140, 212
Pearl River, 1, 363, 383
Philippines
- as part of MSEA, 325
- Austronesian expansion through, 331, 333
- linguistic area with Taiwan, 267

Phnom Penh, 97, 466, 480
Pyin U Lwin, 171
Rakhine Province (Burma), 124
Rangoon, 97
Red River, 1
Sagaing, 124, 167
Salween River, 1
Salween Valley, 203
Sen Monorom, 480
Shanghai, 379, 406
Siang River, 217
Sichuan, 36, 37, 38, 39
Singapore, 84, 252, 294, 328
Sittwe (Akyab), 599
Solomon Islands, 285
South America, 29, 32
Subansari River, 217
Sulawesi, 46, 267, 268, 289, 325, 327, 328
Sumatra, 267, 278, 289, 304, 307, 314, 327, 328, 339
Sumba, 275
Sumbawa, 269
Sunda, 46, 304, 339
Taiwan, 266-355, 363, 400, 561
Taiwan Strait, 285, 363

Place index — **645**

Thailand, 175
– as part of MSEA, 1, 6, 84, 212, 441, 500
– map, 2, 3
– northern Thailand, 95, 213
Tibet, 38, 218
Togo, 560
Tripura, 6, 127, 214, 215
Vanuatu, 285
Vientiane, 97
Vietnam
– as part of MSEA, 1, 6, 84, 212, 441, 500
– central highlands, 5, 61, 494
– map, 2, 3
– northern Vietnam, 96, 107, 575
– population movement, 336
– southern Vietnam, 33, 88, 90
Wèi River Valley, 360
West Papua, 1, 269
Yangon, 599
Yangtze River, 1, 2, 6, 360, 364
Yellow River, 358
Yunnan, 6, 125, 339, 360, 383
Zhejiang, 6, 359
Zomia, 5

Language index

A-Hmao/ A-Hmø, 36, 377
A-Hmyo dialects, 376
Abun, 269, 286, 288
Acehnese, 289
Achang, 112, 376
Adamawa languages, 576, 577, 578
African languages, 29, 325, 577-582; see also individual language entries
Aka languages; see Hruso; Koro
Ahi, 572
Akan, 589
Akha, 141, 572, 574
Alak, 42
Altaic, 361, 362, 399
Amdo Tibetan, 38, 43, 571
Andro, 124, 131, 135, 145
Angami Naga; see Naga
Angkorian Khmer, 377, 570; see also Khmer
Angkuic, 52, 53-61
– Proto Angkuic, 56, 57, 60
Anong, 10, 13, 115, 116, 118, 119, 120, 135, 572
Ao (Chungli), 574
Ao (Mongsen), 10, 182, 183, 571
Apatani, 218, 220, 221, 222, 233, 234-235, 239, 566, 572, 574
Arabic, 451
Arakanese; see also Marma
– relationship with Sak, 134
– relationship with Burmese, 598, 599, 624
– motion expressions in, 600-602, 608, 614, 618, 623
– serial verb constructions in, 604, 606, 616
Arandic languages, 594
Arawan, 560
Arem, 10

Asakian, 124, 144, 145, 146
Aslian languages, 10, 11; see also individual language entries
– as an Austroasiatic family, 35, 533,
– linguistic properties of the family, 103, 202, 534, 535-536, 538, 540, 541, 544, 546
Athapaskan languages, 105
Atlantic languages, 578
Atong/A'tong, 10, 215, 571; see also A'tong
Atsi; see Zaiwa
Australian languages; see also individual language entries
– as a linguistic area, 266, 267, 310
– influencing other languages, 285
– Mekong-Mamberamo properties of, 272, 282, 284, 287, 288, 294-295, 319, 323, 325, 340
– noun classification in, 559, 560, 576, 582, 594
– polysynthetic languages, 317
Austroasiatic; see also individual language entries
– and areal features, 283
– and contact, 256
– and tone, 86, 87, 99, 103, 106, 444
– and causatives, 158, 176, 294
– as a family, 85
– derivational morphology, 8
– historical aspects, 12, 43
– homeland, 330
– in MSEA area, 213, 6, 9, 29, 33, 153, 212, 215, 269, 313
– phonological aspects, 34, 35, 39, 42, 43, 52, 509, 562
– population movements, 363, 399

– Proto Austroasiatic, 4, 12, 43, 75, 76, 283, 444, 530, 569
– substrate, 284, 364
– vocabulary, 7
– word structure, 563-585
Austronesian; see also individual language entries
– and contact, 287, 283, 289, 294, 546, 549, 569
– and convergence, 212
– and the MSEA area, 6, 84, 88, 153, 267, 313
– and TAM marking, 325
– and tone, 87, 90, 99, 102, 103, 106
– and voice, 298, 302, 303, 311, 592
– areal aspects, 33
– cognate sets, 314
– expansion, 4, 270, 275, 286, 289, 290, 303, 309, 328, 329-336, 338
– history of, 46, 363
– homeland, 283
– loan words, 568
– origins, 327
– phonology, 29, 38, 284, 285
– Proto Austronesian, 283, 285, 325, 326, 328, 335
– syllable structure, 444, 520
– vocabulary, 7
Awju-Dumut languages, 276
Bahing, 572
Bahnar, 533, 538, 549
Bahnaric languages
– as members of Austroasiatic, 35, 569, 570
– morphology in, 535, 536, 538, 540, 542, 552, 563
– Proto Bahnaric, 563, 570
Bahnaric, Northern, 61-70
– Proto North Bahnaric, 64, 65, 66, 67, 69
Bahnaric, Southern, 71, 474, 495
Bahnaric, West, 70

– Proto West Bahnaric, 71, 72
Bai, Bái languages, 11, 132, 359, 373, 388, 390, 394
– Proto Bái, 359, 373
Bajau, 289
Balinese, 297
Balsas Nahuatl, 105, 109
Baltic languages, 143, 268
Bangru, 216, 219, 566, 567
Barai, 295
Bargam, 276
Barish, 111, 113, 127; see also Bodo-Garo
Bauzi, 285
Bawm, 127
Bengali, 127, 215
Bengni, 574; see also Bokar
Benue-Congo languages, 578, 581, 582
Bhramu, 571
Biāo, 364
Biat, 569
Bima, 334
Bird's Head languages, 269, 274, 278, 289, 332,
Bisu, 119, 275
Bodic languages, 218, 219, 361, 566, 567, 571
Bodo, 219
Bodo-Garo, 111, 112-114, 115, 142-143, 571; see also Barish
– as a Northeast Indian language, 214, 215, 219
– linguistic influence on other languages, 216, 256
– morphology, 138
– phonological development, 140
Bokar, 217, 218, 220, 251, 567, 574
Bori, 217, 218
Bru/Bruu, 42, 520, 533, 539, 542, 544, 545, 547, 549, 550, 563
Bugan/Bugun, 216, 533, 546, 571

Buli, 291
Bunaq, 282
Bunong, 441-499, 508; see also Mnong
Burmese; see also Lolo-Burmese
– as a major language, 13, 29, 181
– as part of MSEA, 153, 365, 367, 428, 429
– associated motion in, 595-596
– examples, 162, 390, 595, 596, 600-605, 607, 615, 617-622
– historical aspects, 250
– influenced by other languages, 157, 176, 203
– influence on other languages, 112, 121, 122, 123, 125, 126, 129, 133, 136, 204
– motion events in, 598-606
– Old Burmese, 173, 570
– path satellites in, 606-607, 614-625
– phonological features of, 384
– preverbal negator, 240
– syllable structure, 446, 508, 520
– tone, 376
– typological features of, 368, 369
– with 'give' and 'get' constructions, 156, 167-168, 177-179, 186, 191-193, 199-200, 202
– word order, 356, 389, 392, 397, 427
– written Burmese, 127, 134, 373, 572
Burmish languages, 112, 114, 117, 123, 376, 429, 572; see also individual language entries
Buxing, 533, 544
Bwe, 194
Càijiā, 359
Cak, 127-128
Cambodian, 10, 13, 510; see also Khmer
Cantonese; see also Nánníng Cantonese; Yue
– adnominal attributes in, 297
– as a MSEA language, 366-367, 368, 369
– as a standard language, 47
– examples, 296, 387, 396, 402, 405, 407, 409, 413, 425, 613
– influence from other languages, 363
– influencing other languages, 361, 383, 410
– morphology, 396
– motion verbs in, 613
– numeral classifiers in, 286
– phonological features in, 384
– syntax in, 412-415, 420, 421, 612
– tone in, 374
– word order in, 387, 388, 395, 399, 400, 405, 407-410, 425, 427-428
Cao Lan, 102
Caodeng, 572
Car Nicobarese, 533, 548,
Cara, 581
Celtic languages, 143
Central American languages, 32
Central Jukunoid languages, 581
Central Nyah Kur, 35, 42, 520, 533, 569
Chairel, 112, 113, 124, 143, 145
Chak; see Cak
Chakku; see Cak
– Proto Cak, 145
Chakma, 127
Cham dialects, 10, 11, 13, 69, 102, 165, 313, 314, 466, 569
Chamic languages, 38, 39, 61, 70, 356, 365, 373, 389, 522
Chaozhou, 37
Chatong, 569
Chepang, 574
Chimbu languages, 276
Chin languages, 102, 170, 566, 567, 571, 574
Chinbon, 567
Chinese
– areal features, 36, 37, 340
– as an official language, 181
– contact, 73, 83, 551
– converbs, 610

- external possession, 242
- history of, 12, 84, 573
- loans from, 44, 117, 119
- phonology, 43, 46, 47, 356-439
- reduplication, 534-535
- resultative constructions, 187, 197
- serial verb constructions, 590, 610, 613
- syllable structure, 448
- tone, 105, 106
- word order, 243, 356-439

Chinese, Old, 357, 570, 572, 574
- and proto Sinitic, 12
- and sesquisyllables, 501
- difficulty with morphemic representation, 362
- family subgrouping, 359
- reconstructed phonology, 37, 43, 44, 360-361, 368, 393
- reconstructed prefixes, 562
- word order, 395-399

Chittagonian, 390
Cho (Mindat), 571
Chong, 550, 563, 569
Chōngzuǒ Pínghuà; see Pínghuà
Chrau, 520, 533, 549, 563, 569
Chug, 216
Chút, 535, 563; see also Ruc
Cibər (Lopa), 581
Classical Tibetan, 373
cLela, 579, 581
Cua, 447
Czech, 160
Daai, 102, 571
Dabu Hakka, 332
Dakoid languages, 581
Damal, 328
Damu, 218
Dànánshān Hmong, 367, 384
Dani languages, 276
Dānzhōu, 359, 379

Daofu, 572
De'ang, 533, 544; see also Palaung
Deuri, 10
Dhimal, 140
Didayi/Didei, 75, 76, 77
Digarish languages, 216, 217, 251
Digaru, 216, 217, 219
Dirang, 572
Dogon languages, 578
Dolakhali; see Newar
Dravidian, 212
Dulong, 115, 116, 117, 118, 119, 120, 121, 135, 138, 572
Dungan, 414
Dutch, 591
Dyirbal, 559
Eastern Guǎngxī Patois; see Guìdōng Tǔhuà
Eastern Kayah Li, 366, 367, 369, 378, 384, 390, 405; see also Kayah Li
Eastern Miji, 566, 567; see also Miji
Eastern Naga languages; see Naga languages
Enga, 295
Enggano, 289, 314
English
- adnominal attribution, 287, 291, 295
- and schwa, 450
- bare obliques, 322
- influence from, 40, 41, 328
- conventional greetings, 280
- dental clicks, 277
- 'get' construction, 186
- Indian English, 218
- loans into, 568
- marked grammatical categories, 318, 320
- motion expressions, 587
- numeral classifiers, 286, 295
- phonaesthemes, 561
- phonetics/phonology, 455, 480, 504, 521
- reduplication, 538

– translation equivalents, 157, 301
– voice, 305
Ersu, 38, 572
Ese Ejja, 595, 608
Ewe, 589
Fataluku, 282
Fijian, 38
Finnish, 451
Formosan languages, 391
French, 10, 480, 559, 587, 589, 594, 614
Fúqīng Eastern Mǐn, 372, 384, 396, 397, 403, 417, 427; see also Mǐn
Fúquán, 376
Fùyáng Wú, 371, 384, 396, 397, 404, 408, 414, 417, 424, 427; see also Wú
Fúzhōu, 376, 400
Galo, 10, 217, 218, 220-243, 574
– Proto Galo, 230
Gàn/Gan, 37, 332, 370, 371, 377-379, 383, 384, 397, 408, 427
Ganan, 124, 130, 131, 132, 137, 145
Garo, 10, 141
Gayo, 313
Geelvink Bay languages, 269-270, 285
Geman, 38, 43, 46; see also Miju
German, 158-159, 160, 451, 587
Germanic languages, 54, 57
Great Andamanese, 6
Greater Kwerba languages, 270
Greek, 143, 589
Green Hmong, 367, 389, 410, 421
Gta', 52, 75-77
Guìdōng Tǔhuà, 358
Guiqiong, 572
Gumuz, 577, 578, 580
Gur-Adamawa languages, 576, 578
Gurung (Ghachok), 572
Gutob, 75, 76, 77
Gǔzhàng Xiānghuà, 371, 384, 397, 427; see also Xiānghuà

Gwamhi-Wuri, 579
Hainan Cham, 313, 314
Hǎinán Mǐn (Hainanese), 370, 378, 379, 383, 408, 412, 414, 426; see also Mǐn
Hakha; see Lai
Hakka (Kèjiā)
– as a dialect group, 358
– as part of MSEA, 29, 364, 366, 367
– Cantonese influence in, 361
– central macro-zone, 370, 371
– contact, 359, 400
– Hmong-Mien influence in, 363
– 'give' construction, 332
– phonology, 37, 39, 378, 383
– tone, 374
– typological features in, 368, 369
– word order in, 388, 408-409
Halang, 63, 64, 65, 66, 67, 533
Hani (Khatu), 574
Hasha, 581
Hatam, 288, 297
Hebrew, 587
Hindi, 212, 213, 218, 219, 243
Hkauri, 122, 145
Hlai, 275, 374
– Proto Hlai, 35
Hmong; see also Dànánshān Hmong; East Hmongic; Green Hmong; Hmongic; White Hmong
– as part of MSEA, 366, 367
– 'give' constructions, 165
– phonology, 44
– Proto Hmongic, 36
– reconstruction, 135
– serial verb constructions, 596, 609, 615
– typological features, 368, 369
– word order, 397, 427
Hmongic, 36, 37, 40, 41, 134, 363, 364, 367, 376-377, 384
– East Hmongic, 36, 41,

– Northern Hmongic languages, 36
– Western Hmongic languages, 36, 40, 41, 367, 376, 377, 384
Hmong-Mien/Hmong-Mien languages; *see also* individual language entries
– and loans, 37, 44
– as part of MSEA, 6, 29, 84, 153, 212, 269, 283, 356, 365
– historical aspects, 12, 41
– influence by, 363
– influence on, 361, 367
– nominal classification, 559, 560
– phonological aspects, 34, 35
– population movements of speakers, 95
– Proto Hmong-Mien, 35, 40, 43, 44, 83, 106, 373
– reconstruction, 135
– syllable structure, 42, 560-561
– tone, 87, 88, 99, 100, 102, 103, 106
– word length, 313
– word order, 87, 399
– word structure, 562
Ho Ne/She, 36, 37
Hruso, 132, 564, 565, 576
Hu, 53, 54, 55, 56, 57, 564, 60
Huĭ, 358, 359, 370, 377, 403, 428
Huĭ'ān Southern Mĭn, 371, 384, 423; *see also* Mĭn
Huishu, 567
Hyamic (Plateau), 579, 581
Idu, 215, 216, 217, 219, 254, 571
Iha, 281, 288, 325
Iha Pidgin, 313
Ijoid languages, 578
Ikann, 581
Inanwatan, 269, 288, 325
Indic languages, 51, 77, 123, 134, 216, 373, 391; *see also* Indo-Aryan
Indo-Aryan, 122, 127, 158, 212-216, 229, 256, 624; *see also* Indic languages

Indo-European languages, 143, 144, 209, 218, 242, 559, 562, 587, 592; *see also* individual language entries
Indonesian; *see also* Malay
– bare-oblique constructions, 321, 322
– dental clicks, 278-279
– 'eye day' > 'sun' lexicalizations, 282-283
– isolating, 311
– on periphery of MSEA area, 365
– past tense, 318
– periphrastic causatives, 294
– phonology, 284
– verbless sentences, 592, 594
– voice, 298-299, 301-304, 305, 306, 307, 309
– 'where' greeting, 281
– word length, 314-315, 317
Iranian languages, 391
Italian, 589
Italic languages, 143
Ivatan, 285
Jah-Hut, 533, 538
Jahai
– nominalization, 543
– onsets, 517, 524
– passing gesture (lack of), 275
– plural affixes, 546
– syllable structure, 446, 501, 503, 508-509, 510, 512, 518, 519
– word structure, 563
Jakaltek popti', 609
Japanese
– case affixes (lack of), 323
– consonant clusters, 451
– converb constructions, 591, 621
– motion satellites, 612, 613, 622
– phonology of loans, 37
– 'where' greeting, 282
– word order, 390
Jarai, 520

Javanese, 38, 276, 294, 299-302, 307, 310, 311, 314, 318
Jeh, 103, 504, 507, 533
Jìn, 360, 362, 370, 374
Jinghpaw/Jingpho, 111-151, 160, 170, 179-182, 200, 202, 204; see also Singpho
Jiongnai, 36
Jīxī Huī, 372, 384, 397, 401, 403, 418, 419, 427
Jju cluster, 581
Jru'/Jruq, 43, 46, 563; see also Laven
Kaalak – Domurik languages, 578
Kachai, 138
Kachin, 33, 111, 112, 113, 114, 135; see also Jinghpaw/Jingpho
Kachinic languages, 250, 251
Kaera, 281
Kaike, 571
Kainji languages, 579, 580, 581
– Northwest Kainji languages, 579, 580, 581
Kam-Sui languages, 164, 294, 364
– Proto Kam-Sui, 35, 43
Kam-Tai languages, 35
Kamang, 281
Kamarupan languages, 38, 42
Kambari, 581
Kambera, 38, 286
Kamengic, 571
Kammu, 278, 501, 503, 504, 508, 514-518, 520, 524; see also Khmu
– Kammu Yùan, 10
– Northern Kammu, 5, 452, 453
Kana, 577, 581
Kanauri, 571
Kantu-Sak, 124
Karbi, 10, 214, 571; see also Mikir
Karen, Karenic
– as part of MSEA, 213, 248, 364-365
– 'get' construction, 193-194
– 'give' construction, 169, 170

– nominal classification, 571, 572
– proto Karen, 373
– phonology, 378
– syllable structure, 520
– word order, 248, 366-367, 388, 390, 404
Kashmiri, 388, 391
Kasong, 543
Katu, 42, 72, 533, 538, 539, 543, 546
Katuic languages
– areal influence, 61
– as Austroasiatic, 35
– aspect, 538, 539
– mood categories marked, 544
– morphology, 534, 535, 536
– nominal classification, 563, 569, 570
– plural subject marking, 547
– pronominal case marking, 541-542
– Proto Katuic, 569
– semantic role marking, 540
– sesquisyllables, 70
Kayah Li, 169, 170, 193, 194, 313, 503, 608, 618; see also Eastern Kayah Li; Northern Kayah Li
Kayan (Pekon), 572
Kaytej, 594
Kehu, 270
Kei, 334
Kèjiā; see Hakka
Kemie, 533
Kenaboi, 7
Kensiu / Kensiw, 103
Kentakbong, 533, 545
Kesui, 285
Kham, 182, 183, 184, 201, 203, 240
Khamti Tai, 215, 216, 255
Khasi, Khasic/Khasian languages
– as part of MSEA, 330
– morphology, 536, 540, 544, 545, 550, 568
– nominal classification, 570
– prenasalized stops, 39

- similarity to Sino-Tibetan, 575
- speakers, 215
- subgrouping problems, 213
- word order, 216, 390

Khatu; see Hani

Khmer; see also Angkorian Khmer; Cambodian
- animal prefixes, 568, 569, 570
- areal influences, 61
- as part of MSEA, 365, 367
- aspect, 291
- consonantal codas, 377, 378, 384
- dental discrepancies, 285
- examples, 399, 410
- 'give' and 'get' constructions, 156, 157, 160, 162, 168, 176, 293
- grammatical categories in, 551
- interrupted transmission, 551
- loans, 328
- morphology, lack of, 535
- nominal classification, 546
- phonological aspects, 29, 46, 71, 72, 73
- serial verb constructions, 423
- sesquisyllables, 441, 499, 313
- syllable structure, 500, 501, 508, 510-513, 514, 515, 518, 519, 520, 524
- tone and register, 68, 70, 103, 376
- typological features, 368, 369
- word order, 392, 397, 399, 410, 423, 426, 427

Khmeric languages, 35, 510, 533, 536, 546, 547, 549, 550, 569, 570

Khmu, Khmuic languages; see also Kammu
- as Austroasiatic, 35
- nominal classification, 569
- dental clicks, 278
- historical phonology, 568
- morphology, 534, 536, 538, 544, 547, 549, 549
- Proto Khmuic, 568

- syllable structure, 537
- tone, 103, 539

Kmhmu Cwang, 189
Khoirao, 574
Khumi, 127, 571
Khyang, 127
Kim Mun, 374
Kiowan, 560
Kiranti languages, 129, 227, 572
Kiwai, 295
Kmhmu; see Khmu; Kammu
Koho, 103, 533, 542, 544, 547, 548,
Köho; see Sre
Kok-Borok/Kokborok, 127, 215, 571; see also Tripura
Kómnzo, 276
Kon Keu, 53
Konda-Yahadian languages, 269
Konyak; see Naga
Kordofanian languages, 580
Korean, 105, 362, 390, 611
Koro, 216, 219, 564, 571, 576
Korowai, 276
Kra languages, 35
Kra-Dai languages; see also individual language entries
- as part of MSEA, 356, 364, 429
- influence from other languages, 365
- influence on other languages, 363, 370
- linguistic situation of, 363
- Proto Kra-Dai, 373
- syllable structure, 377-378
- tone, 374
- typology of, 356
- word order, 371, 389

Kri, 10, 15,1 6, 90, 533, 544
Krongo, 577
Kuay, 520
Kucong, 574
Kui, 35

654 — Language index

Kuki, Kuki-Chin languages, 215, 390, 567
Kuot, 277
Kwa languages, 578
Lahu
– as part of MSEA, 213
– diphthongs, 248-249
– 'give' constructions, 183, 293
– historical phonology, 118, 119, 120, 123, 127, 132, 133, 141
– negation, 240
– passing gesture, 275
– serial verb constructions, 250
– typology, 213-214
Lai (Hakha), 571
Lakher (Mara), 566, 571, 574
Lalo, 572
Lamalera, 282
Lamet, 54, 57
Lampung, 289
Lango, 297
Langsu; see Maru
Lao
– as a national language, 29
– bare-oblique constructions, 322
– descriptive work on, 10, 13, 14
– 'give' constructions, 159, 292, 293
– "elaborate expressions", 605
– final verbal particle, 618
– historical aspects, 74
– influence on other languages, 61, 70, 73, 75, 84
– labile verbs, 8
– noun classes, 559
– phonology and tone, 35, 373
– syllable structure, 70
– voice, 300-301
– word order, 299, 392, 395, 398, 416, 421, 422, 425, 615
Lare, 218, 220, 221, 227, 228, 238, 240, 241, 242, 243

Lashi, 112, 114, 123, 376
Latin, 290, 357
Laven, 52, 65, 66, 67, 70-75, 563; see also Jru'/Jruq
Lawa, 43, 520
Lepcha; see Rong
Leti, 282
Limbu, 572
Lish, 216
Loi, 124, 145; see also Luish
Lolo-Burmese; see also Burmese
– relationships to other languages, 111-151, 219, 248, 251
– as part of MSEA, 248, 257, 365
– cognate sets, 563-564, 571, 572
– Proto Lolo-Burmese, 119, 123, 141, 373
Lolo-Burmese-Naxi family, 41
Loloish languages, 38, 41, 114, 117, 119, 133, 376, 571, 572, 574
– Proto North Loloish, 572
Lotha Naga; see Naga
Lower Cross languages, 581
Luish languages, 17, 111-151, 572
– Proto Luish, 130, 131, 132, 141
Luo, 293
Luóbóhé, 376
Lushai (Mizo), 567, 571, 574
Lüsu, 38
Madang languages, 276, 293
Madurese, 303
Magar, 140, 572, 574
Mairasi, Mairasi languages, 269, 288
Makasae, 282
Mal, 533
Malagasy, 38, 277, 329, 330, 333
Malay; see also Indonesian
– and creolization, 334
– as part of the Austronesian expansion, 4, 325
– bare-oblique constructions, 321

– dental clicks, 278-279
– 'give' and 'get' constructions, 202, 294
– loans from, 534, 546, 549, 551, 569
– Papuan Malay, 300, 301, 316
– periphrastic undergoer construction, 300-302
– phonology, 83, 284
– "second passive", 299
– Sri Lankan Malay, 202, 294
– Tanjung Raden Malay, 279
– Ternate Malay, 279
– voice, 303, 307
– word length, 314-317
Malayic languages, 335
Mambay, 577
Mambila, Mambiloid, 577, 581
Mandarin, including varieties
– adverbs, 402, 408
– affixes, 396
– as part of MSEA, 365, 429
– history of speakers, 360
– Huàngshuǐ Mandarin, 362
– influence on other languages, 54
– influenced by other languages, 362
– left-headedness, 356, 397
– locative postpositions, 405
– macro-areas, 370-371
– object marking construction, 413-415
– phonology, 37, 39, 46-47, 383, 384
– Pingli Central Mandarin, 403
– possession, 242
– serial verb constructions, 591, 610, 613, 614
– Suīníng Central Mandarin, 372
– tone, 54, 374, 377
– typology, 368, 369
– word order, 388, 397, 399, 411, 412, 419, 427, 428
– Zhōukǒu Central Plains Mandarin, 371
Mande languages, 578

Mang, Mangic languages
– tone, 103, 376,
– morphology, 536, 538, 539, 540, 358, 542, 544, 545, 546, 550, 568,
Mangap Mbula, 621
Manggarai, 299, 313
Mangshi, 35; see also Shan
Maniq, 275
Maonan, 35, 164, 165, 293
Mara; see Lakher
Maraic, 566
Marma, 112, 127, 134, 140, 572; see also Arakanese
Maru (Langsu), 114, 123, 376
Matu, 571
Mayan languages, 609
Maybrat, 269, 288, 296, 297, 313
Mee, 276
Meithei, 124, 141, 215, 571, 574
Memba, 566, 572
Mentawai (including Muarasiberut Mentawai), 292, 293, 294, 307, 308, 309, 314, 322
Mey (Sherdukpen), 216, 567, 568
Mey (Shergaon) languages, 571
Meyah, 278, 288, 299, 310, 311, 318, 321, 322
Meyor, 572
Mien, Mienic languages
– as part of MSEA, 366-367
– historical phonology, 36, 41, 135, 374
– phonology, 384
– typological features, 368, 369, 374
– word order, 397, 427
Miji, Miji languages, 216, 219, 564, 565, 566, 567, 571, 576; see also Eastern Miji ; Nafra Miji; Western Miji
Miju, Mijuish languages, 216, 571
Mikir, Mikir languages, 119, 137, 185, 571

Milang, 216, 217, 218, 219, 221, 245, 252, 254, 571
Mǐn, Mǐn languages, 360, 361, 363, 370, 371, 372, 374, 376, 378, 379, 383, 384, 279, 400; see also Fúqīng Eastern Mǐn; Hǎinán Mǐn; Huì'ān Southern Mǐn
– Proto Mǐn 37, 373
Minangkabau, 286, 287, 289, 290, 296, 297, 308
Mindat; see Cho
Minyong
– as a Tani language, 217, 218, 220, 221
– pronouns, 235
– syntax, 223-234
– verbal morphology, 239
Mishmic languages, 571
Mising, 214, 218, 220, 233, 236, 239, 240, 574
Mizo, 127, 137, 141, 215, 216, 571, 574; see also Lushai
Mlabri, 503, 533, 550
Mnong, 35, 533, 569; see also Bunong
Modang, 314
Mon
– and conversation analysis, 13
– 'give' construction, 164, 167, 168, 172-175, 176, 203
– 'get' construction, 196-198, 200, 203
– influence on other languages, 156-157, 177-179, 182, 204
– word order, 161, 162
Mon-Khmer,
– as part of MSEA, 85, 364
– history of, 12, 373, 376
– influence on other languages, 121, 390
– morphology, 530-557
– prosody, 216
– Proto Mon-Khmer, 12, 54, 76, 535, 544, 549, 568, 569
– syllable structure, 72, 75

– tone and register, 54, 86, 88, 90
– typological features, 356, 364
– word order, 387, 389
Mongsen Ao, 10, 182, 183, 571
Monic, 35, 42, 533, 536, 549, 569, 570
– Proto Monic, 570
Monpa, 570, 571
Mor, 269
Morehead and Upper Maro River languages, 276
Mosetén, 297
Moshang, 113, 141, 143
Motuo Menba. 571
Mpi, 120, 572
Mpur, 269
Mru, 127, 390
Muak (Sa-aak), 53, 54, 57, 58, 59, 60, 61
Muna, 38, 289, 328
Munda, Munda languages
– as part of MSEA, 213, 575
– history of, 12, 52, 568
– influenced by other languages, 330,
– syllable structure, 75-77, 561,
Muong, 533, 550
Muya, 38
Na/Bangni, 218
Nafra Miji, 565
Naga languages 39, 215
– Angami Naga, 184
– Eastern, 38, 42
– Konyak, 111, 112
– Lotha, 574
– Northern/Northeastern, 111, 113, 114, 138, 140, 142, 143, 566, 571
– Rengma 38, 42
Nage, 322
Nah, 572
Namsang, 113, 143
Namuyi, 38, 572
Nancowry Nicobarese, 533, 555

Language index —— 657

Nánníng Cantonese, 412, 425; see also Cantonese
Nánníng Southern Pínghuà; see Pínghuà
Nasu, 572
Navajo, 558
Naxi, 41, 572
New Caledonian languages, 105
New Guinea languages; see also individual language entries; non-Austronesian languages
– as part of MSEA area, 33, 46, 266-270, 272, 273, 285, 326
– as part of Mekong-Mamberamo area, 321-322, 328, 329, 336, 339
– dental clicks, 278-279
– drift, 340
– 'give' construction, 293-295
– isolating structure, 311
– low grammatical morpheme density, 319-323
– passing gesture, 275-277
– periphrastic undergoer construction, 302
– phonology, 29, 32, 39, 284
– syllable structure, 313
– TAM marking, 291-292, 325
– verby adjectives, 287-289
– voice (lack of), 299, 309-310
– 'where' greeting, 282-283
– word length, 314-317
Newar, Newaric (Dolakhali) languages 213, 214, 253, 571
Ngarnic languages, 560
Ngeq, 42, 533, 563
Ngizim, 297
Nias, 289
Niger-Congo languages, 558, 559, 560, 561, 576, 578, 579, 580, 582
– Proto Niger-Congo, 578
Nilo-Saharan languages, 55, 560, 561, 577, 578, 580, 582

Níngbō Wú, 400, 406, 407
Nivkh, 365
Non-Austronesian languages; see also New Guinea languages
– contact, 270, 287
– Mekong-Mamberamo areal features, 276, 283, 285
– substrate, 267
North Halmahera languages, 269, 283, 288, 289, 294; see also Sahu
Northern Kammu; see Kammu
Northern Khmer; see Surin Khmer
Northern Roglai, 502
Northern Zhuang, 387, 404, 409, 425
Northwest Kainji; see Kainji
Nung, Nungish
– and Jingpho, 121-122, 142
– and Luish, 134-135
– as a Tibeto Burman group, 111, 114-121
– historical phonology, 140, 141
– influenced by Burmese, 112
– nominal classification, 569, 572, 574
– Proto Nungish, 115, 116
– syllable structure, 138
Nusu, 376, 572
Nyah Kur, 35, 42, 520, 533, 569
Nyaheun, 52, 55, 70-75
Nyhmoye, 571
Oceanic languages, 330, 333, 561
– Proto Oceanic, 330
Oi, 278
Old Chinese; see Chinese, Old
Ong Be, 379, 421, 426
Pacoh
– clitics, 540
– morphosyntax, 540, 541, 542, 545, 546, 547, 549
– nominal classification, 569, 570
– register, 61
– syllable structure, 446, 507, 520

Padam, 218, 220, 230, 254, 574
Padam-Mising (Abor-Miri), 574
Palauan, 388
Palaung, Palaungic languages
– dental discrepancies, 285
– 'give' and 'get' constructions, 175-176, 198-200
– (historical) phonology, 35, 54, 57
– morphology, 536, 539, 544, 545, 546, 549
– nominal classification, 568, 570
– Proto Palaungic, 53, 54
– syllable structure, 500
– tone, 103
Palu'e, 285, 299
Pamiri languages, 391
Pangkhua, 127
Pasi, 218, 225
Pazeh, 285
Pearic languages, 35, 103, 533, 536, 537, 543, 550, 563, 569, 570
Phan Rang Cham, 165
Phnong; see Bunong; Mnong
Phom, 571
Pínghuà, 357, 358, 359, 370, 408, 412, 428
– Chōngzuǒ Pínghuà, 396, 412
– Nánníng Southern Pínghuà, 372
– Northern Pínghuà, 359, 363,
– Southern Pínghuà, 374, 378, 383
Piro, 451
Ple-Temer, 546
Pnar, 278
Polish, 160, 587, 588
Pong, 569
Proto Heiban, 580
Proto North Loloish; see Loloish
Proto Tani, 217-223, 262
– and MSEA, 256
– creoloid typology, 211, 257
– migration of speakers, 251, 253, 254, 256
– reconstructed morphology, 42, 247, 248

– reconstructed phonology, 244, 247, 248
– reconstructed pronouns, 235
– reconstructed word classes, 226, 244, 248
– reconstructed words, 138, 231, 239, 244, 566
– reconstructed syntax, 233-234, 240, 244, 248
– shared features with Tibeto-Burman, 250
Proto West Papuan, 289
Pugo, 218, 221
Puroik (Sulung), 216, 219, 566, 567, 571
Pwo Karen, 194, 388
Pyu, 173
Qiang (Mawo), Qiangic languages, 38, 42, 132, 572
Rade, 39, 480
Rakhine languages, 390
Rawang, 112, 115-122, 132, 134, 138, 141, 574
Remo, 75, 76, 77
Rengao, 62-63, 64, 65, 66, 67, 533, 549
Rengma; see Naga languages
rGyalrong, rGyalrongic languages, 572
Riang-Liang, 533
Rölöm Mnong, 35
Romance languages, 357, 587, 589
Rong, 568, 575
Rongmei, 571, 574
Roon, 276, 278, 290, 291, 293, 314, 322
Rote, 334
Rotinese, 38
Ruc 533, 538, 539, 541, 546, 548, 550; see also Chút
Russian, 160
Sa-aak; see Muak
Sa'ban, 314
Sahu (North Halmaheran), 283
Sahu (Tamangic); see Tamang
Sak, 102, 112, 113, 114, 124, 126, 127-131, 132-141, 144-146; see also Cak
Sakai, 570

Sal, 112-114, 115, 146
Samre, 103, 570
Sangkong, 38, 43
Sanskrit, 86, 122, 451
Sapuan, 42
Sarikoli, 391
Sartang, 216
Saweru, 269-270, 294, 328
Sawu, 286
Sedang, 29, 56, 64-68, 520, 533, 547, 563, 569-570
Semai/Sengol, 533
Semelai, 10, 519, 533, 534, 545, 549
Sengmai, 124, 131, 135, 145
Sgaw, 169, 170, 194, 378, 520
Shan (Tai)
– as a regionally dominant language, 156, 176, 179, 181, 214
– 'give' construction, 166, 170-172
– 'get' construction, 194-196, 199
– loans into other languages, 58, 122, 125, 126, 130, 136, 176
– loans into Shan, 122
– phonology, 35
– tone, 54
Shanghainese, 47, 376, 407
Shàntóu/ Swatow, 379
Shàowǔ Mǐn-Gàn, 372, 384, 396, 397, 420, 421, 427
Sháozhōu Patois, 358
Shen, 581
Sherdukpen cluster (Mey), 216, 567, 568
Shinman, 570
Siamese, 116, 117, 122, 123, 133; *see also* Thai
Siang, Siangic languages, 216, 218, 251, 571
– Proto Siang, 216
Sika, 334
Singpho, 111, 145, 214, 215, 216, 257, 512; *see also* Jinghpaw/Jingpho

Sinitic, 356-439; *see also* individual language entries
– and MSEA, 29, 244
– and Sino-Tibetan phylum, 564
– contact and, 51, 213, 218, 575
– 'give' construction, 332
– nominal classification, 570, 572, 574
– phonology, 34, 35, 36, 37, 39, 43, 573
– Proto-Sinitic, 12
Sino-Tibetan; *see also* individual language entries
– as part of MSEA, 6, 84, 85, 269, 356, 365, 428
– contact, 575
– controversy of 'Sino-Tibetan' term, 562, 564
– 'eye day ' > 'sun', 283
– nominal classification, 560, 576, 580, 582
– subgrouping, 12
– syllable structure, 99-101, 444
– tone, 87, 88, 90, 102, 103
– word length, 313
– word structure, 561, 562, 563-574
Siroi, 293
Slavic languages, 143
So, 570
Somali, 293
South American languages, 29
South West Halmahera / West New Guinea languages, 278
Southwestern Gelao, 35
Spanish, 120, 505, 506, 587, 588, 589
Sre, 55, 533, 539, 544, 569
Stieng, 42, 71, 446, 507, 569
Subansiri, 217, 218
Sui, 35, 46, 164, 294, 364
Sundanese, 278, 285, 291, 308, 321, 322
Sundic, 298, 304-309
Surin Khmer, 29, 72
Sūzhōu Wú, 406

Tabare, 276
Tacanan languages, 608
Tagalog, 305, 311-312, 314, 318, 319, 323, 325, 326, 592-594
Tagin, 218, 221
Tai; see Shan
– Proto Tai, 106, 501, 559
Tai languages of Assam, 10, 216
Tai Lue, 54, 58
Tai-Kadai languages,
– as part of MSEA, 6, 153, 209, 212, 269
– causatives, 164
– 'eye day ' > 'sun' lexicalization, 283
– 'give' construction, 294
– phonology, 29, 34, 35, 39, 43, 46
– syllable structure, 42
– tone, 83, 84, 87, 88, 99-103, 106
– word length, 313
Takia, 294, 332
Tamang, 572
Tambora, 269
Tanahmerah, 269
Tangam, 218, 221, 225, 230, 233, 251
Tangkhul, Tangkhulic, 126, 138, 141, 567, 571
– Proto Tangkhulic 115, 116, 117, 118, 119, 120, 138
Tangut, 361, 572
Tani languages, 114, 143, 209, 210, 214, 216, 217-259, 567, 572, 574; see also Proto Tani
Taoih, 540, 541
Taraon, 571
Tawang, 572
Tehit, 286
Temiar, 533, 534, 538, 541, 546, 551, 569
Thado, 566, 567
Thai; see also Siamese
– as a national language, 29
– as part of MSEA, 14, 365
– coverbs, 612

– "elaborate expressions", 605
– 'get' construction, 187-190
– 'give' construction, 157, 161-164, 166, 293
– go/come, 617-618
– grammatical morpheme density, 317-318
– influence on other languages, 61, 74, 624
– interrupted transmission, 551
– isolating, 158, 310, 311
– loans, 328
– nominal classification, 559, 570
– phonology, 35
– Proto Southwestern Tai, 12
– serial verb constructions, 238, 589, 590, 591
– syllable structure, 503
– tone, 84, 374, 384, 447-448
– typological features, 368, 369
– "verb-loving", 607
– word length, 313, 314
– word order, 160, 397, 402, 410, 425, 427
Thakali, 572
Thavung, 504, 519, 533, 550, 569
Thulung, 572
tHun, 579
Tibetan (Alike), 571
Tibetan (Amdo: Bla-brang), 571
Tibetan (Balti), 571
Tibetan (Sherpa), 571
Tibeto-Burman
– agreement in, 227
– and creolization, 257
– as a part of MSEA, 29, 209
– as "Indospheric", 216, 217, 219
– convergence, 212
– 'give' and 'get' constructions, 158, 170, 184, 201, 202
– homeland of, 254
– influence by other languages, 111, 359
– influence on other languages, 111, 214
– intra-TB contact, 102, 112, 113

- negation, 240
- nominal classification, 566, 567, 570, 571, 572, 573-574
- nominalization, 223
- phonology, 34, 37, 39, 42, 44-45, 140-142
- Proto Tibeto-Burman, 113, 116-120, 129-131, 137, 138, 139, 217, 257, 501
- subgrouping, 114, 124, 133, 135, 215
- syllable structure, 126
- tone, 86
- typological division in subgroups, 213
- verb pronominalization, 139-140
- word formation in, 230-231
- word order, 153, 248, 288, 389, 390, 391, 397

Timor-Alor-Pantar languages, 269, 282, 288
Tivoid languages, 560, 581
Toba Batak, 289, 328
Tobelo, 288
Tokharian languages, 391
Trans New Guinea languages, 269, 270, 276, 288, 289
Tripura (Kokborok), 6, 127, 214, 215
Trung, 115, 116, 117, 118, 119, 120, 134
Tsat, 105
Tshangla, 566, 567
Tshona (Mama), 571
Tujia, 572
Tukang Besi, 289, 325
Turkish, 587
Turung, 10, 180, 200-201, 257, 447, 508, 512-514, 517-520, 524
U, 53, 54, 56-57, 59, 60
Uab Meto, 278
Ujir, 275
Upper Cross languages, 581
Ut-Ma'in, 579
Utsat, 373, 389
Uyghur, 391
Viet-Muong/ Việt-Mường, 103, 104, 535

- Proto Việt-Mường, 373

Vietic languages
- as Austroasiatic, 35
- case on pronouns, 540-541, 552
- morphology, 536
- nominal classification, 563, 568, 569
- isolating structure, 535
- Proto Vietic, 569
- syllable structure, 522
- tone, 86, 103

Vietnamese
- adnominal attribution, 297
- as a national language, 29
- as part of MSEA, 365
- bare oblique constructions, 321, 322
- contact-induced change, 61, 73, 83, 84, 102, 569
- 'eye day' > 'sun', 283
- 'give' constructions, 163, 168, 176, 293
- iamitives, 290
- interrupted transmission, 551
- motion expressions, 610
- nominal classification, 563
- Northern Vietnamese, 86
- morphology, 534, 536, 537, 539, 540, 544, 545, 548, 550
- phonology, 29, 35, 378
- population movements of speakers, 4
- syllable structure, 70, 522, 537
- tone, 83, 84, 85, 90, 105, 373, 384
- "verb-loving", 607
- 'where' greeting, 281
- word order, 397, 402, 416, 427

Wa, 10, 68
- Proto Wa, 43

Wa-Lawa
- Proto Wa-Lawa, 43

Waijewa, 275
Waima'a, 282
Wakhi, 391

War Jaintia, 570
Warembori, 294
Wǎxiāng(huà); see Xiānghuà
Wēnzhōu Wú, 395, 403
Wersing, 281
West Bomberai languages, 269
Western Himalayish languages, 213, 571
Western Lugbara, 55
Western Malayo-Polynesian languages, 283, 561, 592
Western Miji, 564, 566
Western Nilotic, 577, 578
White Hmong, 36, 332, 367, 415, 609, 613; see also Hmongic
Wissel Lakes – Termandoga languages, 276
Wú 358, 364, 370, 374, 377, 379, 403, 405, 406-408, 428; see also Fùyáng Wú; Níngbō Wú; Sūzhōu Wú; Wēnzhōu Wú
Wǔtún, 362
Xiāndǎo, 376
Xiāng, Xiang, 37, 39, 358, 360, 370, 371, 374, 377
Xiānghuà, 358, 359, 370, 371, 377, 384, 396, 402, 403, 408, 424; see also Gǔzhàng Xiānghuà

Xiāngnán Tǔhuà, 358
Xiong, 36, 358
Xixia, 38, 43, 572
Xong, see Xiong
Yali, 276
Yami, 285
Yanyuwa, 560
Yáo, 364
Yawa-Saweru languages, 270
Yi; see Loloish
Yíchūn Gàn, 371, 384, 397, 408, 427
Yimas, 295
Yue / Yuè; see also Cantonese
– as a major dialect group, 358
– as part of MSEA, 357
– history of, 364
– influence on other languages, 359
– part of southern zone of Sinitic, 370, 371
– phonology, 37, 39, 41, 379, 383
– syllable structure, 378
– tone, 374, 377
– word order, 408
Yuèběi Tǔhuà, 358
Zaiwa, 114, 123, 376
Zhaba, 38

www.ingramcontent.com/pod-product-compliance
Lightning Source LLC
Chambersburg PA
CBHW060747230426
43667CB00010B/1468